Frommer's 96

Arizona

by Karl Samson
with Jane Aukshunas

Macmillan • USA

ABOUT THE AUTHORS

Karl Samson likes to flee the soggy Northwest to dry out in the Arizona sun and has been exploring the state's deserts, mountains, cities, and towns for the past decade. He is also the author of several other Frommer guidebooks.

Jane Aukshunas enjoys experiencing the unique regional style of Arizona's hotels and restaurants, and is always interested in discovering more about the stimulating landscapes of prehistory and contemporary art she finds there.

MACMILLAN TRAVEL

A Simon & Schuster Macmillan Company
1633 Broadway
New York, NY 10019

Find us online at **http://www.mcp.com/mgr/travel** or
on America Online at Keyword: **SuperLibrary.**

ISBN 0-02-860875-5
ISSN 1053-2471

Editor: Alice K. Thompson
Production Editor: Matt Hannafin
Design by Michele Laseau
Digital Cartography by Geographix Inc.

Maps copyright © Simon & Schuster, Inc.

SPECIAL SALES

Bulk purchases (10+ copies) of Frommer's travel guides are available to corporations at special discounts. The Special Sales Department can produce custom editions to be used as premiums and/or for sales promotion to suit individual needs. Existing editions can be produced with custom cover imprints such as corporate logos. For more information write to: Special Sales, Simon & Schuster, 1633 Broadway, New York, NY 10019.

Manufactured in the United States of America

Contents

List of Maps

An Invitation to the Reader

In researching this book, we discovered many wonderful places—hotels, restaurants, shops, and more. We're sure you'll find others. Please tell us about them, so we can share the information with your fellow travelers in upcoming editions. If you were disappointed with a recommendation, we'd love to know that, too. Please write to:

Karl Samson
Frommer's Arizona '96
Macmillan Travel
1633 Broadway
New York, NY 10019

An Additional Note

Please be advised that travel information is subject to change at any time—and this is especially true of prices. We therefore suggest that you write or call ahead for confirmation when making your travel plans. The authors, editors, and publisher cannot be held responsible for the experiences of readers while traveling. Your safety is important to us, however, so we encourage you to stay alert and be aware of your surroundings. Keep a close eye on cameras, purses, and wallets, all favorite targets of thieves and pickpockets.

What the Symbols Mean

✪ Frommer's Favorites

Hotels, restaurants, attractions, and entertainment you should not miss.

⑤ Super-Special Values

Hotels and restaurants that offer great value for your money.

The following abbreviations are used for credit cards:

AE	American Express	EU	Eurocard
CB	Carte Blanche	JCB	Japan Credit Bank
DC	Diners Club	MC	MasterCard
DISC	Discover	V	Visa
ER	enRoute		

The Best of Arizona

Planning a trip to a state as large and diverse as Arizona involves making lots of decisions, so in this chapter we've tried to give you some direction. Below we've chosen what we feel are the very best the state has to offer—the places and experiences you won't want to miss. Most are written up in more detail elsewhere in this book; this chapter should serve to give you an overview of Arizona's highlights and get you started planning your trip.

1 The Best Places to Experience the Desert

- **Arizona-Sonora Desert Museum:** The name is misleading as this is actually more of a zoo and botanical garden than a museum in the traditional sense. Naturalistic settings house dozens of species of desert animals, including a number of desert critters you might hope *not* to meet in the wild (rattlesnakes, tarantulas, scorpions, black widows, gila monsters). See Chapter 9 for details.
- **Saguaro National Park:** Lying both east and west of Tucson, this national monument is a literal forest of saguaro cacti. This is the very essence of the desert as so many people imagine it. You can hike it or you can drive it. See Chapter 9 for details.
- **Organ Pipe Cactus National Monument:** The organ pipe cactus is a smaller, multi-trunked relative of the giant saguaro and lives only along the Mexican border about 100 miles west of Tucson. This remote national monument has hiking trails, scenic drives, even a large natural spring. What it doesn't have is the crowds you may encounter at Saguaro National Park. See Chapter 9 for details.
- **Desert Botanical Garden:** There's no better place in the state to learn about the plants of Arizona's Sonora Desert and the many other deserts of the world. Displays at this Phoenix botanical garden explain plant adaptations and how Native Americans once utilized many of the wild plants of this region. The gardens stay open until after dark so you can see how the desert changes as it cools off. See Chapter 5 for details.
- **Tucson Botanical Gardens:** Though it's small, this garden has extensive cactus gardens and also has displays on what it takes to garden in the desert. One area grows rare crops that are in danger of disappearing from the botanical gene pool. See Chapter 9 for details.

2 The Best Scenic Drives

- **Apache Trail:** Much of this winding road, which passes just north of the Superstition Mountains, is unpaved and follows a rugged route once ridden by Apaches. This is some of the most remote country you'll find in the Phoenix area, with far-reaching desert vistas and lots to see and do along the way. See Chapter 5 for details.
- **Schnebly Hill Road:** It can be rough going at times, but this gravel road rising up through the red rocks outside Sedona may be the single most spectacular drive in the state. The twists and turns yield ever-changing perspectives on one of the most otherworldly landscapes in the country. See Chapter 6 for details.
- **Up Mount Lemmon:** Sure the views of Tucson are great from the foothills to the north of the city, but the views from Mount Lemmon are even better. With a ski area at its summit, Mount Lemmon rises up from the desert like an island rising from the sea. Along the way the road climbs from cactus country to cool pine forests. See Chapter 9 for details.
- **Through Monument Valley:** This valley of sandstone buttes and mesas is one of the most photographed spots in America and is familiar to people all over the world from the many movies, TV shows, and commercials that have been shot here. A 17-mile dirt road winds through the park giving visitors closeups of such landmarks as Elephant Butte, the Mittens, and Totem Pole. See Chapter 8 for details.
- **Oak Creek Canyon:** Slicing down from the pine country outside Flagstaff to the red rocks of Sedona, Oak Creek Canyon is a cool oasis. From the scenic overlook at the top of the canyon to the swimming holes and hiking trails at the bottom, this canyon road provides a rapid change in climate and landscape. See Chapter 6 for details.

3 The Best Active Vacations

- **Rafting the Grand Canyon:** Whether you go for three days or two weeks, no other active vacation in the state comes even remotely close to matching the excitement of a raft trip through the Grand Canyon. Sure the river is crowded with rafting groups in the summer, but the grandeur of the canyon is more than enough to make up for seeing other adventurous souls during your trip. See Chapter 7 for details.
- **Riding the Range at a Guest Ranch:** Yes, Virginia, there are still cowboys. They ride ranges all over the state, and so can you if you book a stay at one of the many guest ranches (these used to be called dude ranches in the old days). After a long or short day in the saddle, you can usually soak in a hot tub, go for a swim, or play a game of tennis, before chowing down.
- **Staying at a Golf or Tennis Resort:** If horseback riding and cowboy cookouts aren't your thing, how about golf or tennis to your heart's content? The Phoenix/Scottsdale area has the greatest concentration of resorts in the country, and Tucson and Sedona add even more. There's something very satisfying about swinging a racquet or club with the state's spectacular scenery in the background, and the climate means you can do it practically year-round.
- **Hiking into the Grand Canyon:** Not for the unfit or the faint of heart, a hike down into the Grand Canyon is a hike through millions of years of time set in

stone. This trip takes plenty of advance planning just to get a permit, and then requires some very strenuous hiking. With both a campground and a lodge at the bottom of the canyon, you can choose to make this trip either with a fully loaded backpack or just a light daypack. See Chapter 7 for details.

- **Hiking into Havasu Canyon:** Turquoise waters at the foot of cascading waterfalls, strange terraces formed by limestone deposits, and a cottonwood-shaded stream are what lure backpackers the 11 miles down to the campground in Havasu Canyon. This is the heart of the Havasupai Indian Reservation, and, aside from the narrow ribbon of greenery along the canyon floor, is a landscape of sandstone and cacti. See Chapter 7 for details.

- **Hiking into Betatakin or Keet Seel:** While it's possible to drive right up to many of the Native American ruins in Arizona, there's something much more rewarding about coming upon cliff dwellings after a long hike. These two ruins in Navajo National Monument in northern Arizona can only be reached on foot or on horseback: Betatakin is a day hike and Keet Seel an overnight trip. See Chapter 8 for details.

4 The Best Day Hikes & Nature Walks

- **Bright Angel Trail:** Sure it's a human highway near the top, but this, the most popular trail into the Grand Canyon, offers everyone the chance to say that they've hiked the Grand Canyon. Despite its popularity, Bright Angel Trail is a strenuous hike even if you only go a mile or so down the trail. The trip back is all uphill. See Chapter 7 for details.

- **Picacho Peak Trail:** The hike up this central Arizona landmark is short but strenuous, and from the top there are superb views out over the desert. The best time of year to make the hike is in spring when the peak comes alive with wildflowers. Picacho Peak is between Casa Grande and Tucson just off I-10.

- **Camelback Mountain:** For many Phoenicians the trail up to the top of Camelback Mountain is a ritual, a Phoenix institution. Sure there are those who make this a casual but strenuous hike, but many more turn it into a serious workout by jogging to the top and back. We prefer a more leisurely approach, the better to enjoy the views. See Chapter 5 for details.

- **The White House Ruins Trail at Canyon de Chelly:** There's only one Canyon de Chelly hike that the general public can do without a Navajo guide, and that's the 2¹/₂-mile trail to White House Ruins. The trail leads from the canyon rim across bare sandstone, through a tunnel, and down to the floor of the canyon. Though it seems as though you've left the modern world behind, when you finally reach the ruins, you'll likely find quite a few four-wheel-drive vehicles parked near the ancient Anasazi cliff dwelling. See Chapter 8 for details.

- **The Boynton Canyon Trail Near Sedona:** Any walk among the red rocks around Sedona is rewarding, but the 6-mile round-trip hike into Boynton Canyon provides views as well as a chance to see ancient Sinagua ruins. See Chapter 6 for details.

- **Hikes and walks in the Petrified forest:** Few visitors to the Petrified Forest National Park venture far from their cars, which is understandable when you consider how much petrified wood there is to see near the road. More adventurous visitors, however, should venture farther afield (with plenty of water, of course). Back-country camping is also permitted here. See Chapter 8 for details.

5 The Best Swimming Holes

- **Sabino Canyon:** When the summer heats up, this is where Tucson cools off. With a cool stream running its length and forming pools and beaches, Sabino Canyon is an idyllic oasis (at least it would be without the crowds). See Chapter 9 for details.
- **Slide Rock State Park:** Water is at a premium in the desert, and when it's available people take full advantage of it. Set on the banks of Oak Creek near Sedona, this park really does have a natural water slide, as well as a great little swimming hole. See Chapter 6 for details.
- **Havasu Canyon:** Though it's an 11-mile hike to the turquoise waters and waterfalls of this swimming hole, hundreds of people make the trek and camp out at the nearby campground. The contrast of turquoise waters and sandstone cliffs make this one of the most striking settings in Arizona. See Chapter 7.
- **Lake Powell:** This is Arizona's biggest swimming hole, so big that it stretches all the way into Utah. Hundreds of miles of sandstone canyons are there to be explored by boat, with a quick dip right off the bow. See Chapter 7 for details.
- **The Salt River:** When Phoenicians want to cool off on a scorching summer day, they quite frequently head for the Salt River with inner tubes in tow. There are few better ways to beat the heat than lazing away the day floating downstream. See Chapter 5 for details.

6 The Best Resort Swimming Pools

- **Hyatt Regency Resort at Gainey Ranch, Scottsdale:** This Scottsdale resort boasts a 10-pool, 2^1/$_2$-acre water playground complete with sand beach, waterfalls, sports pool, lap pool, adult pool, three-story water slide, massive whirlpool, and lots of waterfalls. See Chapter 5 for details.
- **The Phoenician, Scottsdale:** This system of seven pools is as impressive as the Hyatt's but has a much more sophisticated air about it. Waterfalls, water slides, play pools, a lap pool, and—the crown jewel—a mother-of-pearl pool, all add up to plenty of aquatic fun. See Chapter 5 for details.
- **The Pointe Hilton at Squaw Peak, Phoenix:** They don't just have a pool here, they have a River Ranch, with an artificial tubing river, water slide, and a waterfall pouring into the large, free-form main pool. See Chapter 5 for details.
- **Red Lion's La Posada Resort, Scottsdale:** With its swim-through grotto, artificial pink-rock outcropping, and cascading waterfalls, La Posada's pool is straight out of Disneyland. The kids will love it. See Chapter 5 for details.
- **Arizona Biltmore, Phoenix:** The main pool here, which was added only recently, mixes old and new with its private cabanas (available for a fee) and its Frank Lloyd Wright–inspired water-slide tower. See Chapter 5 for details.
- **The Buttes, Tempe:** A lush stream cascading over desert rocks seems to feed this free-form pool; it's a desert oasis fantasy world unmatched in the state. A narrow canal connects the two halves of the pool and tucked in among the rocks are several whirlpools. See Chapter 5 for details.
- **Arizona Inn, Tucson:** The pool here isn't large, but the private little courtyard that surrounds it is planted with jasmines, gardenias, and fragrant, flowering orange trees. The garden setting gives the pool a homey, old-Arizona feel. See Chapter 9 for details.

7   The Best Bird-Watching

- **Ramsey Canyon:** Nearly 200 species of birds—including 14 species of hummingbirds—frequent this canyon, making it one of the top birding hot spots in the country. See Chapter 10 for details.
- **Cave Creek Canyon:** Though there are other rare birds to be seen in this remote canyon, most people come in hopes of spotting the rare elegant trogon, which reaches the northernmost limit of its range here. See Chapter 10 for details.
- **San Pedro Riparian National Conservation area:** With water such a scarce commodity in the desert, it tends to attract a lot of animal life, including more than 300 bird species. This is a life-list bonanza spot. See Chapter 10 for details.
- **Madera Canyon:** The mountain canyons of southern Arizona tend to attract a variety of birdlife, from species common in the lowland deserts to those that prefer thick forest settings. Madera is a good place to experience this variety. See Chapter 9 for details.
- **Patagonia:** With a year-round stream and a Nature Conservancy preserve on the edge of town, Patagonia is one of the best spots in the state for sighting various flycatcher species. See Chapter 10 for details.
- **Willcox Ponds:** Wading birds in the middle of the desert? You'll find them at the Willcox sewage-treatment ponds south of town. Avocets, sandhill cranes, and a variety of waterfowl all frequent these shallow bodies of water. See Chapter 10 for details.

8   The Best Offbeat Travel Experiences

- **Sleeping in a Wigwam:** Back in the heyday of Route 66, the Wigwam Motel in Holbrook lured passing motorists with its unusual architecture—concrete wigwam-shaped cabins. Today this little motel is still a great place for anyone who enjoys the unusual.
- **Touring Walpai Village:** Of the Hopi villages that stand atop the mesas of northeastern Arizona, only Walpai, one of the oldest, offers guided tours. The young Hopi guides share information on the history of the village and the Hopi culture. See Chapter 8 for details.
- **Visiting a Quartzite Gem and Mineral Show:** Every winter, the community of Quartzite becomes a sea of RVs as tens of thousands of rock hounds flock to the area for the many gem and mineral shows. These shows include hundreds of vendors selling everything from uncut geodes to beautiful jewelry. See Chapter 11 for details.
- **Taking a Vortex Tour in Sedona:** Crystals and pyramids are nothing compared to the power of the Sedona vortexes, which just happen to be in the middle of some very beautiful scenery. Organized tours shuttle believers from one vortex to the next. See Chapter 6 for details.
- **Digging for Artifacts at Ravensite Ruin:** Looking at Anasazi ruins is all well and good, but how would you like to get your hands dirty digging for ancient artifacts? At the White Mountain Archaeological Center near St. Johns, you can—for a fee—participate in an ongoing archaeological dig. See Chapter 8 for details.

- **Walking Across the London Bridge:** The famous bridge *was* falling down until a far-sighted (perhaps slightly daft) developer transported it to the middle of the Arizona desert. You'll find the bridge in Lake Havasu City and, if it's not too blazingly hot, you can stroll across it and admire all the surrounding pseudo-Tudor architecture. See Chapter 11 for details.
- **Touring the Queen Mine in Bisbee:** You can descend deep into the earth outside Bisbee and see how copper was once mined in the Copper State. Beginning in the late 1800s, copper mines turned Bisbee into the wildest boom town this side of New Orleans. This is also where Bisbee blue turquoise was once mined. See Chapter 10 for details.
- **Shake and Bake Tours into Canyon de Chelly:** There are only a few ways the public can visit this scenic canyon on the Navajo Reservation, and truck tours, known as "shake and bake" tours by the locals, are by far the least strenuous. See Chapter 8 for details.
- **Gazing at the Stars:** Insomniacs and stargazers will find plenty to keep them sleepless in the desert as they peer at the stars through telescopes at Lowell Observatory in Flagstaff or Kitt Peak National Observatory near Tucson. See Chapters 7 and 9 for details.
- **A Visit to Biosphere 2:** This giant terrarium, in which humans are the residents, is purportedly a research center for understanding how the earth's ecosystems operate. The giant greenhouses in the middle of the desert are straight out of post-apocalyptic sci-fi. See Chapter 9 for details.

9 The Best Family Experiences

- **Wild West Restaurants:** No family should visit Arizona without spending an evening at a "genuine" cowboy steakhouse. With gunslingers and gimmicks (one will cut off your necktie, another has a slide from the bar to the dining room), cowboy bands, and false-fronted buildings, these Arizona eateries are all entertainment and loads of fun. See Chapters 5 and 9 for details.
- **Arizona-Sonora Desert Museum:** This is actually a zoo featuring the animals of the Sonora Desert. There are rooms full of snakes, a prairie dog town, mountain goats, mountain lions, an aviary full of hummingbirds, even the best zoo restaurant we've ever eaten at. Kids and adults love this place. See Chapter 9 for details.
- **Shootouts at the O.K. Corral:** Tombstone may be "the town too tough to die," but poor Ike Clanton and his buddies the McLaury boys have to die over and over again at the frequent reenactments of the famous gunfight. See Chapter 10 for details.
- **Tubing down the Salt River:** If an aquatic amusement park is just too contrived for you and your family, how about a relaxing float down the Salt River. There are tube-rental companies and shuttle buses to make this an easy and fun outing. See Chapter 5 for details.
- **Riding the Grand Canyon Railway:** Not only is this train excursion a fun way to get to the Grand Canyon, but it also lets you avoid the parking problems and congestion that can prove so wearisome. Shootouts and train robberies are to be expected in this corner of the Wild West. See Chapter 7 for details.
- **Visit the Pioneer Arizona Living History Museum:** Located north of Phoenix, this museum features old buildings and costumed interpreters who show and

tell what life was like for Arizona pioneers 100 years ago. See Chapter 5 for details.

- **Spend a Week on a Houseboat:** Renting a floating vacation home on Lakes Powell, Mead, Mohave, or Havasu is a summer tradition for many Arizona families. With a houseboat, you aren't tied to one spot and can cruise from one scenic beach to the next. See Chapters 7 and 11 for details.

10   The Most Interesting Architectural Landmarks

- **Arcosanti:** This funky, futuristic city in the middle of the desert is the brain-child of a former student from Frank Lloyd Wright's Taliesin West. Organically shaped poured-concrete structures sprout from the desert like so many giant fungi. See Chapter 5 for details.
- **Arizona Biltmore:** Though Frank Lloyd Wright was not the official architect of this historic hotel, his influence and work can be seen throughout, in the distinctively concrete-block walls, the stained glass in the lobby, the sculptures by the front door. See Chapter 5 for details.
- **Chapel of the Holy Cross:** Built upon the rocks outside Sedona, this non-denominational chapel is an intriguing work of devotion that melds with its surroundings. See Chapter 6 for details.
- **Mission San Xavier del Bac:** Known as the "White Dove of the Desert," this 18th-century Spanish church is a primitive yet amazingly detailed building, and is considered the finest mission church in the United States. See Chapter 9 for details.
- **Taliesin West:** This was Frank Lloyd Wright's winter home and desert architecture school. The buildings are classic examples of Wright's work and tours are offered. See Chapter 5 for details.

11   The Best Art Communities

- **Tubac:** This is the oldest town in Arizona and dates to 1691 when the Spanish founded this northern outpost of New Spain. Today the many old adobe homes in Tubac have been turned into art galleries, artist's studios, and shops selling southwestern crafts. See Chapter 9 for details.
- **Jerome:** Perched high on the slopes of Cleopatra Hill on Mingus Mountain, Jerome is a former mining town that has become one of Arizona's most popular artists' communities. The streets are lined with interesting galleries and the views are some of the best in the state. See Chapter 6 for details.
- **Bisbee:** Once the largest town between New Orleans and San Francisco, Bisbee made its fortune on copper. When the copper ran out, the town was almost left to the ghosts. Today, Bisbee is once again making a name for itself, but this time as southern Arizona's liveliest arts community. Galleries and shops line the narrow winding streets. See Chapter 10 for details.
- **Sedona:** This was Arizona's original artists' community and today is second only to Scottsdale in number of galleries. Artists came, and still come, for the breath-taking scenery which has found its way onto countless canvases. See Chapter 6 for details.
- **Scottsdale:** Only New York and Santa Fe have more art galleries than Scottsdale, which has become one of the nation's centers for western and

Native American art. Bronzes and large paintings are most popular here. With street after street lined with almost nothing but art galleries, the art aficionado will need plenty of time for a visit to Scottsdale. See Chapter 5 for details.

12 The Best Museums

- **Heard Museum:** This is one of the nation's premier museums devoted to Native American culture. In addition to historical exhibits, a huge kachina collection, and an excellent museum store, there are annual exhibits of contemporary Native American art as well as performances of traditional dances and demonstrations of traditional skills. Chapter 5 for details.
- **Museum of Northern Arizona:** The geology, ethnography, and archaeology of this region are all explored in fascinating detail at this Flagstaff museum, and throughout the year there are excellent special exhibits and festivals focusing on the region's different tribes. Chapter 7 for details.
- **Amerind Foundation:** Though located in the remote southeast corner of the state near Willcox, this museum and research center houses a superb collection of Native American artifacts. Displays focus on tribes of the Southwest, but other tribes are also represented. See Chapter 10 for details.
- **Phoenix Art Museum:** This museum has been the process of building a new home for several years, and new building or not, has an outstanding collection of contemporary art as well as a fascinating exhibit of miniature rooms. See Chapter 5 for details.
- **University of Arizona Museum of Art:** This Tucson museum displays works dating from the Renaissance to the present, with a set of 15th-century Spanish religious panels the focus of the collection. Georgia O'Keeffe and Pablo Picasso are among the artists whose works are on display here. See Chapter 9 for details.

13 The Best Places to Discover the Old West

- **Old Tucson Studios:** Though many of the original movie sets burned in a fire in 1995, this combination back lot and amusement park provides visitors with a glimpse of the most familiar old West—the Hollywood West. Sure the shootouts and cancan reviews are silly, but it's all in fun, and everyone gets a thrill out of seeing film crews in action. See Chapter 9 for details.
- **Guest Ranches:** The Old West lives on at guest ranches all over the state, where rugged wranglers lead city slickers on horseback rides through desert scrub and mountain meadows. Campfires, cookouts, and cattle are all part of a stay at many guest ranches.
- **Tombstone:** This is the *real* Old West in that Tombstone is a real town, unlike Old Tucson. However, "the town too tough to die" long ago was reincarnated as a major tourist attraction with gunslingers in the streets, stagecoach rides, and shootouts at the O.K. Corral. See Chapter 10 for details.
- **Rodeos:** Any rodeo will give you a glimpse of the Old West, but Arizona has two that claim title to being the oldest in the country. Whether you head for the rodeo in Prescott or the one in Payson, you'll see plenty of bronco-busting, bull riding, and beer drinking. See Chapters 6 and 8 for details.

- **Trappings of the American West:** This annual exhibition at the Coconino Center for the Arts in Flagstaff displays contemporary western art as well as crafts and accouterments of cowboy life. See Chapter 7 for details.
- **Monument Valley:** John Ford made it the hallmark of his western movies, and today the starkly beautiful and unbelievably shaped buttes and mesas of this valley are the quintessential western landscape. You'll recognize it the moment you see it. See Chapter 8 for details.

14 The Most Interesting Native American Ruins

- **Besh Ba Gowah:** These reconstructed ruins in the town of Globe have been set up to look the way they might have appeared 700 years ago. This gives these ruins a bit more cultural context than other ruins in the state. See Chapter 5 for details.
- **Canyon de Chelly:** Small cliff dwellings up and down the length of Canyon de Chelly can be seen from overlooks. A trip into the canyon itself offers a chance to see some of these ruins close up. See Chapter 8 for details.
- **Casa Grande:** Unlike most of the other ruins in the state, this large and unusual structure is built of packed desert soil. Inscrutable and perplexing, Casa Grande rises seems to rise from nowhere. See Chapter 5 for details.
- **Keet Seel/Betatakin:** Although both of these ruins located in Navajo National Monument are at the end of long hikes, their size and state of preservation make them among the finest examples of Anasazi cliff dwellings. See Chapter 8 for details.
- **Montezuma Castle:** This is the most easily accessible cliff dwelling in Arizona, and though it cannot be entered, it's just off I-17. Nearby Montezuma's Well also has some small ruins. See Chapter 6 for details.
- **Tonto National Monument:** Located east of Phoenix on the Apache Trail, this is one of the only easily accessible cliff dwellings in Arizona that you can still visit, rather than just look at from a distance. See Chapter 5 for details.
- **Wupatki:** Not nearly as well known as the region's Anasazi cliff dwellings, these ruins are set on a wide plain. A ball court similar to those found in Central America hints at cultural ties with the Aztecs. See Chapter 7 for details.

15 The Best Guest Ranches

- **Grapevine Canyon Ranch:** If you already know a heifer from a steer and can keep a horse under control even when it smells the barn, then maybe you're ready to help with the spring cattle roundup at this ranch in southeastern Arizona. See Chapter 10 for details.
- **Kay El Bar Ranch:** This Wickenburg guest ranch is just about the smallest in the state, which means personal attention. It also incorporates a historic adobe building and vintage ranch furnishings that together create an ambience unique in the state. See Chapter 6 for details.
- **Rancho de los Caballeros:** Actually far more than just a guest ranch, this luxurious Wickenburg resort has its own 18-hole golf course, tennis courts, pool, and plenty of excellent food. Guests who aren't interested in riding horses will find plenty to do. See Chapter 6 for details.

- **Tanque Verde Inn:** Although there are other guest ranches that are more luxurious, no other offers such a superb setting, authentic ranch feel, creature comforts, and excellent food. See Chapter 9 for details.
- **Wickenburg Inn:** So maybe you like to ride horses, but your spouse prefers tennis, your daughter lives for ponies, and your son wants to see rattlesnakes. No problem. The Wickenburg Inn, a combination guest ranch and tennis resort that doubles as a nature preserve, should keep the whole family happy. See Chapter 6 for details.

16 The Best Luxury Hotels & Resorts

- **Arizona Biltmore:** Combining discrete service and the architectural styling of Frank Lloyd Wright, the Arizona Biltmore has long been one of the most popular resorts in the state. Recent renovations have done much to improve the quality of the rooms and a new pool has become a big hit with families. See Chapter 5 for details.
- **Arizona Inn:** This Tucson resort dates back to Arizona's earliest days as a vacation destination and prides itself on its personal service. The gardens are a fragrant and colorful oasis. This is a low-key operation and the only historic resort in the state. See Chapter 9 for details.
- **The Boulders:** Taking its name from the massive blocks of eroded granite that are scattered about the grounds of this resort, the Boulders is among the most exclusive and expensive resorts in the state. Pueblo architecture fits seamlessly with the landscape, and the golf course is the most breathtaking you'll find in Arizona. See Chapter 5 for details.
- **Enchantment Resort:** A dramatic setting in a red-rock canyon outside Sedona makes this the most stunningly situated resort in the state. Guest rooms are for the most part quite large and are constructed in a pueblo architectural style. If you want to feel as if you're vacationing in the desert, this place fills the bill. See Chapter 6 for details.
- **Hyatt Regency Scottsdale Resort at Gainey Ranch:** Contemporary desert architecture, dramatic landscaping, a water playground with its own beach, a staff that's always at the ready to assist you, several good restaurants that aren't overpriced, and even gondola rides make this one of the "funnest" and most smoothly run resorts in Arizona. See Chapter 5 for details.
- **Loews Ventana Canyon:** With the Santa Catalina Mountains rising up in the backyard of this resort and an almost-natural waterfall only steps away from the lobby, this is Tucson's most dramatic resort. Contemporary styling throughout makes constant reference to the desert setting. See Chapter 9 for details.
- **Marriott's Camelback Inn:** Of Scottsdale's many resorts, this is one of the few that retains an old Arizona atmosphere without sacrificing comfort or modern conveniences. A full-service spa caters to those who crave pampering, while two golf courses provide plenty of challenging fairways and greens. See Chapter 5 for details.
- **The Phoenician:** This Xanadu of the resort world is brimming with marble, crystal, and works of art. With staff seemingly around every corner, the hotel offers its guests impeccable service. Two of the resort's dining rooms are among the finest restaurants in the city, and the views are hard to beat. See Chapter 5 for details.

- **Scottsdale Princess:** The Moorish styling and numerous fountains and waterfalls of this Scottsdale resort create a setting made for romance. Two superb restaurants—one serving Spanish cuisine and one serving gourmet Mexican fare—top it off. See Chapter 5 for details.
- **Sheraton El Conquistador:** The craggy ramparts of Pusch Ridge rising to the east and some of the best sunsets in the state are two of the outstanding features of this resort. Add to that three golf courses, several good restaurants, riding stables, and plenty of other exercise facilities, and you have the makings of thoroughly enjoyable resort stay. See Chapter 9 for details.

17 The Best Moderately Priced Hotels

- **San Carlos:** Arizona doesn't have many historic hotels, and downtown Phoenix doesn't have many hotels of any kind. Consequently this restored Phoenix hotel is a welcome choice for anyone looking for character, economical rates, and a downtown location. See Chapter 5 for details.
- **Bright Angel Lodge:** Located right on the rim of the Grand Canyon, this hotel offers a wide variety of room types and a wide range of rates. If you can get a reservation here, you'll get to experience the best hotel deal in Grand Canyon National Park. See Chapter 7 for details.
- **Sky Ranch Lodge:** Accommodations in Sedona tend to be pricey, but at this motel you get your money's worth in the form of spectacular mesa-top views of the red rocks and the city far below. See Chapter 6 for details.
- **Goulding's Lodge:** Anyone planning on staying the night near Monument Valley should try to get a reservation here first. From your balcony, you'll be able to see the buttes and mesas of the valley. See Chapter 8 for details.
- **Best Western Ghost Ranch Lodge:** This older motel isn't in a very attractive neighborhood, but a sign designed by Georgia O'Keeffe, a superb cactus garden, and a guest ranch feel make this a good economical choice in Tucson. See Chapter 9 for details.
- **Cameron Trading Post:** It's tough finding accommodations anywhere near the Grand Canyon in the summer months, so if you're turned away at the park and don't mind a bit of a drive, this former trading post makes a good choice. See Chapter 8 for details.
- **Fiesta Inn:** This Tempe hotel offers many of the amenities and facilities of much more expensive Scottsdale resorts. The grounds are shady and there are plenty of athletic facilities. It's close to the airport, which is both good and bad (easy to get to but a bit noisy). See Chapter 5 for details.
- **Smuggler's Inn:** Set around a shallow pond full of fish, this Tucson hotel has the feel of a small resort. Tropical landscaping and a Caribbean theme restaurant contrive to transport guests out of the desert. See Chapter 9 for details.
- **Hotel St. Michael:** Situated right on rowdy Whiskey Row in downtown Prescott, this historic hotel offers small rooms (one of which is said to be haunted) and an Old West atmosphere. See Chapter 6 for details.
- **Tanque Verde Inn:** It doesn't look like much from the outside, but shady courtyards give this small hotel a very peaceful atmosphere. It also happens to stand in the middle of one of Tucson's restaurant rows. See Chapter 9 for details.

18   The Best Historic Inns & Hotels

- **Arizona Inn:** This small resort near downtown Tucson dates to 1930 and is built in the Southwest pueblo style with lush, fragrant gardens. Many rooms have original furniture that was built by disabled World War I veterans. See Chapter 9 for details.
- **El Tovar:** This classic mountain lodge stands in Grand Canyon Village only feet from the South Rim of the Grand Canyon, and although the rooms sport incongruous American colonial furniture, the lodge immerses guests in the history of the area. See Chapter 7 for details.
- **Gadsden Hotel:** Though it isn't the most comfortable of the state's historic hotels, the Gadsden in Douglas still wears an early 19th-century air. The Grand Lobby is unique in the state and features a large Tiffany stained-glass window. See Chapter 10 for details.
- **Grand Canyon Lodge:** This, the Grand Canyon's other grand lodge, sits right on the North Rim of the canyon. Rooms are primarily in cabins which aren't quite as impressive as the main lodge building, but guests tend to spend a lot of time sitting on the lodge's two viewing terraces or in the sunroom. See Chapter 7 for details.
- **Hassayampa Inn:** Built as a luxury hotel in 1927, the Hassayampa is Prescott's premier historic inn and sits only a block off Courthouse Plaza. Many of the rooms, which vary considerably in size, have original furnishings, and one is said to be haunted. See Chapter 6 for details.

19   The Best B&Bs

- **Briar Patch Inn:** Oak Creek Canyon, near Sedona, where this collection of cottages is located, is an oasis in the desert. Few experiences are more restorative than breakfast on the shady banks of the creek. See Chapter 6 for details.
- **Casa Tierra:** This modern adobe home is located close to Saguaro National Park west of downtown Tucson and is an ideal choice for anyone who really wants to feel as if they're staying in the desert. See Chapter 9 for details.
- **El Presidio Inn:** Located in the El Presidio historic district in downtown Tucson, this is one of the only 19th-century adobe homes in the state that operates as a B&B. Victorian architectural details have, however, hidden the adobe styling quite effectively. See Chapter 9 for details.
- **Inn at the Citadel:** Located north of downtown Scottsdale, this modern inn features rooms full of European antiques (most of which are for sale) and equipped with large luxurious bathrooms. Designer touches place this inn solidly ahead of the vast majority of B&Bs. See Chapter 5 for details.
- **Saddle Rock Ranch:** With some of the best views in Sedona, this stone-and-adobe home dates to 1926 and has its own little swimming pool. Of the three available rooms, the little cottage, with its peeled-log bed and flagstone floors, has the most western character. See Chapter 6 for details.

20   The Best Restaurants

- **The Arizona Kitchen:** Spicy and flavorful southwestern dishes and unique pizzas made with jalapeño-and-corn fry bread are the draw here in Litchfield Park, and the piki bread shouldn't be missed. See Chapter 5 for details.

- **Cafe Poca Cosa:** It's small, it's hip, and it's very reasonably priced. In Tucson's Park Inn Santa Rita, the Cafe Poca Cosa serves some of the most creative and complex Mexican food since *Like Water for Chocolate*. See Chapter 9 for details.
- **Christopher's:** With his skillful renditions of traditional French fare and flavorful new American dishes, Phoenix's chef Christopher Gross has kept his clientele loyal for more than a few years now. See Chapter 5 for details.
- **El Tovar Dining Room:** It would be hard to match the setting, a historic mountain lodge in Grand Canyon Village on the rim of the Grand Canyon, but this restaurant does its best. The menu features a mix of continental and southwestern flavors, though those dishes showing a regional flavor are the better choices. See Chapter 7 for details.
- **Heartline Cafe:** Combining the zesty flavors of the Southwest with the best of the rest of the world, Sedona's Heartline Cafe frequently comes up with some surefire winners guaranteed to please jaded palates. See Chapter 6 for details.
- **Janos:** Housed in an old adobe building in the El Presidio historic district of Tucson, this popular restaurant serves a combination of French and southwestern dishes. See Chapter 9 for details.
- **Marquesa:** Located amid the Moorish architecture of the Scottsdale Princess resort, this Spanish restaurant specializes in Catalonian dishes. To dine here is to be totally immersed in a Mediterranean experience. See Chapter 5 for details.
- **Mary Elaine's:** Located in Scottsdale's posh Phoenician resort, Mary Elaine's is where the elite dine in the Valley of the Sun. The menu focuses primarily on Mediterranean flavors, though the chef doesn't limit himself. See Chapter 5 for details.
- **Such Is Life:** This elegant little Mexican restaurant serves the sort of meals you might expect to find in a luxurious Mexico City restaurant, and service is excellent. Don't look for any standard Mexican fare covered in melted cheese here—Phoenix's Such Is Life has higher standards. See Chapter 5 for details.
- **The Tack Room:** Superb service, creative southwestern dishes, and an authentic Arizona atmosphere make Tucson's Tack Room one of the finest restaurants in the West. Though the steaks are the traditional favorite here, other dishes are well worth consideration. See Chapter 6 for details.

2 Getting to Know Arizona

Despite the searing summer temperatures of the deserts that cover much of the state, people have been lured to Arizona for centuries. The Spanish came looking for gold—but settled for saving souls. Cattle ranchers came for Arizona's miles of excellent rangeland. In the mid-19th century miners scoured the hills for gold (and found more than the Spanish did), but their boom towns soon went bust—the mother lode was copper, which Arizona has in such abundance that it's called the Copper State.

In the 1920s and 1930s Arizona struck a new vein of gold. The railroads made travel to Arizona easy, and wintering here became fashionable with wealthy Northerners.

Today it's still the golden sun that lures people to Arizona. Scottsdale, Phoenix, Tucson, and Sedona together are home to some of the most luxurious and expensive resorts in the world. The state has also seen a massive influx of retirees, many of whom have found the few pockets of Arizona where the climate is absolutely perfect—not too hot, not too cold, and plenty of sunshine.

But it's the Grand Canyon that attracts most visitors to Arizona. Though not the deepest or the widest canyon on earth, the Grand Canyon is without a doubt the most spectacular. However, it's only one of the natural wonders of Arizona—the largest natural bridge in the world, the largest meteorite crater, the spectacular red-rock country of Sedona, and Monument Valley are just a few of the state's other natural spectacles.

The human hand has also left its mark on Arizona. More than 1,000 years ago Anasazi, Sinagua, and Hohokam Native American tribes built villages on mesas, in valleys, and in the steep cliff walls of deep canyons. In more recent years, it has been such huge structures as the Hoover and Glen Canyon dams along the Colorado River, creating the largest man-made reservoirs in the country, that have attracted millions of visitors each year.

In addition to its sunshine, resorts, and reservoirs, Arizona's fascinating history makes a visit unique. This is the Wild West, the land of cowboys and Indians, of prospectors and ghost towns, coyotes and rattlesnakes. Scratch the glossy surface of modern, urbanized Arizona and you'll strike real gold—the history of the American West.

1 The Natural Environment

Though the very mention of Arizona may cause some people to break out in a sweat, this state is much more than a searing landscape of cactus and creosote bush. From the baking shores of the lower Colorado River to the snow-capped heights of the San Francisco Peaks, Arizona offers virtually every climatic zone. Cactus flowers bloom in the spring, and in summer mountain wildflowers have their turn. In autumn, the aspens color the White Mountains golden, and in winter, snows blanket mountaintops throughout the state.

But it's the Sonora Desert, with its massive saguaro cacti, that most people associate with Arizona. The Sonora Desert surrounds Phoenix and Tucson and is among the most biologically diverse deserts on the planet, in part because it's one of the wettest deserts. Rain here falls in the winter months as well as during the late-summer monsoon season, when clamorous thunderstorms send flash floods surging down arroyos. Before the coming of dams and deep wells, many rivers and streams flowed year-round here and nurtured a huge variety of plants and animals. Today only a few rivers still flow unaltered through the desert, among them the San Pedro, Verde, and Hassayampa rivers and Sonoita Creek. The green riparian areas along these watercourses serve as magnets for wildlife and harbor rare birds and fish species that are unique to Arizona.

The Sonora Desert's most conspicuous natural inhabitant is the saguaro cactus, which can stand 40 feet tall and weigh several tons. Massive and many-armed, these are the cacti of comic strips and Hollywood westerns. But there are also many other lesser-known species of cactus, such as the organ pipe cactus (closely related to the saguaro), the barrel cactus, and various species of prickly pears and chollas, all of which have adapted to this harsh environment by storing water in their stems, growing without leaves, and protecting themselves with spines. Despite spiny defenses, cactus are still relied upon by many desert animals for food and protection. Bats sip the nectar from saguaro flowers (and in the process, act as pollinators). Javelinas, similar to wild pigs and also known as collared peccaries, chow down on the prickly pear fruit—spines and all. Gila woodpeckers nest in holes in saguaro trunks, while cactus wrens build their nests in the branches of the cholla cactus.

Just as cacti have adapted to the desert, so, too, have the animals that live here. Many desert animals spend the sweltering days in burrows and only venture out in the cool of the night. Under cover of darkness, rattlesnakes and great horned owls hunt kangaroo rats, coyotes howl, and javelinas root about for anything edible. Gila lizards, among the only poisonous lizards in the world, drag their ungainly bodies though the dust, while tarantulas tiptoe silently in search of unwary insects.

Outside the desert regions there is great diversity as well. In the southern part of the state, solitary mountains and small mountain ranges rise abruptly from the

Impressions

Do nothing to mar its grandeur. . . . keep it for your children, your children's children, all who come after you, as the one great sight which every American should see.
—President Theodore Roosevelt, after visiting the Grand Canyon in 1903

Arizona

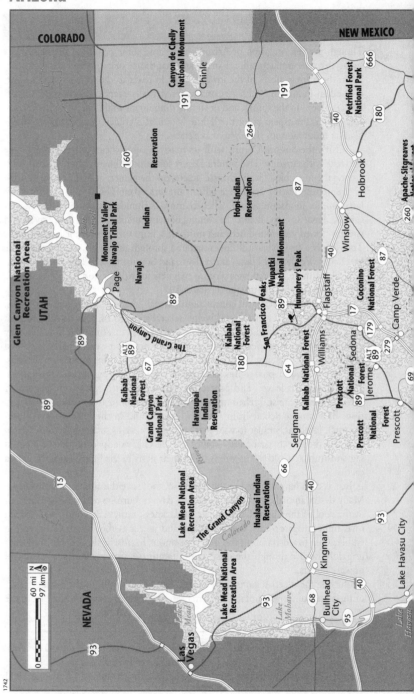

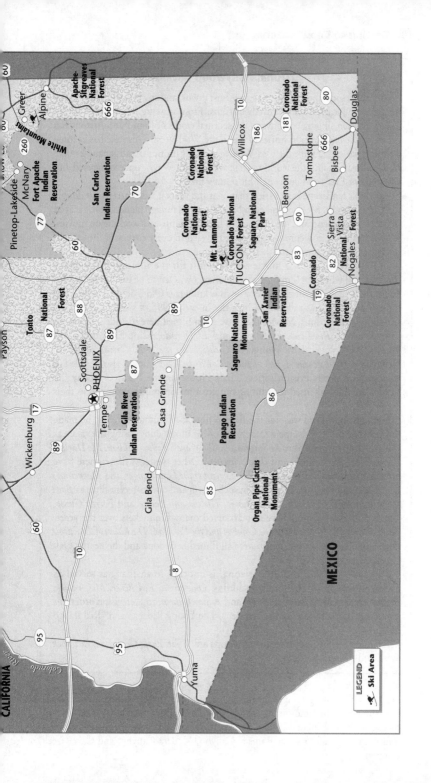

Arizona: Hollywood Backlot

Spectacular landscapes, rugged deserts, ghost towns, and cowboy ethos have made Arizona the location for hundreds of films. From obscure B westerns starring long-forgotten singing cowboys to the seminal works of John Ford, Arizona has provided the backdrop to stories of life in the Wild West. This state has become so much associated with the Old West that even Europeans and Japanese come from halfway around the world to walk where John Wayne once swaggered and where Clint Eastwood cultivated his outlaw image.

Arizona's landscape is so varied that over the years it has managed to double for Texas, Kansas, Mexico, and even New York and foreign planets. It has played the past, the present, and the future. Production companies working on movies, television shows, and commercials have traveled to every corner of the state to find just the right setting for their productions.

In Tucson, in 1939, a movie set was built for the filming of the movie *Arizona,* and when the filming was over, the set was left to be used in other productions. Today this mock-western town is known as Old Tucson Studios, and though much of it was destroyed by a fire in early 1995, it's still used for film and video productions. Movies that have been filmed here include *Tombstone,* John Wayne's *Rio Lobo, Rio Bravo,* and *El Dorado;* Clint Eastwood's *The Outlaw Josey Wales;* Kirk Douglas's *Gunfight at the O.K. Corral;* and Paul Newman's *The Life and Times of Judge Roy Bean.* Old Tucson also doubled as Mankato on the television series "Little House on the Prairie." Today the studios are not only used for filming but are a major tourist attraction in their own right.

Though John Ford was not the first to film at Monument Valley, he made this otherworldly landscape a trademark of his filmmaking, using the valley as the backdrop for such films as *Stagecoach, She Wore a Yellow Ribbon, My Darling Clementine, Rio Grande,* and *The Searchers.* Other westerns filmed here have included *How the West Was Won, The Legend of the Lone Ranger,* and *Mackenna's Gold.* The valley has also shown up in such recent and not-so-recent films as *Back to the Future III, 2001: A Space Odyssey, Thelma and Louise,* and *Forrest Gump.* The red rocks of Sedona have also attracted many filmmakers over the years. *Broken Arrow, 3:10 to Yuma, The Cowboy and the Redhead, The Riders of the Purple Sage,* and *The Call of the Canyon* were all filmed in Sedona and the nearby Oak Creek Canyon.

Patagonia, in southeastern Arizona, is another town that has served as backdrop for quite a few films, including *Oklahoma, Red River, McClintock, Broken Lance, David and Bathsheba,* and *A Star Is Born,* and television programs including "Little House on the Prairie," "The Young Riders," and "Red Badge of Courage."

Among the films shot recently in Arizona are *Wyatt Earp, Geronimo, Red Rock West,* and *Maverick.*

desert floor, creating refuges for plants and animals that require cooler climates. It is these so-called mountain islands that harbor the greatest varieties of bird species in the continental United States. Birds from both warm and cold climates find homes in such oases as Ramsey Canyon, Madera Canyon, and Cave Creek Canyon.

Although rugged mountain ranges crisscross the state, only a few rise to such heights that they support actual forests. Among these are the Santa Catalinas outside Tucson, the White Mountains along the state's eastern border, and the San Franciscos north of Flagstaff. However, it's atop the Mogollon Rim and the Kaibab Plateau that these ponderosa pine forests cover the greatest areas. The Mogollon Rim is a 2,000-foot-high escarpment that stretches from central Arizona all the way into New Mexico. The ponderosa pine forest here is the largest in the world and is dotted with lakes well known for their fishing. At over 8,000 feet in elevation, the Kaibab Plateau is much higher than the Mogollon Rim, and it is through this plateau that the Grand Canyon cuts.

This then is the natural environment of Arizona, a land of extremes where summer temperatures in the Sonora Desert top 120° Fahrenheit while snow still lies atop the San Francisco Peaks. Life here has adapted to these extremes in fascinating ways that are still being deciphered by biologists throughout the state.

2 The Regions in Brief

The Valley of the Sun   This name refers to the sprawling metropolitan Phoenix area, which covers 420 square miles and includes more than 20 cities and communities surrounded by several distinct mountain ranges. It's the economic and population center of modern Arizona.

The Sonora Desert   Extending from Sonora, Mexico, in the south to central Arizona in the north, the Sonora Desert is surprisingly green and characterized by the massive saguaro cactus. It's in the Sonora Desert that most of Arizona's cities are found.

The Four Corners   The point where Arizona, Utah, Colorado, and New Mexico come together, it's the only place in the United States where four states share a common boundary. The Four Corners region of Arizona is almost entirely Hopi and Navajo reservation land. This high-plateau region of spectacular canyons and towering mesas and buttes includes Canyon de Chelly, the Painted Desert, and the Petrified Forest.

The White Mountains   Located in eastern Arizona, the White Mountains are laced with trout streams, covered by a huge pine forest, and home to far more wildlife than people. Arizona's largest and most popular ski area is located on the Apache Reservation near the town of McNary. Cooler temperatures make this region a very popular summer-vacation destination.

Arizona's West Coast   Though Arizona is a landlocked state, its western region is referred to as the West Coast because of the hundreds of miles of lakeshore that were created by the damming of the Colorado River. The low-lying stretches of the Colorado River are the hottest places in Arizona.

Canyon Country   From the Grand Canyon in the north to Oak Creek Canyon in the south, the rugged north-central part of the state alternates high, forested mountains with deep canyons. Through this region cuts the Mogollon Rim, a 2,000-foot-high escarpment that stretches for hundreds of miles from central Arizona into New Mexico.

The Arizona Strip   Located north of the Grand Canyon and bordering on southern Utah, this is one of the most remote and untraveled sections of Arizona. The Grand Canyon acts as a natural boundary between this region and the rest of the state.

Southeastern Arizona   Mile-high elevations make this one of the most temperate climates in the world. Tucson is at the northern edge of this region (and not so temperate), but otherwise there are few towns of any size. Mountain "islands" that rise out of the desert are home to more than 200 species of birds, and the wide grassy valleys make this a ranching region.

3 Arizona Today

Combining aspects of Native American, Hispanic, and European cultures, Arizona is one of the most culturally diverse states in the country. Here the Old West and the "New West" coexist. While the wealthy residents of Scottsdale raise Arabian horses as investments, the Navajos of the Four Corners region still raise sheep for sustenance and wool. Vacationers on Lake Powell waterski through flooded canyons while cowboys in the southeast corner of the state still ride the range mending fences and rounding up cattle.

Although Arizonans are today more likely to ride Hondas and Toyotas than pintos and appaloosas, western wear is still the preferred fashion of rich and poor alike. Cowboy boots, cowboy hats, blue jeans, and bola ties are acceptable attire at almost any function in Arizona. Horses are still used on ranches around the state, but most are kept simply for recreational or investment purposes. In Scottsdale, one of the nation's centers of Arabian horse breeding, horse auctions attract a well-heeled (read lizard-skin boots) crowd, and horses sell for tens of thousands of dollars. Even the state's dude ranches, which now call themselves "guest ranches," have changed their images and many are as likely to offer tennis and swimming as horseback riding.

A long legacy of movies being filmed here has further blurred the line between the real West and the Hollywood West. More city slickers wander the streets of the Old Tucson movie set and videotape shootouts at the O.K. Corral than ever saddle up a palomino or ride herd on a cattle drive. Dinner itself has been raised to a cowboy entertainment form at Arizona's many Wild West steakhouses, where families are entertained by cowboy bands, staged gunfights, hayrides, and singalongs, all in the name of reliving the glory days of "cowboys and Indians."

For Arizona's many Native Americans, those were days of hardship and misery, and today the state's many tribes continue to strive for the sort of economic well-being enjoyed by the state's non-Native population. At the same time, these tribes are also struggling to preserve their own unique cultures, which are reflected in language, religious beliefs and ceremonies, livelihoods, and architecture.

Arizona is home to the largest Native American reservation in the country—the Navajo Nation—as well as nearly two dozen other smaller reservations. As elsewhere in the United States, poverty and alcoholism are major problems on Arizona reservations. However, several of the state's tribes have, through their arts and crafts, managed to both preserve some of their traditional culture and share it with non-Natives. Among these tribes are the Navajo, known for their rugs and silver jewelry; the Hopi, known for their pottery and kachinas; the Zuñi, known for their inlaid stone jewelry; and the Tohono O'odham, known for their baskets.

Lately, however, many non-Natives have been visiting reservations not out of an interest in learning about another culture but rather to gamble. Throughout the state, casinos have opened on reservation land, and despite the controversies surrounding such enterprises, many Native peoples are finally seeing some income on their once-impoverished reservations.

> ## ❷ Did You Know?
>
> - Arizona has more mountainous regions (19,280 square miles) than Switzerland, and more forest land (19,902,000 acres) than Minnesota.
> - Arizona sided with the South during the American Civil War.
> - Arizona was the last territory in the continental United States to become a state.
> - The Four Corners, in the northeast corner of Arizona, adjoins Utah, Colorado, and New Mexico, the only spot where four states come together.
> - The Grand Canyon is one of the seven natural wonders of the world.
> - Some rocks in the Grand Canyon are more than two *billion* years old.
> - The Hopi village of Oraibi (along with Acoma, New Mexico) is the oldest continuously inhabited settlement in the United States.
> - Wyatt Earp, Ike Clanton, and the McLaury brothers really did have a shootout at the O.K. Corral in Tombstone.
> - Arizona has the highest per capita boat ownership of any state.
> - The Spanish were in Arizona a quarter century before St. Augustine, Florida, was founded and 70 years before the British founded Jamestown, Virginia.
> - The bola tie is the official state neckwear of Arizona.
> - Arizona produces more cotton per acre than any other state.
> - Arizonan Lorna Lockwood was the first woman chief justice of a state supreme court.
> - Arizonan Sandra Day O'Connor was the first woman appointed to the United States Supreme Court.

Many of the people who visit these new casinos are senior citizens, who are among the fastest-growing segment of Arizona's population. The mild winter climate in Arizona has attracted tens of thousands of retirees to the state over the past few decades. Many of these winter residents, known as "snowbirds," park their RVs outside such warm spots as Yuma and Quartzite. Others, however, have come to stay and have settled in such retirement communities as Sun City and Green Valley.

This graying of the population, combined with strong ranching and mining industries, has made Arizona one of the most conservative of states. Though by today's standards Barry Goldwater could almost be considered a liberal, his conservative politics were so much a part of the Arizona mind-set that the state kept him in the senate for 30 years.

This conservative legacy continues to the present. Recent years have been characterized by numerous political controversies. When Arizona, under Gov. Evan Mecham, chose not to recognize the Martin Luther King, Jr., holiday, the state was branded racist and lost millions of dollars in potential income from sporting events and conventions that chose not to be held in Arizona. The state finally acquiesed to public opinion and agreed to observe the holiday, which is perhaps one reason why Phoenix will finally be hosting the Super Bowl in 1996.

The controversial Governor Mecham was convicted in 1988 of illegally loaning state funds to his automobile dealership and of trying to block an investigation into charges that an aide made a death threat against a grand jury witness. (Mecham, by the way, was succeeded by Rose Mofford, the state's first woman governor.)

Within three years controversy again threw Arizona into the national limelight as Charles Keating was convicted of defrauding Lincoln Savings & Loan customers of $250 million. Among other places this money went was into the ostentatious Phoenician resort in Scottsdale and a smaller sister hotel, the Crescent, in Phoenix.

In 1995 the state legislature angered environmentalists the world over by voting to exempt itself from both federal law and an international agreement to ban the manufacture of freon, which is used in air-conditioning and may be partly responsible for the thinning of the ozone layer. Gov. Fife Symington, who signed this legislation, is a state's rights advocate who seems to be currying favor with those in the federal government with similar beliefs.

Though to many people the desert is a wasteland in need of transformation, others see it as a fragile ecosystem that has been endangered by the encroachment of civilization. Although saguaro cacti throughout the state are protected by law, the deserts they grow in are not. In Tucson, environmentalists have for several years been fighting to stop the suburban sprawl that's pushing farther and farther into saguaro country.

Way up at the north end of the state, remote Grand Canyon National Park is suffering from its own popularity. With more than five million visitors a year, the park now sees summer traffic jams and parking problems that have made a visit to the park an exercise in patience. Plans are currently under way to try to save the park from being loved to death.

These efforts at preserving the state's environment make it clear that Arizonans value the outdoors. However, a ski boat in every driveway doesn't mean that the arts are ignored. Although it hasn't been too many years since evening entertainment in Arizona meant dance-hall girls or a harmonica by the campfire, Phoenix and Tucson have become centers for both the visual and the performing arts. The two cities share both an opera company and a ballet company, and the Valley of the Sun is also home to a number of symphony orchestras and theater companies.

Even in small cities, local arts centers and festivals attract performers of national renown: Sedona stages jazz and classical music festivals, Flagstaff's Coconino Center for the Arts offers a full season of performances by musicians and dance companies from around the country, and even Grand Canyon Village, on the South Rim of the Grand Canyon, hosts an annual chamber music festival.

Small towns around the state are also supporting the arts. Whole communities such as Jerome, Tubac, and Bisbee, all nearly ghost towns at one time, have been reborn as arts communities. Where miners and outlaws once walked, artists now offer their creations for sale.

In Arizona today, the New West and the Old West are coming to grips with each other. Hopi perform their ages-old dances atop their mesas, urban cowboys and cowgirls line dance in nightclubs around the state, the grizzled wrangler leads a family of vacationing Germans on a horseback ride across open range, and ranchers find that they have something in common with environmentalists—saving Arizona's ranch lands.

4 A Look at the Past

Arizona is the site of North America's oldest cultures and the longest continuously inhabited settlement (Oraibi). Over the past five centuries it has been Native American territory and part of New Spain, Mexico, and the United States. Early explorers and settlers saw little to profit from in the desert wasteland, but time proved them wrong: mineral resources, cattle grazing, and particularly cotton (after dams began providing irrigation water) all became important income sources. In this century the economy has moved from the three Cs (copper, cattle, and cotton) to a service industries–based economy, with tourism one of its major resources.

EARLY HISTORY More than 11,000 years ago Paleo-Indians known as the Clovis people lived in southeastern Arizona, where stone tools and arrowheads have been found as evidence of their presence. A mammoth-kill site has also been discovered and has proved to be an important source of information about these people who were some of the earliest inhabitants of North America.

Few records exist of the next 9,000 years of Arizona's history, but by about A.D. 200, wandering bands of hunters and gatherers began living in Canyon de Chelly in the north. These people would come to be known as the Anasazi, a Navajo word that means "the ancient ones." The earliest Anasazi period, from A.D. 200 to 700, is called the Basketmaker period because of the numbers of baskets that have been found in Anasazi ruins from this time. During this period the Anasazi gave up hunting and gathering and took up agriculture, growing corn, beans, squash, and cotton on the canyon floors in northern and northeastern Arizona.

During the Pueblo period, between 700 and 1300, the Anasazi began building multistory pueblos (villages) and cliff dwellings. It's unknown why the Anasazi began living in niches and caves high on the cliff walls of the canyons. It may have been to conserve farmland as their population grew and required larger harvests, or for protection from flash floods or attacks by hostile neighbors. Whatever the reason, the Anasazi cliff dwellings were all abandoned by 1300. It's also unknown why the villages were abandoned, but a study of tree rings

Dateline

- **9700 B.C.** Paleo-Indians (the Clovis people) in southeastern Arizona are the earliest recorded inhabitants in North America.
- **A.D. 200** The Anasazi people move into Canyon de Chelly.
- **450** Hohokam peoples farm the Salt and Gila river valleys, eventually building 600 miles of irrigation canals.
- **650** The Sinagua cultivate land northeast of present-day Flagstaff.
- **1100s** Hopi tribes build Oraibi village, the oldest continuously occupied village in the U.S.; the Anasazi build cliff dwellings in Canyon de Chelly; the Sinagua build Wupatki.
- **1250** The Sinagua abandon Wupatki and other pueblos.
- **1300** The Anasazi abandon cliff dwellings in Canyon de Chelly and Tsegi Canyon.
- **1350** The Hohokam build Casa Grande in the Gila River valley.
- **1400s** The Navajo peoples migrate south from Canada to northeastern Arizona.
- **1450** The Hohokam abandon lowland desert villages; the Sinagua abandon Verde Valley villages.
- **1539** Marcos de Niza ventures into present-day Arizona from Mexico (New Spain) in search of the Seven Cities of Cibola.

continues

- 1540s Francisco Vásquez de Coronado leads an expedition to Arizona in search of gold.
- 1691 Jesuit Fr. Eusebio Kino begins converting Native Americans.
- 1751 The mission of Tumacacori and the presidio of Tubac are established, the first European settlement in Arizona.
- 1776 A Spanish garrison is posted in Tucson to protect the mission of San Xavier del Bac.
- 1821 Mexico gains independence from Spain and takes control of Arizona.
- 1848 Most of present-day Arizona ceded to the U.S. following the Mexican War.
- 1853 In the Gadsden Purchase, U.S. acquires the remainder of Arizona from Mexico.
- 1862 Arizona becomes the Confederate Territory of Arizona, but is reclaimed by the Union later that same year.
- 1863 Arizona becomes a U.S. territory.
- 1886 Geronimo surrenders to the U.S. Army.
- 1911 Theodore Roosevelt Dam, on the Salt River, enables irrigation and development of the desert.
- 1912 Arizona becomes the 48th state.
- 1919 Grand Canyon National Park established.
- 1936 Hoover Dam completed.
- 1948 Arizona Native Americans receive the right to vote.
- 1963 U.S. Supreme Court upholds Arizona's claim to Colorado River water.

continues

indicates that the region experienced a severe drought between 1276 and 1299, which suggests that the Anasazi left in search of more fertile farmland. Keet Seel and Betatakin, at Navajo National Monument, and the many ruins in Canyon de Chelly are Arizona's best-preserved Anasazi ruins.

During the Anasazi Basketmaker period, another culture was beginning to develop in the fertile plateau northeast of present-day Flagstaff and southward into the Verde River valley. The Sinagua, a Spanish name that means "without water," built their stone pueblos primarily on hills and mesas such as those at Tuzigoot near Clarkdale and Wupatki near Flagstaff. They also built some cliff dwellings at such places as Walnut Canyon and Montezuma Castle. By the mid-13th century Wupatki had been abandoned by the Sinagua, and by the early 15th century they had also abandoned Walnut Canyon and the lower Verde Valley region.

By A.D. 450 the Hohokam culture, from whom the Sinagua learned irrigation, had begun to farm the Gila and Salt river valleys between Phoenix and Casa Grande. Over a period of 1,000 years they constructed a 600-mile network of irrigation canals, some of which can still be seen today. Because the Hohokam built their homes of earth, few Hohokam ruins remain. However, one building, the Casa Grande, has been well preserved. Throughout this desert region the Hohokam carved many petroglyphs. By the 1450s the tribe had abandoned its villages and disappeared without a sign, hence the name Hohokam, a Tohono O'odham Native American word meaning "all used up" or "the people who have gone." Archaeologists believe that the irrigation of desert soil for hundreds of years had left a thick crust of alkali on the surface, and this made farming no longer possible.

HISPANIC HERITAGE The first Europeans to visit the region may have been a motley crew of shipwrecked Spaniards (and one Moor named Estévan) who spent eight years wandering from a beach in Florida to a Spanish village in Mexico. These wanderers arrived back in Spanish territory with a fantastic story of seven cities filled with goldsmiths, where doorways were encrusted with jewels. No one is sure whether they actually passed through Arizona, but their story convinced the viceroy of New Spain (Mexico) to send a small expedition, led by Fr. Marcos de Niza and Estévan. Father de Niza's report of finding the fabled Seven Cities of Cibola also inspired Don Francisco Vásquez de Coronado to set off in search of wealth. However, instead of fabulously wealthy cities, Coronado found only pueblos of stone and mud. A subordinate expedition led by Garcia Lopez de Cárdenas stumbled upon the Grand Canyon, while another group of Coronado's men, led by Don Pedro de Tovar, visited the Hopi mesas.

In the 150 years that followed, only a handful of Spaniards visited Arizona. In the 1580s and 1600s, Antonio de Espejo and Juan de Oñate explored northern and central Arizona and found indications that there were mineral riches in the region. In the 1670s the Franciscans founded several missions among the Hopi pueblos, but the Pueblo Revolt of 1680 obliterated this small Spanish presence.

In 1687 Fr. Eusebio Francisco Kino, a German-educated Italian Jesuit, began establishing missions in the Sonora Desert region of northern New Spain. In 1691 he visited the Pima village of Tumacacori. Father Kino taught the inhabitants European farming techniques, planted fruit trees, and gave the natives cattle, sheep, and goats to raise. However, it was not until 1751, in response to a Pima rebellion, that the permanent mission of Tumacacori and the presidio (military post) of Tubac were built, which became the first European settlement in Arizona.

- **1974** Construction begins on the Central Arizona Project aqueducts.
- **1975** Raul Castro becomes the first Hispanic governor of Arizona.
- **1981** Arizona judge Sandra Day O'Connor becomes the first woman appointed to the U.S. Supreme Court.
- **1985** The Central Arizona Project begins delivering water to Phoenix.
- **1988** Gov. Evan Mecham removed from office.
- **1991** A California jury finds Charles Keating guilty of defrauding Arizona investors who had deposited funds with Lincoln Savings & Loan.
- **1992** A Tucson jury awards $3 billion in damages to investors who were defrauded in the failed Lincoln Savings & Loan.
- **1995** The Arizona state legislature refuses to ban the manufacture and sale of freon.

In 1775 a group of settlers led by Juan Bautista de Anza set out from Tubac to find an overland route to California, and in 1776 founded the city of San Francisco. That same year the Tubac presidio was moved to Tucson. Father Kino had visited the Tucson area in 1692 and in 1700 had laid out the foundations for the first church at the mission of San Xavier del Bac. However, construction of the present church, known as the White Dove of the Desert, probably did not begin until 1783.

In 1821 Mexico won its independence from Spain, and Tucson, with only 65 inhabitants, became part of Mexico. Mexico at that time extended all the way to northern California, but in 1848 most of this land, except for a small section of southern Arizona that included Tucson, became U.S. territory in the wake of the Mexican-American War. Five years later, in 1853, Mexico sold the remainder of southern Arizona to the United States in a transaction known as the Gadsden Purchase.

INDIAN CONFLICTS   At the time that the Spanish arrived in Arizona, the tribes living in the southern lowland deserts were peaceful farmers, while in the mountains of the east lived the Apache, a hunting-and-gathering tribe that frequently raided neighboring tribes. In the north, the Navajo, relatively recent immigrants to the region, fought with the neighboring Hopi and Ute over land, and the Hopi even fought among themselves.

Coronado's expedition through Arizona and into New Mexico and Kansas was to seek gold. To that end he attacked one pueblo, killed the inhabitants of another, and forced still others to abandon their villages. Spanish-Indian relations were never to improve, and the Spanish were forced to occupy their new lands with a strong military presence. Around 1600, 300 Spanish settlers moved into the Four Corners region, which at the time supported a large population of Navajo. The Spanish raided Navajo villages to take slaves, and angry Navajo responded by stealing Spanish horses and cattle.

For several decades in the mid-1600s missionaries were tolerated in the Hopi pueblos, but the Pueblo tribes revolted in 1680, killing the missionaries and destroying the missions. Encroachment by farmers and miners moving into the Santa Cruz Valley in the south caused the Pima people to stage a similar uprising in 1751, attacking and burning the mission at Tubac. This revolt led to the establishment of the presidio at Tubac that same year. When the military garrison moved to Tucson, Tubac was quickly abandoned because of frequent raids by Apaches. The Yuman tribe, whose land at the confluence of the Colorado and Gila rivers had become a Spanish settlement, staged a similar uprising that wiped out the Spanish settlement at Yuma in 1781.

By the time Arizona became part of the United States, it was the Navajo and the Apache who were proving most resistant to white settlers. In 1864 the U.S. Army, under the leadership of Col. Kit Carson, forced the Navajo to surrender by destroying their winter food supplies, then shipped them to an internment camp in New Mexico. Within five years they were returned to their land, though they were now forced to live on a reservation.

The Apache resisted white settlement 20 years longer than the Navajo. Skillful guerrilla fighters, the Apache were able to attack settlers, forts, and towns despite the presence of U.S. Army troops sent to protect the white settlers. Geronimo and Cochise were the leaders of the last resistant bands of rebellious Apache. Cochise eventually died in his Chiracahua Mountains homeland and Geronimo was finally forced to surrender in 1886. Geronimo and many of his followers were subsequently relocated to Florida by the U.S. government. Open conflicts between whites and Native Americans finally came to an end.

TERRITORIAL DAYS   In 1846 the United States went to war with Mexico, which at the time extended all the way to northern California and included parts of Colorado, Wyoming, and New Mexico. When the war ended, the United States claimed almost all the land extending from Texas to northern California; called the New Mexico Territory, it had its capital at Santa Fe. The land south of the Gila River, which included Tucson, was still part of Mexico, but when surveys determined that this land was the best route for a railroad from southern Mississippi to southern California, the U.S. government negotiated the Gadsden Purchase. In 1853 this land purchase established the current Arizona-Mexico border.

When the California gold rush began in 1849, many hopeful miners crossed Arizona en route to the goldfields, and some stayed to seek mineral riches in Arizona. However, despite the ever-increasing numbers of settlers, the U.S. Congress refused to create a separate Arizona Territory. When the Civil War broke out, Arizonans, angered by Congress's inaction on their request to become a separate territory, sided with the Confederacy; in 1862 Arizona was proclaimed the

Confederate Territory of Arizona. Although Union troops easily defeated the Confederate troops who had occupied Tucson, this dissension convinced Congress, in 1863, to create the Arizona Territory.

The capital of the new territory was temporarily established at Fort Whipple near Prescott, but later the same year the capital was moved to Prescott, and in 1867 to Tucson. Ten years later Prescott again became the capital, which it remained for another 12 years before the seat of government moved finally to Phoenix, which is today the Arizona state capital.

During this period mining flourished, and though small amounts of gold and silver were discovered, copper became the source of Arizona's economic wealth. With each new mineral strike a new mining town would boom, and when the ore ran out the town would be abandoned. These towns were infamous for their gambling halls, bordellos, saloons, and shootouts in the street. Tombstone and Bisbee became the largest towns in the state, and were known as the wildest towns between New Orleans and San Francisco.

In 1867 farmers in the newly founded town of Phoenix began irrigating their fields using canals that had been dug centuries earlier by the Hohokam peoples. In the 1870s ranching became another important source of revenue in the territory, particularly in the southeastern and northwestern parts of the state. In the 1880s the railroads finally arrived and life in Arizona began to change drastically. Suddenly the mineral resources and cattle of the region were accessible to the East.

STATEHOOD & THE 20TH CENTURY   By the turn of the 20th century Arizonans were trying to convince Congress to make the territory a state. Congress balked at the requests, but finally, in 1910, allowed the territorial government to draw up a state constitution. Territorial legislators were progressive thinkers and the draft of Arizona's state constitution included clauses for the recall of elected officials. President William Howard Taft vetoed the bill that would have made Arizona a state because he opposed the recall of judges. Arizona politicians removed the controversial clause, and, on February 14, 1912, Arizona became the 48th state. One of the new state legislature's first acts was to reinstate the clause providing for the recall of judges.

Much of Washington's opposition to Arizona's statehood had been based on the belief that Arizona could never support economic development. This belief was changed in 1911 by one of the most important events in Arizona history—the completion of the Roosevelt Dam (later to be renamed the Theodore Roosevelt Dam) on the Salt River. The dam provided irrigation water to the Valley of the Sun and tamed the violent floods of the river. The introduction of water to the heart of Arizona's vast desert enabled large-scale agriculture and industry. Over the next decades more dams were built throughout Arizona. Completed in 1936, the Hoover Dam on the Colorado River became the largest concrete dam in the western hemisphere and formed the largest man-made reservoir in North America. Arizona's dams would eventually provide not only water and electricity but recreational areas.

Impressions

If the world were searched over, I suppose there could not be found so degraded a set of villains as then formed the principal society of Tucson.
—J. Ross Browne, a visitor to Tucson in 1863

Despite labor problems, copper mining increased throughout the 1920s and 1930s, and with the onset of World War II the mines boomed as military munitions manufacturing increased demand for copper. However, within a few years after the war many mines were shut down. Arizona is still littered with old mining ghost towns that boomed and then went bust. A few towns, such as Jerome, Bisbee, and Chloride, managed to hang on after the mines shut down and were eventually rediscovered by artists, writers, and retirees. Bisbee and Jerome have now become artists' colonies and major tourist attractions.

World War II also created demand for cotton (which became the state's most important crop), beef, and leather. Clear desert skies were ideal for training pilots, and several military bases were established in the state. Phoenix's population doubled during the war years, and after the war many veterans returned with their families. However, it would take the invention of air-conditioning to truly open up the desert to major population growth.

During the postwar years Arizona attracted a number of large manufacturing industries and slowly moved away from its agricultural economic base. Today, electronics manufacturing, aerospace engineering, and other high-tech industries provide employment for thousands of Arizonans. The largest segment of the economy, however, is now in the service industries, with tourism playing a crucial role.

Even by the 1920s Arizona had become a winter destination for the wealthy, and the Grand Canyon, declared a national park in 1919, lured more and more visitors every year. The clear dry air attracted people suffering from allergies and lung ailments, and Arizona became known as a healthful place. Guest ranches of the 1930s gave way to the resorts of the 1980s. Today Scottsdale and Phoenix together have the greatest concentration of resorts in the United States. In addition, tens of thousands of retirees from as far north as Canada make Arizona their winter home and now play a crucial role in Arizona's economy.

Continued population growth throughout the 20th century created greater demand for water. However, despite the damming of virtually all of Arizona's rivers, the state still suffered from insufficient water supplies in the south-central population centers of Phoenix and Tucson. It would take the construction of the controversial and expensive Central Arizona Project (CAP) aqueduct to carry water from the Colorado River, over mountains and deserts, and deliver it where it was wanted. Construction on the CAP began in 1974, and in 1985 water from the project finally began irrigating fields near Phoenix. In 1992, the CAP finally reached Tucson. However, with the populations of Phoenix, Tucson, and Las Vegas skyrocketing, the future of Colorado River water usage may again become a question for hot debate.

By the 1960s Arizona had become an urban state with all the problems confronting cities around the nation. The once-healthful air of Phoenix now rivals that of Los Angeles for the thickness of its smog. Allergy sufferers are plagued by pollen from the nondesert plants that have been planted to make this desert region look more lush and inviting. Resistance to construction of interstate freeways in the Phoenix area caused that city to become one of the most congested in the nation, and today major highway construction projects are only just beginning to relieve the congestion. In the early 1980s, as industry fled from the North to the Sunbelt states, Arizona experienced an economic boom that by the end of the decade had turned to a bust. Today, however, the state's economy is once again growing. High-tech companies continue to locate within the state, and the continued influx of both retirees and Californians fleeing earthquakes and urban

Impressions

O yes, I have heard of that country—it is just like hell. All it lacks is water and good society.

—A 19th-century senator from Ohio

problems is giving the state new energy and new ideas. The signing of the North American Free Trade Agreement (NAFTA) also gave the state an economic shot in the arm and companies have been taking full advantage of the increased trade with Mexico, the state's southern neighbor.

5 Southwestern Cuisine

In the past decade regional cuisines have become all the rage with chefs and diners across the United States. Southwestern cuisine, whose hallmarks are the spices of Mexico (especially chile peppers), the unusual fruit-and-meat pairings of nouvelle cuisine, and flame-broiling over mesquite, has become one of the most popular cuisines in the country. The blue corn industry has been thriving as creative chefs in Arizona, New Mexico, and around the country try their hand at concocting new dishes from ingredients both familiar and foreign.

Southwestern cuisine has become so much a part of the dining scene in Arizona that even in small-town restaurants you'll probably encounter dishes like mesquite-grilled breast of chicken served with a fresh-fruit salsa. In the cities, meanwhile, chefs are still dreaming up new creations such as pistachio-crusted breast of duckling with a fig-and-orange chutney. Pacific salmon might be served with smoked yellow-pepper sauce and roasted black-bean and corn relish, while roast squab might be served with twice-cooked bacon and chipotle pepper and cider sauce. Other dishes might include marinated ahi with avocado-papaya salsa and cilantro-scallion aïoli, or southwestern bouillabaisse with grilled nopal cactus. Even desserts get the desert treatment as shown in such an outlandish, though tasty, concoction as chile-chocolate cake.

A new trend is that many of the restaurants that once served such dishes as those mentioned above have now moved on to milder, more subtle flavors. What with all the chile peppers, southwestern just isn't for everyone. It's still the realm of expensive gourmet restaurants where you can expect to pay at least $30 per person for dinner. In the Phoenix and Tucson chapters of this book, you'll find several restaurants specializing in southwestern cuisine.

Arizona also offers some of the best Mexican food in the country. A few years back the mayor of Tucson even declared that the city was the Mexican restaurant capital of the universe. One specialty that you're likely to encounter at Arizona's Mexican restaurants, especially in Tucson, is *carne seca*, which is air-dried beef that's shredded and added to various sauces. It has a very distinctive texture and shouldn't be missed.

6 Local Arts & Crafts

Though Santa Fe has claimed the Southwest's arts spotlight in recent years, Arizona, too, is a mecca for artists. The Cowboy Artists of America, an organization of artists dedicated to capturing in their art the lives and landscapes of the Old

West, was formed in a tavern in Sedona in 1965 by Joe Beeler, George Phippen, Bob McLeod, Charlie Dye, John Hampton, and a few other local artists. Working primarily in oils and bronze, members of this organization depicted the lives of cowboys and Native Americans in their art, and today their work is sought after by collectors throughout the country.

As more and more artists and craftspeople headed for Arizona, the towns in which they congregated came to be known as artists' colonies, and galleries sprang up to serve a growing numbers of visitors. Although Sedona is probably the best known of these colonies, others include Jerome and Bisbee, both mining towns that came close to becoming ghost towns before being discovered by artists, and Tubac, the first Spanish settlement in Arizona. All three of these towns have numerous art galleries and crafts shops.

Red-rock canyons, pensive Native Americans, hardworking cowboys, desert wildflowers, majestic mesas, and stately saguaros have been the themes of this century's representational artists of Arizona. Although contemporary abstract art can be found in museums and galleries, the style pioneered by Frederic Remington and Charles M. Russell in the early 20th century still dominates the Arizona art scene. Remington, Russell, and those who followed in their footsteps romanticized the West, imbuing their depictions of cowboys, Indians, settlers, and soldiers with mythic proportions that would be taken up by Hollywood.

Further back, even before the first Spanish explorers arrived in Arizona, the ancient Anasazi were creating an artistic legacy in their intricately woven baskets, painted pottery, and cryptic petroglyphs and pictographs. In recent years both contemporary Native American and non-Native artists have been drawing on Anasazi designs for their works. Today's Hopi, Navajo, and Zuñi artisans have become well known for their jewelry, which is made of silver and semiprecious stones, primarily turquoise. The Hopi now carve images of their traditional kachina for distribution in the marketplace, and the Navajo continue to weave traditional patterns in their rugs. The Zuñi, noted for their skill in carving stone, have focused on their traditional animal fetishes. However, since the founding of the Santa Fe Indian School in 1932, and later the Institute of American Indian Art, Native American artists have also ventured into the realm of painting. Hopi artist Fred Kabotie and his son, Michael Kabotie, are among the best-known Native American painters.

Collectors and those with a casual interest in southwestern art will find local arts and crafts available in every corner of the state. From exclusive Scottsdale galleries to roadside stands on the Navajo reservation, Arizona arts and crafts are ubiquitous. The best places to look for southwestern and the cowboy (or western) art are in Scottsdale, Tucson, Sedona, Tubac, and Jerome. Native American crafts can be found in these same towns, but it's somewhat more rewarding to visit trading posts and reservation galleries.

The best known of these are the Hubbell Trading Post in Ganado and the Cameron Trading Post in Cameron, but there are trading posts all over the state and almost all offer excellent selection and quality. Keep in mind that no matter where you shop for Native American arts and crafts, you'll find that prices are high.

The Native American tribes of Arizona tend to have one or two specialty crafts that they produce with consummate skill. Many of these crafts were disappearing when the first traders came to the reservations a century ago. Today most of the crafts are alive and well, but primarily as sale items. Prices are high because of the many hours that go into producing these crafts. However, keep in mind that what you're buying is handmade using a skill that has been handed down for generations.

If you're a price-conscious shopper, you'll be interested to know that museum gift shops do not charge sales tax. You can also avoid paying sales tax if you live outside Arizona and have your purchase shipped directly to your home. On a high-ticket item such as a Navajo rug, you could save quite a bit. Also keep in mind that it's a good idea to make your jewelry purchases from reputable stores rather than from roadside stalls, of which there are many in the Four Corners region of the state. Many of these stalls sell cheap imitation jewelry.

Following are brief discussions of individual Native crafts (see also "A Native American Crafts Primer" in Chapter 8):

NAVAJO RUGS   Rugs have been made only since traders came to the Navajo reservation. Prior to that the Navajo had woven only blankets. Women are the weavers in the Navajo tribe, with the skill passed down from mother to daughter. A single rug only a few feet square takes hundreds of hours to make, much of the time spent in preparing the wool, dyeing it, and setting up the primitive loom. The best rugs are those made from hand-spun wool from local Navajo sheep and goats. Vegetal dyes, which generally produce very muted colors, are considered superior to chemical dyes, but are of course more time-consuming to prepare. When shopping for a rug, check the fineness of the weave and the amount of detail in the design. Finer weave and detail mean higher prices because of the additional time required to produce such a rug. Be prepared to spend $1,000 or more for even a small Navajo rug; even at this price the women who make the rugs are making less than minimum wage for their labor. At the Hubbell Trading Post in Ganado you can see Navajo women weaving rugs.

HOPI KACHINAS   Kachinas, the colorful and often-grotesque dolls of the Hopi people, are representations of the spirits of animals, ancestors, places, and other things. Styles of kachinas vary from village to village. Carved from cottonwood root or other wood, kachinas are then colorfully painted and decorated with feathers, leather capes, and bits of yarn. The finished doll is meant to resemble closely the costume and mask worn by kachina dancers during the annual religious ceremonies held in Hopi villages. Traditionally, kachina dolls have been given to young Hopi girls to help them learn about the different kachina spirits. Today, however, many carvers are creating kachinas specifically for sale. Among the more popular kachinas are the humorous *tsuku* or clown kachinas, which are often painted with bold black and white stripes. A detailed kachina will cost several hundred dollars.

ZUÑI FETISHES   The Zuñi have long been known for their stone-carving skills, which are best demonstrated in their small carved animal fetishes. A fetish is an object in which a spirit dwells, and such objects have always been important to the Zuñi people. Carved from various types of stone, including turquoise and jet, Zuñi fetishes traditionally depict eagles, bears, wolves, mountain lions, horses, and goats, each of which is associated with a particular compass direction. Often fetishes are decorated with turquoise and coral beads, feathers, and miniature arrowheads, all of which are tied to the body of the fetish with gut. Bear fetishes often feature inlaid heartlines, arrow-shaped lines running from the mouth down the side to the center of the body.

Before buying a fetish, it's a good idea to look at enough of them so that you can see the difference between one that's crudely carved and one that exhibits fine detail. Fetish prices start as low as $30 but most are at least $100.

TOHONO O'ODHAM BASKETS   Although virtually all the Arizona tribes produce some sort of basketry, the Tohono O'odham tribe, which has its reservation near Tucson, has come to be known for its baskets. Most Tohono O'odham baskets are made using the coil method. Bear grass is used as the center of the coil, which is then stitched together with bleached yucca and the dark outer covering of the devil's claw seedpod. The Tohono O'odham also make miniature baskets from horsehair. These baskets require all the skill of full-size baskets but are often no more than 2 inches across. One of the most common Tohono O'odham designs shows a human figure in the middle of a maze. This figure is I'itoi (Elder Brother) and the maze represents the route to his home in the Baboquivari Mountains. Simple small baskets can be purchased for less than $50, but a basket that's finely woven and has a complex design may cost several hundred dollars.

JEWELRY   The Navajo, Hopi, and Zuñi all make jewelry, and each tribe has its own distinctive style. The Navajo are well known for heavy silver jewelry that's made primarily by sand casting. The squash-blossom necklace, which is based on an old Spanish symbol, actually features pomegranate blossoms rather than squash blossoms, but was adapted to Navajo tastes. The Navajo tend to place the emphasis on fine silverwork accented by turquoise stones.

The Zuñi, on the other hand, use silver primarily as a setting for their stone carvings. Using turquoise, jet, coral, other semiprecious stones, and seashells, the Zuñi create colorful inlaid images. Another style of Zuñi jewelry features tiny pieces of cut and polished turquoise individually set in delicate grid and starburst patterns.

The Hopi are known for their overlay silverwork, which uses two sheets of silver fused together. The upper sheet of silver has a design cut into it with a tiny saw, while the lower sheet is treated to produce a contrasting black background to the upper layer. In recent years Hopi jewelry has featured ancient Anasazi designs taken from baskets and pottery.

Prices for jewelry vary widely depending on the amount of detail, the amount of silver, and the number of stones.

POTTERY   Although the tribes of New Mexico are much better known for their pottery, Arizona tribes such as the Hopi, Navajo, and Tohono O'odham also make pottery. For years Navajo pottery was crudely made and not very attractive, but in recent years Navajo potters have begun experimenting with new and ancient designs and have begun to produce appealing pottery for sale.

Hopi pottery is almost all made in the village of Hotevilla on First Mesa. It's an orange color and is sometimes incised or decorated with geometric designs in black.

Tohono O'odham pottery is very simple and not as well known as their basketry.

Pottery prices vary considerably, but generally are not nearly as high here as they are in the New Mexico pueblos.

7 Desert Architecture: From Pueblos to Frank Lloyd Wright

Centuries before the first Europeans arrived in Arizona, the Anasazi people were building elaborate villages, which have come to be known by their Spanish name—pueblos. Many, but not all, of the Anasazi pueblos were built high on cliff walls in the rugged canyon lands of northern Arizona. Constructed of cut stones mortared together and roofed with logs and earth, the pueblo dwellings had thick walls that provided insulation from heat and cold, and the tops of flat roofs provided a place to do chores. Pueblo architecture was characterized by small rooms with no windows. Some rooms were used for living, while others served as grain-storage rooms.

Earlier, the Anasazi developed a type of shelter known as a pit house, which was partially dug into the ground. Eventually these flat-roofed stone houses were adapted to apartment-style construction techniques when they moved up into the canyon walls. The pit-house style of architecture was retained in the form of the *kiva*, a round ceremonial room that's still used by the Hopi, Arizona's contemporary pueblo dwellers.

The Sinagua, a culture that developed at the same time as the Anasazi, built similar stone pueblos, but most Sinagua pueblos were on hills rather than in the canyons. At the Wupatki ruins, near Flagstaff, there are two unusual stone structures that were built by the Sinagua. One is a ball court similar in many ways to the ball courts of central Mexico and Central America. The other unusual building is a low-walled round structure that may have been an amphitheater or large kiva.

Many Hopis still live in pueblos similar to those built by the Sinagua and Anasazi, with stone-walled rooms and round kivas that have ladders sticking through the roof (entrance to a kiva is prohibited to non-Hopis). The *hogan*, the traditional home of the Navajo people, displays a very different type of architecture. Usually built with six sides, hogans are constructed of logs and earth and resemble ancient dwellings of central Asia.

When the Spanish arrived in Arizona, they turned to sun-baked adobe bricks as their primary construction material. Because adobe walls must be made very thick, they provide excellent insulation. Very few adobe homes have survived from territorial days because, when not maintained, adobe quickly decays. The best place to see adobe homes is in Tucson, where several have been preserved in that city's downtown historic districts. However, when the railroads arrived in Arizona, many owners modified their adobe homes by adding slanted roofs, Victorian porches, and even siding. In the Barrio Historico district of Tucson, town-house architecture characteristic of Sonora, Mexico, has been preserved. These buildings have no front yards but instead have walls right at the sidewalk. This style of architecture was common during the Mexican and early territorial periods of Arizona history.

With only the two mission churches of San Xavier del Bac and Tumacacori, the Spanish did not leave as great an ecclesiastical architectural legacy in Arizona as they did elsewhere in the New World. However, mission-revival architecture has been popular for much of this century. A somewhat idealized concept of the style—with stucco walls, arches, and courtyards—has come to epitomize the ideal of Arizona living.

In the mid-20th century, architect Frank Lloyd Wright established his winter home and school, called Taliesin West, north of Scottsdale, and eventually designed several buildings around the Phoenix area. The architect of the Biltmore Hotel, one of the state's oldest resorts, relied on Wright for assistance in designing the hotel, and the hand of Wright is evident throughout. One of Wright's students, an Italian architect named Paolo Soleri, decided to settle in Arizona, and has for many years pursued his dream of building an environmentally sensitive, ideal city in the desert north of Phoenix. He calls this city Arcosanti and has partially financed its construction by selling wind-bells at his Cosanti foundry in Paradise Valley. Arcosanti, the Cosanti foundry, and Taliesin West are open to the public.

8 Recommended Books

GENERAL   Few places on earth have inspired as much writing as Arizona's Grand Canyon. John Wesley Powell's *Down the Colorado: Diary of the First Trip Down the Grand Canyon* (E. P. Dutton, 1969), which was first published in 1869, and David Lavendar's *River Runners of the Grand Canyon* (University of Arizona, 1985), an illustrated history of river exploration, provide the explorers' and adventurers' view of the canyon. *The Grand Canyon: Early Impressions* (Pruett, 1989), edited by Paul Schullery, is a collection of first impressions by famous writers including John Muir and Zane Grey. *The Man Who Walked Through Time* (Random House, 1972), by Colin Fletcher, is a narrative of one man's hike through the rugged inner canyon. Even Barry Goldwater, a rather accomplished writer, had his say on the Grand Canyon in his book *Delightful Journey: Down the Green and Colorado Rivers* (Arizona Historical Foundation, 1970). In *Grand Canyon* (Morrow, 1968), Joseph W. Krutch, a brilliant observer of nature, distills his observations of the canyon into expressive prose.

Water rights and man's impact on the deserts of the Southwest have raised many controversies this century, none more heated than those centering around the Colorado River. *Cadillac Desert: The American West and Its Disappearing Water* (Penguin, 1987), by Marc Reisner, focuses on the West's insatiable need for water, while *A River No More: The Colorado River and the West* (Knopf, 1981), by Philip L. Fradkin, addresses the fate of just the one river.

The famous Lost Dutchman Mine has inspired at least two books: *Fool's Gold* (Golden West, 1983), by Robert Sihorsky, and *The Treasure of the Superstitions* (Norton, 1973), by Gary Jennings.

Arizona, A Bicentennial History (Norton, 1976), by Lawrence Clark Powell, provides a thorough history of the state. *Arizona Memories* (University of Arizona, 1984), edited by Anne H. Morgan and Rennard Strickland, is an engaging collection of historical recollections by cowboys, miners, an Apache scout, a frontier doctor, a soldier's wife, and many other Arizonans. In *Home Is the Desert* (University of Arizona, 1984), Ann Woodin addresses the mental and spiritual development that her family experienced when they moved to the desert outside Tucson. In his book *The Desert Year* (Viking, 1963), naturalist Joseph W. Krutch combines his observations of Arizona's deserts with his own personal philosophical observations. Another book well worth searching out is *Cactus Country* (Time-Life Books, 1973), which is full of beautiful photos of the Sonora Desert, but which is more notable for its text by Edward Abbey, who was one of the desert's most outspoken and controversial supporters. Abbey is well known as a brilliant, though cynical, observer of the desert, and captures the desert's many moods in *Desert Solitaire* (McGraw-Hill, 1968), a nonfiction work based on his time spent in southern Utah's Arches National Monument.

Southwestern Indian Arts & Crafts (current edition by Tom Bahti's son, Mark Bahti), *Southwestern Indian Ceremonials,* and *Southwestern Indian Tribes* (all KC Publications) is a trio of softcover books illustrated with color photos by Southwest Native American authority Tom Bahti, and provides an accessible source of information on several aspects of Southwest tribal life. Other books on Arizona's Native American tribes include *The Navajo* (Harvard University Press, 1974), by Clyde Kluckhohn and Dorothea Leighton; *The People Called Apache* (Prentice-Hall, 1974), by Thomas E. Mails; and *Anasazi: Ancient People of the Rock* (Crown, 1974), with text by Donald G. Pike and photos by David Muench.

FICTION   Arizona's rugged landscape, colorful history, and rich Native American culture have long served as backdrops for fiction writers. Tony Hillerman is perhaps the best-known contemporary author whose books rely on Arizona settings. Hillerman's murder mysteries are almost all set on the Navajo Reservation in the Four Corners area, and include many references to actual locations that can be seen by visitors to the area. Among Hillerman's Navajo mysteries are *Sacred Clowns, Coyote Waits, Thief of Time, The Blessing Way, Listening Woman,* and *The Ghostway.*

Barbara Kingsolver, a Tucson resident, biologist, and social activist, sets her novels either partly or entirely in Arizona. *The Bean Trees, Pigs in Heaven,* and *Animal Dreams* are peopled by Anglo, Native American, and Hispanic characters and their traditions, allowing for a quirky and humorous narrative with social and political overtones that allow insight into the cultural melange of Arizona.

Edward Abbey's *The Monkey Wrench Gang* and *Hayduke Lives!* are tales of an unlikely gang of "eco-terrorists" determined to preserve the wildernesses of the Southwest. The former book helped inspire the founding of the radical Earth First movement.

Laughing Boy (Buccaneer Books, 1981), by Oliver LaFarge, is a somewhat-idealized narrative of Navajo life that won the Pulitzer Prize in 1929. Many novels of pioneer life in Arizona have been made into popular films. These include *Foxfire* (Houghton, 1950), by Anya Seton, the story of a young woman from the East who moves to Arizona to marry a part-Apache mining engineer, and Henry Will's *Mackenna's Gold* (Random House, 1963), a story of the search for a lost mine in the Arizona mountains.

Zane Grey spent many years living in north-central Arizona and based many of his western novels on life in this region of the state. Among his books are *Riders of the Purple Sage, West of the Pecos, The Vanishing American, The Arizona Clan,* and *To the Last Man.*

TRAVEL   *Arizona Highways* is a monthly magazine published by the Arizona Department of Transportation. The magazine has been known for decades for its outstanding photographs and stories on history and attractions.

3

Planning a Trip to Arizona

Whether you're headed to Arizona to raft the grand canyon or play golf in Phoenix, you probably have a few questions you'd like answered. When should I go? What shouldn't I miss? What's the best way to get there? How much is it going to cost? These are the kinds of questions that this chapter addresses.

1 Visitor Information & Money

VISITOR INFORMATION

If you have more questions than we can answer in this book, there are a number of places that may have the answers for you. For statewide travel information, contact the **Arizona Office of Tourism,** 1100 W. Washington St., Phoenix, AZ 85007 (☎ **602/ 542-TOUR** or 800/842-8257; fax 602/542-4068). Also keep in mind that every city and town in Arizona has either a tourism office or chamber of commerce that can provide you with information. See the individual chapters for addresses of these sources.

If you're a member of the **American Automobile Association (AAA),** remember that you can get a map and guidebook covering Arizona and New Mexico.

MONEY

What will a vacation in Arizona cost? That depends on your comfort needs. If you drive an RV or carry a tent, you can get by very inexpensively and find a place to stay almost anywhere in the state. If you don't mind staying in motels that date back to the Great Depression and can sleep on a sagging mattress, you can stay for less money in Arizona than almost anyplace else in the United States (under $25 a night for a double). On the other hand, you can easily spend several hundred dollars a day on a room at one of the state's world-class resorts. If you're looking to stay in clean, modern motels at Interstate highway off-ramps, expect to pay $40 to $65 a night for a double room in most places.

When it comes time to eat, you can get a great meal almost anywhere in the state for under $25, but if you want to spend more—or less—that's also possible.

What Things Cost in Phoenix	U.S. $
Taxi from the airport to Scottsdale	14.00
Local telephone call	.25
Double room at the Phoenician (expensive)	300.00
Double room at Scottsdale's Fifth Avenue Inn (moderate)	82.00
Double room at the Travelodge Metrocenter (inexpensive)	47.00
Lunch for one at Malee's on Main (moderate)	12.00
Lunch for one at Ed Debevic's (inexpensive)	7.00
Dinner for one, without wine, at Christopher's (expensive)	50.00
Dinner for one, without wine, at Rawhide (moderate)	21.00
Dinner for one, without wine, at Oregano's Pizza Bistro (inexpensive)	13.00
Bottle of beer in a restaurant	2.00
Coca-Cola in a restaurant	1.00
Cup of coffee	1.00
Roll of ASA 100 Kodacolor film, 36 exposures	5.50
Admission to the Heard Museum	5.00
Movie ticket	6.00
Theater ticket to Gammage Auditorium	free–$40.00

What Things Cost in Flagstaff	U.S. $
Taxi from the airport to the city center	10.00
Local telephone call	.25
Double room at the Woodlands Plaza (moderate)	69.00
Double room at the Monte Vista Hotel (inexpensive)	40.00
Lunch for one at the Brix Grill & Wine Bar (moderate)	12.00
Lunch for one at the Café Espress (inexpensive)	8.00
Dinner for one, without wine, at Chez Marc Bistro (expensive)	30.00
Dinner for one, without wine, at Sakura (moderate)	22.00
Dinner for one, without wine, at the Beaver Street Brewery (inexpensive)	13.00
Bottle of beer in a restaurant	2.00
Coca-Cola in a restaurant	1.00
Cup of coffee	.75
Roll of ASA 100 Kodacolor film, 36 exposures	5.35
Admission to the Museum of Northern Arizona	4.00
Movie ticket	6.00
Theater ticket to the Flagstaff Symphony	11.00–22.00

TRAVELER'S CHECKS, ATMS & CREDIT/CHARGE CARDS   Traveler's checks are accepted at hotels, motels, restaurants, and most stores, as are credit and charge cards. Cities and towns throughout the state have banks with automatic teller machines (the Star, Plus, Arizona Interchange Network, Master Teller, and American Express networks are widely available), so you can get cash as you travel. If you plan to rent a car, you'll need a credit or charge card for the deposit.

2 When to Go—Climate & Events

Arizona is a year-round tourist destination, though people head to different parts of the state at different times of year. In Phoenix, Tucson, and other parts of the desert, the high season runs from October to mid-May, with the highest hotel rates in effect during January and February. However, up at the Grand Canyon the busy season is during the summer months, and it's then that hotel room rates are the highest and crowds are the largest.

The all-around best times to visit are in spring and autumn, when temperatures are cool in the mountains and warm in the desert, but without extremes (although you shouldn't be surprised to get a bit of snow as late as Memorial Day in the mountains and thunderstorms in the desert in August and September). These are also good times to come if you wish to save money, because summer rates are in effect at the desert resorts and the crowds aren't as great at the Grand Canyon. This time period sometimes also coincides with the spring wildflower season, which begins in mid-spring and extends until April and May, when the tops of saguaro cacti become covered with waxy white blooms.

If for some reason you happen to be visiting the desert in August, be prepared for sudden thunderstorms. These storms often cause flash floods that make many roads in the state briefly impassable. Road signs warning motorists not to enter low areas when flooded are meant to be taken very seriously.

CLIMATE

The first thing you should know is that the desert can be cold as well as hot. Although winter is the prime tourist season in Phoenix and Tucson, night temperatures can be below freezing and days can even be too cold for sunning or swimming. However, on the whole, winters in Arizona are positively delightful.

In the winter, sunseekers flock to the deserts, where temperatures average in the high 60s by day. In the summer, when desert temperatures are topping 110°F, the mountains of eastern and northern Arizona are pleasantly warm with daytime averages in the low 80s. Yuma is one of the desert communities where winter temperatures are the highest in the state, and Prescott and Sierra Vista, in the 4,000- to 6,000-foot elevation range, are two cities that claim to have among the best climates in the world—not too cold, not too hot.

The accompanying climate charts will give you an idea of the state's climatic diversity.

Phoenix's Average Temperatures (°F) & Days of Rain

	Jan	Feb	Mar	Apr	May	June	July	Aug	Sept	Oct	Nov	Dec
Avg. High	65	69	75	84	93	102	105	102	98	88	75	66
Avg. Low	38	41	45	52	60	68	78	76	69	57	45	39
Days of Rain	4	4	3	2	1	1	4	5	3	3	2	4

Flagstaff's Average Temperatures (°F) & Days of Rain

	Jan	Feb	Mar	Apr	May	June	July	Aug	Sept	Oct	Nov	Dec
Avg. High	41	44	48	57	67	76	81	78	74	63	51	43
Avg. Low	14	17	20	27	34	40	50	49	41	31	22	16
Days of Rain	7	6	8	6	3	3	12	11	6	5	5	6

ARIZONA CALENDAR OF EVENTS

February

- **Tubac Festival of the Arts,** Tubac. Exhibits by North American artists and craftspeople. For more information, call 520/398-2704. Early February.
- **Flagstaff Winterfest,** Flagstaff. Sled-dog races, sleigh rides, music and dance performances. For details, call 520/774-9541 or 800/842-7293. Early to mid-February.
- **O'odham Tash,** Casa Grande. Tohono O'odham tribal festival featuring rodeos, crafts shows, and dance performances. For further details, call 520/836-4723 or 800/836-8169. Mid-February.

March

- **Territorial Days,** Tombstone. Tombstone's birthday celebration. For more information, call 800/457-3423. First weekend in March.

May

- **Cinco de Mayo,** Tucson, Phoenix, and other cities. Celebration of the Mexican victory over the French in a famous 1862 battle. May 5.
- **Trappings of the American West,** Flagstaff. Exhibition of cowboy art and crafts at the Coconino Center for the Arts. Cowboy poetry readings and music performances. Call 520/779-6921 for details. Early May to mid-June.
- **Phippen Western Art Show & Sale,** Prescott. This is the premier western art sale. For more information, call 520/778-1385. Memorial Day weekend.
- **Wyatt Earp Days,** Tombstone. Gunfight reenactments in memory of the shootout at the O.K. Corral. Call 520/457-9317 for further details. Memorial Day weekend.
- **A Celebration of Native American Art,** Flagstaff. Native American market, dances, and art exhibition at the Museum of Northern Arizona. For more details, phone 520/774-5211. May to September.

June

- **Route 66 Festival,** Flagstaff. This carnival, car show, and more, centers around the theme of historic Route 66. For additional information, call 520/774-9541 or 800/842-7293. Early June.
- **Sedona Chamber Music Festival,** Sedona. Chamber music is performed by companies from around the world at various venues. Phone 520/204-2415 for details. Early to mid-June.

July

- **Prescott Frontier Days,** Prescott. This is the oldest rodeo in the U.S. Phone 520/445-3103 or 800/266-7534 for details. First week of July.
- **Annual Hopi Artists Exhibition,** Flagstaff. Exhibition and sale at the Museum of Northern Arizona. Call 520/774-5211 for more details. First weekend in July.

- **Annual Navajo Artists Exhibition,** Flagstaff. Exhibition and sale at the Museum of Northern Arizona. For details, call 520/774-5211. Last weekend in July.
- **Flagstaff Festival of the Arts,** Flagstaff. One of the largest arts festivals in Arizona, featuring concerts, theater, and films. For more information, call 520/774-7750 or 800/266-7740. All month.

August

- **Cowboy Poets,** Prescott. Not just traditional and contemporary poetry, but yodeling and storytelling that centers around the cowboy lifestyle. For more information, call 520/445-3122. Mid-August.
- **Payson Rodeo,** Payson. The second of Arizona's rodeos claiming to be the world's oldest. For details, call 520/474-4515. Mid-August.

September

- **Navajo Nation Fair,** Window Rock. A rodeo, dances, a parade, and food. Call 520/871-6702 or 520/871-6478 for more information. Early September.
- **Jazz on the Rocks,** Sedona. Open-air jazz festival. For details, call 602/282-1985. Late September.

October

- **Sedona Arts Festival,** Sedona. One of the best arts festivals in the state. For additional information, phone 520/282-7722 or 800/288-7336. Mid-October.
- **Helldorado Days,** Tombstone. 1880s fashion show, tribal dancers, and street entertainment. Call 800/457-3423 for details. Late October.

December

- **Festival of Lights,** Sedona. Thousands of *luminarias* are lit at dusk at the Tlaquepaque Arts & Crafts Village. For details, call 520/282-7722 or 800/288-7336. Mid-December.

PHOENIX CALENDAR OF EVENTS

January

- **Fiesta Bowl Football Classic,** Sun Devil Stadium, Tempe. College football classic. For additional information, call 602/350-0900. January 1 or 2.
- **Phoenix Open Golf Tournament,** Tournament Players Club. Prestigious PGA golf tournament. Phone 602/870-0163 for details. Mid- to late January.
- **Parada del Sol Parade and Rodeo,** Scottsdale. The state's longest horse-drawn parade, plus a street dance and rodeo. For more information, call 602/945-8481 or 800/877-1117. Late January.

February

- **Arizona Renaissance Festival,** Apache Junction. This 16th-century English country fair has costumed participants and includes tournament jousting. Phone 602/463-2700 for details. Weekends from early February to March.
- **All-Arabian Horse Show,** Scottsdale's Westworld. A celebration of the Arabian horse. For additional information, call 602/951-1180. Mid-February.

March

- **Heard Museum Guild Indian Fair,** Heard Museum. Showcase of Native American arts and heritage, with more than 200 artists displaying their work. Call 602/252-8840 for details. First weekend in March.

- **Scottsdale Arts Festival,** Scottsdale Mall. This visual- and performing-arts festival has free concerts, an art show, and children's events. For more information, phone 602/994-ARTS. Second weekend in March.
- **Chandler Ostrich Festival,** Chandler. Live country and big-band music, Irish and Hispanic entertainment, and, of course, ostrich races. For more details, call 602/963-4571. Early to mid-March.
- **Phoenix Jaycee's Rodeo of Rodeos,** Arizona Veterans Memorial Coliseum. One of the biggest and most popular indoor rodeos in the world. Call 602/252-6771 for more information. Mid-March.
- **Spring Festival of the Arts,** Mill Avenue, Tempe. This large arts and entertainment festival features local and traveling artists and artisans. For details, phone 602/967-4877. Late March to early April.

April

- **Scottsdale All-Indian Days Annual Pow-Wow,** Scottsdale Community College. More than 50 tribes from all over North America perform music and dances and exhibit arts and crafts. Call 602/423-6000 for more information. Second weekend in April.
- **Maricopa County Fair,** Arizona State Fairgrounds. There's a midway, agricultural and livestock exhibits, and entertainment. For details, phone 602/252-0717. Late April.

May

- **Cinco de Mayo,** all over the city. Celebration to commemorate the victory of the Mexicans over the French. Call 602/262-5025 for details. May 5.

July

- **Fourth of July Fireworks,** in front of the State Capitol, Phoenix. Big booms are accompanied by food and crafts booths, less flamboyant entertainment, and a children's area. For information, call 602/495-5025. July 4.

September

- **Fiesta Patrias,** Patriot's Park. Celebration of Mexican Independence Day. For details, call 602/255-0980. Mid-September.
- **Scottsdale Center for the Arts Annual Gala,** Scottsdale Center for the Arts. Jazz, ballet, music, art exhibits, and special events. Phone 602/443-8950 or 602/994-ARTS for further information. Late September.

October

- **Coors Rodeo Showdown,** America West Arena. Top rodeo stars from the U.S. and Canada compete in this annual event. For details, call 602/379-7800. Early October.
- **Arizona State Fair,** Arizona State Fairgrounds. Featuring rodeos, top-name entertainment, and ethnic food. Phone 602/252-6771 for more information. Mid- to late October.
- **Annual Cowboy Artists of America Exhibition,** Phoenix Art Museum. This is the most prestigious and best-known western art show. For details, call 602/257-1880. Late October to late November.
- **Desert Botanical Garden Landscape Plant Sale,** Desert Botanical Garden. Display and sale of desert plants during blooming season. Call 602/941-1225 for information. Late October (and late March).

November

- **Hot Air Balloon Race & Thunderbird Balloon Classic,** Scottsdale. More than 100 hot-air balloons fill the Arizona sky. Call 602/978-7208 for details. Early November.

December

- **Fall Festival of the Arts,** Mill Avenue, Tempe. Hundreds of artists and artisans, featuring free entertainment and plenty of food. For additional information, call 602/967-4877. Early December.
- **Fiesta Bowl Events,** Phoenix area. All manner of sports competitions, parades, and cultural events. Phone 602/350-0900 for more information. All month.

3 The Active Vacation Planner

Arizona is known the world over for active, adventure-oriented vacations for the sole reason that the state is home to the Grand Canyon—the most widely known white-water-rafting spot in the world. For others, Arizona is known mostly for its winter golf and tennis. Whichever category of active vacationer you fall into, you'll find information below to help you arrange your trip to Arizona.

ACTIVITIES A TO Z

BICYCLING   With its wide range of climates, Arizona offers good biking somewhere in the state every month of the year. In the winter months there's good road biking around Phoenix and Tucson, while from the spring through the fall, the southeastern corner of the state offers some good routes. Also in the summer months, the White Mountains and Kaibab National Forest between Flagstaff and Grand Canyon National Park offer good mountain biking. For more information contact the **Arizona Bicycle Club,** P.O. Box 7191, Phoenix, AZ 85011-7191 (☎ 602/264-5478), or the **Mountain Bike Association of Arizona,** P.O. Box 32728, Phoenix, AZ 85064 (☎ 602/956-3870).

BIRD-WATCHING   Arizona is a birder's bonanza. Down in the southeastern corner of the state, many species of birds found primarily south of the border reach the northern limits of their territories. Combine this with several mountains that rise up like islands from out of the desert and provide an appropriate habitat for hundreds of species of birds and you some of the best bird-watching in the country. Birding hot spots include Ramsey Canyon Preserve (known for its many species of hummingbirds), Cave Creek Canyon (nesting site for elegant trogons), Patagonia-Sonoita Creek Sanctuary (home to 22 species of flycatchers, kingbirds, and phoebes, as well as Montezuma quails), Madera Canyon (another "mountain island" that attracts many of the same species seen at Ramsey Canyon and Sonoita Creek), and the sewage ponds outside the town of Willcox (known for its avocets and sandhill cranes).

FISHING   The fishing scene in Arizona is as diverse as the landscape. Large and small lakes around the state offer excellent fishing for warm-water game fish such as largemouth, smallmouth, and striped bass, while up on the Mogollon Rim and in the White Mountains there is good trout fishing. There's also good trout fishing in the Grand Canyon, and the more easily accessible sections of the free-running Colorado River between Glen Canyon Dam and Lees Ferry.

Fishing licenses for nonresidents are available for one day, five days, four months, and one year. There are also various special stamps and licenses that may apply. Nonresident fishing licenses are quite a bit more expensive than those for residents. Also keep in mind that if you're heading for an Indian reservation, you'll have to get a special permit for that reservation. For more information, contact the **Arizona Game & Fish Department,** 2222 W. Greenway Rd., Phoenix, AZ 85027 (☎ **602/942-3000**).

GOLFING For many of Arizona's winter visitors, golf is the main reason to visit the state. The state's hundreds of golf courses range from easy public courses to PGA championship links that have challenged the best. In Phoenix and Tucson, greens fees, like room rates, are seasonal. In the popular winter months, fees at resort courses range from $90 to $125 for 18 holes, though this usually includes a mandatory golf cart rental. In the summer months fees often drop to less than half this amount. Almost all resorts also offer special golf packages as well. For information on some of the state's top courses, see "Hot Links," the special golf feature in this chapter.

For more information on golfing in Arizona, contact the **Arizona Golf Association,** 7226 N. 16th St., Suite 200, Phoenix, AZ 85020 (☎ **602/ 944-3035** or 800/458-8484). You can also contact *Golf Arizona,* 15704 Cholla St., Suite 100, Fountain Hills, AZ 85268 (☎ **800/942-5444**), which publishes a guide to where to play golf in Arizona.

HIKING & BACKPACKING Despite its reputation as a desert state, a large percentage of Arizona is forest land, and within these forests are wilderness areas and countless miles of hiking trails.

In northern Arizona, there are good day hikes in Grand Canyon National Park, in the San Francisco Peaks north of Flagstaff, outside Page (near Lake Powell), and in Navajo National Monument. In the Phoenix area, popular day hikes include the trail up Camelback Mountain and the many trails in South Mountain Park. In the Tucson area, there are good hikes on Mount Lemmon and in Saguaro National Park, Sabino Canyon, and Catalina State Park. In the southern part of the state, there are good day hikes in Chiricahua National Monument, Coronado National Forest, in the Nature Conservancy's Ramsey Canyon Preserve and Patagonia-Sonoita Creek Sanctuary, in Cochise Stronghold, and in Organ Pipe National Monument. See the individual chapters for details on these areas.

The state's two most popular overnight backpack trips are the hike down to Phantom Ranch and the hike into Havasu Canyon, a side canyon off the Grand Canyon. Another popular multiday backpack trip is through Paria Canyon, beginning in Utah and ending in Arizona at Lees Ferry. There are also backpacking opportunities in the San Francisco Peaks north of Flagstaff and in the White Mountains of eastern Arizona.

HORSEBACK RIDING All over Arizona there are stables where you can saddle up for short rides. Among the more scenic spots for riding are the Grand Canyon, the red-rock country around Sedona, Phoenix's South Mountain Park, at the foot of the Superstition Mountains east of Phoenix, and at the foot of the Santa Catalina Mountains outside Tucson. See the individual chapters for listings of riding stables. See below for information on overnight guided horseback rides.

Ranch vacations are also immensely popular in the state, and Arizona boasts many outstanding guest ranches accommodating visitors of all riding abilities. For more information you can contact the **Arizona Dude Ranch Association,** Box 603, Cortaro, AZ 85652 or call the Arizona Office of Tourism (☎ **602/ 542-8687**) for brochures.

Hot Links

You don't have to be a hotshot golfer to get all heated up over the prospect of a few rounds of golf in Arizona. Combine near-perfect golf weather with great views—and some very unique challenges—and you've got all the makings of a great game. Phoenix and Tucson are well known as winter golf desinations, but the state also offers golfing opportunities throughout the year at higher-altitude courses in such places as Prescott, Flagstaff, and the White Mountains.

State legislation aimed at conserving water now limits golf courses in Arizona to no more than 90 acres of irrigated land, far less than is found on most traditional golf courses. What this legislation has done, in addition to conserving both water and the desert, is give the state some of the most distinctive and difficult courses in the country. These desert or "target" courses are characterized by minimal fairways surrounded by natural desert landscapes. You might find yourself teeing off over the tops of cacti and searching for your ball amid boulders and mesquite (actual encounters with rattlesnakes are few). If your ball comes to lie in the desert, you can play the ball where it lies or drop the ball within two club lengths of the nearest point of grass, but no nearer the hole, with a one-stroke penalty.

Keep in mind that resort courses are not cheap. For most of the year, greens fees, which include golf cart rentals, range from around $90 to $125 or more. Greens fees at semiprivate clubs are often about the same as at resort courses. Public courses, on the other hand, offer very reasonable greens fees of around $20 for 18 holes, with golf cart rental costing extra (around $15).

You may not think so at first, but summer is really a good time to visit many of Arizona's golf resorts. Why? No, they don't have air-conditioned golf carts or indoor courses. It's because in summer greens fees can be less than half what they are in winter. How does $28 for a round on the famous Gold Course at the Wigwam sound? Plus, most resorts charge next to nothing for rooms in the summer, and those rooms *do* have air-conditioning.

With more golf courses per capita than any other state—over 250 in all—Arizona is a golfing paradise. Now the only problem is choosing where you'd like to play. The information below may help you make some decisions.

The Phoenix/Scottsdale area, known as the Valley of the Sun, has the greatest concentration of golf courses in the state. Whether you're looking to play one of the area's challenging top-rated resort courses or an economical but fun municipal course, you'll find plenty of choices.

For spectacular scenery at a resort course, it's just plain impossible to beat **The Boulders** (☎ **800/553-1717**), located north of Scottsdale in the town of Carefree. Elevated tee boxes beside giant balanced boulders are enough to distract anyone's concentration. Way over on the east side of the valley in Apache Junction, the **Gold Canyon Golf Club** (☎ **602/982-9090**) has what have been rated as three of the best holes in the state (the 11th, 12th, and 13th). Jumping over to Litchfield Park, on the far west side of the valley, you'll find the **Wigwam Golf & Country Club** (☎ **602/935-3811**) and its three 18-hole courses; the

Gold Course here is legendary. Other noteworthy resort courses in the area include the links at **The Phoenician** (☎ 800/888-8234), mixing traditional and desert-style holes. This course is currently undergoing expansion. The **Hyatt Regency Scottsdale Resort at Gainey Ranch** (☎ 602/991-3388) offers three decidedly different nine-hole courses (the Dunes, the Arroyo, and the Lakes courses), each with its own set of challenges.

The area's favorite public course is the **Papago Golf Course** (☎ 602/275-8428), which has a killer 17th hole. The semiprivate **Troon North Golf Club** (☎ 602/585-5300), however, a course that seems only barely carved out of raw desert, garners the most local accolades. If you want to swing where the pros do, beg, borrow, or steal a tee time on the Stadium Course at the **Tournament Players Club of Scottsdale** (☎ 602/585-3600). The **Superstition Springs Golf Club** (☎ 602/962-GOLF) is another popular course and also a PGA Tour qualifying site.

With nearly 40 courses, Tuscon has been giving the Valley of the Sun some golf competition in recent years. Among the city's resort courses, the Mountain Course at the **Ventana Canyon Golf & Racquet Club** (☎ 520/577-6258) is legendary and has been ranked among Arizona's top 10 by *Golf Digest*. A spectacular 107-yard par-3 hole here is the most talked-about hole in the city. If you want to play where the pros play, book a room at the **Tucson National Golf & Conference Resort** (☎ 520/575-7540), home of the Northern Telecom Open. The eighth hole at the Sunrise Course of the **Sheraton El Conquistador Resort and Country Club** (☎ 520/544-1800) has been rated the toughest par 3 in Tucson.

Of Tucson's public courses, **Randolph North** (☎ 520/325-2811) gets the nod for best municipal course and is the site of an annual LPGA tournament. The **Silverbell Municipal Course** (☎ 520/743-7284) boasts a bear of a par-5 17th hole. The **Starr Pass Golf Club** (☎ 520/622-6060) has been garnering a lot of praise the past few years and now co-hosts the Northern Telecom Open; the 15th hole is the signature hole here and plays through a pass.

Courses worth trying in other parts of the state include the 18-hole course at **Rancho de los Caballeros** (☎ 602/684-5484), a luxury ranch resort outside Wickenburg. *Golf Digest* has rated its course one of Arizona's top 10. For concentration-taxing scenery, there are few courses to compare with the **Sedona Golf Resort** (☎ 520/284-9355), which is surrounded by red-rock cliffs; try this course at sunset. In mile-high Prescott, the **Antelope Hills North & South Golf Club** (☎ 520/445-0583) offers two 18-hole courses that offer a respite from the summer heat in the lowlands. Even higher and cooler in summer, the **Silver Creek Golf Club** (☎ 520/537-2744) offers golfing among the pine trees of the White Mountains. South of Tucson near Nogales, the **Rio Rico Resort & Country Club** (☎ 800/288-4746) offers a challenging back nine as well as cooler temperatures and lower greens fees than you'll find in Tucson.

One last tip: If your ball should happen to land in the coils of a rattlesnake, consider it lost and take your penalty. Rattlesnakes make lousy tees.

HOT-AIR BALLOONING For much of the year the desert provides the perfect environment for hot-air ballooning—cool, still air and wide-open spaces. Consequently, there are dozens of hot-air-balloon companies operating here. Most are to be found in the Phoenix and Tucson areas, but there are also several that operate near Sedona, which is by far the most picturesque spot in the state for a balloon ride. See the individual chapters for specific information.

HOUSEBOATING With the Colorado River turned into a long string of lakes, houseboat vacations are a natural in Arizona. Though this doesn't have to be an active vacation, fishing, hiking, and swimming are usually part of a houseboat vacation. Rentals are available on Lake Powell, Lake Mead, Lake Mohave, and Lake Havasu. However, the canyonlands scenery of Lake Powell make this lake the hands-down best spot for a houseboat vacation. See Chapters 7 and 11 for more information on houseboat rentals.

RAFTING The desert doesn't support a lot of roaring rivers, but with the white water in the Grand Canyon you don't need too many other choices. Day-long white-water-rafting trips are available on the upper Salt River and more leisurely inner-tube floats are popular on the lower Salt River. Plenty of waterproof sunscreen is a must for either of these trips. See below and in Chapter 7 for further discussion or rafting and lists of rafting companies.

ROCK CLIMBING With views down to Tucson far below, the climbs on Mount Lemmon are among the most popular in the state. Though hot, the Superstition Mountains also offer some climbing opportunities, as do many of the state's other remote and rugged desert mountain ranges. To learn more about rock climbing spots in Arizona or to find some partners for a climb, contact the **Arizona Mountaineering Club** (☎ 602/867-1487).

SKIING Although Arizona is better known as a desert state, it does have plenty of mountains and even a few ski areas. The two biggest and most popular ski areas are **Arizona Snowbowl** (☎ 520/779-1951) outside Flagstaff and **Sunrise Park** (☎ 800/554-6835) on the Apache reservation outside the town of McNary in the White Mountains. Snowbowl is the more popular because of the ease of the drive from Phoenix and its proximity to good lodging and dining options in Flagstaff. When it's a good snow year, Tucsonans head up to **Mount Lemmon Ski Valley** (☎ 520/576-1321), the southernmost ski area in the United States. Snows here aren't as reliable as they are farther north. One last ski hill, the **Bill Williams Ski Area** (☎ 520/635-9330), is located just outside Williams. Although Arizona Snowbowl has more vertical feet of skiing, Sunrise offers almost twice as many runs and the same snow conditions. All of these ski areas offer ski rentals and lessons.

Cross-country skiers will find plenty of snow-covered forest roads to ski around Flagstaff (there's a nordic center at Arizona Snowbowl), at the South Rim of the Grand Canyon, in the White Mountains around Greer and Alpine, outside Payson on the Mogollon Rim, and on Mount Lemmon outside Flagstaff. However, the state's premier cross-country ski area is the North Rim of the Grand Canyon, which is closed to vehicles in the winter. See "Outfitters and Adventure-Tour Operators," below, for information on the North Rim's Kaibab Lodge, which is accessible only on skis or by snow-van and caters to avid cross-county skiers. The book *Ski Touring Arizona* (Northland Press, 1987) by Dugald Bremner covers the state's major cross-country ski areas.

TENNIS   Resorts all over Arizona have tennis courts; after golf, this is the most popular winter sport in the desert. Many resorts require you to wear traditional tennis attire and don't include court time in the room rates. Although there may be better courts in the state, none can match the views you'll have from the courts at Enchantment Resort outside Sedona. Just don't let the scenery ruin your game.

OUTFITTERS & ADVENTURE-TOUR OPERATORS

BICYCLING   **Backroads,** 1516 Fifth St., Berkeley, CA 94710-1740 (☎ **510/ 527-1555** or 800/245-3874), offers a five-day, inn-to-inn mountain-bike trip through the red-rock country of central Arizona. Mountain-bike trips are also offered by **Southern Arizona Offroad Adventures,** P.O. Box 3339, Tucson, AZ 85722 (☎ **520/882-6567** or 800/689-BIKE), which does two-day camping trips and weeklong trips that stay at hotels. This company also does half-day and full-day trips, and even has a ride for expert mountain bikers.

HIKING/BACKPACKING   Guided backpack trips of various durations and levels of difficulty are offered by the **Grand Canyon Field Institute,** P.O. Box 399, Grand Canyon, AZ 86023 (☎ **520/638-2485**).

If you like to hike but don't want to carry a load, contact the **Delli Llamas,** P.O. Box 1416, Show Low, AZ 85901 (☎ **520/537-0274**). This company operates llama pack trips in the White Mountains. Trips range in length from half a day to several days.

HORSEBACK RIDING/WESTERN ADVENTURES   Among the most popular guided adventures in Arizona are the mule rides down into the Grand Canyon. These trips vary in length from one to three days; for more information, contact **Grand Canyon National Park Lodges,** Reservations Department, P.O. Box 699, Grand Canyon, AZ 86023 (☎ **520/638-2401**). It's also possible to do overnight horseback rides, wagon-train rides, and cattle drives. For more information, contact **Don Donnelly Stables,** 6010 S. Kings Canyon Rd., Gold Canyon, AZ 85219 (☎ **602/982-7822** or 800/346-4403), which does overnight horseback trips in Monument Valley among other places; **Arizona Trail Tours,** P.O. Box 1218, Patagonia, AZ 85624 (☎ **520/394-2701**), which offers a five-day trip through Coronado National Monument in southern Arizona; **C&S Cattle Company** (☎ **800/877-4555**), which does cattle drives; or **Double D Ranch & Wagon Train Company,** P.O. Box 334, Paulden, AZ 86334-0334 (☎ **520/ 636-0418**), which does a wagon-train trip.

ROCK CLIMBING   If you're interested in learning some rock-climbing techniques or want to do some guided mountaineering or canyoneering, contact **Ascend Arizona Mountain Sports,** Arizona Center, 455 N. 3rd St., Suite 244, Phoenix, AZ 85004 (☎ **602/495-9428** or 800/2-ASCEND); **Venture Up,** 2415 E. Indian School Rd., Phoenix, AZ 85016 (☎ **602/955-9100**); or **Wilderness Adventures,** P.O. Box 63282, Phoenix, AZ 85082 (☎ **602/708-6786** or 800/462-5788).

SKI TOURING   **Kaibab Lodge,** P.O. Box 2997, Flagstaff, AZ 86003 (☎ **520/ 638-2389** or 520/526-0924 or 800/525-0924), near the North Rim of the Grand Canyon, is the state's premier cross-country ski lodge. During ski season this lodge is only accessible by skis or in a snow van. In addition to miles of trails and guide trips, the lodge offers yurt-to-yurt overnight trips.

WHITE-WATER RAFTING Rafting the Grand Canyon is the dream of nearly every white-water enthusiast. For a discussion of and list of companies that run trips down the canyon, see Chapter 7. For one- and two-day trips on the Colorado below the Grand Canyon, contact **Hualapai River Runners,** P.O. Box 246, Peach Springs, AZ 86434 (☎ **520/769-2210** or 800/622-4409). For a half-day float on the Colorado above Grand Canyon, contact **Wilderness River Adventures,** P.O. Box 717, Page, AZ 86040 (☎ **520/645-3279** or 800/ 992-8022), which runs its trips from the Glen Canyon Dam to Lees Ferry. **Salt River Rafting** (☎ **520/577-1824** or 800/242-6335) runs half-day, full-day, overnight, and two-day trips (conditions permitting) down the Upper Salt River. **Salt River Canyon Raft Trips** (☎ **602/966-7878** or 800/964-RAFT) also runs trips down the Salt.

4 Educational & Volunteer Vacations

A number of opportunities exist in Arizona for those wishing to combine a vacation with an educational or volunteer experience.

If you'd like to turn a trip to the Grand Canyon into an educational vacation, contact the **Grand Canyon Field Institute,** P.O. Box 399, Grand Canyon, AZ 86023 (☎ **520/638-2485**). Programs are offered from late spring to early fall and include writing, drawing, painting, and photography classes; programs on Native American history and culture; hands-on archeology programs; birding trips; storytelling classes; and plenty of guided hikes and backpacking trips.

The **Nature Conservancy,** 300 E. University Blvd., Suite 230, Tucson, AZ 85705 (☎ **520/622-3861**), is a nonprofit organization dedicated to the global preservation of natural diversity. It does this by identifying and purchasing land that is home to endangered plants, animals, and natural communities. The organization has several preserves in Arizona to which they operate educational field trips of one to four days. Trips are listed in the Conservancy's Arizona chapter newsletter; information about trips and membership ($25 annually) is also available by phone.

If you enjoy the wilderness and want to get more involved in preserving it, consider a Sierra Club Service Trip. These trips are for the purpose of building, restoring, and maintaining hiking trails in wilderness areas. It's a lot of work, but it's also a lot of fun. For more information on service trips, contact the **Sierra Club Outing Department,** 730 Polk St., San Francisco, CA 94109 (☎ **415/ 923-5630**).

Another sort of service trip is being offered by the National Park Service. It accepts volunteers to pick up garbage left by thoughtless visitors to Glen Canyon National Recreation Area. In exchange for picking up trash, you'll get to spend five days on a houseboat called the *Trash Tracker*, cruising the gorgeous canyonlands scenery of Lake Powell. Volunteers must be at least 18 years old, and must provide their own food and sleeping bag. For more information, contact **Glen Canyon National Recreation Area,** P.O. Box 1507, Page, AZ 86040 (☎ **520/645-2471**).

If you'd like to lend a hand at an archaeological dig, contact the **White Mountain Archeological Center** (☎ **602/333-5857**), which is located near Springerville on the edge of the White Mountains.

Older travelers who want to learn something from their trip to Arizona or who simply prefer the company of like-minded older travelers should look into programs by **Elderhostel,** 75 Federal St., Boston, MA 02110 (☎ **617/426-7788**). To participate in an Elderhostel program, either you or your spouse must be at least 60 years old. In addition to one-week educational programs, Elderhostel also offers short getaways with interesting themes.

5 Health & Insurance

HEALTH PRECAUTIONS   If you've never been to the desert before, you should be sure to prepare yourself for this harsh environment. No matter what time of year it is, the desert sun is strong and bright. Use sunscreen when you're outdoors—particularly if you're up in the mountains, where the altitude makes sunburn more likely. The bright sun also makes sunglasses a necessity.

Even if you don't feel hot in the desert, the dry air still steals moisture from your body, so drink plenty of fluids. You may want to use a body lotion as well. The desert air quickly dries out skin.

It's not only the sun that makes the desert a harsh environment. There are poisonous creatures out there too, but with a little common sense and some precautions you can avoid them. Rattlesnakes are very common in the desert, but your chances of meeting one are slight (except during the mating season in April and May) because they tend not to come out in the heat of the day. However, never stick your hand into holes among the rocks in the desert, and look to see where you're going to step before putting your foot down.

Arizona also has a large poisonous lizard called the Gila monster. These black-and-orange lizards are far less common than rattlesnakes and your chances of meeting one are slight.

Although the tarantula has developed a nasty reputation, the tiny black widow is more likely to cause illness. Scorpions are another insect danger of the desert. Be extra careful whenever turning over rocks or logs that might harbor either black widows or scorpions.

INSURANCE   Before going out and spending money on various sorts of travel insurance, check your existing policies to see if they'll cover you while you're traveling. Make sure your health insurance will cover you when you're away from home. Most credit and charge cards offer automatic flight insurance when you purchase an airline ticket with that card. These policies insure against death or dismemberment in the case of an airplane crash. Also, check your cards to see if any of them pick up the collision-damage waiver (CDW) when you rent a car. The CDW can run as much as $12 a day and can add 50% or more to the cost of renting a car. Check your automobile insurance policy too; it might cover the CDW as well. If you own a home or have renter's insurance, see if that policy covers off-premises theft and loss wherever it occurs. If you're traveling on a tour or have prepaid a large chunk of your travel expenses, you might want to ask your travel agent about trip-cancellation insurance.

If, after checking all your existing insurance policies, you decide that you need additional insurance, a good travel agent can give you information on a variety

Impressions

From the hygienic point of view, whiskey and cold lead are mentioned as the leading diseases at Tombstone.

—A Tombstone visitor in the 1880s

of different options. **Teletrip Company (Mutual of Omaha),** at Mutual of Omaha Plaza, Floor 7, Teletrip, Omaha, NE 68175 (☎ **800/228-9792**), offers four different types of travel insurance policies for one day to six months. These policies include medical, baggage, trip-cancellation or interruption insurance, and flight insurance against death or dismemberment.

6 Tips for Special Travelers

FOR TRAVELERS WITH DISABILITIES   When making airline reservations, always mention your disability. Airline policies differ regarding wheelchairs and Seeing Eye dogs. Most hotels now offer wheelchair-accessible accommodations, and some of the larger and more expensive resorts also offer TDD telephones and other amenities for the hearing and sight impaired.

If you plan to visit many of Arizona's national parks or monuments, you can avail yourself of the **Golden Access Passport.** This lifetime pass is issued free to any U.S. citizen or permanent resident who has been medically certified as disabled or blind. The pass permits free entry into national parks and monuments and also provides a 50% discount on campgrounds and recreational activities provided by the federal government (but not those provided by private concessionaires).

Rick Crowder of the **Travelin' Talk Network,** P.O. Box 3534, Clarksville, TN 37043-3534 (☎ **615/552-6670** Monday through Friday between noon and 5pm central time), organizes a network for disabled travelers. An eight-page newsletter is available for any contribution. A directory listing people and organizations around the world who are networked to provide the disabled traveler with firsthand information about a chosen destination is available for $35.

FOR GAY MEN & LESBIANS   To get in touch with the Phoenix gay community, you can contact the **Gay and Lesbian Community Center,** 3136 N. Third Ave. (☎ **602/234-2752**). At the community center and at gay bars around Phoenix, you can pick up various community publications, including *The Western Express, Echo,* and *Women's Center, Inc.* **Wingspan,** Tucson's lesbian, gay, and bisexual community center, is at 422 N. Fourth Ave. (☎ **520/624-1779**).

FOR SENIORS   When making airline reservations, always mention that you're a senior citizen—many airlines offer discounts. You should also carry some sort of photo ID card (driver's license, passport, etc.) to avail yourself of senior-citizen discounts on attractions, hotels, motels, and public transportation, as well as one of the best deals in Arizona for senior citizens—the **Golden Age Passport,** which is available for $10 to U.S. citizens and permanent residents age 62 and older. This federal government pass allows lifetime entrance privileges and a 50% discount on campground and recreation fees in national parks, forests, and other federal recreation areas. You can apply in person for this passport at a national park, national forest, or other location where it's honored, and you must show reasonable proof of age.

Impressions

If this was my lake, I'd mow it.
> —Will Rogers to former President Calvin Coolidge about
> San Carlos Lake, which was formed by the Coolidge Dam

If you aren't a member of the **American Association of Retired Persons (AARP),** 601 E St. NW, Washington, DC 20049 (☎ **800/424-3410**), you should consider joining. This association provides discounts at many lodgings and attractions throughout Arizona, although you can sometimes get a similar discount simply by showing your ID.

If you'd like to do a bit of studying on vacation, consider **Elderhostel** (see "Educational & Volunteer Vacations," earlier in this chapter).

Phoenix and the Valley of the Sun have long been popular with retirees. Over the years entire cities (such as Sun City) have developed for senior citizens. *Arizona Senior World Newspaper* (☎ **602/438-1566**) is a monthly newspaper with information relevant to senior citizens. You can find it in supermarkets and convenience stores.

FOR FAMILIES Arizona offers something for everyone and is a popular family vacation destination. Kids love the "cowboy and Indian" lore of Arizona, and there are plenty of opportunities for them to explore this aspect of American history. Dude ranches (now known as guest ranches) are popular with families. The kids can go off for a day of horseback riding while the parents relax by the pool, or vice versa. Cookouts and wagon rides are geared as much toward kids as adults. Old Tucson and Tombstone are two attractions that kids find fascinating (though parents may be less than enchanted with all the souvenir shops).

Keep in mind that most hotels and motels allow kids to sleep free in their parents' room as long as a crib or extra bed is not necessary.

Last, remember that Arizona is a very large state. Driving times are long, so bring plenty to keep the kids entertained if your vacation plans require covering large distances. Looking out the window at the desert for hours and hours is boring even for adults.

FOR STUDENTS Because Arizona is a popular destination with young European travelers, it has quite a few youth hostels. You can purchase a Youth Hostel membership card from **Hostelling International–American Youth Hostels (HI–AYH),** 733 15th St. NW, Suite 840, Washington, DC 20013 (☎ **202/783-6161** or 800/444-6111 in the U.S.). You can also get special student discounts on admission to many attractions if you show a current student ID card from your college. Arizona's three major **universities**—Arizona State University in Tempe, the University of Arizona in Tucson, and Northern Arizona University in Flagstaff—all have an active nightlife in the surrounding neighborhoods. At Arizona State University in Tempe, east of downtown Phoenix, Mill Avenue is the center of activity for ASU students. Here you'll find inexpensive restaurants, cafés, unusual shops, and numerous bars and nightclubs featuring nightly live and recorded music. Available on the ASU campus, the *University Guide* (☎ **602/820-0768**) is a student-oriented directory with information on everything from apartments to student aid, from concerts to where to go skiing. Student unions at the universities can also offer some assistance to traveling students.

7 Getting There

BY PLANE

Arizona is served many airlines flying to both Phoenix and Tucson from around the United States. Dozens of car-rental companies are located both at Sky Harbor International Airport in Phoenix and at Tucson International Airport.

THE MAJOR AIRLINES

Phoenix and Tucson are both served by the following airlines: Aero México (☎ 800/237-6639), America West (☎ 800/235-9292), American (☎ 800/433-7300), Continental (☎ 800/525-0280), Delta (☎ 800/221-1212), Northwest (☎ 800/225-2525), Southwest (☎ 800/435-9792), and United (☎ 800/241-6522). The following airlines serve Phoenix but not Tucson: Alaska Airlines (☎ 800/426-0333), TWA (☎ 800/221-2000), and USAir (☎ 800/428-4322).

FINDING THE BEST AIRFARE

REGULAR FARES   At press time fares from New York to Phoenix averaged about $460 for a nonrefundable, minimum seven-day advance-purchase round-trip ticket, to $1,280 for a full-fare round-trip coach ticket to $1,630 for a first-class round-trip ticket.

GOOD-VALUE CHOICES   You may be able to fly for less than the standard fare by contacting a **ticket broker** (also known as a bucket shop). These companies advertise in the Sunday travel sections of major city newspapers with small ads listing numerous destinations and ticket prices. You won't always be able to get the low price they advertise, but you're likely to save a bit of money off the regular fare. Call a few and compare prices, making sure you find out about all the taxes and surcharges that may not be included in the initial fare quote. In general, the more restrictions there are attached to an airfare, the lower it will be. However, when an airline runs a special deal, you won't always do better at the ticket brokers.

Also be sure to check fares at **smaller airlines,** some of which are not on travel-agent computer systems. These small, often new, airlines often offer the lowest available fares.

For last-minute bookings, contact **Ridgewood Macs & Olsen** (☎ **800/FLY-ASAP**), which can often get you tickets at significantly less than full fare.

FLIGHTS FROM THE U.K.

From London, there are flights **to Phoenix** from Heathrow Airport on United, American, and British Airways and from Gatwick Airport on American, British Airways, Continental, Delta, Northwest, and TWA. There are flights to **Tucson** from Heathrow on American, Delta, and United, and from Gatwick on American, Continental, Delta, and Northwest.

BY TRAIN

Phoenix and Flagstaff have **Amtrak** (☎ **800/872-7245** in the U.S. and Canada for information and reservations) service from Los Angeles to the west and Albuquerque, Santa Fe, Kansas City, and Chicago to the east aboard the *Southwest Chief.* The *Sunset Limited* connects New Orleans, Houston, San Antonio, El Paso, and Los Angeles with Phoenix and Tucson. At press time, the fare from Los Angeles to Phoenix was $85 one way and $170 round-trip. This trip takes about nine hours. Lower fares are possible depending on availability; that is, earlier bookings mean better discounts.

BY BUS

Greyhound Lines (☎ **800/231-2222**) offers service to several Arizona cities from Los Angeles, San Diego, Las Vegas, and Albuquerque. Travel by bus is economical, especially if you're planning on doing a lot of traveling and purchase a special un-limited-travel pass. The trip from Los Angeles to Phoenix takes about seven hours. The fare is $29 one way, $58 round-trip.

BY CAR

The distance to Phoenix from Los Angeles is approximately 369 miles; from San Francisco, 778 miles; and from Albuquerque, N.M., 455 miles.

If you're planning to travel through northern Arizona anytime in the winter, carry chains.

PACKAGE TOURS

If you prefer to let someone else do all your travel preparations, then a package tour might be for you—whether you just want to lie by the pool at a resort for a week or see the whole state in two weeks. The best way to find out about pack-age tours to Arizona is to visit a travel agent, who will likely have several booklets about different tours and airfare/hotel-room packages being offered by different airlines.

Gray Line of Phoenix, P.O. Box 21126, Phoenix, AZ 85036 (☎ **602/495-9100** or 800/732-0327), offers excursions lasting 1 to 13 days. Tours include the Grand Canyon by way of Sedona and Oak Creek Canyon; and a canyonlands tour that includes the Grand Canyon and Lake Powell, with stops in Utah and at Las Vegas.

Maupintour, 1515 St. Andrews Dr., Lawrence, KS 66047 (☎ **913/843-1211** or 800/255-4266), one of the largest tour operators in the world, offers several Arizona itineraries that cover the Grand Canyon, the Four Corners region, Phoenix, and Tucson.

8 Getting Around

BY CAR

A car is by far the best way to see Arizona. There just isn't any other way to get to many of the more remote natural spectacles and historic sites. Remember, though, that this is a big state, and distances are large. For driving distances between cities in Arizona, see the map "Arizona Driving Times and Distances," in this chapter.

RENTALS   Because Phoenix and Tucson are major resort destinations, they both have dozens of **car-rental agencies.** Prices at rental agencies elsewhere in the state tend to be higher, so if at all possible, try to rent your car in either Phoenix or Tucson. Major rental-car companies with offices in Arizona include Alamo (☎ 800/327-9633), Avis (☎ 800/331-1212), Budget (☎ 800/527-0700), Dollar (☎ 800/800-4000), Hertz (☎ 800/654-3131), National (☎ 800/227-7368), and Thrifty (☎ 800/367-2277).

Rates for rental cars vary considerably between companies and with the model you wish to rent. Also, keep in mind that the rate for any given date will fluctu-ate depending on availability and demand. If you call the same company three times and ask about renting the same model car, you may get three different quotes. It pays to start shopping early. At press time, Budget was charging $114 per week or $25 per day for a compact car with unlimited mileage.

If you're a member of a frequent-flyer program, check to see which rental-car companies participate in the program. Also, when making a reservation be sure to mention any discount you might be eligible for, such as corporate, military, or AAA, and any specials offered. Beware of coupons offering discounts on rental-car rates—often these discount the highest rates only. It's always cheaper to rent by the week, so even if you don't need a car for seven days, you might find that it's still cheaper than renting for four days only.

One last tip: Check with your credit/charge-card and auto-insurance companies to see if you can decline the collision-damage waiver (CDW). Many credit and charge cards now cover the charges if you decline the CDW, and your insurance may already be sufficient to pay for any damage you do to the rental car. CDW insurance can add $12 or more per day to the price of renting a car, so you'll save quite a bit if you're renting for a week or more.

GASOLINE   Always be sure to keep your gas tank topped off. It's not unusual for it to be 60 miles between gas stations in many parts of Arizona.

DRIVING RULES   A right turn on a red light is permitted after a complete stop. Seat belts are required for the driver and any other passenger, and children four years and younger, or who weigh 40 pounds or less, must be in a children's car seat. General speed limits are 25 to 35 m.p.h. in towns and cities, 15 m.p.h. in school zones, and 55 m.p.h. on highways, except rural Interstates where the speed limit is 65 m.p.h.

BREAKDOWNS/ASSISTANCE   It's a long way between towns in Arizona and a breakdown in the desert can be more than just an inconvenience—it can be dangerous. Always carry drinking water with you while driving through the desert, and if you plan to head off on back roads, it's a good idea to carry extra water for the car as well.

If you're a member of the **American Automobile Association (AAA)** and your car breaks down, call 800/633-3222 or 800/AAA-HELP for 24-hour emergency road service.

MAPS   The best road maps of Arizona are produced by the American Automobile Association (you have to be a member to get these) and by *Arizona Highways* (☎ **800/543-5432**), a local magazine. Other maps are available from tourist information offices in Phoenix and Tucson. You can also pick up state road maps at almost any gas station.

BY PLANE

Arizona is a big state (the sixth largest), so if your time is short, you might want to consider flying between cities. Several small commuter airlines offer service within the state. These include America West (☎ 800/235-9292), Arizona Airways (☎ 800/274-0662), Scenic Airlines (☎ 800/535-4448), Skywest (☎ 800/453-9417), and United Express (☎ 800/241-6522). Cities served by these airlines include Phoenix, Tucson, Flagstaff, Sedona, Showlow, Prescott, Fort Huachuca, Bullhead City, Lake Havasu City, Yuma, and Page.

BY TRAIN

The train is not really a viable way of getting around much of Arizona because there is no Amtrak train service between Flagstaff in the north and Phoenix in the south. However, you can travel between Phoenix and Tucson by train. There's also an excursion train that runs from Williams (30 miles west of Flagstaff) to Grand Canyon Village at the South Rim of the Grand Canyon (see Chapter 7 for details).

Arizona Driving Times & Distances

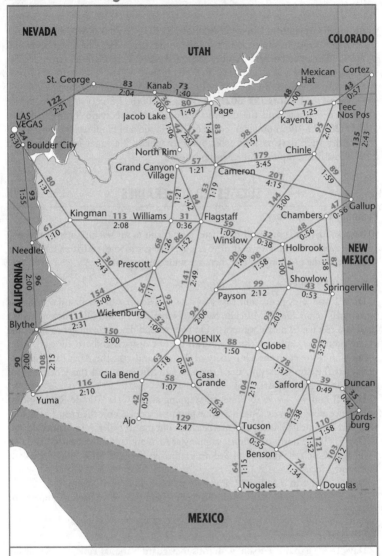

Black numbers *indicate driving times*
Red numbers *indicate distances in miles*
In this schematic we assume 100 miles *will take an average of* 1 hour, 49 minutes *(excluding stops) at an average speed of 55 miles per hour*

BY BUS

Although **Greyhound Lines** (☎ 800/231-2222) offers bus service to quite a few cities in Arizona, its routes don't cover the entire state. Cities served by Greyhound include Phoenix, Tucson, Tempe, Mesa, Chandler, Casa Grande, Green Valley, Nogales, Sierra Vista, Douglas, Prescott, Camp Verde, Flagstaff, Williams, Seligman, Kingman, Bullhead City/Laughlin, Houck, Holbrook, and Winslow.

Nava-Hopi Tours (☎ 602/774-5003 or 800/892-8687) offers bus service between Flagstaff and the Grand Canyon, and the **Navajo Transit System** (☎ 520/729-4002) provides service on the Navajo and Hopi reservations, which includes such destinations as Canyon de Chelly National Monument and Window Rock, capitol of the Navajo Nation.

SUGGESTED ITINERARIES

Planning Your Itinerary

Because Arizona is such a diverse state, it's difficult to suggest an itinerary that will fit everyone's needs. However, if your goal is to get to know Arizona rather than just lie by the pool or play golf, here are some suggestions:

If You Have 1 Week

Days 1 and 2   Spend your first two days in Tucson. On the first day, visit the Arizona-Sonora Desert Museum, Saguaro National Park, and Old Tucson Studios (if you're a fan of movie westerns). On your second day in town, get to know the city proper by exploring the downtown historic districts and arts districts. After lunch, head over to the University of Arizona and visit the Arizona Historical Society Tucson Museum, the Arizona State Museum, and the University of Arizona Museum of Art.

Days 3 and 4   Drive to Phoenix, stopping at the Casa Grande Ruins and in Florence along the way. Spend a day exploring Phoenix: Visit the Heard Museum, Desert Botanical Garden, and maybe check out the art galleries in Scottsdale.

Day 5   Drive north to Sedona, stopping at Arcosanti and Montezuma Castle on the way. Catch the sunset over Sedona's red rocks from Schnebly Hill overlook or Airport Mesa.

Day 6   Drive to the Grand Canyon by way of Oak Creek Canyon.

Day 7   Wake up for sunrise on the canyon, and then drive back to Phoenix or Tucson.

If You Have 2 Weeks

Days 1–3   Explore Tucson, with trips to Saguaro National Park, San Xavier del Bac, Tubac/Tumacacori, Tombstone, and Bisbee.

Days 4 and 5   Drive to Phoenix, stopping at the Casa Grande Ruins and in Florence along the way.

Days 6 and 7   Drive to Sedona by way of Prescott and Jerome.

Days 8 and 9   Explore the Flagstaff area and the Grand Canyon.

Days 10–13   Explore the Four Corners region, including Navajo National Monument, Monument Valley, Canyon de Chelly, the Painted Desert, and the Petrified Forest.

Day 14   Return to Phoenix or Tucson, stopping at Montezuma Castle and Arcosanti on the way back.

If You Have 3 Weeks

With this much time you can indulge in whatever your personal interest happens to be. Spend several days or even the whole week at a resort or guest ranch. Rent a houseboat on Lake Powell, Lake Mead, Lake Mohave, or Lake Havasu. Raft the Grand Canyon. Hike or ride a mule down into the Grand Canyon and spend several days exploring the inner canyon.

FAST FACTS: Arizona

American Express   There are offices or representatives in Phoenix, Tucson, Green Valley, Flagstaff, Sun City, and Scottsdale. For more information, call American Express at 800/528-4800.

Area Code   The telephone area code for the Phoenix area is 602. For the rest of Arizona it's 520.

Banks and ATM Networks   ATMs in Arizona generally use the following systems: Star, Plus, Arizona Interchange Network, Master Teller, and American Express.

Business Hours   The following are general open hours; specific establishments may vary. **Banks:** Monday through Friday from 9am to 5pm (some are also open on Saturday from 9am to noon). **Offices:** Monday through Friday from 9am to 5pm. **Stores:** Monday through Saturday from 10am to 6pm and on Sunday from noon to 5pm (malls usually stay open until 9pm Monday through Saturday). **Bars:** Although they generally open around 11am, bars in Arizona are legally allowed to be open Monday through Saturday from 6am to 1am and on Sunday from 10am to 1am.

Camera/Film   Because the sun is almost always shining in Arizona, you can use a slower film—that is, one with a lower ASA number. This will give you sharper pictures. If your camera accepts different filters, and especially if you plan to travel in the higher altitudes of the northern part of the state, you'd do well to invest in a polarizer, which reduces contrast, deepens colors, and eliminates glare. Also, be sure to protect your camera and film from heat. Never leave your camera or film in a car parked in the sun—temperatures inside the car can climb to more than 130°, which is plenty hot enough to damage sensitive film.

Car Rentals   See "Getting Around," earlier in this chapter.

Climate   See "When to Go," earlier in this chapter.

Driving Rules   See "Getting Around," earlier in this chapter.

Drugstores   Call 800/WALGREENS for the Walgreens pharmacy that's nearest you or that's open 24 hours a day.

Emergencies   Throughout Arizona, **911** is the number to call in case of a fire, police, or medical emergency.

Fruits, Vegetables, and Live Plants   Because Arizona is one of the main citrus-growing states in the United States, there are restrictions on what fruits, vegetables, and live plants can be brought into the state. These restrictions are designed to protect local crops from imported insects and plant diseases and apply primarily to citrus fruits, but other plant matter may also be confiscated. If you'd like to find out more about restrictions, phone 602/255-4933.

Information   See "Visitor Information" in "Visitor Information and Money," earlier in this chapter, and individual city chapters and sections for local information offices.

Legal Aid   If you're in need of legal aid, first look in the white pages of the local telephone book under "Legal Aid." You may also want to contact the Travelers Aid Society, which may also be found in the white pages. In Phoenix, the phone number for Community Legal Services is 602/258-3434. In Tucson, the number for Southern Arizona Legal Aid is 520/623-9465 or 800/248-6789, and for Travelers Aid of Tucson it's 520/622-8900.

Liquor Laws   The legal age for buying or consuming alcoholic beverages is 21. Only 1 liter per month can be brought in from a foreign country. You cannot purchase any alcoholic drinks from 1 to 6am Monday through Saturday and from 1 to 10am on Sunday.

Newspapers/Magazines   Arizona supports dozens of daily and weekly newspapers. Among these are the morning and evening dailies of Phoenix and Tucson, and those two cities' weekly arts and entertainment newspapers. *Arizona Highways* is nationally known for its stunning color photography that shows Arizona at its best.

Pets   Many hotels and motels in Arizona accept pets, though there is sometimes a small fee charged to allow the pet to stay in your room. Others don't allow pets at all, especially bed-and-breakfast inns. If you plan to travel with a pet, it's always best to check when making hotel reservations. At Grand Canyon Village, there's a kennel where you can board your pet while you hike down into the canyon.

Police   In most places in Arizona, phone **911**. A few small towns have not adopted this emergency phone number, so if 911 doesn't work, dial 0 (zero) for the operator and state the type of emergency.

Safety   When driving long distances, always carry plenty of drinking water, and if you're heading off onto dirt roads, extra water for your car's radiator is also a good idea. When hiking or walking in the desert, keep an eye out for rattlesnakes; these poisonous snakes are not normally aggressive unless provoked, so give them a wide berth and they'll leave you alone. Black widow spiders and scorpions are also desert denizens that can be dangerous, though the better-known tarantula is actually much less of a threat. If you go turning over rocks or logs, you're likely to encounter one of Arizona's poisonous residents.

Taxes   There's a state sales tax of 5% (local communities levy additional taxes), a car-rental tax of 5% (Tucson) to 9.5% (Phoenix), and a hotel room tax of 6.05% to 14.05%.

Time Zone   Arizona is in the mountain time zone. However, the state does *not* observe daylight saving time, and so time differences between Arizona and the rest of the country vary with the time of year. From the last Sunday in October until the first Sunday in April, Arizona is one hour later than the West Coast and two hours earlier than the East Coast. The rest of the year Arizona is on the same time as the West Coast and is three hours earlier than the East Coast. There is an exception, however—the Navajo Reservation observes daylight saving time. However, the Hopi Reservation, which is completely surrounded by the Navajo Reservation, does not.

Weather   For current weather information, call 602/265-5550.

For Foreign Visitors

4

The American West is well known and well loved in many countries. Arizona's images are familiar from western novels, movies, television shows, and advertisements. And of course, the Grand Canyon is one of the wonders of the world. However, despite Arizona's being the Wild West, there will likely be typically American situations that you'll encounter in Arizona, and this chapter should help you prepare for your trip.

1 Preparing for Your Trip

ENTRY REQUIREMENTS

DOCUMENT REGULATIONS   Canadian citizens may enter the United States without visas; they need only proof of residence.

British subjects and citizens of New Zealand, Japan, and most Western European countries traveling on valid passports may not need a visa for less than 90 days of holiday or business travel to the United States, providing that they hold a round-trip or return ticket and enter the country on an airline or cruise line participating in the visa-waiver program.

(Note that citizens of these visa-exempt countries who first enter the United States may then visit Mexico, Canada, Bermuda, and/or the Caribbean islands and then reenter the United States, by any mode of transportation, without needing a visa. Further information is available from any U.S. embassy or consulate.)

Citizens of countries other than those stipulated above, including citizens of Australia, must have two documents: (1) a valid passport, with an expiration date at least six months later than the scheduled end of the visit to the United States; and (2) a tourist visa, available without charge from the nearest U.S. consulate.

To obtain a visa, the traveler must submit a completed application form (either in person or by mail) with a 1½-inch-square photo and demonstrate binding ties to a residence abroad.

Usually you can obtain a visa at once or within 24 hours, but it may take longer during the summer rush from June to August. If you cannot go in person, contact the nearest U.S. embassy or consulate for directions on applying by mail. Your travel agent or airline office may also be able to provide you with visa applications and instructions. The U.S. consulate or embassy that issues your visa will determine whether you will be issued a multiple- or single-entry visa and any restrictions regarding the length of your stay.

MEDICAL REQUIREMENTS No inoculations are needed to enter the United States unless you're coming from, or have stopped over in, areas known to be suffering from epidemics, especially of cholera or yellow fever.

If you have a disease requiring treatment with medications containing narcotics or drugs requiring a syringe, carry a valid signed prescription from your physician to allay any suspicions that you're smuggling drugs.

CUSTOMS REQUIREMENTS Every adult visitor may bring in free of duty: 1 liter of wine or hard liquor; 200 cigarettes *or* 100 cigars (but no cigars from Cuba) *or* 3 pounds of smoking tobacco; and $100 worth of gifts. These exemptions are offered to travelers who spend at least 72 hours in the United States and who have not claimed them within the preceding six months. It's altogether forbidden to bring into the country foodstuffs (particularly cheese, fruit, cooked meats, and canned goods) and plants (vegetables, seeds, tropical plants, and so on). Foreign tourists may bring in or take out up to $10,000 in U.S. or foreign currency with no formalities; larger sums must be declared to Customs on entering or leaving the country.

INSURANCE

There is no national health-care system in the United States. Because the cost of medical care is extremely high, we strongly advise every traveler to secure health insurance coverage before setting out. You may want to take out a comprehensive travel policy that covers (for a relatively low premium) sickness or injury costs (medical, surgical, and hospital); loss or theft of your baggage; trip-cancellation costs; guarantee of bail in case you are arrested; and costs associated with accident, repatriation, or death. Such packages (for example, "Europe Assistance" in Europe) are sold by automobile clubs at attractive rates, as well as by insurance companies and travel agencies.

MONEY

CURRENCY & EXCHANGE The U.S. monetary system has a decimal base: one American **dollar** ($1) = 100 **cents** (100¢).

Dollar bills commonly come in $1 ("a buck"), $5, $10, $20, $50, and $100 denominations (the last two are not welcome when paying for small purchases and are not accepted in taxis). There are also $2 bills (seldom encountered).

There are six denominations of coins: 1¢ (one cent, or a "penny"), 5¢ (five cents, or a "nickel"), 10¢ (ten cents, or a "dime"), 25¢ (twenty-five cents, or a "quarter"), 50¢ (fifty cents, or a "half dollar"), and the rare $1 piece.

Note: The "foreign-exchange bureaus" so common in Europe are rare even at airports in the United States, and nonexistent outside major cities. Try to avoid having to change foreign money, or traveler's checks not denominated in U.S. dollars, at a small-town bank, or even a branch bank in a big city. In fact, leave any currency other than U.S. dollars at home—it may prove more nuisance to you than it's worth.

TRAVELER'S CHECKS Traveler's checks denominated in U.S. dollars are readily accepted at most hotels, motels, restaurants, and large stores, but the best place to change traveler's checks is at a bank. Do not bring traveler's checks denominated in other currencies.

CREDIT & CHARGE CARDS   The method of payment most widely used is credit and charge cards: Visa (BarclayCard in Britain), MasterCard (EuroCard in Europe, Access in Britain, Chargex in Canada), American Express, Diners Club, Discover, and Carte Blanche. You can save yourself trouble by using "plastic money" rather than cash or traveler's checks in most hotels, motels, restaurants, and retail stores (a growing number of food and liquor stores now accept credit/charge cards). You must have a credit or charge card to rent a car. It can also be used as proof of identity (it often carries more weight than a passport) or as a "cash card," enabling you to draw money from banks and automated-teller machines (ATMs) that accept it.

SAFETY

GENERAL   While tourist areas are generally safe, crime is on the increase everywhere, and U.S. urban areas tend to be less safe than those in Europe or Japan. Visitors should always stay alert. This is particularly true in large U.S. cities. It is wise to ask the city's or area's tourist office if you're in doubt about which neighborhoods are safe. Avoid deserted areas, especially at night. Don't go into any city park at night unless there is an event that attracts crowds. Generally speaking, you can feel safe in areas where there are many people and many open establishments.

Avoid carrying valuables with you on the street, and don't display expensive cameras or electronic equipment. Hold on to your pocketbook, and place your billfold in an inside pocket. In restaurants, theaters, and other public places, keep your possessions in sight.

Remember also that hotels are open to the public, and in a large hotel, security may not be able to screen everyone entering. Always lock your room door—don't assume that once inside your hotel you are automatically safe and no longer need be aware of your surroundings.

DRIVING   Safety while driving is particularly important. Question your rental agency about personal safety, or ask for a brochure of traveler safety tips when you pick up your car. Obtain from the agency written directions, or a map with the route marked in red, to show you how to get to your destination. If possible, arrive and depart during daylight hours.

Recently more and more crime has involved cars and drivers. If you drive off a highway into a doubtful neighborhood, leave the area as quickly as possible. If you have an accident, even on the highway, stay in your car with the doors locked until you assess the situation or until the police arrive. If you are bumped from behind on the street or are involved in a minor accident with no injuries, and the situation appears to be suspicious, motion to the other driver to follow you. *Never* get out of your car in such situations. You can also make and keep in your car a sign that reads: PLEASE FOLLOW THIS VEHICLE TO REPORT THE ACCIDENT. Show the sign to the other driver and go directly to the nearest police precinct or store—at night, to a well-lit service station or all-night store.

If you see someone on the road who indicates a need for help, *don't stop*. Take note of the location, drive on to a well-lit area, and telephone the police by dialing 911.

Park in well-lit, well-traveled areas if possible. Always keep your car doors locked, whether the vehicle is attended or unattended. Look around you before you get out of your car, and never leave any packages or valuables in sight. If someone attempts to rob you or steal your car, do *not* try to resist the thief/carjacker—report the incident to the police department immediately.

Also, make sure that you have enough gasoline in your tank to reach your intended destination, so that you're not forced to look for a service station in an unfamiliar and possibly unsafe neighborhood—especially at night.

You may wish to contact the tourist information bureau in Phoenix or Tucson, or the Arizona state tourism office, before you arrive. They may be able to provide you with a safety brochure. Contact information for those offices are: **Phoenix & Valley of the Sun Convention & Visitors Bureau,** One Arizona Center, 400 E. Van Buren St., Suite 600, Phoenix, AZ 85004-2290 (☎ **602/ 254-6500**); **Metropolitan Tucson Convention & Visitors Bureau,** 130 S. Scott Ave., Tucson, AZ 85701 (☎ **520/624-1817** or 800/638-8350); or the **Arizona Office of Tourism,** 1100 W. Washington St., Phoenix, AZ 85007 (☎ **602/ 542-TOUR** or 800/842-8257).

2 Getting To & Around the U.S.

GETTING TO THE U.S.

Travelers from overseas can take advantage of the **APEX (advance-purchase excursion)** fares offered by the major U.S. and European carriers. Aside from these, attractive values are offered by Icelandair on flights from Luxembourg to New York and by Virgin Atlantic Airways from London to New York/Newark.

From London, there are flights to Phoenix from Heathrow Airport on United, American, and British Airways and from Gatwick Airport on American, British Airways, Continental, Delta, Northwest, and TWA. There are flights to Tucson from Heathrow on American, Delta, and United, and from Gatwick on American, Continental, Delta, and Northwest.

From Canada there are flights to Phoenix from Toronto on American, Delta, Northwest, United, and USAir, and from Vancouver on Alaska, United, and America West. There are flights to Tucson from Toronto on American, Delta, and United, and from Vancouver on Delta.

From New Zealand and Australia, there are flights to Los Angeles on Quantas and New Zealand Air. Continue on to Phoenix or Tucson on a regional airline such as America West or Southwest. If you're heading to the Grand Canyon, take a flight from Los Angeles to Las Vegas.

The visitor arriving by air, no matter what the port of entry, should cultivate patience before setting foot on U.S. soil. Getting through Immigration control may take as long as two hours on some days, especially summer weekends. Add the time it takes to clear Customs and you'll see that you should make very generous allowance for delay in planning connections between international and domestic flights—an average of two to three hours at least.

In contrast, travelers arriving by car or by rail from Canada will find border-crossing formalities streamlined practically to the vanishing point. And air travelers from Canada, Bermuda, and some places in the Caribbean can sometimes go through Customs and Immigration at the point of departure, which is much quicker.

GETTING AROUND THE U.S.

For information specific to travel to and around Arizona, see "Getting There" and "Getting Around" in Chapter 3.

BY PLANE Some large airlines (for example, American, Delta, Northwest, TWA, and United) offer travelers on their transatlantic and transpacific flights special discount tickets under the name **Visit USA,** allowing travel between any U.S. destinations at minimum rates. They are not on sale in the United States—they must be purchased before you leave your foreign point of departure. This system is the best, easiest, and fastest way to see the United States at low cost. You should obtain information well in advance from your travel agent or the office of the airline concerned, since the conditions attached to these discount tickets can be changed without advance notice.

BY TRAIN   Long-distance trains in the United States are operated by **Amtrak** (☎ **800/872-7245**), the national rail passenger corporation. International visitors can buy a **USA Railpass,** good for 15 or 30 days of unlimited travel on Amtrak. The pass is available through many foreign travel agents. The price at press time for a 15-day pass was $340; a 30-day pass was $425. With a foreign passport, you can also buy passes at any staffed Amtrak station in the United States. Reservations are generally required and should be made for each part of your trip as early as possible. Amtrak also offers an **Air/Rail Travel Plan** that allows you to travel both by train and plane; for information call 800/321-8684.

Visitors should be aware of the limitations of long-distance rail travel in the United States. With a few notable exceptions (for instance, the Northeast Corridor line between Boston and Washington, D.C.), service is rarely up to European standards: delays are common, routes are limited and often infrequently served, and fares are rarely significantly lower than discount airfares. Thus, cross-country train travel should be approached with caution. See "Getting Around" in Chapter 3 for specific information on Amtrak service in Arizona.

BY BUS   The cheapest way to travel in the United States is by bus. **Greyhound** (☎ **800/231-2222**), the nationwide bus line, offers an **Ameripass** for unlimited travel. At press time, a 7-day pass was $179, a 15-day pass was $289, and a 30-day pass was $399. Bus travel in the United States can be both slow and uncomfortable, so this option is not for everyone.

BY CAR   The United States is a nation of car drivers, and the most cost-effective, convenient, and comfortable way to travel through the country—particularly through the western states—is by car. The Interstate highway system connects cities and towns all over the country, and in addition to these high-speed, limited-access roadways, there's an extensive network of federal, state, and local highways and roads. Travel by car gives visitors the freedom to make—and alter—their itineraries to suit their own needs and interests. And it offers the possibility of visiting some of the off-the-beaten-path locations, places that cannot be reached easily by public transportation. Another convenience of traveling by car is the easy access it offers to inexpensive motels at Interstate highway off-ramps. Such motels are almost always less expensive than hotels and motels in downtown areas.

FAST FACTS: For the Foreign Traveler

Accommodations   It's always a good idea to make hotel reservations as soon as you know the dates of your travel. To make a reservation, you'll usually need to leave a deposit of one night's payment. Some of the major hotels listed in this book maintain overseas reservation networks and can be booked either directly or through travel agents.

Phoenix, Scottsdale, and Tucson are particularly busy during the winter months, and hotels book up in advance. The Grand Canyon is busy all year. If you want to stay at one of the lodges in Grand Canyon National Park, you should make a reservation at least a year in advance. Also, because distances in Arizona are so great (it might be 60 miles or more to the next town), it's crucial to have a room reservation before heading off to remote yet very popular sections of the state such as the Four Corners region. If you don't have a room reservation, it's best to look for a room in the midafternoon. If you wait until later in the evening you run the risk that all the hotels will be full.

In the United States, major downtown hotels, which cater primarily to business travelers, commonly offer weekend discounts of as much as 50% to entice vacationers to fill up the empty hotel rooms. However, resorts and hotels near tourist attractions tend to have higher rates on weekends.

Hotel room rates in most of Arizona tend to go up in the winter months when there's a greater demand. If you wish to save money and don't mind hot weather, you should consider visiting sometime other than winter. The really unbearable temperatures usually don't hit until mid-May and are over by the end of September.

Automobile Organizations   Auto clubs will supply maps, suggested routes, guidebooks, accident and bail-bond insurance, and emergency road service. The major auto club in the United States, with 955 offices nationwide, is the **American Automobile Association (AAA).** Members of some foreign auto clubs have reciprocal arrangements with the AAA and enjoy its services at no charge. If you belong to an auto club in your home country, inquire about AAA reciprocity before you leave. The AAA can provide you with an **International Driving Permit** validating your foreign license. You may be able to join the AAA even if you're not a member of a reciprocal club. To inquire, call 800/AAA-HELP. In addition, some automobile rental agencies now provide these services, so you should inquire about their availability when you rent your car.

Automobile Rentals   To rent a car you need a major credit or charge card and a valid driver's license. Sometimes a passport or an international driver's license is also required if your driver's license is in a language other than English. You usually need to be at least 25 years of age, although some companies do rent to younger people (they may add a daily surcharge). Be sure to return your car with the same amount of gasoline you started out with, as rental companies charge excessive prices for gas. Keep in mind that a separate motorcycle driver's license is required in most states. See "Getting Around" in Chapter 3 for specifics on auto rental in Arizona.

Business Hours   The following are general open hours; specific establishments may vary. **Banks:** Monday through Friday from 9am to 5pm (some are also open on Saturday from 9am to noon); there's usually 24-hour access to the automatic-teller machines (ATMs) at most banks and other outlets. **Offices:** Monday through Friday from 9am to 5pm. **Stores:** Monday through Saturday from 10am to 6pm and on Sunday from noon to 5pm (malls usually stay open until 9pm Monday through Saturday). **Bars:** Although they generally open around 11am, bars in Arizona are legally allowed to be open Monday through Saturday from 6am to 1am and on Sunday from 10am to 1am.

Climate   See "When to Go," in Chapter 3.

Currency   See "Preparing for Your Trip," earlier in this chapter.

Currency Exchange   You'll find currency-exchange services in major airports with international service (there's a bank that offers this service at Sky Harbor Airport in Phoenix, but not at Tucson International Airport). Elsewhere, they may be quite difficult to come by. In Arizona, you can call the following banks to find the nearest bank branch that can change money for you: **In Phoenix,** Thomas Cook, 3164 E. Camelback Rd. (☎ 602/954-0800); Norwest Bank, 3300 N. Central Ave. (☎ 602/263-5936); or Bank of America, 101 N. First Ave. (☎ 602/594-2891). **In Tucson,** call Bank One of Arizona, 2 E. Congress St. (☎ 520/792-7200 or 520/792-7431).

Drinking Laws   The legal drinking age in Arizona—and most other states in the country—is 21. The penalties for driving under the influence of alcohol are stiff.

Electricity   The United States uses 110–120 volts, 60 cycles, compared to 220–240 volts, 50 cycles, as in most of Europe. In addition to a 110-volt tranformer, small appliances of non-American manufacture, such as hairdryers or shavers, will require a plug adapter with two flat, parallel pins.

Embassies and Consulates   All embassies are located in the national capital, Washington, D.C.; some consulates are located in major cities, and most nations have a mission to the United Nations in New York City.

Listed here are the embassies and consulates of the major English-speaking countries—Australia, Canada, Ireland, New Zealand, and the United Kingdom. If you're from another country, you can get the telephone number of your embassy by calling "information" in Washington, D.C. (dial 202/555-1212).

The embassy of **Australia** is at 1601 Massachusetts Ave. NW, Washington, DC 20036 (☎ **202/797-3000**). There is no consulate in Arizona; the nearest is at 611 N. Larchmont Blvd., Los Angeles, CA 90004 (☎ **213/469-4300**). Other Australian consulates are in Chicago, Honolulu, Houston, New York, and San Francisco.

The embassy of **Canada** is at 501 Pennsylvania Ave. NW, Washington, DC 20001 (☎ **202/682-1740**). There is no consulate in Arizona; the nearest is at 300 S. Grand Ave., 10th Floor, Los Angeles, CA 90071 (☎ **213/346-2700**). Other Canadian consulates are in Atlanta, Buffalo (N.Y.), Chicago, Cleveland, Dallas, Detroit, Miami, Minneapolis, New York, San Francisco, and Seattle.

The embassy of the **Republic of Ireland** is at 2234 Massachusetts Ave. NW, Washington, DC 20008 (☎ **202/462-3939**). There is no consulate in Arizona; the nearest is at 655 Montgomery St., Suite 930, San Francisco, CA 94111 (☎ **415/392-4214**). Other Irish consulates are in Boston, Chicago, and New York.

The embassy of **New Zealand** is at 37 Observatory Circle NW, Washington, DC 20008 (☎ **202/328-4800**). The only consulate is in Los Angeles, in the Tishman Building, 10960 Wilshire Blvd., Suite 1530, Los Angeles, CA 90024 (☎ **310/477-8241**).

The embassy of the **United Kingdom** is at 3100 Massachusetts Ave. NW, Washington, DC 20008 (☎ **202/462-1340**). There is no consulate in Arizona; the nearest is at 11766 Wilshire Blvd., Suite 400, Los Angeles, CA 90025 (☎ **310/477-3322**). Other British consulates are in Atlanta, Chicago, Houston, Miami, and New York.

Emergencies   Call 911 to report a fire, call the police, or get an ambulance. This is a toll-free call (no coins are required at a public telephone).

If you encounter traveler's problems, check the local telephone directory to find an office of the **Traveler's Aid Society,** a nationwide nonprofit social-service organization geared to helping travelers in difficult straits. Their services might include reuniting families separated while traveling, providing food and/or shelter to people stranded without cash, or even emotional counseling. If you're in trouble, seek them out.

Gasoline (Petrol)   One U.S. gallon equals 3.8 liters, while 1.2 U.S. gallons equals one imperial gallon. You'll notice there are several grades (and price levels) of gasoline available at most gas stations. And you'll also notice that their names change from company to company. The unleaded ones with the highest octane rating are the most expensive (most rental cars take the least expensive "regular" unleaded); leaded gas is the least expensive, but only older cars can take this anymore, so check if you're not sure. And often the price is lower if you pay in cash instead of by credit or charge card. Also, many gas stations now offer lower-priced self-service gas pumps—in fact, some gas stations, particularly at night, are all self-service.

Holidays   On the following legal national holidays, banks, government offices, post offices, and many stores, restaurants, and museums are closed: January 1 (New Year's Day), third Monday in January (Martin Luther King, Jr., Day), third Monday in February (Presidents' Day/Washington's Birthday), last Monday in May (Memorial Day), July 4 (Independence Day), first Monday in September (Labor Day), second Monday in October (Columbus Day), November 11 (Veterans Day/Armistice Day), third Thursday in November (Thanksgiving Day), and December 25 (Christmas). The Tuesday following the first Monday in November is Election Day, and is a legal holiday in presidential-election years (1996 is an election year).

Languages   Major hotels may have multilingual employees. Unless your language is very obscure, they can usually supply a translator on request.

Legal Aid   The foreign tourist will probably never become involved with the American legal system. If, however, you are pulled up for a minor infraction (for example, of the highway code, such as speeding), never attempt to pay the fine directly to the police officer; you may wind up arrested on the much more serious charge of attempted bribery. Pay fines by mail, or directly into the hands of the clerk of the court. If you're accused of a more serious offense, it's wise to say and do nothing before consulting a lawyer. Under U.S. law, an arrested person is allowed one telephone call to a party of his or her choice. Call your embassy or consulate.

Mail   If you want to receive mail on your vacation and you aren't sure of your address, your mail can be sent to you, in your name, **[c/o] General Delivery** (Poste Restante) at the main post office of the city or region where you expect to be. The addressee must pick it up in person and produce proof of identity (driver's license, credit or charge card, passport, etc.).

Generally to be found at intersections, **mailboxes** are blue with a red-and-white stripe and carry the designation U.S. MAIL. If your mail is addressed to a U.S. destination, don't forget to add the five-digit **postal code,** or ZIP (Zone Improvement Plan) code, after the two-letter abbreviation of the state to which the mail is addressed (AZ for Arizona, CA for California, NY for New York, and so on).

Domestic **postage rates** are 23¢ for a postcard and 32¢ for a letter. Check with any local post office for current international postage rates to your home country.

Medical Emergencies   To call an ambulance, dial **911** from any phone. No coins are needed.

Newspapers/Magazines   National newspapers include the *New York Times, USA Today,* and the *Wall Street Journal.* National news weeklies include *Newsweek, Time,* and *U.S. News & World Report.* In large cities most newsstands offer a small selection of the most popular foreign periodicals and newspapers, such as *The Economist, Le Monde,* and *Der Spiegel.* For information on local publications, see the "Fast Facts" sections for Phoenix and Tucson.

Post   See "Mail," above.

Radio and Television   Audiovisual media, with four coast-to-coast networks—ABC, CBS, NBC, and Fox—joined in recent years by the Public Broadcast System (PBS) and the cable network CNN, play a major part in American life. In big cities, televiewers have a choice of about a dozen channels (including the UHF channels), most of them transmitting 24 hours a day, not counting the pay-TV channels showing recent movies or sports events. All options are usually indicated on your hotel TV set. You'll also find a wide choice of local radio stations, both AM and FM, each broadcasting particular kinds of talk shows and/or music—classical, country, jazz, pop, gospel—punctuated by news broadcasts and frequent commercials. You'll usually find the affiliates of the National Public Radio system at the bottom of the radio dial, broadcasting in-depth news programs as well as talk shows and other eclectic programming.

Safety   See "Safety" in "Preparing for Your Trip," earlier in this chapter.

Taxes   In the United States there is no VAT (value-added tax) or other indirect tax at a national level. Every state, and each county and city in it, is allowed to levy its own local tax on purchases (including hotel and restaurant checks, airline tickets, and so on) and services. Taxes are already included in the price of certain services, such as public transportation, cab fares, telephone calls, and gasoline. The amount of sales tax varies from about 4% to 12%, depending on the state and city, so when you're making major purchases, such as photographic equipment, clothing, or stereo components, it can be a significant part of the cost.

In Arizona, the state sales tax is 5%, but communities can add local sales tax on top of this. There's a car-rental tax of 5% (Tucson) to 9.5% (Phoenix), and a hotel room tax of 6.05% to 14.05% (travelers on a budget should keep this hotel tax in mind when making accommodations choices).

Telephone, Telegraph, Telex, and Fax   The telephone system in the United States is run by private corporations, so rates, especially for long-distance service and operator-assisted calls, can vary widely—even on calls made from public telephones. Local calls in the United States usually cost 25¢ (they're 25¢ throughout Arizona).

Generally, hotel surcharges on long-distance and local calls are astronomical. You're usually better off by calling collect, using a telephone charge card, or using a **public pay telephone,** which you'll find clearly marked in most public buildings and private establishments as well as on the street. Outside metropolitan areas, public telephones are more difficult to find. Stores and gas stations are your best bet.

Most **long-distance and international calls** can be dialed directly from any phone (stock up on quarters if you're calling from a pay phone or use a telephone charge card). For calls to Canada and other parts of the United States, dial 1 followed by the area code and the seven-digit number. For international calls, dial 011 followed by the country code (Australia, 61; Republic of Ireland, 353; New Zealand, 64; United Kingdom, 44), then the city code (for example, 171 or 181 for London, 21 for Birmingham) and the telephone number of the person you wish to call.

Note that all calls to area code 800 are toll free. However, calls to numbers in area codes 700 and 900 (chat lines, bulletin boards, "dating" services, etc.) can be very expensive—usually a charge of 95¢ to $3 or more per minute, and they sometimes have minimum charges that can run as high as $15 or more.

For **reversed-charge or collect calls,** and for **person-to-person calls,** dial 0 (zero, *not* the letter "O") followed by the area code and number you want; an operator will then come on the line, and you should specify that you are calling collect, or person-to-person, or both. If your operator-assisted call is international, ask for the overseas operator.

For **local directory assistance** ("information"), dial 411; for **long-distance information,** dial 1, then the appropriate area code and 555-1212.

Like the telephone system, **telegraph** and **telex** services are provided by private corporations like ITT, MCI, and, above all, Western Union, the most important. You can bring your telegram in to the nearest Western Union office (there are hundreds across the country) or dictate it over the phone (a toll-free call, 800/325-6000). You can also telegraph money (using a major credit or charge card), or have it telegraphed to you, very quickly over the Western Union system. (Note, however, that this service can be very expensive—the service charge can run as high as 15% to 25% of the amount sent.)

Many hotels have **fax** machines available for guest use (be sure to ask about the charge to use it), and many hotel rooms are even wired for guests' fax machines. Almost all shops that make photocopies offer fax service as well.

Telephone Directory   There are two kinds of telephone directories available to you. The general directory is the so-called *White Pages,* in which private and business subscribers are listed in alphabetical order. The inside front cover lists the emergency number for police, fire, and ambulance, and other vital numbers (like the Coast Guard, poison-control center, crime-victims hotline, and so on). The first few pages are devoted to community-service numbers, as well as a guide to long-distance and international calling, complete with country codes and area codes.

The second directory, printed on yellow paper (hence its name, *Yellow Pages*), lists all local services, businesses, and industries by type of activity, with an index at the back. The listings cover not only such obvious items as automobile repairs by make of car, or drugstores (pharmacies) often by geographical location, but also restaurants by type of cuisine and geographical location, bookstores by special subject and/or language, places of worship by religious denomination, and other information that the tourist might otherwise not readily find. The *Yellow Pages* also include city plans or detailed area maps, often showing postal ZIP codes and public transportation routes.

Time   The United States is divided into six time zones. From east to west these are eastern standard time (EST), central standard time (CST), mountain standard time (MST), Pacific standard time (PST), Alaska standard time (AST), and Hawaii standard time (HST). Always keep the changing time zones in mind if you are traveling (or even telephoning) long distances in the United States. For example, noon in New York City (EST) is 11am in Chicago (CST), 10am in Phoenix (MST), 9am in Los Angeles (PST), 8am in Anchorage (AST), and 7am in Honolulu (HST).

Arizona is in the mountain time zone, but it does *not* observe daylight saving time (summertime). Consequently, from the first Sunday in April until the last Sunday in October, there is no time difference between Arizona and California and other states on the West Coast. However, there is a two-hour difference to Chicago, and three hours to New York.

Tipping   This is part of the American way of life, on the principle that you must expect to pay for any service you get (many service personnel receive little direct salary and must depend on tips for their income). Here are some rules of thumb:

In **hotels,** tip bellhops $1 per piece and tip the chamber staff $1 per day. Tip the doorman or concierge only if he or she has provided you with some specific service (for example, calling a cab for you or obtaining difficult-to-get theater tickets).

In **restaurants, bars, and nightclubs,** tip the service staff 15% of the check, tip bartenders 10% to 15%, tip checkroom attendants $1 per garment, and tip valet-parking attendants $1 per vehicle. Tip the doorman only if he has provided you with some specific service (such as calling a cab for you). Tipping is not expected in cafeterias and fast-food restaurants.

Tip **cab drivers** 15% of the fare.

As for **other service personnel,** tip redcaps at airports or railroad stations $1 per piece and tip hairdressers and barbers 15% to 20%.

Tipping ushers in cinemas, movies, and theaters and gas-station attendants is not expected.

Toilets   Foreign visitors often complain that public toilets (or "restrooms") are hard to find in most U.S. cities. True, there are none on the streets, but the visitor can usually find one in a bar, restaurant, hotel, museum, department store, or service station—and it will probably be clean (although service-station restrooms sometimes leave much to be desired). Note, however, that a growing number of restaurants and bars display a notice like RESTROOMS ARE FOR THE USE OF PATRONS ONLY. You can ignore this sign, or better yet, avoid arguments by paying for a cup of coffee or soft drink, which will qualify you as a patron. The cleanliness of toilets at railroad stations and bus depots may be more open to question. Some public places are equipped with pay toilets, which require you to insert one or more coins into a slot on the door before it will open. In restrooms with attendants, leaving at least a 25¢ tip is customary.

THE AMERICAN SYSTEM OF MEASUREMENTS

Length

1 inch (in.)			=	2.54cm			
1 foot (ft.)	=	12 in.	=	30.48cm	=	.305m	
1 yard	=	3 ft.			=	.915m	
1 mile (mi.)	=	5,280 ft.					
					=	1.609km	

To convert miles to kilometers, multiply the number of miles by 1.61 (for example, 50 miles × 1.61 = 80.5km). Also use to convert from miles per hour (m.p.h.) to kilometers per hour (kmph).

To convert kilometers to miles, multiply the number of kilometers by .62 (example, 25km × .62 = 15.5 miles). Also use to convert from kilometers per hour to miles per hour.

Capacity

1 fluid ounce (fl. oz.)			=	.03 liter		
1 pint	=	16 fl. oz.	=	.47 liter		
1 quart	=	2 pints	=	.94 liter		
1 gallon (gal.)	=	4 quarts	=	3.79 liter	=	.83 Imperial gal.

To convert U.S. gallons to liters, multiply the number of gallons by 3.79 (for example, 12 gal. × 3.79 = 45.48 liters).

To convert liters to U.S. gallons, multiply the number of liters by .26 (for example, 50 liters × .26 = 13 U.S. gal.).

To convert U.S. gallons to Imperial gallons, multiply the number of U.S. gallons by .83 (for example, 12 U.S. gal. × .83 = 9.95 Imperial gal.).

To convert Imperial gallons to U.S. gallons, multiply the number of Imperial gallons by 1.2 (for example, 8 Imperial gal. × 1.2 = 9.6 U.S. gal.).

Weight

1 ounce (oz.)			=	28.35g			
1 pound (lb.)	=	16 oz.	=	453.6g	=	.45kg	
1 ton	=	2,000 lb.			=	907kg	=	.91 metric ton

To convert pounds to kilograms, multiply the number of pounds by .45 (for example, 90 lb. × .45 = 40.5kg).

To convert kilograms to pounds, multiply the number of kilos by 2.2 (for example, 75kg × 2.2 = 165 lb.).

Temperature

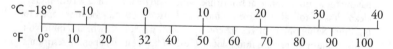

To convert degrees Fahrenheit to degrees Celsius, subtract 32 from °F, multiply by 5, and then divide by 9 (for example, 85°F − 32 × 5 ÷ 9 = 29.4°C).

To convert degrees Celsius to degrees Fahrenheit, multiply °C by 9, divide by 5, and add 32 (for example, 20°C × 9 ÷ 5 + 32 = 68°F).

Phoenix 5

Like the phoenix of ancient mythology, Arizona's capital city of Phoenix has risen from its own ashes, in this case the ruins of an ancient Native American village. The name Phoenix, given to the city by an early settler from Britain, has proven repeatedly to be very appropriate. Rising from the dust of the desert, this city has become one of the largest metropolitan areas in the country.

Though the city has had its economic ups and downs, Phoenix right now is booming. The Camelback Corridor that leads through north-central Phoenix has become the corporate heartland of the city and shiny glass office towers keep pushing up toward the desert sky. Along this burgeoning stretch of road, new restaurants (including both a Planet Hollywood and a Hard Rock Cafe) are opening, malls are being refurbished and expanded, and Phoenicians are flocking both for work and for play.

Throughout the metropolitan area the population is growing and at such a rapid pace that an alarm has been raised: Slow the pace before we become another Los Angeles! Why the phenomenal growth? In large part it's due to the climate. More than 300 days of sunshine a year is a powerful attraction. Sure, summers are hot, but the mountains, and cooler air, are only two hours away. However, it's in the winter that Phoenix truly shines. When most of the country is frozen solid, Phoenix is sunny and warm. This great winter climate has helped make Phoenix and Scottsdale the resort capitals of the United States.

Golf, tennis, and lounging by the pool are only the tip of the iceberg (so to speak). With the cooler winter weather comes the cultural season, and between Phoenix and the neighboring city of Scottsdale, there's an impressive array of music, dance, and theater to be enjoyed. Scottsdale is also well known as a center of the visual arts, ranking only behind New York and Santa Fe in the number of its art galleries.

Over the years, Phoenix has enjoyed the benefits and suffered the problems of rapid urban growth. It has gone from tiny agricultural village to sprawling cosmopolitan metropolis in little more than a century. Along the way it has lost its past amid urban sprawl and unchecked development, while at the same time it has forged a city that's quintessentially 20th-century American. Shopping malls, the gathering places of America, are raised to an art form in Phoenix.

What's Special About Phoenix

Architecture

- Arcosanti, Paolo Soleri's fascinating city of the future in the desert north of Phoenix (you can also visit the Cosanti Foundation, a smaller-scale complex by Soleri in Paradise Valley).
- Taliesin West, Frank Lloyd Wright's school of architecture and the architect's former winter residence.
- Pueblo Grande Museum and Cultural Park, excavated Hohokam ruins dating as far back as A.D. 1.

Museums

- The Heard Museum, one of the country's finest collections of Native American artifacts, arts, and crafts.

Parks/Gardens

- Desert Botanical Garden, devoted to the plants of the desert with a special section on historical uses of Sonora Desert plants.
- Phoenix South Mountain Park, a desert wilderness said to be the largest city park in the country.

Natural Spectacles

- Camelback Mountain, said to look like a camel lying down.
- Mummy Mountain, from the north vaguely resembling the sarcophagus of an Egyptian mummy.
- Papago Buttes, a park northeast of downtown Phoenix with a natural window through the sandstone rock of the buttes.

Shopping

- Old Scottsdale and the Fifth Avenue Shops, an area of old western-style buildings filled with boutiques, Native American arts and crafts stores, and art galleries; considered the Rodeo Drive of Phoenix.
- The Borgata, also in Scottsdale, a shopping mall built to resemble a medieval European village that's filled with expensive boutiques.

Great Neighborhoods

- Mill Avenue in Tempe, a hangout for Arizona State University students and site of unusual little shops, numerous bars, and frequent live-music performances.

Offbeat Oddities

- Mystery Castle, a bizarre and sprawling home in south Phoenix built by one man for his daughter.
- The world's tallest water fountain, in the town of Fountain Hills, 30 miles northeast of Phoenix.

Luxurious resorts create fantasy worlds of waterfalls and swimming pools. Wide boulevards stretch for miles across land that was once desert but has been made green through irrigation. Perhaps it's this willingness to create a new world on top of an old one that attracts people to Phoenix. Then again, maybe it's all that sunshine.

As the mythical phoenix rose reborn from its ashes, so shall a great civilization rise here on the ashes of a past civilization. I name thee Phoenix.
—"Lord" Bryan Philip Darrel Duppa, the British settler who named Phoenix

1   Orientation

ARRIVING

BY PLANE   Centrally located 3 miles from downtown Phoenix, **Sky Harbor Airport** has recently undergone major renovation and expansion. The airport has three terminals—2, 3, and 4—and in these three terminals you'll find car-rental desks, information desks, hotel-reservation centers with direct lines to various valley hotels, and a food court. There's a free 24-hour shuttle bus operating every six minutes between the three terminals. For general airport information, call 602/273-3300; for airport paging, call 602/273-3455; for lost and found, call 602/273-3307.

Getting to and from the Airport   There are two entrances to the airport. The west entrance can be accessed from either the Squaw Peak Parkway (Ariz. 51) or 24th Street, and the east entrance can be accessed from the Hohokam Expressway, which is an extension of 44th Street. If you're headed downtown, leave by way of the 24th Street exit, and if you're headed to Scottsdale, Tempe, or Mesa, take the 44th Street exit.

The **SuperShuttle** (☎ **602/244-9000** or 800/331-3565 outside Arizona) and **Courier Transportation** (☎ **602/232-2222**) offer 24-hour door-to-door van service between Sky Harbor Airport and resorts, hotels, and homes throughout the valley. Fares average about $7 to $10 to the downtown and Tempe area, and about $16 to $20 to the Scottsdale and northern area of the city (each additional person is charged $5). When heading back to the airport for a departure, call 602/244-9000.

Taxis can also be found waiting outside all three airport terminals, or you can call **Yellow Cab** (☎ **602/252-5252**) or **Checker Cab** (☎ **602/257-1818**).

Valley Metro provides **public bus service** throughout the valley with the Red Line (R) operating between the airport and downtown Phoenix, Tempe, and Mesa and the no. 13 (Buckeye) bus operating between the airport and downtown. Note that the Red Line operates only Monday through Friday between 5am and 9:30pm. Bus no. 13 operates similar hours, with Saturday service as well. You can pick up a copy of *The Bus Book*, a guide to using the local bus system that includes detailed information on all routes, at either downtown tourist information center or at the downtown bus terminal at the corner of First Street and Washington Street.

BY CAR   Phoenix is connected to Los Angeles and Tucson by I-10 and to Flagstaff via I-17. If you're headed to Scottsdale, the easiest route is to take the Squaw Peak Freeway north to Highland Avenue, continue a block north to Camelback Road, and then head east to Scottsdale Road. The Superstition Freeway (U.S. 60) leads to Tempe, Mesa, and Chandler.

BY TRAIN   Amtrak's *Southwest Chief* connects Phoenix (via a bus connection from Flagstaff) with Los Angeles in the west and Dallas, St. Louis, and Chicago in the east. The *Sunset Limited* connects Miami, New Orleans, Houston,

Phoenix at a Glance

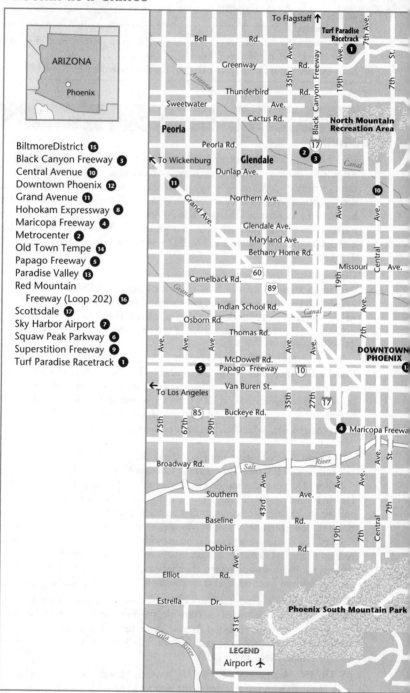

BiltmoreDistrict **15**
Black Canyon Freeway **3**
Central Avenue **10**
Downtown Phoenix **12**
Grand Avenue **11**
Hohokam Expressway **8**
Maricopa Freeway **4**
Metrocenter **2**
Old Town Tempe **14**
Papago Freeway **5**
Paradise Valley **13**
Red Mountain
   Freeway (Loop 202) **16**
Scottsdale **17**
Sky Harbor Airport **7**
Squaw Peak Parkway **6**
Superstition Freeway **9**
Turf Paradise Racetrack **1**

ARIZONA

Phoenix

To Flagstaff ↑

Turf Paradise
Racetrack **1**

Bell   Rd.

Greenway

Thunderbird   Ave.

Sweetwater

Cactus Rd.

**North Mountain
Recreation Area**

Peoria

Peoria Rd.

← To Wickenburg   **Glendale**   **2** **3**   Canal

Dunlap Ave.

11

Northern Ave.

10

Glendale Ave.

Maryland Ave.

Bethany Home Rd.

Camelback Rd. **60**

89   Missouri   Ave.

Grand

Indian School Rd.   Canal

Osborn Rd.

Thomas Rd.

Ave. Ave. Ave.

McDowell Rd.
Papago Freeway **10**

**DOWNTOWN
PHOENIX**

5

Van Buren St.

← To Los Angeles

85   Buckeye Rd.

75th 67th 59th

4 Maricopa Freewa

Broadway Rd.   Salt   River

Southern   Ave.

43rd

Baseline   Rd.

Dobbins   Rd.

Elliot   Rd.

Estrella   Dr.

Phoenix South Mountain Park

51st

Gila River

LEGEND
Airport ✈

1744

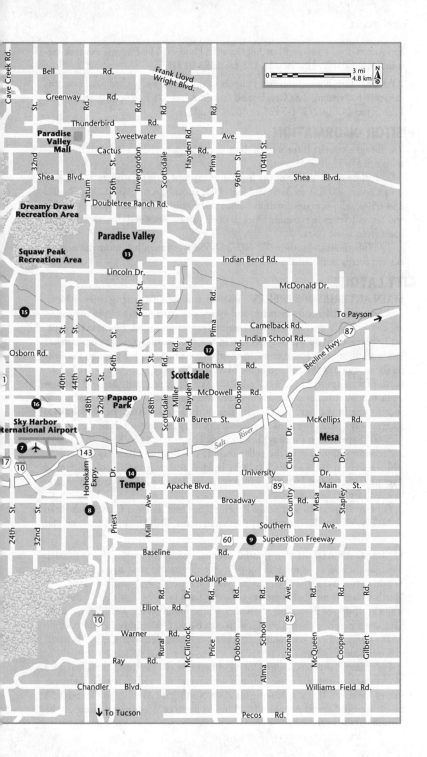

San Antonio, El Paso, and Los Angeles with Phoenix. The Phoenix **Amtrak terminal** is at 401 W. Harrison St. (☎ **602/253-0121**).

BY BUS   Greyhound connects Phoenix to the rest of the United States with its extensive bus system. The **Greyhound terminal** is at 525 E. Washington St., near Fifth Street (☎ **602/271-7426** or 800/231-2222).

VISITOR INFORMATION

You'll find a **tourist information desk** in the baggage claim area of all three terminals at Sky Harbor Airport.

The **Phoenix & Valley of the Sun Convention & Visitors Bureau,** One Arizona Center, 400 E. Van Buren St., Suite 600, Phoenix, AZ 85004-2290 (☎ **602/ 254-6500**), also operates a visitors bureau at the northwest corner of Adams Street and Second Street in the same block as the Hyatt Regency and directly across the street from Civic Plaza.

The **Information Hotline** (☎ **602/252-5588**) has recorded information about current events in Phoenix.

CITY LAYOUT

MAIN ARTERIES & STREETS   Phoenix and the surrounding cities of Mesa, Tempe, Scottsdale, and Chandler, and even those cities farther out in the valley, are laid out in a grid pattern with major avenues and roads about every mile. **I-17 (Black Canyon Freeway)** comes in from the north, curves to the east just south of downtown, and then merges with I-10. Known as the **Papago Freeway** on the west side of the city and as the **Maricopa Freeway** to the south, **I-10** passes north of the airport. At the west end of the Sky Harbor Airport, **Ariz. 51 (Squaw Peak Freeway)** heads north through the center of the city and is the best north-south route in the city. On the east side of the airport, **Ariz. 143 (Hohokam Expressway)** heads north but doesn't yet go very far. Just south of the airport, **U.S. 60 (Superstition Freeway)** heads east to Tempe, Chandler, Mesa, and Gilbert.

Secondary highways in the valley include the **Beeline Highway (Ariz. 87)**, which starts out as Country Club Drive in Mesa and leads to Payson, and **Grand Avenue (U.S. 60 and U.S. 89),** which starts downtown and leads to Sun City and Wickenburg.

For traveling east to west across Phoenix, your best choice is **Camelback Road** or **McDowell Road.** For traveling north and south, 44th Street, 24th Street, and Central Avenue are good choices.

FINDING AN ADDRESS   **Central Avenue,** which runs north to south through downtown Phoenix, is the starting point for all east and west street numbering. **Washington Street** is the starting point for north and south numbering. North-to-south numbered streets are to be found on the east side of the city, while north-to-south numbered avenues will be found on the west. For the most part, street numbers change by 100 with each block. Odd-numbered addresses are on the south and east sides of streets, while even-numbered addresses are on north and west sides of streets.

For example, if you're looking for 4454 East Camelback Road, you'll find it 44 blocks east of Central Avenue between 44th Street and 45th Street on the north side of the street. If you're looking for 2905 North 35th Avenue, you'll find it 35 blocks west of Central Avenue and 29 blocks north of Washington Street on the east side of the street.

STREET MAPS The street maps handed out by rental-car companies are almost useless for finding anything in Phoenix. However, the **Phoenix Chamber of Commerce** sells a detailed map for $2.50 at their office at Bank One Plaza, 201 N. Central Ave., Suite 2700, Phoenix, AZ 85073 (☎ **602/254-5521**). You can also get a simple map at either the airport tourist information desks or at the downtown visitors' information center. Local gas stations also sell maps.

NEIGHBORHOODS IN BRIEF

Because of urban sprawl, Phoenix has yielded its importance to the Valley of the Sun, an area encompassing Phoenix and its metropolitan area of more than 20 cities. Consequently, neighborhoods, per se, have lost significance as outlying cities take on regional importance.

Downtown Phoenix Roughly bordered by Thomas Road on the north, Buckeye Road on the south, 19th Avenue on the east, and Seventh Street on the west, downtown Phoenix is primarily a business, financial, and government district, where both the city hall and state capitol are located. However, there are also a number of tourist attractions, including several art museums, Heritage Square, the Civic Plaza, and Symphony Hall.

Biltmore District The Biltmore District, also known as the Camelback Corridor, centers along Camelback Road between 24th Street and 44th Street and is Phoenix's upscale shopping, residential, and business district. The area is characterized by modern office buildings and is anchored by the Biltmore Hotel and Biltmore Fashion Park shopping mall.

Scottsdale A separate city of more than 130,000 people, Scottsdale extends from Tempe in the south to Carefree in the north, a distance of more than 20 miles, much of which is still desert. "Resort Row" is the name given to Scottsdale Road between Indian School Road and Shea Boulevard. Along this section of road are more than a dozen major resorts. Old Scottsdale capitalizes on its cowboy heritage and has become the valley's main shopping district, with boutiques, jewelers, Native American crafts stores, and numerous restaurants.

Tempe Tempe is the home of Arizona State University and has all the trappings of a university town. The presence of so many young people keeps a very active nightlife going year-round. The center of activity, both day and night, is Mill Avenue, which has dozens of unusual shops along a stretch of about four blocks.

Paradise Valley If Scottsdale is Phoenix's Beverly Hills, then Paradise Valley is its Bel-Air. The most exclusive neighborhood in the valley is almost exclusively residential, but you won't see too many of the more expensive homes because they're set on large tracts of land.

Mesa This eastern suburb of Phoenix has in recent years become something of a high-tech area. Large shopping malls, several inexpensive motels, and a museum attract both locals and visitors to Mesa.

Carefree and Cave Creek Located about 20 miles north of Scottsdale, these two communities represent the Old West and the New West. Carefree is a planned community and is home to the prestigious Boulders resort and El Pedregal shopping center. Cave Creek plays up its western heritage in its architecture and preponderance of bars, steakhouses, and shops selling western crafts and other gifts.

2 Getting Around

BY PUBLIC TRANSPORTATION

Unfortunately the Phoenix **public bus system** is not very useful to tourists. It's primarily meant for use by commuters, and most routes stop running before 9pm at night. There's no bus service on Sunday, and some buses don't run on Saturday either. However, if you decide that you want to take the bus, you should pick up a copy of *The Bus Book* at one of the tourist information desks in the airport (where it's sometimes available), at either downtown tourist office, or at the Downtown Bus Terminal at the corner of First Street and Washington Street. There are both local and express buses. Local bus fare is $1 and express bus fare is $1.50. Monthly passes are also available.

Of more value to visitors is the **Downtown Area Shuttle (DASH),** which provides free bus service within the downtown area. These purple buses with orange racing stripes operate Monday through Friday between 6:30am and 6pm. The buses stop at regular bus stops every 6 to 12 minutes. Attractions along the bus's route include the state capitol, the tourist information center, the Arizona Museum of Science and Technology, Heritage Square, America West Arena, and the Arizona Center shopping mall.

BY TAXI

Because distances in Phoenix are so large, the price of an average taxi ride can be quite high. However, if you haven't got your own wheels and the bus isn't running because it's late at night or the weekend, you don't have any choice but to call a cab. **Yellow Cab** (☎ **602/252-5252**) or **Checker Cab** (☎ **602/257-1818**) provide service throughout the valley. Fares start at $2.40 for the first mile and then increase by $1.40 for each additional mile.

BY CAR

Phoenix and the surrounding cities that together make up the Valley of the Sun sprawl over 420 square miles, so if you want to make the best use of your time, it's fairly essential to have a car to get around.

RENTALS   All the major rental-car companies have offices in Phoenix, with desks inside the airline terminals at Sky Harbor Airport, and because this is a major tourist destination, there are often excellent rates. The best rates are those reserved at least a week in advance, but car-rental companies change what they charge for their cars as the demand goes up and down. If you book far enough in advance, you might get a compact car for less than $100 per week. To save money on your rental, check to see if your credit- or charge-card company picks up the tab for the collision-damage waiver; if not, you'll have to pay an extra $12 or so for this insurance coverage. The state tax on car rentals is 9.5%, so if you want to know what your total rental cost will be before making a reservation, be sure to ask about the tax and the collision-damage waiver. Frequent flyers may get bonus miles for renting a car from a particular company—check with your airline plan to find out. If you happen to be making a last-minute reservation, ask if there are any weekend rates or other specials in effect.

All the major rental-car companies have offices in Phoenix. Among them are the following: **Alamo,** 2246 E. Washington St. (☎ **602/244-0897** or 800/327-9633); **Avis,** Sky Harbor Airport (☎ **602/273-3222** or 800/331-1212); **Budget,**

Sky Harbor Airport (☎ **602/267-1717** or 800/527-0700) and several other locations; **Dollar,** Sky Harbor Airport (☎ **602/275-7588** or 800/800-4000); **Hertz,** Sky Harbor Airport (☎ **602/267-8822**, or 800/654-3131) and many other locations around the area; **National,** Sky Harbor Airport (☎ **602/275-4771** or 800/227-7368); and **Thrifty,** 4114 E. Washington St. (☎ **602/990-9556** or 800/367-2277).

PARKING Phoenix is a new city and has grown up around the automobile. Outside downtown Phoenix, there's almost always plenty of free parking around wherever you go.

DRIVING RULES See "Getting Around," in Chapter 3.

ON FOOT

Unless you happen to be in downtown Phoenix on business or out in Scottsdale shopping, there really isn't anywhere in the valley that's suitable for exploring on foot. Distances are large and the heat and bright sun can make walking a chore rather than a pleasure.

FAST FACTS: Phoenix

American Express There are American Express offices at 2508 E. Camelback Rd. (☎ 602/468-1199), open Monday through Saturday from 10am to 6pm; and at 6900 E. Camelback Rd., Scottsdale (☎ 602/949-7000), open Monday through Saturday from 9:30am to 5:30pm.

Airport See "Arriving" in "Orientation," earlier in this chapter.

Area Code The telephone area code is 602.

Babysitters First check with your hotel, and if they can't recommend or provide a sitter, contact Golden Grandmas (☎ 602/843-4533) or the Granny Company (☎ 602/264-5454).

Camera Repair See "Photographic Needs," below.

Car Rentals See "Getting Around," earlier in this chapter.

Climate See "When to Go," in Chapter 3.

Dentist Call the Dental Referral Service at 602/256-7588 for a referral.

Doctor Call the Maricopa County Medical Society at 602/252-2844 for doctor referrals.

Drugstores See "Pharmacies," below.

Embassies/Consulates See the "Fast Facts: For Foreign Visitors," in Chapter 4.

Emergencies For police, fire, or medical emergency, phone **911.**

Eyeglass Repair The Nationwide Vision Center has 10 locations around the valley, including 933 E. University Dr., Tempe (☎ 602/966-4992), 5130 N. 19th Ave. (☎ 602/242-5294), and 4615 E. Thomas Rd. (☎ 602/952-8667).

Hospitals The Good Samaritan Regional Medical Center, 1111 E. McDowell Rd. (☎ 602/239-2000), and the Desert Samaritan Medical Center, 1400 S. Dobson Rd., Mesa (☎ 602/835-3000), are two of the largest hospitals in the valley.

Hotlines   The Information Hotline (☎ 602/252-5588) provides recorded tourist information on Phoenix and the Valley of the Sun. Pressline (☎ 602/271-5656) provides access to daily news, the correct time, and other topics.

Information   See "Visitor Information" in "Orientation," earlier in this chapter.

Libraries   The Phoenix Central Library is at 1221 N. Central Ave. (☎ 602/262-4636).

Lost Property   If you lost something in the airport, call 602/273-3307; on a bus, call 602/261-8549.

Luggage Storage/Lockers   You'll find luggage-storage lockers at the Greyhound bus station at 525 E. Washington St. (☎ 602/271-7425).

Maps   See "City Layout" in "Orientation," earlier in this chapter.

Newspapers/Magazines   *The Arizona Republic* is Phoenix's morning daily newspaper, and the *Phoenix Gazette* is the afternoon daily. You'll find both in newspaper boxes, convenience stores, grocery stores, and other places. The Friday papers have special sections with schedules of the upcoming week's movie, music, and cultural performances. *New Times* is a free weekly news and arts journal with comprehensive listings of cultural events, film, and rock-music club and concert schedules. The best place to find *New Times* is at Circle K convenience stores all over the valley. An extensive selection of newspapers and magazines can be found at Mill Avenue News, 1 E. Sixth St., Tempe (☎ 602/921-1612).

Pharmacies   Check the *Yellow Pages* of the local telephone directory for the location of a drugstore near you, or call 800/WALGREENS for the Walgreens pharmacy that's nearest you or that's open 24 hours a day.

Photographic Needs   Photomark, 1916 W. Baseline Rd., Mesa (☎ 602/897-2522); 2202 E. McDowell Rd. (☎ 602/244-1133); 204 E. University Dr., Tempe (☎ 602/894-8337); or 5719 W. Northern Ave., Glendale (☎ 602/934-4441), can supply camera needs or repairs.

Police   For police emergencies, phone **911.**

Post Office   The Phoenix General Mail Facility (main post office) is at 4949 E. Van Buren St. (☎ 602/407-2049 or 602/225-3158).

Safety   Don't leave valuables in view in your car, especially when parking in downtown Phoenix. Put anything of value in the trunk or under the seat if you're driving a hatchback. The south-central Phoenix area and downtown are two areas of the city that visitors should take extra precautions in after dark. Angry freeway drivers here in Phoenix have been known to pull guns, so it's a good idea to be polite when driving. Aggressive drivers should be given plenty of room.

Many hotels now provide in-room safes, for which there's a daily charge. Others will be glad to store your valuables in a safety-deposit box at the front office. For additional information, see "Safety" in "Preparing for Your Trip," in Chapter 4.

Taxes   There's a 5% state sales tax (plus variable local taxes), hotel room taxes ranging from 10.25% to 12.05%, and a car-rental tax of 9.5%.

Taxis   See "Getting Around," earlier in this chapter.

Television   Valley of the Sun stations are Channels 3 (independent), 5 (CBS), 8 (PBS), 10 (Fox), 12 (NBC), and 15 (ABC).

Transit Information For Phoenix Transit System public bus information, call 602/253-5000. For Greyhound intercity bus information, call 602/271-7426 or 800/231-2222. For Amtrak intercity train information, call 602/253-0121 or 800/872-7245. For general airport information at Sky Harbor Airport, call 602/273-3300.

Weather The phone number for weather information is 602/265-5550.

3 Accommodations

Because Phoenix has long been popular as a winter refuge from cold and snow, it now has the greatest concentration of resorts in the continental United States. The city also has some of the highest room rates during its winter season. There are also plenty of moderately priced motels. However, during the winter, even these tend to jack up their prices high above what you might expect to pay. No matter where you stay, even in a budget motel, you're likely to find a pool and whirlpool on the premises.

With the exception of valet parking services, parking is free at the majority of Phoenix hotels. If there is a parking charge, we have noted it. You'll find that almost all hotels now have no-smoking and wheelchair-accessible rooms. Also, keep in mind that most resorts offer a variety of weekend, golf, and tennis packages, as well as special discounts in the off-season.

Finally, in the hostelries recommended below all accommodations come with private bath unless otherwise indicated.

BED & BREAKFAST ACCOMMODATIONS If you're the kind of person who likes to stay in bed-and-breakfast inns, you may be surprised that, rather than being housed in historic buildings, the B&Bs of Phoenix are in modern homes. **Mi Casa–Su Casa**, P.O. Box 950, Tempe, AZ 85280-0950 (☎ **602/990-0682** or 800/456-0682), is a reservation service that offers accommodations in homes in Phoenix and across the state. Rates range from $50 to $150 for a double room, depending on the location and luxury of the home. The **Arizona Association of Bed & Breakfast Inns**, P.O. Box 7186, Phoenix, AZ 85011 (☎ **602/277-0775**), is another organization representing B&Bs across the state. Contact it for a list of members. One other option is to contact **Bed & Breakfast Inn Arizona**, P.O. Box 11253, Glendale, AZ 85318-1253 (☎ **602/561-0335** or 800/266-STAY), which represents B&Bs all over the state.

PRICE CATEGORIES In the following listings, price categories are based on the rate for a double room in high season (most resorts and hotels charge the same for a single or double room), and are as follows: "Very Expensive," $125 or more per night; "Expensive," $90 to $125 per night; "Moderate," $60 to $90 per night; and "Inexpensive," under $60 per night.

PHOENIX
VERY EXPENSIVE

✪ Arizona Biltmore

24th St. and Missouri Ave., Phoenix, AZ 85016. ☎ **602/955-6600** or 800/950-0086. Fax 602/954-2571. 498 rms, 45 suites. A/C TV TEL. Early Sept to early June, $280–$360 double; from $500 suite. Early June to early Sept, $120–$145 double; from $300 suite. AE, CB, DC, DISC, EURO, JCB, MC, V.

Phoenix Accommodations

Arizona Biltmore **9**
The Buttes **41**
Crown Sterling Suites **12**
Crowne Plaza–Phoenix **16**
Days Inn–Mesa **45**
Days Inn–Scottsdale Resort **25**
Days Inn–Tempe **39**
Fiesta Inn **40**
Fountain Suites **1**
Hampton Inn Airport **42**
Hermosa Inn **14**
Holiday Inn Hotel &
   Conference Center **21**
Hyatt Regency Phoenix **17**
Hyatt Regency Scottsdale Resort
   at Gainey Ranch **34**
John Gardiner's Tennis Ranch
   on Camelback **28**
Maricopa Manor Bed &
   Breakfast Inn **10**
Marriott's Camelback Inn **31**
Marriott's Mountain Shadows **30**
Motel 6–Mesa North **44**
Motel 6–Scottsdale **24**
Motel 6–Thunderbird **2**
The Phoenician **27**
Pointe Hilton at Squaw Peak **8**
Pointe Hilton at Tapatio Cliffs **3**
Pointe Hilton on
   South Mountain **43**
Radisson Resort Scottsdale **32**
Radisson Tempe Mission
   Palms Hotel **36**
Ramada/Camelback **11**
Red Lion's La Posada Resort **29**
Regal McCormick Ranch **33**
Ritz-Carlton Phoenix **13**
Rodeway Inn–Airport **18**
Rodeway Inn–Phoenix/
   Scottsdale **23**
San Carlos Hotel **15**
Scottsdale Marriott Suites **22**
Scottsdale Princess **35**
Scottsdale's Fifth Avenue Inn **20**
Sheraton Crescent Hotel **5**
Sheraton Mesa Hotel **46**
Super 8–Phoenix/Metro **7**
Super 8–Tempe/Scottsdale **37**
Travelodge Metrocenter **6**
Travelodge–Tempe **38**
Wyndham Garden Hotel **19**
Wyndham Metrocenter Hotel **4**
Wyndham Paradise
   Valley Resort **26**

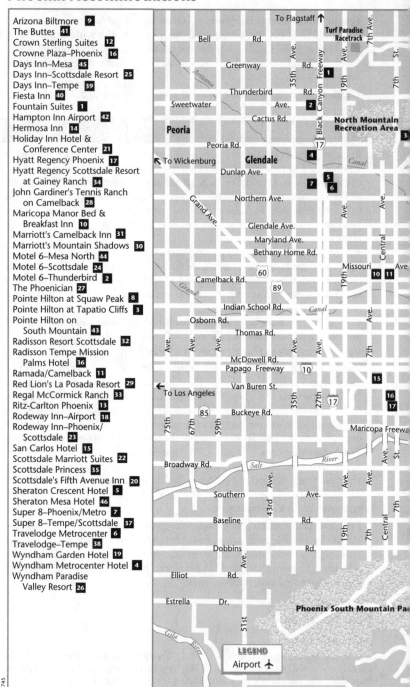

1745

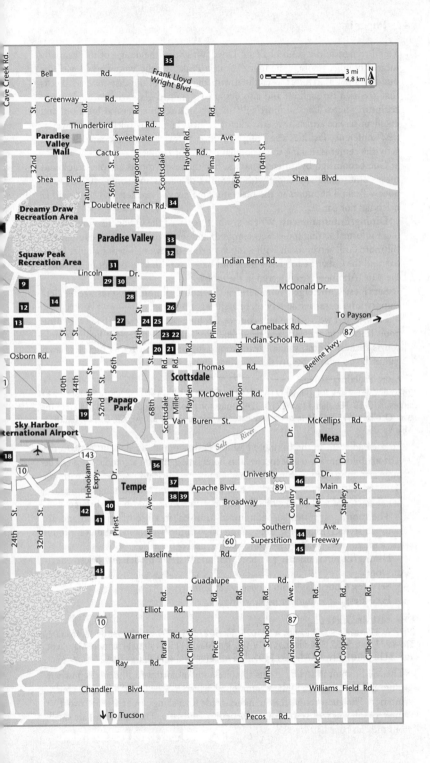

You'll recognize the hand of Frank Lloyd Wright in the design of this centrally located premier resort at the foot of Squaw Peak. Wright, who worked with the building's main architect, is credited with the design of the cast-concrete blocks that are used throughout and also designed a stained-glass window and several sculptures here. The Biltmore's distinctive architecture, central location, and excellent service attract a wealthy clientele, including many celebrities. However, new conference facilities also bring in corporate travelers and the new children's activities center is making this a popular choice for families.

Guest rooms go by different names, but the resort rooms are the largest and most comfortable and come with balconies or patios and some offer views of Squaw Peak. The rooms in the main building are the smallest and have neither balconies nor patios.

Dining/Entertainment: Wright's, which replaced the Orangerie, now offers a more informal setting (no jackets required) and serves new American cuisine. The Biltmore Grill serves meals with a touch of the Southwest. There's a quiet lobby bar, and the Cabaña Club Restaurant and Bar serves drinks and light meals beside the pool. Afternoon tea is served in the lobby.

Services: Concierge, room service (24-hour), limousine, massages, valet/laundry service, car-rental service, babysitting, physician.

Facilities: Two 18-hole golf courses, 18-hole putting course, five swimming pools (including one with a water slide), two whirlpool spas, eight lighted tennis courts, fitness center, sauna, steam room, jogging paths, rental bicycles, lawn games, board games, beauty salon, several shops.

Crown Sterling Suites

2630 E. Camelback Rd., Phoenix, AZ 85016. ☎ **602/955-3992** or 800/433-4600. 232 suites. A/C TV TEL. Jan–May, $210–$240 suite for two. May–Sept, $115–$145 suite for two. Oct–Dec, $154–$194 suite for two. Rates include full breakfast. AE, CB, DC, DISC, EURO, MC, V.

Located adjacent to the Biltmore Fashion Park shopping center and close to the Arizona Biltmore's two golf courses, this hotel is designed on a grandiose scale. The huge atrium is filled with tropical greenery, waterfalls, and ponds filled with koi (Japanese carp). Tucked in and around the lush atrium are a dining room and a bar. The curved wall of glass that forms the atrium looks out on a fairly large pool.

The rooms, all suites, are done in an unusual mixture of art deco and art nouveau styles. There are marble countertops in the bathrooms, and every room has a microwave, small refrigerator, wet bar, and coffeemaker.

Dining/Entertainment: The hotel restaurant serves moderately priced Mexican food.

Services: Concierge, room service, valet/laundry.

Facilities: Large outdoor pool, whirlpool.

Ⓢ Fountain Suites

2577 W. Greenway Rd., Phoenix, AZ 85023. ☎ **602/375-1777** or 800/338-1338. Fax 602/375-1777, ext. 5555. 314 suites. A/C TV TEL. Jan–May, $115–$180 suite for two. May–Sept, $65–$118 suite for two. Oct–Dec, $105–125 suite for two. AE, CB, DC, DISC, MC, V.

The Mediterranean styling at this all-suite hotel in northwest Phoenix is nowhere more eye-catching than in the atrium lobby, which has the feel of a Spanish church interior. The guest rooms feature motel-grade furnishings, but there are two TVs in every suite, as well as wet bars, refrigerators, and safes. The bathrooms are small, but they do have hairdryers.

Dining/Entertainment: The restaurant in the atrium lobby is a casual place with moderately priced meals. Also in the lobby is a piano lounge, and beside the pool, there's the Cabaña Bar.

Services: Room service, valet/laundry service.

Facilities: Large outdoor pool and an adjacent garden court, exercise facility, whirlpool, sauna, tennis court, volleyball court, racquetball court.

Hyatt Regency Phoenix at Civic Plaza

122 N. Second St., Phoenix, AZ 85004. ☎ **602/252-1234** or 800/233-1234. Fax 602/254-9472. 712 rms, 44 suites. A/C TV TEL. $109–$235 double; $250–$1,000 suite. AE, CB, DC, DISC, MC, V. Valet parking $8; self-parking $6.

Located directly across the street from the Phoenix Civic Plaza, this high-rise Hyatt is almost always packed with conventioneers and consequently does not offer the sort of seasonal price breaks of other area hotels. The rooms are fairly standard, though comfortably furnished.

Dining/Entertainment: The Compass Room is Arizona's only rotating rooftop restaurant and serves southwestern dishes at the sort of prices you'd expect. There's also the more casual and inexpensive Theater Terrace Café in the hotel's atrium.

Services: Concierge, room service, valet/laundry service, car-rental desk.

Facilities: Small outdoor pool, exercise room, whirlpool, tennis courts, several gift shops.

⊛ The Pointe Hilton at Squaw Peak

7677 N. 16th St., Phoenix, AZ 85020-9832. ☎ **602/997-2626** or 800/876-4683 or 800/572-7222. Fax 602/997-2391. 564 suites, studios, and casitas. A/C MINIBAR TV TEL. Jan–May, $169–$259 suite, studio, or casita for two. June–Sept, $89–$149 suite, studio, or casita for two. Sept–Jan, $169–$229 suite, studio, or casita for two. AE, CB, DC, DISC, EURO, JCB, MC, V.

Located at the foot of Squaw Peak, this is a lushly landscaped family- and convention-oriented resort in north Phoenix. Spanish villa styling surrounds you with large courtyards with Mexican fountains. All the guest rooms here are suites, studios, or two-story casitas with stucco walls and a mixture of Spanish colonial-style and contemporary furnishings. There are wet bars with marble counters and marble vanities in all the rooms.

Dining/Entertainment: Aunt Chilada's Mexican restaurant is housed in an old adobe building that was built in 1880. Hole-in-the-Wall, the resort's western-theme restaurant, is housed in a building that dates to the 1930s. Beside the Pointe provides a garden setting, and also has a sports lounge. There are poolside cabanas as well.

Services: Concierge, room service, valet/laundry service, massages, rental-car desk, no-smoking rooms, complimentary afternoon cocktails, babysitting.

Facilities: The River Ranch aquatic playground, with its tubing river, water slide, and waterfalls, is the resort's star attraction. Other facilities include an 18-hole golf course, four other swimming pools, whirlpool spas, four tennis courts, jogging trails, table tennis, 18-hole putting course, games room, bike rentals, shops. A fitness center includes racquetball courts, aerobics classes, free weights, exercise machines, a lap pool, sauna, steam room, and exercise instructors.

The Pointe Hilton at Tapatio Cliffs

11111 N. Seventh St., Phoenix, AZ 85020. ☎ **602/866-7500** or 800/876-4683 or 800/572-7222. Fax 602/993-0276. 584 suites. A/C MINIBAR TV TEL. Jan–Apr, $199–$255 suite for two. May–Sept, $79–$215 suite for two. Sept–Dec, $165–$215 suite for two. AE, CB, DC, DISC, EURO, JCB, MC, V.

Situated on the shoulder of North Mountain, this resort offers the steepest and lushest grounds of the three Pointe resorts and the same Spanish villa architecture. The grounds here are so steep that many people leave their cars in the parking lot and get shuttled around in golf carts. The resort backs up to a nature preserve where guests can hike in the desert. If you're not a hiker, you can still avail yourself of the golf course, which is a short distance from the guest rooms. One of the most outstanding features here, however, is a full-service spa offering numerous health and beauty treatments.

As at other Pointe resorts, all rooms here are spacious suites. Furnishings reflect the Southwest, and some have high ceilings. Corner rooms, with their extra windows, are particularly bright.

Dining/Entertainment: The hilltop Different Pointe of View offers stupendous views from lounge and dining room. The menu is international, and the wine cellar is one of the largest in the Southwest. For Wild West dining, there's the Waterin' Hole, in an old house with sawdust on the floor and steaks on the grill. Marble floors and mahogany paneling give Pointe in Tyme a classic clublike atmosphere. For light poolside meals there's La Cabaña.

Services: Concierge, room service, complimentary afternoon cocktails, massages, rental-car desk, free shuttle between Pointe Hilton properties, horseback riding, babysitting.

Facilities: 18-hole golf course, 15 lighted tennis courts, seven swimming pools, whirlpool spas, fitness room, steam room, sauna, gift shop, tennis shop, golf shop, beauty salon, full-service spa.

The Pointe Hilton Resort on South Mountain

7777 S. Pointe Pkwy., Phoenix, AZ 85044. ☎ **602/438-9000** or 800/876-4683 or 800/572-7222. Fax 602/431-6535. 638 suites. A/C MINIBAR TV TEL. Jan–May, $205–$235 suite for two. June–Sept, $89–$139 suite for two. Sept–Dec, $159–$215 suite for two. AE, CB, DC, DISC, EURO, JCB, MC, V.

Located on the flanks of South Mountain, this Pointe Hilton resort is surrounded by a 16,000-acre nature preserve, though the resort's manicured grounds keep nature at a distance. The lobby, with its high ceiling, sweeping stairs, and crystal chandeliers, is calculated to impress. The size here accommodates conventions rather than makes individual travelers feel at home. However, if you are an active type, you'll find enough to keep you busy here for days. Golfers get great views, urban cowboys can ride right into South Mountain Park, and the fitness center is among the biggest and best I've ever seen at a resort.

All the guest rooms are suites and feature contemporary southwestern furnishings. Even the smallest suites are quite roomy. Mountainside suites offer the best views of the golf course and South Mountain.

Dining/Entertainment: Another Pointe in Tyme features a mahogany-paneled interior and continental cuisine, with live jazz Wednesday through Saturday evenings. Rustler's Rooste is a western-theme restaurant featuring cowboy bands, rattlesnake appetizers, and a slide from the lounge to the dining room. Aunt Chilada's serves Mexican food, and Sports Club Dining provides light and healthy meals.

Services: Concierge, room service, valet/laundry service, massages, rental-car desk, complimentary afternoon cocktails, babysitting.

Facilities: 18-hole golf course, 10 lighted tennis courts, five racquetball courts, seven swimming pools, two volleyball courts, riding stables, beauty salon, gift shop, pro shop. A complete health club offers aerobics classes, fitness equipment, free weights, and a lap pool.

⊙ The Ritz-Carlton Phoenix

2401 E. Camelback Rd., Phoenix, AZ 85016. ☎ **602/468-0700** or 800/241-3333. Fax 602/468-9883. 281 rms, 14 suites. A/C MINIBAR TV TEL. Sept–May, $190–$260 double; $250–$1,500 suite. May–Sept, $105–$165 double; $195–$1,500 suite. AE, CB, DC, DISC, EURO, JCB, MC, V. Valet parking $9.50.

Located directly across the street from the Biltmore Fashion Park shopping center in the heart of the Camelback Corridor business and shopping district, the Ritz-Carlton is the city's finest nonresort hotel. The service is impeccable, the public areas are filled with European antiques, and crystal chandeliers hang from the ceiling. Though this decor may seem a bit out of place in Phoenix, it's still utterly sophisticated. In the guest rooms you'll find reproductions of antique furniture. The marble bathrooms have ornate fixtures and good assortments of toiletries.

Dining/Entertainment: The Grill offers a clubbish atmosphere and a good steaks and seafood. For southwestern cuisine there's the more casual Restaurant. The elegant lobby lounge serves afternoon tea as well as cocktails.

Services: Concierge, room service, valet/laundry service, babysitting, car-rental desk, massages, complimentary golf shuttle.

Facilities: Small outdoor pool, tennis court, fitness center, saunas.

Sheraton Crescent Hotel

2620 W. Dunlap Ave., Phoenix, AZ 85021. ☎ **602/943-8200** or 800/423-4126. Fax 602/371-2856. 342 rms, 12 suites. A/C TV TEL. Jan–May, $179–$259 double; $300–$500 suite. May–Sept, $109–$129 double; $300–$500 suite. Sept–Dec, $179–$199 double; $300–$500 suite. AE, CB, DC, DISC, EURO, JCB, MC, V.

Located in the north-central high-tech district and across I-17 from the Metrocenter mall, this business hotel is a sister property of the Phoenician and displays much the same decorative style, albeit on a more subdued level. Marble abounds in the lobby and also shows up in guest-room bathrooms. Sadly, the maintenance here seems to be suffering and the lobby furnishings are in need of replacement. However, the guest rooms offer plenty of space, comfort, and convenience, with dual-line phones, irons and ironing boards, hairdryers, and shaving mirrors.

Dining/Entertainment: Charlie's Grill is a big, casual restaurant with a rather uncreative southwestern menu and an adjacent bar.

Services: Concierge, room service, valet/laundry service.

Facilities: The hotel's small pool is in a lush garden setting. Other facilities include a fitness center, whirlpool spa, sauna, two tennis courts, two squash courts, volleyball and basketball courts.

Wyndham Garden Hotel–Phoenix Airport

427 N. 44th St., Phoenix, AZ 85018. ☎ **602/220-4400** or 800/822-4200 in the U.S. or 800/631-4200 in Canada. Fax 602/231-8703. 214 rms, 24 suites. A/C TV TEL. Sept–May, $159–$216 double; $169–$226 suite. May–Sept, $83 double; $93 suite. AE, CB, DC, DISC, MC, V.

Located only a mile from the east exit from the airport, this is a comfortable modern hotel. The "king" rooms are particularly well designed, with a comfortable chair, a work desk, and a bureau that separates the sleeping area from the sitting/

working area. Other room amenities include hairdryers, coffeemakers, and two telephones.

Dining/Entertainment: There's a clublike lounge to one side of the lobby, and an inexpensive casual restaurant as well.

Services: Complimentary airport shuttle, room service, valet/laundry service.

Facilities: The outdoor pool is surrounded by an attractive patio with desert-style landscaping.

EXPENSIVE

✪ Crowne Plaza–Phoenix

111 N. Central Ave., Phoenix, AZ 85004. ☎ **602/257-1525** or 800/227-6963. Fax 602/253-9755. 532 rms, 70 suites. A/C MINIBAR TV TEL. Oct–Apr, $149 double; $189–$609 suite. Apr–Oct, $89 double; $129–$249 suite. AE, CB, DC, DISC, MC, V. Valet parking $7.

Fresh from an extensive renovation that, unfortunately, did nothing to improve this hotel's dated facade, this business and convention hotel is now the best choice in downtown. A Mediterranean villa theme has been adopted throughout the public areas with slate flooring and walls painted to resemble cracked stucco. Guest rooms continue the Mediterranean feel and are designed with the business traveler in mind. Dual-line phones with modem ports, hairdryers, safes, irons and ironing boards, and coffeemakers all add up to a high level of convenience.

Dining/Entertainment: The Cactus Café serves light fare amid casual surroundings. The Adams Lounge is a quiet bar that also serves a lunch buffet.

Services: Room service, massages, airport shuttle, valet/laundry service, car rental desk.

Frommer's Smart Traveler: Hotels

1. Consider traveling during the shoulder seasons of late spring and late summer. Temperatures are not at their midsummer peak nor are room rates at their midwinter heights. If you can stand the heat of summer you'll save more than 50% on room rates.

2. Be flexible when making reservations. Unless you ask, you may not find out that rates are scheduled to go down a week before or after you've planned your vacation. Changing your dates by a few days or a few weeks may save you hundreds of dollars.

3. Always ask about possible discounts or packages that you might be able to take advantage of. Phoenix hotels often offer weekend rates and golf packages that can save you money.

4. Be sure to find out if the hotel you'll be staying at offers free airport transfers. This can save you an expensive taxi or shuttle-bus ride.

5. Request a room with a view of the mountains whenever possible. You can overlook a swimming pool anywhere, but one of the main selling points of Phoenix hotels is the views of Mummy Mountain, Camelback Mountain, and Squaw Peak.

6. If you'll be traveling with children, always ask what the age cutoff is if children get to stay for free, and whether there's a limit to the number of children who can stay for free.

🅐 Family-Friendly Hotels

Hyatt Regency Scottsdale Resort at Gainey Ranch *(see p. 91)*   Not only is there a totally awesome water playground complete with sand beach and water slide, but the Kamp Hyatt Kachina program provides supervised structured activities.

The Phoenician *(see p. 93)*   The Funicians Club is a supervised activities program for children ages 5 to 12. Kids get to play games, make crafts, and burn up lots of excess energy.

Marriott's Mountain Shadows *(see p. 92)*   Kids age 5 to 15 can participate in the Kactus Kids Klub, a recreation program that includes field trips, hay rides, games, pool activities, and arts and crafts activities.

Facilities: Fitness room, swimming pool, whirlpool spa, jogging track, beauty salon and barbershop, gift shop.

✪ Hermosa Inn

5532 N. Palo Cristi Rd., Paradise Valley, AZ 85253. ☎ **602/955-8614** or 800/2412-1210. Fax 602/955-8299. 17 rms, 18 suites. A/C TV TEL. June–Sept, $60 double; $69–$195 suite. Sept–Jan, $125–$175 double; $160–$350 suite. Jan–May, $195–$225 double; $245–$475 suite. AE, DC, MC, V.

This renovated guest ranch is one of the few hotels in the Phoenix area to offer a bit of old Arizona atmosphere. Originally built as the home of western artist Lon Megargee in 1930, the inn is situated in a quiet residential neighborhood and is set on over 6 acres of neatly landscaped gardens. Situated around the grounds are a small outdoor pool, a couple of whirlpools (one in a shady garden setting), and three tennis courts.

The least expensive guest rooms have gas fireplaces but don't have the stunning designer styling of the more expensive suites. These latter accommodations incorporate a mixture of contemporary and antique southwestern furnishings and accent pieces and have more southwestern flavor than any other rooms in the area.

Dining/Entertainment: The dining room, which is located in the original adobe home, serves new American and southwestern cuisine in a rustic setting.

Wyndham Metrocenter Hotel

10220 N. Metro Pkwy. E., Phoenix, AZ 85051. ☎ **602/997-5900** or 800/WYNDHAM. Fax 602/997-1034. 284 rms, 18 suites. A/C TV TEL. Jan–Apr, $99–$159 double; $198 suite. May–Dec, $70–$140 double; $118 suite. AE, CB, DC, DISC, MC, V.

Under new management, the former Hotel Westcourt is undergoing extensive renovation that will give this hotel a Mediterranean look similar to that at the above-mentioned Crowne Plaza. This hotel benefits from its location in the heart of Phoenix's north-central business district and adjacent to the largest shopping mall in Arizona. Facilities here include an Olympic-size swimming pool, whirlpool spa, tennis court, exercise room, and sauna. The guest rooms, though with new furniture, aren't always in top shape. Hairdryers, coffeemakers, and dual-line phones are definite pluses.

Dining/Entertainment: Trumps Bar & Grill offers both indoor and patio dining at reasonable prices and a bar area with lots of polished brass and varnished oak.

Services: Room service, airport shuttle, concierge floor, valet/laundry service, car-rental desk.

A Bed & Breakfast Inn

⑤ Maricopa Manor

15 W. Pasadena Ave. (P.O. Box 7186), Phoenix, AZ 85011-7186. ☎ **602/274-6302.** Fax 602/266-3904. 5 suites. A/C TV TEL. Sept–May, $109–$159 suite for two. June–Aug, $89 suite for two. AE, DISC, MC, V.

Centrally located between downtown Phoenix and Scottsdale, this elegant B&B is just a block off busy Camelback Road. However, the orange trees, palms, and large yard all lend an air of the country. The inn's main home was built in 1928 and is designed to resemble a Spanish manor house. All the guest rooms are large suites, two of which are located in a separate guesthouse. One suite has a sunroom and kitchen, while another has two separate sleeping areas. Breakfast is delivered to your door each morning in a basket and can be eaten in the room or at one of the tables in the garden. For relaxing, there's a hot tub in a gazebo. This B&B is particularly popular with business travelers.

MODERATE

In addition to the moderately priced hotel listed below, some of the better moderately priced chain motels around Phoenix include the following (rates are for the high season; for toll-free phone numbers, see the Appendix): **Ramada/Camelback**, 502 W. Camelback Rd., Phoenix, AZ 85013 (☎ **602/264-9290**), charging $85 to $140 double; **Hampton Inn–Phoenix Airport**, 4234 S. 48th St., Phoenix, AZ 85040 (☎ **602/438-8688**), charging $95 double; and **Rodeway Inn–Airport West**, 1202 S. 24th St., Phoenix, AZ 85034-4899 (☎ **602/273-1211**), charging $65 to $80 double.

⑤ San Carlos Travelodge Hotel

202 N. Central Ave., Phoenix, AZ 85004. ☎ **602/253-4121** or 800/528-5446. Fax 602/253-6668. 111 rms, 7 suites. A/C TV TEL. $69–$99 double; $129–$199 suite. AE, CB, DC, DISC, MC, V.

Built in 1928 and listed on the National Register of Historic Places, the San Carlos is a small European-style hotel that provides that touch of elegance and charm missing from the other standardized high-rise hotels downtown. You're close to shopping, the Phoenix Convention Center, sightseeing, and theaters, which makes this a good choice for both vacationers and conventioneers. Crystal chandeliers, a travertine check-in desk, and comfortable couches give the small lobby sophistication. The rooms, though smaller than today's standard hotel room, feature wingback chairs, ceiling fans, and coffeemakers.

Il San Carlino, with its sunken dining room just off the lobby, serves good Italian meals. An Irish pub, small bar, and the café add up to plenty of dining and drinking options. The hotel also features valet/laundry service, complimentary coffee, a rooftop pool, and an exercise room.

INEXPENSIVE

Among the better budget chain motels around Phoenix are the following: **Motel 6–Thunderbird,** 2735 W. Sweetwater Ave., Phoenix, AZ 85029 (☎ **602/942-5030**), charging $45 double; **Super 8–Phoenix Metro/Central,** 4021 N. 27th Ave., Phoenix, AZ 85017 (☎ **602/248-8880**), charging $46 to $49 double; and **Travelodge Metrocenter,** 8617 N. Black Canyon Hwy., Phoenix, AZ 85021 (☎ **602/995-9500**), charging $47 to $65 double.

SCOTTSDALE

VERY EXPENSIVE

✪ Hyatt Regency Scottsdale Resort at Gainey Ranch

7500 E. Doubletree Ranch Rd., Scottsdale, AZ 85258. ☎ **602/991-3388** or 800/233-1234. Fax 602/483-5550. 493 rms, 7 casitas, 25 suites. A/C MINIBAR TV TEL. Jan–May, $285–$395 double; $1,125–$2,000 casita; $460–$2,200 suite. May–Sept, $130–$260 double; $775–$1,800 casita; $275–$1,900 suite. Sept–Dec, $260–$335 double; $875–$1,550 casita; $375–$1,900 suite. AE, DC, DISC, MC, V.

Located north of Scottsdale resort row, this is a visually compelling resort, with a 2¹/₂-acre water playground serving as focal point. Surrounded by a lake, gardens, fountains, and fishponds, this extravagant complex of 10 swimming pools includes a water slide, a sand beach, water volleyball pool, waterfalls, and a whirlpool spa. As if this weren't enough, the resort also offers 27 holes of golf, 8 tennis courts, and trails for jogging and cycling. The grounds are abundantly planted with tall palm trees. Original works of art are on display throughout the resort, and for those who prefer nature, there are gorgeous views of the McDowell Mountains. The guest rooms are everything you'd expect in this price range, with robes, hairdryers, scales, marble-top tables, and attractive pastel color schemes.

Dining/Entertainment: The Golden Swan, serving southwestern cuisine, extends into out a fishpond. The Squash Blossom provides a casual atmosphere and also serves southwestern cuisine. Ristorante Sandolo is an Italian café that also offers after-dinner gondola rides. A lobby bar features nightly piano music and there are two bars and a grill near the pool.

Services: Concierge, room service (24-hour), valet parking, valet/laundry service, children's programs, gondola rides, massages.

Facilities: 27-hole golf course, 10 pools, whirlpools, eight tennis courts, croquet court, jogging and bicycling trails, and a health spa with exercise equipment, aerobics classes, and sauna.

✪ Inn at the Citadel

8700 E. Pinnacle Peak Rd., Scottsdale, AZ 85255. ☎ **602/585-6133** or 800/927-8367. Fax 602/585-3436. 11 suites. A/C TV TEL. Jan–May, $265 suite for two. May–Sept, $89 suite for two. Sept–Jan, $195 suite for two. Rates include continental breakfast. AE, DC, DISC, MC, V.

This small inn is located about 20 minutes north of downtown Scottsdale in an upscale shopping-and-business complex. Throughout the rooms are antiques and original works of art that give the inn a unique atmosphere. Some of the antique furnishings, which tend toward Spanish colonial pieces, are even for sale. Some suites have fireplaces while others have small balconies. Many also have good views of the surrounding desert and mountains. The bathrooms, which are huge, are done in marble and have lace shower curtains. The guest rooms also have safes, terry robes, coffeemakers, and hairdryers. In the same building that houses the inn you'll find several exclusive shops, a beauty salon, a shady courtyard with a beautiful little pond, and 8700, one of the area's best restaurants (see "Dining," later in this chapter, for details).

John Gardiner's Tennis Ranch on Camelback

5700 E. McDonald Dr., Phoenix, AZ 85253-5268. ☎ **602/948-2100** or 800/245-2051. Fax 602/483-7314. 100 rms and suites. Dec–May, $245 double; $345–$585 suite. May–June and Sept–Dec, $195 double; $295–$485 suite. Tennis packages available. AE, MC, V. Closed July–Aug.

If tennis is your game, you'll definitely want to consider making this resort your address while vacationing in the Phoenix area. Located on the north slope of Camelback Mountain, John Gardiner's has long been helping tennis players improve their game. The resort is small and, with its gated entry, has the feel of a private country club. There are plenty of courts, and with eight pools, there are plenty of places to cool off as well. The rooms are individually decorated condominium units. Some have large balconies, while in others the balconies have been turned into sunrooms. The resort also has houses for rent, and some of these have their own private pool or tennis court. Fresh-squeezed orange juice and the newspaper at your doorstep each morning is a nice touch.

Dining/Entertainment: There's a great view of Mummy Mountain from the dining room and bar. The menu includes a very tempting mix of southwestern and continental dishes.

Services: Room service, valet/laundry service, tennis lessons.

Facilities: 20 tennis courts, eight pools, whirlpools, fitness center.

Marriott's Camelback Inn

5402 E. Lincoln Dr., Scottsdale, AZ 85253. ☎ **602/948-1700** or 800/24-CAMEL. Fax 602/951-8469. 423 rms, 23 suites. A/C MINIBAR TV TEL. Jan–May, $295–$380 double; $450–$1,550 suite. June–Sept, $109–$190 double; $200–$700 suite. Sept–Dec, $225–$275 double; $350–$975 suite. AE, CB, DC, DISC, MC, V.

The Camelback Inn opened in 1936 and later became the first Marriott resort. Today it's one of the oldest and most traditionally southwestern of the area's many resorts and attracts a well-heeled and conservative crowd. Set at the foot of Mummy Mountain and overlooking Camelback Mountain, the resort offers a tranquil setting only five minutes from downtown Scottsdale. Although the two nearby 18-hole golf courses are the main attraction for guests here, the spa is among the finest in the state and would be a reason to visit in its own right. The guest rooms are decorated with contemporary southwestern furnishings and art. All have balconies or patios, and some have their own sundecks. The bathrooms are well lit and come with hairdryers, a large basket of toiletries, and a shaving mirror.

Dining/Entertainment: The Chaparral, serving continental fare, is one of the best restaurants in the valley. The Navajo Room is a more casual place. Light snacks are available at Dromedary's or the Oasis Lounge, and you'll find healthy meals at Sprouts. Golfers can dine at the 19th Hole. For a quiet drink, there's the Chaparral Lounge.

Services: Concierge, room service, babysitting, valet/laundry service, car-rental desk; spa services include numerous body and skin treatments.

Facilities: Two 18-hole golf courses, eight tennis courts, three pools, three whirlpools, full-service health spa with beauty salon, lap pool, aerobics room, saunas, steam rooms, whirlpool, fitness room.

Marriott's Mountain Shadows

5641 E. Lincoln Dr., Scottsdale, AZ 85253. ☎ **602/948-7111** or 800/228-9290. Fax 602/951-5430. 336 rms, 19 suites. A/C MINIBAR TV TEL. Jan–May, $225–$340 double; $255–$1,050 suite. June–Sept, $89–$125 double; $119–$1,050 suite. Sept–Dec, $185–$245 double; $215–$1,050 suite. AE, CB, DC, DISC, MC, V.

Located across the road from the Camelback Inn, Mountain Shadows offers better views of Camelback Mountain, but the ambiance is entirely different. Mountain Shadows was built in the late 1950s and its architecture may seem dated; still, the property is well maintained and appeals to families and younger travelers looking for a less formal atmosphere than is found at the Camelback Inn. An 18-hole resort course on the premises keeps most guests happy, but for the more serious golfer, there is access to the Camelback Inn's two outstanding courses. Guests here can also use the Inn's spa facilities.

Standard rooms are large and have high ceilings, wet bars, king-size beds, and balconies. The rooms around the main pool can be a bit noisy and should be avoided by those seeking peace and quiet. Those rooms in the Palm section offer the best views of the mountain. Some suites include whirlpool tubs, brass beds, and private patios.

Dining/Entertainment: Shell's Oyster Bar & Seafood Restaurant offers both indoor and terrace dining. Family dining can be had at the moderately priced Cactus Flower. There's casual dining at the Country Club Dining Room.

Services: Concierge, room service, valet/laundry service, car-rental desk, baby-sitting, guided mountain hikes, golf and tennis lessons, massages.

Facilities: Three 18-hole golf courses, eight tennis courts, three pools, two whirlpools, saunas, fitness center (and access to the Camelback Inn's spa), volleyball court, games areas, beauty shop, pro shop.

✪ The Phoenician

6000 E. Camelback Rd., Scottsdale, AZ 85251. ☎ **602/941-8200** or 800/888-8234. Fax 602/947-4311. 440 rms, 31 suites. A/C MINIBAR TV TEL. Jan–June, $300–$435 double; $900–$1,500 suite. June–Sept, $160–$280 double; $425–$800 suite. Sept–Dec, $320–$455 double; $1,000–$1,600 suite. AE, CB, DC, DISC, EURO, JCB, MC, V.

Situated on 130 acres at the foot of Camelback Mountain, the Phoenician is this city's most ostentatious resort, with a shimmering expanse of polished marble and sparkling crystal for a lobby. Service is the best in town, with uniformed employees waiting around every corner. Some may find the formality of the resort a bit out of place in casual Arizona. Still, you can't deny that the pool complex is one of the finest in the state and is a fabulous place to while away a day. The Center for Well Being, the resort's spa, offers all the pampering anyone could ever need, and for the more active types, there is a challenging 18-hole golf course.

The guest rooms here continue the elaborate style of the public areas and include sunken bathtubs for two, Berber carpets, muted color schemes, three phones, large patios, two closets, terry robes, bathroom scales, hairdryers, and wall safes. And this is just the standard room.

Dining/Entertainment: Mary Elaine's, featuring Mediterranean cuisine, offers elegant dining and great views. In the Terrace Dining Room the atmosphere is less formal and Italian dishes are served. Windows on the Green features southwestern cuisine and a view of the golf course. For quick snacks, there are the poolside Oasis and the Café & Ice Cream Parlor. The Lobby Tea Court serves afternoon tea. The Thirsty Camel, with its view of the Valley, is the resort's most popular place for a drink, especially after sunset when the city's lights sparkle on the horizon.

Services: Concierge, room service (24-hour), valet/laundry service, tour desk, car-rental desk, children's program.

Facilities: Seven pools (including one lined with mother-of-pearl tiles and a water slide), 18-hole golf course, putting green, 12 lighted tennis courts, whirlpool, lawn games, volleyball court, shopping arcade. The Center for Well Being is a spa that includes a fitness center, saunas, steam rooms, whirlpools, aerobics room, beauty salon, and barbershop.

Radisson Resort Scottsdale

7171 N. Scottsdale Rd., Scottsdale, AZ 85253-3696. ☎ **602/991-3800** or 800/333-3333. Fax 602/948-1381. 318 rms, 41 suites. A/C TV TEL. Jan–May, $195–$215 double; $295–$1,500 suite. May–Sept, $90–$100 double; $160–$1,500 suite. Sept–Jan, $175–$190 double; $250–$1,500 suite. AE, CB, DC, DISC, MC, V.

Located in the heart of resort row, the Radisson has recently undergone remodeling, with the lobby receiving a complete face-lift that added a touch of elegance to the large room. Unfortunately, not all of the rooms were updated, and many still have old furnishings. Studio rooms are the smallest here and come with Murphy beds, daybeds, and sunken bathtubs. Regular rooms feature marble bathrooms with two sinks, marble-top tables with comfortable chairs, and private patios. The bilevel suites feature kitchenettes, sleeping lofts, second-floor decks, and two bathrooms. The golf-course rooms are our favorites simply because of the views of the McDowell Mountains. The focus at this classic resort is on tennis and golf, and with 21 courts and two 18-hole golf courses, you'll have no trouble getting tee or court times.

Dining/Entertainment: Andre's, a conservative French provincial dining room, serves continental fare. Markers Lounge has pool tables and a lively atmosphere at night. During the day the Cabaña Bar caters to swimmers and sunbathers.

Services: Concierge, room service (24-hour), valet/laundry service, car-rental desk, massages and other body and skin treatments, tennis lessons.

Facilities: Two 18-hole golf courses, 21 lighted tennis courts, pro shop, three pools, whirlpool, volleyball court, health club.

Red Lion's La Posada Resort

4949 E. Lincoln Dr., Scottsdale, AZ 85253. ☎ **602/952-0420** or 800/547-8010. Fax 602/852-0151. 264 rms, 10 suites. A/C TV TEL. Jan–May, $209–$259 double; $325–$450 suite. May–Sept, $99–$169 double; $175–$300 suite. Sept–Jan, $169–$209 double; $300–$375 suite. AE, CB, DC, DISC, MC, V.

If you prefer to spend your time by the pool rather than on the courts or the fairways, you'll love the pool at La Posada. It covers half an acre and features its own two-story waterfall that cascades over artificial pink boulders. Connecting the two halves of the pool is a swim-through grotto with its own bar. The resort also offers tennis and racquetball facilities and a pitch-and-putt golf course.

The resort features Mediterranean styling, and the lobby is a grand high-ceilinged affair that incorporates a bit of French country decor. The guest rooms are larger than average and feature southwestern-style furnishings. The bathrooms have two sinks, plenty of counter space, and tile floors.

Dining/Entertainment: The Garden Terrace restaurant features continental cuisine with many southwestern touches; there's a view of Camelback Mountain and a pianist plays during dinner on weekends. Mangia Bene is an upscale Italian restaurant located across the parking lot from the lobby. The Terrace Lounge features a big-screen TV and occasional live music.

Services: Concierge, room service, laundry/valet service.

Facilities: Two pools, four whirlpools, sauna, six tennis courts, two racquetball courts, volleyball court, horseshoe pits, pitch-and-putt green, pro shop, beauty salon.

⑤ Regal McCormick Ranch

7401 N. Scottsdale Rd., Scottsdale, AZ 85253. ☎ **602/948-5050** or 800/243-1332. 125 rms, 3 suites, 51 condominium villas. A/C MINIBAR TV TEL. Jan–Apr, $169–$259 double; from $299 suite; from $340 villa. May–Sept, $59–$195 double; from $130 suite; from

$140 villa. Sept–Jan, $120–$195 double; from $230 suite; from $240 villa. AE, CB, DC, DISC, MC, V.

This low-rise resort, surrounded by green lawns and a golf course, is smaller than many in the area and consequently has a more personal feel. However, understaffing problems crop up with regularity. The focal point of this resort is its lake, where you can rent boats if you like. More traditional resort activities are available at the two 18-hole golf courses and on the four tennis courts.

The lobby is a jewel of southwestern decor, with huge amphoras, tables of cast stone, and rustic mission-style furniture. The guest rooms are done in pastel hues and each has its own private balcony or patio. More than half the rooms overlook the lake, while others overlook the pool or the mountains.

Dining/Entertainment: The Piñon Grill features bold southwestern decor and a menu to match. Diamondbacks Bar and Grill continues the southwestern theme.

Services: Concierge, room service, valet/laundry service, tennis lessons and clinics, golf-course shuttle.

Facilities: Two 18-hole golf courses, four lighted tennis courts, pool, whirlpool, boat rentals, walking and jogging paths, tennis pro shop.

Scottsdale Marriott Suites

7325 E. Third Ave., Scottsdale, AZ 85251. ☎ **602/945-1550** or 800/228-9290. Fax 602/945-2005. 251 suites. A/C TV TEL. Jan–May, $149–$170 suite for two. June–Sept, $79–100 suite for two. Sept–Jan, $149–$170 suite for two. AE, CB, DC, DISC, EURO, JCB, MC, V.

If shopping is your raison d'être and you're in Scottsdale on a pilgrimage, this hotel is an excellent base for making shopping forays. Though this is primarily a business hotel, it's located only two blocks from the famous Fifth Avenue Shops, and Scottsdale Fashion Square is only slightly farther. All the rooms here are suites and have two telephones and two TVs, as well as refrigerators, wet bars, and coffee makers. In the marble bathrooms you'll find separate showers and tubs.

Dining/Entertainment: Allie's American Grille is a casual restaurant serving moderately priced meals.

Services: Room service, valet/laundry service.

Facilities: Outdoor pool, whirlpool, exercise room, saunas.

✪ Scottsdale Princess

7575 E. Princess Dr., Scottsdale, AZ 85255. ☎ **602/585-4848** or 800/344-4758. Fax 602/585-0086. 400 rms, 125 casitas suites, 75 villa suites. A/C MINIBAR TV TEL. Jan–May, $285–$380 double; $480–$2,200 suite. May–Sept, $125–$170 double; $225–$1,160 suite. Sept–Dec, $215–$285 double; $410–$1,700 suite. AE, CB, DC, DISC, MC, V.

Located a 20-minute drive from downtown Scottsdale, this resort is a Moorish fantasy, and is home to the Phoenix Open golf tournament and a professional tennis tournament. As you can imagine, the resort has top golf and tennis facilities, in addition to a full-service spa and fitness center. With its royal palms, tiled fountains, waterfalls, and classical art and antiques, the resort is also perfect for romantic getaways. The truly exotic atmosphere is unmatched by any other valley resort.

The guest rooms all have distinct living and work areas, wet bars, refrigerators, and private balconies. The decor is elegant southwestern, and the bathrooms, roomy enough for even the most fastidious guest, include two sinks, a separate shower and tub, a vanity, and a telephone.

Dining/Entertainment: The Marquesa is a highly acclaimed—and high-priced—Spanish restaurant. Equally highly praised is La Hacienda, a gourmet Mexican restaurant with strolling mariachis. More casual dining is available in the main building, in the golf clubhouse, and by the pool. Lounge options include a quiet spot and a rowdy saloon with country dance music.

Services: Concierge, room service, valet/laundry service, babysitting, health and beauty treatments.

Facilities: Two 18-hole golf courses, nine tennis courts, three pools, whirlpools, and racquetball, squash, basketball courts, complete spa and fitness center, boutiques, tennis and golf pro shops.

Ⓢ Wyndham Paradise Valley Resort

5401 N. Scottsdale Rd., Scottsdale, AZ 85250. ☎ **602/947-5400** or 800/WYNDHAM. Fax 602/481-0209. 387 rms, 17 suites. A/C MINIBAR TV TEL. Jan–May, $145–$275 double; $220–$425 suite. June–Aug, $59–$109 double; $109–$209 suite. Sept–Dec, $129–$225 double; $204–$375 suite. AE, CB, DC, DISC, MC, V.

This lushly landscaped resort gives a bow to the pioneering architectural style of Frank Lloyd Wright, and for this reason stands out from many other comparable Scottsdale resorts. Built around several courtyards containing swimming pools, bubbling fountains, palm trees, and desert gardens, the resort has much the look and feel of Hyatt's nearby Gainey Ranch megaresort, but on a more human scale.

The guest rooms are all quite large and are distinctively styled with art deco armoires, marble vanities, glass-block accents, travertine entries, flagstone patios, and beamed ceilings. Wet bars, comfortable chairs, and a work desk provide comfort and convenience.

Dining/Entertainment: Off to one side of the lobby is a skylit dining room serving southwestern dishes. There are also a lobby lounge for drinks and light meals and a patio bar adjacent to the main pool.

Services: Concierge, room service, valet/laundry service, car-rental desk.

Facilities: The two outdoor pools, which have small waterfalls, are set in palm-shaded courtyards. There are also four tennis courts, a fitness center, two racquetball courts, saunas, steam room, whirlpools, and a beauty salon.

EXPENSIVE

Holiday Inn Hotel & Conference Center

7353 E. Indian School Rd., Scottsdale, AZ 85251. ☎ **602/994-9203** or 800/695-6995. Fax 602/941-2567. 206 rms, 6 suites. A/C TV TEL. Jan–May, $160 double; $300–$450 suite. May–Sept, $79 double; $92–$138 suite. Sept–Jan, $115 double; $170–$255 suite. AE, CB, DC, DISC, MC, V.

If you're a shopaholic or a culture vulture, this recently renovated Holiday Inn is worth considering. The low-rise hotel is located on the beautifully landscaped Scottsdale Civic Center Mall (a park, not a shopping center) and is adjacent to the Scottsdale Center for the Arts and the popular Fifth Avenue Shops. The guest rooms have been renovated, though the bathrooms don't seem to have been upgraded. The best rooms are those opening onto the mall.

Dining/Entertainment: Bola's Grill features regional dishes and patio dining overlooking the park. In the evening there's dancing to live and recorded popular music.

Services: Room service.

Facilities: Small outdoor pool, tennis court, whirlpool.

MODERATE/INEXPENSIVE

In addition to the hotel listed below, Scottsdale does have a few inexpensive and moderately priced chain motel options, although during the winter season prices are a bit higher than you might expect. These include the following (rates are for the high season; see the Appendix for toll-free telephone numbers): **Days Inn–Scottsdale Resort at Fashion Square Mall,** 4710 N. Scottsdale Rd., Scottsdale, AZ 85251 (☎ **602/947-5411**), charging $69 to $119 double; **Motel 6–Scottsdale,** 6848 E. Camelback Rd., Scottsdale, AZ 85251 (☎ **602/946-2280**), charging $30 to $49 double; and **Rodeway Inn–Phoenix/Scottsdale,** 7110 E. Indian School Rd., Scottsdale, AZ 85251 (☎ **602/946-3456**), charging $89 to $138 double.

Scottsdale's Fifth Avenue Inn

6935 Fifth Ave., Scottsdale, AZ 85251. ☎ **602/994-9461** or 800/528-7396. Fax 602/947-1695. 92 rms. A/C TV TEL. Jan–Apr, $82–$87 double. May–Sept, $40–$45 double. Oct–Dec, $52–$57 double. Rates include continental breakfast. AE, CB, DC, DISC, MC, V.

Located at the west end of Scottsdale's Fifth Avenue Shops, this motel is within walking distance of some of the best shopping and dining in Scottsdale. The guest rooms are large and have held up well since their last renovation. The three-story building is arranged around a central courtyard where you'll find the pool and a whirlpool.

MESA

EXPENSIVE

Sheraton Mesa Hotel

200 N. Centennial Way, Mesa, AZ 85201. ☎ **602/898-8300** or 800/325-3535. Fax 602/964-9279. 274 rms, 5 suites. A/C MINIBAR TV TEL. Jan–May, $119–$150 double. May–Sept, $55–$79 double. Sept–Dec, $89–$119 double. AE, CB, DC, DISC, MC, V.

Located in the heart of downtown Mesa and convenient to the convention center, amphitheater, and area businesses, this high-rise convention hotel offers great views of the valley from its upper floors. The guest rooms are comfortable in a corporate sort of way but don't offer much local flavor.

Dining/Entertainment: The hotel's main dining room is a warehouselike space serving unremarkable fare. There's also a large Mexican theme bar.

Services: Concierge, room service, valet/laundry service, free airport shuttle, free golf-course transportation.

Facilities: Small outdoor pool, whirlpool, small fitness room, business center.

INEXPENSIVE

Mesa has quite a few budget chain motels. These include the following (rates are for the high season; for toll-free phone numbers, see the Appendix): **Days Inn–Mesa,** 333 W. Juanita Ave., Mesa, AZ 85210 (☎ **602/844-8900**), charging $61 to $91 double; **Motel 6–Mesa North,** 336 W. Hampton Ave., Mesa, AZ 85210 (☎ **602/844-8899**), charging $42 double; and **Super 8–Mesa,** 6733 E. Main St., Mesa, AZ 85205 (☎ **602/981-6181**), charging $66 to $72.

TEMPE

VERY EXPENSIVE

✪ The Buttes

2000 Westcourt Way, Tempe, AZ 85282. ☎ **602/225-9000** or 800/843-1986. Fax 602/431-8433. 355 rms, 7 suites. A/C MINIBAR TV TEL. Jan–May, $195–$235 double; $475–$1,500 suite. May–Sept, $100–$130 double; $295–$1,500 suite. Sept–Dec, $170–$205 double; $395–$1,500 suite. AE, CB, DC, DISC, JCB, MC, V.

Located 3 miles from Sky Harbor Airport, this spectacular resort makes the most of its hilltop location. From its circular restaurant to its free-form swimming pool and desert landscaping, every inch of the resort is calculated to take your breath away. The flagstone-floored lobby is built into the hillside and has an artificial stream that flows through a cactus garden before cascading down to a fishpond in a dining room.

The guest rooms have shutters on the windows, and almost all have good views (marred slightly by the adjacent freeway). The coffee tables are built with artificial stone bases, and the TV cabinets and minibars are built into the walls beneath the picture windows. The bathrooms have oval tubs.

Dining/Entertainment: The resort's restaurant snags the best view around, and sunset dinners are always packed. An informal dining room is located below the lobby. There are bars in the lobby, the main restaurant (with live popular dance music), and by the pool.

Services: Concierge, room service (24-hour), valet/laundry service, complimentary airport shuttle, rental-car desk.

Facilities: Two free-form pools with waterfalls and a connecting swim-through canal, four whirlpools tucked into the rocks, four tennis courts, fitness center.

Radisson Tempe Mission Palms Hotel

60 E. Fifth St., Tempe, AZ 85281. ☎ **602/894-1400** or 800/333-3333. Fax 602/968-7677. 303 rms, 6 suites. A/C TV TEL. Dec–May, $209–$229 double; $345 suite. May–Sept, $99–$109 double; $215 suite. Sept–Dec, $149–$159 double; $320 suite. AE, CB, DC, DISC, EURO, MC, V.

College students and their families and anyone else who wants to be close to Tempe's nightlife will find this an ideal, though overpriced, location. Situated right in the heart of the Mill Avenue shopping, restaurant, and nightlife district, the Radisson sports a hip contemporary style. The courtyard poolside patio, with its turquoise and purple lounge chairs, is a great place to hang out on a hot day. The guest rooms are scheduled to be redone this year and will get dark-stained wood furniture with a Southwest look.

Dining/Entertainment: The restaurant serves southwestern meals at reasonable prices, and in the aptly named Monster Bar, a large alligator sculpture hangs from the ceiling.

Services: Room service, valet/laundry service.

Facilities: Medium-size outdoor pool, two tennis courts, fitness center, whirlpool, sauna.

EXPENSIVE

⑤ Fiesta Inn

2100 S. Priest Dr., Tempe, AZ 85282. ☎ **602/967-1441** or 800/528-6481. Fax 602/967-0224. 270 rms, 4 suites. A/C TV TEL. Jan–May, $120–$140 double; $210–$275 suite. May–Sept, $70–$85 double; $110–$150 suite. Sept–Jan, $100–$125 double; $160–$205 suite. AE, CB, DC, DISC, MC, V.

When you see the luxurious grounds of this conveniently located hotel, you may be as surprised as we were at the reasonable rates and extensive recreational facilities, including three tennis courts, a putting green, and driving range. The rooms are large and all have refrigerators, coffeemakers, and hairdryers. Local phone calls are free.

Dining/Entertainment: The restaurant serves reliable American fare, and the lounge features a copper bar and a big-screen TV.

Services: Concierge, room service, free airport shuttle, complimentary morning paper, valet/laundry service.

Facilities: In addition to those mentioned above, you'll find a pool, health club with sauna and whirlpool, and jogging trails.

MODERATE/INEXPENSIVE

Budget chain motel options in the Tempe area include the following (rates are for the high season; for toll-free phone numbers, see the Appendix): **Days Inn–Tempe,** 1221 E. Apache Blvd., Tempe, AZ 85281 (☎ **602/968-7793**), charging $40 to $79 double; **Super 8–Tempe/Scottsdale,** 1020 E. Apache Blvd., Tempe, AZ 85281 (☎ **602/967-8891**), charging $66 to $75 double; and **Travelodge–Tempe,** 1005 E. Apache Blvd., Tempe, AZ 85281 (☎ **602/968-7871**), charging $42 to $59 double.

NEARBY ACCOMMODATIONS

○ The Boulders

34631 N. Tom Darlington Dr. (P.O. Box 2090), Carefree, AZ 85377. ☎ **602/488-9009** or 800/553-1717. Fax 602/488-4118. 160 casitas. A/C MINIBAR TV TEL. $225–$450 casita for two. Rates vary from month to month. AE, CB, DC, MC, V. Closed July–Aug.

Set amid a jumble of giant rocks 45 minutes north of Scottsdale, the Boulders epitomizes the Southwest aesthetic and is the state's premier resort. Adobe buildings blend unobtrusively into the desert, as do the two golf courses, which feature the most breathtaking tee boxes in Arizona. If you can tear yourself away from the greens, you can relax around either of two pools, play tennis (no boulders on the courts), or take advantage of the facilities and treatments at a full-service spa.

The lobby is an organic adobe structure with tree-trunk pillars, a flagstone floor, and a collection of Native American artifacts on display. The guest rooms continue the adobe styling with stucco walls, beehive fireplaces, and beamed ceilings. The bathrooms are large and luxuriously appointed with tubs for two, separate showers, and double sinks. The rooms vary in size, with the smallest being a bit cramped (what with all the attractive furnishings). The best views are from second-floor rooms.

Dining/Entertainment: The resort's premier restaurant serves innovative American cuisine; jackets are required for men at dinner. A less formal room serving regional dishes features a tile-front exhibition kitchen. At the country club is a dining room that emphasizes grilled meats and seafoods. A fourth restaurant, serving Mexican food, is in the resort's upscale shopping plaza.

Services: Concierge, room service, valet/laundry service, airport shuttle, bike rentals.

Facilities: Two 18-hole golf courses, six tennis courts, two pools, jogging and hiking trails, a pro shop. There's a new full-service spa as well as a fitness center with a lap pool, sauna, and exercise machines.

Gold Canyon Ranch

6100 S. Kings Ranch Rd., Apache Junction, AZ 85219. ☎ **602/982-9090** or 800/624-6445. Fax 602/830-5211. 57 rms. A/C TV TEL. Jan–May, $150–$230 double. May–Sept, $106–$155 double. Sept–Dec, 146–$205 double. AE, DC, DISC, MC, V.

Although this resort is a long ways out of town, it's popular with golfers who come to play some of the most scenic holes in the state. The Superstition Mountains are the backdrop for the 18-hole course, and even nongolfers will appreciate the scenery. The small outdoor pool here is meant for cooling off after a round of golf, not as a place to lounge away the day. You can also soothe your aches in a whirlpool or play some tennis on the two lighted courts. The guest rooms here are large and are housed in pueblo-influenced buildings painted a bright white that fairly jumps out of the surrounding brown desert landscape. Some rooms have fireplaces while others have whirlpools.

Dining/Entertainment: If you don't like chiles or the vibrant flavors of southwestern cuisine, your choices are very limited here. Although the food is quite good, a fair number of people end up eating in the bar and grill, which serves basic burgers and sandwiches.

Services: Room service, valet/laundry service.

Facilities: Pool, whirlpool, two lighted tennis courts, horseback riding.

The Wigwam

Indian School Rd. at Litchfield Rd., Litchfield Park, AZ 85340. ☎ **602/935-3811** or 800/327-0396. Fax 602/935-3737. 331 rms, 70 suites. A/C MINIBAR TV TEL. Jan–May, $280–$310 double; $380–$430 suite. May–Sept, $120–$140 double; $129–$149 suite. Sept–Jan, $230–$260 double; $320–$360 suite. AE, DC, MC, V.

Located 20 minutes west of downtown Phoenix, this golf resort opened its doors to the public in 1929 and has kept pace with the times ever since, and a complete renovation a few years ago gave guest rooms and public areas a contemporary southwestern look. Three challenging golf courses are the main reason most people choose this resort, which, though elegant, lacks the scenery of its competitor, the Boulders.

Most of the guest rooms are in small pueblo-style buildings and are surrounded by green lawns and colorful gardens. All the rooms have contemporary southwestern furniture and offer plenty of space. Some rooms have fireplaces, but the most popular rooms are those along the golf course.

Dining/Entertainment: The resort's traditional gourmet restaurant serves continental cuisine indoors or on the terrace beside the pool. The equally elegant Arizona Kitchen serves acclaimed southwestern cuisine and features an exhibition grill. Golfers have their own conveniently located restaurant in the clubhouse. Afternoon tea and evening cocktails are served in a lobby lounge, and sports fans can retreat to the Arizona Bar to catch the games on big-screen TVs.

Services: Concierge, room service, valet/laundry service, massages, golf lessons, tennis lessons.

Facilities: Three golf courses, putting green, nine tennis courts, two pools, bicycles, volleyball, croquet, trap and skeet shooting range, exercise room, sauna, pro shop.

4 Dining

Just as the Valley of the Sun is full of excellent resorts, so, too, is it full of excellent restaurants. Scottsdale and the Biltmore District are home to most—but not all. If you can afford only one expensive meal while you're here, be sure to make it at one of the resort restaurants that offers a view of the city lights. Other meals not to be missed are the cowboy dinners served amid Wild West decor at such places as Pinnacle Peak and Rustler's Rooste. Mexican food and southwestern cuisine are two other Phoenix specialties.

If you're looking to save money on your meals, consider eating between 5 and 6pm, when many restaurants offer early-bird or sunset dinner specials. These dinner deals are more common in the summer months. And finally, if a restaurant is out of your budget at night, try having lunch there instead. Lunch prices can be half those at dinner.

Price categories are as follows, based on the average cost of a three-course meal, exclusive of drinks, tip, and tax: "Very Expensive," more than $35; "Expensive," $25 to $35; "Moderate," $15 to $25; and "Inexpensive," under $15.

PHOENIX
VERY EXPENSIVE

Christopher's
In the Biltmore Financial Center, 2398 E. Camelback Rd. ☎ **602/957-3214.** Reservations required. Main courses $29; menu prestige $75 ($115 with wines). AE, CB, DC, DISC, MC, V. Summer, Thurs–Sat 6–10pm; winter, Tues–Sun 6–10pm. FRENCH/NOUVELLE AMERICAN.

Plush burgundy carpeting and brocade-upholstered chairs set a tone of traditional elegance at Christopher's, which is located in a modern office building at the corner of Camelback Road and 24th Street. The dining room is small with only a handful of tables. Conversation tends to be in hushed tones, and the clientele sport top-of-the-line suits and multicarat diamonds.

Chef Christopher Gross calls his creations contemporary French cuisine, and his versions of traditional dishes (such as poached lobster in red-wine sauce with a lobster flan) are truly memorable. His wife, sommelier Paola Gross, has assembled what may be the best wine collection in Phoenix. The house smoked salmon with ahi tuna and caviar and Christopher's own foie gras are both signature appetizers. The menu changes regularly. For those who crave the full treatment whatever the cost, there's a *menu dégustation* with seven courses and wines from around the world. If the prices here are beyond your means, don't despair. Christopher's also operates the Bistro (see below), where prices are more down to earth.

EXPENSIVE

The Bistro
In the Biltmore Financial Center, 2398 E. Camelback Rd. ☎ **602/957-3214.** Reservations recommended. Main courses $6–$15 at lunch, $16–$23 at dinner. AE, CB, DC, MC, V. Mon–Sat 11am–10pm, Sun 5–10pm. FRENCH/INTERNATIONAL.

The meals here are created in the same kitchen that prepares the pricey dishes for Christopher's, the adjacent restaurant. Some of the same dishes, such as Christopher's tender alder-smoked salmon, are also available at the Bistro (and nearly a requirement of dining here). So what's the difference other than price? Well, noise level for one. This is a bistro, with marble floors and cherrywood paneling, and the customers tend to be young, upwardly mobile types who most certainly do not converse in hushed tones. The main courses are frequently straightforward and paired with sauces designed to bring out the flavor of the dish, such as grilled prime beef with pepper sauce or grilled halibut with plum tomato and niçoise olive sauce. Desserts run the gamut from soufflés to a banana split made with homemade ice cream and fresh seasonal fruits. More than 70 wines are available by the glass.

Roxsand
2594 E. Camelback Rd. ☎ **602/381-0444.** Reservations recommended. Main courses $19.95–$23.95. AE, DC, MC, V. Mon–Thurs 11am–3:30pm and 5–10pm, Fri–Sat 11am–3pm and 5–10:30pm, Sun noon–3pm and 5–9:30pm. NEW AMERICAN.

Phoenix Dining

Arena Cantina ㉝
Big Wong ⑧
The Bistro ⑰
Bobby McGee's ②
Café Terra Cotta ㉕
The Chaparral ㉒
Christopher's ⑪
Ed Debevic's Short
   Orders Deluxe ⑭
Eddie's Grill ⑩
El Chorro Lodge ㉔
Etienne's Different
   Pointe of View ③
The Farm at South
   Mountain ㊹
The Fish Market ⑤
5 & Diner ⑥
Garcia's Mexican
   Restaurant ⑲
The Great Wall ⑨
Guedo's Taco Shop ㊵
House of Tricks ㊱
Ill San Carlino Restaurant ㉞
Jean Claude's Petit Café ㉙
Malee's on Main ㉚
Mancuso's ㉖
Mary Elaine's ㉗
Mikado ㉓
Monti's La Casa Vieja ㉟
Mr. Sushi Japanese
   Restaurant ①
Oregano's Pizza Bistro ㊸
Pepin ㉛
Pho Bang Restaurant ⑦
Planet Hollywood ⑮
Rancho Pinot Grill ⑫
Richardson's ④
Roxsand ⑯
Sam's Cafe ㊶
San Carlos Bay Seafood
   Restaurant ㉑
6th Avenue Bistro ㊷
The Stockyards Restaurant ㉜
Such is Life ⑳
T-Bone Steakhouse ㊴
Tucchetti ⑬
Rustler's Rooste ㊳
Top of the Rock ㊲
Vincent Guerithault
   on Camelback ⑱
Windows on the Green ㉘

1746

Located on the second floor of the exclusive Biltmore Fashion Park shopping mall, Roxsand serves what it calls "fusion" cuisine, a creative combination of international influences. We attempted to choose between Morrocan b'stilla (braised chicken in phyllo with roasted eggplant purée), Japanese sea-scallop salad, and rice tamales with lamb and Thai peanut sauce. And those were just the appetizers. Perhaps because of the diversity of the menu, some of the dishes can be hit or miss. Sauces sometimes lack complexity, but we can recommend the air-dried duck with Szechuan black-bean sauce, evil jungle prince sauce, plum sauce, and moo-shu pancakes. After dinner, get some exercise and walk to the dessert case to select a dessert, which will be served to you on a dinner plate adorned with additional cookies and perhaps a dollop of sorbet. Service can be on the pretentious side.

Vincent Guerithault on Camelback

3930 E. Camelback Rd. ☎ **602/224-0225.** Reservations highly recommended. Main courses $19.25–$22. AE, DC, MC, V. Mon–Fri 11am–2:30pm and 6–10pm, Sat 5:30–10pm, Sun 6–10pm. Closed Sun in summer. SOUTHWESTERN.

Vincent Guerithault has long been a local restaurant celebrity, and his restaurant serves southwestern cuisine in an intimate, unpretentious French country atmosphere. Despite the continental decor, the cuisine is solidly southwestern, with chiles appearing in numerous guises. For a starter, it's hard to beat the aggressive flavors of a smoked-salmon quesadilla with horseradish cream. Moving on to the main course, grilled meats and seafoods are the specialty here and might come accompanied by an ancho-chili and honey glaze or by habañero pasta. The extensive wine list is equally divided between Californian and French wines. There's a valet parking attendant at the door, and the number of Mercedeses here should tip you off that this is one of Phoenix's top restaurants.

MODERATE

✪ Big Wong

616 W. Indian School Rd. ☎ **602/277-2870.** Reservations accepted only for parties of five or more. Main courses $5–$14. MC, V. Mon–Thurs 11am–9:30pm, Fri 11am–11:30pm, Sat noon–11:30pm, Sun noon–9:30pm. CANTONESE/MANDARIN/HUNANESE.

What you won't find here is standard watered-down Chinese food; what you'll get are memorable dishes such as garlic-imbued yu-choi greens on a ginger-studded sizzling plate with oysters and green onions. Two menus, one more Americanized and the other more tailored to an authentic Chinese dining experience, offer sizzling dishes, hot pots, and soups. You'll find unusual dishes for adventurous palates (shark-fin soup, sea cucumber and duck feet hot pot, jellyfish). The small room is always busy, and you might have to wait for a table. If you take along a crowd, you'll get a chance to sample an abundance of these interesting dishes.

Bobby McGee's

8501 N. 27th Ave. ☎ **602/995-5982.** Reservations recommended. Main courses $6–$20; early dinner (5–6pm) $6–$10. AE, DC, DISC, MC, V. Mon–Thurs 5–10pm, Fri–Sat 5–11pm, Sun 5–10pm (lounge stays open until 1am). AMERICAN.

Bobby McGee's isn't just a restaurant, it's an event. This is where local families head for special occasions and where Phoenicians take their out-of-town guests. The restaurant is always full, so be sure to make a reservation or you may be in for a long wait. From the outside Bobby McGee's looks a bit like an old, dilapidated warehouse, but on the inside it's crammed full of antiques and old photos that give it the feel of a Wild West saloon. Waiters and waitresses are dressed in

😊 Family-Friendly Restaurants

Ed Debevic's *(see p. 108)*   This classic 1950s diner is full of cool stuff, including little jukeboxes in the booths. You can tell your kids about hanging out in places like this when you were a teenager.

Pinnacle Peak Patio *(see p. 117)*   Way out in north Scottsdale, this restaurant is a Wild West steakhouse complete with cowboys, shootouts, hayrides, and live western music nightly.

Rustler's Rooste *(see p. 117)*   Similar to Pinnacle Peak, but closer in, Rustler's Rooste has a slide from the lounge to the main dining room, a big patio, and live cowboy bands nightly. See if you can get your kids to try the rattlesnake appetizer—it tastes like chicken.

costumes that range from antebellum gowns to Boy Scout uniforms. Steaks and prime rib are the specialties here, but also on the menu is lighter fare such as pastas and fresh fish of the day.

Other branches are at 1320 W. Southern Ave., Mesa (☎ **602/969-4600**), and 7000 E. Shea Blvd., Scottsdale (☎ **602/998-5591**).

Eddie's Grill

4747 N. Seventh St. ☎ **602/241-1188.** Reservations recommended. Main courses $12–$20. AE, DC, MC, V. Mon–Thurs 11:30am–2:30pm and 5–11pm, Fri 11:30am–2:30pm and 5pm–midnight, Sat 5pm–midnight, Sun 4–9pm. NEW AMERICAN.

At Eddie's Grill in downtown Phoenix, there's a high-tech bistro upstairs, a more formal wine-cellar atmosphere downstairs, and a patio with a pond and gazebo outside. Chef Eddie Matney offers a long menu as diverse as the setting, with mo' rockin' shrimp in a spicy beer sauce one of his specialties. Sesame-seared ahi tuna with a pasta combining artichokes, spinach, and feta cheese, and grilled shrimp with vegetable lasagne are two of our favorites. The crust on the crème brûlée we shared for dessert was a trifle too thick, although the velvety custard inside met our expectations. Service is friendly and competent.

The Fish Market

1720 E. Camelback Rd. ☎ **602/277-3474.** Reservations recommended. Main courses $7.75–$31 downstairs, $8.50–$35 upstairs. AE, DISC, MC, V. Downstairs, Mon–Thurs 11am–9:30pm, Fri–Sat 11am–10pm, Sun noon–9:30pm. Upstairs, Sun–Thurs 5–9:30pm, Fri–Sat 5–10pm. SEAFOOD.

The Fish Market is divided into two restaurants: the large and casual downstairs dining room and the smaller, tonier, and slightly more expensive Top of the Market upstairs. If you feel more comfortable in jeans than in a suit and tie, stay downstairs. The Fish Market offers seafood from around the world, including fish caught by the restaurant's own boats. In the tin-ceilinged and tile-floored oyster bar you can start your evening with some Puget Sound oysters. Mesquite charcoal-broiling is the specialty downstairs, though there are a few blackened or fried dishes as well. Upstairs you'll find delicious seafood pastas and a greater variety of preparation styles.

Il San Carlino Restaurant

12 W. Monroe St. ☎ **602/252-7242.** Reservations recommended for dinner. Main courses $14.95–$18.50. AE, DISC, MC, V. Daily 10am–11pm. NORTHERN ITALIAN.

Downtown Phoenix doesn't have very many restaurants worth seeking out, but if you're in the area and want to get away from the crowds at Arizona Center, this Italian restaurant in the historic San Carlos Hotel makes a good choice. The setting is very Old World (a far cry from the rest of modern, downtown Phoenix), and Il San Carlino could hold its own even out in toney Scottsdale. The menu is relatively short and very traditional. Artichoke salad and melon with prosciutto appear as antipasti and gnocchi Gorgonzola and lobster risotto are among the pasta offerings. Entrees range from the familiar chicken marsala to the more surprising prawns cooked in orange juice.

Mr. Sushi Japanese Restaurant

8041 N. Black Canyon Hwy., Suite 112. ☎ **602/864-9202.** Reservations accepted for parties of six or more. Sushi $1.50–$6; main courses $6.45–$14. AE, MC, V. Tues–Thurs 11:30am–2pm and 5–9:30pm, Fri 11:30am–2pm and 5–10pm, Sat 5–10pm, Sun 4–9pm. JAPANESE.

This little sushi place is tucked into a nondescript office complex away from the tourist track, but it's worth searching out. The sushi chefs don't speak much English, but they can whip up some outrageous concoctions—the best of which aren't even on the menu. Of course, there are also plenty of cooked dishes for those who haven't developed a taste for sea urchin roe, raw quail eggs, or thinly sliced octopus. Prices are quite moderate if you stick to the cooked dishes, but your bill can escalate if you start ordering off the sushi menu.

Planet Hollywood

2402 E. Camelback Rd. ☎ **602/954-7827.** Main courses $6.50–$17. AE, DC, MC, V. Daily 11am–midnight. (Bar, daily 11am–1am.) INTERNATIONAL.

It's big, it's brash, it's Planet Hollywood. If you haven't yet caught the cinephile's version of the Hard Rock Cafe, then by all means stand in line for a seat here. The restaurant is all glitz and glamour from start to finish, and is decked out with an abundance of Hollywood memorabilia. With the likes of a Terminator cyborg and the dress worn by Marilyn Monroe in *Bus Stop* to distract you, who cares how the food tastes? Luckily, you won't be too disappointed by your meal if glorified diner fare suits your mood.

Richardson's

1582 E. Bethany Home Rd. ☎ **602/265-5886** or 602/230-8718. Reservations accepted only for parties of four or more. Main courses $7–$13. AE, DC, MC, V. Sun–Wed 11am–11pm, Thurs 11am–midnight, Fri–Sat 8:30am–midnight. SOUTHWESTERN.

Tucked into an older corner shopping center with far too few parking spaces, Richardson's is almost invisible amid the glaring lights and flashing neon of this otherwise unmemorable neighborhood. However, if you enjoy creative and spicy cookery, you'll be glad you found this place. Downstairs a bar and a dozen or so booths and tables are usually crowded and noisy, so you might want to ask for a table upstairs where it's quieter. If you're in the mood for a light meal, try the Taos club sandwich made with turkey, bacon, and avocado wrapped in a flour tortilla with melted cheese and salsa. A more substantial appetite may be assuaged by baked chicken stuffed with spinach, sun-dried tomatoes, poblano chile, and asiago cheese, accompanied by green-chile potatoes. For dessert, prickly-pear-syrup flan is as creamy as a good crème brûlée.

Sam's Cafe

In the Arizona Center, 455 N. Third St. ☎ **602/252-3545.** Reservations recommended. Main courses $9–$15. AE, DC, DISC, MC, V. Sun–Thurs 11am–10pm, Fri–Sat 11am–midnight. SOUTHWESTERN.

Sam's Cafe, one of only a handful of decent downtown restaurants, serves food that's every bit as imaginative—but not nearly as expensive—as that served at other (often-overrated) southwestern restaurants in Phoenix. Breadsticks served with picante-flavored cream cheese, grilled eggplant tacos, and penne pasta in a spicy peanut sauce with black beans and goat cheese all have a nice balance of flavors and are not too spicy—but spicy enough. The salad and dipping sauces are complex and interesting. The downtown Sam's has a large patio that stays packed with the lunchtime, after-work, and convention crowd and overlooks a fountain and palm garden.

There is another Sam's in the Biltmore Fashion Park at 2566 E. Camelback Rd. (☎ **602/954-7100**).

San Carlos Bay Seafood Restaurant

1901 E. McDowell Rd., just west of the Squaw Peak Parkway (Ariz. 51). ☎ **602/340-0892.** Reservations not accepted. Main courses $6.25–$20. No credit cards. Daily 10am–9pm. MEXICAN.

If you've ever spent time in a Mexican beach town, you probably have fond memories of fish dinners, but unfortunately you rarely get great Mexican seafood dishes north of the border. This basic little place remedies that problem. From whole fried fish to octopus in garlic to shrimp stew, San Carlos Bay does seafood and it does it right. This restaurant is very popular with the area's Hispanic population (you'll probably be the only outsider here), so you might want to practice your Spanish before making a foray to Bahía San Carlos.

The Stockyards Restaurant

5001 E. Washington St. ☎ **602/273-7378.** Reservations recommended. Main courses $10–$29. AE, CB, DC, DISC, MC, V. Mon–Fri 11am–2pm and 5–10pm, Sat 5–10pm, Sun 4:30–9pm. STEAK/SEAFOOD.

Once surrounded by 200 acres of feedlots and frequented almost exclusively by cattlemen in town to sell a few thousand head of cattle, this steakhouse knows its business. Today it attracts the Arizona gentry, who come to enjoy perfectly cooked steaks and cowboy beans amid an 1889 decor. There are several dining rooms, two of which have muraled walls.

✪ Such Is Life

3602 N. 24th St. ☎ **602/955-7822.** Reservations recommended. Main courses $12–$19. AE, DC, DISC, MC, V. Mon–Fri 11:30am–2pm and 5:30–9pm, Sat 5:30–9pm. MEXICAN.

If you're tired of unidentifiable Mexican food smothered in melted cheese and sour cream, then you're a candidate for Such Is Life. This is simply the best Mexican food in Phoenix. The three salsas alone are enough to justify a visit: Each has its own distinctive flavor and none is too hot. There are daily specials, but we suggest trying one of the Mexican casseroles known as *guisados*. The mole poblano guisado was made with one of the best mole sauces we've ever had. Fresh juices and flan cheesecake also excel.

T-Bone Steakhouse

10037 S. 19th Ave. ☎ **602/276-0945.** Reservations recommended. Main courses $8.50–$20. AE, MC, V. Sun–Thurs 5–10pm, Fri–Sat 5–11pm. STEAK.

With some of the best steaks in Phoenix and a great view north across the valley, the T-Bone Steakhouse is hard to beat. Though there are checkered tablecloths, sawdust on the floor, and a barbecue grill out front, this place is more a locals' hangout than a tourist attraction. To reach the restaurant, head south on 19th

Avenue until it seems to dead-end, hang a right for about 100 feet, and then turn left and continue on 19th Avenue for a mile or so. The road will turn to gravel before you reach the restaurant.

Tucchetti

2135 E. Camelback Rd. ☎ **602/957-0222.** Reservations recommended. Main courses $8–$14. AE, DISC, MC, V. Mon–Thurs 11:15am–10pm, Fri 11:15am–11pm, Sat noon–11pm, Sun 4:30–9pm. SOUTHERN ITALIAN.

Located in the parking lot of the Town & Country Shopping Center and looking like a Hollywood rendition of an old Mexican cantina, Tucchetti is one of Phoenix's most popular Italian restaurants. The food here is your basic no-frills, no-fancy-ingredients, southern Italian fare, and no one goes away hungry.

INEXPENSIVE

Arena Cantina

142 E. Washington St. (at the northwest corner with Second St). ☎ **602/495-9969.** Salads and Mexican specialties $3–$5. AE, DC, MC, V. Mon–Sat 11am–9pm (also on Sun if there's a game). HEALTHY MEXICAN.

Located near the America West Arena, this small eatery with high stools and exposed brick walls is popular with businesspeople and conventioneers during weekday lunch hours. The specialties here are health-conscious choices like chicken burritos and enchiladas, red-chile pasta salad, and Caesar salad topped with Cajun-grilled mahimahi. They'll easily put up an order to go.

ⓢ Ed Debevic's Short Orders Deluxe

2102 E. Highland Ave. ☎ **602/956-2760.** Reservations not accepted. Burgers and blue-plate specials $5–$6.50. MC, V. Sun–Thurs 11am–10pm, Fri–Sat 11am–11pm. AMERICAN.

Hidden away behind the Smitty's supermarket in the Town & Country Shopping Center, Ed's is a classic 1950s diner right down to the little jukeboxes in the booths. Not only do they make their own burgers, chili, and bread, but they serve the best malteds in Phoenix. The sign in the front window that reads WAITRESSES WANTED—NO PEOPLE SKILLS NECESSARY should give you a clue that service here is unique. This place stays busy and the waitresses are overworked (though they do break into song now and again), so don't be surprised if your waitress sits down in the booth with you to wait for your order. That's just the kind of place Ed runs, and as Ed says, "If you don't like the way I do things—buy me out."

The Farm at South Mountain

6106 S. 32nd St. ☎ **602/276-6360.** Sandwiches and salads $4–$6. No credit cards. Tues–Sat 8am–5pm. Take Exit 151A off I-10 and go south on 32nd Street. SANDWICHES & SALADS.

If being in the desert has you dreaming of shady trees and green grass, you'll enjoy this little oasis reminiscent of a New England orchard or midwestern farm. A rustic outbuilding surrounded by potted flowers has been converted to a stand-in-line restaurant where you can order a real turkey sandwich with cranberry relish on whole-grain bread or have a choice of fresh salads such as haricots verts with organic spinach, red potatoes, black olives, and feta cheese with a lemon vinaigrette dressing. The grassy lawn is ideal for a picnic on a blanket under the pecan trees.

Filiberto's

10802 N. 32nd St. ☎ **602/971-7015.** Combination plates $4.40–$5. No credit cards. Daily 24 hours. FAST FOOD/MEXICAN.

We're always on the lookout for the city's best fish taco, and Filiberto's manages to turn out a delectable one: stuffed with batter-fried fish, drizzled with a good tartar sauce, and accented by crunchy chopped cabbage. We enjoyed these little goodies while sitting on the outside patio on a warm spring night, with Phoenix traffic rushing by.

Here are several other locations; call for additional locations throughout the Valley of the Sun: 4014 N. 43rd Ave., Phoenix (☎ **602/352-0697**); 2240 W. Indian School Rd., Phoenix (☎ **602/277-4334**); 3433 W. Camelback Rd., Phoenix (☎ **602/973-3390**).

5 & Diner
5220 N. 16th St. ☎ **602/264-5220.** Reservations not accepted. Full meals $4.50–$9. AE, MC, V. Daily 24 hours. AMERICAN.

If it's 2am and now you just have to have a big burger and a side of fries after a night of dancing, head for the 24-hour 5 & Diner. You can't miss it; it's the classic streamlined diner that looks as if it just materialized from New Jersey.

There's another one in Scottsdale at Scottsdale Pavillions at Pima Road and Indian Bend Road (☎ **602/949-1957**).

Garcia's Mexican Restaurant
4420 E. Camelback Rd. ☎ **602/952-8031.** Reservations recommended. Main courses $6.25–$9.95. AE, CB, DC, DISC, MC, V. Sun–Thurs 11am–10pm, Fri–Sat 11am–11pm. MEXICAN/SONORAN.

For more than 30 years Garcia's has been serving Mexican food in Phoenix, where the lively atmosphere, large portions, and low prices attract a family-oriented crowd. Located next to a tennis complex on busy Camelback Road, this Garcia's looks like a corporate-style hacienda from the outside. Inside, you're transported to an Mexican colonial home with a sunken courtyard. We'll give you a couple of tips on the menu—try the espinaca con queso, a concoction of spinach, jalapeño cheese, and onions served with tortilla chips. After that fresh start, skip to the house specialties or try one of the traditional Sonoran combination dinners.

Other branches of this popular restaurant are at 3301 W. Peoria Ave. (☎ **602/866-1850**); 5509 N. Seventh St., at Missouri Avenue (☎ **602/274-1176**); 1940 E. University Ave., Mesa (☎ **602/844-0023**); 2394 N. Alma School Rd., Chandler (☎ **602/963-0067**); and 17037 N. 59th Ave., Glendale (☎ **602/843-3296**).

⑤ The Great Wall
5055 N. 35th Ave. ☎ **602/973-1112.** Reservations not accepted. Main courses $4.50–$10. MC, V. Daily 11am–11pm (dim sum, daily 11am–3pm). CHINESE.

Located south of Bethany Home Road, the Great Wall is just about large enough to double as a hangar for Boeing 747s, and on weekend afternoons it seems as though Phoenix's entire Chinese community packs in here to savor the best dim sum in Phoenix. We particularly like the broccoli, which wasn't on the cart the last time we went, so we ordered it from a waiter. Consider coming after 1:30pm when the crowds begin to thin out.

⑤ Pho Bang Restaurant
1702 W. Camelback Rd. ☎ **602/433-9440.** Reservations not accepted. Main courses $4.25–$13. MC, V. Daily 10am–10pm. VIETNAMESE.

Sure, the names are unpronounceable and the decor leaves a lot to be desired, but after you've had your first taste of the summer rolls, you'll know you've come to the right place for Vietnamese food. The hot-and-sour fish soup is a real winner, as is the marinated shrimp and beef that's cooked at your table. If you're daring, try some pickled lemonade or dried longan in syrup. Lunch specials are offered Monday through Friday.

SCOTTSDALE
VERY EXPENSIVE

Mary Elaine's
At the Phoenician, 6000 E. Camelback Rd., Scottsdale. ☎ **602/423-2530.** Reservations highly recommended. Jacket required for men. Main courses $29–$34. AE, CB, DC, DISC, MC, V. Mon–Thurs 6–10pm, Fri–Sun 6–11pm. MEDITERRANEAN/ASIAN.

Located on the top floor of the Phoenician's main building, Mary Elaine's is one of the finest hotel restaurants in the valley and boasts one of the city's best views as well. The restaurant is the height of Phoenician elegance and sophistication, with original artwork and soft jazz performed live in the lounge. The tables are set with fine German crystal, Reed & Barton silver, and a custom-pattern china by Mikasa. Patios with firepits provide a more relaxing setting for those who'd like to enjoy the Arizona evening outdoors. Executive chef Alessandro Stratta focuses on the flavors of the Mediterranean but also makes forays into the Far East, with such recent offerings as applewood-smoked salmon with tuna tartare and wasabi-chili, beluga caviar, and celery crème fraîche; sesame-seared sturgeon with smoked yellow-tomato coulis, water chestnuts, and daikon sprouts; and crispy salmon skin with roasted tomatillo sauce. Some dishes are particularly low in sodium, fat, and cholesterol. There's an extensive wine list that has won several awards.

EXPENSIVE

The Chaparral
At Marriott's Camelback Inn, 5402 E. Lincoln Dr. ☎ **602/948-1700** or 602/948-6644. Reservations highly recommended. Main courses $18–$28. AE, CB, DC, DISC, MC, V. Sun–Thurs 6–10pm, Fri–Sat 6–11pm. CONTINENTAL.

The Camelback Inn was built in 1936, and ever since its opening it has been known as the home of some of the valley's finest restaurants. The Chaparral is possibly the most consistently reliable continental restaurant in the valley. The decor is southwestern, with a view of Camelback Mountain through the curving glass wall and a carved silhouette of the mountain on the back of each chair. Tableside cooking is one of the specialties of the house, so be sure to ask your waiter what you can have cooked at your table. The menu features a balanced mixture of exquisitely prepared old standards and nouvelle offerings displaying the chef's creative flair. For a bit of culinary showmanship, try the wilted-spinach salad, which is prepared and flamed at your table. The beef Wellington with périgourdine and Dijon sauces is tender and juicy, while the Muscovy duck with a passionfruit sauce offers adventurous diners an unusual combination of flavors. Call for summer hours.

8700 Restaurant
8700 E. Pinnacle Peak Rd. (at Pima Rd.). ☎ **602/994-8700.** Reservations highly recommended. Main courses $17–$32. AE, DC, DISC, MC, V. Daily 6–10pm. SOUTHWESTERN.

You'll find 8700 in an office complex 20 minutes north of downtown Scottsdale. The restaurant has a large lounge and balcony seating area on the second floor, where the views are worth coming early to enjoy. However, it's the creative cuisine and artistic surroundings that keep people coming back. Meals are presented with artistic flair in a genteel atmosphere, and the desserts in particular are veritable works of art. Most of the menu is southwestern and adventurous in slant. For a starter we're partial to the roasted chile stuffed with grilled corn, goat cheese, wild mushrooms, chayote (a squashlike vegetable), black beans, and cilantro. Unusual flavor combinations appear on the menu, such as mesquite-grilled shrimp raviolis with tomatillos, jicama, and roasted red peppers in a pasta flavored with cilantro, chipotle, saffron, and mushrooms—with a vanilla-bean sauce.

El Chorro Lodge

5550 E. Lincoln Dr. ☎ **602/948-5170.** Reservations recommended. Full dinner $14–$27. AE, CB, DC, MC, V. Mon–Fri 11am–2:30pm and 5:30–11pm, Sat 9am–2:30pm and 5:30–11pm, Sun 9am–3pm (brunch) and 5:30–11pm. CONTINENTAL.

Built in 1934 as a school for girls and converted to a lodge and restaurant three years later, El Chorro Lodge is a valley landmark set on its own 22 acres of desert. At night spotlights shine on the palo verdes and cacti and the restaurant takes on a timeless tranquillity, even if the interior is a little dowdy. The adobe building houses several dining rooms, but on a chilly night the patio, with its crackling fireplace, is the place to sit. Both decor and menu offerings are traditional and popular with old-timers and families, with such classic dishes as chateaubriand and rack of lamb. In addition to the favorites, there are several dishes that are low in salt and fat. El Chorro's sticky buns are legendary, so you might want to save room.

✪ La Hacienda

At the Scottsdale Princess Resort, 7575 E. Princess Dr. (about 12 miles north of downtown Scottsdale). ☎ **602/585-4848.** Reservations recommended. Main courses $15–$24. AE, DC, DISC, MC, V. Sun–Thurs 6–10pm, Fri–Sat 6–11pm. MEXICAN.

This is not your local neighborhood Mexican restaurant, but an upscale, glamorous-but-rustic rendition of an early 1900s Mexican ranch house replete with stone tiled floor, Mexican glassware and crockery, and a beehive fireplace. The entrees are not your local north-of-the-border burritos either. Offerings include such dishes as cochinillo asado, suckling pig (carved at the table) with bitter orange, black pepper, and tamarind; and costillas de cordero, charcoal-broiled lamb chops in a pumpkin-seed crust, sauced with roasted tomatoes and mint. The rendition of tortilla soup here—a fragrant assemblage of spicy chicken broth dotted with avocado, cheese, chiles, and tortilla strips—is almost as good as ones we've had in Mexico. Grilled shrimp and baked sea bass are simpler dishes but just as delicious, as is the flan dessert.

Mancuso's

At the Borgata, 6166 N. Scottsdale Rd. ☎ **602/948-9988.** Reservations recommended. Pastas $13–$17; complete dinner $15–$24. AE, CB, DC, DISC, MC, V. Daily 5–10pm. ITALIAN/ CONTINENTAL.

The Borgata is built in the style of a medieval European village with ramparts, towers, stone walls, and narrow, uneven alleyways leading through the complex. When you reach your castle banquet hall for a repast of gourmet Italian cuisine, a pianist will be playing soft jazz (alas, no Gregorian chants) amid a soaring ceiling, stone walls, arched windows, and huge roof beams and walls of mirrors (which make the restaurant seem far larger than it really is). If you lack the means to start your meal with the beluga caviar, perhaps carpaccio di manzo—sliced raw beef with mustard sauce and capers—will do. Although there's an extensive selection of main courses, including an entire page of veal dishes, we find it difficult to get past the pasta offerings: Mancuso's serves no fewer than 10 different types in

16 different sauces. If you want something other than pasta, there are dozens of meat and seafood dishes. The professional service will have you feeling like royalty by the time you finish your dessert and coffee.

✪ Marquesa

At the Scottsdale Princess Resort, 7575 E. Princess Dr. (about 12 miles north of downtown Scottsdale). ☎ **602/585-4848.** Reservations recommended. Main courses $19.50–$27; champagne brunch $24.95. AE, DC, DISC, MC, V. Mon–Thurs 6–10pm, Fri–Sat 6–11pm, Sun 10:30am–2:30pm (brunch) and 6–10pm. SPANISH/CATALONIAN.

Located at the Scottsdale Princess, a resort designed with Moorish influences in mind, the Marquesa is a romantic dining splurge. High-backed chairs, chandeliers, muted lighting, and large classic Spanish paintings create an ambience reminiscent of an 18th-century Spanish villa. The cuisine that appears on the tables, however, is Catalonian with a contemporary interpretation by chef Reed Groban. Sea scallops wrapped in Serrano ham with tomato coulis, or crabmeat and fontina cheese in baked sweet red peppers with garlic aïoli are elegant starters, and paella with lobster, chicken, pork, shellfish, chistora, and saffron rice is the restaurant's signature dish. Some dishes are prepared to be especially low in fat and sodium, but desserts on the carts that flank the entryway, such as a crème fraîche flan with a black-walnut crust, are tempting works of art definitely to be considered. There's a separate tapas bar outside the main dining area, and brunch is served on Sunday on the outdoor patio.

Rancho Pinot Grill

6208 N. Scottsdale Rd. ☎ **602/468-9463.** Reservations recommended. Main courses $16–$21.50. MC, V. Summer, Thurs–Sun 5:30–10pm; winter, Tues–Sat 5:30–10pm. NEW AMERICAN.

Located south of Lincoln Drive, Rancho Pinot combines fun and kitschy 1950s cowboy memorabilia with an airy setting in the back of a shopping mall. The menu is short and changes regularly, which keeps fashionable Scottsdalites coming back for more. On a recent visit we tried a salad of shaved fennel, red onion, orange, and parsley with lemon and parmesan, and an entree of chicken with mixed greens, grilled asparagus, mushrooms, and polenta croûtons. Although the flavors are not as exciting and punchy as the southwestern fare here used to be, the food is well prepared and the staff is friendly and treats you like a regular even if it's your first visit.

✪ Windows on the Green

At the Phoenician, 6000 E. Camelback Rd., Scottsdale. ☎ **602/423-2530.** Reservations recommended. Main courses $17–$28; lunch/brunch $6–$16. AE, CB, DC, DISC, MC, V. Mon 11am–3pm, Tues–Sat 11am–3pm and 6–10pm, Sun 10am–3pm (brunch) and 6–10pm. SOUTHWESTERN.

Slightly more casual than the Phoenician's premier Mary Elaine's (shirts with collars are required for men), but no less elegant, Windows on the Green has a sweeping view of the resort's golf course. Chef Robert McGrath combines ingredients of the region, such as jicama, Nopales cactus, and cilantro, with meats (sometimes including wild game), fowl, fish, and vegetables to produce a menu that runs the gamut from mild to very spicy. A sampling of the menu includes lobster and roasted corn chile, roasted chicken with avocado-and-orange salad, and swordfish grilled with achiote and served with a rock shrimp tamale and cucumber salsa. The wine list is chosen to complement these regional flavors. Lunch and Sunday brunch provide an opportunity to sample the kitchen's creations at reduced prices.

MODERATE

○ Café Terra Cotta

At the Borgata, 6166 N. Scottsdale Rd., Suite 100. ☎ **602/948-8100.** Reservations recommended for dinner. Main courses $7–$19. AE, CB, DC, MC, V. Mon–Thurs 11:30am–9:30pm, Fri–Sat 11:30am–10pm. SOUTHWESTERN/INTERNATIONAL.

Café Terra Cotta started out in Tucson, where it has been a perennial favorite, so it should come as no surprise that Phoenix has beaten a path to the door of this casually sophisticated and low-key restaurant. The menu is long and includes wood-oven pizzas, sandwiches, and smaller meals as well as full-size main courses. Imaginative combinations are the rule here, so you'll want to take your time with the menu before ordering. Just for example, roll this one over on your imaginary taste buds: grilled chicken breast with achiote-sherry glaze on mole verde with chipotle whipped potatoes. Preparation can sometimes be uneven, although the last time we ate here everything was well prepared.

○ Jean Claude's Petit Cafe

7340 E. Shoeman Lane. ☎ **602/947-5288.** Reservations recommended. Main courses $7–$11.50 at lunch, $14–$19 at dinner. AE, CB, DC, MC, V. Mon–Fri 11:30am–2:30pm and 6–10pm, Sat 6–10pm. FRENCH.

It's small and quiet, and those who know about it prefer to keep it a secret. Shoeman Lane runs parallel to Camelback Road east of Scottsdale Road, and you'll find the restaurant a few blocks east of the latter. There are several small dining rooms, the nicest of which overlook the lighted fountain in the courtyard. Other than this little fountain, there's nothing in the simple decor to distract you from the well-prepared French food. All the favorites of the French kitchen are here— escargots bourguignons, pâté, Brie with apples and pears—but for an hors d'oeuvre you can't miss with the steamed mussels in a cream sauce liberally sprinkled with fennel seeds. For a main dish, try the fragrant grilled loin of lamb with rosemary-and-ginger sauce or poached trout stuffed with seafood mousse in a lobster sauce. The desserts are as tempting as the rest of the menu; crème caramel à l'orange is our favorite choice.

Malee's on Main

7131 E. Main St. ☎ **602/947-6042.** Reservations recommended for dinner. Main courses $8.25–$12.50. AE, DC, MC, V. Mon–Wed 11:30am–2:30pm and 5–9pm, Thurs 11:30am–2:30pm, Fri 11:30am–2:30pm and 5–9:30pm, Sat noon–2:30pm and 5–9:30pm, Sun 5–9pm. THAI.

The casual comfort of soft Southwest colors and the delicious aroma of Thai food is an enticing combination at downtown Scottsdale's Malee's. One of our barometers of good Thai cooking is pad thai noodles, which here were saucy and tangy. Among the many specialties at Malee's are fish filet topped with a sweet-and-hot ginger-garlic sauce and red curry with bamboo shoots and shrimp. (Unfortunately, on our visit there wasn't a sprig of cilantro in any dish.) Those who like spicy food can order dishes "Thai hot," somewhere on the other side of very hot. The outside patio and streetside seating are quiet in the evenings when downtown shuts down.

Mikado

7111 E. Camelback Rd. ☎ **602/481-9777.** Reservations recommended on weekends. Main courses $12.50–$35; sushi $2–$10. AE, MC, V. Mon–Thurs 11:30am–2:30pm and 5–10pm, Fri 11:30am–2:30pm and 5–11pm, Sat 5–11pm, Sun 5–10pm. JAPANESE/ SUSHI BAR.

Near downtown Scottsdale and set in a big 1950s-style building with a wall of glass at the front, Mikado is a serene scene with a dining area downstairs and a large U-shaped sushi bar upstairs. The sushi chef greets you in Japanese, and then you sit down to the bowl of soothing miso soup and a spot of delicate tuna salad that comes with your sushi order. The ingredients that make up the sushi, maki, handrolls, and sashimi are tender and subtly flavored in a way that only the freshest can be, and they're beautifully presented. Sushi specials and combination dinners, as well as a variety of à la carte entrees, including tempura and tonkatsu (deep-fried pork cutlet), are served downstairs. Reservations aren't taken for the sushi bar, but in spite of the fact that Phoenicians love this restaurant, you'll usually get a seat.

Pepin

7363 Scottsdale Mall. ☎ **602/990-9026.** Reservations recommended. Main courses $9–$25. AE, CB, DC, DISC, MC, V. Tues–Sat 11:30am–3pm and 5–11pm, Sun 5–11pm. (Happy hour, Tues–Fri 4:30–6:30pm.) SPANISH.

Located on the Scottsdale Mall, this elegant little Spanish restaurant offers such a wide selection of tapas that you can easily have dinner without ever glancing at the main-course list. However, if you should limit your tapas consumption, there are several different styles of paella or zarzuela de marisco, most of which are seafood extravaganzas. Thursday through Saturday evenings there are live flamenco performances, and from 9pm on Friday and Saturday there's Latin dancing.

6th Avenue Bistro

7150 E. Sixth Ave. ☎ **602/947-6022.** Reservations recommended. Main courses $16.25–$17.25. AE, MC, V. Mon 5:30–10pm, Tues–Fri 11:30am–2pm and 5:30–10pm, Sat 5:30–10pm, Sun 5:30–9pm (shorter hours in July). CLASSIC FRENCH.

Who says French has to be fussy? This little bistro less than a block off Scottsdale Road is as casual as a French restaurant gets. Stucco walls and a concrete floor are the antithesis of Scottsdale chic, though lace curtains soften the interior a bit. The draw here is a simple menu of reliable dishes at very reasonable prices. A bit of country pâté, seared salmon dijonnaise, a hearty beaujolais, all topped off with crème caramel and you have a perfect French dinner.

INEXPENSIVE

✪ Oregano's Pizza Bistro

3622 N. Scottsdale Rd. (south of Indian School Rd.). ☎ **602/970-1860.** Main courses $6–$17. AE, DC, DISC, MC, V. Mon–Thurs 11am–10pm, Fri–Sat 11am–11pm, Sun 4–10pm. PIZZA.

The originator of Oregano's has created a restaurant based on his father's recipes and expertise in the kitchen. The prices are very reasonable, and both the thin-crust pizzas—spread with the likes of pesto and Cajun chicken (and, by the way, too much for one person)—and the Chicago stuffed pizza are all the good things pizza should be. But pizza isn't all they have here—there's artichoke lasagne with both a cream and a marinara sauce, barbecue wings, a variety of Caesar salads, and more. This place is enormously popular with the young Scottsdale set, so if you want to get a table quickly you may have to sit inside rather than on the outdoor patio.

TEMPE/CHANDLER

⑤ House of Tricks

114 E. Seventh St., Tempe. ☎ **602/968-1114.** Reservations recommended. Main courses $11.25–$14. AE, CB, DC, DISC, MC, V. Mon 11am–4pm, Tues–Fri 11am–9pm, Sat 5–9pm. NEW AMERICAN.

Arizona State University is surrounded by neighborhoods of old Craftsmen bungalows, and in one of them is the area's trendiest restaurant. There are only a few tables inside the tiny dining room, which has a cozy fireplace, and slightly more outside on the grape arbor–covered patio. The clientele tends to be students and professors who know a good value when they taste it. The menu changes regularly and consists of a single page of tempting salads, appetizers, and main dishes. Besides a garlic-inspired Caesar salad, what stood our on our last visit was grilled chicken with corn-and-red-pepper pudding with ancho-chile sauce. The fresh fruit and cheese appetizer is a favorite, too.

Monti's La Casa Vieja

3 W. First St. (at the corner with Mill Ave.), Tempe. ☎ **602/967-7594.** Reservations recommended for dinner. Main courses $5.75–$22. AE, CB, DC, DISC, MC, V. Sun–Thurs 11am–11pm, Fri–Sat 11am–midnight. AMERICAN.

If you're tired of the glitz and glamour of the Valley of the Sun and are looking for Old Arizona, head down to Tempe to Monti's La Casa Vieja. The adobe building was constructed in 1873 (*casa vieja* means old house in Spanish) on the site of the Salt River ferry in the days when the Salt River flowed year-round and Tempe was nothing more than a ferry crossing. Today local families who have been in Phoenix for generations know Monti's well and rely on the restaurant for solid meals and low prices. You can get a filet mignon for under $10—or even less when it's the Monday-night special. The dining rooms are dark and filled with memorabilia of the Old West.

⑤ Guedo's Taco Shop

71 E. Chandler Blvd., Chandler. ☎ **602/899-7841.** Reservations not accepted. Main dishes $1–$4.05. No credit cards. Tues–Sat 11am–9pm. MEXICAN.

We have friends who will drive 40 miles to eat at Guedo's. The freshness of the ingredients and the authenticity of the recipes here have made this place the best little taco house in Phoenix. There are no sides of tasteless rice or beans, so be sure to order at least two tacos—three if you're hungry. Wash it all down with fresh horchata, a creamy drink made from rice and spices.

A second Guedo's is at 108 W. Broadway Rd., Mesa (☎ **602/461-3660**).

NEARBY RESTAURANTS

The Arizona Kitchen

At the Wigwam Resort, W. Indian School Rd., Litchfield Park. ☎ **602/935-3811.** Reservations highly recommended. Main courses $11.50–$27. AE, CB, DC, DISC, MC, V. Tues–Sat 6–10:30pm. Closed five weeks in the summer. SOUTHWESTERN.

It's a long way out to Litchfield Park and the Wigwam Resort, but if you have succumbed to the spicy flavors of southwestern cuisine and want to taste some of the best, you may want to make the drive. In the Arizona Kitchen, the Wigwam's southwestern ambience takes the guise of a blue-and-white-tiled exhibition kitchen in a dining room paved with bricks and filled with Spanish colonial–style furnishings. Here you'll find true regional offerings. Don't miss the opportunity to sample the traditional mainstay of the Hopi diet, piki bread. This paper-thin cornmeal bread is served with various creative fillings. Rattlesnake fritters are another specialty. Innovative pizzas are an inexpensive dinner choice and are made with a jalapeño-and-corn fry breadcrust. However, once you encounter such pricier main dishes as quinoa-and-wild-rice-stuffed pheasant glazed with chipotle pomegranate honey, you may forget your budget.

Diane Carr's Cowboy Cook Shack

26725 N. Extension Rd. (a 20-minute drive north of downtown Scottsdale). ☎ **602/ 585-4362.** Burgers $4.25–$6.75. No credit cards. Summer, Sun–Thurs 11am–10pm; winter, daily 11am–10pm. BURGERS.

On the edge of the desert, just past Pinnacle Peak Patio, is this rustic restaurant with old cable-spool tables and some firepits strewn amongst the saguaro cacti. We enjoyed an evening high in the hills out here, contemplating the sunset and experiencing the arrival of the cool desert night. We started out with some cheese crisps, stuffed flour tortillas, and after a brief wait (the staff consists of only one or two people) we chowed down on big juicy burgers by the light of a kerosene lantern. If you like things unpretentious, this is the place. To bring your own beer or wine, you need to call ahead to make a reservation.

SPECIALTY DINING
DINING WITH A VIEW

Etienne's Different Pointe of View

At the Pointe Hilton Resort at Tapatio Cliffs, 11111 N. Seventh St. ☎ **602/863-0912.** Reservations highly recommended. Main courses $19–$42. AE, CB, DC, DISC, MC, V. Mon–Thurs 6–9:30pm, Fri–Sat 6–10pm (lounge open later), Sun 10am–1:30pm (brunch) and 6–9:30pm. FRENCH.

The lounge at Etienne's faces north and the restaurant faces south, but both have curving walls of glass that let in sweeping vistas of the city, mountains, and desert. The building is built right into the top of the mountain (the road to the restaurant is incredibly steep, so we advise leaving your car at the bottom of the hill and taking the free shuttle up to the front door). The restaurant has all the glimmer and glitz of Las Vegas, and there's a Vegas-style floor show most nights. Classical French cuisine, such as onion soup gratinée and shrimp provençal, is featured, but there's also a separate menu with more adventurous sauces and preparations such as smoked pork loin with a mushroom salad and pan-fried yucca root. However, despite the excellent food, award-winning wine list, and live entertainment, it's still the view that's the star of the show here.

✪ Top of the Rock

At the Buttes, 2000 Westcourt Way, Tempe. ☎ **602/225-9000.** Reservations recommended. Main courses $8.50–$12 at lunch, $15–$25 at dinner. AE, CB, DC, DISC, MC, V. Mon–Thurs 5–10pm, Fri–Sat 5–11pm, Sun 10am–2pm (brunch) and 5–10pm. NEW AMERICAN/SOUTHWESTERN.

All the best views in Phoenix are from resorts and their restaurants, so if you want to dine with a view of the valley, you're going to have to pay the price. Luckily, quality accompanies the high prices here at the Top of the Rock in the Buttes resort. And in addition to the stunning setting of the resort, you can enjoy some very creative cuisine. There's no question as to which appetizer to order on your first visit: Get the appetizer assortment, so you can sample such delicacies as duck roulade, marinated shrimp, and crab ravioli. Sauces on the entree menu offer a good range of mellow as well as bold flavors, so even those who aren't chile fanatics can enjoy a dinner here.

COWBOY STEAKHOUSES

Though Arizona doesn't claim to have invented the steakhouse or cow towns, the state certainly has cornered the market on combining the two. Wild West theme-town restaurants abound here in the Phoenix area. These family restaurants generally provide big portions of grilled steaks and barbecued ribs, outdoor and "saloon" dining, live country music, and various sorts of entertainment, including stagecoach rides and shootouts in the street.

Pinnacle Peak Patio

10426 E. Jomax Rd. ☎ **602/967-8082** or 602/585-1599 after 5pm and on weekends. Reservations recommended on weekends. Main courses $5.50–$23. AE, MC, V. Mon–Thurs 4–10pm, Fri–Sat 4–11pm, Sun noon–10pm. Take Scottsdale Road north to Pinnacle Peak Road, turn right, and continue to Pima Road, where you turn left; at this point just follow the signs. STEAK.

Businessmen beware! Wear a tie into this restaurant and you'll have it cut off and hung from the rafters. The casual dress code is strictly enforced at this Wild West restaurant about 20 minutes north of downtown Scottsdale up in the hills overlooking the valley. A meal at the Pinnacle Peak Patio is more an event than an opportunity to satisfy your hunger. Though you can indulge in mesquite-broiled steaks (they even have a 2-pound porterhouse monster) with all the traditional trimmings, the real draw here is all the free Wild West entertainment—gunfights, cowboy bands, two-stepping, cookouts.

◯ Rawhide Western Town & Steakhouse

23023 N. Scottsdale Rd. (4 miles north of Bell Rd.), Scottsdale. ☎ **602/502-5600.** Reservations not accepted. Main courses $11–$19. AE, DC, DISC, MC, V. June–Sept, daily 5–10pm; Oct–May, Mon–Thurs 5–10pm, Fri–Sun 11am–10pm. STEAKS.

There's plenty of entertainment here, including country-music bands, shootouts, stagecoach rides, and a petting zoo. Kids love dancing to the country music and pretending they're in a real old western town, which isn't difficult, since Rawhide, with its big wide street, looks pretty authentic. Along with mesquite-broiled steaks you'll find a few barbecue items and fruit pie à la mode.

Rockin' R Ranch

6136 E. Baseline Rd., Mesa. ☎ **602/832-1539.** Reservations recommended on weekends. Main courses $13–$20. MC, V. Steakhouse, winter, Mon–Sat 5:30–9pm; summer, Wed–Sat 5:30–9pm. Theater, winter, Mon–Sat at 5pm; summer, Sat–Sun at 5pm. STEAKS.

Two different venues—one a steakhouse and the other a cowboy dinner theater—both dish out big juicy steaks with all the fixin's, including a smattering of gunfights and wagon rides. You enter this place through an artificial cave.

◯ Rustler's Rooste

At the Pointe on South Mountain, 7777 S. Pointe Hwy. ☎ **602/431-6474.** Reservations recommended. Main courses $11–$22. AE, CB, DC, DISC, MC, V. Sun–Thurs 5–10pm, Fri–Sat 5–11pm. STEAKS.

This location doesn't exactly seem like cowboy country. However, up at the top of the hill you'll find one of our favorite Phoenix restaurants. How many other restaurants do you know where you can slide from the bar down to the main dining room? The view north across Phoenix is entertainment enough for most people, but there are also western bands playing for those who like to kick up their heels. If you've ever been bitten by a snake, you can exact your revenge here by ordering the rattlesnake appetizer. Follow that (if you've got the appetite of a hardworking cowpoke) with the enormous cowboy "stuff" platter consisting of, among other things, broiled sirloin, barbecued pork ribs, cowboy beans, beer-batter shrimp, barbecued chicken, and swordfish kebabs.

CAFÉS & COFFEEHOUSES

Although it's more difficult to find a cup of good espresso in Arizona than in the Northwest (perhaps because of all that sun, caffeine isn't such a necessity here), there are a few establishments that are worth mentioning:

At Central Avenue and Camelback Road in the Uptown Plaza, the **Orbit Café** (☎ 602/265-2354) is a big trendy space with large colorful artwork, live music, and poetry slams. Call for the schedule. **Coffee Plantation** has several locations, but two of the largest are at the corner of Sixth Street and Mill Avenue in Tempe (☎ 602/829-7878), one of the happening places in Tempe; and at Biltmore Fashion Park, East Camelback Road and 24th Street (☎ 602/553-0203). **Dos Estrellas,** at the Town & Country Shopping Center, 4745 N. 20th St. (☎ 602/957-0662), has good days and bad days when it comes to serving java. **Coffee Grinders,** 7373 E. Second St., Scottsdale (☎ 602/990-8384), is a small place located next to the park at Scottsdale Center for the Arts and serves a pretty good cup. **Jamaican Blue,** tucked into a small mall at 4017 N. Scottsdale Rd., Scottsdale (☎ 602/947-2160), has live performances in the evening. **The Willow House,** 149 W. McDowell Rd. (☎ 602/252-0272), is unusual in that it isn't located in a mall, but in a 1920s house with a somewhat-bohemian atmosphere.

AFTERNOON TEA

Between 3 and 5pm every afternoon, a genteel full tea including scones with Devonshire cream is served in the lobby at **The Phoenician,** 6000 E. Camelback Rd., Scottsdale (☎ 602/423-2530). The setting, which looks out over the manicured lawns and palm trees of the resort, is comfortably elegant.

BRUNCH/BREAKFAST

Most of Phoenix's best Sunday brunches are to be had at the major hotels. Among the finest are the Golden Swan at Gainey Ranch, the Marquesa at the Hyatt Regency Scottsdale, and the Terrace Dining Room at the Phoenician (see "Accommodations," earlier in this chapter, for more information). The best continental breakfast I can think of is at **Pierre's Pastry Café,** 7119 E. Shea Blvd., Scottsdale (☎ 602/443-2510), where the croissants and brioche have a luxurious, buttery texture. Almost two dozen different kinds of bagels are sold at **Chompie's,** 3202 E. Greenway Rd. (☎ 602/971-8010), plus inexpensive and big breakfasts.

5 Attractions

Few would argue that spectacular views, some of the country's top resorts and spas, and fabulous outdoor activities and sports opportunities are the city's top draw. But a number of exceptional museums and historic sites around town and just outside will undoubtedly pull you away from the pool or off the greens.

SUGGESTED ITINERARIES

If You Have One Day

Head downtown to the Heard Museum and Pueblo Grande Museum and Ruins. After lunch, visit the Desert Botanical Gardens, then cross town to Scottsdale for some shopping in old Scottsdale. Have dinner at a restaurant with a view of the valley.

If You Have Two Days

Spend your first day as suggested above. On the second day, take an early morning hike up one of the Phoenix mountains (Squaw Peak, Mummy Mountain, Camelback Mountain), and afterward visit the Phoenix Art Museum. In the afternoon, visit the ASU Art Museum or play golf. Have dinner at Pinnacle Peak Patio for a bit of western kitsch along with your steak, or seek out some of the area's excellent southwestern or Mexican fare.

If You Have Three Days

Spend your first two days as suggested above. On Day 3, drive the Apache Trail or head north from Phoenix to the Pioneer Arizona Living History Museum to see what life was like in Arizona 100 years ago, and then continue north to Arcosanti to see what life would be like in Paolo Soleri's future. In the late afternoon, go for a horseback ride in the desert, and return to your hotel in time to wash up and head out for a late dinner.

If You Have Five Days or More

For the first three days, follow the suggestions above. On Days 4 and 5, you can opt to spend a couple of days by the pool, play tennis or golf, or take an overnight trip out from Phoenix. Two days is enough time to visit the Grand Canyon, Sedona and Oak Creek Canyon, Tucson, the White Mountains, or one of the lakes on the Colorado River.

THE TOP ATTRACTIONS

✪ Heard Museum

22 E. Monte Vista Rd. ☎ **602/252-8840.** Admission $5 adults, $4 seniors and students, $3 children 13–18, $2 children 4–12; free for everyone Wed 5–9pm. Mon–Tues and Thurs–Sat 9:30am–5pm, Wed 9:30am–9pm, Sun noon–5pm. Closed some hols. Bus: 0.

Considered one of the finest museums that deals exclusively with Native American cultures in the country, the Heard Museum makes an informative first stop before heading out to explore the Native American cultures of Arizona. "Native Peoples of the Southwest" is an extensive exhibit that examines the culture of each of the major tribes of the region. Included in the exhibit are a Navajo hogan, an Apache wickiup, and a Hopi corn-grinding display. A large kachina doll gallery will give you an idea of the number of different kachina spirits that populate the Hopi and Zuñi religions. *Our Voices, Our Land* is an audiovisual presentation in which contemporary Native Americans express their thoughts on their heritage. "Old Ways, New Ways" is an unusual interactive exhibit that's aimed at children, but is also interesting to adults. You can join a drumming group on a video, duplicate a Northwest tribal design, or set up a miniature tepee. On weekends there are performances by Native American singers and dancers, and throughout the week artists demonstrate their work. Guided tours of the museum are offered daily.

The biggest event of the year is the **Guild Indian Fair & Market,** which is held on the first weekend in March and includes performances of traditional dances as well as arts and crafts demonstrations and sales.

Desert Botanical Garden

1201 N. Galvin Pkwy. ☎ **602/941-1225.** Admission $6 adults, $5 senior citizens, $1 children 5–12, free for children 4 and under. Oct–Apr, daily 8am–sunset; May–Sept, daily 7am–10pm. Closed Dec 25. Bus: 3.

Phoenix Attractions

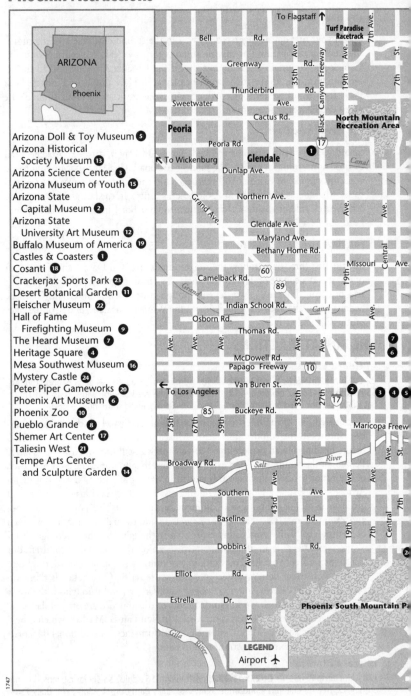

Arizona Doll & Toy Museum **5**
Arizona Historical
   Society Museum **13**
Arizona Science Center **3**
Arizona Museum of Youth **15**
Arizona State
   Capital Museum **2**
Arizona State
   University Art Museum **12**
Buffalo Museum of America **19**
Castles & Coasters **1**
Cosanti **18**
Crackerjax Sports Park **23**
Desert Botanical Garden **11**
Fleischer Museum **22**
Hall of Fame
   Firefighting Museum **9**
The Heard Museum **7**
Heritage Square **4**
Mesa Southwest Museum **16**
Mystery Castle **24**
Peter Piper Gameworks **20**
Phoenix Art Museum **6**
Phoenix Zoo **10**
Pueblo Grande **8**
Shemer Art Center **17**
Taliesin West **21**
Tempe Arts Center
   and Sculpture Garden **14**

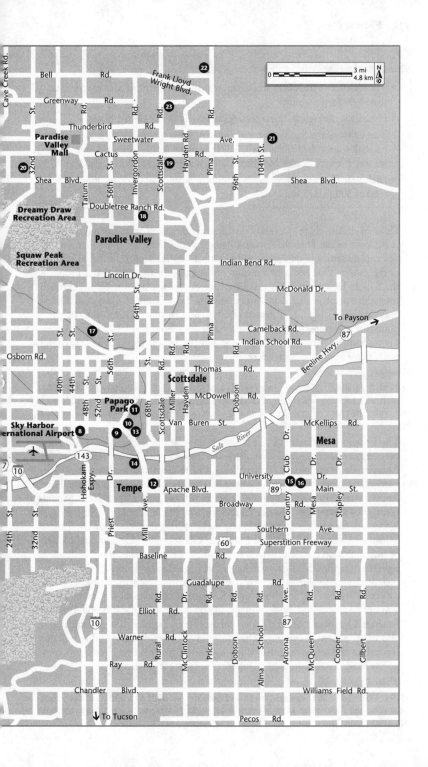

❷ Did You Know?

- The Phoenix metropolitan area has more than 100 major golf courses and more than 1,000 tennis courts.
- Phoenix is the eighth-largest metropolitan area in the United States.
- The Valley of the Sun hosts the spring-training camps of seven major-league baseball teams: the Oakland A's, San Francisco Giants, Chicago Cubs, Milwaukee Brewers, Seattle Mariners, California Angels, and San Diego Padres.
- Each year Phoenix enjoys sunshine during 86% of all daylight hours, for a total of 300 to 315 sunny days.

Devoted exclusively to cacti and other desert plants, the Desert Botanical Garden is adjacent to the Phoenix Zoo and Papago Park. There are more than 20,000 desert plants from all over the world on display throughout the different sections of the garden. One fascinating section of the garden is the "Plants and People of the Sonora Desert" trail. This trail explains the science of ethnobotany through interactive displays that demonstrate how the inhabitants of the Sonora Desert once utilized wild and cultivated plants. You can practice grinding corn and pounding mesquite beans, or make a yucca-fiber brush. The Center for Desert Living features demonstration gardens and the Desert House, an energy- and water-conservation research house.

Phoenix Art Museum

1625 N. Central Ave. (at the northeast corner with McDowell Rd.). ☎ **602/257-1222.** Admission $4 adults, $3 senior citizens, $1.50 students and children 6–12, free for children 5 and under; free for everyone Wed. Tues and Thurs–Sat 10am–5pm, Wed 10am–9pm, Sun noon–5pm. Closed major holidays. Bus: 0.

The Phoenix Art Museum is the largest art museum in the Southwest and has a very respectable collection that spans the major artistic movements from the Renaissance to the present. The collection of modern and contemporary art is particularly good, with works by Diego Rivera, Frida Kahlo, Pablo Picasso, Karel Appel, Mark Rothko, Willem de Kooning, Alexander Calder, Henry Moore, Georgia O'Keeffe, Henri Rousseau, and Auguste Rodin. The large first-floor gallery is used for special exhibits including major touring retrospectives. The Thorne Miniature Collection is one of the museum's most popular exhibits, and consists of tiny rooms on a scale of 1 inch to 1 foot. The rooms are exquisitely detailed, right down to the leaded-glass windows of an English lodge kitchen. Other exhibits include historic fashions in a gallery used by the Arizona Costume Institute, a large collection of Asian art, Spanish colonial furnishings and religious art, and of course, a western American exhibit featuring works by members of the Cowboy Artists of America. One-hour tours of the museum are offered Tuesday through Sunday and also on Wednesday evening. The museum is currently undergoing a major renovation and remodeling that will give it and its grounds a much more contemporary look. If you visit in 1996, expect to see work in progress.

Pueblo Grande Museum and Cultural Park

4619 E. Washington St. (between 44th St. and 48th St.). ☎ **602/495-0901.** Admission 50¢ for anyone age 7 and older. Mon–Sat 9am–4:45pm, Sun 1–4:45pm. Closed major holidays. Bus: Yellow Line (Y).

Located not far from the Sky Harbor Airport and downtown Phoenix, the Pueblo Grande Museum and Cultural Park houses the ruins of an ancient Hohokam village. This was one of several villages located along the Salt River between A.D. 300 and 1400. Sometime around 1450, this and other villages were mysteriously abandoned. One speculation is that drought and a buildup of salts from irrigation water reduced the fertility of the soil and forced the people to leave their homes and seek more fertile lands. Before touring the grounds to view the partially excavated ruins, you can walk through the small museum, which exhibits many of the artifacts that have been dug up on the site. There are also changing exhibits focusing on different aspects of ancient and contemporary Native American cultures. The Pueblo Grande Museum also sponsors interesting workshops, demonstrations, and tours throughout the year. Past programs have included a bow-and-arrow workshop, a basketry workshop, and a hide-tanning demonstration. A major effort is on the way to expand this museum.

✪ Arizona State University Art Museum

In the Nelson Fine Arts Center, 10th St. and Mill Ave., Tempe. ☎ **602/965-ARTS**. Admission free. Tues 10am–9pm, Wed–Sat 10am–5pm, Sun 1–5pm. Closed major holidays. Bus: Red Line (R).

Though it isn't very large, the Arizona State University Art Museum is memorable for its innovative architecture and excellent exhibitions. The building, stark and angular, captures the colors of sunset on desert mountains with its purplish gray stucco facade and pyramidal shape. The museum entrance is down a flight of stairs that lead to a cool underground garden area. Inside are galleries for crafts, prints, contemporary art, Latin American art, a temporary exhibition gallery, and two outdoor sculpture courts. The museum's collection of American art includes works by Georgia O'Keeffe, Edward Hopper, and Frederic Remington. The Matthews Center, at the corner of Cady and Taylor malls, is also part of the museum and contains American ceramics, glasswork, works by Arizona artists, and the Experimental Gallery.

MORE ATTRACTIONS
HISTORIC BUILDINGS/MONUMENTS

Heritage Square

115 N. Sixth St., at Monroe. ☎ **602/262-4734** or 602/262-5071. Rosson House tours, $3 adults, $2 senior citizens, $1 children 6–12, free for children 5 and under. Wed–Sat 10am–3:30pm, Sun noon–3:30pm (shorter hours in summer); other hours vary. Arizona Doll and Toy Museum closed Aug. Bus: Red or Yellow Line (R or Y).

Though the city of Phoenix was founded as recently as 1870, much of its history has been obliterated. Heritage Square is a collection of some of the few remaining houses in Phoenix that date to the last century and the original Phoenix townsite. All the buildings here are listed on the National Register of Historic Places and most display Victorian architectural styles popular just before the turn of the century. Among the buildings on Heritage Square are the ornate Eastlake Victorian Rosson House, which is open for tours; the Silva House, a neoclassical revival–style home that now houses historical exhibits on turn-of-the-century life in the Valley of the Sun; the Burgess Carriage House; the Bouvier-Teeter House; an 1899 bungalow; an 1897 mule barn; the Stevens-Haustgen House; and the Arizona Doll and Toy Museum, housed in a 1912 schoolhouse.

Frommer's Favorite Phoenix Experiences

Hiking up Camelback Mountain. Hiking up to the top of Camelback Mountain very early on Sunday morning is a tradition among the city's more active residents. It's a steep climb, but the views from up top are superb.

Having Dinner with a View. There's something bewitching about gazing down at the twinkling lights of the city while enjoying a delicious meal at one of Phoenix's restaurants with a view.

Lounging by the Pool. Nothing is more relaxing than lounging by one of the spectacular pools and gazing up at the desert mountains from a world-class Valley of the Sun resort.

Tubing down the Salt River. The best way to see the desert is from an inner tube as you float downriver. A few companies provide inner tubes and shuttles.

Taking the Scottsdale Art Walk. Thursday evening from October to May is the chance for dilettantes and connoisseurs to visit nearly 60 art galleries in downtown Scottsdale, often with complimentary refreshments and artists on hand.

Attending a Spring Training Baseball Game. Get a head start on all your fellow baseball fans by going to a spring-training game while you're in Phoenix.

Arizona State Capitol Museum

1700 W. Washington St. ☎ **602/542-4581.** Admission free. Mon–Fri 8am–5pm. Closed state hols. Bus: Yellow Line (Y).

In the years before Arizona became a state, the territorial capital moved from Prescott to Tucson, then back to Prescott, and finally to Phoenix. In 1898 a stately territorial capitol building was erected with a copper roof to remind the local citizenry of the importance of that metal in the Arizona economy. A statue, *Winged Victor,* stands atop the polished copper. This building no longer serves as the actual state capitol, but has been restored to the way it appeared in 1912, the year Arizona became a state. Among the rooms on view are the senate and house chambers, as well as the governor's office and historical exhibits.

MUSEUMS/GALLERIES

Arizona Science Center

147 E. Adams St. ☎ **602/256-9388.** Admission $4.50 adults, $3.50 senior citizens and children 4–12, free for children 4 and under. Mon–Sat 9am–5pm, Sun noon–5pm. Bus: Red Line (R), Yellow Line (Y), or O.

Aimed primarily at children, the Arizona Museum of Science and Technology is a hands-on museum with more than 100 interactive exhibits. There are frequent physics, biology, and chemistry demonstrations, and a small collection of reptiles. Throughout the year there are different traveling exhibits on display. Recent exhibits have included a weather station, a momentum machine, and a beautiful collection of minerals and fossils. For several years the museum has been in the process of constructing a new building on Washington Street between Fifth Street and Seventh Street. Be sure to call first to find out if they have made the move and reopened at the new location.

Arizona Historical Society Museum

1300 N. College Ave., Tempe. ☎ **602/929-0292.** Bus: Red Line (R).

This museum, at the new headquarters for the Arizona Historical Society, was still under construction at publication time, but was expected to open in early 1996. The museum will cover the history of central Arizona during the 20th century, and focus on the lives and works of the people who have shaped this region of the state. You'll find the museum just off Curry Road in Papago Park. Hours and admission prices were not available at press time, so call before you try visiting.

Mesa Southwest Museum

53 N. Macdonald St. (at the corner of First St.), Mesa. ☎ **602/644-2230.** Admission $4 adults, $3.50 senior citizens and students, $2 children 5–12, free for children 4 and under. Tues–Sat 10am–5pm, Sun 1–5pm. Closed major holidays. Bus: Red Line (R).

Located in downtown Mesa, this museum appeals mostly to children, but its exhibits on prehistoric Native American cultures in the region are particularly interesting. Kids will love the fossils and animated dinosaurs, and they can even pan for gold. The mine and jail (this really *was* the old jail) displays are also a lot of fun for kids. There are usually a couple of different temporary exhibits at any given time, and these may include displays of contemporary art or regional history.

Fleischer Museum

At Perimeter Center, 17207 N. Perimeter Dr., Scottsdale. ☎ **602/585-3108.** Admission free. Daily 10am–4pm. Closed major holidays.

This is the only museum in the United States devoted exclusively to the California school of American impressionism, which drew extensively on French impressionist styles and holds a quiet place in American art history. You'll find this small museum in a business park off Pima Road near the intersection with Frank Lloyd Wright Boulevard, which is an extension of Bell Road.

Shemer Art Center

5005 E. Camelback Rd. ☎ **602/262-4727.** Admission free. Tues 10am–9pm, Wed–Fri 10am–5pm, Sat 9am–1pm, Sun 1–5pm. Bus: 50.

Housed in a historic Santa Fe mission–style home built in the 1920s, the Shemer Art Center stages changing exhibits of traditional and contemporary art. The center also offers classes, concerts, sales, and lectures.

Tempe Arts Center and Sculpture Garden

Tempe Beach Park, Mill Ave. and First St., Tempe. ☎ **602/968-0888.** Admission free; suggested donation $2 adults, $1 students, free for children 11 and under; free for everyone Sun. Tues–Sun noon–5pm. Bus: Red Line (R).

Though this arts center is tiny, it often stages very interesting exhibits of contemporary art and crafts by living artists. Outside the gallery, in an area that was once a public swimming pool, is a small sculpture garden with contemporary pieces by local, regional, and national artists. There's also a small gift shop full of one-of-a-kind crafts and art.

Champlin Fighter Museum

4636 Fighter Aces Dr., Mesa. ☎ **602/830-4540.** Admission $6 adults, $3 children 14 and under. Daily 10am–5pm. From U.S. 60, take the Greenfield exit and go north to McKellips Boulevard.

This aeronautical museum is dedicated exclusively to fighter planes and the men who flew them. Aircraft from World Wars I and II, the Korean War, and the Vietnam

War are on display, with a strong emphasis on the wood-and-fabric biplanes and triplanes of World War I. There are several Sopwiths and Fokkers. From World War II, there's a Spitfire, a Messerschmitt, and a Goodyear Corsair. Jet fighters from more recent battles include a MiG-15, a MiG-17, and an F4 Phantom. In addition to the restored fighter planes, there is memorabilia of famous fighter aces.

Buffalo Museum of America

10261 N. Scottsdale Rd. (at the southeast corner with Shea Blvd.), Scottsdale. ☎ **602/ 951-1022.** Admission $3 adults, $2.50 senior citizens, $2 children 6–17, free for children 5 and under. Mon–Fri 9am–5pm. Closed major holidays. Bus: 72 or 106.

Scottsdale may not be the home where the buffalo roam, but it does have a fascination with the Old West, so it seems appropriate to find a museum dedicated to the beasts here. This small museum is the culmination of one man's infatuation with the American bison, which is commonly known as the buffalo. The museum houses stuffed buffaloes, bronze buffaloes, buffalo paintings, and all manner of buffalo memorabilia, including a rifle that once belonged to Buffalo Bill Cody.

Hall of Flame Firefighting Museum

6101 E. Van Buren St. ☎ **602/275-3473.** Admission $4 adults, $3 senior citizens, $1.50 children 6–17, free for children 5 and under. Mon–Fri 9am–5pm, Sat 9am–4pm, Sun noon–4pm. Closed Jan 1, Thanksgiving, and Dec 25. Bus: 3.

The world's largest firefighting museum houses a fascinating collection of vintage fire trucks. The displays date back to a 1725 hand-pumper from England, but also include several classic fire engines from this century. All are beautifully restored and, of course, fire-engine red. In all, there are more than 100 vehicles on display.

Mystery Castle

800 E. Mineral Rd. ☎ **602/268-1581.** Admission $3 adults, $1 children 5–15. Tues–Sun 11am–4pm. Closed July–Sept (but sometimes open Sat–Sun).

Built for a daughter who longed for a castle more permanent than those built in sand at the beach, Mystery Castle is a work of folk-art architecture. Boyce Luther Gulley, who had come to Arizona in hopes of curing his tuberculosis, constructed the castle during the 1930s and early 1940s using stones from the property. The resulting 18-room fantasy has 13 fireplaces, a wedding chapel, parapets, and many other unusual touches. This castle is a must for fans of folk-art constructions.

A ZOO

Phoenix Zoo

455 N. Galvin Pkwy. (in Papago Park in central Phoenix). ☎ **602/273-1341.** Admission $7 adults, $6 senior citizens, $3.50 children 4–12, free for children 3 and under. May–Labor Day, daily 7am–4pm; Labor Day–Apr, daily 9am–5pm. Closed Dec 25. Bus: 3.

Home to more than 1,200 animals, the Phoenix Zoo is known for its 4-acre African veldt exhibit and its baboon colony. The southwestern animal exhibits are also of particular interest. All the animals in the zoo are kept in naturalistic enclosures and can be viewed from a train that makes a 30-minute circuit of the grounds. Narrators aboard the train explain each exhibit. Kids will love the 11-acre children's zoo, where they can see baby animals and pet some of the more friendly residents.

ESPECIALLY FOR KIDS
MUSEUMS

Arizona Doll & Toy Museum

602 E. Adams St. ☎ **602/253-9337.** Admission by donation. Tues–Sat 10am–4pm, Sun noon–4pm. Closed Aug. Any downtown bus.

Located in the Stevens House on Heritage Square in downtown Phoenix, the Arizona Doll & Toy Museum is as interesting to adults as it is to kids. There's a 1912 schoolroom display in which the children are all antique dolls.

Arizona Museum for Youth

35 N. Robson St. (at the corner of Pepper Place, between Main St. and First St.), Mesa. ☎ **602/644-2467** or 602/644-2468. Admission $2, free for children under 2. Fall–spring, Sun and Tues–Fri 1–5pm, Sat 10am–5pm; summer, Tues–Fri 9am–5pm, Sat 10am–5pm, Sun 1–5pm. Closed for two weeks between exhibits.

This museum has received kudos for the innovative way it presents creativity and fine arts to children, using both traditional displays and participatory activities. It's housed in a refurbished grocery store, which may be transformed into a zoo, a farm, or a foreign country depending on the theme of the show. A recent exhibit was titled "Weather or Not," and used borrowed museum-quality works of art from different time periods and media to communicate ideas about weather. Activities that reinforced the idea of weather were then suggested to children so that they could express the concepts that they saw. Exhibits are geared mainly to toddlers through 12-year-olds, but all ages can work together to make an object or experience the activities.

AMUSEMENT PARKS

Castles & Coasters

9445 E. Metro Pkwy. ☎ **602/997-7576.** Park, free; ride or game, varies. Summer, Sun–Thurs 10am–10 or 11pm, Fri–Sat 10am–midnight; fall–spring, Fri–Sun 10am–10 or 11pm.

Located adjacent to Metrocenter, Arizona's largest shopping mall, this amusement park boasts a very impressive roller coaster and plenty of tamer rides as well. There are also four 18-hole miniature-golf courses.

Crackerjax Family Fun & Sports Park

16001 N. Scottsdale Rd. (one-quarter mile south of Bell Rd.), Scottsdale. ☎ **602/998-2800.** Park, free; activity, varies. Mon–Thurs 10am–10pm, Fri–Sat 10am–midnight, Sun 10am–9pm.

Three miniature-golf courses are the main attraction here, but you'll also find a driving range, batting cages, go-cart tracks, sand volleyball courts, and a video-game arcade.

Peter Piper Gameworks

10620 N. 32nd St. ☎ **602/404-2200.** Admission varies. Mon–Fri 11am–10pm, Sat 10am–midnight, Sun 10am–10pm (shorter hours in winter).

This fun park is aimed at the younger set and features bumper boats, bumper cars, a small roller coaster, a moon walk, and a video-game arcade.

CHILDREN'S THEATER

The **Phoenix Children's Theatre** (☎ 602/265-4142), which stages its plays at the Performing Arts Center, 1202 N. Third St., and the **Great Arizona Puppet**

Theater (☎ 602/277-1275), which performs at 3302 N. Seventh St., provide lots of theatrical fun for kids. Call for schedules.

SPECIAL SIGHTS FOR ARCHITECTURE BUFFS

Cosanti

6433 Doubletree Ranch Rd. (1 mile west of Scottsdale Rd.), Scottsdale. ☎ **602/948-6145.** Admission: $1 donation. Daily 9am–5pm. Closed major hols.

This complex of cast-concrete structures served as a prototype and learning project for architect Paolo Soleri's much grander Arcosanti project currently under construction north of Phoenix (see "Easy Excursions from Phoenix," later in this chapter, for details). It's here at Cosanti that Soleri's famous bells are cast.

Taliesin West

114th St. and Frank Lloyd Wright Blvd., Scottsdale. ☎ **602/860-8810** or 602/860-2700. Admission Oct–May, $10 adults, $8 senior citizens and students, $3 children 4–12, free for children 3 and under; June–Sept, $8 adults, $6 students and senior citizens, $3 children 4–12, free for children 3 and under. Oct–May, daily 9am–4pm; June–Sept, daily 8–11am. Closed Easter, Thanksgiving, Christmas, and occasional special events. Go east on Shea Boulevard to 114th Street, then north 1 mile.

Architect Frank Lloyd Wright fell in love with the Arizona desert and in 1937 opened a winter camp here that served as his office and school. Today Taliesin West is the headquarters of the Frank Lloyd Wright Foundation and School of Architecture. Tours cover a general background introduction to Wright and his theories of architecture, and the buildings of this campus. Wright believed in us-ing local materials in his designs and this shows up at Taliesin West in the use of local stone for building foundations. Wright developed a number of innovative methods for dealing with the extremes of the desert climate, such as sliding wall panels to let in varying amounts of air and light. Architecture students, and anyone interested in the work of Wright, will find the gift shop full of excellent books. Behind-the-scenes tours ($25 per person), guided desert hikes ($12 per person), and night hikes ($25 per person) are also available at certain times of year.

6 Organized Tours

There are numerous companies offering guided tours of both the Valley of the Sun and the rest of Arizona. Tours of the valley tend to include only brief stops at high-lights. **Gray Line of Phoenix** (☎ 602/495-9100 or 800/732-0327), is one of the largest tour companies in the valley. They offer a three-hour tour of Phoenix and the Valley of the Sun for $27 per adult. The tour points out such local landmarks as the state capitol, downtown Phoenix, Barry Goldwater's home, the Wrigley Mansion, and Camelback Mountain. There's also a stop in Scottsdale for lunch and shopping.

Far more fun are the desert Jeep tours. **Desert Mountain Jeep Tours** (☎ 602/860-1777) has been leading Jeep tours through the desert for longer than any other company in the valley. The trips include a bit of six-gun shooting practice, nature walks, horseback riding, and Native American folklore as told by cowboy guides. They'll pick you up at your resort or hotel. **Arizona Awareness Desert Jeep Tours** (☎ 602/947-7852) offers nature tours, Native American mythology tours, expe-ditions to ghost towns, and cookouts in the desert. History-laden Jeep tours are given by **Old West Trails** (☎ 602/945-5251).

7 Outdoor Activities

BALLOONING   The still morning air of the Valley of the Sun is perfect for hot-air ballooning and, not surprisingly, there are quite a few companies offering balloon rides around Phoenix. **A Aerozona Adventure** (☎ 602/991-4260 or 800/421-3056) offers daily sunrise flights, and between November and March they also have sunset flights. They charge about $100 per person if you meet them at the launch site and $135 with hotel pickup. The **Unicorn Balloon Company** (☎ 602/991-3666 or 800/468-2478) and **Sky Climber Balloon Adventures** (☎ 602/483-8208 or 800/854-1798) offer similar trips.

BICYCLING   Though the Valley of the Sun is a sprawling place, it's mostly flat, which makes bicycling a breeze as long as it isn't windy or in the heat of summer. **Wheels & Gear,** 7607 E. McDowell Rd., Scottsdale (☎ 602/945-2881), rents mountain bikes for between $15 and $20 per day.

FISHING   There are six large lakes in the mountains northeast of Phoenix, and all offer good fishing. You'll need a fishing license from the Arizona Game & Fish Commission. These licenses are generally available wherever fishing gear is sold.

GOLF   With more than 100 courses in the Valley of the Sun, golf is the most popular sport in Phoenix. Many of the golf resorts around the valley are open to the public. You can get more information on Valley of the Sun golf courses from the **Phoenix & Valley of the Sun Convention & Visitors Bureau,** One Arizona Center, 400 E. Van Buren St., Suite 600, Phoenix, AZ 85004 (☎ 602/254-6500). You can also pick up a copy of the *Phoenix and Valley of the Sun Golf Guide* at the Visitors Bureau, golf courses, and many hotels and resorts. **Resorts Tee Time** (☎ 602/962-GOLF, or 800/GO-TRY-18) will make reservations for you at various courses around the valley.

Among the valley's favorite golf courses are **Papago Municipal Golf Course,** 5595 E. Moreland St. (☎ 602/275-8428); **Encanto Golf Course,** 2705 N. 15th Ave. (☎ 602/253-3963); **Troon North Golf Club,** 10320 E. Dynamite Blvd., Scottsdale (☎ 602/585-5300); the **Pointe Golf Club at Lookout Mountain,** 11111 N. Seventh St. (☎ 602/866-6356); the **Arizona Biltmore,** 24th Street and Missouri Avenue (☎ 602/955-9655); and **Tournament Players Club (TPC) of Scottsdale,** 17020 N. Hayden Rd., Scottsdale (☎ 602/585-3939).

HIKING   Mummy Mountain, Camelback Mountain, and Squaw Peak all have a portion of land that's a public park. However, the city's largest park is **Phoenix South Mountain Park,** said to be the largest city park in the world. There are many nature, hiking, and horseback-riding trails in South Mountain Park, and the views of Phoenix are spectacular, especially at sunset. To reach the park, simply drive south on Central Avenue.

Another popular spot for hiking is **Camelback Mountain,** near the boundary between Phoenix and Scottsdale. This is the highest mountain in Phoenix, and the 1.2-mile trail to the summit is very steep. Don't attempt this one in the heat of day, and take at least a quart of water with you. The reward for your effort is the city's finest view. To reach the trailhead for Camelback Mountain, drive up 44th Street until it becomes McDonald Drive, then turn right on East Echo Canyon Drive and continue up the hill until the road ends.

Squaw Peak in the Phoenix Mountains Preserve offers a slightly less strenuous hike and views that are almost as spectacular as those from Camelback Mountain.

Squaw Peak is reached from Squaw Peak Drive off Lincoln Drive between 22nd Street and 23rd Street.

Farther afield there are numerous hiking opportunities in the Superstition Mountains to the east and the McDowell Mountains to the north.

HORSEBACK RIDING   There are plenty of places around Phoenix to rent a horse. On the south side of the city, try **Ponderosa Stables,** 10215 S. Central Ave. (☎ 602/268-1261), which leads rides into South Mountain Park and charges $12 per hour. Up on the north side, there's **Blackhawk Stables,** 11111 N. Seventh St. (☎ 602/867-3780), which charges $20 for a 1¹/₂-hour ride.

IN-LINE SKATING   In the Scottsdale area, you can rent in-line skates at **Scottsdale Bladez,** 10155 E. Via Linda (☎ 602/391-1139), for $4 per hour, including all protective equipment. You can also rent equipment at **Scottsdale Sidewalk Surfer,** 2602 N. Scottsdale Rd., Scottsdale (☎ 602/994-1017). The folks at these shops can point you in the direction of nearby spots that are good for skating, or call the hotline listed below. Some of these places include the Indian Bend Wash green belt, an 8-mile multi-use path. It runs parallel to Hayden Road in Scottsdale, and can be accessed at Hayden and Indian School Road. The sidewalks in Tempe are 8 feet wide and in good shape, and if you skate with consideration for others, no one will bother you. For more information on the Phoenix skate scene, call the **Valley Inline Hotline** (☎ 602/831-2166).

SOARING   The thermals that form above the mountains in the Phoenix area are ideal for sailplane (glider) soaring. **Estrelia Sailport,** on Ariz. 238, 6 miles west of Maricopa (☎ 602/568-2318), offers sailplane rides as well as instruction.

TENNIS   Tennis is second only to golf in popularity in the Phoenix area. Most major hotels have a few tennis courts and there are several tennis resorts around the valley. Other places to play include the **City Center Tennis Courts,** 121 E. Adams St. (at the top of the Hyatt Regency Parking Garage), Phoenix (☎ 602/256-4120); **Scottsdale Ranch Park,** 10400 E. Via Linda, Scottsdale (☎ 602/994-7774); **Encanto Park,** 15th Avenue and Encanto Boulevard (☎ 602/495-5458); and the **Phoenix Tennis Center,** 6330 N. 21st Ave. (☎ 602/249-3712).

WATER PARKS   At **Waterworld Safari Water Park,** 4243 W. Pinnacle Peak Rd. (☎ 602/581-1947), you can free-fall 6¹/₂ stories down the Avalanche speed water slide or catch a gnarly wave in the wave pool. Other water slides offer tamer times. Admission is $12.50 for adults, $10.25 for children 4 to 11. Waterworld is open from Memorial Day to Labor Day only, Monday through Saturday from 10am to 9pm and on Sunday from 11am to 7pm. **Sunsplash-Golfland,** 155 W. Hampton, Mesa (☎ 602/834-8318), has a wave pool and a tunnel called "the Black Hole." Admission is $11.75 plus tax for adults, $9.60 plus tax for children. Sunsplash is open spring to fall only, Monday through Saturday from 10am to 9pm and on Sunday from 11am to 7pm. **Big Surf,** 1500 N. McClintock Rd. (☎ 602/947-SURF), also has a wave pool, underground tube slides, and more. Admission is $12.50 for adults over 12, $10.25 for children 4 to 11, and free for children 3 and under. Big Surf is open spring to fall only, Monday through Saturday from 10am to 6pm and on Sunday from 11am to 7pm.

WHITE-WATER RAFTING & TUBING ON THE SALT RIVER   The desert may not seem like the place for white-water rafting, but up in the mountains to the northeast of Phoenix, the Upper Salt River still flows wild and free and offers some exciting rafting. **Salt River Rafting** (☎ 602/577-1824 in Tucson, or

800/242-6335) runs half-day, full-day, overnight, and two-day trips (conditions permitting) down the Upper Salt River. Prices range from $49 to $199. **Salt River Canyon Raft Trips** (☎ **602/966-7878** or 800/964-RAFT) also runs trips down the Salt.

Tamer river trips can be had from **Salt River Recreation** (☎ **602/984-3305**), which has its headquarters 20 miles northeast of Phoenix on the Bush Highway at the intersection with Usery Pass Road in the Tonto National Forest. For $8 they'll rent you a large inner tube and shuttle you by bus upriver for the float down.

8 Spectator Sports

Call **Dillard's Box Office** (☎ **602/678-2222**) or **Ticketmaster** (☎ **602/784-4444**) for tickets to the events below. For tickets to sold-out events, try **Danny's Tickets Unlimited** (☎ **602/840-2340** or 800/289-8497) or **Ticket Exchange** (☎ **602/254-4444** or 800/800-9811) or check in the Friday edition of *The Arizona Republic* in the Weekend section.

AUTO RACING   At the **Firebird International Raceway Park,** at 20000 Maricopa Rd., at Exit 162A off I-10 (☎ **602/268-0200**), you can see NHRA races and amateur drag racing. At the **Phoenix International Raceway,** 115th Avenue and Baseline Road, Avondale (☎ **602/252-3833**), there is NASCAR racing in the autumn and Indy car racing in the spring on the world's fastest 1-mile oval. Tickets are available at Dillard's Box Office or through Ticketmaster (see phone numbers above).

BASEBALL   Seven major-league baseball teams have spring-training camps in the Valley of the Sun during March and April. You can catch **major-league exhibition games** by the San Francisco Giants, Oakland A's, California Angels, Chicago Cubs, San Diego Padres, Seattle Mariners, and Milwaukee Brewers several nights a week. You can get a schedule from the convention and visitors bureau, or check the *Arizona Republic* while you're in town.

In addition, the **Phoenix Firebirds** play AAA Pacific Coast League professional ball at Scottsdale Stadium, 7408 E. Osborn Rd. (☎ **602/275-0500**). This is a farm club of the San Francisco Giants. Tickets cost $4 to $7 and can be gotten at Scottsdale Stadium or Dillard's Box Office locations.

BASKETBALL   The NBA's **Phoenix Suns** play at America West Arena, 201 E. Jefferson St. (☎ **602/379-7867** or 602/379-7800). Tickets are $10 to $75 and are available at the America West Arena box office and Dillard's Box Office locations. The Suns are a very hot team at the moment, so tickets are hard to come by. Your best bet is to contact the box office the day before or the day of a game to see if tickets have been returned.

FOOTBALL   The **Arizona Cardinals,** 8701 S. Hardy Rd., Tempe (☎ **602/379-0102**), became Phoenix's NFL football team in 1988. Games are played at the Arizona State University's Sun Devil Stadium, which is also home to the Fiesta Bowl Football Classic. Tickets are $25 to $50. Excepting a few specific games each season, it is generally possible to get Cardinals tickets.

GOLF TOURNAMENTS   Among the many PGA events held in the Valley of the Sun, the **Phoenix Open Golf Tournament** in January is the largest. Other major tournaments include the **Standard Register Turquoise Classic,** an LPGA tournament played in March, and **The Tradition,** a Senior PGA Tour event also held in March.

HOCKEY The **Phoenix Road Runners** professional ice-hockey team plays October to April at Veterans' Memorial Coliseum, 1826 W. McDowell Rd. (☎ **602/340-0001**). Call Ticketmaster (see number above) for tickets, which cost $8 to $14.

HORSE/GREYHOUND RACING The **Phoenix Greyhound Park,** East Washington Street and 38th Street (☎ **602/273-7181**), is one of the nation's premier greyhound tracks. The large, fully enclosed, and air-conditioned facility offers seating in various grandstands, lounges, and restaurants. There's racing nightly throughout the year, and tickets are $1.50 to $3.

    Turf Paradise, 1501 W. Bell Rd. (☎ **602/942-1101**), is Phoenix's horse-racing track. The season runs from September to May, with post time at 12:30pm. Admission ranges from $2 to $4, but many hotels give out complimentary passes.

TENNIS TOURNAMENTS Top international tennis players compete at the **Arizona Men's Tennis Championships** held in Scottsdale in February (☎ **602/381-6600**).

9 Shopping

Phoenix and Scottsdale have long been winter meccas for the moneyed classes, so it's no surprise that the same fashionable shopping establishments you're likely to find in Beverly Hills, New York, London, and Paris are also here. In addition to these are the many boutiques and shops of local designers who have gained a dedicated following in the Southwest, where a very distinctive style has emerged in recent years.

THE SHOPPING SCENE

For the most part, shopping in the valley means malls. They're everywhere and they're air-conditioned, which, we're sure you'll agree, makes shopping in the desert far more enjoyable than in the 100° heat. Scottsdale and the Biltmore District of Phoenix are the valley's main upscale shopping areas. Old Scottsdale (one of the few outdoor shopping areas) plays host to hundreds of boutiques, galleries, jewelry stores, and Native American crafts stores. The western atmosphere of Old Scottsdale is partly real and partly a figment of the local merchants' imaginations, but nevertheless it's the single most popular tourist shopping area in the valley. It also happens to be the heart of the valley's art market, with dozens of art galleries along Main Street.

    Shopping hours are usually Monday through Saturday from 10am to 6pm and on Sunday from noon to 5pm, and malls usually stay open until 9pm Monday through Saturday.

SHOPPING A TO Z
ANTIQUES

Glendale is antique central for the valley, with the highest concentration of shops in downtown Glendale and Glendale Avenue between the 5000 and 6000 blocks.

The Antique Gallery
In Uptown Plaza, Central Ave. and Camelback Rd. ☎ **602/241-1174.**

This antique mall houses about 70 antiques dealers under one roof and offers a wide variety of collectibles and antiques.

✪ Antique Trove
2020 N. Scottsdale Rd., Scottsdale. ☎ **602/947-6074.**

This is one of the biggest antiques malls in the valley and, though it isn't as clean and modern as the Antique Gallery, it has a larger selection. If you make only one antiques mall stop, make it here.

Arizona West Galleries
7149 E. Main St., Scottsdale. ☎ **602/994-3752.**

Nowhere else in Scottsdale will you find such an amazing collection of cowboy collectibles and western antiques. There are antique saddles and chaps, old rifles and six-shooters, sheriff's badges, spurs, and the like.

✪ Bo's Funky Stuff
5605 W. Glendale Ave., Glendale. ☎ **602/842-0220.**

Billing itself the "wildest shop north of the border," Bo's is a repository of midcentury modern collectibles, including Beatles memorabilia, 1950s furniture, neon signs, old advertisements, bakelite jewelry, western collectibles, and generally odd and unusual stuff.

ART

The galleries mentioned below are all within walking distance of each other in downtown Old Scottsdale. For a more extensive listing of galleries and exhibitions in the area, pick up a copy of *The Official Valley of the Sun Gallery Guide*, available at art galleries.

✪ The Art of the Toy
4151 N. Marshall Way, Scottsdale. ☎ **602/423-2911.**

If you're a child at heart, be sure to visit this unusual gallery where artistic toys for grownups are the raison d'être. There are fanciful puppets, found-object robots, colorful and complex whirligigs, and other fun things you won't ever find at your local Toys "R" Us.

Art One
4120 N. Marshall Way, Scottsdale. ☎ **602/946-5076**.

If you appreciate wacky art, don't miss this gallery, which specializes in works by students and local artists. Where else can you find a table lamp made from a bowling pin and a toaster?

Fagen-Peterson Fine Art
7077 E. Main St., Scottsdale. ☎ **602/941-0089.**

This gallery features primarily colorful, offbeat art with a sense of humor. Works are often tongue-in-cheek.

Feathers Gallery
7100 E. Main St., Scottsdale. ☎ **602/423-8119.**

Here you'll find Native American and Southwest art, including ceramics, colorful paintings, bronzes, home furnishings, and unusual sculptures.

Leona King Gallery
7171 Main St., Scottsdale. ☎ **602/945-1209.**

This gallery offers contemporary art with Native American themes. There are also painted leather Apache war shields, Zuñi fetishes, ceramics, stone statuettes, and portraits.

Leslie Levy Fine Art
7135 E. Main St., Scottsdale. ☎ **602/947-2925.**

This gallery tends to take chances with offbeat contemporary art from outside the mainstream. Perhaps because of this fringe aesthetic, quality is high.

✪ Lisa Sette Gallery
4142 N. Marshall Way, Scottsdale. ☎ **602/990-7342.**

If you aren't a fan of cowboy or Native American art, you may think that Phoenix has little serious art to offer. Think again, then stop by Lisa Sette. Premier glass artist William Morris recently showed his "Artifact" series here. Other international, national, and local artists all share wall space, with a wide mix of media represented.

Molinar
4151 N. Marshall Way, Scottsdale. ☎ **602/990-1416.**

Sharing space with the Art of the Toy (see above), this gallery specializes in graphics by such artists as Claes Oldenburg, Robert Rauschenburg, David Hockney, and Andy Warhol.

Overland Gallery
7155 Main St., Scottsdale. ☎ **602/947-1934.**

Traditional western paintings and a collection of Russian impressionist paintings form the backbone of this gallery's collection.

BOOKS

Borders
In Biltmore Fashion Park, 2402 E. Camelback Rd. ☎ **602/957-6660.**

Aisles of books, magazines and newspapers, a café, author signings, kid's storytime, and musical presentations are what you'll find at this large bookstore. It's a good place to browse.

Changing Hands Bookstore
414 Mill Ave., Tempe. ☎ **602/966-0203.**

Located in the heart of the Arizona State University district, this bookstore satisfies the cravings for an intellectual collegiate atmosphere. It's not big—only three small floors—but there are books both new and used on all kinds of topics and easy chairs to relax in.

CRAFTS

Mind's Eye Craft Gallery
4200 N. Marshall Way, Scottsdale. ☎ **602/941-2494.**

You'll find the finest contemporary crafts from around the nation at this Scottsdale gallery. There's an emphasis on American craftspeople in the collection of jewelry, ceramics, wood, clothing, paper, and glass.

FASHIONS

Western Wear

Boot Barn
2949 N. Scottsdale Rd., Scottsdale. ☎ **602/946-1381.**

These boots are made for walking . . . and riding. Arizona's largest selection of cowboy boots.

Hollywood Cowboy

8700 E. Pinnacle Peak Rd., Scottsdale. ☎ **602/585-4300.**

If I wanted to treat myself to a buckskin jacket with oodles of fringe (and costing about that many dollars), I'd head out to this very small boutique with a choice selection of high-end cowgirl and cowboy leather trappings.

Saba's Western Stores

7254 Main St., Scottsdale. ☎ **602/949-7404.**

Since 1927 this store has been outfitting Scottsdale's cowboys and cowgirls, visiting dude ranchers, and anyone else who wants to adopt the look of the Wild West. Call for other locations around Phoenix.

✪ Sheplers Western Wear

9201 N. 29th Ave. ☎ **602/870-8085.**

This just may be the largest western-wear store in the valley. If you can't find it here, it just ain't available in these parts. Another location is at 8979 E. Indian Bend Rd., Scottsdale (☎ **602/948-1933**).

Stockman's Cowboy & Southwestern Wear

23587 N. Scottsdale Rd., Scottsdale. ☎ **602/585-6142.**

This is one of the oldest western-wear businesses in the valley, though the store is now housed in a new shopping plaza. You'll find swirly skirts for cowboy dancing, denim jackets, and flashy cowboy shirts. The store is at the corner of Pinnacle Peak Road.

Women's Wear

✪ Carol Dolighan

At the Borgata, 6166 W. Scottsdale Rd., Scottsdale. ☎ **602/922-0616.**

The hand-painted, handwoven, and handmade dresses, skirts, and blouses here abound in rich colors. Each is unique. There's another Carol Dolighan store in El Pedregal shopping plaza (☎ **602/488-4505**) in Carefree.

Children's Wear

Lil'People

At the Arizona Center, Third St. and Van Buren St. in downtown Phoenix. ☎ **602/252-2241.**

Cute and bright cotton playwear for children newborn to six years old.

The Moushka Bambino Co.

8700 E. Pinnacle Peak Rd., Scottsdale. ☎ **602/585-4300.**

If you like to have only the best for the baby in your life, drive out to this upscale children's fashion boutique. The clothing is primarily for the under-five set and includes lace and crocheted dresses and darling hats. (It's in the same location as Hollywood Cowboy; see above.)

GIFTS/SOUVENIRS

✪ Arizona State University Gift Shop

In the Arizona State University Art Museum, Nelson Fine Arts Center, 10th St. and Mill Ave., Tempe. ☎ **602/965-9076.**

A selection of not-too-expensive and pretty good stuff in the way of Mexican folk art, pottery, children's toys, jewelry, books, T-shirts, and greeting cards can be found here.

Heard Museum Gift Shop

In the Heard Museum, 22 E. Monte Vista Rd. ☎ **602/252-8344,** or 800/252-8344.

As museum stores go, this place is pretty big, and there's no better place to buy Native American arts and crafts. The museum sells only the best, with prices to prove it.

Phoenix Art Museum Store

In the Phoenix Art Museum, 1625 N. Central Ave. (at the northeast corner with McDowell Rd.). ☎ **602/257-1880.**

Crafts, greeting cards, unique photo frames and other decorative items, and a wide selection of art-related books make up a large portion of the choices available here.

✪ Shades of the West

7253 Main St., Scottsdale. ☎ **602/945-3289.**

One-stop shopping for all things southwestern is the name of the game in this sprawling store. From T-shirts to regional foodstuffs, Shades of the West has it all. It's got a good selection of wrought-iron cabinet hardware that can give your kitchen a western look, and there are imported Turkish rugs and Mexican crafts that all fit in with a Southwest interior decor.

The UNICEF Shop

At the Town & Country Shopping Center, 4741 N. 20th St. ☎ **602/956-0781.**

If you're looking for unusual gifts and crafts from around the world, take a look in this interesting little shop. They've got a lot of pieces you won't find anywhere else, and the profits go to UNICEF.

JEWELRY

Alizes Exclusive Creations

At the Borgata, 6166 N. Scottsdale Rd., Scottsdale. ☎ **602/948-6166.**

Stunning beaded necklaces and other unique works of wearable art fill the display cases in this shop. Designs draw on various current trends in jewelry design.

Chief Dodge Indian Jewelry Store

1332 N. Scottsdale Rd., Scottsdale. ☎ **602/970-1133.**

You can watch Native American craftspeople create beautiful silver jewelry, sand paintings, rugs, and other crafts right in the store, and then peruse the cases searching for a kachina, bowl, or basket to take home.

Gilbert Ortega's Indian Arts

7150 E. Fifth Ave. ☎ **602/945-8912.**

You'll find cases and cases of Native American jewelry at Gilbert Ortega shops. Some of the many other branches are located at the Hyatt Regency Hotel, 122 N. Second St. (☎ **602/265-9923**); 7237 E. Main St., Scottsdale (☎ **602/481-0788**); 7252 E. First Ave., Scottsdale (☎ **602/945-1819**); 7155 E. Fifth Ave. (☎ **602/941-9281**); and at Koshari in the Borgata, 6166 N. Scottsdale Rd. (☎ **602/998-9699**).

✪ Heard Museum Gift Shop

In the Heard Museum, 22 E. Monte Vista Rd. ☎ **602/252-8344** or 800/252-8344.

The Heard Museum has an awesome collection of very aesthetic, extremely well crafted, and very expensive Native American jewelry.

S. A. Gaulthier

4164 N. Marshall Way, Scottsdale. ☎ **602/941-1707.**

Very stylish, modern designs using precious stones make every piece of jewelry in this shop a miniature work of art.

MALLS/SHOPPING CENTERS

Arizona Center

455 N. Third St. ☎ **602/271-4000.**

Revitalizing downtown Phoenix, this mall houses several nightclubs as well as shops and a food court. The gardens and fountains are a peaceful oasis amid downtown's asphalt.

Biltmore Fashion Park

E. Camelback Rd. and 24th St. ☎ **602/955-8400.**

Since this is a "fashion park" and not just a shopping mall, it comes as no surprise that the shops bear the names of international designers and exclusive boutiques. Saks Fifth Avenue anchors the mall, with the likes of Gucci, Louis Vuitton, Williams-Sonoma, I. Magnin, and Laura Ashley filling the smaller stores. Limousine service from certain hotels and valet parking are both available.

✪ The Borgata of Scottsdale

6166 N. Scottsdale Rd. ☎ **602/998-1822.**

Designed to resemble a medieval Italian village with turrets, stone walls, and ramparts, the Borgata is far and away the most architecturally interesting shopping mall in the valley. There are about 50 upscale boutiques, art galleries, and restaurants, including Dos Cabezas, a store with fun and colorful designs in women's clothing and home furnishings.

El Pedregal Festival Marketplace

Scottsdale Rd. and Carefree Hwy. ☎ **602/488-1072.**

Located adjacent to the spectacular Boulders Resort north of downtown Scottsdale, El Pedregal is the most self-consciously southwestern shopping center in the valley. It's worth the long drive out here just to see the new pueblo architecture and colorful accents. The shops offer high-end merchandise, fashions, and art, including the Imagine Gallery and Conrad Leather Boutique, which carry upscale southwestern fashions.

Metrocenter

9617 Metro Pkwy. W. ☎ **602/997-2641.**

This is the largest shopping center in the Southwest, with more than 200 specialty shops, four major department stores (Dillard's, Broadway Southwest, Robinson's, and Sears), and about 40 eating establishments.

Scottsdale Fashion Square

7000 E. Camelback Rd., Scottsdale. ☎ **602/990-7800.**

Scottsdale has long been the valley's shopping mecca, and for years this huge mall was the reason why. It houses three major department stores—Dillard's, Neiman Marcus, and Bullock's—and smaller stores like the Nature Company and a Godiva Chocolatier.

Superstition Springs Center

Superstition Frwy. at Power Rd., Mesa. ☎ **602/396-2570.**

Located out on the east side of the city just off Ariz. 360, the Superstition Springs Center is one of the valley's newest malls. Stores include Dillard's, Sears, Mervyn's, and J. C. Penney, as well as more than 120 others.

Town & Country

20th St. and Camelback Rd. ☎ **602/955-6850.**

This one of Phoenix's newer shopping plazas, and acts as a sort of western anchor for the Camelback Corridor, which is currently the shopping, business, dining, and nightlife center for Phoenix. You'll find high fashion as well as bargains, kitsch gifts, the UNICEF Shop, a Bookstar discount bookstore, and many other small shops.

NATIVE AMERICAN ARTS & CRAFTS

Grey Wolf

7101 Stetson Dr., Scottsdale. ☎ **602/423-0004.**

You'll find the valley's largest selection of Native American artifacts—everything from shields to war bonnets—plus handcrafted kachina dolls, sterling silver jewelry, music, rugs, and pottery. There are Northwest and Plains Indians artifacts here as well.

✪ John C. Hill

6962 E. First Ave., Scottsdale. ☎ **602/946-2910.**

This store is for collectors, and has one of the finest selections of Navajo rugs in the valley, including quite a few older ones. There are also kachinas, Navajo and Zuñi silver-and-turquoise jewelry, baskets, and pottery. They sell only the highest quality here, so you can familiarize yourself with what the best looks like.

Old Territorial Shop

7220 E. Main St., Scottsdale. ☎ **602/945-5432.**

There's good value and a lot of selection here—jewelery, sand paintings, concha belts, kachinas, fetiches, pottery, and Navajo rugs.

SWAP MEETS

American Park 'n' Swap

3801 E. Washington St. ☎ **602/273-1258.**

This is Phoenix's oldest and largest swap meet and takes place weekends in the parking lot of the Phoenix Greyhound Park.

Swapmart

5115 N. 27th Ave. ☎ **602/246-9600.**

If it's the middle of summer, or Friday or Saturday, and you still want to hit a swap meet (flea market), try this 3-acre indoor market. You'll find plenty of southwestern crafts at prices lower than in the gift shops around town.

10   Phoenix After Dark

The best place to look for nightlife listings is in the *Phoenix New Times,* a weekly newspaper that tends to have the most comprehensive listings of what's going on. This is also the publication to check for club listings and schedules of rock concerts at various concert halls. *The Arizona Republic* is another good place to look for entertainment listings, though you won't find as many club listings as in the *New Times.* The Weekend section, which appears on Friday, and the Arts Plus section, which appears on Sunday, have listings of upcoming events and performances. Other publications to check for abbreviated listings are the *Arizona Quick Guide* and *Key to the Valley,* both of which are free and can usually be found at hotels and resorts.

Another way to find out what's going on this week in Phoenix is to call the **Visitors Information Hotline** (☎ 602/252-5588).

Tickets to many concerts, theater performances, and sporting events are available through **TicketMaster** (☎ 602/784-4444), which has outlets at Zia, Wherehouse, and Tower Records, as well as May-Robinson department stores. Tickets are also available at all **Dillards** department store box offices (☎ 602/678-2222). For tickets to sold-out events try **Danny's Tickets Unlimited** (☎ 602/840-2340 or 800/289-8497), **Ticket Exchange** (☎ 602/254-4444 or 800/800-9811), or check in the Weekend section of the Friday edition of *The Arizona Republic.*

THE PERFORMING ARTS

The performing-arts scene in Phoenix could be said to lack direction. There's no main district in the Phoenix area for performing arts, although Phoenix proper has several venues downtown. Instead, major performing-arts venues are scattered across the area. Consequently, Phoenicians find themselves crisscrossing the valley to attend this concert or that dance performance.

There are surprisingly few performing-arts companies in the valley, but the area's performing-arts centers book a wide variety of acts throughout the year. These national and international acts give the valley just the diversity of performers you would expect to find in a city of this size.

Groups of 15 or more may want to contact **Curtain Call** (☎ 602/997-6409) for priority, discount seating to a number of the Valley of the Sun's major performing-arts events. They can also arrange special pretheater dinner packages.

MAJOR PERFORMING ARTS CENTERS   Phoenix's premier performance venue is the **Phoenix Symphony Hall,** 225 E. Adams St. (☎ 602/262-7272 or 800/AT-CIVIC), which is home to the Phoenix Symphony and the Arizona Opera Company and also hosts classical music performances, touring Broadway shows, and various other concerts and theatrical productions. The box office is at the entrance to the Phoenix Convention Center, Lobby 2, Plaza South, and is open Monday through Friday from 9:30am to 5pm.

In Scottsdale, the **Scottsdale Center for the Arts,** 7380 E. Second St., Scottsdale (☎ 602/994-2787), on the Scottsdale Mall, hosts a wide variety of performances and series ranging from African dance to classical music. It may be the wealth of the local population, but for whatever reason, this center seems to get the best of the touring performers who come through the valley. The box office

The Major Concert & Performance Halls

Chandler Center for the Arts, 250 N. Arizona Ave., Chandler (☎ **602/786-3954**).

Blockbuster Desert Sky Pavilion, North 83rd Avenue and Encanto Boulevard (☎ **602/254-7200**).

Grady Gammage Memorial Auditorium, Mill Avenue and Apache Boulevard, Tempe (☎ **602/965-3434**).

Herberger Theater Complex, 222 E. Monroe St. (☎ **602/252-8497**).

Kerr Cultural Center, 6110 N. Scottsdale Rd., Scottsdale (☎ **602/965-5377**).

Phoenix Civic Plaza and Symphony Hall, 225 E. Adams St. (☎ **602/262-7272**).

Scottsdale Center for the Arts, 7380 E. Second St., Scottsdale (☎ **602/994-2787**).

Sundome Center for the Performing Arts, 19403 R. H. Johnson Blvd., Sun City West (☎ **602/584-3118**).

and galleries are open Monday through Saturday from 10am to 5pm (to 8pm on Thursday) and on Sunday from noon to 5pm.

The Frank Lloyd Wright–designed **Grady Gammage Memorial Auditorium,** at Mill Avenue and Apache Boulevard on the Arizona State University campus in Tempe (☎ **602/965-3434**), is at once massive and graceful. This 3,000-seat hall hosts everything from barbershop quartets to touring Broadway plays. The box office is open Monday through Friday from 10am to 6pm and on Saturday from 10am to 4pm.

Several other halls around the valley also schedule interesting performances throughout the year. The **ASU Kerr Cultural Center,** 6110 N. Scottsdale Rd. (☎ **602/965-KERR**), offers up an eclectic season that includes music from around the world. The **Chandler Center for the Arts,** 250 N. Arizona Ave., Chandler (☎ **602/786-3954**), books a few name entertainers each year and fills out its season with a variety of other acts. The **ASU Sundome Center for the Performing Arts,** 19403 R. H. Johnson Blvd., Sun City West (☎ **602/975-1900**), seats more than 7,000 people and stages shows that will appeal to Sun City's older residents. The **Tempe Performing Arts Center,** 132 E. Sixth St., Tempe (☎ **602/966-3391**), is small but manages to book a good range of performances.

OUTDOOR VENUES   With all those days of sunshine each year, it should come as no surprise that Phoenicians like to go to performances under the stars. The city's top outdoor venue is the **Blockbuster Desert Sky Pavilion** (☎ **602/254-SKYY**), located half a mile north of I-10 between 79th Avenue and 83rd Avenue. This 20,000-seat amphitheater is open year-round and hosts everything from Broadway musicals to rock concerts; tickets run $10 to $45. The **Scottsdale Center for the Arts** (☎ **602/994-2787**) heads outdoors for many of its summer concerts, which are held in the Scottsdale Amphitheater, which is on the Scottsdale Mall. The **Mesa Amphitheater,** at the corner of University Drive and Center Road in Mesa (☎ **602/644-2178**), is a much smaller amphitheater that holds rock concerts throughout the summer; tickets run $12 to $25. In Tempe, the small **Hayden**

Square Amphitheatre, at Fourth Street and Mill Avenue (☎ **602/966-1300**), schedules frequent rock concerts throughout the year.

Outdoor concerts are also held at various parks and plazas during the summer months. In downtown Phoenix, there are evening concerts on the grass at the **Arizona Center** (☎ **602/949-4353**), while way up in Carefree, the **El Pedregal Festival Marketplace** (☎ **602/488-1072**) stages summer evening concerts as well. Both these series host jazz, blues, country, and rock concerts.

OTHER VENUES   When big-name music stars come to town, they often perform at the **America West Arena,** 201 E. Jefferson St. (☎ **602/379-7800**), which is known locally as the Purple Palace; tickets run $10 to $75. This arena is also home to the NBA's Phoenix Suns basketball team.

If your tastes run to country music, you may want to consider a night at the **Red River Opry,** 730 N. Mill Ave., Tempe (☎ **602/829-OPRY**). This theater just across the Salt River from ASU presents western variety shows similar to those of the Grand Ole Opry. There are also frequent pop, rock, jazz, and country music concerts; tickets are $13.50 to $30.

One venue that defies categorization but that often holds interesting events is **Westworld of Scottsdale,** 16601 N. Pima Rd., Scottsdale (☎ **602/483-8800**). This sprawling complex provides an amazing variety of entertainment and sporting events. There are rodeos, polo matches, and an Arabian horse show, but there are also country music concerts, hot-air balloon races, a steakhouse, horse rentals, and horseback-riding instruction. Ticket prices vary with the event.

CLASSICAL MUSIC, OPERA & DANCE

There are a few high-quality classical music options in the valley. The **Phoenix Symphony** (☎ **602/264-6363** or 800/776-9080), the Southwest's leading symphony orchestra, performs at the Phoenix Symphony Hall (tickets run $10 to $36), while the **Scottsdale Symphony Orchestra** (☎ **602/945-8071**) performs at the Scottsdale Center for the Arts (tickets go for $12 to $15).

Opera buffs may want to see what the **Arizona Opera Company** (☎ **602/ 266-7464**) has scheduled. This company splits its time between Phoenix and Tucson; tickets cost $14 to $61).

Ballet Arizona (☎ **602/381-1096**) performs at the Phoenix Symphony Hall and the Herberger Theater Center and stages both familiar and innovative ballets; tickets run $17.25 to $65. The **Center Dance Ensemble** (☎ **602/482-6410**), which performs at various venues around the area, is the city's contemporary dance ensemble; tickets go for $13.25 to $16.25. **Southwest Dance** (☎ **602/482-6410**) brings to Phoenix acclaimed dance companies from around the world (the Bolshoi Ballet will be performing here in April 1996), with most performances staged at the Chandler Center for the Arts (tickets range from about $14 to $28, higher for outstanding performances; discounts are available for students, seniors, and children).

THEATER

Phoenix is not much of a theater city and supports only a handful of professional theater companies and series. Theater in Phoenix also tends to be pretty conservative, so don't expect the latest avant-garde production.

The city's main hall for live theater is the **Herberger Theater Center,** 222 E. Monroe St. (☎ **602/252-8497**), which is located downtown and vaguely resembles a Spanish colonial church. Its two Broadway-style theaters together host more than 600 performances each year, including productions by the **Actors Theatre of Phoenix (ATP)** (☎ **602/253-6701** or 602/252-8497) and the **Arizona Theatre Company (ATC)** (☎ **602/256-6899** or 602/252-8497). ATP has, in less than 10 years, become one of Phoenix's premier acting companies. Plays tend to be smaller, lesser-known works, with musicals, dramas, and comedies equally represented; tickets go for $6.50 to $21. ATC splits its performances between Phoenix and Tucson and tends toward big productions and well-known works. Founded in 1967, the ATC has grown into a major force in the Arizona thespian scene; tickets run $20 to $30.

The **Phoenix Theatre,** Central Avenue and McDowell Road (☎ **602/258-1974** or 602/254-2151), has been around for more than 70 years and stages a wide variety of productions on three different stages; tickets are $18 to $22. If your interest lies in Broadway plays, see what the **Valley Broadway Series** (☎ **602/965-3434**) has scheduled; their focus is mostly on comedies and musicals. This series is held at the Gammage Auditorium in Tempe; tickets cost $25 to $60. The **Theater League** (☎ **602/262-7272**) is another series that brings in Broadway musicals; tickets cost $26.50 to $32.50.

Smaller companies around the valley include **Theater Works** (☎ **602/486-8636**), which performs primarily well-known works such as the comedies of Neil Simon; tickets go for $10 to $14. The **Unlikely Theater Company,** 414 S. Mill Ave., Tempe (☎ **602/952-1955**), tucked into the back of a shopping plaza on busy Mill Avenue, is the most outrageous theater company in the valley; tickets run $5 to $10.

THE CLUB & MUSIC SCENE

The Valley of the Sun has a very diverse club and music scene that's spread out across the length and breadth of the valley. However, there are a few concentrations of clubs and bars. **Phoenix Live!** at Arizona Center, 455 N. Third Ave. (☎ **602/252-2112**), is playing a big part in the renaissance of downtown Phoenix. With three different bars and clubs side by side in the modern shopping mall, Phoenix Live! offers downtown barhoppers a chance to do all their hopping under one roof. Another place to wander around until you hear your favorite type of music is **Mill Avenue** in Tempe. Because Tempe is a college town, there are plenty of clubs and bars on this short stretch of road. Looking for a more upscale crowd and more sophisticated surroundings? Head for **Scottsdale.** Both the Old Scottsdale neighborhood and resort row along Scottsdale Road have plenty of choices for evening entertainment. Bars are allowed to stay open until 1am.

NIGHTCLUBS/CABARET/COMEDY

The Improvisation
930 E. University Dr., Tempe. ☎ **602/921-9877.** Cover $8–$12; dinner $8–$15.

With the best of the national comedy circuit harassing the crowds and rattling off one-liners, the Improv is the valley's most popular comedy club. Weekend lines are long, but your reward is a chance to see the same folks that appear on TV stand-up comedy shows. Dinner is served and reservations are advised.

Yesterday's
9035 N. Eighth St. ☎ **602/861-9080.** No cover; $10-per-person minimum.

Singing waiters and waitresses perform Broadway show tunes and other songs from the 1920s to the 1960s. There's no cover charge but there is a $10 minimum per person. Meals range from $13 to $18, and reservations are required. In the winter you should book at least a week in advance.

FOLK & COUNTRY

Handlebar-J
7116 E. Becher Lane, Scottsdale. ☎ **602/948-0110.** No cover Sun–Thurs, $3 Fri–Sat.

We're not saying that this is a genuine cowboy bar, but cowpokes do make this one of their stops when they come in from the ranch. You'll hear live git-down two-steppin' music and can even get free dance lessons on Wednesday and Thursday. Great lunches also.

The Rockin' Horse
7000 E. Indian School Rd., Scottsdale. ☎ **602/949-0992.** No cover to $12.

A honky-tonk this ain't, and the music doesn't always come straight from Nashville, but for cowboys and cowgirls with a taste for new country, the Rockin' Horse is the place to be.

Toolie's Country Saloon and Dance Hall
4231 W. Thomas Rd. (at SE 43rd Ave.). ☎ **602/272-3100.** No cover to $5.

Once a Safeway supermarket, Toolie's is now the best country-and-western bar in the valley. A false-front cow-town facade beckons enthusiasts of all ages to come on in and git down. Nationally known acts make this their Phoenix stop, and when they aren't on stage Toolie's books the best of the local C&W bands. They offer dance lessons, too.

ROCK

Anderson's Fifth Estate
6820 Fifth Ave., Scottsdale. ☎ **602/994-4168.** Cover $2–$5.

Phoenix has a thriving scene for alternative music and this is where a lot of it gets played. Most nights there's a DJ spinning the dance music, but there are also occasional live shows.

Gibson's
410 S. Mill Ave., Tempe. ☎ **602/967-1234.** Cover $3–$12.

Overlooking the Hayden Square Amphitheatre in the heart of Tempe's Mill Avenue college hangout district, Gibson's is a glossy club that stays packed. Step through the door and you almost trip onto the dance floor. High above you is the stage and higher still is a huge video screen. Local bands perform on weekends with touring groups filling up the weeknight slots.

Long Wong's
701 S. Mill Ave. ☎ **602/966-3147.** No cover to $3.

This club is scruffy and tiny and stays packed most nights with college students who come to hear the best of the local rock bands and eat great buffalo wings.

The Roxy
2110 E. Highland Ave. ☎ **602/954-7838.** No cover to $20.

This huge place, dark and partially underground, is behind the Town & Country shopping plaza just off Camelback Road, and books both the best touring bands and name acts that have seen more popular days. Because of the setup of the stage, it's possible to get a pretty decent view of the performers.

JAZZ & BLUES

Call the **Arizona Jazz Hotline** (☎ **602/254-4545**) for a schedule of jazz performances all over the state. In Sedona in September, the **Jazz on the Rocks** festival (☎ **520/282-1985**) features nationally known jazz musicians.

Char's Has the Blues

4631 N. Seventh Ave. ☎ **602/230-0205**. Cover $3 weekends.

Yes, indeed, Char's does have those mean-and-dirty, lowdown blues, and if you want the blues too, this is where you head when you're in Phoenix. All the best blues brothers and sisters from around the city and around the country make the scene here to the enjoyment of hard-drinkin' crowds.

The Rhythm Room

1019 E. Indian School Rd. ☎ **602/265-4842**. No cover to $15.

This blues club books quite a few national acts as well as the best of the local scene, and has a dance floor if you want to move to the beat.

Timothy's

6335 N. 16th St. ☎ **602/277-7634**. No cover, but there's a food-and-drink minimum.

For an elegant evening of dining and listening to lively jazz, Timothy's is hard to beat. The restaurant and lounge both attract a well-off crowd. Live jazz is performed nightly.

DANCE CLUBS/DISCOS

Bobby McGee's

8501 N. 27th Ave. ☎ **602/995-5982**. Cover $3 Wed and Fri–Sun.

A wacky family restaurant with costumed waitresses may not seem like the place for a hot singles bar, but the bar in back is known throughout the valley for luring a young and attractive crowd. There's a strict dress code to keep out questionable types, so be sure to dress up a bit (no torn jeans or open-toed shoes, etc.).

Club Rio

430 N. Scottsdale Rd., Tempe. ☎ **602/894-0533**. Cover $4.

This cavernous club has a dance floor big enough for football practice. From barely legal ASU students to the Porsche-and-pony set from Scottsdale, everyone agrees that Club Rio is *de rigueur* if you want to dance to the latest Top 40, alternative, and R&B. Plenty of live shows, too.

Jetz/Stixx

7077 E. Camelback Rd., Scottsdale. ☎ **602/970-6001**. Cover $5.

Located across from the Scottsdale Fashion Square mall, Jetz is currently one of Phoenix's hottest singles' scenes. If you can't pick someone up here, you might as well give up. Deep tans, blond hair, and hard bodies seem to be *de rigueur*. Bands from Los Angeles and Las Vegas are featured. Stixx is Jetz's upscale pool hall.

Studebakers

10345 N. Scottsdale Rd. (at Shea Blvd.), Scottsdale. ☎ **602/443-3222** or 602/443-0303. Cover $2 Sun–Thurs, $3 Fri–Sat.

A sort of Hard Rock Cafe imitation with an old Studebaker coupe parked in the middle of the club, this spot attracts singles and couples from 25 to 50 years old. Disc jockeys play music from 1950s to contemporary, and there's a free happy-hour buffet weekdays from 5 to 8pm.

The Works
7223 E. Second St., Scottsdale. ☎ **602/946-4141.** Cover $2–$10.

This cavernous neo-industrial building looks distinctly out of place in Old Scottsdale, but that doesn't prevent it from being one of the most popular dance clubs in the valley, throbbing with the latest in techno-industrial and alternative vibes. There are several different areas in the club, including a terrace with a swimming pool and a huge patio. The Works is well known as a gay hangout, but is also very popular with straights.

THE BAR & PUB SCENE

Another Pointe in Tyme
In the Pointe Hilton on South Mountain, 7777 S. Pointe Pkwy. ☎ **602/438-9000.**

If you feel most comfortable when surrounded by walls of mahogany and sitting on brocade or velvet, or if a little light jazz or piano music is your idea of the perfect music to drink by, then you'll be content at Another Pointe in Tyme.

AZ88
7353 Scottsdale Mall, Scottsdale. ☎ **602/994-5576.**

Located across the park from the Scottsdale Center for the Arts, this sophisticated bar has a cool ambience that's right for a martini before or after a performance.

Durants
2611 N. Central Ave. ☎ **602/264-5967.**

If you prefer martinis to beer, and all your friends prefer martinis too, then you probably belong at Durants. For many years this has been *the* place for downtown money merchants to stop on their way back to their rooms with a view.

COCKTAILS WITH A VIEW

The Valley of the Sun has more than its fair share of spectacular views. Unfortunately, most of them are in expensive restaurants. Fortunately, however, all these restaurants have lounges where, for the price of a drink (and perhaps valet parking), you can sit back and ogle a crimson sunset and the purple mountains' majesty. Your choices include **Etiennes's Different Pointe of View** at the Pointe Hilton at Tapatio Cliffs, **Rustler's Rooste** at the Pointe on South Mountain, and the **Top of the Rock** at the Buttes. All these restaurants can be found in the restaurant section of this chapter. One other choice is **The Thirsty Camel** at the Phoenician resort. You may never drink in more ostentatious surroundings than here at Charles Keating's Xanadu.

SPORTS BARS

America's Original Sports Bar
455 N. Third St. ☎ **602/252-2112.**

Located in the Arizona Center, this huge sports bar (nearly an acre) is a sort of fun center for grown-ups. There's a huge back deck, 60 TVs, 10 giant-screen TVs, a sand volleyball court, and a small video-games arcade.

Majerle's Sports Grill
24 N. Second St. ☎ **602/253-9004.**

If you're a Phoenix Suns basketball fan, you won't want to miss this sports bar only a couple of blocks from the America West Arena where the Suns play. Suns memorabilia covers the walls.

✪ Max's

6727 N. 47th Ave., Glendale. ☎ **602/937-1671.**

These days it seems that sports bars are as common as knee injuries on the football field. Most are little more than a bar with a big-screen TV, but Max's is the real thing. In fact, it's a sports museum, restaurant, dinner theater, and off-track betting parlor all wrapped up in one. Yes, after perusing the glass cases full of football helmets and other sports memorabilia, you can sit down to some prime ribs and a cold glass of beer, and wager on the horses or greyhounds.

GAY & LESBIAN BARS

Ain't Nobody's Business

3031 E. Indian School Rd. ☎ 602/224-9977.

This bar, with a DJ and dartboards and located in a shopping plaza, caters exclusively to women and is the city's most popular lesbian bar. Sometimes there's live music by local musicians.

Charlie's

727 W. Camelback Rd. ☎ **602/265-0224.**

This nondescript bar just a dozen or so blocks off I-17 is a good bet if you're staying in the Camelback corridor area.

Nu Towne Saloon

5002 E. Van Buren St. ☎ **602/267-9959.**

A big red truck parked inside this bar acts as a visual focal point, but the real draws are the food-and-drink specials every Sunday. After 20 years of popularity it's obvious that the friendly, funky atmosphere here works.

307 Lounge

222 E. Roosevelt St. ☎ **602/252-0001.**

Drag shows and talent contests keep this gay bar lively on weekends and make it one of the funniest scenes in the valley. Serious drag-show aficionados won't want to miss *The Golden Girl Revue.*

BREW PUBS

Bandersnatch Brew Pub

125 E. Fifth St., Tempe. ☎ **602/966-4438.**

With good house brews and a big patio in back, Bandersnatch is a favorite of those unusual ASU students who prefer quality to quantity when it's beer-drinking time. There's live music here most nights.

✪ Coyote Springs Brewing Company

4883 N. 20th St. ☎ **602/468-0403.**

This brew pub in the Town & Country Shopping Plaza on Camelback Road is a casual, friendly place, and on any given night it has the valley's largest selection of handcrafted beers and ales on tap, sometimes including apricot or raspberry ale. There's also live music, mostly blues and R&B, on weekends.

Hops! Bistro & Brewery

7000 E. Camelback Rd., Scottsdale. ☎ **602/945-4677.**

Take a down-home idea—brewing your own beer—and mix it up with a bit of Scottsdale chic (by way of San Diego) and you get Hops!, an upscale brew pub that includes a patio with live acoustic music, a bar, a separate sports-bar area, and a dining room that serves creative contemporary American cuisine.

There's also a branch at the Biltmore Fashion Park, at 2584 E. Camelback Rd. (☎ **602/468-0500**).

MORE ENTERTAINMENT
FILMS

IMAX Theater Scottsdale

Scottsdale Rd. and Civic Center Blvd. ☎ **602/945-4629**. Tickets $6–$8.50 adults, $4.50–$7 senior citizens and children 12 and under.

The massive IMAX screen puts you in the midst of the action. There are usually two different films showing here on any given day.

A CASINO

Fort McDowell Casino

Ariz. 87, 2 miles east of Shea Blvd. ☎ **800/THE-FORT**.

Phoenicians, once the mainstay clientele of casinos in Nevada, now need drive only to the east side of the valley to throw their hard-earned dollars at the slot and video-poker machines. The casino's open 24 hours a day, and there's even free transportation from Phoenix.

11   Easy Excursions from Phoenix

THE APACHE TRAIL

There isn't a whole lot of desert or history left in Phoenix, but only an hour's drive to the east you'll find quite a bit of both. The Apache Trail, a winding, partially unpaved road that snakes its way around the north side of the Superstition Mountains, offers some of the most scenic desert driving in central Arizona. Along the way there are ghost towns and legends, saguaros and century plants, ancient ruins and man-made lakes.

To start this drive, head east on U.S. 60 to the town of Apache Junction and then head north on Ariz. 88. Just north of Apache Junction, you'll come to **Goldfield ghost town,** 4650 N. Mammoth Mine Rd. (☎ **602/983-0333**), a reconstructed 1890s gold-mining town. Though it's a bit of a tourist trap—gift shops, an ice-cream parlor, and the like—it's also home to the **Superstition Mountain / Lost Dutchman Museum** (☎ **602/983-4888**) with interesting exhibits about the history of the area. Of particular note is the exhibit on the Lost Dutchman gold mine, perhaps the most famous mine in the country despite the fact that its location is unknown. Admission to the museum is $2 for adults and $1 for children. While in Goldfield, you can also take a tour of an underground gold mine ($4 for adults, $2 for children). A saloon here in Goldfield also has live country music several nights a week.

Not far from Goldfield is **Lost Dutchman State Park** (☎ **602/982-4485**), where you can hike into the rugged Superstition Mountains and see what the region's gold seekers have been up against. Park admission is $3 per vehicle.

Continuing northeast, you'll next come to **Canyon Lake,** the first of three reservoirs on the Salt River. The three lakes provide much of Phoenix's drinking water, without which the city would never have been able to grow as large as it is

Lost Dutchman in the Superstitions

The Superstition Mountains rise up to the east of Phoenix, dark and ominous, jagged and hot. Cacti bristle across the mountains' flanks and water is almost nonexistent. Yet for more than a century gold-crazed prospectors have been scouring these forbidding mountains for a gold mine that may not even exist. The power of a legend is strong, and few legends are as well documented as the legend of the Lost Dutchman gold mine.

The year was 1870 when two German miners, Jacob Waltz and Jacob Weiser, set off into the Arizona wilderness east of Phoenix in hopes of striking it rich. When these two "Dutchmen" (an appelation derived from German word *Deutsch*) next returned to civilization, they carried with them pouches filled with gold nuggets. Though unsavory prospectors tried to track them to their motherlode in hopes of claim jumping, none was successful. Through visits to saloons and brothels, the two Jacobs remained tight-lipped about their mine's whereabouts.

Jacob Weiser eventually disappeared from the scene amid speculation that his partner did him in so as to keep all the gold to himself. Waltz eventually gave up prospecting in the Superstitions in 1889 at the age of 80. On his deathbed in 1891, he gave detailed directions to a Phoenix woman he had befriended. She and her foster son and the foster son's father and brother spent the next 40 years searching fruitlessly for Waltz's Lost Dutchman mine. Waltz's dying directions just weren't good enough to lead the searchers through these rugged, uncharted mountains.

Clues to the mine's location abound, and hopeful prospectors and treasure hunters have followed every possible lead in their quest for the mine, many losing their lives in this harsh wilderness in the process. While skeptics say that there's no proof there ever was a Lost Dutchman mine, others see in the mine's continued elusiveness hope that they might one day be the prospector to find this fabled motherlode.

today. Here at Canyon Lake you can go for a swim or take a cruise on ***Dolly's Steamboat*** (☎ **602/827-9144**). A 90-minute cruise on this reproduction paddlewheeler costs $12 for adults and $8 for children 6 to 12. You can also rent powerboats at the Canyon Lake Marina. If you're hungry, you can grab a bite at the Lakeside Restaurant, which overlooks the marina. However, for a taste of the Old West, hold out for **Tortilla Flat** (☎ **602/984-1776**), an old stagecoach stop that has a restaurant, saloon, and general store, all of which are papered with more than $35,000 worth of dollar bills and business cards left by travelers who have stopped here. The prickly pear ice cream served here is worth a try (guaranteed no spines).

A few miles past Tortilla Flat, the pavement ends and the truly spectacular desert scenery begins. Among the rocky ridges, arroyos, and canyons of this stretch of road, you'll see saguaro cacti and century plants (a type of agave that sends up a 15-foot-tall flower stalk once, after years and even decades of slow growth, and then dies). Next you'll come to **Apache Lake,** which is in a deep canyon flanked by colorful cliffs and rugged rock formations. This lake also has a marina, as well as a campground, motel, restaurant, and general store.

Shortly before reaching pavement again you'll come to the **Theodore Roosevelt Dam.** This dam, which forms Roosevelt Lake, is the largest masonry dam in the world and was built in 1911. A recent renovation has given it a facelift.

Continuing on Ariz. 88, you'll next come to **Tonto National Monument** (☎ 520/467-2241), which preserves the southernmost cliff dwellings in Arizona. These pueblos were built between 1100 and 1400 by the Salado people, and are some of the few remaining traces of the Salado people who once cultivated lands now flooded by Roosevelt Lake. The lower ruins are half a mile up a steep trail from the visitor center, and the upper ruins are a 3-mile round-trip hike from the visitor center. The latter ruins are only open on Saturday and Sunday by reservation. The park is open daily from 8am to 4pm, and the admission is $4 per car.

Continuing on Ariz. 88 will bring you to the copper-mining town of **Globe.** The mines here are open pits, and though you can't see the mines themselves, the tailings (remains of rock removed from the copper ore) can be seen piled high all around the town. In Globe, be sure to visit **Besh Ba Gowah Archaeological Park** (☎ 602/425-0320), which is on the eastern outskirts of town. This Salado Indian pueblo site has been partially reconstructed, and several rooms are set up to reflect the way they might have looked when they were first occupied about 700 years ago. These are among the most fascinating ruins in the state. To reach Besh-Ba-Gowah, head out of Globe on South Broad Street to Jesse Hayes Road.

From Globe, head east on U.S. 60. On the west side of Superior, you'll come to **Boyce Thompson Southwestern Arboretum** (☎ 520/689-2811), which is dedicated to researching and propagating desert plants. The cactus gardens here are quite impressive, as are the two bizarre boojum trees. The arboretum is open daily from 8am to 5pm, and admission is $4 for adults and $2 for children 5 to 12, free for children 4 and under.

If it's not too late, you can finish your day with a horseback ride at **Don Donnelly Stables,** 6010 S. Kings Ranch Rd. (☎ 602/982-7822), in the community of Gold Canyon. A two-hour ride costs $30 per person. These stables also do overnight rides, cookouts, and hayrides.

If after a long day on the road you're looking for a good place to eat, stop in at **Gold Canyon Ranch** (☎ 602/982-9090), which has a good, though expensive, dining room serving creative southwestern cuisine. There's also a bar and grill serving basic burgers and sandwiches.

THE OLD WEST & THE NEW WEST

A drive north from Phoenix can give you glimpses both into how pioneers once lived and how cities of the future might look. Head north out of Phoenix on I-17 for about 20 miles and take the Pioneer Road exit. Here you'll find the **Pioneer Arizona Living History Museum** (☎ 602/993-0212). This museum includes more than 20 original and reconstructed buildings, and inside (or near) these buildings you'll find costumed interpreters practicing traditional frontier activities. Among the buildings here are a carpentry shop, a blacksmith shop, a miner's cabin, a stagecoach station, a one-room schoolhouse, an opera house, a church, farmhouses, and a Victorian mansion. Each November there are Civil War battle reenactments and a gathering of modern-day mountain men here. The museum is open between October and June only, daily from 9am to 5pm. Admission is $5.75 for adults, $5.25 for senior citizens and students, and $4 for children 4 to 12, free for children 4 and under.

Continuing north another 40 miles or so will bring you to Cordes Junction and Italian architect Paolo Soleri's vision of the future. **Arcosanti** (☎ **520/632-7135**) is the slow realization of Soleri's dream of a city that merges architecture and ecology. Soleri, who came to Arizona to study with Frank Lloyd Wright at Taliesin West, envisions a compact, energy-efficient city that disturbs the natural landscape as little as possible—and that's just what's rising out of the Arizona desert here at Arcosanti. The organic design of this city built of cast concrete will fascinate both students of architecture and those with only a passing interest in the discipline. Arcosanti has been built primarily with the help of students and volunteers who come and live here for various lengths of time.

To help finance the construction, Soleri designs and sells wind bells that are cast in bronze or made of ceramic. These distinctive bells are available at the gift shop here.

If you'd like to stay overnight, there are basic accommodations available, and you'll also find a bakery and café on the premises. Arcosanti is open daily from 9am to 5pm, and tours are held hourly from 10am to 4pm ($5 suggested donation).

On your way back south to Phoenix you may want to take Exit 223 and head east to the funky community of **Cave Creek** and its more polished neighbor—Carefree. Cave Creek clings to its Wild West image, and is home to several western steakhouses and shops selling western and Native American crafts and antiques. At **Crazy Ed's Satisfied Frog,** 6245 E. Cave Creek Rd. (☎ **602/253-6293**), you can sample Cave Creek chili beer, each bottle of which has a chile pepper in it. **Carefree** is a much more subdued place, and is home to the exclusive Boulders resort, which has a couple of excellent restaurants and one of the most spectacular settings of any resort in Arizona. Carefree is a planned community popular with retirees, and street names such as Ho and Hum roads and Easy Street reflect the sedate nature of the town.

FLORENCE & CASA GRANDE

Driving southeast from Phoenix on I-10 for about 60 miles will bring you to the Florence and Casa Grande area, where you can learn about Native American cultures both past and present and view the greatest concentration of historic buildings in Arizona. At Exit 175 (Ariz. 587), you'll find the **Gila River Indian Arts & Crafts Center & Heritage Museum** (☎ **520/963-3981**), which is located on the Gila River Indian Reservation. The center has a museum with historical photos and artifacts, including beautiful Pima baskets. In the Heritage Park are replicas of five different types of Native American villages—Tohono O'odham, Pima, Maricopa, Apache, and Hohokam. During the winter months, there are frequent dance performances here at the center. The biggest performances are during the **Pima-Maricopa Arts Festival,** the first weekend in November, and the **Native American Dance Festival,** the weekend after Thanksgiving. The center is open daily from 9am to 5pm, and admission is free.

To reach Florence, continue south on I-10 to Exit 185 (Ariz. 387) and head east. Before reaching Florence, near the town of Coolidge, you'll come to **Casa Grande Ruins National Monument** (☎ **520/723-3172**). In Spanish, the name means "Big House," and that's exactly what you'll find. In this instance, the big house is an earth-walled ruin that was built 650 years ago by the Hohokam people. Although it's still not known what purpose this unusual structure served, the building provides a glimpse of a style of ancient architecture rarely seen. Instead of using adobe bricks or stones, the people who built this structure used layers of hard-packed soil that have survived the ravages of the weather. The Hohokam people who once occupied this site began farming the valleys of the Gila and Salt rivers about 1,500 years ago, and eventually built an extensive network of irrigation canals for watering their fields. By the middle of the 15th century, however, the Hohokam had abandoned both their canals and their villages and disappeared without a trace. The monument is open daily from 7am to 6pm, and admission is $2 for adults.

Continuing east, you'll soon come to the farming community of **Florence**. Though at first glance this town may seem like any other small town, closer inspection turns up more than 150 buildings on the National Register of Historic Places. The majority of these buildings are constructed of adobe and were originally built in the Sonoran style, a style that was influenced by Spanish architectural ideas. Most buildings were altered over the years and now display aspects of various architectural styles popular during territorial days in Arizona.

Before touring the town, stop in at the **Pinal County Historical Society Museum** on South Main Street to learn more about the history of the area. The museum is open Wednesday through Sunday from noon to 4pm (11am to 4pm from December to March). At the corner of Main Street and Ruggles Street, you'll find the **McFarland State Historic Park** (☎ **520/868-5216**), which is housed in a former Pinal County Courthouse that was built in 1878. The current county courthouse, built in 1891, rises above the center of town and displays an unusual combination of different architectural styles. To find out more about the buildings of Florence, stop in at the **Pinal County Visitors Center,** 912 N. Pinal St. (☎ **520/868-4331**), or the **Florence Chamber of Commerce,** 291 N. Bailey St. ☎ **520/868-9433** or 800/868-3821), which is housed in a historic 1889 grocery store in the center of town. Each year in February there's a tour of historic buildings. Contact the chamber of commerce for more information.

From Florence, head back the way you came. If you're interested, there are a couple of **factory-outlet shopping malls** in the town of Casa Grande at Exit 194 (Ariz. 287 / Florence Boulevard).

6 Central Arizona

No other region of Arizona packs so much into so little space. Encompassing the Mogollon Rim, the fertile Verde River valley, Oak Creek Canyon, the red rocks of Sedona, the pine-forested mountains around Prescott, and the desert in the Wickenburg area, central Arizona has played an important role in Arizona history for more than 1,500 years. Ancient Hohokam and Sinagua peoples, as well as early settlers, were drawn to the fertile valley of the Verde River. Though these tribes had disappeared by the time the first white settlers arrived in the area, hostile Apache and Yavapai tribes inhabited the area, so the U.S. Army established Fort Verde to protect the settlers.

When Arizona became a U.S. territory in 1863, Prescott was chosen as its capital because of its central location. Though Prescott would later lose that title to Tucson and then to Phoenix, for part of the late 19th century it was the most important city in Arizona, as stately Victorian homes and an imposing county courthouse show.

Settlers were lured to this region not only by fertile land, but by the mineral wealth that lay hidden in the ground. Miners founded a number of communities in central Arizona, among them Jerome. When the mines shut down, Jerome was almost completely abandoned, but artists and craftspeople moved in to reclaim and revitalize the old mining town.

Artists also found their way to Sedona, but only after the movie industry had hit upon Sedona's red-rock country as a striking backdrop for exciting westerns. Situated at the mouth of Oak Creek Canyon, one of Arizona's major recreational areas, Sedona now attracts artists, retirees, and New Agers (who come to visit Sedona's mystical vortexes).

Once called the dude ranch capital of the world, Wickenburg clings to its western roots and has restored much of its downtown to its 1880s appearance. There are even a few dude ranches—now called guest ranches—still in business.

1 Wickenburg

53 miles NW of Phoenix, 61 miles S of Prescott, 128 miles SE of Kingman

Wickenburg was once the "Dude Ranch Capital of the World" and attracted celebrities and families from all over the country. Today

What's Special About Central Arizona

Native American Ruins
- Sinagua cliff dwellings at Montezuma Castle National Monument.
- A Sinagua pueblo atop a hill at Tuzigoot National Monument.

Great Towns/Villages
- Jerome, almost a ghost town until discovered by artists and craftspeople, in a spectacular setting on a steep mountainside.
- Prescott, the former territorial capital of Arizona.

Shopping
- Sedona and Jerome, two of Arizona's arts communities, with dozens of art galleries as well as upscale shops.

Natural Spectacles
- The red rocks surrounding Sedona.
- Oak Creek Canyon, a small but beautiful canyon that has a year-round stream.

Activities
- The Verde Valley Railroad, a scenic train ride.
- Searching out vortexes around Sedona.
- Jeep tours through Sedona's red-rock country.
- Riding the range at a guest ranch.

Museums
- The Native American artifacts collection at the Smoki Museum in Prescott.
- Prescott's Bead Museum, dedicated to beads and ornamentation.
- Phippen Museum of Western Art in Prescott, where paintings and statues capture the lives of the West.

TV & Film Locations
- Sedona's red-rock country.

there are still several dude ranches, now known as guest ranches, in the area, ranging from the rustic to the luxurious.

Located on the northern edge of the Sonora Desert in central Arizona, Wickenburg stands on the banks of the Hassayampa River, one of the last clear, free-flowing rivers in the Arizona desert. The town was founded in 1863 by Prussian gold prospector Henry Wickenburg, who discovered what would eventually become the most profitable gold and silver mine in Arizona. Today the abandoned mine can be toured.

When the dude ranches flourished back in the 1920s and 1930s, Wickenburg realized that visitors wanted a taste of the Wild West, so the town gave the tenderfoots what they wanted—trail rides, hayrides, cookouts, the works. Wickenburg still likes to play up its western heritage and has preserved one of its downtown streets much as it may have looked in 1900. If you've come to Arizona searching for the West the way it used to be, Wickenburg is a good place to look.

ESSENTIALS
GETTING THERE

By Bus　Greyhound Lines, 412 Wickenburg Way, provides service to Wickenburg from Phoenix and Las Vegas. Call 520/684-2601 for schedule information.

By Car　From Phoenix, take U.S. 60, which heads northwest and becomes Ariz. 93/U.S. 89. U.S. 89 also comes down from Prescott in the north, while U.S. 60 comes in from I-10 in western Arizona. Arizona 93 comes down from I-40 in northwestern Arizona.

VISITOR INFORMATION

For more information about Wickenburg, contact the **Wickenburg Chamber of Commerce,** 215 Frontier St. (P.O. Drawer CC), Wickenburg, AZ 85358 (☎ **520/684-5479**).

WHAT TO SEE & DO

A **stroll around the old section of downtown Wickenburg** provides a glimpse of the Old West. Most of the buildings here were built between 1890 and the 1920s, although a few are older. **Frontier Street** is preserved as it looked in the early 1900s. The covered sidewalks and false fronts are characteristic of old western architecture, which often disguised older adobe buildings. The old **Santa Fe train station** is now the Wickenburg Chamber of Commerce, which should be your first stop in town. They'll give you a map that tells a bit about the history of the town's older buildings. The brick **post office** building almost across the street from the train station once had a ride-up window providing service to people on horseback. The oldest building in town is the **Etter General Store,** adjacent to the Gold Nugget Restaurant. The old adobe-walled store was built in 1864 and has long since been disguised with a false wooden front.

Two of the town's most unusual attractions aren't buildings at all. The **Jail Tree,** behind the Circle K store at the corner of Wickenburg Way and Tegner Street, is an old mesquite tree that served as the local hoosegow. Outlaws were simply chained to the tree. Their families would often come to visit and have a picnic in the shade of the tree. The second, equally curious, town attraction is the **Wishing Well,** which stands beside the bridge over the Hassayampa. Legend has it that anyone who drinks from the Hassayampa River will never tell the truth again, and so drinking water was always drawn from this well. How it became a wishing well is unclear.

Desert Caballeros Western Museum

21 N. Frontier St. ☎ **520/684-2272.** Admission $4 adults, $3.50 senior citizens, $1 children 6–16; under 6 free. Mon–Sat 10am–4pm, Sun 1–4pm.

Inside this museum you'll find western art depicting life on the range in the days of "cowboys and Indians." Though it's not too large, the museum manages to convey a great deal about the history of this part of Arizona. There's an excellent display of colorful minerals and a small collection of Native American artifacts. Branding and barbed-wire exhibits cover the ranching history of the area. On the main floor, dioramas depict important scenes from the history of the Wickenburg region. Downstairs, a 1900 street scene from a western town is re-created, complete with general store. Rooms from a Victorian home are also on display.

Central Arizona

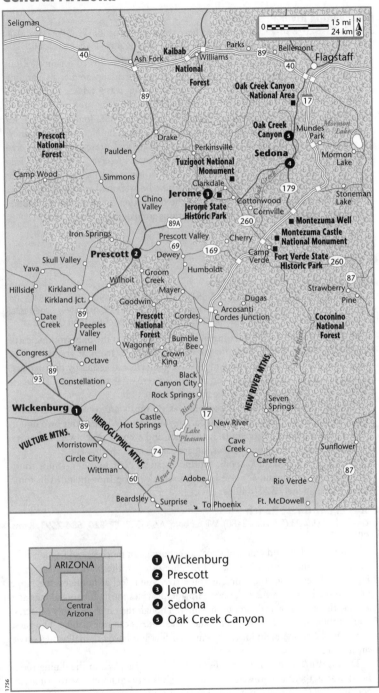

0 — 15 mi
24 km
N

Seligman

Kaibab
National
Forest

Parks
89
Bellemont
Flagstaff
40

Ash Fork
Williams

89

Oak Creek Canyon
National Area
17

Prescott
National
Forest

Drake

Paulden

Perkinsville

Oak Creek
Canyon **5**

Mundes
Park

Mormon
Lake

Camp Wood

Simmons

Tuzigoot National
Monument

Sedona 4

Mormon
Lake

Clarkdale

Stoneman
Lake

Chino
Valley

Jerome 3

Cottonwood
179

Iron Springs

Jerome State
Historic Park
89A

Cornville

■ Montezuma Well

Prescott Valley
69

260

**Montezuma Castle
National Monument**

Prescott 2

Dewey
169

Cherry

Camp
Verde

**Fort Verde State
Historic Park** 260

Skull Valley

Humboldt

Yava

Groom
Creek

Mayer

Dugas

Strawberry
87

Hillside

Kirkland

Pine

Kirkland Jct.

Goodwin

Cordes

Arcosanti
Cordes Junction

Coconino
National
Forest

Date
Creek
89

Peeples
Valley

**Prescott
National
Forest**

Bumble
Bee

Congress

Yarnell

Wagoner

93

Octave

Crown
King

Constellation

Black
Canyon City

Rock Springs

NEW RIVER MTNS.

Seven
Springs

Wickenburg 1

Castle
Hot Springs

VULTURE MTNS.

89

HIEROGLYPHIC MTNS.

Morristown

74

Lake
Pleasant

New River

Cave
Creek

Sunflower

Circle City

Wittman

60

Carefree

87

Beardsley

Surprise

To Phoenix

Adobe

Rio Verde

Ft. McDowell

ARIZONA

Central
Arizona

1 Wickenburg
2 Prescott
3 Jerome
4 Sedona
5 Oak Creek Canyon

1756

Hassayampa River Preserve

U.S. 60. ☎ **520/684-2772.** Admission free; suggested donation $5. Sept–May, daily 6am–noon; May–Sept, Wed–Sun 6am–noon. Drive 3 miles south of town on U.S. 60.

At one time the Arizona desert was laced with rivers that flowed for most, if not all, of the year. In the past 100 years these rivers have disappeared at an alarming rate because of the damming of rivers and lowering water tables. The riparian (waterside) habitat supports trees and plants that require more water than is usually available in the desert, and this lush growth provides food and shelter for hundreds of species of birds, mammals, and reptiles. The Nature Conservancy, a nonprofit organization dedicated to purchasing and preserving endangered habitats, owns and manages the Hassayampa River Preserve. Nature trails lead along the river beneath cottonwoods and willows and past the spring-fed Palm Lake. More than 230 species of birds have been spotted within the preserve. Naturalist-guided walks are offered; call the reservation for the current schedule. Though the guided walks are free, reservations are required.

WHERE TO STAY

GUEST RANCHES

Flying E Ranch

U.S. 60 (P.O. Box EEE), Wickenburg, AZ 85358. ☎ **520/684-2690.** Fax 520/684-5304. 17 rms. A/C TV. $190–$250 double. Rates include all meals. A 15% gratuity is added to all bills. No credit cards. Closed May to mid-Oct. Drive 4 miles west of town on U.S. 60.

Of the guest ranches still operating in Wickenburg, this is the only working cattle ranch. There are 20,000 acres for you and the cattle to roam, if you want. The main lodge features a spacious lounge where guests like to gather by the fireplace. The guest rooms vary in size, but all have western-style furnishings. There are either twin or king-size beds in the rooms.

Dining/Entertainment: Three family-style meals are served in the wood-paneled dining room, but there's no bar, so you'll need to bring your own liquor. There are also breakfast cookouts, lunch rides, and evening chuck-wagon dinners.

Services: Hayrides, guest rodeos, square dances in the barn.

Facilities: Small outdoor pool, whirlpool, sauna, exercise room, tennis court, shuffleboard, table tennis, horseshoes, horseback riding (not included in room rates; approximately $20–$30 per day).

⑤ Kay El Bar Guest Ranch

Rincon Rd., off U.S. 93 (P.O. Box 2480), Wickenburg, AZ 85358. ☎ **520/684-7593.** 8 rms, 1 cottage.

This is the smallest and oldest of the Wickenburg guest ranches, and its old adobe buildings, built between 1914 and 1925, are listed in the National Register of Historic Places. From the moment you arrive, you'll feel at home on the range here. In the lodge is a rustic lounge. A piano provides music for sing-alongs and a stone fireplace warms the room in winter. Though the ranch has only 60 acres, it abuts thousands of acres of public lands where guests can ride or hike. The guest rooms in the adobe main lodge are much smaller but have original western-style furnishings.

Dining/Entertainment: A tile floor and beehive fireplace in the dining room provide an authentic southwestern feel. The meals vary from Chinese to prime rib, and are served in heaping portions. There's also a fully stocked bar.

Services: Horseback riding (included in rates).
Facilities: Small outdoor pool.

Rancho de los Caballeros

1551 S. Vulture Mine Rd. (off U.S. 60 west of town), Wickenburg, AZ 85390. ☎ 520/
684-5484. Fax 520/684-2267. 74 rms. A/C TV TEL. $254–$372 double. Rates include all
meals. A 14% gratuity is added to all bills. No credit cards. Closed mid-May to Oct.

Located on 20,000 acres 2 miles west of Wickenburg, Rancho de los Caballeros
is part of an exclusive country club resort community. Peace and quiet are the key-
notes of a stay at this ranch, with golfing and horseback riding the most popular
activities. The lobby is a classic southwestern lodge, with sandstone floors, brick
walls, open ceiling beams, a large copper fireplace, and a painting by Frederic
Remington. The guest rooms have either tile floors or carpeting and rustic
Spanish colonial furnishings. Exposed-beam ceilings and Native American rugs
complete the southwestern motif. Some rooms have their own fireplaces.

Dining/Entertainment: The dining room features traditional southwestern furnishings, and the dinner menu includes a choice of five main dishes. At lunch
there's a poolside buffet.

Services: Children's programs, babysitting.

Facilities: Small outdoor pool, four tennis courts, 18-hole golf course, pro shop,
horseback riding ($29 to $38 per ride), trap and skeet shooting.

Wickenburg Inn

P.O. Box P (off U.S. 89 north of town), Wickenburg, AZ 85358. ☎ **520/684-7811** or
800/942-5362. Fax 602/684-2981. 22 rms and studios, 31 suites. A/C TV TEL. Nov–Apr,
$275–$310 double; $330–$370 suite. May–Nov, $185–$205 double; $225–250 suite. Rates
include all meals. MC, V.

Located 8 miles north of Wickenburg and calling itself a tennis and guest ranch,
the Wickenburg Inn caters both to those who want to perfect their backhand and
those who want to become trail hands. Wranglers provide riding instruction, while
tennis pros give private lessons and group clinics. Unlimited tennis privileges and
daily horseback rides are included in room rates.

Suites are in cottages built to resemble old Spanish colonial adobes, with
red-tile roofs and porches made from rough-hewn logs. Inside are kitchenettes with
tile counters, fireplaces, high beamed ceilings, and wet bars. Deluxe suites have sun
decks, and studios have similar styling to suites. Lodge rooms have rough-hewn
wood walls and furniture and a deck or balcony.

Dining/Entertainment: Meals are a combination of southwestern and
continental fare, and on Saturday nights there are campfire cookouts in the desert.

Services: Horseback riding and lessons, tennis lessons, holiday children's
programs, babysitting, guided nature hikes.

Facilities: Outdoor pool, whirlpool, nine tennis courts, self-service laundry,
volleyball court, playground, arts-and-crafts center, nature center, jogging trail.

A MOTEL

Best Western Rancho Grande

293 E. Wickenburg Way (P.O. Box 1328), Wickenburg, AZ 85358. ☎ **520/684-5445** or
800/528-1234. Fax 602/684-7380. 80 rms, 6 suites. A/C TV TEL. $55–$95 double, $85 suites.
AE, CB, DC, DISC, MC, V.

Right in the heart of downtown Wickenburg, this Best Western motel is built in
Spanish colonial style, with tile roofs, stucco walls, arched colonnades, and tile

murals on the walls. There's a wide range of room types and prices. At the higher end you get a larger room, a larger bathroom (with a phone), large towels, and a coffeemaker. The suites are housed in 120- and 150-year-old buildings, one of which is an old adobe. However, remodeling has updated these buildings completely. The motel's restaurant and lounge are across the street. The hotel also offers an outdoor pool, a whirlpool, and a tennis court.

WHERE TO DINE

Armando's at Wickenburg Inn

U.S. 89 (Prescott Hwy.). ☎ **520/684-7811.** Reservations required. Complete dinner $18.75; cookout $23. MC, V. Sun and Wed–Fri 5:30–8 or 8:30pm, Tues and Sat 5–10pm (cookout). AMERICAN/CONTINENTAL.

The Wickenburg Inn is north of town in a picturesque setting of rolling desert hills. The dining room, which is open to the public with advance reservations, has the feeling of an old-fashioned southwestern lodge. Stone and raw wood give it a rugged feeling, but creature comforts are not overlooked. For the fixed price of $18.75 you get soup, salad, a choice of main dish, beverages, and dessert. Main-course choices include steaks, seafood, chicken, pasta, and various southwestern specialties. Cookouts are offered on Tuesday and Saturday nights.

Charley's Steakhouse

1187 W. Wickenburg Way. ☎ **520/684-2413.** Reservations recommended. Complete dinners $10–$17. DISC, MC, V. Tues–Sun 5–9pm. Closed in summer. STEAKS.

Out on the west side of town is Wickenburg's favorite steakhouse. Though the building looks quite modern from the outside, the interior is done in rustic pine paneling, and collectors' whiskey bottles are lined up all over the dining room. Dinners come with salad, baked potato, cowboy beans, rolls and butter, tea, and dessert—so bring a hearty appetite.

Rancho de los Caballeros

1551 S. Vulture Mine Rd. ☎ **520/684-5484.** Reservations required. Jackets required for men. Complete dinner $23. No credit cards. Daily 6:30–8:30pm. Closed May 16–Sept. CONTINENTAL/SOUTHWESTERN.

Wickenburg's most exclusive guest ranch also opens its excellent restaurant to the public. The menu changes daily. However, you always have a choice of two soups, two salads, five main courses, and desserts. If none of the regular main dishes appeals to you, there are slightly more expensive alternatives. Men are required to wear a jacket, and women must also dress appropriately.

2 Prescott

100 miles N of Phoenix, 60 miles SW of Sedona, 87 miles SW of Flagstaff

In 1863 the Walker party discovered gold in the mountains of central Arizona, and soon miners were flocking to the area to seek their own fortunes. In 1864 Arizona became a U.S. territory and the new town of Prescott, located right in the center of Arizona, was made the territorial capital. Prescott lost its statewide influence when the capital moved to Phoenix, but because of the importance of ranching and mining in central Arizona, Prescott continued to be a very important regional town.

A stately courthouse on a tree-shaded square in the middle of town, a well-preserved historic downtown business district, and quite a few old Victorian homes give Prescott a timeless American hometown atmosphere. Several small museums, a couple of historic hotels, and the nearby Prescott National Forest assure that visitors with a diverse range of interests spend time here.

In summer, when Phoenix is baking, Prescott is generally 20° cooler, which makes this a popular weekend destination with Phoenicians. Prescott is also gaining importance as a retirement community, as retirees from California rediscover Arizona's once-bustling territorial capital.

ESSENTIALS
GETTING THERE

By Plane   There is regularly scheduled service between Prescott's Ernest A. Love Airport, on U.S. 89, and the Phoenix Sky Harbor Airport on America West airlines (call 800/235-9292 for schedule information). The round-trip airfare is $99 or $109, depending on how far in advance you buy your ticket.

Shuttle "U" provides shuttle service between Prescott and the Phoenix Sky Harbor Airport. The fare is $29 one way and $52 round-trip. Phone 520/772-6114 for schedule information.

By Bus   Prescott is served by Greyhound Lines. The bus station is at 820 E. Sheldon St. (call 520/445-5470 for further details).

By Car   Prescott is at the junction of U.S. 89, U.S. 89A, and Ariz. 69. If you're coming from Phoenix, take the Cordes Junction exit (Exit 262) from I-17. If you're coming from Flagstaff, the most direct route is to take I-17 to Ariz. 169 to Ariz. 69. From Sedona, just take U.S. 89A all the way.

ORIENTATION

U.S. 89 comes into Prescott on the northeast side of town, where it joins with Ariz. 69 coming in from the east. The main street into town is **Gurley Street,** which forms the north side of the Courthouse Plaza. **Montezuma Street,** also known as Whiskey Row, forms the west side of the plaza. If you continue south on Montezuma Street, you'll be on U.S. 89 heading toward Wickenburg.

VISITOR INFORMATION

For more information on Prescott, contact the **Prescott Chamber of Commerce,** 117 W. Goodwin St. (P.O. Box 1147), Prescott, AZ 86302 (☎ **520/445-2000** or 800/266-7534). The visitor information center here is open Monday through Saturday from 9am to 5pm and on Sunday from 10am to 4pm.

GETTING AROUND

If you need to rent a car, contact **Budget** (☎ **520/778-3806** or 800/527-0700). If you need a taxi, call **Ace City Cab** (☎ **520/445-1616**).

SPECIAL EVENTS

The World's Oldest Rodeo is held each year in early July as part of the city's **Prescott Frontier Days** celebration. Also included in this celebration is a western art show, a golf tournament, a carnival, a 10km run, and a parade. **Territorial Days,** held in early to mid-June, is another big annual festival with special art exhibits, performances, tournaments, races, and lots of food and free entertainment.

WHAT TO SEE & DO

A walk around the **Courthouse Plaza** should be your first introduction to Prescott. The stately old courthouse in the middle of a tree-shaded plaza captures the former importance of Prescott. The building, far too large for a small regional town such as this, dates from the days when Prescott was the capital of the Arizona Territory. Surrounding the courthouse and extending north for a block is Prescott's **historic business district.** Stroll around admiring the brick buildings and you'll get an idea that Prescott was once a very important city. Duck into an old saloon or the lobby of one of the town's two historic hotels. After you've gotten a taste of Prescott, there are several museums, listed below, you might like to visit.

If you'd like to learn more about the history of Prescott, contact **Prescott Historical Tours,** 815 Bertrand Ave. (☎ 520/445-4567).

MUSEUMS

Sharlot Hall Museum

415 W. Gurley St. ☎ **520/445-3122.** Admission free; donation $2 adults, free for children. Mar–Oct, Mon–Sat 10am–5pm, Sun 1–5pm; Nov–Feb, Tues–Sat 10am–4pm, Sun 1–5pm.

At the age of 12, Sharlot Hall traveled to the Arizona territory with her parents in 1882. From an early age she was fascinated by frontier life. As an adult, she became a writer and historian and began collecting artifacts from Arizona's pioneer days. From 1909 to 1911 she was the territorial historian, an official government position. In 1928 she opened this museum in Prescott's **Old Governor's Mansion,** a log home that had been built in 1864. Eventually, through the donations of others and the activities of the local historical society, the museum grew into the present complex of historic buildings and gardens. In addition to the Old Governor's Mansion, which is furnished much as it might have been when it was built, there are several other interesting buildings that can be toured. The **John C. Frémont House** was built in 1875 for the fifth territorial governor. Its traditional wood-frame construction shows how quickly Prescott grew from a remote logging and mining camp into a civilized little town. The 1877 **William Bashford House** reflects the Victorian architecture that was popular throughout the country around the turn of the century. The **Sharlot Hall Building** was built of stone and pine logs in 1934 and now houses museum exhibits on prehistoric and historic Native American artifacts and the history of Prescott.

Other buildings of interest include a blacksmith's shop, a schoolhouse, a gazebo, a ranch house built by Sharlot Hall, and an old windmill. The museum's rose garden honors famous women of Arizona. Every year in late spring, artisans, craftspeople, and costumed exhibitors participate in the **Folk Arts Fair.**

Prescott's Phippen Museum of Western Art

4701 U.S. 89N. ☎ **520/778-1385.** Admission $2 adults, $1.50 senior citizens, $1 students. Mar–Dec, Mon and Wed–Sat 10am–4pm, Sun 1–4pm; Jan–Feb, Wed–Mon 1–4pm.

Located on a hill a few miles north of town, the Phippen Museum of Western Art is named after the first president of the prestigious Cowboy Artists of America. The museum exhibits works by both established western artists and newcomers. Each year on Memorial Day weekend the museum sponsors the **Phippen Western Art Show.** In the museum store, more than 100 Arizona artists are represented.

The Smoki Museum

147 N. Arizona St. ☎ **520/445-1230** or 520/778-7554. Admission $2. May–Sept, Thurs–Tues 10am–4pm; Oct, Fri–Sat 10am–4pm, Sun 1–4pm. Closed Nov–Apr.

There never was a real Smoki tribe. The Smoki organization was founded in 1921 by a group of non–Native Americans who wanted to inject some new life into

Prescott's July Fourth celebrations. Despite its non–Native American origins, the museum contains genuine artifacts from many different tribes.

✪ The Bead Museum

140 S. Montezuma St. ☎ **520/445-2431.** Admission free. Mon–Sat 9:30am–4:30pm, Sun by appointment.

This small museum in downtown Prescott is one of the only museums in the country dedicated to beads and body ornamentation. There are cases full of unusual beads from around the world, and half the museum is a bead shop selling many interesting beads.

PARKS, NATURAL AREAS & RECREATION

Prescott's most readily recognizable feature is **Thumb Butte,** a rocky outcropping that towers over the forest just outside town. If you'd like to go hiking on Thumb Butte, head west out of town on Gurley Street, which becomes Thumb Butte Road. A few miles north of town is an unusual and very scenic area known as the **Granite Dells.** Jumbled hills of rounded granite suddenly jut up from the landscape, creating a maze of huge boulders and smooth rock. Set in this strange geological feature is a man-made lake that makes the scene even more picturesque. This is a great place to go for a walk or shoot some photos.

Prescott is situated on the edge of a wide expanse of high plains with the pine forests of **Prescott National Forest** at its back. There are hiking trails, several lakes, and campgrounds within the national forest. For maps and information, stop by the Prescott National Forest Office, 344 S. Cortez St. (☎ **520/445-1762**).

Granite Mountain Stables (☎ **520/771-9551**), 7 miles north of downtown Prescott, offers trail rides, sunset steak rides, and hayrides. Rates are about $15 for a one-hour ride, $35 for the sunset cookout, and $180 for an overnight ride.

Reasonably priced golfing is available at the **Antelope Hills Golf Course,** 19 Clubhouse Dr. (☎ **520/445-0583** or 800/972-6818 in Arizona). Prescott bills itself as the "Softball Capital of the World," and on summer weekends it's hard to argue with this claim. At parks all over town, teams from around the world play **championship softball.**

WHERE TO STAY

EXPENSIVE

Prescott Resort & Conference Center

1500 Ariz. 69, Prescott, AZ 86301. ☎ **520/776-1666** or 800/967-4637. Fax 520/776-8544. 160 rms, 82 suites. A/C TV TEL. $99–$140 double; $129–$170 suite. AE, CB, DC, DISC, MC, V.

Prescott's only full-service resort hotel is built high on a hill overlooking the city and the surrounding valley and mountains. The lobby, with its soaring ceiling and wall of glass, is a mixture of urban sophistication and western chic. Red recessed lights and modern furnishings are offset by a baby grand piano, and western art is on display throughout the resort. The guest rooms are spacious and comfortable, and each room has its own balcony overlooking the valley.

Dining/Entertainment: The Thumb Butte Room, serving American dishes, offers a stunning panorama to accompany the fine meals. For a drink and conversation, there's a lobby lounge. There's also a 24-hour casino, which is the resort's biggest draw for many guests.

Services: Room service, valet/laundry service.

Facilities: Outdoor pool, tennis courts, racquetball courts, exercise room, art gallery, beauty salon.

MODERATE

✪ Hassayampa Inn

122 E. Gurley St., Prescott, AZ 86301. ☎ **520/778-9434,** or 800/322-1927 in Arizona. 70 rms, 10 suites. A/C TV TEL. Apr–Oct, $89–$109 single or double; $135–$160 suite. Nov–Mar, $80–$99 single or double; $120–$140 suite. Rates include full breakfast. AE, CB, DC, DISC, MC, V.

Listed on the National Register of Historic Places, the Hassayampa Inn was built as a luxury hotel in 1927 and evokes the time when Prescott was the bustling capital of the Arizona Territory. Stenciled exposed ceiling beams, wrought-iron chandeliers, and arched doorways all reflect a southwestern heritage. There are even two pianos, one of which guests may play.

All the guest rooms are a bit different, and feature either original furnishings or antiques. One room here is even said to be haunted, and any hotel employee will be happy to tell you the story of the ill-fated honeymooners.

Dining/Entertainment: The Peacock Room (see "Where to Dine," below) exudes the same classic elegance as the rest of the hotel. A small lounge provides a quiet place to have a drink in the evening.

Bed & Breakfast Inns

Hotel Vendome–Clarion Carriage House Inn

230 S. Cortez St., Prescott, AZ 86303. ☎ **520/776-0900.** Fax 520/776-0901. 21 rms, 4 suites. TEL TV. $70–$85 double; $85–$100 suite. Rates include continental breakfast. AE, CB, DC, DISC, MC, V.

Built in 1917 as a lodging house, this restored two-story brick building is only two blocks from the action of Whiskey Row but far enough away from the noise that you'll get a good night's sleep. The guest rooms are outfitted with new furnishings, but some still have original clawfoot tubs in the bathrooms. Others have modern oval tubs, and all have built-in water filters, air filters, and overhead fans. Of course, this hotel has its own resident ghost as well. Not quite as luxurious as the Hassayampa, yet not as basic as the St. Michael, this hotel offers a good middle-price choice for anyone who wants to stay in a historic hotel.

Mount Vernon Inn

204 N. Mount Vernon Ave., Prescott, AZ 86301. ☎ **520/778-0886.** 4 rms, 3 cottages. TEL. $70–$80 double in the inn, $90–$110 double in the cottages. Inn rates include full breakfast. AE, DISC, MC, V.

Built in 1900 by a local bootlegger, the Mount Vernon Inn is located on one of the most attractive tree-lined streets in Prescott. The location is quiet, yet convenient to the bustle of downtown. The rooms vary from comfortable rooms in the main house to spacious cottages—one of which was the tack house and one of which was the carriage house. The cottages have full kitchens, and consequently, breakfast is not included in cottage rates.

The Prescott Country Inn

503 S. Montezuma St. (U.S. 89), Prescott, AZ 86303. ☎ **520/445-7991.** 12 rms. TV TEL. $95–$129 double. Rates include continental breakfast. DISC, MC, V.

If you've traveled any sections of old highway in Arizona, you've seen the aging motel courts that sprang up in the 1930s and 1940s to cater to travelers heading to California. Before being totally renovated, the Prescott Country Inn was just such a motel. Today it's a surprisingly comfortable place to stay. Despite the name, this bed-and-breakfast inn is located only a few blocks from Courthouse Plaza. All the rooms here feature country decor and have their own kitchenettes. Some also have small gas fireplaces.

Prescott Pines Inn

901 White Spar Rd. (U.S. 89), Prescott, AZ 86303. ☎ **520/445-7270.** 13 rms. TV TEL. $59–$139 double. MC, V.

Just as the name implies, this inn is located amid the pines in the mountains to the south of downtown Prescott. The main house is a 1902 Victorian homestead, and the country Victorian theme is continued throughout the several cottages that comprise this inn. There are modern furnishings in the guest rooms, all of which have private bathrooms. Numerous porches and verandas and a garden patio invite guests to sit back and relax in the cool shade of the pines. An A-frame chalet sleeping up to four couples is available for large families and groups. It comes with its own deck, a woodstove, and a kitchen. A full breakfast is available for $5 per person.

Victorian Inn of Prescott

246 S. Cortez St., Prescott, AZ 86303. ☎ **520/778-2642** or 800/704-2642. 3 rms, 2 with bath; 1 suite. $90–$135 double. Rates include full breakfast. AE, DISC, MC, V.

In the blocks surrounding Courthouse Plaza are dozens of beautifully restored Victorian homes, including this bed-and-breakfast inn. There are only four guest units here, and each features a different decor. There's the Garden of Eve with its wicker furnishings and mosquito net over the bed, the Teddy Bear Room, the Rose Room, and the Victorian Suite, which has a sitting area, private bathroom, and two large bay windows. Breakfasts are large and include such dishes as cheese soufflés and Swedish pancakes.

INEXPENSIVE

In addition to the following hotel, Prescott has several budget chain motels. These include the following (see the Appendix for toll-free phone numbers): **Super 8 Motel,** 1105 E. Sheldon St., Prescott, AZ 86301 (☎ **520/776-1282**), charging $46 to $48 double; and **Motel 6,** 1111 E. Sheldon St., Prescott, AZ 86301 (☎ **520/776-0160**), charging $42 double.

⑤ Hotel St. Michael

205 W. Gurley St., Prescott, AZ 86301. ☎ **520/776-1999** or 800/678-3757. Fax 520/776-7318. 72 rms, 3 suites. A/C TV TEL. $36–$52 double; $52–$72 suite or family unit. Rates include continental breakfast. AE, MC, V.

Located on Whiskey Row, this restored hotel offers a historic setting at budget prices. The Hotel St. Michael even has its own resident ghost and features the oldest elevator in Prescott. All rooms are different, and some have only bathtubs (no showers) in their bathrooms. If you're a light sleeper, be sure to get a room away from the wall separating the hotel from the adjacent cowboy bar. Among the St. Michael's past guests have been Teddy Roosevelt and Barry Goldwater. The casual Café St. Michael, where the complimentary breakfast is served, has brick walls and a pressed-tin ceiling and overlooks Courthouse Square.

WHERE TO DINE
MODERATE

✪ The County Seat Café & Bar

214 S. Montezuma St. ☎ **520/778-9570.** Reservations recommended on weekends. Main courses $10–$18. AE, MC, V. Mon–Sat 11am–2:30pm and 5:30–9pm, Sun noon–8pm. SOUTHWESTERN/INTERNATIONAL.

Situated half a block from the Courthouse and frequented by a well-dressed crowd and retirees who know delicious food, this place is quite busy and gets good marks for both comestibles and service. We bolted down the chunky and piquant salsa and ordered lunch. A good range of dishes with various regional references are on the menu, including crab cakes, tortilla soup, a large taco salad on a dinnerplate, and a Cajun grilled-chicken sandwich with chili mayonnaise. Dinner fare consists of similar flavors, plus the likes of tornados of beef and fish of the day. The chef's wife turns out cappuccino/amaretto ice-cream pie and other desserts worth devouring. The interior has sort of a fern bar feeling, with high-backed wooden booths and brick walls. A lounge and a patio are located in back, where on Sunday a barbecue is served.

Murphy's

201 N. Cortez St. ☎ **520/445-4044.** Reservations recommended for parties of five or more. Main courses $11–$21; Sun brunch $5–$14. AE, DISC, MC, V. Mon–Thurs 11am–3pm and 4:30–10pm, Fri–Sat 11am–3pm and 4:30–11pm, Sun 11am–3pm (brunch) and 4:30–10pm. AMERICAN.

"All goods guaranteed to be first class." That was the motto of the store that once occupied this location and it's now the motto of Prescott's most popular restaurant. Located a block from Courthouse Plaza, Murphy's is housed in the oldest mercantile building in the Southwest. The building, which is on the National Register of Historic Places, was built in 1890, and many of the shop's original shelves can be seen in the restaurant's lounge area. Sparkling leaded-glass doors usher diners into a high-ceilinged room with fans turning slowly overhead. In keeping with the historical nature of the building, antiques are on display throughout the restaurant. The appetizer list features such varied dishes as escargots and buffalo wings. Mesquite-broiled prime rib is the specialty of the house, and there's a daily fresh menu, so the steaks and seafood cooked over the same fire are equally tasty.

The Peacock Room

In the Hassayampa Inn, 122 E. Gurley St. ☎ **520/778-9434.** Reservations recommended. Main courses $15–$17. AE, DC, DISC, MC, V. Mon–Tues 7am–1pm and 5–9pm, Wed–Fri 7am–2pm and 5–9pm, Sat 7am–2pm and 5–9:30pm, Sun 7am–1pm and 5–9:30pm. CONTINENTAL.

Located in the elegant Hassayampa Inn just off Courthouse Plaza, the Peacock Room evokes a period of history when Prescott played an important role as the capital of the Arizona Territory. High ceilings, frosted-glass windows, tiny bistro lamps, and spacious tapestry-upholstered booths give the restaurant a grand and elegant old style. The short menu with about five entree choices is as traditional as the decor, with such continental standards as escargots and steak au poivre making appearances. The wine list is extensive, and the dessert tray always has a few irresistible treats on it.

INEXPENSIVE

⑤ Gurley St. Grill

230 W. Gurley St. ☎ **520/445-3388.** Reservations recommended on weekends. Main courses $5.50–$15. AE, DISC, MC, V. Daily 11am–10pm; bar menu until midnight. ITALIAN/AMERICAN.

Run by the same people who brought Prescott Murphy's, the Gurley Street Grill is located a block off Courthouse Plaza. Brick walls, ceiling fans, and beveled glass reflect the building's historic heritage. Pastas and pizzas are the most popular dishes, but there are also steaks and burgers. At lunch, try the Sonoran black-bean turkey chili. The service is fast and friendly, and the roast chicken with asiago cheese and pasta was not only delicious but plentiful. A bar called Margaritaville has lots of microbrews on tap and attracts a lively, professional crowd.

Kendall's Famous Burgers and Ice Cream

113 S. Cortez St. ☎ **520/778-3658.** Burgers $4–$6. No credit cards. Mon–Sat 11am–8pm, Sun 11am–6pm. BURGERS.

"Do I have to eat all this?" asked a customer once when we were here. "Either that or use it for art," answered the server at the counter. Ask anyone in town where to get the best burger in Prescott and you'll be sent to Kendall's on Courthouse Plaza. This bright and noisy luncheonette serves juicy burgers with a choice of toppings and breads. A basket of fries is a mandatory accompaniment.

✪ TJ's BBQ

234 S. Cortez St. ☎ **520/776-7224.** Main courses $4.50–$13. MC, V. Mon–Thurs 11am–9pm, Fri–Sat 11am–10pm, Sun noon–8pm. BARBECUE.

This casual restaurant is a block off Courthouse Plaza, and though it's short on atmosphere, it serves up the best barbecue in town. On cool evenings, the front porch is the place to eat.

SHOPPING

Downtown Prescott, especially along the historic Whiskey Row section of Montezuma Street, has numerous interesting shops selling Native American arts and crafts, antiques, and gifts. There are also a few art galleries to be seen. One of the most interesting shopping areas here is the brick-paved alley beneath the Hotel St. Michael. You'll find stores selling imports and exclusive fashions.

Prescott makes a lot of superlative claims. Accordingly, it calls itself the "Antiques Capital of Arizona." Whether or not this is true, there are plenty of antiques stores downtown. Most of the shops are concentrated along Cortez Street in the block north of Gurley Street and the courthouse. The **Merchandise Mart Mall,** 205 N. Cortez St. (☎ **520/776-1728**), houses several dealers under one roof, and is the largest antiques store in town.

EVENING ENTERTAINMENT

Back in the days when Prescott was the territorial capital and a booming mining town, it supported dozens of rowdy saloons, most of which were concentrated along Montezuma Street on the west side of Courthouse Plaza. This section of town was known as **Whiskey Row,** and legend has it that there was a tunnel from the courthouse to one of the saloons so lawmakers wouldn't have to be seen ducking into the saloons during regular business hours. On July 14, 1900, a fire consumed most of Whiskey Row, including 25 saloons and bawdy houses. However, concerned cowboys and miners managed to drag the tremendously heavy bar of the Palace Saloon across the street before it was damaged by the fire. The saloon continued to do business in its new open-air location. Today Whiskey Row is no longer the sort of place where respectable women shouldn't be seen, although it does still have a few noisy saloons with genuine Wild West flavor. The **Prescott Brewing Company,** 130 W. Gurley St. (☎ 520/771-2795), across from the Courthouse, is today's answer to the saloons of yore, serving microbrews and traditional pub victuals.

THE PERFORMING ARTS   The **Prescott Fine Arts Association,** 208 N. Marina St. (☎ 520/445-3286), sponsors plays, music performances, children's theater, and art exhibits. The association's main building is a former church that was built in 1899 and is on the National Register of Historic Places. The **Yavapai College Performance Hall,** 1100 E. Sheldon St. (☎ 520/776-2033), schedules quite a few performances throughout the year. Check with the performance halls or the chamber of commerce for a schedule of upcoming events. The Phoenix Symphony Orchestra does several performances annually in Prescott; for information on the schedule, contact the **Yavapai Symphony Association** (☎ 520/776-4255).

RODEO   Prescott claims to be the home of the world's oldest rodeo, held each year in early July.

3 Jerome

35 miles NE of Prescott, 28 miles W of Sedona, 130 miles N of Phoenix

Clinging to the slopes of Cleopatra Hill high on Mingus Mountain, Jerome beckons to the traveler today just as it once did to miners. The town's fortune was made and lost on copper from several mines that operated between 1882 and 1950. Over the years Jerome experienced an economic roller-coaster ride as the price of copper rose and fell, and when it was finally no longer profitable to mine the ore, the last mining company shut down its operations and almost everyone left town. By the early 1960s Jerome looked as if it was on its way to becoming just another ghost town. But about that same time, artists discovered the phenomenal views and dirt-cheap rents to be had here. Before long the town was being called an artists' colony and tourists were beginning to visit to see—and buy—the artwork that was being created.

Today Jerome is far from a ghost town, and on summer weekends the streets are packed with visitors shopping at galleries and crafts shops. The same remote and rugged setting that once made it difficult and expensive to mine copper here has now become one of the town's main attractions. Jerome is divided into two sections by an elevation of 1,500 vertical feet, with the upper part of town 2,000 feet above the Verde Valley. On a clear day (of which there are quite a few), the view from up here is stupendous—it's possible to see for more than 50 miles, with the red rocks of Sedona, the Mogollon Rim, and the San Francisco Peaks all visible in the distance.

Because Jerome is built on a 30° slope, the two streets through town are switchbacks from one level of houses to the next. Old brick and wood-frame buildings built into the side of the mountain have windows gazing out into the distance. Narrow streets, alleys, and stairways connect the different levels of town.

Jerome is so steep that in the 1920s a dynamite blast loosened the town jail from its foundations and the building slid 225 feet down the hill to its present location.

In recent years the artists who have moved into town have been restoring and renovating the old houses. Residences, studios, shops, and galleries all stand side by side looking (externally, anyway) much as they did when Jerome was an active mining town. The entire town has been designated a national historic landmark.

ESSENTIALS
GETTING THERE
By Car Jerome is on Ariz. Alt 89 roughly halfway between Sedona and Prescott. Coming from Phoenix, take Ariz. 260 from Camp Verde.

VISITOR INFORMATION
For information on Jerome, contact the **Jerome Chamber of Commerce,** P.O. Drawer K, Jerome, AZ 86331.

WHAT TO SEE & DO
Simply wandering through town soaking up the atmosphere and shopping are the main pastimes in Jerome, but for those interested in learning more about the town's mining history there's the **Jerome State Historic Park,** off U.S. 89A in the lower section of town (☎ 520/634-5381). Located in a mansion that was built in 1916 as a home for mine owner "Rawhide Jimmy" Douglas and as a hotel for visiting mining executives, the Jerome State Historic Park contains both exhibits on mining and many of the mansion's original furnishings. Built on a hill above Douglas's Little Daisy Mine, the mansion overlooks Jerome and, dizzyingly far below, the Verde Valley. Constructed of adobe bricks made on the site, the mansion contained a wine cellar, billiard room, marble shower, steam heat, and a central vacuum system. The mansion's library has been restored as a period room, while other rooms contain exhibits on copper mining and the history of Jerome. Various types of colorful ores are on display, along with the tools that were once used to extract the ore from the mountain. Admission is $2 for adults, $1 for children 12 to 17, and free for children 11 and under. It's open daily from 8am to 5pm, except Christmas Day.

Jerome's shops offer an eclectic blend of urban art, chic jewelry, one-of-a-kind handmade fashions, and unusual imports and gifts. **Sky Fire,** 140 Main St. (☎ 520/634-8081), has a fascinating collection of southwestern gifts and furnishings and Central American imports. The **Raku Gallery** and **Downhill Clay Company,** both at 250 Hull Ave. (☎ 520/639-0239), are places to see and buy interesting art. **The Shaman,** on Main Street (☎ 520/639-3577), carries the ceremonial art of the Huichol people of Mexico.

Many of the old storefronts in downtown Jerome have now become **artists' studios.** You can watch the artists at work and then have a look at some of the completed pieces being offered for sale.

And what would an old mining town be without a saloon? The **Spirit Room,** at 166 Main St. (☎ 520/634-8809), is an old-fashioned high-ceilinged saloon with mannequins in Gay Nineties attire overlooking the bar. This big, open saloon becomes a dance hall on weekends when regional rock and country bands perform.

NEARBY ATTRACTIONS & ACTIVITIES

Tuzigoot National Monument

Off U.S. 89A near Clarkdale. ☎ **520/634-5564.** Admission $2 adults, free for children 16 and under. Summer, daily 8am–7pm; winter, daily 8am–5pm.

Perched atop a hill overlooking the Verde River, this Sinagua ruin was inhabited between 1125 and 1400. The Sinagua people, whose name is Spanish for "without water," were contemporaries of the better-known Anasazi, who lived in the canyonlands of northeastern Arizona. The Sinagua were traditionally dry-land farmers relying entirely on rainfall to water their crops. When the Hohokam, who had been living in the Verde Valley since A.D. 600, moved on to more fertile land around 1100, the Sinagua moved in. Their buildings progressed from individual homes called pit houses to communal pueblos. Here at Tuzigoot they built atop a hill, but in other areas they built into the cliffs, just as the Anasazi were doing at that same time. A Sinagua cliff dwelling can be seen at nearby Montezuma Castle National Monument (see above).

Inside the visitor center at Tuzigoot is a small museum displaying many of the artifacts unearthed at Tuzigoot. An interpretive trail leads through the ruins, explaining different aspects of Sinaguan life. Desert plants, many of which were utilized by the Sinagua, are also identified along the trail.

Verde River Canyon Excursion Train

300 N. Broadway. ☎ **520/639-0010** or 800/293-7245. Admission $34.95 adults, $19.95 children 12 and under; first class $52.95. Senior discounts available. Daily; call for schedule and reservations.

When the town of Jerome was busily mining copper, a railway was built to link the booming town with the territorial capital at nearby Prescott. Because of the rugged mountains between Jerome and Prescott, the railroad was forced to take a longer but less difficult route north along the Verde River before turning back south toward Prescott. The route through the Verde River Canyon traverses unspoiled desert that's inaccessible by car and is part of the Prescott National Forest. The views of the rocky canyon walls are quite dramatic, and if you look closely, you can even see traces of ancient Sinagua cliff dwellings in the canyon.

WHERE TO STAY

Ghost City Inn

541 N. Main St. (P.O. Box 382), Jerome, AZ 86331. ☎ **520/63-GHOST.** 6 rms, none with bath. TV. $75–$95 double. Rates include full breakfast. DISC, MC, V.

With its long verandas on both floors, this restored old house is hard to miss as you drive into Jerome from Cottonwood. Most of the rooms here have great views across the Verde River Valley and all are furnished with antiques.

The Inn at Jerome

309 Main St., Jerome, AZ 86331. ☎ **520/634-5094** or 800/634-5094. 8 rms, 2 with bath. TV. $55–$85 double. AE, DISC, MC, V.

Operated by the same people who run the Ghost City Inn, this B&B has similar styling, with antiques in most rooms. One room has a rustic log bed so tall that you have to climb up into it. Other rooms have equally attractive beds, including a wrought-iron bed, a spool bed, and a sleigh bed. All the rooms have terry robes, ceiling fans, and evaporative coolers (almost as good as air-conditioning). Reception is at the restaurant downstairs. Note that breakfast does not come with rooms.

WHERE TO DINE

Flatiron Café

In the Flatiron Building, at the corner of Main St. and Hull Ave. ☎ **520/634-2733.** Breakfast and sandwiches $4.95–$6.95. No credit cards. Daily 8am–5pm. BREAKFAST/ LIGHT MEALS.

The tiny Flatiron Café serves breakfast and light food such as black-bean humous, sandwiches, fresh juices, and coffee drinks. It looks as though you could hardly squeeze in here, but there's more seating across the street.

House of Joy

Hull Ave. ☎ **520/634-5339.** Reservations required. Main courses $20–$25. No credit cards. Sat–Sun 3–9pm. CONTINENTAL.

If you know exactly when you'll be in town, and it happens to be a Saturday or Sunday, you might want to make a reservation for dinner at the House of Joy. This excellent continental restaurant is housed in a building that was once a bordello, and the interior decor is reminiscent of its colorful history. Reservations are an absolute necessity and must be made several weeks in advance because there are only seven tables in the restaurant.

4 Sedona & Oak Creek Canyon

106 miles S of the Grand Canyon, 116 miles N of Phoenix, 56 miles NE of Prescott

Though the first settler didn't arrive in the Sedona area until 1877 and the city wasn't incorporated until 1987, it has become one of the most popular destinations in Arizona. The city was named for Sedona Schnebly, one of the first residents of the area, because her name was short enough to fit on a postal cancellation stamp and the postmaster didn't like any of the other names that were suggested for this new town at the mouth of Oak Creek Canyon. Hollywood producers of western movies were among the first people to discover the beauty of Sedona. Next came artists lured by the red-rock landscapes and desert light. More recently the spectacular views and mild climate were discovered by retirees, and when a New Age channeler discovered the "Sedona vortexes," a whole new group descended on the town. This unusual history has created an ideal destination for lovers of the arts as well as lovers of nature. However, an unfortunate side effect of Sedona's popularity has been unchecked suburban sprawl, which detracts from the beauty of the red rocks.

The waters of Oak Creek Canyon that first lured settlers, and native peoples before them, still lure visitors to Sedona. Two of Arizona's finest swimming holes are located on Oak Creek only a few miles from Sedona; one, Slide Rock, has been made into a state park.

Sedona is also a good base for exploring much of central Arizona. Within easy driving distance are several ancient Native American ruins, including an impressive cliff dwelling.

ESSENTIALS

GETTING THERE

By Plane   Scenic Airlines has several flights daily between Phoenix and Sedona Airport. The fare is $79 one way, $158 round-trip. Call the airport at 520/ 282-4409 at the airport, or 520/282-7935 or 800/535-4448 at the airline, for schedule information.

Vortex Power

In recent years Sedona has become one of the world's centers for the New Age movement and attracts ever-growing numbers of people who come to experience the "power vortexes" of the surrounding red-rock country. You'll see local bulletin boards and publications advertising such diverse New Age services as past-life regressions, crystal healing, astrology readings, reiki, axiatonal therapy, electromagnetic field balancing, soul retrieval, channeling, aromatherapy, myofacial release, and holographic kinesiology.

A vortex is a site where the earth's unseen lines of power intersect to form a particularly powerful energy field. Page Bryant, a member of the New Age movement, determined through channeling that there were four vortexes around Sedona. Scientists may scoff, but Sedona's vortexes have become so well known that the chamber of commerce visitor center has several handouts to explain them and guide you to them. (Many of the most spectacular geological features of the Sedona landscape also happen to be vortexes.)

The four main vortexes include Bell Rock, Cathedral Rock, Airport Mesa, and Boynton Canyon. **Bell Rock** and **Airport Mesa** are both said to contain masculine or electric energy that boosts emotional, spiritual, and physical energy. **Cathedral Rock** is said to contain feminine or magnetic energy, good for facilitating relaxation. The **Boynton Canyon** vortex is considered an electromagnetic energy site, which means it has a balance of both masculine and feminine energy.

If you're not familiar with vortexes and want to learn more about the ones here in Sedona, consider a vortex tour. These are offered by several companies around town including **Sedona Nature Excursions** (☎ 520/282-6735), **Dorian Tours** (☎ 520/282-4562 or 800/728-4562), and **Sacred Earth Tours** (☎ 520/282-6826 or 800/848-7728). All offer vortex tours that combine aspects of Native American and New Age beliefs. Tours last about three hours and cost $50 to $55 per person.

You can also stock up on books, crystals, and other spiritual supplies at such stores as **Crystal Magic,** 2978 W. Hwy. 89A (☎ 520/282-1622); or **The Eye of the Vortex Book Center,** 1405 W. Hwy. 89A (☎ 520/282-5614).

By Bus   Sedona Phoenix Shuttle operates several trips daily between the Phoenix Sky Harbor Airport and Sedona. The one-way fare is $30 and the round-trip fare is $55. Phone 520/282-2066 or 800/448-7988 in Arizona, for schedule information.

By Car   Sedona is on Ariz. 179 at the mouth of scenic Oak Creek Canyon. From Phoenix, take I-17 to Ariz. 179 north. From Flagstaff, head south on I-17 until you see the turnoff for Ariz. 179 and Sedona. U.S. 89A connects Sedona with Prescott.

VISITOR INFORMATION

For more information on Sedona, contact the **Sedona–Oak Creek Chamber of Commerce,** P.O. Box 478, Sedona, AZ 86339 (☎ 520/282-7722), which also operates a Tourist Information Center on the corner of U.S. 89A and Forest Road near uptown Sedona.

GETTING AROUND

Budget Rent-a-Car (☎ 520/282-4602 or 800/527-0700) is located at the Sedona Airport. Jeeps can be rented at **Canyon Jeep Rentals** (☎ 520/282-6061 or 800/224-2229) or **Sedona Jeep Rentals** (☎ 520/282-2227 or 800/879-JEEP). For a taxi, call **Bob's Taxi of Sedona** (☎ 520/282-1234).

SPECIAL & FREE EVENTS

With its cosmopolitan population, Sedona is host to a wide variety of annual events. You can find out what will be happening during your visit by contacting the **City of Sedona Department of Arts & Culture,** 2940 Southwest Dr., Sedona, AZ 86336 (☎ 520/282-9738). Each year in May, Hopi artists gather for the **Hopi-Tu Tsootsvolla** (☎ 520/282-6428), which takes place in uptown Sedona and includes Hopi art, dances, food, and cultural exhibits. One of the year's big events is the **Sedona Chamber Music Festival,** held each June; contact the Sedona Chamber Music Society, P.O. Box 153, Sedona, AZ 86339 (☎ 520/204-2415), for details. **Jazz on the Rocks,** held each year in September, usually features nationally known jazz musicians who perform at the Verde Valley School Campus. For more information contact Sedona Jazz on the Rocks, Inc., P.O. Box 889, Sedona, AZ 86339-0889 (☎ 520/282-1985). In mid-December each year Sedona celebrates the **Festival of Lights** at Tlaquepaque (☎ 520/282-4838) by the lighting of thousands of luminárias (paper bags partially filled with sand and containing a single candle each) beginning at sunset.

WHAT TO SEE & DO

EXPLORING THE RED ROCKS

Rugged cliffs, needlelike pinnacles, and isolated buttes rise up from the green forest floor at the mouth of Oak Creek Canyon in Sedona. Layers of different-colored stone deposited during various prehistoric ages form bands through the cliffs above, the most prominent of these bands being the layer of red sandstone called the Schnebly Hill Formation. Because this rosy sandstone predominates around Sedona, the region has come to be known as the red-rock country. Each evening at sunset the red rocks put on a sunset light show that's reason enough for visiting Sedona.

Days can be spent exploring the red-rock country in any of half a dozen different modes of transport. There are Jeep tours, hot-air-balloon flights, horseback rides, mountain-bike trails, hiking trails, and scenic drives suitable for standard cars. (See "Organized Tours" and "Recreation," below.) For a relatively easy and yet spectacular red-rock viewing excursion, head south out of Sedona on Ariz. 179, turn left after you cross the bridge over Oak Creek, and head up the unpaved **Schnebly Hill Road.** The road climbs up into the hills above town and every turn yields a new and breathtaking view. The road eventually climbs to the top of the Mogollon Rim. At the rim is the Schnebly Hill overlook, which offers the very best view in the area.

Just south of Sedona, on Ariz. 179, you'll see the aptly named **Bell Rock** on the east side of the road. There's a parking area at the foot of Bell Rock and trails leading up to the top. From Bell Rock, you can see **Cathedral Rock** to the west. This rock is the most photographed formation in Sedona. Adjacent to Bell Rock is **Courthouse Rock,** and not far from Bell Rock and visible from Chapel Road, are **Eagle Head Rock** (from the front door of the Chapel of the Holy Cross—see "Other Attractions," below—look three-quarters of the way up the mountain to see the eagle's head), the **Twin Nuns** (two pinnacles standing side by side), and **Mother and Child Rock** to the left of the Twin Nuns.

If you head west out of Sedona on U.S. 89A and turn left onto Airport Road, you'll drive up onto **Airport Mesa,** which consists of three small hills commanding an unobstructed panorama of Sedona and the red rocks.

One of the most beautiful areas around Sedona is **Boynton Canyon.** To reach this spectacular canyon, drive west out of Sedona on U.S. 89A, turn right on Dry Creek Road, take a left at the T intersection, and at the next T intersection take a right. On the way to Boynton Canyon, look north from U.S. 89A and you'll see **Coffee Pot Rock,** which is also known as Rooster Rock, rising 1,800 feet above Sedona. Three pinnacles, known as the **Three Golden Chiefs** by the Yavapai tribe, stand beside Coffee Pot Rock. As you drive up Dry Creek Road, you'll see on your right **Capitol Butte,** which resembles the U.S. Capitol building. Just outside the gates of the Enchantment Resort is a parking area for the Boynton Canyon trailhead. From the parking area the trail leads 3 miles up into the canyon. The ancient Sinagua people once lived in Boynton Canyon, and the ruins of their homes can still be seen.

On the south of U.S. 89A and just beyond the turnoff for Boynton Canyon is Lower Red Rock Loop Road. Near the end of this road and on the banks of Oak Creek, you'll find **Red Rock State Park** (☎ **520/282-6907**). The views here take in many of the rocks listed above, and you have the additional bonus of being right on the creek. The park admission is $4 per vehicle.

OAK CREEK CANYON

The **Mogollon Rim** is a 2,000-foot escarpment cutting diagonally across central Arizona and on into New Mexico. At the top of the Mogollon Rim are the ponderosa pine forests of the high mountains, while at the bottom the lowland deserts begin. Among the canyons cutting down from the rim, Oak Creek Canyon is the best known. Ariz. 179 runs down through the canyon from Flagstaff to Sedona, winding its way down from the rim and paralleling Oak Creek. Along the way there are overlooks, parks, picnic areas, campgrounds, cabin resorts, and small inns.

If you have a choice of how to first see Oak Creek Canyon, come at it from the north. Your first stop after traveling south from Flagstaff will be the Oak Creek Canyon overlook, which provides a view far down the valley to Sedona and beyond. The overlook is at the edge of the Mogollon Rim, and the road suddenly drops in tight switchbacks just south of the overlook. You may notice that one rim of the canyon is lower than the other. This is because Oak Creek Canyon is on a geologic fault line; one side of the canyon is moving in a different direction from the other.

Though the top of the Mogollon Rim is a ponderosa pine forest and the bottom is a desert, Oak Creek Canyon supports a forest of sycamores and other deciduous trees. In the autumn the canyon is ablaze with red and yellow leaves. **Arizona 179** is considered the most beautiful road in Arizona, and there's no better time to drive it than between late September and mid-October, when the leaves are usually changing.

At the **Cave Spring Campground** is a self-guided nature walk that describes the riparian environment of Oak Creek. (A riparian area is one along a body of water.) Different plants live in this moist environment, and the plants and water attract a wide variety of animals. Riparian habitats are especially crucial in deserts.

The most popular spot in all of Oak Creek Canyon is **Slide Rock State Park** (☎ **520/282-3034**). Located 7 miles north of Sedona on the site of an old homestead, this park preserves a natural water slide. On hot summer days the park is jammed with people splashing in the water and sliding over the algae-covered sandstone bottom of Oak Creek. Sunbathing and fishing are other popular pastimes here. Admission is $5 per vehicle. There's another popular swimming area at **Grasshopper Point,** several miles closer to Sedona.

Within Oak Creek Canyon several hikes of different lengths are possible. By far the most popular is the 6-mile round-trip hike up the **West Fork of Oak Creek.** This is a classic canyon-country hike with steep canyon walls rising up from the creek. At some points the canyon is no more than 20 feet wide with walls rising up more than 200 feet. Stop by the Sedona–Oak Creek Chamber of Commerce to pick up a free map listing hikes in the area. The **Coconino National Forest** ranger station (☎ 520/282-4119) on Brewer Road, just west of the intersection of U.S. 89A and Ariz. 179, is also a good source of hiking information.

OTHER ATTRACTIONS

Sedona's most notable architectural landmark is the **Chapel of the Holy Cross,** a small church built right into the red rock on the south side of town. If you're driving up from Phoenix, you can't miss the chapel. It sits high above the road just off Ariz. 179. With its very contemporary styling, the chapel is considered one of the most architecturally important modern churches in the country. Marguerite Brunswig Staude, a devout Catholic painter, sculptor, and designer, had the inspiration for the chapel in 1932, but it wasn't until 1957 that her dream was finally realized here in Sedona. The chapel's design is dominated by a simple cross forming the wall that faces the street. The cross and the chapel seem to grow directly from the rock. The stark beauty of the church leaves the natural beauty of the red rock to speak for itself. The chapel is open daily from 9am to 5pm.

Another Sedona attraction is the **Sedona Museum of Art,** 310 Apple Ave. (☎ 520/282-7021). The museum houses a small collection of fine art and contemporary works by local artists and artists who have been inspired by Sedona. The **Sedona Arts Center,** U.S. 89A at Art Barn Road (☎ 520/282-3865 or 520/282-3809), near the north end of town, serves both as a gallery for art-works by local and regional artists and as a theater for plays and music perfor-mances. In April and September the center holds its annual Fine Arts and Crafts Exhibitions.

ORGANIZED TOURS

Two different 45 minute tours of Sedona are offered by **City & Scenic Tours** (☎ 520/282-5400); the cost is $9 for both tours. **Roadrunner Tours** (☎ 520/282-4696) offers tours to Oak Creek Canyon and Jerome in a military Humvee, as well as two-hour tours of Sedona. A half-day tour will set you back $50.

The red-rock country surrounding Sedona is the city's greatest natural attrac-tion, and for more than 30 years **Pink Jeep Tours,** P.O. Box 1447, Sedona, AZ 86339 (☎ 520/282-5000 or 800/8-SEDONA), has been sharing it with the curious. There's no better way to explore the red-rock country than in a four-wheel-drive vehicle. This company heads deep into the Coconino National Forest on four different tours ranging in length from one hour ($18) to three hours ($42). You can travel the Sedona backcountry or simply visit the best views in the area. **Sedona Red Rock Jeep Tours,** 270 N. U.S. 89A (P.O. Box 10305), Sedona, AZ 86339 (☎ 520/282-6826 or 800/848-7728), offers similar tours at comparable prices.

RECREATION

Red Rock Balloon Adventures (☎ **520/284-0040** or 800/258-3754) and **Northern Light Balloon Expeditions** (☎ **520/282-2274** or 800/230-6222) offer peaceful hot-air-balloon rides over the canyons and sculpted buttes. **Action Helicopter of Arizona** (☎ **520/282-7884**), **Arizona Helicopter Adventures** (☎ **520/282-0904** or 800/282-5141), and **Skydance Helicopters** (☎ **520/ 282-1651** or 800/882-1651) all offer short flights to different parts of this colorful region.

The **Sedona Golf Resort** (☎ **520/284-9355**) is located south of town on Ariz. 179. The views of the red rocks are magnificent. Sedona's other 18-hole course is the **Oak Creek Country Club,** 690 Bell Rock Blvd. (☎ **520/284-1660**), which is also south of town and offers equally stunning views from the course.

Kachina Stables, Lower Red Rock Loop Road (☎ **520/282-7252**), offers guided horseback trail rides. Prices range from $25 for a one-hour ride to $98 for an all-day ride. There are also breakfast, full-moon, lunch, sunset, and Indian ceremony rides. Lower Red Rock Trail is west of Sedona on U.S. 89A.

You can rent a mountain bike from **Sedona Sports,** 245 U.S. 89A (☎ **520/ 282-6956**). If you want to take the family fishing, try the **Rainbow Trout Farm,** 4 miles north of Sedona (☎ **520/282-3379**). The **tennis courts** at Poco Diablo Resort, on the south side of Sedona, are open to the public for $12 per hour. To make reservations, call the resort at 520/282-7333.

WHERE TO STAY
VERY EXPENSIVE

✪ Briar Patch Inn

Star Route 3, Box 1002, Sedona, AZ 86336. ☎ **520/282-2342.** Fax 520/282-2399. 17 rms. $135–$195 double. Rates include full breakfast. MC, V.

Located 3 miles north of Sedona on the banks of Oak Creek, this inn's cottages are set amid beautiful shady grounds where birdsong and the babbling of the creek set the mood. The cottages date back to the 1930s but have all been very attractively renovated and updated. A western style predominates, and some rooms have a fireplace and kitchenette. Breakfast is often served on a terrace above the creek. All in all, the Briar Patch offers a delightful combination of solitude and sophistication.

✪ Enchantment Resort

Boynton Canyon, 525 Boynton Canyon Rd., Sedona, AZ 86336. ☎ **520/282-2900** or 800/ 826-4180. Fax 520/282-9249. 162 rms and suites. A/C TV TEL. $160–$240 double; $260–$385 one-bedroom suite; $380–$575 two-bedroom suite. AE, DISC, MC, V.

Located at the mouth of Boynton Canyon, this resort more than lives up to its name. The setting is breathtaking and the pueblo-style architecture of the hotel blends in with the canyon landscape. The individual casitas (little houses) of this resort can be booked as two-bedroom suites, as one-bedroom suites, or as single rooms. It's worth booking a suite just so you can enjoy a casita living room, which features high, beamed ceilings, beehive fireplaces, and built-in shelves set with Native American crafts. The large patios provide dramatic views of the canyon, while skylights brighten the large bathrooms.

Dining/Entertainment: The resort's restaurant (the Yavapai Dining Room; see "Where to Dine," below) and lounge offer terrace tables as well as indoor dining and drinking. At lunch there's a casual buffet, while at dinner the dining room is dressed up with pink linens for a more formal atmosphere. The menu features innovative American cuisine.

Services: Room service, tennis lessons, guided hikes, complimentary morning juice and newspaper, local airport shuttle.

Facilities: Four pools, 12 tennis courts, croquet court, whirlpools, fitness center, hiking trails, putting green, spa (with aerobics classes, personal training, fitness programs, massages, facials, and aromatherapy).

Junipine Resort

8351 N. U.S. 89A, Sedona, AZ 86336. ☎ **520/282-3375** or 800/742-PINE. 50 condos. TV TEL. $180–$220 one-bedroom condo; $210–$250 two-bedroom condo. AE, DC, DISC, MC, V.

If you're coming up this way with the family and are looking for a place in the cool depths of Oak Creek Canyon, consider this condominium resort. All the condos have loads of space (some with lofts), skylights, decks, stone fireplaces, decorative quilts on the walls, full kitchens, and contemporary styling. Best of all, the creek is right outside the door of most condos. The resort's dining room serves a surprisingly sophisticated continental menu at reasonable prices, so there's no need to drive all the way into Sedona for a good meal.

L'Auberge de Sedona

301 L'Auberge Lane (P.O. Box B), Sedona, AZ 86339. ☎ **520/282-1661** or 800/272-6777. Fax 520/282-2885. 99 rms and cottages. A/C TEL. $130–$250 double in the inn, $275–$385 double in cottages. AE, CB, DC, DISC, MC, V.

Located in the heart of uptown Sedona, this romantic getaway offers a variety of room types, all of which are done in an incongruous country French decor (the desert doesn't really conjure images of France). If you want spectacular views and sunsets, opt for the Orchards rooms, which face the red rocks. Our personal favorites are the rooms with gas fireplaces. If you crave a creekside cottage set beneath shady sycamores, opt for one of the cottages on the banks of Oak Creek. These are decorated in a frilly, country French style, with canopy beds and fireplaces but no TVs. If the atmosphere of a French hunting lodge appeals, try a lodge room, which will have a few rustic furnishings. With two restaurants and only a pool and whirlpool for activities, this resort definitely aims for the less active guest who prefers fine dining to working up a sweat.

Dining/Entertainment: L'Auberge Restaurant (see "Where to Dine," below) is one of Sedona's finest and most expensive restaurants. Pink linens and bone china set the tone for the five-course French dinners. A more casual restaurant in the Orchards section serves simpler meals.

Services: Room service.

Facilities: Small outdoor pool, whirlpool, French boutique.

Los Abrigados

160 Portal Lane, Sedona, AZ 86336. ☎ **520/282-1777** or 800/521-3131. Fax 520/282-2614. 172 suites. A/C MINIBAR TV TEL. $210–$275 one-bedroom suite for two; $395 two-bedroom suite for two. AE, CB, DC, DISC, MC, V.

If you were born to shop, this might be your idea of heaven; the famous Tlaquepaque shopping center is just across the parking lot from this mission-revival resort on the banks of Oak Creek. The resort attempts to be an architectural extension of the shopping center, but doesn't quite succeed.

The suites, though spacious, are spartanly furnished with a blend of Spanish colonial and inexpensive contemporary pieces. Stocked minibars and microwave ovens provide convenience, and in the bathrooms you'll find hairdryers and lighted shaving/makeup mirrors. Many of the suites also have fireplaces, whirlpool tubs, and views of the red rocks.

Dining/Entertainment: With four restaurants, the resort tries to cater to all tastes. Southern Italian and burgers and ribs are the fare at two of the restaurants. The two formal dining rooms focus on steaks and continental fare. Lounge areas include a billiard-and-cigar room and a more lively space with nightly entertainment

Services: Concierge, room service.

Facilities: Outdoor pool, three tennis courts, hair salon, sauna, whirlpools, health spa (with massages, facials, and other treatments).

Poco Diablo

1752 S. Ariz. 179 (P.O. Box 1709), Sedona, AZ 86339. ☎ **520/282-7333** or 800/528-4275. Fax 520/282-2090. 109 rms, 3 suites. A/C TV TEL. $135–$185 double; $240–$360 suite. AE, DC, DISC, MC, V.

This golf and tennis resort is located on the southern outskirts of Sedona, with Oak Creek running right through the 25-acre grounds. The green fairways of the nine-hole golf course provide a striking contrast to the red rocks and blue skies. The small lobby exudes Arizona sophistication with mission-style furnishings, contemporary southwestern art, and Native American baskets and pottery. The guest rooms, unfortunately, don't live up to the promise of the setting and many are in need of renovation. The views here are also not as good as at other comparable properties in the area, but the staff is courteous and helpful.

Dining/Entertainment: The restaurant offers views of the golf course and red rocks and a menu that features southwestern and continental dishes. The small dark lounge sports a golf-and-tennis theme and offers live dance music on weekends.

Services: Room service, valet/laundry service.

Facilities: Two small pools, three whirlpools, four tennis courts, racquetball courts, nine-hole golf course.

EXPENSIVE

⑤ Best Western Arroyo Roble Hotel

400 N. U.S. 89A (P.O. Box NN), Sedona, AZ 86339. ☎ **520/282-4001,** 602/252-4483 in Phoenix, or 800/7-SEDONA. 53 rms, 1 cottage, 7 villas. A/C TV TEL. Feb–Nov, $100–$125 double; $155–$195 cottage; $250–$275 villa. Dec–Feb, $70–$85 double; $155–$195 cottage; $250–$275 villa. AE, CB, DC, DISC, MC, V.

This five-story hotel crowding up against U.S. 89A in uptown Sedona perches above Oak Creek with views of the red rocks and provides many of the amenities of a more expensive resort. All rooms come with king- or queen-size beds and a private balcony or patio. Surrounded by Oak Creek Canyon's shady sycamores, the villas are below the main hotel building and consists of two-bedroom condominiums with two fireplaces, $2^1/_2$ bathrooms, two TVs, a stereo, a VCR, and two private patios or balconies. Facilities include an outdoor and an indoor/outdoor pool, whirlpools, two tennis courts, handball and racquetball courts, a billiard room, an exercise room, a steam room and sauna, and a video-games room. The hotel doesn't have its own restaurant, but there are plenty within walking distance.

The Lodge at Sedona

125 Kallof Place, Sedona, AZ 86336. ☎ **520/204-1942** or 800/619-4467. Fax 520/204-2128. 11 rms, 2 suites. A/C. $95–$145 double; $175–$205 suite. Rates include full breakfast. MC, V.

Located on the newer, west side of Sedona, this large B&B is surrounded by desert landscaping that includes rock gardens, waterfalls, and pine trees. The rooms are all individually decorated, but our personal favorites are the Lariat Room and the Master Suite, which is absolutely huge and has a stone fireplace. With 13 rooms and suites, this lodging may seem large for a bed-and-breakfast inn, but size doesn't limit the hospitality of the owners, who make all their guests feel very much at home.

✪ Saddle Rock Ranch

255 Rock Ridge Dr., Sedona, AZ 86336. ☎ **520/282-7640.** Fax 520/282-6829. 3 rms. A/C. $115–$135 double. Rates include full breakfast. No credit cards.

With a breathtaking view and classic western ranch styling, this vintage 1926 home makes a superb bed-and-breakfast inn. Walls of stone and adobe, a flagstone floor in the living room, huge exposed beams, and plenty of windows to take in the views are enough to enchant guests even before they reach their rooms. And the rooms don't disappoint either. In one you'll find Victorian elegance, in another an English canopy bed and stone fireplace. Dressing areas and private gardens add to the charm. The third room is a separate little western cottage with a lodgepole-pine bed, flagstone floors, and beamed ceiling. The pool and whirlpool are surrounded by a flagstone terrace and enjoy one of the best red-rock views in town. Stunning views combined with reasonable rates make this one of Sedona's best lodging choices.

MODERATE

Matterhorn Motor Lodge

230 Apple Ave., Sedona, AZ 86336. ☎ **520/282-7176.** Fax 520/282-0727. 23 rms. A/C TV TEL. Mar–Nov, $74–$84 double. Dec–Feb, $49–$64 double. AE, MC, V.

Located in the heart of the uptown shopping district, the Matterhorn is convenient to restaurants and shopping and all rooms have excellent views of the red-rock canyon walls. The motel has had a complete make-over in the past few years and now has an adobe-style exterior and modern furnishings in the guest rooms. In-room amenities include coffeemakers, hairdryers, and refrigerators, and an outdoor pool and whirlpool provide recreation. Although the hotel overlooks busy U.S. 89A, if you lie in bed and keep your eyes on the rocks, you won't notice the traffic below you.

Quality Inn King's Ransom

771 Ariz. 179 (P.O. Box 180), Sedona, AZ 86339. ☎ **520/282-7151** or 800/221-2222. 65 rms. A/C TV TEL. $80–$116 double. Lower rates available in winter. AE, CB, DC, DISC, EURO, MC, V.

Situated on the outskirts of Sedona on Ariz. 179, the King's Ransom doesn't have the breathtaking views of some of Sedona's other hotels, but it does have a peaceful courtyard garden with a pool and elegant Mediterranean-style covered spa. Some of the guest rooms are a bit cramped, but others have lots of space. The bathrooms have plenty of counter space and an assortment of toiletries, but some rooms have showers only. A casual dining room and terrace on the second floor offers continental and Middle Eastern dishes. There's a tiny bar off to one side of the main dining room.

Rose Tree Inn

376 Cedar St., Sedona, AZ 86336. ☎ **520/282-2065.** 5 rms. TV. $85–$115 double. MC, V.

This little inn is located only a block from Sedona's uptown shopping district and is tucked amid pretty gardens on a quiet street. The inn consists of an eclectic cluster of older buildings that have all been renovated and are now quite attractive. Four of the rooms have kitchenettes, which makes these good choices for families, or for a longer stay. All the rooms are furnished a little bit differently—one Victorian, one southwestern, another with a gas fireplace. There's also a whirlpool here, and complimentary coffee and tea are available.

⑤ Sedona Motel

P.O. Box 1450, Sedona, AZ 86339. ☎ **520/282-7187.** 16 rms. A/C TV TEL. $64–$95 double. AE, DISC, MC, V.

Located almost at the intersection of Ariz. 179 and U.S. 89A, the Sedona Motel looks like any other older motel from the outside, but once you check in, you'll find a few surprises. First and foremost is the view across the parking lot. You can pay twice as much in Sedona and not have this good a view. The windows are double-paned so the rooms stay cool and quiet. New carpets, wallpaper, and pine furniture, as well as contemporary bathroom fixtures, all add up to comfort and a good value.

⑤ Sky Ranch Lodge

Airport Rd. (P.O. Box 2579), Sedona, AZ 86339. ☎ **520/282-6400.** Fax 520/282-7682. 94 rms. A/C TV TEL. $60–$145 double. MC, V.

This motel is located just down the street from Sedona's airport, which makes it convenient. But what makes it special is its stupendous setting on the edge of Airport Mesa. From here you can see the entire red-rocks country, with Sedona filling the valley below. Of course, the rooms with the best views are also the most expensive ($90 to $145), but if you're willing to walk a few feet for your view, you can stay here for much less. The rooms are fairly standard motel style.

WHERE TO DINE
VERY EXPENSIVE

L'Auberge

In L'Auberge de Sedona, 301 L'Auberge Lane. ☎ **520/282-7131.** Reservations recommended. Main courses $28–$36; fixed-price five-course dinner $49. AE, CB, DC, MC, V. Daily 7–10:30am, 11:30am–2pm, and 5:30–9pm. FRENCH.

L'Auberge—the name conjures up an image of a French country inn, and though this L'Auberge happens to be in the red-rock country of central Arizona, it manages to live up to its name. Oak Creek and a terrace are just outside the windows, and sycamores shade the banks. Inside, all is country elegance in the fairly fussy French decor. The menu is changed daily, but you'll always have a choice of several hors d'oeuvres and main dishes. Among the main-course choices on a recent evening were filet of sole with sea-scallop ravioli and vermouth sauce, and rack of lamb with couscous and sautéed eggplant. For dessert there was an array of delicate pastries.

EXPENSIVE

René at Tlaquepaque

Tlaquepaque, Ariz. 179. ☎ **520/282-9225.** Reservations highly recommended. Main courses $15–$27. AE, CB, DC, MC, V. Mon–Thurs 11:30am–2:30pm and 5:30–9pm, Fri–Sat 11:30am–2:30pm and 5:30–9:30pm, Sun 11:30am–2:30pm. CONTINENTAL/AMERICAN.

Located in Tlaquepaque, the city's upscale south-of-the-border-theme shopping center, René's is the quintessential Sedona dining experience. Original works of art by southwestern artists hang from the walls, reminding you while you dine that Sedona is an art community. Virtually any dish made with lamb is sure to be tender and juicy, but the rack of Colorado lamb (served for two people), though expensive, is superb.

✪ Yavapai Dining Room

In the Enchantment Resort, 525 Boynton Canyon Rd. ☎ **520/282-2900.** Reservations highly recommended. Main courses $17–$25; pastas $15.50–$17.50. AE, DISC, MC, V. Daily 7am–10:30am, 11:30am–2:30pm, and 6pm–9:30pm. NOUVELLE AMERICAN.

If you crave a taste of the good life, make a reservation for dinner at the Enchantment Resort's dining room. Put on your best clothes and ensconce yourself in the realm of the rich and famous. It may be expensive, but where else can you dine inside a genuine power vortex? The best time for dinner is at sunset, when the desert sun paints the red rocks in fiery hues—and the food is as spectacular as the view. For an appetizer, try the pan-seared duck with ginger, cilantro, and a jicama salad. The salads are made with the finest produce of the season, and even simple black-bean soup gets a special touch with applewood-smoked bacon and cumin-scented tortilla strips. The menu changes regularly, but if you're lucky you might get to try the Sonoran chicken breast sautéed with spinach, red onion, leeks, piñon pine nuts, and southwestern spices. The dessert tray is, of course, enchantingly decadent.

MODERATE

⑤ Cowboy Club

241 N. U.S. 89A. ☎ **520/282-4200.** Reservations recommended. Main courses $9–$23. MC, V. Daily 11am–10pm. SOUTHWESTERN.

With its big green booths, huge steer horns over the bar, and saddles and guns adorning the walls, this place looks like a cowboy diner, so it shouldn't surprise you that even the bread is branded. Choose from a list of chicken, venison, fish, or shrimp dishes served with sauces such as smoked-Gouda cream, cherry-sage chutney, or ancho-chili syrup; or pick a dish from the list of daily specials. Standards such as fried chicken, steaks, burgers, and pasta are also on the menu. Desserts are hearty, the atmosphere is relaxed and friendly, and there's live country music on the weekends.

✪ Fournos Restaurant

241 N. U.S. 89A. ☎ **520/282-3331.** Reservations required. Main courses $13–$14. No credit cards. Thurs–Sat seatings at 6 and 8pm, Sun (brunch), seating at noon. GREEK.

Pots and ladles hang from the kitchen ceiling in this tiny place where chef Demetrios cooks up a storm, preparing such dishes as Greek salads with homemade kalamata olives, and shrimp flambéed in ouzo and baked with feta cheese. Greek music plays and his engaging wife, Shirley, seats guests at tables. A lot of the people who come here know each other, but you won't feel out of place because Shirley has a way of making everybody feel at home. The menu is written on a chalkboard and includes such specialties as Colorado lamb Cephalonian with herbs and potatoes, and baked fish Mykonos with a sauce of yogurt, onions, mayonnaise, and butter. Greek pastry such as a flourless semolina-honey sponge cake comes with ice cream and fruit for a textural and decadent dessert.

✪ The Heartline Cafe

1610 W. U.S. 89A. ☎ **520/282-0785.** Reservations recommended. Main courses $9.25–$21. AE, CB, DISC, MC, V. Mon–Sat 11am–2:30pm and 5–9pm, Sun 5–9pm. SOUTHWESTERN/INTERNATIONAL.

The heartline, from Zuñi mythology, is a symbol of health and longevity, and also a symbol for the food here—healthy, and very creative as well. Service is good, and crusty bread appears on the table immediately. At lunch we tried sandwiches of tuna with wasabi and balsalmic vinegar served with yam fries, and grilled chicken with ginger mayonnaise and avocado, and were wowed by the flavor combinations. Other unexpected dishes are fettuccine and shrimp with anise-cream sauce, and seared halibut with pear-walnut chutney. A beautiful courtyard outside and an elegant bar inside are both places to savor a meal and enjoy a selection from the wine list, or a dessert of white-chocolate mousse, crème brûlée, or caramel-raspberry cheesecake.

Pietro's Restaurant & Cafe

2445 W. U.S. 89A. ☎ **520/282-2525.** Reservations highly recommended. Main courses $15–$22; pasta $14–$16. AE, CB, DC, MC, V. Spring–fall, daily 5:30–9:30pm; winter, daily 5–9pm. ITALIAN.

While visiting Sedona several years ago, the owner of Pietro's couldn't find a good place to eat. He decided to open his own restaurant, and created this New York–style bistro with New York attitude. You'll find appetizers such as mushrooms stuffed with crab and shrimp, and other classic Italian dishes that include a deliciously rich lasagne bolognese or a more innovative fettuccine with smoked salmon and roasted peppers in vodka-cream sauce. For seafood lovers, there are always plenty of choices. This place is small, so make reservations.

Samba! Café

2321 W. U.S. 89A. ☎ **520/282-5219.** Reservations recommended. Main courses $12–$19. AE, DC, DISC, MC, V. Sun–Thurs 11:30am–3pm and 5–9pm, Fri–Sat 11:30am–3pm and 5–10pm. Tapas, daily 9pm–midnight. SPANISH/INTERNATIONAL.

This rather tropical ambience is pleasantly colorful in the daytime, and at night, when there's frequently live music, flickering candles cast romantic shadows on the yellow walls. The salads we had were not your usual drab lettuce and cucumber, but colorful and flavorful plates composed of lots of fresh little greens. Side servings of veggies were also treated kindly. Although the menu has a Spanish leaning, it also includes favorite dishes from hot spots around the world, such as a chunky, spicy-smokey jerked-chicken salad and piquant coconut shrimp. For late-night small meals, the tapas menu is served until late.

Sedona Swiss Restaurant & Cafe

350 Jordan Rd. ☎ **520/282-7959.** Reservations recommended. Main courses $11–$25. MC, V. Restaurant, Mon–Sat 11am–2pm and 5:30–9:30pm. Pastry shop, Mon–Sat 7:30–9pm. SWISS/FRENCH.

Chef Robert Ackermann, formerly the executive chef at the Swiss embassy in Washington, D.C., is the raison d'être for this authentically Swiss restaurant located in a quiet spot near old-town Sedona. You'll find classic Swiss and French fare such as Rahmschnitzel (sautéed pork scaloppine in a mushroom-cream sauce), rack of lamb provençal, and the house specialty, Galgenspiess—beef tenderloin dramatically flambéed at your table. You can dine inside the cozy restaurant or outside on the patio. Visit the café and pastry shop for dessert and coffee that are truly a European experience. When we were last here at lunchtime, it was crowded with European tour groups.

INEXPENSIVE

Cups Bistro and Gallery

1670 W. U.S. 89A. ☎ **520/282-2531.** Main courses $6.25–$9. CB, DC, MC, V. Aug–May, daily 8am–4pm; June–July, daily 8am–10pm. ORGANIC.

Basically a vegetarian restaurant (that also serves seafood), the attempt here is to present organic grains and vegetables. They have good daily specials, and the menu includes such offerings as stuffed grape leaves, a goat-cheese sandwich on rosemary-walnut bread, pasta with pesto sauce, and vegetable quiche. This is a place for a tasty breakfast of blueberry pancakes or couscous with fruit compote.

SHOPPING

Sedona is well known as an arts community, and it was here that the highly respected Cowboy Artists of America was founded in 1965. You'll see their works in some of the nearly 50 art galleries in town. Most of these galleries specialize in traditional western, contemporary southwestern, and Native American art. You'll find the greatest concentration of galleries and shops in the many shopping centers around town. Unfortunately many of Sedona's shops now specialize in cheap Southwest gifts that have little to do with art, and it can be difficult weeding through the tacky gift shops to find the real art galleries.

✪ Garland's Navajo Rugs

411 Ariz. 179. ☎ **520/282-4070.**

With a very large collection of both contemporary and antique Navajo rugs, Garland's is the premier Navajo rug shop in Sedona. It also carries a line of Native American baskets and pottery, Hopi kachina dolls, and Navajo sandpaintings.

Hillside Courtyard

671 Ariz. 179. ☎ **520/282-4500.**

This is a shopping center dedicated to art galleries, retail shops, and a couple of restaurants. Carol Dolighan, carrying artistic women's fashions, and Acrey's Gallery of the West, featuring large-format photographs of red rock, are located here.

✪ Hoel's Indian Shop

9440 N. U.S. 89A. ☎ **520/282-3925.**

Located in Oak Creek Canyon 10 miles north of Sedona past Hoel's Cabins in a private residence, this Native American arts-and-crafts gallery is one of the finest in the region, and sells pieces of the highest quality almost exclusively to collectors.

Hozho

431 Ariz. 179. ☎ **520/282-1038.**

There are about 10 shops in this small shopping center, including the Dinéthah Silver Gallery, which has an interesting selection of Native American–style belts, bracelets, button covers, and more. Most of the shops are galleries selling paintings and sculpture.

Sedona Southwest Store

Ariz. 179 and Schnebly Hill Rd. ☎ **520/204-1312.**

This store has good prices on southwestern and Native American furnishings, art, and crafts.

Sinagua Plaza

320 N. U.S. 89A. ☎ **520/282-0641.**

Located in old town Sedona, this shopping center includes shops such as Joe Wilcox Western Wear, galleries, and restaurants.

✪ Son Silver West

1476 Ariz. 179 (outside Sedona on the south side). ☎ **520/282-3580.**

For those who love all things southwestern, this shop is a treasure trove of all kinds of interesting stuff, from Native American and Hispanic arts and crafts to antique santo (saint) carvings and rifles, to big imported pots, chile strings, and garden art.

✪ Tlaquepaque Arts & Crafts Village

Ariz. 179 (on the south side of Sedona). ☎ **520/282-4838.**

This premier shopping center, with over 40 stores and restaurants, is named after a famous arts-and-crafts neighborhood in the suburbs of Guadalajara, Mexico, and is designed to resemble an old Mexican village. The maze of narrow alleys, connecting courtyards, fountains, and even a chapel and a bell tower, are worth a visit even if you aren't in a buying mood. Occasionally you'll see artists working here in their combination gallery-studios.

Touchstone

25 Schnebly Hill Rd. (at Ariz. 179). ☎ **520/282-2380.**

Western designers provide the drapey Sedona look in handwovens, hand-dyed silk, rayon, cotton, and linen, done up in dresses and matching separates. Colors and textures are beautiful.

EVENING ENTERTAINMENT

The **Sedona Arts Center,** U.S. 89A at Art Barn Road (☎ **520/282-3865** or 520/282-3809), has frequent performances of music and plays. If you're searching for the best margarita in town, head for **El Rincon** (☎ **520/282-4648**), a Mexican restaurant in Tlaquepaque Village. For a more sophisticated ambience, try a resort hotel lounge. **On the Rocks Bar & Grill,** at Los Abrigados, beside Tlaquepaque, is one of the nicest lounges in town.

EASY EXCURSIONS FROM SEDONA
CAMP VERDE

For thousands of years people have been drawn to the Verde (Spanish for "green") Valley, which was named by the Spanish because of the lushness of the valley compared to the surrounding desert. The Verde River has served as a source of irrigation waters for ancient Hohokam and Sinagua peoples, for the Yavapai and Apache, and most recently, for white settlers. With its headwaters in the Juniper Mountains of the Prescott National Forest, the Verde River flows down through a rugged canyon before meandering slowly across the wide Verde Valley plains. These plains are today one of Arizona's richest agricultural and ranching regions, but long before the first white explorers entered the Verde Valley, the Sinagua were living by the river. Sinagua ruins can still be seen at Tuzigoot and Montezuma national monuments. Later, when white settlers and the Yavapai and Apache tribes clashed, the U.S. Army established Fort Verde to protect settlers.

Historic Sites

Fort Verde State Historic Park

3 miles east of I-17. ☎ **520/567-3275**. Admission $2 adults, $1 children 12–17, free for children 11 and under. Daily 8am–5pm.

Established in 1871, Fort Verde was the third military post in the Verde Valley and was occupied until 1891, by which time tensions with the Native American population had subsided and made the fort unnecessary. The military had first come to the Verde Valley in 1865 at the request of settlers who wanted protection from the local Tonto Apache and Yavapai. The tribes, traditionally hunters and gatherers, had been forced to raid the settlers' fields for food after their normal economy was disrupted by the sudden influx of whites and Mexicans into the area. Between 1873 and 1875 most of the Native Americans in the area were rounded up and forced to live on various reservations. An uprising in 1882 led to the last clash between Native Americans and Fort Verde's soldiers.

Today the state park, which covers 10 acres, preserves three officers' quarters, an administration building, and some ruins. The buildings that have been fully restored house exhibits on the history of the fort and what life was like here in the 19th century. With their white lattices and picket fence, gables, and shake-shingle roofs, the buildings of Fort Verde suggest that life at this remote post was not so bad, at least for officers.

Montezuma Castle National Monument

Exit 289 from I-17. ☎ **520/567-3322**. Montezuma Castle, $2 adults, free for children 16 and under; Montezuma Well, free. Summer, daily 8am–7pm; winter, daily 8am–5pm.

Neither a castle nor an Aztec dwelling, as the name implies with its reference to the Aztec ruler Moctezuma (traditionally Montezuma), this Sinagua cliff dwelling is still very impressive. **Montezuma Castle** is perhaps the best preserved of all the cliff dwellings in Arizona and consists of two stone pueblos. The more intriguing of the two is set in a shallow cave 100 feet up in a cliff overlooking Beaver Creek. Construction on this five-story, 20-room village began sometime in the early 12th century. For more than 600 years Montezuma Castle has been protected from the elements by the overhanging roof of the cave in which it was built—the original adobe mud that was used to plaster over the stone walls of the dwelling is still intact. Another structure, containing 45 rooms on a total of six levels, stands at the base of the cliff. This latter dwelling is not nearly as well preserved as the cliff dwelling because it has been subjected to rains and floods over the years. For some as-yet-unknown reason these buildings were abandoned in the early 14th century by the Sinagua people, who disappeared without a trace. In the visitor center are artifacts that have been unearthed at the ruins.

Deserts are supposed to be dry places where water is scarce, so **Montezuma Well** comes as quite a surprise. Located 11 miles north of Montezuma Castle, Montezuma Well is another prehistoric Native American site. Occupied by both the Hohokam and Sinagua at different times in the past, this desert oasis measures 368 feet across and 65 feet deep. The rock of this area is porous limestone, which is often laced with caverns and underground streams, and Montezuma Well resulted when a cavern in the limestone rock collapsed to form a sinkhole. Springs that still flow today soon filled the sinkhole, and eventually local tribes discovered this reliable source of year-round water. The water was used for irrigation by both the Hohokam and Sinagua, and their irrigation channels can still be seen. An excavated Hohokam pithouse, built around 1100, and Sinagua houses and pueblos stand around the sinkhole.

Other Attractions & Activities

If you have an interest in 19th-century reenactments or antique cowboy and military gear, stop in at **Kicking Mule Outfitters,** 545 S. Main St., Camp Verde (☎ 520/567-2501). This store specializes in making reproduction western leather holsters, gun belts, saddles, and the like. They also sell western antiques, and rent equipment to movie companies.

The Verde River is a designated Wild and Scenic River and is one of the only rivers in the state that's good for canoeing and leisurely boating activities. **River Otter Canoe Co.,** 458 S. First St., Camp Verde (☎ 520/567-4116), rents canoes and kayaks and also offers shuttles to anywhere in the Verde Valley. Prices start at $35 a day for canoes and $30 for shuttles.

Other options for exploring this area include guided hikes with **Montezuma Outback Tours,** P.O. Box 2074, Camp Verde, AZ 86322 (☎ **520/567-9519**), and trail rides with **Blazing Trails** (☎ **520/567-6611**).

The Grand Canyon & Northern Arizona

The Grand Canyon—the name is at once apt and inadequate. How can words sum up the grandeur of two billion years of the earth's history sliced open by the power of a single river? Once a barrier to explorers and settlers, today the Grand Canyon attracts visitors from all over the world who gaze wonderstruck into its seemingly infinite depths.

Yet, other parts of northern Arizona also contain worthwhile—and less crowded—attractions. Only 60 miles south of the great yawning chasm stand the San Francisco Peaks, the tallest of which, Humphreys Peak, stands 12,643 feet above sea level. These peaks, sacred to the Hopi and Navajo, are ancient volcanoes. Smaller volcanoes in this region once made the land fertile enough to support an ancient Sinagua culture that has long since disappeared, leaving only the ruins of its ancient villages.

Amid northern Arizona's miles of windswept plains and ponderosa pine forests is the city of Flagstaff, which at 7,000 feet in elevation is one of the highest cities in the United States. It's also home to Northern Arizona University, whose students ensure that it's a lively town. Born of the railroads, Flagstaff has preserved its western heritage in its restored downtown historic district.

In the name of progress and developing the desert, the great river canyons of Arizona have been dammed. Their sometimes quiet, sometimes angry waters have been turned into vast lakes. Among these is Lake Powell, created by the construction of the Glen Canyon Dam. The bitter fight to preserve Glen Canyon has is a thing of the past, and today the lake is popular with boaters, anglers, and water-skiers. This lake, with its miles of water mirroring steep canyon walls hundreds of feet high, is one of northern Arizona's curious contrasts—a vast man-made reservoir in the middle of barren desert canyons.

1 Flagstaff

150 miles N of Phoenix, 32 miles E of Williams, 80 miles S of Grand Canyon Village

Flagstaff is the best all-around staging point for explorations of the Grand Canyon and the rest of northern Arizona, and its university supports a lively cultural community and is also home to one of the finest museums in Arizona—the Museum of Northern Arizona. The

What's Special About Northern Arizona

Indian Ruins
- The ancient Sinagua pueblos of Wupatki National Monument.
- The Sinagua cliff dwellings of Walnut Canyon National Monument.

Museums
- The Museum of Northern Arizona in Flagstaff.

Events/Festivals
- Hopi, Navajo, and Zuñi festivals at the Museum of Northern Arizona.

Natural Spectacles
- The Grand Canyon, one of the earth's greatest natural wonders.
- Sunset Crater, a colorful cinder cone near Flagstaff.
- The beautiful waterfalls of Havasu Canyon, an oasis in the desert.
- Meteor Crater, the world's largest and best-preserved meteorite crater, located east of Flagstaff.

Activities
- Rafting through the Grand Canyon on the Colorado River.
- Riding a mule to the bottom of the Grand Canyon.
- Hiking into Havasu Canyon.
- Houseboating on Lake Powell, the best way to explore this huge man-made lake and water-sports paradise in the middle of the desert.

San Francisco Peaks, just outside the city, are one of Arizona's winter playgrounds, with the Arizona Snowbowl attracting thousands of skiers to the slopes. In summer, sightseers ride the lift to the top of the mountain for the views and hikers come to explore the miles of mountain trails. Hikers and photographers also enjoy exploring Sunset Crater National Monument, a colorful cinder cone created by a volcanic eruption hundreds of years ago.

Situated at 7,000 feet above sea level, Flagstaff is one of the highest cities in the country, and is the county seat of Coconino County, the second-largest county in the United States. The town has done much to preserve its pioneer heritage, but its history goes much farther back. Within a short drive of the city are ancient Sinagua cliff dwellings and the ruins of large pueblos that were built more than 700 years ago.

ESSENTIALS
GETTING THERE

By Plane Flagstaff's Pulliam Airport is served by America West Express (call 800/235-9292 for flight information). The airport is located 3 miles south of town off I-17.

By Train Flagstaff is served by Amtrak (call 520/774-8679, or 800/872-7245, for schedule information) from Chicago and Los Angeles. The train station is at 1 E. Rte. 66.

By Bus Flagstaff is served by Greyhound Bus Lines. The bus station is at 399 S. Malpias Lane; call 520/774-4573 for schedule information.

By Car Flagstaff is on I-40, one of the main east-west Interstates in the United States. I-17 also starts here and heads south to Phoenix. U.S. 89A connects

Flagstaff to Sedona by way of Oak Creek Canyon. U.S. 180 connects Flagstaff with Grand Canyon Village, and U.S. 89 with Page.

VISITOR INFORMATION

The **Flagstaff Visitors' Center,** at 1 E. Rte. 66 (☎ **520/774-9541** or 800/842-7293), is open Monday through Saturday from 8am to 7pm (to 6pm in winter) and on Sunday from 8am to 5pm.

GETTING AROUND

By Car Car rentals are available from **Budget** (☎ **520/779-0307** or 800/527-0700) and **Hertz** (☎ **520/774-4452** or 800/654-3131).

By Taxi For a taxi, call **Friendly Cab** (☎ **520/774-4444**).

By Bus **Pine Country Transit** (☎ **520/779-6624**), provides public bus transit around the city; the fare is 75¢ for adults. In summer, **Flagstaff Trolleybuses** operate between many of Flagstaff's hotels, the downtown area, the university, and most of the city's museums. A day pass costs $4. Phone **Nava-Hopi Tours** (☎ **520/774-5003**) for more information.

ORIENTATION

Downtown Flagstaff is located just north of I-40. Milton Road, which at its southern end becomes I-17 to Phoenix, leads past the Northern Arizona University on its way into downtown. Santa Fe Avenue runs parallel to the railroad tracks. Downtown's main street is San Francisco Street, while Humphreys Street leads north out of town toward the San Francisco Peaks and the south rim of the Grand Canyon.

Foreign currency can be exchanged at **Bank One,** which has offices at 100 W. Birch St. (☎ **520/779-7411**) and 2520 N. Fourth St. (☎ **520/779-7351**).

WHAT TO SEE & DO

Downtown Flagstaff along Santa Fe Avenue, San Francisco Street, Aspen Avenue, and Birch Avenue is the city's **historic district.** The old brick buildings of this neighborhood are now filled with interesting little shops selling Native American handcrafts, art and crafts by local artisans, and various other Arizona souvenirs such as rocks, minerals, and crystals. This historic area is worth a walk through even if you aren't shopping.

MUSEUMS, PARKS & CULTURAL ACTIVITIES

✪ Museum of Northern Arizona

3001 N. Fort Valley Rd. (U.S. 180). ☎ **520/774-5211.** Admission $4 adults, $3 seniors, $2 children. Daily 9am–5pm. Closed Jan 1, Thanksgiving, and Dec 25.

Located 2 miles north of downtown Flagstaff on U.S. 180, this small but surprisingly thorough museum is a good first stop to acquaint yourself with the Flagstaff area. Here you'll learn in state-of-the-art exhibits about the archeology, ethnology, geology, biology, and fine arts of the region. The cornerstone exhibit of the museum is "Native Peoples of the Colorado Plateau," an exploration of life on the Colorado Plateau from 15,000 B.C. to the present. Among the other displays are a life-size kiva ceremonial room and an small but interesting collection of kachinas. The large gift shop is full of contemporary Native American arts and crafts. Throughout the summer there are special exhibits focusing on Hopi, Navajo, and Zuñi arts and crafts.

The museum building itself is made of native stone and incorporates into its design a courtyard featuring vegetation from the six life zones of northern Arizona. Outside the museum is a short self-guided nature trail that leads through a narrow canyon strewn with boulders.

Coconino Center for the Arts

2300 N. Fort Valley Rd. (U.S. 180). ☎ **520/779-6921.** Exhibits, free; performances, $5–$14. Oct–Mar, Tues–Sat 10am–5pm; Apr–Sept, Tues–Sun 10am–5pm. Evening hours for performances vary. Closed Easter Sun, Thanksgiving, and Dec 25–Jan 6.

Throughout the year various exhibits and performances are held at this well-designed center north of downtown. The center offers visual and performing arts, and literary programs, with the focus on regional artists.

Lowell Observatory

1400 W. Mars Hill Rd. ☎ **520/774-2096.** Admission $2.50 adults, $1 children. Visitor center, Apr–Oct, daily 9am–5pm; Nov–Mar, Mon–Sat 10am–5pm, Sun noon–5pm. Evening viewing through telescope more frequent in summer than in winter.

Located atop aptly named Mars Hill is one of the oldest astronomical observatories in the Southwest. Founded in 1894 by Percival Lowell, the observatory has played important roles in contemporary astronomy. Among the work carried out here was Lowell's study of the planet Mars and his calculations that led him to predict the existence of the planet Pluto. It wasn't until 13 years after Lowell's death that Pluto was finally discovered, almost exactly where he had predicted it would be. Today this is still an important research facility, but most astronomical observations are now carried out at Anderson Mesa, which is 10 miles farther away from the lights of Flagstaff.

The facility consists of several observatories, a large new visitor center, and outdoor exhibits. Keep in mind that the telescope domes are not heated, so if you come up to observe the stars on a wintry night be sure to dress appropriately.

Arizona Historical Society/Pioneer Museum

2340 N. Fort Valley Rd. (U.S. 180). ☎ **520/774-6272.** Admission $1 donation. Mon–Sat 9am–5pm. Closed Jan 1, Thanksgiving, and Dec 25.

Located next door to the Coconino Center for the Arts, this museum houses a historical collection from northern Arizona's pioneer days. The main museum building is a large stone structure that was built in 1908 as a hospital for the indigent. Among the exhibits are pieces of camera equipment used by Emery Kolb at his studio on the South Rim of the Grand Canyon. Many of Kolb's photos are also on display. Several small exhibit rooms cover various aspects of life in northern Arizona during the pioneer days and later. You'll see a doctor's office filled with frightening instruments, barbed wire and brands, dolls, saddles, and trapping and timber displays.

Riordan Mansion State Park

1300 Riordan Ranch Rd. ☎ **520/779-4395.** Admission $3 adults, $2 students, free for children. May–Sept, daily 8am–5pm; Oct–Apr, daily 12:30–5pm. Closed Dec 25.

Built in 1904 for local timber barons Michael and Timothy Riordan, this 13,000-square-foot mansion is unusual in that it's actually two houses connected by a large central hall. Each Riordan brother and his family occupied one half. The two halves of the mansion have different rooflines, so visitors can tell the two apart. The home is built in the Craftsmen style and though it looks like a log cabin, it's

The Grand Canyon & Northern Arizona

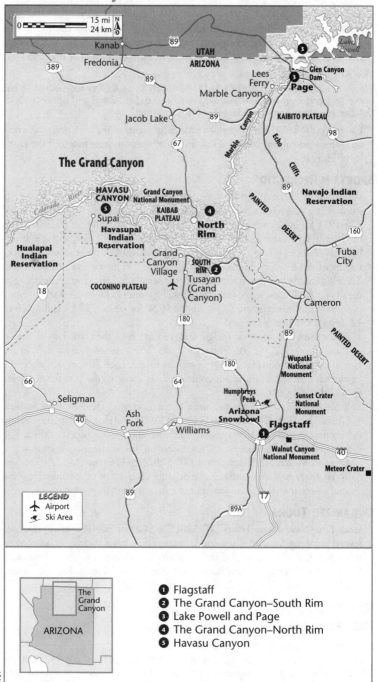

1 Flagstaff
2 The Grand Canyon–South Rim
3 Lake Powell and Page
4 The Grand Canyon–North Rim
5 Havasu Canyon

actually only faced with log slabs. The Riordans played important roles in the early history of Flagstaff. They helped establish the first Roman Catholic church, the first library, the power company, and the phone company. You'll find the Riordan Mansion off Milton Road (U.S. 89A) just north of the junction of I-40 and I-17.

The Arboretum at Flagstaff

Woody Mountain Rd. ☎ **520/774-1441.** Admission $3 adults, free for children 18 and under. May and Sept, Mon–Sat 10am–3pm; June–Aug, Sat 10am–3pm, Sun noon–3pm. Oct–Dec 23, 10am–3pm. Guided tours at 11am and 1pm.

Covering 200 acres, this arboretum focuses on plants of the high desert, coniferous forests, and alpine tundra, all of which are environments found in the vicinity of Flagstaff.

Sports & Recreation

Flagstaff is northern Arizona's center for outdoor activities. Chief among these is snow skiing at **Arizona Snowbowl** on the slopes of Mount Agassiz (☎ **520/ 779-1951** for information or 520/779-4577 for a snow report, or 602/957-0404 in Phoenix for a snow report). There are four chair lifts, 32 runs, and 2,300 vertical feet of slopes. There are also ski rentals and a children's ski program. Lift tickets range from $18 for a half-day midweek pass to $30 for a weekend all-day pass. There's a shuttle bus that operates from highway U.S. 180, as well as parking at the top for 1,000 cars. In the summer the ski lift carries anyone who wants to enjoy the views. Summer rates are $9 for adults, $6.50 for seniors, $5 for children 6 to 12, free for children 5 and under.

When there's no snow on the ground, you can **hike the trails** here at the ski area and throughout the San Francisco Peaks. Many national forest trails in the area are open to mountain bikes as well as hikers. Late September, when the aspens have turned to a brilliant golden yellow, is one of the best times of year for a hike in Flagstaff's mountains.

If you feel like saddlin' up and hittin' the trail, contact **Hitchin' Post Stables,** 448 Lake Mary Rd. (☎ **520/774-1719** or 520/774-7131). This horseback-riding stable offers guided trail rides, sunset steak rides, and cowboy breakfast rides. The most popular trail ride goes into Walnut Canyon, site of ancient cliff dwellings.

Arizona Mountain Bike Tours (☎ **520/779-4161** or 800/277-7985 in Arizona) offers guided mountain-bike rides for all levels of experience. Trips are around Flagstaff or to the canyons and volcanos of northern Arizona.

Organized Tours

Gray Line/Nava-Hopi Tours (☎ **520/774-5003** or 800/892-8687) operates several day-long tours of northern Arizona. These tours include excursions to the South Rim of the Grand Canyon; Wupatki and Sunset Crater; Monument Valley and the Navajo Indian Reservation; the Petrified Forest, Painted Desert, and Meteor Crater; and the Hopi Indian Reservation.

WHERE TO STAY
Very Expensive

Residence Inn Flagstaff

3440 N. Country Club Rd., Flagstaff, AZ 86004. ☎ **520/526-5555** or 800/331-3131. Fax 520/527-0328. 102 studios and suites. May–Sept, $159–$199 studio or suite for two; Oct–Apr, $69–$159 studio or suite for two. Rates include continental breakfast. AE, CB, DC, MC, V.

Located on the eastern outskirts of Flagstaff, this hotel is designed to resemble an apartment complex, and though it's a bit of a drive to downtown, the surroundings are quieter and less congested. Directly across the street is a golf course. The rooms are either studios or two-bedroom suites, and all have kitchenettes. Services include complimentary cocktail hour, morning newspaper, airport shuttle, and a grocery shopping service. Facilities include an outdoor pool, whirlpool spa, exercise room, and coin laundry.

MODERATE

Arizona Mountain Inn

685 Lake Mary Rd., Flagstaff, AZ 86001. ☎ **520/774-8959.** 3 rms, 16 cabins. $75–$105 double. DISC, MC, V.

Located just a few minutes south of downtown Flagstaff, the Arizona Mountain Inn is a quiet mountain retreat set beneath shady pine trees. Though there are three bed-and-breakfast rooms in the main building, all the rest of the accommodations here are cabins that can sleep anywhere from 2 to 16 people. Many of the rustic cabins are A-frames or chalets and each is a little bit different from the others. The family-oriented inn has 13 acres surrounding it, and beyond this are miles of national forest. Facilities include volleyball, horseshoes, basketball court, playground, coin laundry.

✪ Best Western Woodlands Plaza Hotel

1175 W. Rte. 66, Flagstaff, AZ 86001. ☎ **520/773-8888** or 800/528-1234. Fax 520/773-0597. 183 rms, 2 suites. A/C TV TEL. $69–$139 double or suite. AE, CB, DC, DISC, MC, V.

With its elegant marble-floored lobby, the Woodlands Plaza would easily fit in on Scottsdale's resort row. A baby grand piano, crystal chandelier, traditional European furnishings, and contemporary sculpture all add to the unexpected luxury, as do intricately carved pieces of furniture and architectural details from different Asian countries. Traditional European styling, with southwestern touches, is used in the guest-room decor.

One of the two restaurants here serves Japanese meals with tableside cooking and a sushi bar, while the other features traditional American fare with a few international and southwestern dishes. The hotel also offers room service, an outdoor pool, two whirlpools, a sauna, steam room, and fitness center.

Embassy Suites

706 S. Milton Rd., Flagstaff, AZ 86001. ☎ **520/774-4333** or 800/EMBASSY. Fax 520/774-0216. 102 suites. A/C TV TEL. $99–$190 suite for two. Rates include full breakfast. AE, DC, DISC, ER, JCB, MC, V.

Conveniently located near the Northern Arizona University and downtown Flagstaff, this all-suite hotel is a good choice for families or business travelers. Plenty of space and a convenient in-town location may give this more appeal than the Marriott Residence Inn. Breakfast is served in a bright, plant-filled room, and in the evening complimentary cocktails are served in a librarylike lounge. The guest rooms are all divided into sleeping rooms and living rooms, with wet bar, refrigerator, microwave oven, two TVs, two phones, and an AM/FM stereo. The hotel also has a pool and whirlpool.

Little America

2515 E. Butler Ave., Flagstaff, AZ 86003. ☎ **520/779-2741** or 800/352-4386. Fax 520/779-7983. 248 rms, 9 suites. A/C TV TEL. $65–$109 double; $125–$225 suite. AE, CB, DC, DISC, MC, V.

At first it might seem as if Little Americas, of which there are several around the West, are little more than glorified truck stops, but on closer inspection you'll find that this Little America is an excellent economy hotel. It's a spread-out complex beneath the pines on the east side of Flagstaff at Exit 198 from I-40. The rooms vary in size but all have small private balconies. The interior decor is dated but fun, with a French provincial theme throughout the guest rooms. The televisions are absolutely huge.

There's a casual dining room that's open 24 hours a day, plus a more formal restaurant that serves continental dishes and features live piano music in the evenings. The hotel also offers room service, laundry/dry cleaning, courtesy van, a pool, health club passes, badminton, volleyball, croquet, and jogging/hiking trails.

A Bed & Breakfast

✪ The Inn at 410

410 N. Leroux St., Flagstaff, AZ 86001. ☎ **520/774-0088** or 800/774-2008. 8 rms. $90–$135 double. Rates include full breakfast. AE, MC, V.

Located only two blocks from downtown Flagstaff, this restored 1907 bungalow provides convenience, pleasant surroundings, comfortable rooms, and delicious breakfasts. The rooms are all individually decorated (our favorites are the cowboy-theme room and the Santa Fe room). The living room and dining room are very bright, and in addition, you'll find a large front porch with a swing and a patio dining area. Upstairs rooms can have odd layouts, but there are plans to remodel this floor. Some of the rooms are in a new building to one side of the old house, and one of these rooms is wheelchair accessible.

INEXPENSIVE

In addition to the hotel listed below, you'll also find many budget chain motels in Flagstaff. These include the following (rates listed are for summer, which is the high season in Flagstaff): **Econo Lodge,** 2355 S. Beulah Blvd., Flagstaff, AZ 86001 (☎ **520/774-2225**), offering $79 to $95 double; **Motel 6,** 2440 E. Lucky Lane, Flagstaff, AZ 86004 (☎ **520/774-8756**), $44 double; **Motel 6,** 2745 S. Woodlands Village, Flagstaff, AZ 86001 (☎ **520/779-3757**), $38 double; **Super 8 Motel,** 3725 Kasper Ave., Flagstaff, AZ 86004 (☎ **520/526-0818**), $54 to $68 double; and **Travelodge,** 2520 E. Lucky Lane, Flagstaff, AZ 86004 (☎ **520/779-5121**), $54 to $78 double.

✪ Hotel Monte Vista

100 N. San Francisco St., Flagstaff, AZ 86001. ☎ **520/779-6971** or 800/545-3068. Fax 520/779-2904. 65 rms, 58 with bath; 5 suites; 3 dorm beds. TV TEL. $25–$30 double without bath, $40–$85 double with bath; $80–$110 suite. Lower rates in winter. AE, MC, V.

Originally opened in 1927, the Hotel Monte Vista was renovated in the mid-1980s and is today a historic budget hotel with old-fashioned flair. In its heyday the Monte Vista is said to have hosted Clark Gable, John Wayne, Walter Brennan, Alan Ladd, Jane Russell, Spencer Tracy, Lee Marvin, Carole Lombard, and Gary Cooper. In the small, dark lobby (which is still a bit the worse for wear) are painted ceiling beams and Victorian furniture. Shops and a rather noisy bar take up most of the space on the ground floor. The rooms vary in size and many are furnished with oak furniture and ceiling fans. We like the corner rooms best because they have windows on two sides. You'll find a coffee shop and lounge on the first floor. The hotel also has a dormitory for hostelers, with a few beds going for $12 a night.

WHERE TO DINE
EXPENSIVE

Chez Marc Bistro

503 Humphreys St. ☎ **520/774-1343.** Reservations recommended. Main courses $16–$20; four-course *menu dégustation* $32. AE, DC, MC, V. Daily 11:30am–3pm and 5:30–9pm. Closed lunch spring–fall. FRENCH.

If it weren't for the busy street in front, this stone and half-timbered house could pass as a country inn. The renovated old house has a big front porch and inside are several small dining rooms, one of which has a cozy fireplace. Creative combinations are the rule here. Though the menu is ostensibly French, astute observers might notice that the smoked salmon and beluga sturgeon appetizers are prepared with capers and lime juice. Though it might not seem so, tenderloin of pork and duck leg confit with lobster mushrooms and carmelized apple in a sage demi-glace is one of several dishes that appear on the menu that's lower in calories, cholesterol, and sodium than other choices. The wine list is excellent.

MODERATE

Black Bart's

2760 E. Butler Ave. ☎ **520/779-3142.** Reservations recommended. Main courses $11–$24. AE, MC, V. Sun–Thurs 5–9pm, Fri–Sat 5–10pm (until 9pm in winter). STEAK/SEAFOOD.

Arizona is full of odd restaurants and Black Bart's must surely be classified as one of the most unusual. A part of an RV park and antiques store, this warehouse-size restaurant serves gigantic steaks complete with cowboy beans, "leaves-and-weeds" salads, and sourdough biscuits. But the real draw is the entertainment, provided by a player piano and the service staff (local university students), who get up on stage and sing for your supper.

○ Brix Grill & Wine Bar

801 S. Milton Rd. ☎ **520/779-5117.** Reservations recommended. Main courses $11–$16. AE, DC, MC, V. Mon–Thurs 11am–3pm and 5–10pm, Fri–Sat 11am–3pm and 5–10:30pm, Sun 5–10pm. SOUTHWESTERN/MEDITERRANEAN.

Located in a nondescript shopping plaza, Brix is currently Flagstaff's most innovative restaurant. Dishes have a distinctly southwestern slant, and ingredients are always fresh. On our last visit, the chilled avocado soup with smoked salmon and red- and yellow-pepper confetti was almost a meal in itself. Chicken breast was prepared with a slightly sweet Bing-cherry-and-bourbon barbecue sauce. The decor is a surprisingly sophisticated renovation of an old shopping plaza store, with gleaming copper in the open kitchen and wine racks everywhere. There's a little wine bar tucked into one corner. The lunch dishes are quite creative, and prices are much lower than in the evening. The Marketplace Deli is next door, where you can buy wines and food to go.

Cottage Place Restaurant

126 W. Cottage Ave. ☎ **520/774-8431.** Reservations required. Main courses $13–$22.50. AE, MC, V. Tues–Sun 5–9:30pm. CONTINENTAL.

Located in a rather run-down neighborhood between the railroad tracks and the university, Cottage Place is just what its name implies—a little cottage. There are a few tables in each of the dining rooms, so dining here is an intimate affair. We like the front rooms with their walls of windows, especially at sunset on a summer evening. Though the menu is primarily continental, there are French, southwestern, and middle eastern influences as well. The house specialties are chateaubriand and rack of lamb (both served for two), and for vegetarians there's a delicious polenta gratin stuffed with fresh vegetables and chipotle salsa and baked with Cheddar cheese. Every evening there's a different selection of tempting desserts.

Kelly's Christmas Tree Restaurant

5200 E. Cortland Blvd. ☎ **520/526-0776.** Reservations recommended. Main courses $8–$20. MC, V. Mon–Sat 11:30am–3pm and 5–10pm, Sun 4–9pm. AMERICAN.

This oddly named restaurant has long been a Flagstaff favorite of retirees and is located in a shopping center on the east side of town. A festive holiday atmosphere reigns year round in the red, white, and green dining room. The menu runs the gamut from sautéed chicken livers to curried chicken to beef Stroganoff. There are daily seafood specials as well as such menu standards as tender sautéed scallops. Chicken and dumplings is Kelly's most popular dish.

Sakura Restaurant

In the Woodlands Plaza Hotel, 1175 W. Rte. 66. ☎ **520/773-8888.** Reservations recommended. Main courses $10–$18. AE, DC, DISC, MC, V. Mon–Sat 11:30am–2pm and 5–10pm, Sun 5–10pm. JAPANESE.

Though major cities around the world have had teppanyaki Japanese restaurants in the form of Benihanas for years, this style of tableside cooking is fairly new to Flagstaff and it has made quite a hit. Dinner or lunch here is an event, with the chef's culinary floor show at a grill in front of your table. Steaks, grilled seafood, and chicken are the mainstays of the menu, but there's also sushi made with fresh fish flown in from Los Angeles, crispy tempura, and warming miso soup for cold winter nights. Shoji screens give the dining room a Japanese atmosphere.

INEXPENSIVE

Ⓢ Beaver Street Brewery

11 S. Beaver St. ☎ **520/779-0079.** Main courses $6.25–$8. AE, DISC, MC, V. Daily 11:30am–midnight. BURGERS/PIZZA.

This big microbrewery and café located in a former supermarket on the south side of the railroad tracks serves up several good brews, but it also does great pizzas and burgers. We liked the Beaver Street pizza, which is made with roasted garlic pesto, sun-dried tomatoes, fresh basil, and soft goat cheese. There are also good salads, such as a shaved sirloin salad with sesame-ginger dressing, and even fondue. A potbellied stove surrounded by easy chairs and a selection of reading material make this place feel homey.

Café Espress

16 N. San Francisco St. ☎ **520/774-0541.** Dinner $4.50–$8.50. MC, V. Sun–Thurs 7am–10pm, Fri–Sat 7am–11pm. INTERNATIONAL/VEGETARIAN.

Grab an alternative newspaper from the table by the front door, sit down at one of the tables by the front window, and ensconce yourself in college life all over again. If you happen to be still in school, this place will certainly be your favorite dining spot in Flagstaff. You can start the day with granola, move on to tempeh or turkey burgers for lunch, and then have spanakopita for dinner.

Café Olé

119 S. San Francisco St. ☎ **520/774-8272.** Reservations not accepted. Main dishes $5–$8. No credit cards. Mon–Thurs 11am–7:30pm, Fri 11am–8pm. MEXICAN.

This tiny hole-in-the-wall Mexican cantina serves up some of the freshest Mexican food in Flagstaff. The salsa is appropriately fiery and flavorful, but we found our other dishes to be overly spicy. The menu is short and changes regularly, so you can expect to find daily specials and a few surprises whenever you visit.

Macy's European Coffee House and Bakery

14 S. Beaver St. ☎ **520/774-2243.** Meals $4.50–$6.50. No credit cards. Sun–Wed 6am–8pm, Thurs–Sat 6am–10pm. COFFEE/BAKERY.

Good espresso and baked goodies are what draw people in here the first time, but there are also decent pasta dishes, soups, salads, and other old simple, college-town standbys. There are plenty of vegetarian dishes and sandwiches as well. This is a great place to meet local students.

⑤ Pasto

19 E. Aspen St. ☎ **520/779-1937.** Reservations recommended. Main dishes $7–$14. MC, V. Sun–Thurs 5–9:30pm, Fri–Sat 5–10pm (later in summer). ITALIAN.

Operated by the same folks who run Café Espress, Pasto is a health-conscious Italian restaurant in downtown Flagstaff popular with the hip and young-at-heart. The sign outside says FUN ITALIAN DINING, which gives an indication of the flamboyant decor and casual atmosphere here. The menu includes a good assortment of pastas, of course, but there are also dishes such as eggplant parmigiana and artichoke orzo.

FLAGSTAFF AFTER DARK

Check the local newspaper for events taking place on the campus of Northern Arizona University. The university has many musical and theatrical groups that perform throughout most of the year.

Each summer, the **Flagstaff Festival of the Arts,** P.O. Box 1607, Flagstaff, AZ 86002. (☎ **520/774-7750** or 800/266-7740), brings to the city a month's worth of performances that are scheduled at venues around the city. Ticket prices range from $15 to $40 for individual events.

The rest of the year, the **Flagstaff Symphony Orchestra** (☎ **520/774-5107**) provides the city with a full season of classical music. Performances are held at Ardrey Auditorium on Knoles Drive on the campus of Northern Arizona University. Tickets prices range from $11 to $22.

The city's community theater group, **Theatrikos** (☎ **520/774-1662**), performs at the Flagstaff Playhouse, 11 W. Cherry St. Tickets are $7 to $10.

For a livelier scene, check out the **Museum Club,** 3404 E. Rte. 66 (☎ **520/526-9434**). Built in the early 1900s and often called the Zoo Club, this cavernous log saloon is filled with deer antlers, stuffed animals, and trophy heads. There's live music, predominantly country-and-western, with varying admission prices, and country swing dance lessons (call for times). Willie Nelson, John Lee Hooker, Dr. Hook, Asleep at the Wheel, and Mose Allison are some of the musicians who have appeared here in the past. If you call 520/774-4444 you can get a complimentary ride to and from the Museum Club.

EASY EXCURSIONS FROM FLAGSTAFF

Meteor Crater

I-40, 35 miles east of Flagstaff. ☎ **520/289-2362.** Admission $7 adults, $6 senior citizens, $2 children 13–17, $1 children 6–12, free for children 5 and under. May 15–Sept 15, daily 6am–6pm; Sept 16–May 14, daily 8am–5pm.

In the middle of the barren desert east of Flagstaff lies a gaping hole in the earth. Standing on a platform on the crater rim it's difficult to imagine the instant devastation that occurred 49,000 years ago when a meteorite estimated to be about 100 feet in diameter slammed into the ground here at 45,000 miles per hour. Today the Meteor Crater is 570 feet deep and nearly a mile across. Billed as "this planet's most penetrating natural attraction," Meteor Crater is the best-preserved crater in the world. The resemblance of the crater landscape to the surface of the moon prompted NASA to use this area as a training site for Apollo program astronauts. There's a small museum, part of which is dedicated to the exploration of space, and an Apollo space capsule on display. The rest of the museum is devoted to astrogeology and includes a meteorite weighing nearly three-quarters of a ton.

✪ Wupatki National Monument

36 miles north of Flagstaff off U.S. 89. ☎ **520/556-7040.** Admission $4 per car. Daily sunrise–sunset; visitor center, daily 8am–5pm (until 6pm in summer). Closed Dec 25.

The landscape northeast of Flagstaff is desolate and windswept, a sparsely populated region carpeted with volcanic ash deposited in the 11th century. It comes as quite a surprise, then, to learn that this area contains hundreds of prehistoric and historic habitation sites. The most impressive ruins are those left by the Sinagua (the name means "without water" in Spanish) people who inhabited this area from around A.D. 1100 until shortly after A.D. 1200. The Sinagua people built small villages of stone similar to the pueblos on the nearby Hopi reservation, and today the ruins of these ancient villages can still be seen.

The largest of the prehistoric pueblos is **Wupatki ruin** in the southeastern part of the monument. Here the Sinagua built a sprawling three-story pueblo containing nearly 100 rooms. Though the ball court here is quite different from the courts of the Aztec and Maya, there's no doubt that a similar game was played. Another circular stone structure just below the main ruins may have been an amphitheater or dance plaza.

Wupatki ruin is also the site of the **visitor center.** Inside you'll find interesting exhibits on the Sinagua and Anasazi people who once inhabited the region.

The most unusual feature of Wupatki, however, is a natural phenomenon—a blowhole—that may have been the reason for building the pueblo on this site. A network of small underground tunnels and chambers acts as a giant barometer, blowing air through the blowhole when the underground air is under greater pressure than the outside air. On hot days, cool air rushes out of the blowhole with amazing force.

Several **other ruins** within the national monument are easily accessible by car. These include Nalakihu, Citadel, and Lomaki, which are the closest to U.S. 89, and Wukoki, which is near Wupatki. Wukoki ruin is built atop a huge sandstone boulder and is particularly picturesque.

Sunset Crater National Monument

18 miles north of Flagstaff off U.S. 89. ☎ **520/556-7042.** Admission $4 per car (includes admission to Wupatki National Monument). Daily sunrise–sunset; visitor center, daily 8am–5pm (until 6pm in summer). Closed Dec 25.

Dotting the landscape northeast of Flagstaff are more than 400 volcanic craters, of which Sunset Crater is the youngest. Taking its name from the sunset colors of the cinders near its summit, Sunset Crater stands 1,000 feet tall and began forming in A.D. 1064. Over a period of 100 years the volcano erupted repeatedly, creating the red-and-yellow cinder cone we see today and eventually covering an area of 800 square miles with ash, lava, and cinders. There's a mile-long interpretative trail that passes through a desolate landscape of lava flows, cinders, and ash as it skirts the base of Sunset Crater. In the **visitor center** you can learn more about the formation of Sunset Crater and about volcanoes in general.

Near the visitor center at the west entrance to the national monument is a small **campground** that's open from spring to fall.

Walnut Canyon National Monument

Walnut Canyon Rd. ☎ **520/526-3367.** Admission $4 per car. Daily 8am–5pm (until 6pm in summer). Closed Dec 25.

The remains of hundreds of 13th-century Sinagua cliff dwellings can be seen in a dry, wooded canyon 7 miles east of Flagstaff. The undercut layers of limestone in this 400-foot-deep canyon proved ideal for building dwellings well protected both from the elements and from enemies. The Sinagua were the same people who built and then abandoned the stone pueblos found in Wupatki National Monument. It's theorized that when the land to the north lost its fertility, the Sinagua began migrating southward, and settled for 150 years in Walnut Canyon.

A self-guided trail leads from the visitor center on the canyon rim down 185 feet to a section of the canyon wall where 25 cliff dwellings can be viewed and entered. Look closely and you can see handprints in the mud that was used to cement the dwellings' stone walls together. There's also a picnic area near the visitor center.

2 The Grand Canyon: South Rim

60 miles N of Williams, 80 miles NE of Flagstaff, 230 miles N of Phoenix, 340 miles N of Tucson

A strange hush clings to the edge of this mile-deep canyon. It's the hush of reverential awe. For the first-time visitor to the canyon, there's no better approach than from the south, across the barren windswept scrubland of the Colorado Plateau. You hardly notice the elevation gain and the change to pine and juniper forest. Suddenly—it's there. No preliminaries, no warnings. Stark, quiet, a maze of colors and cathedrals sculpted by nature.

A mile deep and 18 miles wide in places, the Grand Canyon is truly one of the great wonders of the world, and it comes as no surprise to learn that the cartographers who mapped the area sensed the spiritual beauty of the canyon. Their reverence is reflected in the names of its formations: Apollo Temple, Venus Temple, Thor Temple, Zoroaster Temple, Horus Temple, Buddha Temple, Vishnu Temple, Krishna Temple, Shiva Temple, Confucius Temple, the Tabernacle, Solomon Temple, Angels Gate.

Banded layers of sandstone, limestone, shale, and schist give the canyon its color, and the interplay of shadows and light from dawn to dusk creates an ever-changing palette of hues and textures. Written in these bands of stone are more than two *billion* years of history. Formed by the cutting action of the Colorado River as it flows through the Kaibab Plateau, the Grand Canyon is an open book exposing the secrets of the geologic history of this region. Geologists believe that it has taken between three and six million years for the Colorado River to carve the Grand Canyon, but the canyon's history extends much further back in time. Millions of years ago vast seas covered this region. Sediments carried by seawater were deposited and over millions of years turned into sedimentary limestone and sandstone. When the ancient seabed was thrust upward to form the Kaibab Plateau, the Colorado River began its work of cutting through the plateau. Today 21 sedimentary layers, the oldest of which is more than a billion years old, can be seen in the canyon. However, beneath all these layers, at the very bottom, is a stratum of rock so old that it has been metamorphosed, under great pressure and heat, from soft shale to a much harder stone called schist. Called Vishnu schist, this layer is the oldest rock in the Grand Canyon and dates back two billion years.

In the more recent past the Grand Canyon has been home to several Native American cultures, including the Anasazi, who are best known for their cliff dwellings in the Four Corners region. About 150 years after the Anasazi and Coconino peoples abandoned the canyon in the 13th century, another tribe, the Cerbat, moved into the area. The Hualapai and Havasupai tribes, descendents of the Cerbat people, still live in and near the Grand Canyon on the south side of the Colorado River. On the North Rim lived the Southern Paiute, and in the west the Navajo.

In 1540 Spanish explorer Garcia Lopez de Cárdenas became the first European to set eyes on the Grand Canyon. However, it would be another 329 years before the first expedition would travel through the entire canyon. John Wesley Powell, a one-armed Civil War veteran, was deemed crazy when he set off to navigate the Colorado River in wooden boats. His small band of men spent 98 days traveling 1,000 miles down the Green and Colorado rivers. Their expedition was not without mishap. When some boats were wrecked by the powerful rapids, part of the group abandoned the journey and set out on foot, never to be heard from again.

Today the Grand Canyon is the last major undammed section of the Colorado River, and the river, which once carried more than half a million tons of sand and silt with it every 24 hours, now flows cold and clear from the bottom of the upriver Glen Canyon Dam. By raft, by mule, on foot, in helicopters and small planes—five million people come to the canyon each year seeking one of nature's meccas.

ESSENTIALS
GETTING THERE

By Plane   The Grand Canyon Airport is 6 miles south of Grand Canyon Village in Tusayan (Grand Canyon). It's served by **Air Nevada Airlines** (☎ 703/736-8900 or 800/634-6377), which charges $109 one way from Las Vegas ($59 if you leave before 6:30am) and $159 round-trip; and **Scenic Airlines** (☎ 702/739-1900 or 800/634-6801), which charges $119 one way and $159 round-trip.

By Train   The **Grand Canyon Railway,** Grand Canyon Railway Depot, Grand Canyon Boulevard (☎ 800/843-8724), operates vintage steam locomotives and 1920s coaches between Williams and Grand Canyon Village. Round-trip fares (including park entrance fees) range from $58 to $113 for adults and $21 to $76 for children 2 to 16. It's possible to ride up one day and return on a different day—just let the reservationist know.

For long-distance connections, **Amtrak** (☎ 520/774-8679 or 800/872-7245) provides service to Flagstaff. From Flagstaff it's then possible to take a bus directly to Grand Canyon Village. Another option is to take a Greyhound bus to Williams and then take the steam train from there to Grand Canyon Village.

By Bus   Bus service between Phoenix, Flagstaff, Williams, and Grand Canyon Village is provided by **Nava-Hopi Tours** (☎ 520/774-5003 or 800/892-8687). A round-trip ticket between Phoenix and Flagstaff is $43, and a round-trip ticket from Flagstaff to Grand Canyon Village is $25.

Greyhound Lines has service to Flagstaff from around the country and also offers service between Flagstaff and Williams.

By Car   In the past few years parking problems, traffic jams, and traffic congestion have become the norm at Grand Canyon Village during the popular summer months. If at all possible, we suggest that you travel into the park by some means *other* than car. (Alternatives include taking the Grand Canyon Railway from Williams, flying into the Grand Canyon Airport and then taking the Tusayan–Grand Canyon Shuttle or a taxi, or taking the Nava-Hopi Tours bus service from either Williams or Flagstaff.) There are plenty of scenic overlooks, hiking trails, restaurants, and lodges in the village area, and a free shuttle operates along the West Rim Drive in summer.

If you do drive, be sure that you have plenty of gasoline in your car before setting out for the canyon; there are few service stations in this remote part of the state. The South Rim of the Grand Canyon is 60 miles north of Williams and I-40 on Ariz. 64 and U.S. 180. Flagstaff, the nearest city of any size, is 78 miles away. From Flagstaff it's possible to take U.S. 180 directly to the South Rim or U.S. 89 to Ariz. 64 and the east entrance to the park.

VISITOR INFORMATION

You can get information on the Grand Canyon before leaving home by contacting the **Grand Canyon National Park,** P.O. Box 129, Grand Canyon, AZ 86023-0129 (☎ **520/638-7888**).

Once there, you should stop by the **Grand Canyon National Park Visitor Center,** located on Village Loop Drive 6 miles north of the south entrance. Here you'll find an information desk, brochures, exhibits about the canyon, and a bookshop selling maps as well as books about the canyon. The center is open daily from 8am to 6pm (later in summer). **The Guide,** a small newspaper crammed full of useful information about the park, is available at all entrances.

ORIENTATION

Village Layout

Grand Canyon Village is built on the South Rim of the canyon and is roughly divided into two sections. At the east end of the village is the visitor center, Yavapai Lodge, Trailer Village, and Mather Campground. At the west end are El Tovar Hotel and Bright Angel, Kachina, Thunderbird, and Maswik lodges, as well as several restaurants and the trailhead for the Bright Angel Trail. Just before the El Tovar Hotel the road becomes one way.

Getting Around

As mentioned earlier, the Grand Canyon Village area can be extremely congested. If possible you may want to use one of the transportation options below to avoid the parking problems and congestion.

By Bus   The **Tusayan–Grand Canyon Shuttle** (☎ **520/638-0821**) operates between the Grand Canyon Airport in Tusayan (Grand Canyon), at the park's south entrance, and Grand Canyon Village, with stops at the Canyon Squire Inn, the IMAX Theater, and the Village Store in Tusayan, and at Yavapai Lodge, Bright Angel Lodge, and Maswik Lodge in Grand Canyon Village. A day pass is $7 and buses leave hourly between 8:15am and 6:15pm.

Trans Canyon (☎ **520/638-2820**) offers shuttle-bus service between the South Rim and the North Rim. The vans leave the South Rim at 1:30pm and arrive at the North Rim at 6:30pm. The return trip leaves the North Rim at 7am, arriving back at the South Rim at 11:30am. The fare is $60 per person one way, $100 per person round-trip.

During the summer months a free shuttle operates between the park's visitor center and village lodges. Also in summer, when the West Rim Drive is closed to private vehicles, another free shuttle covers this route.

By Car   Budget (☎ **520/638-9360** or 800/527-0700) and **Dollar** (☎ **520/638-2625** or 800/800-4000) maintain desks at the Grand Canyon Airport at the south entrance to the park.

There are **service stations** at Grand Canyon Village, in Tusayan, and at Desert View near the east entrance (this station is seasonal). Because of the long distances within the park and to towns outside the park, be sure that you have plenty of gas before setting out on a drive.

By Taxi   There is taxi service available to and from the airport, trailheads, and other destinations. Phone 520/638-2822 or 520/638-2631, ext. 6563.

FAST FACTS: The Grand Canyon

Admission   The Grand Canyon is a national park. Admission to the park is $10 per car or $4 per person if you happen to be coming in on a bus, by taxi, or on foot.

Banks and ATM Networks   There's an ATM at the Bank One at the shopping center near Yavapai Lodge. The bank is open Monday through Friday from 10am to 3pm and on Friday from 4 to 6pm as well.

Climate   The climate at the Grand Canyon is quite different from that of Phoenix, and between the rim and the canyon floor there's also a considerable difference. Because the South Rim is at 7,000 feet, it gets quite cold in the winter. You can expect snow anytime between November and May and winter temperatures can be below 0° Fahrenheit at night, with daytime highs in the 20s or 30s. Summer temperatures at the rim range from highs in the 80s to lows in the 50s. The North Rim of the canyon is slightly higher and stays a bit cooler throughout the year, but is only open to visitors from May to October. On the canyon floor temperatures are considerably higher. In summer the mercury can top 100°F with lows in the 70s, while in the winter temperatures are quite pleasant with highs in the 50s and lows in the 30s. July, August, and September are the wettest months because of frequent afternoon thunderstorms. April, May, and June are the driest months, though it might still rain or even snow. Down on the canyon floor there is much less rain year-round.

Drugstores   There's a drugstore in Grand Canyon Village down Center Road, which runs past the National Park Service rangers office. The drugstore is open Monday through Friday from 8:30am to 5:30pm. Call 520/638-2460 for information.

Emergencies   Dial **911;** from hotel or motel rooms, dial 9-911.

Hospitals/Clinics   The Grand Canyon Medical Clinic (call 520/638-2551 or 520/638-2469 for assistance) is located down Center Road, which runs past the National Park Service rangers office. The clinic is open Monday through Friday

Grand Canyon Village

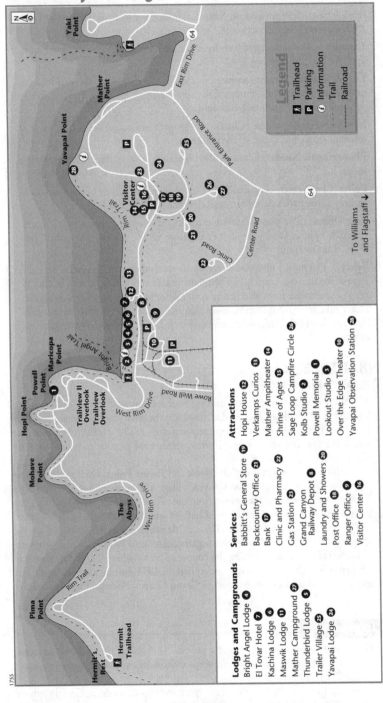

Legend

- Trailhead
- P Parking
- *i* Information
- Trail
- Railroad

Lodges and Campgrounds

- Bright Angel Lodge **4**
- El Tovar Hotel **7**
- Kachina Lodge **6**
- Maswik Lodge **11**
- Mather Campground **27**
- Thunderbird Lodge **5**
- Trailer Village **25**
- Yavapai Lodge **24**

Services

- Babbitt's General Store **19**
- Backcountry Office **21**
- Bank **17**
- Clinic and Pharmacy **22**
- Gas Station **23**
- Grand Canyon Railway Depot **8**
- Laundry and Showers **20**
- Post Office **18**
- Ranger Office **9**
- Visitor Center **16**

Attractions

- Hopi House **12**
- Verkamps Curios **13**
- Mather Ampitheater **14**
- Shrine of Ages **15**
- Sage Loop Campfire Circle **26**
- Kolb Studio **2**
- Powell Memorial **1**
- Lookout Studio **3**
- Over the Edge Theater **10**
- Yavapai Observation Station **28**

from 8am to 5:30pm and on Saturday from 9am to noon. It also provides 24-hour emergency service.

Laundry　A coin-operated laundry is located near Mather Campground in the Camper Services building.

Lost & Found　Report lost items or turn in found items at the visitor center or Yavapai observation station. Call 520/638-7798 Monday through Friday between 8am and noon or 1 and 4pm.

Newspapers/Magazines　Current newspapers and magazines are available at souvenir stores and lodges in the village.

Photographic Needs　Film and film processing are available at all village curio shops.

Police　In an emergency, dial **911**. Ticketing speeders is one of the main occupations of the park's police force, so obey the posted speed limits.

Post Office　The post office is located in the shopping center near Yavapai Lodge. It's open Monday through Friday from 9am to 4:30pm and on Saturday from 11am to 1pm.

Safety　The most important safety tip to remember is to be careful near the edge of the canyon. Footing can be unstable and may give way. Also be sure to keep your distance from wild animals, no matter how friendly they may appear. Don't hike alone, and keep in mind that the canyon rim is more than a mile above sea level (it's harder to breathe up here). Don't leave valuables in your car or tent.

WHAT TO SEE & DO
THE WEST RIM DRIVE

The West Rim Drive is an 8-mile-long road leading west from Grand Canyon Village to Hermits Rest. This road is closed to private automobiles during the summer, but a free shuttle operates frequently and stops at all the scenic overlooks. The rest of the year it's possible to drive this scenic road in your own car, stopping whenever and wherever you wish.

The first stops are **Trailview Overlook** and **Paiute Point.** From either of these points you have a view of Grand Canyon Village to the east with the Bright Angel Trail winding down into the canyon from the village. The trail leads 3,000 feet below the rim to the Tonto Plateau, site of Indian Gardens, a grove of cottonwood trees.

The next stop on the West Rim Drive is **Maricopa Point.** Here you can see the remains of the Orphan Mine, which began operation in 1893. The mine went out of business because transporting the copper to a city where it could be sold was too expensive. Uranium was discovered here in 1954, but in 1966 the mine was shut down and the land became part of Grand Canyon National Park. If you look

Impressions

We are imprisoned three quarters of a mile in the depths of the earth and the great unknown river shrinks into insignificance as it dashes its angry waves against the walls and cliffs that rise to the world above.

—Maj. John Wesley Powell, on his successful trip through the Grand Canyon carefully at the bottom of the canyon you can see some of the black Vishnu schist, which is among the oldest exposed rock on earth.

The **Powell Memorial,** which is the next stop, is dedicated to John Wesley Powell, who, in 1869 with a party of nine men, became the first person to navigate the Colorado River through the Grand Canyon.

Next along the drive is **Hopi Point,** from which you can see a long section of the Colorado River. Because of the great distance, the river seems to be a tiny, quiet stream, but in actuality the section you see is more than 100 yards wide and races through Granite Rapids.

Mojave Point is the next stop. From here you can see (and sometimes hear) Hermit Rapids, another section of white water. As are almost all rapids in the canyon, these are formed at the mouth of a side canyon where boulders loosened by storms and carried by flooded streams are deposited in the Colorado River.

The next pull-off is at **The Abyss,** the appropriately named 3,000-foot drop-off created by the Great Mojave Wall. This vertiginous view is one of the most awe-inspiring in the park. The walls of the Abyss are red sandstone that's more resistant to erosion than the softer shale in the layer below. Other layers of erosion-resistant sandstone have formed the freestanding pillars that are visible from here, the largest of which is called the Monument.

From **Pima Point** it's possible to see the remains of Hermit Camp on the Tonto Plateau. Built by the Santa Fe Railroad, Hermit Camp was a popular tourist destination between 1911 and 1930 and provided cabins and tents. Today only foundations remain.

At the end of the West Rim Drive is **Hermits Rest,** named for Louis Boucher, a prospector who came to the canyon in the 1890s and was known as the Hermit. The log-and-stone Hermits Rest building, designed by Mary Jane Colter and built in 1914, is on the National Register of Historic Places.

THE EAST RIM DRIVE

The East Rim Drive extends for 25 miles from Grand Canyon Village to Desert View. The first stop is **Yaki Point,** which is the trailhead for the Kaibab Trail leading to Phantom Ranch. The spectacular view from here encompasses a wide section of the central canyon. The large flat-topped butte to the northeast is Wotan's Throne, one of the canyon's easily recognizable features.

The next stop, **Grandview Point,** affords a view of Horseshoe Mesa, another interesting feature of the canyon landscape. The mesa was the site of the Last Chance Copper Mine in the early 1890s. Later that same decade the Grandview Hotel was built and served canyon visitors until its close in 1908.

Next along the drive is **Moran Point,** from which you can see a bright red layer of shale in the canyon walls. This point is named for a 19th-century landscape painter named Thomas Moran.

The **Tusayan Museum** is the next stop along the East Rim Drive. Inside this small museum are exhibits on the ancient Anasazi people who once inhabited this region. Outside the museum are the ruins of an Anasazi village.

At **Lipan Point** you can see the Grand Canyon supergroup: several strata of rock that are tilted at an angle to the other layers of rock in the canyon. Their angle indicates that there was a period of geological mountain building prior to the layers of sandstone, limestone, and shale. The red, white, and black rocks of the supergroup are composed of sedimentary rock and layers of lava. From **Navajo Point,** the Colorado River and Escalante Butte are both visible.

Shooting the Canyon: Tips for Photographers

By the time most people leave the Grand Canyon they've shot several rolls of film. This is not at all surprising considering the stunning beauty of this rugged landscape. However, it's not always easy to capture the canyon's spirit on film. Here are some tips to help you bring back the best possible photos from your trip:

A polarizing filter is a great investment if you have the kind of camera that will accept lens filters. A polarizing filter will reduce haze, lessen the contrast between shadowy areas and light areas, and deepen the color of the sky.

The best time to photograph the canyon is at sunrise and sunset, when filtered and sharply angled sunlight paints the canyon walls in beautiful shades of lavender and pink. At these times the shadows are also at their most dramatic. To capture these ephemeral moments it's best to use a tripod and a long exposure. The worst time to photograph the canyon is at noon when there are almost no shadows, and thus little texture or contrast. The National Park Service includes a table with sunrise and sunset times in *The Guide*, the park's official visitor newspaper.

Something else to keep in mind is that the Grand Canyon is immense. A wide-angle lens may leave the canyon looking like a distant plane of dirt on paper. Try zooming in on narrower sections of the canyon to emphasize a single dramatic landscape element. If you're shooting with a wide-angle lens, try to include something in the foreground (people or a tree branch) to give the photo perspective and scale.

When shooting portraits against a sunrise or sunset, use a flash to illuminate your subjects; otherwise your camera meter may expose for the bright light in the background and leave your subjects in shadow.

Desert View, with its trading post, cafeteria, service station, and watchtower, is the end of this scenic drive. However, the road continues east from here. Though the views are breathtaking from anywhere at Desert View, the best lookout is from atop the Desert View Watchtower. This unusual building was designed by Mary Jane Colter and opened in 1932. From the roof, which is the highest point on the South Rim (7,522 feet above sea level) it's possible to see the Painted Desert to the northeast, the San Francisco Peaks to the south, the Colorado River, and Marble Canyon to the north. Coin-operated binoculars provide closeup views of some of the noteworthy landmarks of this end of the canyon. On the roof are several black-mirror "reflectoscopes" that provide interesting darkened views of some of the most spectacular sections of the canyon.

INTERPRETIVE PROGRAMS

Numerous interpretive programs are scheduled throughout the year at various South Rim locations. There are ranger-led walks that explore various aspects of the canyon, geology talks, lectures on the cultural and natural resources of the canyon, nature hikes, trips to fossil beds, and stargazing gatherings. At Tusayan Ruin there are guided tours. Evening programs are held at Mather Amphitheater in the summer and at the Shrine of the Ages the rest of the year. Consult your copy of *The Guide* for information on times and meeting points.

ORGANIZED TOURS

A RAILWAY EXCURSION   In the early part of this century most visitors to the Grand Canyon came by train, and today it's once again possible to travel to the canyon by steam train. The **Grand Canyon Railway** (☎ **800/843-8724**) operates 1906- and 1910-vintage steam engines and 1920s-vintage passenger cars between Williams and Grand Canyon Village. Trains depart from the renovated Fray Marcos Hotel, which was built in 1908 and now houses a railroad museum, gift shop, and café. At Grand Canyon Village, the trains use the 1910 log railway terminal in front of El Tovar Hotel. Passengers have the choice of three grades of service, including coach class, club class (with a full bar), and chief class (a parlor car with plush couches and chairs). Morning and afternoon, actors posing as cowboys provide entertainment, and during the 2^1/$_4$-hour trips, there are music performances aboard the train. Round-trip fares (including park entrance fees) range from $58 to $113 for adults, and $21 to $76 for children 2 to 16. Not only is this a fun trip that provides great scenery and a trip back in time, but by taking the train, you can avoid the traffic congestion and parking problems in Grand Canyon Village.

AIR TOURS   Because the Grand Canyon is so immense and remote, the only way to see it all is from an airplane or helicopter. Several companies operating out of the Grand Canyon Airport offer air tours of the canyon. Tours vary from 30 minutes to about 2 hours and all are quite expensive.

Companies offering air tours by small plane include the following: **Air Grand Canyon** (☎ **520/638-2686** or 800/AIR-GRAND), charging $56 to $136 for adults, $36 to $86 for children; **Grand Canyon Airlines** (☎ **520/638-2407** or 800/528-2413), $60 for adults, $33 for children; and **Windrock Aviation** (☎ **520/638-9591** or 800/24-ROCKY), $56 to $134 for adults, $36 to $86 for children.

Helicopter tours are available from **Airstar Helicopters** (☎ **520/638-2622**), charging $86 to $156 per person; **Kenai Helicopters** (☎ **520/638-2412** or 800/541-4537), $90 to $160 per person; and **Papillon Grand Canyon Helicopters** (☎ **520/638-2419** or 800/528-2418), $90 to $165 for adults, $73 to $133 for children.

BUS TOURS   If you'd rather leave the driving to someone else and enjoy more of the scenery, you can opt for a bus or van tour of one or more sections of the park. The **Fred Harvey Transportation Co.** (☎ **520/638-2631,** ext. 6015) offers several trips ranging in length from 2 to 11 hours. Inside the park, tours visit the East Rim and West Rim, while beyond the park boundaries they raft through Glen Canyon and visit Monument Valley, Wupatki National Monument, Sunset Crater, and Walnut Canyon National Monument. Tours can be booked by calling the above phone number or by stopping at one of the transportation desks, which are located at Bright Angel, Maswik, and Yavapai lodges. Prices range from $7.50 to $105 for adults and $3.75 to $105 for children.

MULE RIDES

After having a look at the steep drop-offs and narrow path of the Bright Angel Trail, you might decide that this isn't exactly the place to trust your life to a mule. However, the trail guides will be quick to reassure you that they haven't lost a rider yet. Mule rides into the canyon are some of the most popular activities at Grand Canyon Village and have been since the turn of the century when the Bright

Angel Trail was a toll road. Trips of various lengths and to different destinations are offered. The one-day trip descends to Plateau Point, where there's a view of the Colorado River 1,320 feet below. This is a grueling trip requiring riders to spend six hours in the saddle. Those who want to spend a night down in the canyon can choose an overnight trip to Phantom Ranch, where there are cabins and dormitories available at the only lodge actually in the canyon. From mid-November to mid-March there's also a three-day/two-night trip to Phantom Ranch.

There are a couple of rider qualifications that you should keep in mind before making a reservation. You must weigh less than 200 pounds fully dressed and stand no less than 4 feet 7 inches tall. Pregnant women are not allowed on mule trips.

Because these trail rides are very popular (especially in summer), make a reservation as soon as you know when you'll be visiting. For more information or to make a reservation, contact the **Grand Canyon National Park Lodges,** Reservations Department, P.O. Box 699, Grand Canyon, AZ 86023 (☎ **520/638-2401**). If you arrive without a reservation and decide that you'd like to go on a mule ride, stop by the Bright Angel Transportation Desk to get your name on the day's waiting list.

HORSEBACK RIDING

Horseback riding is available from **Apache Stables,** P.O. Box 158, Grand Canyon, AZ 86023 (☎ **520/638-2891** or 520/638-2424), at the south entrance to the park. There are rides of various lengths; prices range from $22 for a one-hour ride to $57.50 for a four-hour ride.

RAFTING

Rafting down the Colorado River as it roars and tumbles through the mile-deep gorge of the Grand Canyon is an adventure of a lifetime. Ever since John Wesley Powell ignored everyone who knew better and proved that it was possible to travel by boat down the tumultuous Colorado River, running the big river has become a passion and an obsession with adventurers. Today anyone, from grade schoolers to grandmothers, can join the elite group who have made the run. However, be prepared for some of the most furious white water in the world.

There are 17 companies offering trips through the canyon. You can spend as few as 3 days on the river or as many as 16. You can go down the river in a huge motorized rubber raft, in a paddled- or oar-powered raft, a kayak, or a wooden dory.

Most trips start from Lees Ferry on the Arizona side of the Colorado near Page and Lake Powell. It's also possible to start or finish a trip at Phantom Ranch, hiking in or out from either the North or South Rim. The main rafting season is from April to October, but some companies operate year-round. A six-day trip costs more than $1,000 and a three-day trip costs about $500.

The following are just a few of the 20 companies currently authorized to operate trips through the Grand Canyon: **Arizona Raft Adventures,** 4050-F E. Huntington Dr., Flagstaff, AZ 86004 (☎ **520/526-8200** or 800/786-RAFT); **Arizona**

Impressions

Ours has been the first and will doubtless be the last party of whites to visit this profitless locality.

—Lt. Joseph C. Ives, exploring the Colorado River by steamboat (1857–58)

River Runners, P.O. Box 47788, Phoenix, AZ 85068-7788 (☎ **602/ 867-4866** or 800/477-7238); **Colorado River & Trail Expeditions,** P.O. Box 57575, Salt Lake City, UT 84157-0575 (☎ **801/261-1789** or 800/253-7328); **Grand Canyon Expeditions,** P.O. Box O, Kanab, UT 84741 (☎ **801/644-2691** or 800/544-2691); **Hatch River Expeditions,** P.O. Box 1200, Vernal, UT 84078 (☎ **801/789-3813** or 800/433-8966); **Moki Mac River Expeditions,** P.O. Box 21242, Salt Lake City, UT 84121 (☎ **801/268-6667** or 800/284-7280); **Outdoors Unlimited,** 6900 Townsend Winona Rd., Flagstaff, AZ 86004 (☎ **520/ 526-4546** or 800/637-7238); and **Western River Expeditions,** 7258 Racquet Club Dr., Salt Lake City, UT 84121 (☎ **801/942-6669** or 800/453-7450).

TWO WHITE-WATER ALTERNATIVES   For those not addicted to adrenaline, there are two Colorado River rafting alternatives. **Wilderness River Adventures,** P.O. Box 717, Page, AZ 86040 (☎ **520/645-3279** or 800/992-8022), operates half-day smooth-water raft trips between the Glen Canyon Dam and Lees Ferry. They offer two trips daily May to September at 7:30am and 1:30pm for $39.95 for adults and $34.95 for children, with a more limited schedule in late spring and early fall. It's also possible to arrange this trip through the **Fred Harvey Transportation Co.,** P.O. Box 709, Grand Canyon, AZ 86023 (☎ **520/ 638-2401**), which will transport you between Grand Canyon Village and Page. This trip costs $75 for adults and $50 for children.

West of Grand Canyon Village, on the Hualapai Indian Reservation, **Hualapai River Runners,** P.O. Box 246, Peach Springs, AZ 86434 (☎ **520/769-2219** or 800/622-4409 outside Arizona), operates one- and two-day river trips that include a day of white water and a day of smooth water. These trips can include accommodations the night before and the night after the trip and cost between $250 and $360 per person.

HIKING THE CANYON

There are no roads leading into the Grand Canyon, so if you want to visit the inner canyon you have to fly, float, ride a mule, or hike. The ever-changing views are as spectacular as those from the rim, and up close there are fossils, old mines, petroglyphs, wildflowers, and wildlife to see. Keep in mind, however, that no hike below the rim of the canyon is easy.

The Grand Canyon offers some of the most rugged and strenuous hiking anywhere in the United States, and for this reason anyone attempting even a short walk should be well prepared. Each year several people are injured or killed because they set out to hike the canyon without preparing properly. Most of these injuries and fatalities are suffered by day hikers who set out without sturdy footgear and without food or adequate amounts of water. Don't become another Grand Canyon statistic! Take precautions. Unless you have proper footgear and at least 1 quart of water, you won't even be allowed on the daily ranger-led nature walk along the South Kaibab Trail. Even a short 30-minute hike in the summer can dehydrate you, and a long hike into or out of the canyon in the heat can necessitate drinking more than a gallon of water. Remember while hiking that mules have the right of way; always stay to the inside of the trail when being passed by a mule train. Don't attempt to hike from the rim to the Colorado River and back in one day. Many people who have tried this have suffered injury or death.

DAY HIKES   There are no loop-trail day hikes possible in the Grand Canyon, but the vastly different scenery in every direction makes a return trip on the same trail a totally new experience. The easiest day hikes are those along the rim. There's a 1¹/₂-mile paved trail leading from the Yavapai Museum to the Powell Memorial. From the Powell Memorial the trail becomes dirt and continues another 8 miles to Hermits Rest, from which, in summer, you can take a free shuttle back to Grand Canyon Village.

Trails leading down into the canyon include the Bright Angel Trail, the South Kaibab Trail, Grandview Trail, and the Hermit Trail. If you plan to hike for more than 30 minutes, carry 2 quarts of water per person.

The **Bright Angel Trail** starts just west of Bright Angel Lodge in Grand Canyon Village. It's the main route down to Phantom Ranch and is the most popular trail into the canyon. Day hikes on this trail include the trips to Indian Gardens or Plateau Point. Both these trips are long and very strenuous. There are rest houses at 1¹/₂ and 3 miles (during the summer they have water), which make good turn-around points for a 3-mile or 6-mile round-trip hike.

The **South Kaibab Trail** begins near Yaki Point east of Grand Canyon Village and is the alternative route to Phantom Ranch. This trail offers the best views of any of the day hikes in the canyon. From the trailhead it's a 3-mile round-trip to Cedar Ridge. The hike is very strenuous and there's no water available along the trail.

The **Grandview Trail** is a steep, unmaintained trail that should be attempted only by people with experience hiking in the desert. It's a very strenuous 6-mile round-trip hike to Horseshoe Mesa, and there's no water available along the trail. Allow at least seven hours for this rugged hike.

The **Hermit Trail** begins near Hermits Rest and is also steep and unmaintained. Don't attempt this trail if you don't have some experience hiking in the desert. It's a 5-mile round-trip to Santa Maria Springs and a 6-mile round-trip to Dripping Springs. Water from these springs must be treated before it's safe to drink.

BACKPACKING   There are miles of trails deep in the canyon and several established campgrounds for backpackers. The best times of year to backpack in the canyon are spring and autumn. During the summer, temperatures at the bottom of the canyon are regularly over 100° Fahrenheit, while in the winter ice and snow at higher elevations make footing on trails precarious. Be sure to carry at least 2 quarts, and preferably 1 gallon, of water whenever backpacking in the canyon.

A **Backcountry Use Permit** is required of all hikers planning to overnight in the canyon unless you'll be staying at Phantom Ranch in one of the cabins or in the dormitory. Because a limited number of hikers are allowed into the canyon on any given day, it's important to make reservations by mail as far in advance as possible. Contact the **Backcountry Reservations Office,** Grand Canyon National Park, P.O. Box 129, Grand Canyon, AZ 86023 (☎ **520/638-7888,** or 520/638-7875 for information). Holiday periods are the most popular. The office begins accepting reservations on the first of every month for the following four months. If you want to hike over the Labor Day weekend, be sure you make your reservation on May 1! If you show up without a reservation, go to the Backcountry Reservations Office (open daily from 8am to noon) and put your name on the waiting list. When applying for a permit you'll have to specify your exact itinerary and, once in the canyon, you must stick to this itinerary. There are **campgrounds** at Indian Gardens, Bright Angel Campground (near Phantom Ranch), and at Cottonwood, but hikers are limited to two nights per trip at each of these campgrounds (except from November 15 to February 28 when four nights are allowed at each campground). Other nights can be spent camping at undesignated sites in certain regions of the park. The Backcountry Reservations Office has information available to help you plan your itinerary.

MUSEUMS, HISTORIC BUILDINGS & OTHER ATTRACTIONS

✪ Grand Canyon IMAX Theatre

Ariz. 64/U.S. 180, Grand Canyon. ☎ **520/638-2203.** Admission $7 adults, $4 children 3–11. Mar–Oct, daily 8:30am–8:30pm; Nov–Feb, daily 10:30am–6:30pm.

Located in the village of Grand Canyon at the south entrance to the park, the Grand Canyon IMAX Theatre devotes its seven-story screen to a 34-minute film about the canyon. A reenactment of John Wesley Powell's first navigation of the Colorado River is the central focus of the film, but geology, ancient history, and cultural and natural history are also included. However, the star of the show is, of course, the heart-stopping IMAX cinematography. The huge screen that fills your field of vision and the amazing high definition of the film together create an astoundingly realistic image of the canyon.

Kolb and Lookout Studios

On the Rim, Grand Canyon Village. ☎ **520/638-2771** or 520/638-2631, ext. 6087. Admission free. Kolb Studio, daily 8am–5pm, later in summer. Lookout Studio, Mar–Nov, daily 8am–7pm; Nov–Mar, daily 9am–5pm.

These two buildings cling precariously to the rim of the canyon just west of the Bright Angel Lodge. Though they have very different early histories, both have been listed on the National Register of Historic Places. **Kolb Studio** is named for Ellsworth and Emory Kolb, two brothers who set up a photographic studio on the rim of the Grand Canyon in 1904. The building became the center of a controversy over whether buildings should be allowed on the canyon rim. Because the Kolbs had friends in high places, their sprawling studio and movie theater remained. Emory Kolb lived here until his death in 1976, by which time the building had been listed as a historic building and could not legally be torn down. Today it serves as a bookstore. **Lookout Studio,** built in 1914 from a design by Mary Jane Colter, was the Fred Harvey Company's answer to the Kolb brothers' studio. Photographs and books about the canyon were sold at the studio, which incorporates architectural styles of the Hopi and the Anasazi. The use of native limestone and an uneven roofline allows the studio to blend in with the canyon walls and gives it the look of an old ruin. Today the studio houses a souvenir store and two lookout points.

Over the Edge Theatre

Community Building, Village Loop Dr., Grand Canyon Village. ☎ **520/638-2229.** Admission $4 adults, $3.50 seniors, $2 children 8–15, free for children 7 and under. Mar–Oct, daily 9am–9pm; Nov–Feb, daily 10am–6pm.

Not quite as stunning as the IMAX film, this program is nevertheless informative and visually exciting. Using slides instead of motion pictures, the audiovisual program introduces the visitor to the geology and history of the canyon. The narration is given from the point of view of Capt. John Hance, one of the canyon's first guides.

Tusayan Museum

East Rim Dr. ☎ **520/638-2305.** Admission free. June–Nov, daily 8am–6pm; Nov–May, daily 9am–5pm.

Located 23 miles east of Grand Canyon Village and 3 miles west of Desert View, the Tusayan Museum is dedicated to the Hopi tribe and ancient Anasazi people who inhabited this region 800 years ago. Inside the small museum are artfully displayed exhibits on various aspects of Anasazi life. Outside is a short self-guided trail through actual Anasazi ruins. Free guided tours are available.

Visitor Center

Village Loop Dr. ☎ **520/638-7888.** Admission free. June–Nov, daily 8am–7pm; Nov–May, daily 8am–6pm.

The visitor center, in addition to providing answers to all your questions about the Grand Canyon, also contains exhibits on the canyon's natural history, history, and exploration. Throughout the day, slide and video programs are shown. There's also an excellent little bookstore here where you can find books on all aspects of the canyon. In the center's courtyard are several boats that have navigated the canyon over the years.

The Watchtower

Desert View, East Rim Dr. ☎ **520/638-2736.** Admission: Tower, 25¢; gift shop, free. May–Oct, daily 8am–8pm; Nov–Apr, daily 8am–6pm.

Though the watchtower looks as though it were built centuries ago, it's actually only 60 years old. Architect Mary Jane Colter, who is responsible for much of the park's historic architecture, designed the tower to resemble the prehistoric towers that dot the southwestern landscape. Built as an observation tower and rest stop for tourists, the watchtower incorporates Native American designs and art. The curio shop on the ground floor is a replica of a kiva (sacred ceremonial chamber). The tower's second floor features artwork by Hopi artist Fred Kabotie. Covering the walls are pictographs incorporating traditional designs. On the walls and ceiling of the upper two floors are more traditional images, this time reproductions of petroglyphs from throughout the Southwest by Fred Geary. The gift shop offers a pamphlet describing the watchtower in detail.

Yavapai Observation Station

Village Loop Dr. ☎ **520/638-7890.** Admission free. June–Aug, daily 8am–8pm; Sept–May, daily 8am–6pm.

Located less than a mile east of the visitor center, this historic building features a panoramic view of the canyon through the museum's large windows.

WHERE TO STAY

Keep in mind that the Grand Canyon is one of the most popular national parks in the country and hotel rooms within the park are in high demand. If you want to stay in the park, make your reservations as far in advance as possible. For rim cabins at the Bright Angel Lodge, it's often necessary to make a reservation a year in advance. Hotels outside the park are especially popular with tour groups, which during the busy summer months keep many hotels full. Don't head up here in the summer months without a reservation and expect to find a room. If you do it's more than likely you'll have to drive to Williams or Flagstaff to find a vacancy.

Grand Canyon Village

Expensive

El Tovar Hotel

P.O. Box 699, Grand Canyon, AZ 86023. ☎ **520/638-2401.** Fax 520/638-9247. 65 rms, 12 suites. A/C TV TEL. $111–$166 double; $182–$271 suite. AE, DC, DISC, MC, V.

This is the park's premier lodge and first opened its doors in 1905. Built of native boulders and Oregon pine by Hopi craftsmen, the El Tovar is a rustic yet luxurious mountain lodge that perches on the edge of the canyon with awe-inspiring views (but only from some rooms). The lobby, entered from a veranda set with rustic furniture, has a small fireplace, cathedral ceiling, and log walls from which hang moose, deer, and antelope heads.

The rooms are not, however, done in the same rustic style as the hotel's public rooms. A renovation a few years back added carpets and colonial-style furniture that would be more appropriate in Williamsburg, Virginia. The standard rooms are rather small, as are the bathrooms, which were added after the hotel was built. Deluxe rooms provide more legroom, and the suites, with their private terraces and stunning views, are extremely spacious.

Dining/Entertainment: The El Tovar Dining Room (see "Where to Dine," below) is the best restaurant in the village and serves excellent continental and southwestern cuisine. Just off the lobby is a cocktail lounge with a view by day and live piano music by night.

Services: Concierge, room service, tour desk.

Moderate

Thunderbird & Kachina Lodges
P.O. Box 699, Grand Canyon, AZ 86023. ☎ **520/638-2401.** Fax 520/638-9247. 100 rms. A/C TV TEL. $96–$106 single or double. AE, DC, DISC, MC, V.

These are the two newest lodges on the canyon rim, and though they are both two-story motel-style buildings, the use of native sandstone in their construction helps them blend in a bit with the adjacent historic lodges. Thunderbird Lodge registration is handled by Bright Angel Lodge, and Kachina Lodge registration is handled by El Tovar Hotel.

The rooms in both lodges have large windows, although you'll have to request a canyonside room on the second floor if you want a view of something more than a parking lot or the crowds milling along the rim trail. The canyon-view rooms are only $10 more than those without views and are well worth the extra cost. Neither lodge has its own dining room or lounge, but because they're between the El Tovar and Bright Angel lodges, you don't have to walk far when you get hungry.

Yavapai Lodge
P.O. Box 699, Grand Canyon, AZ 86023. ☎ **520/638-2401.** Fax 520/638-9247. 348 rms. TV TEL. $79–$89 double. AE, DC, DISC, MC, V.

Located in several buildings at the east end of Grand Canyon Village, the Yavapai is the largest lodge in the park. The rooms in the Yavapai East section of the hotel are set under shady pines and are more attractive than the rooms in the Yavapai West section (well worth the $10 price difference). There are no canyon views here, which is why this lodge is less expensive than the Thunderbird and Kachina lodges. It's also a 1-mile hike to the main section of the village.

There's a cafeteria (see "Where to Dine," below) serving burgers, sandwiches, pizza, and salads at relatively economical prices. The lodge also has a tour desk.

Inexpensive

✪ Bright Angel Lodge & Cabins
P.O. Box 699, Grand Canyon, AZ 86023. ☎ **520/638-2401.** Fax 520/638-9247. 34 rms, 10 with sink only, 10 with sink and toilet, 14 with bath; 55 cabins. $37 double with sink only, $43 double with sink and toilet, $53 double with bath; $61–$221 cabin. AE, DC, DISC, MC, V.

Bright Angel Lodge began operation in 1896 as a collection of tents and cabins on the edge of the canyon, but the current lodge didn't open until 1935. With its flagstone floor, huge fireplace, log walls, and soaring ceiling, the lodge's lobby is the epitome of a rustic retreat (albeit a very crowded one).

This is the most economical lodge in the park and offers the greatest variety of accommodations. In addition to rooms with shared bathrooms, there are also roomier cabins, including four rim cabins that have their own fireplaces. These rim cabins are the most popular and are usually booked a year in advance. The other rooms should be booked at least six months in advance. Most of the rooms and cabins feature rustic furnishings, but have been recently renovated. The Buckey Suite, the oldest structure on the canyon rim, is arguably the best room in the park, with a canyon view, fireplace, and a king-size bed.

The Bright Angel Dining Room (see "Where to Dine," below) serves all meals, while the Arizona Steak House (see "Where to Dine," below) is open for dinner only. For snacks, sandwiches, and ice cream, there's the Bright Angel Fountain. The lodge also has a tour desk and museum.

Maswik Lodge
P.O. Box 699, Grand Canyon, AZ 86023. ☎ **520/638-2401.** Fax 520/638-9247. 280 rms. TV TEL. $48–$103 double. AE, DC, DISC, MC, V.

Set back a bit from the rim, the Maswik Lodge offers spacious rooms and rustic cabins. If you crave modern appointments, opt for one of the Maswik North rooms. More rugged types will prefer the less expensive old cabins, which aren't too attractive but are economically priced. The cabins have bathtubs but not showers in their bathrooms.

There's a large cafeteria (see "Where to Dine," below) and a sports lounge with a big-screen TV. There's also a tour desk here.

Campgrounds
On the South Rim, there are two campgrounds, both charging $10 per site, and an RV park charging $17 per site for two people. **Mather Campground** is in Grand Canyon Village and has 320 campsites. For reservations, contact MISTIX, P.O. Box 85705, San Diego, CA 92138-5705 (☎ **800/365-2267**), which takes reservations only for stays between March and November. Reservations are a necessity if you want to be certain to get a campsite in the park and should be made exactly 56 days before the desired date you wish a site.

Desert View Campground, with 50 sites, is located 26 miles east of Grand Canyon Village and is only open from mid-May to early October. No reservations are accepted for this campground.

The **Trailer Village RV park** is located in Grand Canyon Village. Reservations are made through the Fred Harvey Co., P.O. Box 699, Grand Canyon, AZ 86023 (☎ 520/638-2401; fax 520/638-9247). There are 78 full hookup sites here.

TUSAYAN (OUTSIDE THE SOUTH ENTRANCE)
If you can't get a reservation for a room in the park, this is the next closest place to stay. Unfortunately, this area can be very noisy because of the many helicopters and airplanes taking off from the airport and other places around town.

Moderate

Best Western Grand Canyon Squire Inn
P.O. Box 130, Grand Canyon, AZ 86023-0130. ☎ **520/638-2681** or 800/622-6966. Fax 520/638-2782. 250 rms, 4 suites. A/C TV TEL. Mar–Oct and Christmas week, $100–$125

double; $175–$195 suite. Oct–Nov, $80–$100 double; $175 suite. First three weeks of Dec and Jan–Mar, $55–$75 double; $150 suite. AE, DC, DISC, MC, V.

If you prefer playing tennis to riding a mule, this may be the place for you. The rooms are large and come with two double beds and comfortable easy chairs. One wall of each guest room is made of local stones and there are large windows that let in plenty of light.

The dining room here is the best restaurant in the area, and serves continental cuisine and regional American specialties at reasonable prices. Less expensive fare is available in the coffee shop. Before or after dinner you can sit by the fireplace in the lounge. The inn offers free airport shuttle service, a pool, tennis courts, a whirlpool, sauna, bowling alley, pool room, and video arcade.

Moqui Lodge
P.O. Box 699, Grand Canyon, AZ 86023. ☎ **520/638-2401.** Fax 520/638-9247. 127 rms. TV TEL. $79 double. AE, DC, DISC, MC, V. Closed Nov–Mar.

Operated by the Fred Harvey Company but located outside the south entrance to the park, Moqui Lodge, with its tall A-frame construction, has the feel of a ski lodge. Just off the main lobby is a dark lounge with a stone fireplace. The guest accommodations are standard motel-style rooms with large windows that for the most part look out onto wide expanses of parking lot. What this lodge has going for it is its proximity to the park entrance and its riding stables. Moderately priced Mexican and American meals are served in the dining room amid Spanish-colonial decor. There's also a tour desk here.

Quality Inn Grand Canyon
P.O. Box 520, Grand Canyon, AZ 86023. ☎ **520/638-2673** or 800/221-2222. Fax 520/638-9537. 176 rms. A/C TV TEL. $68–$138 double. AE, CB, DC, DISC, MC, V.

This luxurious hotel at the park's south entrance is built around two enclosed skylit courtyards, one of which houses a restaurant serving buffet meals and the other of which has a bar and whirlpool spa. There's also an outdoor whirlpool, as well as an outdoor pool. The rooms are large and comfortable, and have balconies or patios. Most also have minibars. The hotel is located next to the IMAX Theatre and is very popular with tour groups.

IN THE CANYON

Phantom Ranch
P.O. Box 699, Grand Canyon, AZ 86023. ☎ **520/638-2401.** Fax 520/638-9247. 11 cabins, 40 dorm beds. $56 double in the cabins; $21 dormitory bed. Packages available for mule riders. AE, MC, V.

This is the only lodge at the bottom of the Grand Canyon and as such is very popular with both hikers and mule riders. Built in 1922, Phantom Ranch has a classic ranch atmosphere. The accommodations are in rustic stone-walled cabins or 10-bedded sex-segregated dormitories. Evaporative coolers keep both the cabins and the dorms cool in the summer. Make reservations as early as possible (up to a year in advance). It's also possible to get a room on the day of departure if there are any last-minute cancellations. To attempt this, you must be at the Bright Angel Lodge transportation desk before 6am (some people show up at 4am) on the day you wish to stay.

Dining/Entertainment: Family-style meals must be reserved in advance. The menu consists of beef-and-vegetable stew or vegetarian dinner for $16.25, or steak for $26.50. Breakfasts ($11.50) are hearty and sack lunches ($5.50) are available.

Between meals the dining hall becomes a canteen selling snacks, drinks, gifts, and necessities. After dinner the dining hall becomes a beer hall. Services here include a public phone and mule-back baggage transfer between Grand Canyon Village and Phantom Ranch ($43.60 each way).

WILLIAMS

Although it's 60 miles south of the Grand Canyon, Williams is the nearest real town to the canyon. Consequently it has dozens of low-budget motels catering to people who were unable to get a room at the park. The Grand Canyon Railway Depot is also located here.

Moderate

Ramada Inn Mountain Side Inn & Resort

642 E. Bill Williams Ave., Williams, AZ 86046. ☎ **520/635-4431** or 800/462-9381. Fax 520/635-2292. 96 rms. A/C TV TEL. $65–$125 double. AE, CB, DC, DISC, MC, V.

Located at the east end of town, this large motel is popular with tour groups. The rooms are medium size with large windows, some with mountain views. The large restaurant and lobby lounge provide American meals. In summer there's sometimes live music in the lounge. The hotel also offers a pool and whirlpool.

Quality Inn Mountain Ranch

Rte. 1, Box 35 (at Exit 171 from I-40), Williams, AZ 86046. ☎ **520/635-2693** or 800/221-2222. 73 rms. A/C TV TEL. $65–$102 double. AE, DC, DISC, MC, V.

Located 5 miles east of town, this motel is surrounded by 26 acres of forest and meadow that give it a secluded feeling. This seclusion and the activities available here make this the best choice in the Williams area. However, the rooms, though large and mostly with views of forest and mountains, are strictly motel issue. There's a restaurant on the premises, so you don't have to drive into town to eat. The hotel offers horseback riding, a pool, whirlpool, sauna, tennis courts, volleyball, basketball, and a putting green.

Inexpensive

In addition to the motels listed below, budget chain motels in Williams include the following (rates are for the summer high season; see the Appendix for toll-free phone numbers): **Comfort Inn,** 911 W. Bill Williams Ave., Williams, AZ 86046 (☎ **520/635-4045**), charging $42 to $118 double; **Days Inn–Williams,** 2488 W. Bill Williams Ave., Williams, AZ 86046 (☎ **520/635-4051**), $50 to $85 double; and **Super 8,** 2001 E. Bill Williams Ave., William, AZ 86046 (☎ **520/635-4700**), $30 to $60 double.

Canyon Country Inn

442 W. Bill Williams Ave., Williams, AZ 86046. ☎ **520/635-2349** or 800/643-1020. 13 rms. TV TEL. $55–$95 double. Rates include continental breakfast. AE, DISC, MC, V.

This quaint country inn is a cross between a motel and a bed-and-breakfast. Though it's not a historic building and is located in the middle of Williams's motel row, all rooms are individually furnished and feature crafts made by local women, ceiling fans, and plenty of teddy bears to keep guests company.

Norris Motel

1001 W. Bill Williams Ave. (P.O. Box 388), Williams, AZ 86046. ☎ **520/635-2202** or 800/341-8000. Fax 520/635-9202. 33 rms. A/C TV TEL. $48–$74 double. AE, DISC, MC, V.

Run by a British family, the Norris Motel may not look like anything special from the street, but the friendliness of the welcome will immediately let you know that this is not your ordinary motel. Most of the guest rooms have been remodeled and have quilt-patterned bedspreads that give each room a homey feel. Many rooms also have refrigerators. There's even a whirlpool bath to soak away your aches and pains in the evening.

The Red Garter

137 W. Railroad Ave., Williams, AZ 86046. ☎ **520/635-1484.** 4 rms. $45–$85 double. Rates include continental breakfast. Lower rates off-season. AE, DISC, MC, V.

The Wild West lives again at this restored 1897 bordello, but these days the only extras that come with the rooms are breakfasts in the bakery downstairs. Located across the street from the Grand Canyon Railway terminal at the top of a steep flight of stairs, this B&B sports high ceilings, new carpets, attractive wood trim, and reproduction period furnishings. A couple of rooms even have graffiti written by visitors in the early part of this century.

WHERE TO DINE
GRAND CANYON VILLAGE
Expensive

El Tovar Dining Room

In the El Tovar Hotel. ☎ **520/638-2631.** Reservations required at dinner. Main courses $14–$25. AE, DC, DISC, MC, V. Daily 6:30–11am, 1:30am–2pm, and 5–10pm. CONTINENTAL/SOUTHWESTERN.

Rough-hewn ceiling beams and log walls are a surprising contrast to the fine china, crystal, and linen table settings in the El Tovar Dining Room. World-class continental cuisine with touches of southwestern flavor thrown in for good measure is the hallmark of the restaurant's excellent chef. Most of the ingredients used in the El Tovar's kitchen are flown in daily to assure freshness and quality. On a recent visit the dinner menu featured tortilla-crusted shrimp with orange-peppercorn sauce and jicama slaw among the appetizers. For a main course the filet mignon and quail medallions with Gorgonzola polenta was mouthwatering. The view out the picture windows is one of the best in the world. Make reservations as soon as possible to get the dinner time you want.

Moderate

Arizona Steak House

In the Bright Angel Lodge. ☎ **520/638-2631.** Reservations not accepted. Dinner $12–$20. AE, DC, DISC, MC, V. Daily 5–10pm. STEAKS.

If you have a craving for a thick juicy steak or a crisp cool salad, a visit to this steakhouse is in order. The decor is contemporary Southwest with a desert palette of pastel colors. A wall of glass along one side of the restaurant assures everyone of a view of the canyon beyond. Since the restaurant is open only for dinner (although group tours dine here at lunch), you should get here as early as possible to enjoy the sunset view and to avoid a long wait for a table.

Bright Angel Dining Room

In the Bright Angel Lodge. ☎ **520/638-2631.** Reservations not accepted. Main dishes $5–$11. AE, DC, DISC, MC, V. Daily 6:30–10:45am and 11:15am–10pm. AMERICAN.

Muted desert tones, lodgepole pine beams and pillars, and wrought-iron chandeliers give this spacious and casual dining room a distinctive southwestern feel. Waiters in black bolo ties and vests are friendly and efficient. What's on the menu are southwestern favorites such as enchiladas, tamales, and fajitas, and foods comforting to a hungry and tired hiker such as spaghetti and meatballs. Wines are available. If you put your name on the waiting list, the wait usually isn't very long.

Inexpensive

If you're looking for a quick, inexpensive meal, there are plenty of options. In Grand Canyon Village, choices include **cafeterias** at the Yavapai and Maswik lodges and a **delicatessen** at Babbitt's General Store (across from the visitor center). **Hermits Rest Fountain** on the West Rim Drive is a snack bar. At Desert View (on the West Rim Drive) is the **Desert View Trading Post Cafeteria.** All of these places are open daily for all three meals, and all serve meals for about $7 and under.

WILLIAMS

Rod's Steak House

301 E. Bill Williams Ave. ☎ **520/635-2671.** Main dishes $7–$25. DISC, MC, V. Daily 11am–10pm. STEAKS/SEAFOOD.

If you're looking for a good dinner in Williams, just look for the red neon steer at the east end of town. This is the sign that beckons hungry canyon explorers to come on in and have a great steak. The menu is short and comes printed on a paper cutout of a steer, but what Rod's does have is always reliable. Prime rib au jus, the house specialty, comes in three different weights to fit your hunger.

SHOPPING

There are several curio shops along the South Rim of the canyon. The largest and most interesting of these is the **Hopi House** (☎ 520/638-2631, ext. 6383), in front of the El Tovar Hotel. This shop, the first in the park, was built in 1905 to resemble a Hopi pueblo and to serve as a place for Hopi artisans to work and sell their crafts. Today it's full of Hopi and Navajo arts and crafts, including expensive kachinas, rugs, jewelry, and pottery. The nearby **Verkamps Curios** (☎ 520/638-2242) originally opened in a tent in 1898, but after John Verkamp went out of business, it was not reopened until 1905. Today it's the main place to look for souvenirs and crafts. The **Desert View Watchtower** (☎ 520/638-2736), 23 miles east of Grand Canyon Village, is another fascinating shop housed in a historic building. It's full of souvenirs and southwestern crafts.

EVENING ENTERTAINMENT

Most people visiting the Grand Canyon aren't thinking about anything other than a campfire when they think of evening entertainment, but in fact there's quite a bit of nightlife for those who haven't been exhausted by a day of hiking or mule riding. The **Maswik Cafeteria** has a sports bar with big-screen TV. In the lounges of the **El Tovar Hotel** and **Bright Angel Lodge,** there's live music. There's also a lounge at **Moqui Lodge.**

In addition to these lively pursuits, there are more traditional national park evening programs such as stargazing and lecture/slide shows on cultural and natural-history aspects of the Grand Canyon (see *The Guide* for information).

In September there's the **Grand Canyon Chamber Music Festival** (**☎520/ 638-9215**). Most of these programs are held in the Shrine of the Ages near the visitor center.

3 Lake Powell & Page

272 miles N of Phoenix, 130 miles E of the Grand Canyon North Rim, 130 miles NE of Grand Canyon South Rim

Had the early Spanish explorers of Arizona suddenly come upon Lake Powell, they would have either taken it for a mirage or fallen to their knees and rejoiced. Surrounded by hundreds of miles of parched desert land, this man-made lake acts like a magnet, drawing everyone in the region toward its promise of relief from the heat. Though construction began on the Glen Canyon Dam in 1960 and was completed in 1963, Lake Powell did not reach capacity until 1980. Today it's a water playground frequented by boaters, skiers, fishermen, and people who come here to see the Rainbow Bridge, one of the natural wonders of the world. The Rainbow Bridge is called *nonnozhoshi*, or "the rainbow turned to stone," by the Navajo. It's the largest natural bridge on earth and stretches 278 feet across a side canyon in the Glen Canyon National Recreation Area.

Construction of the Glen Canyon Dam came despite the angry outcry of many who felt that this canyon was even more beautiful than the Grand Canyon and should be preserved in its natural state. Preservationists lost this battle, and today houseboats and skiers cruise where birds and waterfalls once filled the canyons with their songs. Page, a work camp constructed to house the workers who built the dam, has now become a town unto itself and, with its many motels and restaurants, is the best place from which to explore Lake Powell.

ESSENTIALS
GETTING THERE

By Plane   The Page Airport, 1 mile east of town on Ariz. 98, is served by Skywest airlines (call 520/645-2494, or 800/453-9417, for flight information).

By Car   Page is connected to Flagstaff by U.S. 89. Ariz 98 leads southeast into the Navajo Indian Reservation and connects with U.S. 160 to Kayenta and Four Corners.

VISITOR INFORMATION

For further information on Page and Lake Powell, contact the **Page/Lake Powell Chamber of Commerce,** P.O. Box 727, Page, AZ 86040 (**☎ 520/645-2741**), or the **John Wesley Powell Memorial Museum,** 6 N. Lake Powell Blvd. (P.O. Box 547), Page, AZ 86040 (**☎ 520/645-9496**).

GETTING AROUND

Rental cars are available at the Page Airport from **Budget** (**☎ 520/645-3977** or 800/527-0700).

WHAT TO SEE & DO
GLEN CANYON NATIONAL RECREATION AREA & RAINBOW BRIDGE NATIONAL MONUMENT

Until the construction of the Glen Canyon Dam and the subsequent formation of Lake Powell, this area was one of the most remote regions in the contiguous 48 states. Today, however, it's one of the nation's most popular national recreation areas and attracts 3.6 million visitors each year. The lake is the main attraction, and its stunning setting amid the slick-rock canyons of northern Arizona and southern Utah makes it one of the most beautiful of Arizona's many reservoirs. More than 500 feet deep in some places, and bounded by nearly 2,000 miles of shoreline, **Lake Powell** is a maze of convoluted canyons. Waterskiing, Jet Skiing, and fishing are the most popular activities, and five marinas (only Wahweap is in Arizona) help boaters explore the lake. There are, however, few roads penetrating the recreation area, so the only way to appreciate this rugged region is by boat. You can bring your own boat or rent one here, and there are houseboats for rent if you want to spend a few days or a week living in comfort on the water.

The most popular destination on the lake is the **Rainbow Bridge,** the world's largest natural bridge, which is preserved as a national monument. Standing 290 feet high and spanning 275 feet, this sandstone arch is an awesome reminder of the powers of erosion that have sculpted this entire region into the spectacle it is today. The Rainbow Bridge is located 50 miles from Glen Canyon Dam and is accessible only by boat or on foot. Traveling there by boat is by far the more popular route. There are daily tours from the Wahweap and Bullfrog marinas (see "Organized Tours," below, for details).

It's the **Glen Canyon Dam,** built across a stretch of the Colorado River less than a third of a mile wide, that impounds the waters of the Colorado River to form Lake Powell. The dam, which stands 710 feet above the bedrock, contains almost five million cubic yards of concrete. Built to provide water for the desert communities of the Southwest and West, the dam also provides hydroelectric power. Self-guided tours of the dam take 30 to 45 minutes. The dam is open for tours daily from 8am to 5pm in winter and from 7am to 7pm in summer. Admission is free. For more information, contact the Carl Hayden Visitor Center (see below).

For more information on the recreation area, visit one of the two visitors centers. The **Carl Hayden Visitor Center,** beside Glen Canyon Dam (☎ 520/608-6405), is open daily from 8am to 5pm (7am to 7pm in summer). The **Bullfrog Visitor Center,** in Bullfrog, Utah (☎ 801/684-7400), is open daily from 8am to 5pm, but may be closed in winter months.

For more information before leaving home, you can contact the **Glen Canyon National Recreation Area,** P.O. Box 1507, Page, AZ 86040 (☎ 520/608-6405).

A MUSEUM

John Wesley Powell Memorial Museum

6 N. Lake Powell Blvd. ☎ **520/645-9496.** Admission free; requested donation, $1 adults, 50¢ children. May–Sept, Mon–Sat 8am–6pm, Sun 10am–6pm; Oct–Apr, Mon–Sat 9am–5pm.

Lake Powell is named after John Wesley Powell, the one-armed Civil War veteran who led the first expedition through the Grand Canyon. In 1869 Powell and a small band of men spent more than three months fighting the rapids of the Green and Colorado rivers in wooden-hulled boats. This small museum is dedicated to the courageous—some said crazy—Powell and his expedition. Besides documenting the Powell expedition with photographs, etchings, and artifacts, the museum displays Native American artifacts from Anasazi pottery to contemporary Navajo and Hopi crafts. The exhibit of fluorescent minerals is particularly interesting. There are also several informative videos that are regularly screened in the museum's small auditorium. The museum also acts as an information center for Page, Lake Powell, and the region, and has a small gift shop.

OUTDOOR ACTIVITIES

HIKING   There also several good, though strenuous, hikes in the area. The most popular is the 7-mile round-trip hike into **Antelope Canyon,** which is one of the most photographed canyons in Arizona. This narrow, sandstone-walled canyon is only a few feet wide in some places and the interplay of shadows and light is transfixing. The trailhead for Antelope Canyon is at milepost 299 on Ariz. 98.

The much shorter hike to the **Horseshoe Bend** viewpoint is also worthwhile. This trail leads to a view of a scenic loop in the Colorado River. The total length of this hike depends on where you park, but plan on a little more than a mile to the viewpoint and back. The trailhead is 5 miles south of the Carl Hayden Visitor Center on U.S. 89 just south of highway marker 545.

WATER SPORTS   By far the most popular activities here are boating, waterskiing, and Jet Skiing. At the **Wahweap Marina** (☎ 520/645-2433, or 800/528-6154) you can rent various types of boats, Jet Skis, and waterskis. Rental rates range from $63 for a 16-foot skiff with a 25-horsepower engine up to $225 per day for a 19-foot boat with a 150-horsepower engine.

ORGANIZED TOURS

The Glen Canyon National Recreation Area covers an immense area, much of it inaccessible to regular automobiles. If you'd like to see more of the area than is visible from the few roads, you might want to consider a tour by Jeep, boat, or small plane. **Lake Powell Jeep Tours** (☎ 520/645-5501) offers trips to photogenic Antelope Canyon in open Jeeps. A 1¹/₂-hour tour costs $21.50 for adults and $10.50 for children. **Photographic Tours** (☎ 520/645-8579 or 801/675-9109) offers photography tours to Antelope Canyon for about $40. **High Mesa Tours** (☎ 520/645-2266) also offers a number of interesting tours of the Page area. These tours range in cost from $10 to $60. If you'd like to explore the area by horseback, contact **Rope & Saddle Promotions,** Vermillion Downs, Haul Road (☎ 520/645-2752 or 520/645-2077), which charges $25 for a one-hour trail ride ($15 for children). Mountain-bike and sea-kayak rentals and tours are available from **Red Rock Cyclery,** 819 N. Navajo Dr. (☎ 520/645-1479).

If you'd like to cool off, try a float trip from Glen Canyon Dam to Lees Ferry. These raft trips are operated by **Wilderness River Adventures** (☎ 520/645-3279 or 800/528-6154) and cost about $40 for adults and $35 for children for a half-day trip.

Scenic Airlines (☎ 520/645-2494 or 800/634-6801) offers several air tours of northern and northeastern Arizona, including flights to the Rainbow Bridge, the Escalante River, the Grand Canyon, Canyonlands, Bryce Canyon, Monument Valley, and the Navajo nation. Rates range from $61 to $252.

Lake Powell Resorts & Marinas (☎ 520/645-2433 or 800/528-6154) offers a variety of boat tours on Lake Powell. Three times daily, the paddlewheeler *Canyon King* embarks on a one-hour tour out of the Wahweap Marina ($9 for adults, $6.45 for children). There are also sunset ($19.65 for adults, $12.95 for children) and dinner cruises ($42.95) aboard the *Canyon King*. There are half-day ($55.50 for adults, $30.60 for children) and full-day ($72 for adults, $39.80 for children) tours to Rainbow Bridge National Monument, 50 miles up Lake Powell from the Wahweap Marina. Colorado River float trips and white-water-rafting trips are also available. The float trips depart March to October from just below the Glen Canyon Dam and cost $39.95 for adults and $34.95 for children for a half day. You can also rent your own powerboat and go exploring on your own. The same company that operates the boat tours rents runabouts, skiffs, and patio boats. Rental rates range from $63 to $225 a day in the high season and $38 to $135 a day in the low season. Weekly rates are also available.

WHERE TO STAY

HOUSEBOATS

Though there are plenty of hotels and motels in and near Page, the most popular accommodations here are not waterfront hotel rooms but houseboats, which function as floating vacation homes. With a houseboat, you can explore Lake Powell's beautiful red-rock country, far from any roads. These powered houseboats are as easy to operate as a car.

○ **Lake Powell Resorts & Marinas–Houseboats,** P.O. Box 56909, Phoenix, AZ 85079 (☎ **520/645-2433,** 602/278-8888 in Phoenix, or 800/528-6154; fax 520/331-5258), has boats that range in size from 36 to 59 feet and sleep anywhere from 6 to 12 people. They come complete with hot showers, refrigerator/freezer, heating system, stove, oven, and gas grill. Kitchens come equipped with everything you'll need to prepare meals. The only things you'll really need to bring are bedding and towels. Seven-night houseboat rentals are $1,241 to $3,495 mid-May to mid-Oct, $931 to $2,621 April to mid-May and mid- to late October; $745 to $2,097 November to March. Rentals also available for two, three, or four nights.

EXPENSIVE

⑤ Courtyard by Marriott

600 Country Club Dr. (P.O. Box 8000-365), Page, AZ 86040-8000. ☎ **520/645-5000** or 800/321-2211. Fax 520/645-5004. 153 rms. A/C TV TEL. Mar–Oct, $89–$119 double. Nov–Feb, $59–$89 double. AE, CB, DC, DISC, MC, V.

Located on the outskirts of Page, this hotel is done in an attractive pueblo motif and is the top in-town choice. The rooms are larger than at most motels and there are king-size beds, separate seating areas, dressing areas, and mirrored closet doors.

Dining/Entertainment: Moderately priced meals are served in a casual restaurant that has a terrace overlooking the distant lake. There's also an adjacent lounge.

Services: Room service, valet/laundry service.

Facilities: A golf course was under construction when we last visited, but for the time being an outdoor pool, whirlpool, and exercise room are the recreational facilities.

Wahweap Lodge

100 Lakeshore Dr. (P.O. Box 56909), Phoenix, AZ 85079. ☎ **520/645-2433,** 602/278-8888 in Phoenix, or 800/528-6154. Fax 520/331-5258. 375 rms, 2 suites. A/C TV TEL. Apr–Oct, $109–$129 double; $189 suite. Nov–Mar, $71–$85 double; $123 suite. AE, DC, DISC, MC, V.

The Wahweap Marina is a sprawling complex 4 miles north of Glen Canyon Dam on the shores of Lake Powell. As the biggest and best hotel in the area, Wahweap features many of the amenities and activities of a resort. The guest rooms are arranged in two long two-story wings. All the rooms have either a balcony or a patio, but only half have lake views. The west wing has the better view (the east wing overlooks the Navajo coal-fired power plant).

Dining/Entertainment: The Rainbow Room (see "Where to Dine," below) offers fine dining with a sweeping panorama of the lake and desert. The menu is equally divided between American standards and southwestern fare. A snack bar near the boat ramp provides light meals, snacks, ice cream, and cookies, and a lounge serves cocktails with a view.

Services: Room service.

Facilities: Two outdoor pools, whirlpool, boat rentals, boat tours, float trips, boat ramp.

MODERATE

Best Western Arizona Inn

716 Rim Dr. (P.O. Box C), Page, AZ 86040. ☎ **520/645-2466** or 800/528-1234. Fax 520/645-2053. 103 rms, 2 suites. A/C TV TEL. Apr–Oct, $79–$92 double; $125 suite. Oct–Mar, $49–$56 double; $75 suite. AE, DC, DISC, MC, V.

Perched right at the edge of the mesa on which Page is built, this modern motel has a fine view across miles of desert. Half the rooms have views, and of course these are more expensive. The hotel's restaurant is across the parking lot from the main building. Large windows take in a view of the desert that's slightly marred by the number of power lines that stretch out from the dam. Steaks and seafood are the menu mainstays. The hotel also offers free coffee in the lobby, an airport shuttle, an outdoor pool with a 100-mile view, and a whirlpool.

Best Western at Lake Powell

208 N. Lake Powell Blvd. (P.O. Box MM), Page, AZ 86040. ☎ **520/645-5988** or 800/528-1234. Fax 520/645-2578. 132 rms. A/C TV TEL. May–Oct, $79–$135 double. Oct–May, $35–$89 double. AE, CB, DC, DISC, MC, V.

This modern hotel lies on the edge of town overlooking Lake Powell. The rooms are comfortable and modern, and there's a pool with a great view. There's no restaurant on the premises, but breakfast is available. The hotel also offers a free airport shuttle.

INEXPENSIVE

Lake Powell Motel

U.S. 89 (P.O. Box 65909, Phoenix, AZ 85079). ☎ **520/645-2477** 602/278-888 in Phoenix, or 800/528-6154. 25 rms. A/C TV TEL. Apr–Nov, $70–$132.50 double. AE, DC, DISC, MC, V. Closed Nov–Mar. Drive 3 miles west of the Wahweap Marina or 4 miles north of the Glen Canyon Dam on U.S. 89.

Located on a barren hill set back from the lake, the Lake Powell Motel offers an alternative away from the traffic and lights of downtown Page and the bustle of activity at the Wahweap Marina. The accommodations are standard motel rooms with two queen-size beds.

Pension at Lake Powell

125 Eighth Ave. (P.O. Box 1077), Page, AZ 86040. ☎ **520/645-3898.** 14 rms, 2 with bath; 50 dormitory beds. $25–$35 double without bath; $50–$70 double with bath; $12–$15 dormitor bed. No credit cards.

Housed in old company apartments built for the construction of the Glen Canyon Dam, these two economical lodgings offer budget travelers a couple of options. With both a pension offering private rooms and a hostel offering small dormitories, this place caters to young travelers, primarily from Europe. The rooms are clean and there's a kitchen available. They even offer free airport pickups.

CAMPGROUNDS & RV PARKS

There are campgrounds and RV facilities at Wahweap and Lees Ferry in Arizona and at Bullfrog, Hite, and Halls Crossing in Utah.

WHERE TO DINE

Rainbow Room

In the Wahweap Lodge, at the Wahweap Marina, Lakeshore Dr. ☎ **520/645-2433.** Reservations not accepted. Main courses $9.75–$19. AE, DC, DISC, MC, V. Daily 6am–2:30pm and 5–10pm. AMERICAN/SOUTHWEST.

Because of the sweeping vistas of Lake Powell through the walls of glass (and not necessarily because of the food), the Rainbow Room at the Wahweap Lodge is Page's best restaurant. There's a good chance you'll run into international tour groups here. The menu features American dishes, such as grilled Cajun catfish and seafood Caesar salad, but there are also specials and such dishes as broiled chicken with roasted Anaheim chiles, red onion, and cilantro to tempt those with a taste for southwestern flavors. If you're heading out on the water for the day, they'll fix you a box lunch.

Stromboli's

711 N. Navajo Blvd. ☎ **520/645-2605.** Main dishes $6.50–$10. MC, V. Sun–Thurs 11am–10pm, Fri–Sat 11am–1am. SOUTHERN ITALIAN.

With its New Orleans–style grillwork and large front terrace, Stromboli's is unmistakable, but it's really nothing fancy. The terrace makes a great dining spot on a warm evening, and is popular with families. The menu includes all the usual Italian dishes, but also includes such items as fresh-baked Tuscany bread with basil pesto, spinach, tomatoes, mozzarella, and parmesan cheese, and several gourmet pizza combinations. There are also calzones and a good assortment of salads.

Zapata's

614 N. Navajo Dr. ☎ **520/645-9006.** Main courses $7–$13. DISC, MC, V. Daily 10:30am–2pm and 5–9pm. SONORAN/MEXICAN.

Zapata's is a little place located in the shopping plaza diagonally across from the intersection at the Powell Museum. We popped in here for lunch and were pleasantly surprised by a spicy chile verde burrito and the somewhat milder, though flavorful, chicken enchilada that we ordered. Rice and beans, which are frequently pretty generic in Mexican restaurants, were tasty too. At lunch there are a limited selection of specials for about $5. The crowd here is usually more locals than tourists.

EN ROUTE TO THE NORTH RIM

Between Page and the North Rim of the Grand Canyon, Alternate U.S. 89 crosses the Colorado River at Lees Ferry in Marble Canyon. Lees Ferry is the starting point for raft trips through the Grand Canyon, and for many years was the only place to cross the Colorado River for hundreds of miles in either direction. There's also a campground here. Lees Ferry is well known among anglers for its trophy trout fishing, and when the North Rim closes and the rafting season comes to an end, about the only folks you'll find up here are fishermen and hunters.

Continuing west, the highway passes under the **Vermillion Cliffs,** so named for their deep red coloring. At the base of these cliffs are huge boulders balanced on narrow columns of eroded soil. The balanced rocks give the area a very otherworldly appearance. Along this remote and unpopulated stretch of road are a couple of very basic lodges. If you don't have a reservation at one of the three lodges at or near the North Rim, you may want to stop at one of the following lodges and continue on to the North Rim the next morning. Lodges near the canyon fill up early if they aren't already fully booked with reservations made months in advance.

West of Marble Canyon 17 miles, you'll see a sign for **House Rock Ranch.** This wildlife area, managed by the Arizona Game and Fish Department, is best known for its herd of American bison (buffalo). From the turnoff it's a 22-mile drive on a gravel road to reach the ranch.

WHERE TO STAY EN ROUTE

Cliff Dwellers Lodge

U.S. 89A (HC67–30), Marble Canyon, AZ 86036. ☎ **520/355-2228** or 800/433-2543. Fax 520/355-2229. 21 rms. Apr–Sept, $57–$67 double. Oct–Mar, $30 double. DISC, MC, V.

To give you some idea of how remote an area this is, the Cliff Dwellers Lodge is marked on official Arizona state maps. There just isn't much else out here, so a single lodge can be as important as a town. The newer, more expensive rooms here are standard motel rooms and have combination bathtub/showers, while the older rooms, in a stone-walled building, have more character but showers only. A small restaurant provides meals. The lodge is close to some spectacular balanced rocks and it's about 11 miles east to Lees Ferry. The views here are great.

Lees Ferry Lodge

U.S. 89A (HC67-Box 1), Marble Canyon, AZ 86036. ☎ **520/355-2231.** 9 rms. A/C. $45 double. MC, V.

Located at the foot of the Vermillion Cliffs, $3^1/_2$ miles west of the Colorado River, the Lees Ferry Lodge, built in 1929 of native stone and rough-hewn timber beams, is a small place with rustic accommodations that could use new carpets. However, the rafters and anglers who stay here don't seem to care much about the condition of the rooms. The views of the Vermillion Cliffs are quite spectacular, and there's a very pleasant patio seating area in front of all the rooms. Unfortunately the highway is only a few yards away, so traffic noises occasionally disturb the tranquillity. A small dining room provides what's reputed to be the best food for miles around.

Marble Canyon Lodge

Marble Canyon, AZ 86036. ☎ **520/355-2225.** 60 rms. A/C. $55–$125 double. DISC, MC, V.

Located just 4 miles from Lees Ferry, the Marble Canyon Lodge was built in the 1920s and is popular with rafters preparing to head down the Grand Canyon. The room styles vary considerably in size and age, with some rustic rooms in old stone buildings and other rooms in newer motel-style rooms as well. You're right at the base of the Vermillion Cliffs here, and the views are great. There's a cozy restaurant and a trading post (be sure to have some Marble Canyon cake).

4 The Grand Canyon: North Rim

42 miles S of Jacob Lake, 216 miles N of Grand Canyon Village (South Rim), 354 miles N of Phoenix, 125 miles W of Page/Lake Powell

Though the North Rim is only 10 miles as the raven flies from the South Rim, it's a 200-mile drive. For this reason many people never make it to this rim of the canyon. In addition to the great distance from the more popular South Rim, the North Rim is only open from mid-May to October or early November. If Grand Canyon Village was too much of a human zoo for you and not the wilderness experience you had expected, then the North Rim will probably be much more to your liking, though crowds, traffic congestion, and parking problems are not unheard of here either.

At 8,000 feet in elevation, the North Rim is 1,000 feet higher than the South Rim and receives considerably more snow in the winter. Arizona 67 is not plowed and consequently the Grand Canyon Lodge is closed down for the winter.

The North Rim is located on the Kaibab Plateau, which takes its name from the Paiute word for "mountain lying down." This plateau averages over 8,000 feet in elevation and is home to a unique white-tailed squirrel called the Kaibab. Keep your eyes open for this large-eared squirrel whenever you're walking in the forest. The higher elevation of the North Rim's Kaibab Plateau produces a different vegetation from what you see at the South Rim. A dense forest of ponderosa pines, Douglas firs, and aspen interspersed with large meadows gives the North Rim an alpine feel that is lacking at the South Rim.

ESSENTIALS
GETTING THERE

By Bus Trans Canyon operates a shuttle between the North Rim and South Rim of the Grand Canyon. The shuttle leaves the South Rim daily at 1:30pm and arrives at the North Rim at 6:30pm. The return trip leaves the North Rim at 7am and arrives at the South Rim at 11:30am. The fare is $60 one way and $100 round-trip. Call 520/638-2820 for more information.

By Car The North Rim is at the end of Ariz. 67 (the North Rim Parkway), which is reached from Alternate U.S. 89.

VISITOR INFORMATION

For information before leaving home, contact **Grand Canyon National Park,** P.O. Box 129, Grand Canyon, AZ 86023-0129 (☎ **520/638-7888**).

There's an **information desk** in the lobby of the Grand Canyon Lodge, open daily from 8am to 5pm. At the entrance gate you'll also be given a copy of *The Guide,* a small newspaper with information on park activities. There's a separate edition of *The Guide* for each of the two rims.

Important Note: The North Rim is only open from mid-May to late October. The park admission fee is $10 per car and is good for one week.

WHAT TO SEE & DO

There are far fewer activities on the North Rim than there are on the South Rim, and not surprisingly there are also fewer people. There's an information desk in the lobby of the Grand Canyon Lodge, but there's no visitor center or museum here.

The best spots for viewing the canyon are Bright Angel Point, Point Imperial, and Cape Royal. **Bright Angel Point** is the closest to Grand Canyon Lodge, and from here you can see and hear Roaring Springs, which is 3,600 feet below the rim and is the North Rim's only water source. From Bright Angel Point you can also see Grand Canyon Village on the South Rim. At 8,803 feet, **Point Imperial** is the highest point on either rim of the Grand Canyon. A short section of the Colorado River can be seen far below, and off to the east the Painted Desert is visible. However, **Cape Royal** is the most spectacular setting on the North Rim.

Along the 23-mile road to Cape Royal are several scenic overlooks. Across the road from the **Walhalla Overlook** are the ruins of an Anasazi structure. Just before reaching Cape Royal you'll come to the **Angel's Window Overlook,** which gives you a breathtaking view of the natural bridge that forms Angel's Window.

Once at Cape Royal, you can follow a trail across this natural bridge to a towering promontory overlooking the valley.

If you'd like to see the North Rim on a guided tour, contact **TW Recreational Services** in the lobby of the Grand Canyon Lodge. They offer three-hour van tours that stop at the overlooks mentioned above. The cost is $19.95 for adults and $6.95 for children 4 to 12.

After simply taking in the views, **hiking along the rim** is the most popular activity. There are quite a few day hikes of varying lengths possible on the North Rim. The shortest is the half-mile paved trail to Bright Angel Point, and the longest is the North Kaibab Trail to Roaring Springs and back, which takes six to eight hours.

If you want to see the canyon from a saddle, contact **Canyon Trail Rides** (☎ **520/638-2292**), which offers mule rides varying in length from one hour to a full day. Prices range from $12 for an hour ride up to $85 for the all-day trip.

WHERE TO STAY

Grand Canyon Lodge

Contact TW Recreational Services, P.O. Box 400, Cedar City, UT 84721. ☎ **801/586-7686.** 209 rms and cabins. $53–$82 double in rooms or cabins. AE, CB, DC, DISC, MC, V. Closed Nov–May.

Perched right on the canyon rim, this classic mountain lodge is listed on the National Register of Historic Places. The stone-and-log main lodge building has a soaring ceiling and a viewing room set up with chairs facing a wall of glass. On either side of this room are flagstone terraces set with rustic chairs that face out toward the canyon.

The guest rooms vary from standard motel rooms to rustic mountain cabins to comfortable modern cabins. Our favorites are the little cabins, which, though cramped and paneled with dark wood, capture the feeling of a mountain retreat better than any of the other rooms. A few rooms have views of the canyon, but most are tucked back away from the rim.

Dining/Entertainment: A large dining hall with two walls of glass serves straightforward American food and is open daily for all three meals. There's also a snack bar outside the lodge's front entrance and a saloon.

Services: Tour desk.

Jacob Lake Inn

Jacob Lake, AZ 86022. ☎ **520/643-7232.** 11 rms, 33 cabins. May 15–Nov, $59–$78 double in rooms or cabins. Nov–May 15, $45 double in rooms or cabins. AE, DC, DISC, MC, V.

Located 30 miles north of the entrance to the North Rim, the Jacob Lake Inn consists of motel rooms and rustic cabins. The motel rooms are quite a bit nicer than the cabins, which have old carpets and cramped bathrooms with showers (no tubs). This lodge stays open in winter and is a base for cross-country skiers and snowmobilers.

Dining/Entertainment: Just off the lobby is a coffee shop, and adjacent is a more formal dining room. A bakery counter sells delicious cookies and fudge, and the general store sells snacks.

Facilities: Gas station, basketball and volleyball courts, playground.

Kaibab Lodge

P.O. Box 2997, Flagstaff, AZ 86003. ☎ **520/638-2389,** 520/526-0924, or 800/525-0924. 24 rms. May 15–Nov, $65–$85 double. Nov–May 15, package rates only. DISC, MC, V.

Located 5 miles north of the entrance to the Grand Canyon's North Rim, the Kaibab Lodge was built around 1926 and is situated on the edge of a large meadow where deer can often be seen grazing. The rooms are in small rustic cabins set back in the pines from the main lodge building. Nights here are cool even in summer and a favorite pastime of guests is to sit by the fireplace in the lobby. Although the highway from Jacob Lake is closed by the first big snow, the lodge stays open for much of the winter as a cross-country ski lodge, shuttling skiers in by snowcoach. This remote setting is ideal for cross-country skiing and makes a very quiet retreat.

Dining/Entertainment: The lodge's dining room serves all meals, and the kitchen also prepares box lunches.

Services: Tour desk, hiking-equipment rentals, mountain-bike rentals, ski lessons, ski tours.

Facilities: Gift shop, whirlpool spa.

CAMPGROUNDS

Located just north of Grand Canyon Lodge, the **North Rim Campground,** with 82 sites and no hookups for RVs, is the only campground at the North Rim. Reservations can be made by calling Mistix (☎ **800/365-2267**). The fee is $10 per site per night.

There are also two campgrounds outside the park in the Kaibab National Forest. These are **DeMotte Park Campground,** which is the closest to the park entrance and has only 25 sites. **Jacob Lake Campground** is 30 miles north of the park entrance. It has 50 sites. Both campgrounds charge $10 per night. You can also camp anywhere in the Kaibab National Forest. So, if you can't find a site in a campground, simply pull off the highway in the national forest and park your RV or pitch your tent.

The **Jacob Lake R.V. Park,** P.O. Box 498, Jacob Lake, AZ 86022 (☎ **520/643-7804**), is a privately owned campground in the crossroads of Jacob Lake, 30 miles north of the park entrance. This campground has 80 RV sites and 50 tent sites.

5 Havasu Canyon

40 miles NW of Grand Canyon Village, 70 miles N of Ariz. 66, 155 miles NW of Flagstaff, 115 miles NE of Kingman

Imagine hiking for hours through a dusty brown landscape of rocks and cacti. The sun overhead is blistering and bright. The air is hot and dry. This is desert canyon country. Rock walls rise up higher and higher as you continue your descent through a mazelike canyon. Eventually the narrow canyon opens up into a wide plain shaded by cottonwood trees—a sure sign of water—and within a few minutes you hear the sound of a babbling stream. The water, when you finally reach it, is cool and crystal clear, a pleasant surprise. Following the stream, you pass through a dusty village of modern homes. Every yard seems to be a corral for horses, not surprising in a village 8 miles beyond the last road. You pass through the village, still following the stream. As the trail descends again, you spot the first waterfall.

The previously crystal clear water is now brilliant turquoise blue at the foot of the waterfall. The sandstone walls look redder than before. No, you aren't having a heat-induced hallucination—the water really is turquoise, and it fills terraces of travertine to form deep pools of cool water at the base of three large waterfalls. Together these three waterfalls form what many claim is the most beautiful spot in the entire Grand Canyon.

This is Havasu Canyon, the canyon of the Havasupai tribe, whose name means "people of the blue-green waters," and who for centuries have called this idyllic desert oasis home.

ESSENTIALS
GETTING THERE

By Car   It isn't possible to reach Supai village or Havasu Canyon by car. The nearest road ends 8 miles from Supai at Hualapai Hilltop. This is the trailhead for the trail into the canyon and is at the end of Indian Route 18, which runs north from Ariz. 66. The turnoff is 6 miles east of Peach Springs and 21 miles west of Seligman. Many Arizona maps show an unpaved road between U.S. 180 and Hualapai Hilltop, but this road is not maintained on a regular basis and is only passable to four-wheel-drive vehicles *when* it's clear of fallen logs.

By Helicopter   The easiest and fastest (and by far the most expensive) way to reach Havasu Canyon is by helicopter from the Grand Canyon Airport. Flights are operated by Papillon Grand Canyon Helicopters, P.O. Box 455, Grand Canyon, AZ 86023 (call 520/638-2419, or 800/528-2418, for flight information). The round-trip airfare is $410 from May to October, and less expensive the rest of the year. This company also offers package tours to Havasu Canyon and 30- to 50-minute Canyon tours.

By Horse   The next-easiest way to get to Havasu Canyon is by horse. Both you and your luggage can ride from Hualapai Hilltop, the trailhead for Supai and Havasu Canyon. Pack and saddle horses can be rented from the Havasupai Tourist Enterprise, Supai, AZ 86435 (call 520/448-2121 for more information). Round-trip rates are $110 from Hualapai Hilltop to the campground, $80 from Hualapai Hilltop to Supai village, and $40 from Supai village to the campground. One-way rates are also available—many people who hike in decide that it's worth the money to ride out, or at least have their backpack packed out. Be sure to confirm your horse reservation a day before driving to Hualapai Hilltop. Sometimes no horses are available and it's a long drive back to the nearest town.

On Foot   The cheapest, slowest, and most difficult way to reach Havasu Canyon is on foot. Start early to avoid the heat of the day. The hike is beautiful—but it's 10 miles to the campground. The steepest part of the trail is the first mile or so from Hualapai Hilltop. After this section it's relatively flat.

AT THE CANYON

There's a $15-per-person entry fee to Havasu Canyon from April to October, $12 the rest of the year. Everyone is required to register at the Tourist Office across from the sports field as you enter the village of Supai. Because it's a long walk in to the campground, be sure you have a confirmed reservation before setting out from Hualapai Hilltop. It's good to make reservations as far in advance as possible, especially for holiday weekends. The tourist enterprises at Supai operate on a cash-only basis, so be sure to bring sufficient cash.

WHAT TO SEE & DO

The waterfalls are the main attraction here and most people are content to sun themselves on the sand, go for dips in the cool waters, and gaze for hours at the turquoise waters. When you tire of these pursuits, you can go for a hike up the small side canyon to the east of Havasu Falls. Another trail leads along the west rim of Havasu Canyon and can be reached by carefully climbing up a steep rocky area near the village cemetery. There's also a trail that leads all the way down to the Colorado River, though this is an overnight hike.

In Supai village is a small museum dedicated to the culture of the Havasupai people. Its exhibits and old photos will give you an idea of how little the lives of these people have changed over the years.

WHERE TO STAY & DINE
IN HAVASU CANYON

Havasu Campground

Havasupai Tourist Enterprise, Supai, AZ 86435. ☎ **520/448-2121.** 400 sites. Apr–Oct, $10 per person per night. Nov–Mar, $9 per person per night.

The campground is located 2 miles below Supai village, between Havasu Falls and Mooney Falls. The campsites are mostly in the shade of cottonwood trees on either side of Havasu Creek. Picnic tables are provided, but no firewood is available at the campground. Cutting any trees or shrubs is prohibited, so be sure to bring a camp stove with you. Spring water is available, and though it's considered safe to drink we advise treating it first.

Havasupai Lodge

General Delivery, Supai, AZ 86435. ☎ **520/448-2111.** 24 rms. A/C. Apr–Oct, $80 double. Nov–Mar, $50 double. No credit cards.

Located in Supai village just past the school, this modern lodge is, aside from the campground, the only accommodation in the canyon. The two-story building features standard motel-style rooms that are lacking only TVs and telephones, neither of which are in demand at this isolated retreat. People come to Havasu Canyon to get away from it all, and the Havasupai Lodge is happy to oblige. The only drawback of this comfortable lodge is that it's 2 miles from Havasu Falls and 3 miles from Mooney Falls. The Havasupai Café, across from the general store, serves breakfast, lunch, and dinner. It's a very casual place, and the prices are high because all ingredients must be packed in by horse.

NEAR HUALAPAI HILLTOP

Grand Canyon Caverns Inn and Campground

P.O. Box 180, Peach Springs, AZ 86434. ☎ **520/422-3223.** 49 rms. A/C TV TEL. $46 double. MC, V.

If you're planning to hike or ride into Havasu Canyon, you'll need to be at Hualapai Hilltop as early in the morning as possible. It's a three- to four-hour drive to Hualapai Hilltop from Flagstaff, so you might want to consider staying here—the only lodging for miles around. As the name implies, this motel is built on the site of the Grand Canyon Caverns, which are open to the public. There's a casual restaurant and cocktail lounge. Facilities include a games room, a gift shop, and a general store with camping supplies and food.

The Four Corners Region & Eastern Arizona

There's only one place in the United States where four states come together at the same point. Arizona, New Mexico, Colorado, and Utah all meet at a spot called the Four Corners. The name also applies to the huge surrounding area and a large piece of northeastern Arizona. Most of the land in the Four Corners region of Arizona is Navajo and Hopi reservation land, and it's also some of the most spectacular countryside in the state, with majestic mesas, rainbow-hued deserts, gravity-defying buttes, cliffs, and canyons. Among the most spectacular of these are the 1,000-foot buttes of Monument Valley. For years these evocative and colorful monoliths have symbolized the Wild West of cowboys and John Wayne movies.

The Navajo and Hopi peoples who have lived on this land for hundreds of years have adapted different means of surviving in the arid Four Corners region. The Navajo have become herders of sheep, goats, and cattle. Their homes, including traditional log-walled hogans, are scattered across the countryside. The Hopi, on the other hand, have congregated in villages atop mesas and built houses of stone. They farm the floors of narrow valleys at the feet of their mesas in much the same way Native Americans of the Southwest have done for centuries.

The Hopi and the Navajo are, however, only the most recent Native Americans to inhabit what many consider to be a desolate, barren wilderness. The ancient Anasazi have left their mark throughout the canyons of the Four Corners region, with cliff dwellings dating back 700 years and more, the most spectacular being those at Canyon de Chelly National Monument and Navajo National Monument. No one is sure why the Anasazi moved up into the cliff walls, but there is speculation that unfavorable growing conditions brought on by drought may have forced them to use every possible inch of arable land. The cliff dwellings were mysteriously abandoned in the 13th century, and with no written record, the disappearance of the Anasazi may forever remain a mystery.

Northern Arizona is bisected by I-40, which runs east and west. The Four Corners region lies to the north of the Interstate, while to the south the landscape changes dramatically; eastern Arizona is a land of mountains and forests, where towns with such names as Alpine and Pinetop have become summer retreats for the people who live in the state's low-lying, sun-baked deserts. In only a few hours

---

What's Special About the Four Corners Region & Eastern Arizona

Native American Ruins
- Canyon de Chelly, full of ancient Anasazi cliff dwellings.
- Keet Seel and Betatakin, at Navajo National Monument, two of the largest and best-preserved Anasazi ruins in Arizona.

Natural Spectacles
- Canyon de Chelly, a narrow canyon that has been home to Native American cultures for 2,000 years.
- Monument Valley, a breathtaking landscape of eroded buttes, mesas, and pinnacles that has served as a backdrop for dozens of movies, television programs, and commercials.
- The Petrified Forest, where trees have turned to stone.
- The Mogollon Rim, a 2,000-foot escarpment that stretches from central Arizona into New Mexico.
- Rainbow Bridge, the largest natural bridge in the world.

Events/Festivals
- Hopi ceremonial dances, held throughout the year at various Hopi villages.
- Navajo tribal fairs, held throughout the year at different Navajo communities.

Activities
- Hiking to the ruins at Betatakin and Keet Seel.
- Exploring Canyon de Chelly by jeep, on foot, or on horseback.
- Skiing at the Sunrise ski area.
- Participating in the excavation of Raven Site ruin at the White Mountain Archaeological Center near St. Johns.

---

you can drive up from the cacti and creosote bushes of Phoenix to the meadows and pine forests of the White Mountains. Along the Mogollon Rim (pronounced "*Mug*-gee-un" by the locals), the climatic and vegetative change is dramatic. This 2,000-foot-high escarpment divides the arid lowlands from the cool mountain forests. Western author Zane Grey made his home near the Mogollon Rim and many of his novels capture the scenic beauty of this often-overlooked part of Arizona.

Trout fishing, hiking, horseback riding, and hunting are the main warm-weather pastimes of eastern Arizona. However, snow skiing at the Sunrise ski area makes this a winter destination as well. Sunrise is operated by the Apache, whose reservations cover a large part of eastern Arizona. There isn't as much to see or do in this region as there is in the Four Corners area, but if you've been down in the heat of the desert for a while and desperately need a respite from the sun, the White Mountains and Mogollon Rim offer quick relief.

1 The Hopi Reservation

250 miles NE of Phoenix, 67 miles N of Winslow, 100 miles SW of Canyon de Chelly, 140 miles SE of Page/Lake Powell

Completely surrounded by the Navajo Reservation, the Hopi Reservation has at its center the grouping of mesas that are home to the Hopi pueblos. This remote

The Four Corners Region

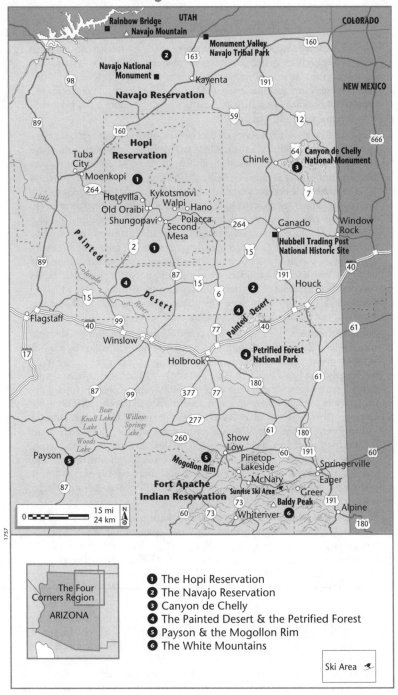

- ❶ The Hopi Reservation
- ❷ The Navajo Reservation
- ❸ Canyon de Chelly
- ❹ The Painted Desert & the Petrified Forest
- ❺ Payson & the Mogollon Rim
- ❻ The White Mountains

Ski Area

A Native American Crafts Primer

The Four Corners region is taken up almost entirely by the Navajo and Hopi reservations, so Native American crafts are ubiquitous here. You'll see jewelry for sale by the side of desolate, windswept roads, Navajo rugs for sale in tiny trading posts, Hopi kachinas being sold out of village homes. If you decide you want to take home a work by a local craftsperson, the information below will help you make an informed purchase.

Hopi Kachinas   These elaborately decorated wooden dolls are representations of spirits of plants, animals, ancestors, and sacred places. Traditionally they have been given to children to initiate them into the pantheon of kachina spirits, who play important roles in ensuring rain and harmony in the universe. In recent years kachinas have become popular with non-Hopi, and Hopi kachina carvers have changed their style to cater to the new market. Older kachinas were carved from a single piece of cottonwood, sometimes with arms simply painted on. This older style of kachina is much simpler and stiffer than the currently popular style that emphasizes action poses and realistic proportions. A great deal of carving and painting goes into each kachina, and prices today are in the hundreds of dollars for even a simple kachina. Currently gaining popularity with tourists and collectors are the *tsuku*, or clown, kachinas, which are usually painted with bold horizontal black and white stripes. The tsukus are often depicted in humorous situations or carrying slices of watermelon.

Navajo Silverwork   While the Hopi create overlay silverwork from sheets of silver and the Zuñi use silverwork simply as a base for their skilled lapidary or stone-cutting work, the Navajo silversmiths highlight the silver itself. Just as rug weaving did not begin until the latter part of the 19th century, silversmithing did not catch on with the Navajo until the 1880s, when Lorenzo Hubbell decided to hire Mexican silversmiths as teachers. When tourists began visiting the area after 1890, the demand for Navajo jewelry increased. The earliest pieces of Navajo jewelry were replicas of Spanish ornaments, but as the Navajo silversmiths became more proficient, they began to develop their own designs. Sand casting, stamp work, repoussé, and file-and-chisel work create the distinctively Navajo jewelry. The squash-blossom necklace, with its horseshoe-shaped pendant, is perhaps the most distinctive Navajo jewelry design. Wide bracelets and concha belts are also popular.

Hopi Overlay Silverwork   Overlay silverwork has come to be considered the characteristic Hopi style of silverwork, but only since World War II have the Hopi been almost exclusively making this sort of jewelry. After the war the G.I. bill provided the funds for Hopi soldiers to study silversmithing at a school founded by the famous Hopi artist Fred Kabotie. The overlay process basically

region of Arizona, with its flat-topped mesas and rugged, barren landscape, is the center of the universe for the Hopi peoples. The handful of villages that together make up the Hopi pueblos are ancient and independent communities that have today been brought together under the guidance of the Hopi Tribal Council. This land has been inhabited by the Hopi and their ancestors for nearly 1,000 years and many aspects of the ancient pueblo culture remain intact. However, much of the uses two sheets of silver, one with a design cut out of it. The two sheets are fused together with heat to form a raised image. Designs used in overlay jewelry are often borrowed from other Hopi crafts such as baskets and pottery, as well as from ancient Anasazi pottery designs. Belt buckles, earrings, bola ties, and bracelets are all popular.

Hopi Baskets   Though the Tohono O'odham of the deserts of central and southern Arizona are better known for their basketry, the Hopi also produce beautiful work. Wicker plaques and baskets are made on Third Mesa from rabbit brush and sumac and are colored with bright aniline dyes. Coiled plaques and baskets are made on Second Mesa from dyed yucca fibers. Yucca-fiber sifters are made by plaiting over a willow ring. This style of basket is made throughout the reservation.

Hopi Pottery   With the exception of undecorated utilitarian pottery that's made in Hotevilla on Third Mesa, most Hopi pottery is produced on First Mesa. Contemporary Hopi pottery comes in a variety of styles including a yellow-orange ware that's decorated with black-and-white designs. This style is said to have been introduced by the potter Nampeyo, a Tewa from the village of Hano who stimulated the revival of Hopi pottery in 1890. A white pottery with red and black designs is also popular. Hopi pottery designs tend toward geometric patterns.

Navajo Rugs   After they acquired sheep and goats from the Spanish, the Navajo learned weaving from the pueblo tribes, and by the early 1800s their weavings were widely recognized as being the finest in the Southwest. The Navajo women primarily wove blankets, but by the end of the 19th century the craft began to die out when it became more economical to purchase a ready-made blanket. When Lorenzo Hubbell set up his trading post, he immediately recognized a potential market in the East for the woven blankets if they could be made heavy enough to be used as rugs. Having great respect for Hubbell, the Navajo adapted his ideas and soon began doing a brisk business. Although today the cost of Navajo rugs, which take hundreds of hours to make, has become almost prohibitively expensive, there are still enough women practicing the craft to keep it alive and provide plenty of rugs for shops and trading posts all over Arizona.

The best rugs are those made with homespun yarn and natural vegetal dyes. However, commercially manufactured yarns and dyes are being used more and more to keep costs down. There are more than 15 regional styles of rugs and quite a bit of overlapping and borrowing. Bigger and bolder patterns are likely to cost quite a bit less than very complex and highly detailed patterns. Navajo rug auctions are held at Window Rock and Crown Point.

Hopi culture is hidden from the view of non-Hopi. Though the Hopi perform elaborate religious ceremonies throughout the year, most of these ceremonies are no longer open to non-Hopi.

Important note: Remember—when visiting the Hopi pueblos that you are a guest of the Hopi and your privileges can be revoked at any time. Respect all posted signs at village entrances, and remember that *photographing, sketching, and recording are all prohibited in the villages and at ceremonies.* Also keep in mind that kivas (ceremonial rooms) and ruins are off-limits.

ESSENTIALS
GETTING THERE

By Train   Amtrak passenger trains stop in Winslow, 67 miles south of Second Mesa. The train station is on East Second Street. Call 800/872-7245 for schedule information.

By Bus   Buses of Greyhound Lines stop in Winslow and Holbrook, but there is no regularly scheduled bus service north to the Hopi pueblos. Phone 800/231-2222 for further information.

The Navajo Transit System operates a bus service Monday through Friday throughout the Navajo and Hopi reservations with service between the following cities: Farmington, Gallup, and Crown Point (all in New Mexico), and Window Rock, Kayenta, Chinle, and Tuba City. The route between Window Rock and Tuba City stops at several of the Hopi villages, including Second Mesa. Call 520/729-4002 for schedule and fare information.

By Car   This section of Arizona is one of the state's most remote regions. Distances are great but the highways are generally in good condition. Arizona 87 leads from Winslow to Second Mesa, while Ariz. 264 runs from Tuba City in the west to the New Mexico state line in the east.

VISITOR INFORMATION

For more information before you leave home, contact the **Hopi Tribal Council,** P.O. Box 123, Kykotsmovi, AZ 86039 (☎ **520/734-2441,** ext. 341 or 360). Because each of the Hopi villages is relatively independent, you might want to contact the **Community Development Office** of a particular village for specific information on that village: Bacavi (☎ 520/734-2404), First Mesa (☎ 520/737-2670), Hotevilla (☎ 520/734-2420), Kykotsmovi (☎ 520/734-2474), Mishongnovi (☎ 520/737-2520), Moenkopi (☎ 520/283-6684), Shungopavi (☎ 520/734-2262), and Shipaulovi (☎ 520/734-2570). These offices are open Monday through Friday from 8am to 5pm.

WHAT TO SEE & DO

The place to start your visit to the Hopi pueblos is at the **Hopi Cultural Center,** on Ariz. 264 (☎ **520/734-6650**) in Second Mesa. This museum, motel, and restaurant is the tourism headquarters for the area. Here you can visit the museum and learn about the Hopi culture and its history. Be sure to take notice of signs indicating when villages are open to visitors. The museum is open Monday through Friday from 8am to 5pm and on Saturday and Sunday from 9am to 3pm (closed Sunday in winter). Admission is $3 for adults and $1 for children.

Though it's possible to get permission to visit most Hopi villages, the easiest to visit is **Walpi,** on First Mesa. Guided tours of this tiny village are offered daily from about 9am to 5pm, and admission is by donation. To sign up for a tour, drive up to the top of First Mesa (in Palacca, take the road that says TO FIRST MESA VILLAGES) and continue driving straight through the village until you see the **information office** (☎ **520/737-2260**) and the signs for the tour. The 40-minute tours are led by young Hopi who will tell you the history of the village and explain a bit about the local culture. Tours usually include a visit to one of the old stone homes.

VILLAGES

The Hopi have for centuries built their villages on the tops of mesas in northeastern Arizona, and claim that Oraibi, on Third Mesa, is the oldest continuously inhabited town in the United States. Whether or not this claim is true, several of the Hopi villages are quite old and for this reason they have become tourist attractions. Most of the villages are built on three mesas, known simply as First, Second, and Third Mesa, which are numbered from east to west. These villages have always maintained a great deal of autonomy, which over the years has led to fighting between villages. The appearance of missionaries and the policies of the Bureau of Indian Affairs have also created conflicts between and within villages. One such conflict led to the division of Oraibi and the formation of Hotevilla.

FIRST MESA   At the foot of First Mesa is **Polacca,** a village founded in the late 1800s by Walpi villagers who wanted to be closer to the trading post and school. At the top of First Mesa is the village of **Walpi,** which was located lower on the slopes of the mesa until the Pueblo Rebellion of 1680 brought on fear of reprisal by the Spanish. The villagers moved Walpi to the very top of the mesa so that they could better defend themselves in the event of a Spanish attack. Walpi looks much like the Anasazi villages of the Arizona canyons, with small stone houses that seem to grow directly from the rock of the mesa top, and ladders jutting from the roofs of kivas. The view stretches for hundreds of miles around. **Sichomovi,** lower down on the mesa, was founded in 1750 as a colony of Walpi, whereas **Hano** was founded by Tewa peoples either seeking refuge from the Spanish or offering aid to the people of Walpi.

SECOND MESA   Second Mesa is today the center of tourism in Hopiland, as the Hopi country is called, and where you'll find the Hopi Cultural Center. Villages on Second Mesa include **Shungopavi,** which was moved to its present site after Old Shungopavi was abandoned in 1680 after the Pueblo Revolt against the Spanish. Below Shungopavi is **Gray Spring.** The Snake Dance is performed here in even-numbered years. **Mishongnovi,** which means "place of the black man," is named for the leader of a clan that came here from the San Francisco Peaks around A.D. 1200. This village was also abandoned in 1680 and moved to its present location. The Snake Dance is held here in odd-numbered years. **Shipaulovi** may also have been founded after the Pueblo Revolt of 1680.

THIRD MESA   **Oraibi,** which the Hopi claim is the oldest continuously occupied town in the United States, is located on Third Mesa. The village dates from 1150 and, according to legend, was founded by people from Old Shungopavi. A Spanish mission was established in Oraibi in 1629 and the ruins are still visible north of the village. For centuries Oraibi was the largest of the Hopi villages, but in 1906 a schism occurred over Bureau of Indian Affairs policies and many of the villagers left to form **Hotevilla.** This latter village is considered the most conservative of the Hopi villages and has had frequent confrontations with the federal government. **Kykotsmovi,** also known as Lower Oraibi or New Oraibi, was founded in 1890 by villagers from Oraibi who wanted to be closer to the school and trading post. **Bacavi** was founded in 1907 by villagers who had helped found Hotevilla but who later decided that they wanted to return to Oraibi. The people of Oraibi would not let them return, and rather than go back to Hotevilla, they founded a new village.

ELSEWHERE One last Hopi village, **Moenkopi,** is located 40 miles to the west. Founded in 1870 by people from Oraibi, Moenkopi sits in the center of a wide green valley where plentiful water makes farming more reliable. Moenkopi is only a few miles from Tuba City off U.S. 160.

DANCES & CEREMONIES

The Hopi, who long ago adopted a farming lifestyle, have developed the most complex religious ceremonies of any of the Southwest tribes. Masked **kachina dances,** for which the Hopi are most famous, are held from January to July, while the equally well-known Snake Dances are held from August through December.

Kachinas, whether in the form of dolls or as masked dancers, are representative of the spirits of everything from plants and animals to ancestors and sacred places. There are more than 300 kachinas that appear on a regular basis in Hopi ceremonies, and another 200 that appear occasionally. The kachina spirits are said to live in the San Francisco Peaks to the south and at Spring of the Shadows in the east. According to legend, the kachinas lived with the Hopi long ago, but the Hopi people made the kachinas angry, causing them to leave. Before leaving, though, the kachinas taught the Hopi how to perform their ceremonies. Today the kachina ceremonies serve several purposes. Most important, they bring clouds and rain to water the all-important corn crop, but they also ensure health, happiness, long life, and harmony in the universe. The kachina season lasts from the winter solstice until shortly after the summer solstice. These months are marked by various kachina dances and ceremonies, with men wearing the elaborate costumes and masks of whichever kachinas have been chosen to appear. Clowns known as *koyemsi, koshares,* and *tsukus* entertain spectators between the more serious dances, with ludicrous and sometimes lewd mimicry, bringing a lighthearted counterpoint to the very serious nature of the kachina dances. Preparations for the dances take place in the kivas (circular ceremonial rooms) that are entered from the roof by means of a ladder. The kachina dancers often bring carved wooden kachina dolls to village children to introduce them to the various kachina spirits.

Despite the importance of the kachina dances, it's the **Snake Dance** that has captured the attention of non-Hopi. The Snake Dance is held only every other year in any given village and involves the handling of both poisonous and nonpoisonous snakes. The ceremony takes place over 16 days with the first 4 days dedicated to collecting all the snakes from the four cardinal directions. Later, footraces are held from the bottom of the mesa to the top. On the last day of the ceremony, the actual Snake Dance is performed. Men of the Snake Society form pairs of dancers—one to carry the snake in his mouth and the other to distract the snake with an eagle feather. When all the snakes have been danced around the plaza, they are rushed down to their homes at the bottom of the mesa to carry the Hopi prayers for rain to the spirits of the underworld.

The best way to find out about attending dances or ceremonies is to call the **Hopi Tribal Council** (☎ **520/734-2441,** ext. 341 or 360). However, as of press time, almost all ceremonies and dances have been closed to non-Hopi because of the disrespectful attitude of some visitors. It's doubtful that these ceremonies and dances will again be open to non-Hopi, but it's certainly worth checking.

SHOPPING

Shopping for Hopi crafts is the main pursuit of visitors to the Hopi Reservation. There are literally dozens of small shops selling crafts and jewelry of different quality, and some homes have signs indicating that they sell crafts—it's alright to stop and inquire. These shops often sell the work of only a few individuals, so you should stop at several to get some idea of the variety of work available. Perhaps the single best place to stop is **Hopi Arts & Crafts–Silvercraft,** 100 yards from the Hopi Cultural Center on Second Mesa. This arts-and-crafts cooperative has more than 300 members, including potters, weavers, basket makers, kachina carvers, painters, and silversmiths.

Other reliable sources of Hopi arts and crafts are **McGee's Indian Art,** at Keams Canyon east of First Mesa (☎ 520/738-2295), and the **Honani Crafts Gallery** (☎520/737-2238), at the intersection of Hwy. 264 and Second Mesa.

WHERE TO STAY & DINE
SECOND MESA

Hopi Cultural Center Restaurant and Motel
P.O. Box 67, Second Mesa, AZ 86043. ☎ **520/734-2401.** 33 rms. TV TEL. $55–$60 double. AE, DC, DISC, MC, V.

This is the only lodging for miles around so be sure you have a reservation before heading up here for an overnight visit. The Hopi Cultural Center is the locus of visitor activities in the Hopi pueblos, and its modern pueblo architecture fits in with its surroundings. The rooms are comfortable and modern. The restaurant serves American and traditional Hopi meals, including piki bread. There's also a museum here.

WINSLOW

Though it's nearly 70 miles south of Second Mesa, this is the next-closest place to stay if you're planning to tour the Hopi pueblos. Budget chain motels in Winslow include the following (see the Appendix for toll-free phone numbers): **Best Western Adobe Inn,** 1701 N. Park Dr., Winslow, AZ 86047 (☎ 520/289-4638), charging $50 to $64 double; **Comfort Inn,** 520 Desmond St., Winslow, AZ 86047 (☎ 520/289-9581), charging $48 to $68 double; **Econo Lodge,** 1706 N. Park Dr., Winslow, AZ 86047 (☎ 520/289-4687), charging $43 to $53 double; and **Super 8 Motel,** 1916 W. Third St., Winslow, AZ 86047 (☎ 520/289-4606), charging $41 to $53 double.

2 The Navajo Reservation

Navajo National Monument: 140 miles NE of Flagstaff, 90 miles E of Page, 60 miles SW of Monument Valley, 110 miles NW of Canyon de Chelly

Monument Valley Navajo Tribal Park: 200 miles NE of Flagstaff, 60 miles NE of Navajo National Monument, 110 miles NW of Canyon de Chelly, 150 miles E of Page

Roughly the size of West Virginia, the Navajo Reservation covers an area of 25,000 square miles of northeastern Arizona, as well as parts of New Mexico, Colorado, and Utah. It's the largest Native American reservation in the United States and is home to nearly 200,000 Navajo. Though there are now modern towns with supermarkets, shopping malls, and hotels on the reservation, many Navajo still follow a pastoral lifestyle—they're herders. As you travel the roads of the Navajo Reservation, you'll frequently encounter flocks of sheep and goats, as well as herds of cattle and horses. These animals have free range of the reservation and often graze beside the highways, so take care when driving, especially at night.

Unlike the pueblo tribes such as the Hopi and Zuñi, the Navajo are relative newcomers to the Southwest. Their Athabascan language is most closely related to the languages spoken by Native Americans in the Pacific Northwest, Canada, and Alaska. It's believed that the Navajo migrated southward from northern Canada beginning around A.D. 1000, arriving in the Southwest sometime after 1400. At this time the Navajo were still hunters and gatherers, but contact with the pueblo tribes, who had long before adopted an agricultural lifestyle, began to change the Navajo into farmers. When the Spanish arrived in the Southwest in the early 17th century, the Navajo acquired horses, sheep, and goats through raids and adopted a pastoral way of life, grazing their herds in the high plains and canyon bottoms.

The continued use of raids, made even more successful with the acquisition of horses, put the Navajo in conflict with the Spanish settlers who were beginning to encroach on Navajo land. In 1805 the Spanish sent a military expedition into the Navajo's chief stronghold, Canyon de Chelly, and killed 115 people, who by some accounts are claimed to have been all women, children, and old men. This massacre didn't stop the conflicts between Navajo and Spanish settlers. In 1846, when this region became part of the United States, American settlers encountered the same problems that the Spanish had. Military outposts were established to protect the new settlers, and numerous unsuccessful attempts were made to establish peace. In 1863, after continued Navajo attacks, a military expedition led by Col. Kit Carson burned crops and homes late in the summer, effectively obliterating the Navajo's winter supplies. Thus defeated, the Navajo were rounded up and herded 400 miles to an inhospitable region of New Mexico near Fort Sumner. This march became known as the Long Walk, and had a profound influence on the Navajo. Living conditions at Fort Sumner were deplorable and the land was unsuitable for farming. In 1868 the Navajo were allowed to return to their homeland.

Upon returning home, and after continued clashes with white settlers, the Navajo eventually settled into a lifestyle of herding. In recent years the Navajo have had to turn to different livelihoods. Though weaving and silverwork have become a lucrative business, the amount of money it garners for the tribe as a whole is not significant. Many Navajo now take jobs as migrant workers; gas and oil leases on the reservation provide more income.

Though the reservation covers an immense area, much of it is of no value other than as scenery. Fortunately, the Navajo are recognizing the income potential of their spectacular land. Monument Valley is operated as a tribal park, and there's also a Navajo-owned marina on Lake Powell in Utah.

As you travel the reservation you may notice small hexagonal buildings with rounded roofs. These are hogans, the traditional homes of the Navajo, and are usually made of wood and earth. The doorway of the hogan always faces east to greet the new day. At the Canyon de Chelly and Navajo National Monument visitor centers you can look inside hogans that are part of the parks' exhibits. If you take a tour at Canyon de Chelly or Monument Valley, you may have an opportunity to visit a hogan that is still someone's home. Most Navajo now live in modest houses or mobile homes, but a family will usually also have a hogan for religious ceremonies.

The Navajo Reservation observes daylight saving time, unlike the rest of Arizona, so remember to set your watch forward an hour if you're visiting in the summer. Also keep in mind that *alcohol is not allowed on the reservation.*

Before taking a photograph of a Navajo, always ask permission. If permission is granted, a tip of $1 or more is expected.

ESSENTIALS
GETTING THERE

By Train   There is Amtrak passenger service to Winslow, south of the reservation. Call 800/872-7245 for schedules and fares.

By Bus   The Navajo Transit System operates bus service Monday through Friday throughout the Navajo nation with service between the cities of Farmington, Gallup, and Crown Point (all in New Mexico), and Window Rock, Kayenta, Chinle, and Tuba City. Call 520/729-4002 for schedule information.

Greyhound Lines stops in Winslow, Holbrook, and Houck. Phone 800/231-2222 for schedules and fares.

By Car   The Navajo Indian Reservation is a vast area and is laced with a network of excellent paved roads as well as many unpaved roads that are not always passable to cars without four-wheel drive. From Flagstaff, Navajo National Monument can be reached by taking U.S. 89 north to U.S. 160; Monument Valley Navajo Tribal Park is a bit farther on U.S. 163. The most direct route to Canyon de Chelly National Monument from Flagstaff is by way of I-40 to U.S. 191 north. Window Rock is east of the north end of U.S. 191 on Ariz. 264.

VISITOR INFORMATION

For more information before visiting, contact the **Navajoland Tourism Department,** P.O. Box 663, Window Rock, AZ 86515 (☎ **520/871-6436** or 520/871-7371).

SPECIAL EVENTS

Unlike the village ceremonies of the pueblo-dwelling Hopi, Navajo religious ceremonies tend to be held in the privacy of family hogans. However, there are numerous fairs, powwows, and rodeos held throughout the year and the public is welcome to attend these. The biggest of these is the **Navajo Nation Fair,** held in Window Rock in early September each year. At this fair there are traditional dances, a rodeo, a powwow, a parade, a Miss Navajo Pageant, and arts-and-crafts exhibits and sales.

Other important fairs include the **Central Navajo Fair** at Chinle, Arizona, in late August; the **Northern Navajo Fair** at Shiprock, New Mexico, in early October; and the **Western Navajo Fair** at Tuba City, Arizona, in mid-October.

WHAT TO SEE & DO
SIGHTS & ATTRACTIONS
Near Kayenta

MONUMENT VALLEY NAVAJO TRIBAL PARK   Nature, in its role as sculptor, has created a garden of monoliths and spires in the north-central part of the Navajo Reservation at Monument Valley, and you may not know it, but you have almost certainly seen Monument Valley before. This otherworldly landscape has been an object of fascination for years, and has served as backdrop for many movies, including *Stagecoach* (1938) by John Ford and *Thelma and Louise* (1992) with Geena Davis, as well as for television shows and commercials.

Located 30 miles north of Kayenta just across the Utah state line, Monument Valley is a vast flat plain punctuated by natural cathedrals of sandstone. These huge monoliths rise up from the sagebrush with sheer walls that capture the light of the rising and setting sun and transform it into fiery hues. Evocative names reflect the shapes the sandstone has taken on as the forces of nature have eroded it: the Mittens, Three Sisters, Camel Butte, Elephant Butte, the Thumb, and Totem Pole being some of the most awe-inspiring natural monuments. A 17-mile unpaved loop road winds among these 1,000-foot-tall buttes and mesas.

Human inhabitation has also left its mark. Within the park there are more than 100 ancient Anasazi archaeological sites, ruins, and petroglyphs dating to before A.D. 1300. The Navajo have been living in the valley for generations, herding their sheep through the sagebrush scrublands, and some families continue to live here today.

At the **valley overlook** parking area you'll find a small museum, gift shop, snack bar, and campground ($10 per night per site), and numerous local Navajo guides who offer tours of Monument Valley. Another option is to book a tour with **Goulding's Tours,** P.O. Box 360001, Monument Valley, UT 84536 (☎ **801/727-3231**). This company has its office on the edge of the valley at Goulding's Lodge, just a few miles from the park entrance. Half-day tours are $30 for adults and $18 for children 11 and under; full-day tours are $60 for adults and $45 for children 11 and under.

One other option is to explore the monument on horseback. **Ed Black's Stables** (☎ **801/739-4285,** or 800/551-4039) is located near the visitor center and charges $25 for a 1¹/₂-hour ride and $60 for an all-day ride. **Bigman's Horseback Riding** (☎ **520/677-3219**) is located on the road to the monument entrance and charges $20 for a one-hour ride and $55 for an all-day ride.

Before leaving the area, you might also want to visit **Goulding's Museum & Trading Post** at Goulding's Lodge. This old trading post was the home of the Gouldings for many years and is set up as they had it back in the 1920s and 1930s. There are also displays about the many movies that have been shot here. The trading post is open daily from 7:30 to 9pm and admission is by donation.

The park is open May to September, daily from 8am to 7pm; October to April, daily from 8am to 5pm. Admission is $2.50 for adults, $1 for seniors, and free for children 6 and under. For more information, contact **Monument Valley Navajo Tribal Park,** P.O. Box 360289, Monument Valley, UT 84536 (☎ **801/727-3287** or 801/727-3353).

NAVAJO NATIONAL MONUMENT   Located 30 miles west of Kayenta and 60 miles northeast of Tuba City, Navajo National Monument encompasses three of the best-preserved Anasazi cliff dwellings in the region—Betatakin, Keet Seel, and Inscription House. It's possible to visit both Betatakin and Keet Seel, but fragile Inscription House is closed to the public. The name Navajo National Monument is a bit misleading. Although the Navajo people do inhabit the area now, it was the ancient Anasazi who built the cliff dwellings. The Navajo arrived centuries after the Anasazi had abandoned the area.

The inhabitants of Tsegi Canyon were ancestral Hopi and Pueblo peoples known as the Kayenta Anasazi. The Anasazi began abandoning their well-constructed homes around the middle of the 13th century for reasons unknown.

Tree rings suggest that a drought in the latter part of the 13th century prevented the Anasazi from growing sufficient crops. However, in Tsegi Canyon there's another theory for the abandonment. The canyon floors were usually flooded each year by spring and summer snowmelt, which made farming quite productive, but in the mid-1200s weather patterns changed and streams running through the canyons began cutting deep into the soil, forming deep, narrow canyons called arroyos, which lowered the water table and made farming much more difficult.

Betatakin, which means "ledge house" in Navajo, is the only one of the three ruins that can be easily seen. Built in a huge amphitheaterlike alcove in the canyon wall, Betatakin was occupied only from 1250 to 1300, and at its height of occupation may have housed 125 people.

A 1-mile round-trip paved trail from the visitor center leads to overlooks of Betatakin. The strenuous 5-mile round-trip hike to Betatakin itself is ranger-led, takes about six hours, and involves descending more than 700 feet to the floor of Tsegi Canyon and later returning to the rim. This hike is conducted from May to September or October and leaves from the visitor center. All hikers are required to carry 2 quarts of water. This hike is very popular and the number of people allowed is limited to 25 per tour; many people line up at the visitor center an hour or more before the center opens. During the summer months there are two hikes a day, while in spring and fall there's only one hike a day.

Keet Seel, which means "broken pieces of pottery" in Navajo, has a much longer history than Betatakin, with occupation beginning as early as A.D. 950 and continuing until 1300. At one point Keet Seel may have housed 150 people.

The 17-mile round-trip hike or horseback ride to Keet Seel is even more strenuous. Hikers may stay overnight at a primitive campground near the ruins. You must carry enough water for your trip since none is available along the trail. Only 20 people a day are given permits to visit Keet Seel, and the trail is only open from Memorial Day to Labor Day.

The visitor center has informative displays on the ancestral Pueblo and Navajo cultures, including numerous artifacts from Tsegi Canyon. You can also watch a 25-minute film or a short slide show. The center is open daily from 8am to 5pm (until 6pm in summer when daylight saving time is observed). There's no lodge at the national monument, but there is a campground that's open year round. There are only 30 campsites here, and an overflow area containing about a dozen more. In summer they're usually full by dark. There's no fee for camping.

For more information, contact **Navajo National Monument,** HC 71, Box 3, Tonales, AZ 86044-9704 (☎ **520/672-2366**).

In Ganado

Hubbell Trading Post National Historic Site
P.O. Box 150, Ganado, AZ 86505. ☎ **520/755-3475**. Admission free. Apr–Oct, daily 8am–6pm; Oct–Apr, daily 8am–5pm.

Located just outside the town of Ganado in the southeastern part of the reservation, the Hubbell Trading Post is the oldest continuously operating trading post on the Navajo Reservation. The trading post was established in 1876 by Lorenzo Hubbell, who did more to popularize the arts and crafts of the Navajo people than any other person. The trading post includes a small museum where you can watch Navajo weavers in the slow process of creating a rug.

The rug room is filled with a variety of traditional and contemporary Navajo rugs. Though it's possible to buy a small 12- by 18-inch rug for around $100, most cost in the thousands of dollars. There are also baskets, kachinas, and several cases of jewelry by Navajo, Hopi, and Zuñi in another room. Glance around the general store and you'll see basic foodstuffs (not much variety here) and bolts of cloth used by Navajo women for sewing their traditional skirts and blouses.

Trading posts have long been more than just a place to trade crafts for imported goods. They were for many years the main gathering spot for meeting people from other parts of the reservation, and served as a sort of gossip fence and newsroom. You can tour the grounds on your own or take a guided tour.

In Ganado, you can get good, inexpensive cafeteria-style food at **Cafe Sage** (☎ 520/755-3411, ext. 294) on the grounds of Ganado's health clinic, which is across Ariz. 264 and half a mile east of the trading post.

In Window Rock

Window Rock, less than a mile from the New Mexico state line, is the capital of the Navajo nation and is named for a huge natural opening in a sandstone cliff just outside town. At one time there was a spring at the base of the rock and water from the spring was used by medicine men performing the Tohee Ceremony, a water ceremony intended to bring the rains. Today Window Rock is preserved as the **Window Rock Tribal Park,** which is located 2 miles off Ariz. 264.

Navajo Tribal Museum

Navajo Arts & Crafts Enterprise, W. Ariz. 264, Window Rock. ☎ **520/871-6673.** Admission free. Summer, Mon–Sat 8am–6pm; winter, Mon–Fri 8am–5pm.

Located in the Navajo Arts & Crafts Enterprise, this small museum contains Navajo artifacts, old photos, and contemporary crafts. They may be moving to a nearby building within the year.

Navajo Nation Zoo & Botanical Park

Ariz. 264, Window Rock. ☎ **520/871-6573.** Admission free. Daily 8am–5pm. Closed Jan 1 and Dec 25.

This zoo and botanical garden features animals and plants that are significant in Navajo history and culture. The zoo includes bears, cougars, and wolves among its small collection. The setting, which includes several sandstone "haystack" rocks, is very striking. Also exhibited are examples of different styles of hogans. You'll find the park east of the Navajo Nation Inn.

St. Michael's Historical Museum

St. Michael's, 3 miles south of Ariz. 264. ☎ **520/871-4171.** Admission free. Memorial Day–Labor Day, daily 9am–5pm. Closed the rest of the year.

This historical museum chronicles the lives and effects of Franciscan friars who started a mission in this area in the 1670s.

Elsewhere on the Reservation

Other attractions you might want to visit while you're in this part of the state include the **Four Corners Monument Navajo Tribal Park,** north of Teec Nos Pos in the very northeast corner of the state. This is the only place in the United States where the corners of four states come together—Arizona, Colorado, Utah, and New Mexico. In the park you'll find a visitor center, a picnic ground, and crafts vendors. The park is open daily: from 7am to 7pm in summer and 8am to 5pm in winter. Admission is $1.50 per person.

West of Tuba City and just off U.S. 160, you can see **dinosaur footprints** preserved in the stone surface of the desert. There are usually a few people waiting at
the site to guide visitors to the best footprints. These guides will expect a tip.

SHOPPING

All over the Navajo Reservation you'll see stalls set up beside the road and at scenic overlooks. Though you might find quality merchandise and bargain prices,
you'd do better to confine your purchases to trading posts, museum and park gift
shops, and established shops where you receive some guarantee of the quality of
the pieces for sale. The **Hubbell Trading Post** (see above) in Ganado has a well-
deserved reputation for having an excellent selection of rugs and jewelry. Prices are
not low, but neither is the quality. The **Cameron Trading Post** (☎ 520/
679-2231, or 800/338-7385), at the crossroads of Cameron where Ariz. 64
branches off U.S. 89 to Grand Canyon Village, is another historic trading post.
The original stone trading-post building now houses a gallery of old and antique
Native American artifacts, clothing, and jewelry. This gallery may be the finest
in the state and offers museum-quality pieces. The main trading post is a more
modern building and is the largest trading post in northern Arizona.

In Window Rock, be sure to visit the **Navajo Arts & Crafts Enterprise**
(☎ 520/871-4090), which is adjacent to the Navajo Nation Inn and has been
operating since 1941. Here you'll find high-quality silver-and-turquoise jewelry,
Navajo rugs, sandpaintings, baskets, pottery, and Native American clothing.

On the west side of the reservation, in Tuba City, you'll find the **Tuba Trading Post** (☎ 520/283-5441) on the corner of Main Street and Moenave Street.
This octagonal trading post was built in 1906 of local stone and is designed to
resemble a Navajo hogan. The trading post serves both as a small market and as
a store selling Native American crafts. On the western outskirts of Tuba City, on
U.S. 160, you'll find **Van's Trading Co.** (☎ 520/283-5343), which has a
dead-pawn auction on the 15th of each month at 3pm. This auction provides
opportunities to buy older pieces of Navajo silver-and-turquoise jewelry.

WHERE TO STAY & DINE
IN & NEAR KAYENTA

Anasazi Inn at Tsegi Canyon
U.S. 160 (P.O. Box 1543), Kayenta, AZ 86033. ☎ **520/697-3793.** Fax 520/697-8249.
56 rms. A/C TV TEL. $80 double. Lower rates available Oct–Apr. AE, CB, DC, DISC, MC, V.
Take U.S. 160 west of Kayenta.

Located about halfway between Kayenta and Navajo National Monument, the
Anasazi Inn at Tsegi Canyon is a simple motel surrounded by wilderness, but it's
the closest lodging to Navajo National Monument. (Note that readers have
recently complained of the motel being less than spotless.) There's a small dining
room attached to the motel.

✪ Goulding's Lodge
P.O. Box 360001, Monument Valley, UT 84536-0001. ☎ **801/727-3231.** Fax 801/
727-3344. 62 rms. A/C TV TEL. Mar–Oct, $88–$108 double. Oct–Mar, $68–$78 double.
AE, DC, MC, V.

This is the only lodge actually located in Monument Valley, and it offers superb
views from the private balconies of the guest rooms, which are furnished with
southwestern decor. A restaurant serves Navajo and American dishes, and the views

from here are enough to make any meal an event. The hotel also has an indoor pool, tour desk, museum, gift shop, coin laundry, and gas station.

Holiday Inn–Kayenta

At the junction of U.S. 160 and U.S. 163 (P.O. Box 307), Kayenta, AZ 86033. ☎ **520/ 697-3221** or 800/HOLIDAY. Fax 520/697-3349. 160 rms. A/C TV TEL. May–Nov, $99–$119 double. Dec–Apr, $79 double. Nov–Apr, $89 double. AE, CB, DC, DISC, MC, V.

Located in the center of Kayenta, 23 miles south of Monument Valley and 29 miles east of Navajo National Monument, this Holiday Inn is very popular with tour groups and is almost always crowded. Though the grounds are dusty and a bit run-down, the rooms are spacious and clean and most have new carpets. We like the poolside rooms best. Part of the motel's restaurant is designed to look like an Anasazi ruin. The menu offers both American and Navajo meals. Room service is available. The hotel also has an outdoor pool and a tour desk.

Wetherill Inn Motel

P.O. Box 175, Kayenta, AZ 86033-0175. ☎ **520/697-3231.** 54 rms. A/C TV TEL. Apr–Oct, $78 double. Oct–Apr, $49.50 double. AE, CB, DC, DISC, MC, V.

Located 1 mile north of the junction of U.S. 160 and U.S. 163 and 20 miles south of Monument Valley, the Wetherill Inn Motel offers modern guest rooms with coffeemakers. The hotel has a tour desk, but there's no restaurant or pool.

IN WINDOW ROCK

Navajo Nation Inn

48 W. Hwy. 264 (P.O. Box 2340), Window Rock, AZ 86515. ☎ **520/871-4108** or 800/ 662-6189. Fax 520/871-5466. 54 rms, 2 suites. A/C TV TEL. $62–$72 double; $72 suite. AE, DC, MC, V.

Located in the center of Window Rock, the administrative center of the Navajo Reservation, the Navajo Nation Inn is a modern motel with rustic pine furniture in the guest rooms. The restaurant and coffee shop are open daily from 6am to 9pm serving American and traditional Navajo dishes. The hotel also offers a tour desk.

CAMERON

✪ Cameron Trading Post Motel

P.O. Box 339, Cameron, AZ 86020. ☎ **520/679-2231** or 800/338-7385. Fax 520/ 679-2350. 62 rms, 4 suites. A/C TV TEL. $69–$79 double; $175–$250 suite. AE, MC, V.

Located 54 miles north of Flagstaff, this motel offers some of the most attractive rooms anywhere in the vicinity of the Grand Canyon. The motel is adjacent to the historic Cameron Trading Post and is built around the old trading post's terraced gardens, which are a shady oasis. The rooms are furnished with southwestern-style pine furniture and are attractively decorated. Most of the rooms have balconies and some have views of the canyon of the Little Colorado River. There are two restaurants here as well as one of the best trading posts in the state.

TUBA CITY

Tuba Trading Post Motel, Restaurant & RV Park

At the junction of U.S. 160 and Ariz. 264 (P.O. Box 247), Tuba City, AZ 86045. ☎ **520/ 283-5441** or 800/644-8383. 80 rms, 2 suites. A/C TV TEL. June–Oct, $80–$90 double; $125 suite. Nov–May, $65–$75 double; $105 suite. AE, DISC, JCB, MC, V.

The Navajo Reservation doesn't have very many motels, so if you expect to be anywhere near the west side of the reservation, this is a good choice. Located adjacent to the historic Tuba City Trading Post, the motel offers comfortable, modern rooms. The motel's restaurant serves Mexican and American meals. There's also an RV park here.

CAMPGROUNDS

If you're headed to Monument Valley Navajo Tribal Park, you can camp in the park at the **Mitten View Campground** (☎ **801/727-3353**) or just outside the park at **Goulding's Monument Valley Campground** (☎ **801/727-3231**). North of Window Rock, there are **Wheatfields Lake Campground** and **Tsaile Lake Campground,** both of which are close to Canyon de Chelly. There's also a campground at **Navajo National Monument** (☎ **520/672-2366**), west of Kayenta. At the **Tuba City Motel** (☎ **520/283-5441**), you'll find an RV park.

3 Canyon de Chelly

222 miles NE of Flagstaff, 68 miles NW of Window Rock, 110 miles SE of Navajo National Monument, 110 miles SE of Monument Valley Navajo Tribal Park

It's hard to imagine narrow canyons less than 1,000 feet deep being more spectacular than the Grand Canyon, but in some ways the canyons of Canyon de Chelly National Monument are just that. Gaze down from the rim of Canyon de Chelly at an ancient Anasazi cliff dwelling as the whinnying of horses and clanging of goat bells drifts up from far below, and you will be struck by the continuity of human life. For more than 2,000 years people have called these canyons home, and today there are more than 100 prehistoric dwelling sites in the area.

Canyon de Chelly National Monument consists of two major canyons—Canyon de Chelly (which is pronounced "Canyon de Shay" and is derived from the Navajo word *tségi,* meaning "rock canyon"), Canyon del Muerto (Spanish for Canyon of the Dead), and several smaller canyons. The canyons extend for more than 100 miles through the rugged slick-rock landscape of northeastern Arizona, draining the seasonal runoff from the snowmelt of the Chuska Mountains.

Canyon de Chelly's smooth sandstone walls of rich reds and yellows sharply contrast with the deep greens of corn, pasture, and cottonwood on the canyon floor. Vast stone amphitheaters form the caves in which the ancient Anasazi built their homes, and as you watch shadows and light paint an ever-changing canyon panorama, it's easy to see why the Navajo consider these canyons sacred ground. With mysteriously abandoned cliff dwellings and breathtaking natural beauty, Canyon de Chelly is certainly as worthy of a visit as the Grand Canyon.

ESSENTIALS
GETTING THERE

By Train   There is Amtrak passenger service to Winslow, south of the Navajo Reservation. The train station is on East Second Street. Call 800/872-7245 for schedule and fare information.

By Bus   Chinle, 3 miles from the entrance to Canyon de Chelly National Monument, is served by the Navajo Transit System; call 520/729-4002 for schedules and fares. Winslow, Holbrook, and Houck are all served by Greyhound Lines; phone 800/231-2222 for schedule and fare information.

By Car   From Flagstaff, the easiest route to Canyon de Chelly is to take I-40 to U.S. 191 to Ganado. At Ganado, drive west on Ariz. 264/U.S. 191 and head north on U.S. 191 to Chinle. If you're coming down from Monument Valley or Navajo National Monument, Indian Route 59, which connects U.S. 160 and U.S. 191, is an excellent road with plenty of beautiful scenery.

VISITOR INFORMATION

Before leaving home you can contact **Canyon de Chelly National Monument,** P.O. Box 588, Chinle, AZ 86503 (☎ **520/674-5500**).

WHAT TO SEE & DO

The **visitor center,** open daily in summer from 8am to 6pm (on daylight savings time) and in winter from 8am to 5pm, should be everyone's first stop at Canyon de Chelly. Out front is an example of a traditional crib-style hogan, a hexagonal structure of logs and earth that Navajo use both as a home and as a ceremonial center. Inside, a small museum acquaints visitors with the history of Canyon de Chelly, and near the front door there's sometimes a silversmith demonstrating Navajo jewelry-making techniques. If you want to drive your own four-wheeler into the canyon, this is where you need to get your permit, and you must hire a guide as well (see below). From May to the beginning of September there are daily programs, including morning coffee talks at the hogan near the visitor center, ranger-led canyon hikes (these are popular, so be sure to sign up at the visitor center), campfire programs, and natural-history programs.

Access to the canyons is restricted, and in order to descend into the canyon *you must be accompanied by either a park ranger or an authorized guide,* unless you're on the White House Ruins trail. To hire a **Navajo guide** to lead you into the canyon on foot or in your own four-wheel-drive vehicle is $10 per hour with a three-hour minimum. Another way to see Canyon de Chelly and Canyon del Muerto is from one of the **four- or six-wheel-drive trucks** that operate out of Thunderbird Lodge (☎ **520/674-5841**). These trucks are equipped with seats in the bed and stop frequently for photographs and to visit ruins, Navajo farms, and rock art. Tours cost $31 per person for a half day ($23 for children 11 and under); all-day tours are $50. Half-day tours leave at 9am and 2pm in summer, at 9am and 1pm in winter; full-day trips leave at 9am and return at 5:30pm.

There are also two stables offering horseback tours into the canyon. **Justin Tso Horse Rental** (☎ **520/674-5678**) and **Twin Trails Tours** (☎ **520/674-8425**) both charge around $8 per hour for a horse and $8 per hour for a guide.

THE RIM DRIVES

A very different view of the canyons is provided by the north and south rim drives. The North Rim Drive overlooks Canyon del Muerto, while the South Rim Drive overlooks Canyon de Chelly. Each of the rim drives is around 20 miles in each direction, and with stops it can easily take three hours to visit each rim.

THE NORTH RIM DRIVE   The first stop on the north rim is the **Ledge Ruin Overlook.** On the opposite wall, about 100 feet up from the canyon floor, you can see the Ledge Ruin. This site was occupied by the Anasazi between A.D. 1050 and 1275. Nearby, at the **Dekaa Kiva Viewpoint,** you can see a lone kiva (circular ceremonial building). This structure was reached by means of toeholds cut into the soft sandstone cliff wall.

The second stop is at the **Antelope House Overlook.** The Antelope House ruin takes its name from the paintings of antelopes on a nearby cliff wall. It's believed that the paintings were done in the 1830s. Beneath the ruins of Antelope House, archeologists have found the remains of an earlier pit house dating back to A.D. 693. Though most of the Anasazi cliff dwellings were abandoned sometime after a drought began in 1276, Antelope House had already been abandoned by 1260, possibly because of damage caused by flooding. Across the wash from Antelope House, an ancient tomb, known as the Tomb of the Weaver, was discovered in the 1920s by archeologists. The tomb contained the well-preserved body of an old man wrapped in a blanket of golden eagle feathers and accompanied by cornmeal, shelled and husked corn, piñon nuts, beans, salt, and thick skeins of cotton. Also visible from this overlook is Navajo Fortress, a red sandstone butte that the Navajo once used as a refuge from attackers. A steep trail leads to the top of Navajo Fortress, and through the use of log ladders that could be pulled up after being used, the Navajo were able to escape their attackers.

The third stop is at **Mummy Cave Overlook,** named for two mummies that were found in burial urns below the ruins. Archaeological evidence indicates that this giant amphitheater consisting of two caves was occupied for 1,000 years from A.D. 300 to 1300. In the two caves and on the shelf between there are 80 rooms, including three kivas. The central structure between the two caves is interesting because it includes a three-story building characteristic of the architecture in Mesa Verde in New Mexico. Archaeologists speculate that a group of Anasazi migrated here from New Mexico. Much of the original plasterwork of these buildings is still intact and indicates that the buildings were colorfully decorated.

The fourth and last stop on the north rim is at the **Massacre Cave Overlook.** The cave received its name after an 1805 Spanish military expedition killed more than 115 Navajo at this site. The Navajo at the time had been raiding Spanish settlements that were encroaching on Navajo territory. Accounts of the battle at Massacre Cave differ. One account claims that there were only women, children, and old men taking shelter in the cave, though the official Spanish records claim 90 warriors and 25 women and children were killed. Also visible from this overlook is Yucca Cave, which was occupied about 1,000 years ago.

If you continue another 10 miles or so from the end of the North Rim Drive to the community of Tsaile, you can visit the **Hatathli Gallery** at Navajo Community College (☎ **520/724-3311**). This modern art gallery has a small but interesting collection of Navajo art, crafts, and artifacts, old photos, and even a collection of Plains Indian regalia and clothing. The gallery is open Monday through Friday from 9am to 4pm, and admission is free.

THE SOUTH RIM DRIVE   The South Rim Drive follows the south rim of Canyon de Chelly and climbs slowly but steadily. At each stop you're a little bit higher above the canyon floor.

The first stop is at **Tségi Overlook.** *Tségi* means "rock canyon" in Navajo, and that's just what you'll see when you gaze down from this viewpoint. A short narrow canyon feeds into Chinle Wash, which is formed by the streams cutting through the canyons of the national monument.

The second stop is at the **Junction Overlook,** so named because it overlooks the junction of Canyon del Muerto and Canyon de Chelly. Visible here is the Junction Ruin, with its 10 rooms and one kiva. The Anasazi occupied this ruin during the great pueblo period, which lasted from around 1100 until the

Anasazi disappeared shortly before 1300. Also visible is First Ruin, which is perched precariously on a long narrow ledge. In this ruin are 22 rooms and two kivas.

The third stop, at **White House Overlook,** provides the only opportunity for descending into Canyon de Chelly without a guide or ranger. The White House Ruins Trail descends 600 feet to the canyon floor, crosses Chinle Wash, and approaches the White House Ruins. These buildings were constructed both on the canyon floor and 50 feet up the cliff wall in a small cave. Though you cannot enter the ruins, you can get close enough to get a good look. You're not allowed to wander off this trail, and please respect the privacy of those Navajo living here. It's a 2¹/₂-mile round-trip hike and takes about two hours. Be sure to carry water. If you aren't inclined to hike the trail, you can view the ruins from the overlook. This is one of the largest ruins in the canyon and contained 80 rooms. It was inhabited between 1040 and 1275. Notice the black streaks on the sandstone walls above the White House Ruins. These streaks were formed by seeping water that reacted with the iron in the sandstone. Iron is what gives the walls their reddish hue. Anasazi artists used to chip away at this black patina to create petroglyphs. Later the Navajo would use paints to create pictographs, painted images of animals, and records of historic events such as the Spanish military expedition that killed 115 Navajo at Massacre Cave. Many of these petroglyphs and pictographs can be seen if you take one of the guided tours into the canyon.

The fourth stop is at **Sliding House Overlook.** These ruins are built on a narrow shelf and appear to be sliding down into the canyon. Inhabited from about 900 until 1200, Sliding House contained between 30 and 50 rooms. This overlook is already more than 700 feet above the canyon floor, with sheer walls giving the narrow canyon a very foreboding appearance.

Wild Cherry Overlook and **Face Rock Overlook,** the next two stops, provide further glimpses of the ever-deepening canyon. Here you are gazing down 1,000 feet to the bottom of the canyon. The last stop on the south rim is one of the most spectacular—**Spider Rock Overlook.** This viewpoint overlooks the junction of Canyon de Chelly and Monument Canyon, and at this wide spot in the canyon stands the monolithic pinnacle called Spider Rock. Rising 800 feet from the canyon floor, the freestanding twin towers of Spider Rock are a natural monument, a geologic wonder. Across the canyon from Spider Rock stands the almost as striking Speaking Rock, which is connected to the far canyon wall.

WHERE TO STAY & DINE

Best Western Canyon de Chelly Inn

P.O. Box 295, Chinle, AZ 86503. ☎ **520/674-5875** or 800/327-0354. Fax 520/3715. 102 rms. A/C TV TEL. $60–$104 double. AE, DC, MC, V.

Located in the center of Chinle, this modern motel is the farthest from the park of the three hotels here in town and should be a last choice. The rooms are medium size to large and have beamed ceilings and coffeemakers. The restaurant is large and the menu features moderately priced American and Navajo meals. There's also an indoor swimming pool.

Holiday Inn–Canyon de Chelly

Indian Rte. 7 (P.O. Box 1889), Chinle, AZ 86503. ☎ **520/674-5000** or 800/23-HOTEL. Fax 520/674-8264. 108 rms. A/C TV TEL. Summer, $79–$95 double. Winter, $49–$69 double. AE, CB, DC, DISC, JCB, MC, V.

This is the newest hotel in Chinle and is located between the town and the entrance to Canyon de Chelly National Monument. The hotel is on the site of an old trading post, which is incorporated into the restaurant and gift shop building. The guest rooms all have patios or balconies and big windows and bathrooms, and most face the cottonwood-shaded pool courtyard. The hotel's restaurant serves moderately priced American and Navajo meals. There's a tour desk here, and room service is available. Native American dance performances are held Monday through Friday evenings here at the hotel.

✪ Thunderbird Lodge
P.O. Box 548, Chinle, AZ 86503. ☎ **520/674-5841** or 800/679-BIRD. Fax 602/674-5844, 72 rms, 1 suite. A/C TV TEL. $79–$84 double; $145 suite. Lower rates Nov–Mar. AE, DC, DISC, MC, V.

Built on the site of an early trading post at the mouth of Canyon de Chelly, the Thunderbird Lodge is the most appealing of the hotels in Chinle. The pink adobe construction is reminiscent of ancient pueblos, and the guest rooms have rustic furniture and Navajo sandpaintings on the walls. The rooms come in two different sizes, with either two double beds or two queen-size beds. Ceiling fans and air conditioners keep the rooms cool in the hot summer months. The original trading post building now serves as the lodge cafeteria, where American and Navajo meals are served. The lodge also has a tour desk, gift shop, and rug room.

CAMPGROUNDS
There's a year-round free campground near Thunderbird Lodge that doesn't take reservations. In the summer the campground has water and restrooms, but in the winter you must bring your own water and only portable toilets are available.

4 The Petrified Forest & Painted Desert

25 miles E of Holbrook, 90 miles E of Flagstaff, 118 miles S of Canyon de Chelly, 180 miles N of Phoenix

Though petrified wood can be found in almost every state, the "forests" of downed logs here in northeastern Arizona are by far the most spectacular. A 27-mile scenic drive winds through the petrified forest and a small corner of the Painted Desert, providing a fascinating desert experience.

Petrified wood has intrigued people for years and when, in the 1850s, it was discovered scattered like kindling across this section of Arizona, enterprising people began exporting it wholesale to the East. By 1900 so much had been removed that in 1906 several areas were set aside as the Petrified Forest National Monument.

It's hard to believe when you drive across this arid landscape, but at one time this area was a vast humid swamp. That was 225 million years ago, when dinosaurs and huge amphibians ruled the earth and giant now-extinct trees grew on the high ground around the swamp. Fallen trees were washed downstream and gathered in piles in still backwaters. There they were eventually covered over with silt, mud, and volcanic ash. Preserved from decay by this burial, the logs lay as they were when they fell until water, bearing dissolved silica that had leached from volcanic ash, seeped into the logs. The dissolved silica filled the cells of the wood and eventually recrystallized into stone to form petrified wood.

This region was later inundated with water, and thick deposits of sediment buried the logs ever deeper. Eventually the land was transformed yet again as a geologic upheaval thrust the lake bottom up above sea level. This upthrust of the land cracked the logs into the segments we see today. Eventually wind and water eroded the landscape to create the many colorful and spectacular features of northern Arizona, including the Painted Desert, and the petrified logs were once again exposed on the surface of the land.

Throughout the region you'll see petrified wood in all sizes and colors, natural and polished, being sold in gift stores. This petrified wood comes from private land. No petrified wood, no matter how small, may be removed from Petrified Forest National Park.

ESSENTIALS
GETTING THERE

By Train   There is Amtrak passenger service to Winslow, 33 miles west of Holbrook. Call 800/872-7245 for schedules and rate information.

By Bus   Holbrook is served by Greyhound Lines; phone 800/231-2222 for schedules and fares.

By Car   The north entrance to Petrified Forest National Park is 25 miles east of Holbrook on I-40. The south entrance is 20 miles east of Holbrook on U.S. 180.

VISITOR INFORMATION

For further information on the Painted Desert or the Petrified Forest, contact the **Petrified Forest National Park,** P.O. Box 2217, Petrified Forest National Park, AZ 86028 (☎ 520/524-6228). For information on Holbrook and the surrounding region, contact the **Holbrook Chamber of Commerce,** 100 E. Arizona St., Holbrook, AZ 86025 (☎ 520/524-6558 or 800/524-2459).

WHAT TO SEE & DO
PETRIFIED FOREST NATIONAL PARK & THE PAINTED DESERT

The park entrances are located 25 miles east of Holbrook on I-40 and 20 miles east of Holbrook on U.S. 180. For park information, call 520/524-6228. Admission is $5 per car and the park is open daily from 8am to 5pm, with longer hours in summer.

The park has two visitor centers. Both have maps and books about the region, and also give out the free permits necessary to backpack and camp in the park's wilderness areas. The **Painted Desert Oasis Visitor Center** is at the north end of the park and is open daily from 8am to 5pm (longer hours in summer). A 17-minute film here explains the process by which wood becomes fossilized. The **Rainbow Forest Museum,** at the south end of the park, is open daily from 8am to 5pm (also with longer hours in summer). Exhibits, including letters written by people who had taken pieces of petrified wood and who later felt guilty and returned the stones, chronicle the area's geologic and human history. Connecting the two visitor centers is a 27-mile scenic road with more than 20 overlooks. The petrified logs are concentrated in the southern part of the park, while the northern section overlooks the Painted Desert.

Starting at the southern end of the park, there is the **Giant Logs self-guided trail.** This trail starts behind the Rainbow Forest Museum and a booklet explaining the numbered stops is available at the front desk. The trail lives up to its name, with huge logs strewn about the hilly area. Almost directly across the parking lot from the Rainbow Forest Museum is the entrance to the Long Logs and Agate House areas. On the Long Logs trail you can see more big trees, while at Agate House you will see the ruins of a pueblo built from wood that was turned into colorful agate. Minerals such as iron, manganese, and carbon are what give petrified wood its distinctive colors.

Heading north, you pass by the unusual formations known as **The Flattops.** These structures are caused by the erosion of softer soil deposits from beneath a harder and more erosion-resistant layer of sandstone. The Flattops area is one of the park's wilderness areas. The **Crystal Forest** is the next stop to the north and is named for the beautiful amethyst and quartz crystals that were once found in the cracks of petrified logs. Concern over the removal of these crystals was what led to the protection of the petrified forest.

At the **Jasper Forest Overlook** you can see logs that include petrified roots, while at **Blue Mesa** pieces of petrified wood form capstones over easily eroded clay soils. As wind and water wear away at the clay beneath a piece of stone, the balance of the stone becomes more and more precarious until it eventually comes toppling down. At the **Agate Bridge** stop, the soil has been washed away under a petrified log creating a natural agate bridge.

Erosion has played a major role in the formation of the Painted Desert, and to the north of Blue Mesa you'll see some of the most interesting erosional features of the area. It's quite evident why these hills of sandstone and clay are known as **The Teepees.** The layers of different color are due to different types of soils and stone and to minerals dissolved in the soil.

Human habitation of the area dates back more than 2,000 years, and at **Newspaper Rock** you can see petroglyphs (rock carvings) left by generations of Native Americans. At **Puerco Indian Ruins** you can see the homes of the people who made the carvings prior to the area's abandonment around 1400.

North of Puerco Ruins, the road crosses the Santa Fe Railroad and then I-40. From here to the Painted Desert Visitor Center there are eight overlooks onto the southernmost edge of the **Painted Desert.** Named for the vivid colors of the soil and stone that cover the land here, the Painted Desert is a Technicolor dreamscape of pastel colors washed across a barren expanse of eroded hills. The colors are created by minerals dissolved in the sandstone and clay soils that were deposited during different geologic periods. There's a picnic area at Chinde Point overlook, and at Kachina Point, where you'll find the **Painted Desert Inn Museum.** From here, there's access to the park's other wilderness area.

At the north end, the **Painted Desert Oasis** provides a full-service cafeteria, and at the south end of the park there's a snack bar serving sandwiches and ice cream.

IN HOLBROOK   Though the Petrified Forest National Monument is the main reason for visiting this area, you may also want to stop in at the **Navajo County Museum** in downtown Holbrook. This old and dusty museum has exhibits on local history, but is most interesting for having the town's old jail cells on display. From June to August, the museum sponsors Native American dancers Monday through Friday evenings from 7 to 9pm on the lawn in front of the museum. There are also several rock shops in Holbrook where you can buy petrified wood and other fascinating stones. Also here in town is **McGee's Beyond Native Tradition Gallery,** 2114 E. Navajo Blvd. (☎ **520/524-1977**), a Native American crafts gallery with a wide selection of typical crafts at reasonable prices.

WHERE TO STAY

Holbrook is the nearest town to Petrified Forest National Monument. Here, in addition to the unique Wigwam Motel listed below, you'll find several budget chain motels, including the following (see the Appendix for toll-free telephone numbers): **Comfort Inn,** 2602 E. Navajo Blvd., Holbrook, AZ 86025 (☎ **520/524-6131**), charging $44 to $68 double; **Days Inn,** 2601 E. Navajo Blvd., Holbrook, AZ 86025 (☎ **520/524-6949**), charging $46 to $68 double; **Motel 6,** 2514 Navajo Blvd., Holbrook, AZ 86025 (☎ **520/524-6101**), charging $34 double; and **Super 8 Motel,** 1989 Navajo Blvd., Holbrook, AZ 86025 (☎ **520/524-2871**), charging $41 to $48 double.

Wigwam Motel
811 W. Hopi Dr., Holbrook, AZ 86025. ☎ **520/524-3048.** 15 rms. A/C TV TEL. $27–$32 double. MC, V.

Here in Holbrook you can have your chance to sleep in a concrete wigwam. This unique motel was built in the 1940s when unusual architecture was springing up all along famous Route 66. Owned by the same family since it was built, the Wigwam was renovated a few years back. However, you'll still find the original rustic furniture and colorful bedspreads in the small wigwam-shaped buildings. There's also a small museum here at the motel.

WHERE TO DINE

Butterfield Stage Co.
609 W. Hopi Dr. ☎ **520/645-2467.** Main courses $7–$18. AE, MC, V. Daily 4–10pm. STEAK/SEAFOOD.

It's natural to assume that finding a decent meal in an out-of-the-way town might be near impossible, so the Butterfield Stage Co. is a pleasant surprise. The owners are from Yugoslavia, and we're not sure how they got to Holbrook, but we do know that meals here are excellent. The soup and salad bar is always fresh and there isn't a better espresso or cappuccino for miles around. The tables have historical panels with amusing information to read while waiting for your peppersteak or filet mignon. The restaurant is named for the famous overland stagecoach line that carried the mail from St. Louis to San Francisco in the mid-19th century.

5 Payson & the Mogollon Rim

94 miles NE of Phoenix, 90 miles SW of Winslow, 90 miles SE of Flagstaff, 100 miles W of Pinetop-Lakeside

Payson, 90 miles from Phoenix and 5,000 feet above sea level, is one of the closest places for Phoenicians to find relief from the summer heat. Summer temperatures are 20° cooler than in the Valley of the Sun, and the surrounding Tonto National Forest provides opportunities for hiking, swimming, fishing, and hunting. It isn't quite high enough to be the mountains, but it certainly isn't the desert. The Mogollon Rim, a 2,000-foot escarpment that runs from central Arizona into New Mexico, is only 22 miles north of town. The Mogollon Rim country was featured in many of the western novels of Zane Grey, who made his home in a cabin near Payson. In recent years, retirees have discovered the nearly perfect climate of Payson. Summer highs are usually in the 80s or 90s while winter highs are usually in the 50° to 60° range.

ESSENTIALS
GETTING THERE

By Bus The Payson Express operates one bus a day between Phoenix and Payson and offers door-to-door service for around $35 to $40 one way; call 520/474-5254 or 602/256-6464 in Phoenix, for further information. The White Mountain Passenger Line also offers service between Phoenix, Payson, and Show Low; phone 520/537-4539 in Show Low or 602/275-4245 in Phoenix for schedule and fare information.

By Car Payson is 94 miles from Phoenix on Ariz. 87, the Beeline Highway. Ariz. 87 also connects Payson to Winslow, which is 90 miles away. Ariz. 260 runs east from Payson, climbing the Mogollon Rim and continuing into the White Mountains.

VISITOR INFORMATION

For more information on Payson, contact the **Payson Chamber of Commerce,** P.O. Box 1380, Payson, AZ 85547 (☎ **520/474-4515** or 800/672-9766).

SPECIAL EVENTS

Payson calls itself the "Festival Capital of the World," and though this claim may be a bit overstated, there certainly are plenty of festivals here. The **world's oldest continuous rodeo** (a claim also made by Prescott's rodeo) takes place each year in August, while an **Old Timers Rodeo** is held in May. In June there's the annual **Blues Festival,** and in July, the **Loggers Sawdust Festival.** In September there's the **State Fiddler's Contest,** and in June and October, the **Payson Art League Exhibit.**

WHAT TO SEE & DO

To learn a bit more about the history of the area, stop in at the **Museum of the Forest,** 1001 W. Main St. (☎ **520/474-1541**), which has displays on the region, as well as a special Zane Grey exhibit. The museum is open weekends from noon to 4pm. You'll also find more Zane Grey memorabilia at the **Zane Grey Museum,** 408 W. Main St., Suite 8 (☎ **520/474-6243**). This tiny museum is open Thursday through Tuesday from 10am to 4pm.

Just north of town, off of Ariz. 87, you can visit the ruins of **Shoofly Village,** in the Tonto National Forest. This village was first occupied nearly 1,000 years ago and contained 87 rooms. Today only rock foundations remain, but an interpretive trail helps bring the site to life.

Outdoor activities are the main pursuit of most visitors to Payson. If you want to do some fishing, stop in at the Payson Chamber of Commerce information center for directions to where the fish might be biting. Anglers might also want to visit the **Tonto Creek Hatchery** (☎ **520/478-4200**), which is off of Ariz. 260 about 20 miles east of Payson. If you'd like to go horseback riding, contact **O.K. Corral Stables** (☎ **520/476-4303**) in Pine, which is 14 miles north of Payson on Ariz. 87. In the winter, cross-country skiers will find ski rentals and groomed trails at **Forest Lakes Touring Center and Cabins,** 36 miles east of Payson on Ariz. 260 (☎ **520/535-4047**).

Tonto Natural Bridge State Park (☎ **520/476-4202**), located 15 miles north of Payson on Ariz. 87, is the largest natural travertine bridge in the world. Discovered in 1877 by a gold prospector named David Gowan, who was being chased by Apache, the bridge is 183 feet high and, at its widest point, is 150 feet across. This state park preserves not only the bridge, but a historic lodge built by Gowan's nephew and the nephew's sons. Today the lodge has been restored to the way it looked in 1927. Admission to the park is $5 per car. The park is open daily: April to October from 8am to 6pm and November to March from 9am to 5pm.

Other attractions in the Payson area include the small **Payson Zoo,** located less than 7 miles east of town on Ariz. 260 (☎ **520/474-5435**). It's a good place to bring the kids, where they'll see animals from around the world, including a tiger. Admission is $4 for adults and $1 for children 12 and under.

The **Highline Trail** is a 51-mile-long hiking trail along the lower slope of the Mogollon Rim. You can find out more about the trail at the Payson Ranger Station on Ariz. 260 at the east end of town. Up on the top of the Mogollon Rim are seven lakes well known for their excellent fishing. The lakes are reached from a forest road that leaves Ariz. 260 just past the top of the Mogollon Rim.

WHERE TO STAY
MODERATE

Best Western Paysonglo Lodge

1005 S. Beeline Hwy. (P.O. Box 620), Payson, AZ 85541. ☎ **520/474-2382** or 800/ 772-9766; 800/872-9766 in Arizona. Fax 520/474-1937. 47 rms. A/C TV TEL. $52–$92 double. Rates include continental breakfast. AE, DC, DISC, MC, V.

Located on the south side of town, this is Payson's best motel. The guest rooms feature contemporary furnishings and several have their own fireplaces. The hotel also offers free coffee and cookies, an outdoor pool, and a whirlpool.

✪ Kohl's Ranch Resort

E. Ariz. 260, Payson, AZ 85541. ☎ **520/478-4211** or 800/331-5645. 41 rms, 8 cabins. A/C TV TEL. $65–$95 double; $115–$170 cabin. AE, DISC, MC, V.

Kohl's Ranch is 17 miles east of Payson on Ariz. 260 and is surrounded by quiet forests. Situated on the banks of Tonto Creek, this casual family resort is an excellent base for exploring the Mogollon Rim region. The lodge's lobby is a towering glass-fronted A-frame with a large stone fireplace and exposed beams. The guest rooms vary from lodge rooms with unusual hardwood-look carpets and log cabin look-alike walls to rustic wood-paneled two-bedroom cabins. Some of the smaller rooms have fireplaces, as do the cabins. The dining room gives the impression that you're eating in the streets of an old Wild West cow town. There's a lounge in the main lodge and a cowboy bar and pool hall across the parking lot. The hotel also offers horseback riding ($20 per hour), hayrides, an outdoor pool, sauna, and video arcade.

INEXPENSIVE

Christopher Creek Lodge

Ariz. 260 (Star Rte., Box 119), Payson, AZ 85541. ☎ **520/478-4300**. 6 rms, 21 cabins. $45– $85 double. MC, V.

Located 23 miles east of Payson on Ariz. 260, the Christopher Creek Lodge is a family-oriented rustic mountain retreat. You can choose between motel-style rooms with sleeping lofts; large spartan creekside cabins complete with full kitchen, woodstove, and sleeping loft; or duplex cabins with woodstoves, sliding glass doors, and picnic tables in the dining areas. All the accommodations are under the trees, and Christopher Creek runs along the edge of the property.

✪ Majestic Mountain Inn

602 E. Ariz. 260, Payson, AZ 85541. ☎ **520/474-0185** or 800/408-2442. 37 rms. A/C TV TEL. $58–$125 double. AE, CB, DC, DISC, MC, V.

This is Payson's newest lodging and is constructed in an attractive, modern mountain-lodge design. There's a large stone chimney and fireplace in the lobby, and several of the deluxe rooms have fireplaces of their own. These deluxe rooms also have tile floors and double whirlpool tubs facing the fireplaces. The standard rooms aren't as spacious or luxurious, but are still quite comfortable. The biggest drawback here is the lack of a pool.

Payson Pueblo Inn

809 E. Ariz. 260, Payson, AZ 85541. ☎ **520/474-5241** or 800/888-9828. 33 rms, 6 suites. A/C TV TEL. $49–$59 double; $95–$125 suite. AE, DC, DISC, MC, V.

This pueblo-style motel is on the right as you're heading east out of town on Ariz. 260. The rooms here are modern and clean, and all have refrigerators. Tile accents on the bathroom counters are a nice touch. There's no pool, but there is free morning coffee. The suites, with whirlpool tubs and fireplaces, are particularly comfortable.

WHERE TO DINE

Heritage House Garden Tea Room

202 W. Main St. ☎ **520/474-5501.** All items $5–$7. MC, V. Mon–Sat 11am–3pm. SALADS/SANDWICHES.

Tucked away in the back of this crafts store is a popular lunch spot and tearoom. The short menu features delicious sandwiches and crisp salads, but for many people the real draw here is the dessert tray. There's always a great selection of tempting cakes, cheesecakes, and mousses, as well as respectable cappuccinos and espressos. You'll find Heritage House only steps away from the Oaks.

The Oaks Restaurant & Lounge

302 W. Main St. ☎ **520/474-1929.** Reservations recommended. Main courses $14–$16. AE, CB, DC, DISC, MC, V. Tues–Thurs 11am–2pm and 5–8pm, Fri–Sat 11am–2pm and 5–9pm, Sun 11am–2pm (brunch) and 5–8pm. AMERICAN.

Taking its name from the grove of oak trees spreading over it, the Oaks Restaurant is a quiet place for a meal in Payson. The large patio dining area beside the grassy front lawn is a great spot for lunch or dinner on a warm night. The dinner menu, which changes monthly, is short and to the point: Steaks and seafood, simply prepared, are the mainstays. The Caesar salad is good, as are the various cakes. The lunch menu features a variety of hot and cold sandwiches as well as several salads.

6 The White Mountains

To Pinetop-Lakeside: 185 miles NE of Phoenix, 140 miles SE of Flagstaff, 50 miles S of Holbrook, 90 miles NE of Payson

When most people think of Arizona, they think of deserts and saguaro cacti. However, Arizona has more mountainous country than Switzerland and more forest than Minnesota. Folks from Phoenix and its surrounding cities long ago discovered how close the desert was to the cool mountain pine forests. And when weather reports from up north have Phoenicians dreaming about snow (it's true, they really do), they head for the White Mountains of eastern Arizona for a bit of skiing. This sparsely populated region of trout streams, ponderosa pine forests, lakes, meadows, and small towns caters primarily to family vacationers, though fishers and hunters also know the White Mountains well. All four seasons can be experienced here, and while summer fishing and hiking and winter skiing may be the main attractions, wildflowers in spring and golden aspen groves in autumn attract vacationers who are simply searching for mountain beauty and tranquillity.

The farther into the White Mountains you journey, the more peaceful and picturesque become the towns. **Pinetop-Lakeside,** two towns that have grown together over the years, is the busiest town in the White Mountains. There are dozens of motels and cabin resorts strung out along Ariz. 260 as it passes through the area. Pinetop-Lakeside is also a sort of ski resort in the winter. Sunrise ski area is only 30 miles away, and on weekends the town is packed with skiers. With Apache Sitgreaves National Forest on one side of town and the Fort Apache Indian Reservation on the other, Pinetop-Lakeside is well situated for those who wish to explore the miles of forests.

Greer is a tiny village of less than 100 permanent residents 8,525 feet up in the White Mountains. It's located 5 miles south of Ariz. 260 in a green valley surrounded by forested mountains. The Little Colorado River flows through the middle of Greer on its way to the Grand Canyon, and though it's little more than a babbling brook up here, it's well known for its trout fishing. Several lakes and ponds in the area also provide good fishing. In winter there are more than 12 miles of cross-country ski trails around Greer; ice skating, ice fishing, and sleigh rides are also popular activities. Greer happens to be the closest town to the Sunrise ski area, and there are several rustic mountain lodges and a number of rental-cabin operations.

Alpine is another small community located not far from the New Mexico state line on U.S. 191 and U.S. 180. This area is known as the Alps of Arizona, and Alpine's picturesque setting in the middle of a wide grassy valley at 8,030 feet certainly lives up to this image. There isn't much to do in Alpine other than enjoy the natural beauty of the area. However, hunting for elk, deer, mountain lion, bobcat, and bear and fishing the 200 miles of nearby trout streams and lakes are very popular. Alpine is surrounded by Apache Sitgreaves National Forest, which has miles of hiking trails and several campgrounds. In spring wildflowers abound and the trout fishing is excellent. In summer there are forest trails to be hiked. In autumn the aspens in the Golden Bowl above Alpine turn a brilliant yellow. In winter, there's cross-country skiing and ice fishing. The Coronado Trail (U.S. 666), a serpentine scenic highway running down the eastern edge of Arizona, passes through Alpine. This road twists and turns its way through miles of forest just waiting to be explored.

ESSENTIALS
GETTING THERE

By Plane   Scenic Airlines flies several times a day from Phoenix to Show Low. The fare is $79 one way, $158 round-trip. Call 800/634-6801 for schedule information.

By Bus   The White Mountain Passenger Line runs regularly scheduled service to Show Low. For fares and schedules, call 520/537-4539 in Show Low or 602/275-4245 in Phoenix.

By Car   Pinetop and Lakeside are both located on Ariz. 260. McNary and Greer are just a few miles south of this highway. Alpine is 27 miles south of the end of Ariz. 260 on U.S. 666 (the Coronado Trail).

VISITOR INFORMATION

For more information on Alpine or Pinetop-Lakeside, contact the **Alpine Chamber of Commerce,** P.O. Box 410, Alpine, AZ 85920 (☎ **520/339-4330**), or the **Pinetop-Lakeside Chamber of Commerce,** 592 W. White Mountain Blvd., Lakeside, AZ 85929 (☎ **520/367-4290**). For more information on the White Mountain Apache Reservation, contact the **White Mountain Apache Tribe,** P.O. Box 700, Whiteriver, AZ 85941 (☎ **520/338-4346**).

WHAT TO SEE & DO

THE APACHE RESERVATION

Fort Apache Historic Park, in Fort Apache (☎ **520/338-4625**), centers around Old Fort Apache, which, along with the Apache reservation, was established in 1870 by the U.S. government. The park now encompasses almost 300 acres, including more than 20 buildings, prehistoric ruins, petroglyphs, and the Apache Culture Center. The park is open Monday through Saturday from 10am to 4pm, and is located approximately 22 miles south of Pinetop on Ariz. 73. Admission is $2 for adults and 50¢ for children. The **Hon-Dah Casino** (☎ **520/369-0299**), owned and operated by the White Mountain Apache Tribe, is open every day around the clock and is located at the junction of Ariz. 73 and Ariz. 260, about 4 miles east of Pinetop.

OUTDOOR ACTIVITIES

There are good opportunities for **cross-country skiing** in Greer, which has 35 miles of developed cross-country trails. At 8,500 feet, the alpine scenery is quiet and serene.

The only downhill ski area is **Sunrise,** P.O. Box 217, McNary, AZ 85930 (☎ **520/735-7335,** or 800/55-HOTEL; for snow conditions, call 800/ 772-SNOW). Located just off Ariz. 260 on Ariz. 273, this ski area is on the White Mountain Apache Reservation and is operated by the Apache people. The ski area usually opens in November and receives more than 20 feet of snow per year. There's also snowmaking equipment to enhance natural snowfall and lights for night skiing on the weekends. Sunrise is one of the largest ski areas in the Southwest and is the most popular in Arizona. Plenty of winter sun makes skiing here almost as pleasant as lounging by the pool down in Phoenix. At the top of 11,000-foot Apache Peak is a day lodge offering meals and a view that goes on forever. There's also a **ski school** (☎ **520/735-7518**) that offers classes for beginners as well as advanced skiers.

If you're interested in fishing, contact **Troutback Flyfishing Guide Service,** in Springerville (☎ **520/333-2371**), where half a day of guided flyfishing will cost $90; or **X Diamond Ranch,** P.O. Box 791, Springerville (☎ **520/333-2286**), which maintains a section of the Little Colorado River as a fishing habitat. Half a day here will cost $25. Also, many lakes in the area offer boat rentals.

Mountain bikes can be rented at **Mountain Outfitters/The Skier's Edge** (☎ **520/367-6200**) for $12 a day. They also rent downhill and cross-country ski equipment. The store is located next to the Pinetop-Lakeside Chamber of Commerce on Ariz. 260.

Several golf courses in the area are open to the public, including **Pinetop Lakes Golf Club** (☎ 520/369-4531), **Silver Creek Golf Club** (☎ 520/ 537-2744), and the **Show Low Country Club** (☎ 520/537-4564).

If you want to get up on a horse, call **Porter Mountain Stable** (☎ 520/ 368-5306) for trail rides. Or for something different, try trekking with a llama. The **Delli Llamas** (☎ 520/537-0274) offer trips ranging in length from half a day ($20 for adults) to several days ($90 per day for adults).

For evening entertainment, **Theatre Mountain,** on Woodland Road in Lakeside (☎ 520/368-8888), stages melodramas and vaudeville shows.

NEARBY ACTIVITIES

If you've ever dreamed about working on site as an archeologist, here in eastern Arizona there are two opportunities. The **White Mountain Archaeological Center & Raven Site Ruin,** H.C. 30, Box 30, St. Johns, AZ 85936 (☎ 520/ 333-5857), operates as a field school and research center on a 5-acre site where Mogollon and Anasazi artifacts have been found. You can participate on a daily or weekly basis in excavating the site and learning about the basics of archaeology. Rooms, tent sites, and food are available at the center. Daily rates are $59 for adults, $37 for children 9 to 17; for 24 hours, $83 for adults, $61 for ages 9 to 17. Children under 9 are not accepted. The ruins at **Casa Malpais Archaeological Park,** 318 Main St. (P.O. Box 390), Springerville, AZ 85938 (☎ 520/333-5375), can be visited on guided tours costing $3 for adults and $2 for students and seniors. There's also a Casa Malpais museum in downtown Springerville. The archaeological park and museum is open in summer, daily from 9am to 5pm; in winter, Wednesday through Sunday from 10am to 4pm.

WHERE TO STAY
PINETOP

Best Western Inn of Pinetop

404 S. White Mountain Blvd. (P.O. Box 1006), Pinetop, AZ 85935. ☎ **520/367-6667** or 800/528-1234. Fax 602/367-6672. 41 rms. A/C TV TEL. $60–$89 double. AE, DC, DISC, MC, V.

Though it's right on busy Ariz. 260, this motel is set back a little from the road so the rooms are as quiet as you'd hope. The rooms feature extra-long beds, and the hotel offers free cider, tea, and coffee in the lobby. There's no pool but there is a whirlpool.

✪ Elk Mountain Lodge

Ariz. 260 (P.O. Box 1254), Pinetop, AZ 85935. ☎ **520/367-0626.** Fax 520/367-2606. 4 suites. TV TEL. $149 suite for two. MC, V.

This modern two-story log building sits right on busy Ariz. 260, but because the rooms face into the pines, you hardly even notice you're in town. In fact the lodge's backyard opens onto the national forest. The rustic architecture makes this small lodge stand out from the many old cabin resorts and motels that clutter this town. Each large suite has two bedrooms, two bathrooms, and two porches, as well as a full kitchen.

✪ Sierra Springs Ranch

H.C. 62, Box 32100, Pinetop, AZ 85935. ☎ **520/369-3900** or 800/247-7590. Fax 520/ 369-0741. 8 cabins. $150–$250 cabin for two. Two-night minimum stay. MC, V.

Located off a gravel road east of Pinetop, the Sierra Springs Ranch is surrounded by forests and is as idyllic a mountain retreat as you'll find in Arizona. Each of the eight cabins is a little bit different, but all are large and comfortable. Our favorite is the honeymoon cottage, which is built of logs and has a stone fireplace. All the cabins have full kitchens, which make up for the lack of a restaurant on the premises. On the ranch grounds you'll find a trout pond and meadows, a tennis court, and a walking/jogging path. Fishing gear, tennis racquets, and bicycles are all available for the use of guests. In the recreation room in the main lodge there's a big-screen TV. In winter cross-country skiing and snowmobiling are both popular, while at other times fly-fishing classes attract guests.

Whispering Pines Resort

Ariz. 260 (P.O. Box 307), Pinetop, AZ 85935. ☎ **520/367-4386** or 800/840-3867. 29 cabins. $30–$89 cabin for two. MC, V.

Situated on $12^1/_2$ wooded acres, the Whispering Pines Resort is a rustic family retreat. The cabins have one or two bedrooms and some are newer and nicer than others. All have fireplaces so you'll stay cozy and warm even in winter. One of the older cabins is a genuine log cabin with a stone fireplace, and though this isn't one of the better cabins, it does have a rustic appeal that may be suitable for the less finicky traveler. Other, more luxurious cabins have their own saunas. Recreational facilities include a whirlpool, volleyball court, and horseshoe pit; there's also a coin laundry.

LAKESIDE

⑤ Lake of the Woods

Off Ariz. 260 (P.O. Box 777), Lakeside, AZ 85929. ☎ **520/368-5353**. 25 cabins, 4 houses. TV. $64–$136 cabin for two; $147–$241 house for two. Lower rates in spring and fall. MC, V.

Located on its own private lake just off Ariz. 260, Lake of the Woods is a rustic mountain resort that caters to families. The kids can fish in the lake, play in the snow, or row a boat. The resort also offers a whirlpool, sauna, exercise equipment, table tennis, pool table, shuffleboard, horseshoes, a playground, and coin-operated laundry. The resort's cabins range from tiny to huge, with rustic and deluxe side byside; the smallest sleep two or three while the largest house sleeps 20 or more. Some have kitchens and fireplaces, and some are on the edge of the lake while others are tucked away under the pines. Be sure to request one away from the busy highway.

MCNARY

Sunrise Park Hotel

Hwy. 273, near intersection with Hwy. 260 (P.O. Box 217), McNary, AZ 85930. ☎ **520/ 735-7676** or 800/55-HOTEL. Fax 520/735-7315. 91 rms. TV TEL. Winter, $59–$110 double. Summer, $48–$68 double. AE, CB, DC, DISC, MC, V. Closed Apr to Memorial Day weekend and Labor Day weekend to early Dec.

This is the closest lodge to the Sunrise ski area and is only open during the winter and summer seasons. About half the rooms overlook Sunrise Lake. The dining room and lounge are a cozy place to gather after a day of skiing or hiking. On weekends there's live popular dance music in the lounge. The hotel also offers a ski area shuttle bus, indoor swimming pool, indoor and outdoor whirlpools, sauna, volleyball, and video arcade.

GREER

☉ Aspen Meadow Guest Ranch

118 Forest Rd., 6¹/₂ miles north of Hwy. 260 (P.O. Box 879), Eagar, AZ 85935. ☎ **520/ 521-0880.** 12 cabins. $95 cabin for two; full guest-ranch experience (with all meals and horseback riding) $600–$1,500 per week cabin for two. AE, MC, V.

Situated on 160 acres about 10 miles north of Greer, this guest ranch is surrounded by meadows and ponderosa pine forest. Accommodations are in modern log cabins with rustic log furniture and kitchenettes. Meals are taken in the main lodge, which is built of spruce logs and has a cathedral ceiling and massive stone fireplace. Ranch activities include horseback riding, fishing, basketball, volleyball, square dancing, table tennis, and crafts making—all of which add up to plenty to keep the whole family occupied for the duration of a stay at this remote ranch.

✪ Greer Lodge

Main Street (P.O. Box 244), Greer, AZ 85927. ☎ **520/735-7216.** 9 rms, 8 cabins. $120 double; $75–$110 cabin for two. MC, V.

The Little Colorado River, which truly lives up to its name here in Greer, runs right past the deck of the largest log lodge in the White Mountains. There are a variety of accommodations here including spacious rooms in the main lodge. These rooms all have views of the mountains or river. Most of the cabins have fireplaces and are quite modern, but there's one rustic log cabin that sleeps six and has a sleeping loft and fireplace. Only 20 minutes from the Sunrise ski area, with its own trout ponds and section of river, the lodge is popular with skiers and anglers both. The hotel also offers ice skating, croquet, volleyball, horseshoes, a barbecue area, fishing ponds, fly-fishing courses, and cross-country ski trails.

ALPINE

Tal-Wi-Wi Lodge

U.S. 191 (P.O. Box 169), Alpine, AZ 85920. ☎ **520/339-4319.** 20 rms. $49–$89 double. MC, V.

Located 3 miles north of Alpine on U.S. 191, the Tal-Wi-Wi Lodge is the best lodging in Alpine. The deluxe rooms here come with their own hot tub and fireplace, both of which are appreciated on cold winter nights. (Alpine is usually the coldest town in Arizona.) The furnishings in the guest rooms are rustic and comfortable, and the wood-paneled walls and large front porches give the lodge country appeal. The lodge's dining room serves country breakfasts and dinners.

WHERE TO DINE

PINETOP/LAKESIDE

In addition to the places mentioned below and a few basic burger and steak places in town, there's **Lauth's Country Store,** on Ariz. 260 in Pinetop (☎ **520/ 367-2161**), where you can get an inexpensive breakfast and a variety of burgers and sandwiches; and a bakery, **Swiss Village, Too,** also on Ariz. 260 (1479 E. White Mountain Blvd.) in Pinetop (☎ **520/367-3737**).

The Christmas Tree Restaurant

455 Woodland Rd. ☎ **520/367-3107.** Reservations recommended on weekends. Main courses $7–$22. DISC, MC, V. Mid-June to mid-Sept, Wed–Mon 5–9pm; mid-Sept to mid-June, Wed–Sun 5–9pm. AMERICAN.

You'll find some good home cooking here, with chicken and dumplings the specialty of the house. There are also straightforward dishes such as steak and scallops and baked sole amandine. Fans of Erma Bombeck, a Christmas Tree regular, may want to dine here on the off chance they might see her.

ⓢ Creasey's at Pinetop

984 E. White Mountain Blvd. (Ariz. 260). ☎ **520/367-1908.** Reservations recommended on weekends. Main courses $8.25–$15.25. CB, DC, MC, V. Labor Day–Memorial Day, Mon–Thurs 5–8:30pm, Fri–Sat 5–9:30pm, Sun 5–8:30pm; Memorial Day–Labor Day, Tues–Fri 11am–2pm, Tues–Sun 5–9:30pm. Sun brunch 11am–2pm year round. ITALIAN/ MEDITERRANEAN.

You'll find this nondescript building toward the east end of town on the main highway. We recommend seeking it out for appetizing culinary creations such as venison stew with tender yet chewy cheese tortellini, or red snapper on a bed of julienned vegetables with pasta. Both aïoli and roasted garlic come with the preliminary bread. The crème brûlée was lighter than others we've tasted, but intoxicatingly good. The service is friendly but professional. We look forward to eating here whenever we come to Pinetop/Lakeside—it seems like money well spent.

The Meadows

453 N. Woodland Rd. ☎ **520/367-8200** or 800/432-2129. Reservations recommended. Main courses $13.50–$18.50. AE, DISC, MC, V. Wed–Sat 11am–2pm and 5–9pm, Sun 10am– 2pm (brunch) and 5–9pm. CONTINENTAL/NEW AMERICAN.

In a woodland setting, this rambling Victorian-style mansion is casually elegant inside, with dark green carpeting and blond furnishings, and has a large shady deck that wraps around the back. The patrons tend to be well-off older people, but anyone can enjoy the surroundings. The menu focuses on continental favorites with a contemporary twist, such as shrimp and scallops Diane with mushrooms, scallions, and Cajun spices, or trout Imperial, baked with hollandaise and stuffed with savory crabmeat. The deck is a charming place for Sunday brunch.

GREER

Greer Lodge

44 Main St. ☎ **520/735-7216.** Reservations suggested. Main courses $13–$18. MC, V. Daily 11am–2:30pm and 5:30–8:30pm. AMERICAN/CONTINENTAL.

You couldn't wish for a prettier location than this one for a meal in the mountains. This multilevel restaurant has walls of glass that look out over a river, meadows, and a trout pond. In the winter there's a cozy fireplace. Unfortunately, the burrito and sandwich we had here at lunch were not up to the quality of the view, which really is the main reason to come here. Dinner fare includes various treatments of chicken, lamb, shrimp, and prime rib, and the wine list has some reasonably priced wines.

9 Tucson

Melding Hispanic, Anglo, and Native American roots, Tucson has become a city with character and awareness of its setting in the desert Southwest, confident in its style. Although the the city is undergoing the same sort of sprawl that many see as having turned Phoenix into a sort of Los Angeles without a beach, advocates for controlled growth are fighting hard to preserve both the city's unique character and its surrounding desert environment. Tucson has also managed to breathe life into its downtown area both by preserving several historic districts and by turning the inner city into an arts district.

Founded by the Spanish in 1775, Tucson is built on the site of a much older Native American village. The city's name comes from the Pima Indian word *chukeson*, which means "spring at the base of black mountain," a reference to the peak now known simply as "A Mountain." From 1867 to 1877 Tucson was the territorial capital of Arizona, but eventually the capital was moved to Phoenix. Consequently, Tucson did not develop as quickly as Phoenix and holds fast to its Hispanic and western heritage.

Tucson supports a very active cultural life, with symphony, ballet, opera, and theater companies, and many festivals celebrating aspects of Tucson life. However, it's the city's natural surroundings that make Tucson truly unique. Four mountain ranges ring the city, and in those mountains and their foothills are giant saguaro cactus, an oasis, one of the finest zoos in the world, a ski area, and miles of hiking and horseback-riding trails. Understandably, the Tucson lifestyle is oriented toward outdoor activities.

History, culture, and nature are the major attractions, but with its mild, sunny climate and mountain vistas, Tucson is a natural for resorts. While it may not yet have as many world-class resorts as the Valley of the Sun, the ones it does have certainly boast the finer views.

1 Orientation

Not nearly as large and spread out as Phoenix and the Valley of the Sun, Tucson is small enough to be convenient, yet large enough to be sophisticated. The mountains ringing the city are bigger and closer than those of Phoenix, and the desert is equally close.

What's Special About Tucson

Historic Buildings
- Mission San Xavier del Bac, called the White Dove of the Desert, a Spanish mission church.
- The ruins of Tumacacori, a nearby Spanish mission.

Cowboy Adventures
- Guest ranches (formerly called dude ranches) for riding the range.
- Cowboy steakhouses, featuring hayrides, staged gunfights, barbecues, and sing-alongs.

Natural Spectacles
- Sabino Canyon Park, an oasis of waterfalls.
- Saguaro National Park, with the massive saguaro cactus, symbol of the American desert.

Activities
- Desert hiking opportunities within a few minutes of downtown.
- Mount Lemmon, a forested mountain with hiking and skiing.
- Excellent golf on the area's numerous public, private, and resort courses.
- Birdwatching at Madera Canyon, one of the best birding spots in the country.

Shopping
- The nearby historic community of Tubac, an enclave of art galleries and artists' studios.

Zoos
- The Arizona–Sonora Desert Museum, one of the leading zoos in the country.

TV and Film Locations
- Old Tucson Studios, where dozens of western movies and television shows have been filmed.

Great Neighborhoods
- El Presidio Historic District (1880s).
- Barrio Historico, the largest concentration of Sonoran-style adobe homes in the U.S.

Offbeat Sites
- The Titan Missile Museum, the world's only ICBM that has become a museum.
- Biosphere II, a huge self-contained airtight greenhouse.

ARRIVING

BY PLANE   Located 6 miles south of downtown, **Tucson International Airport** (☎ **520/573-8100**) is served by many airlines, including Aero México (☎ 800/237-6639), America West (☎ 800/235-9292), American (☎ 800/433-7300), Continental (☎ 800/525-0280), Delta (☎ 800/221-1212), Northwest (☎ 800/225-2525), Southwest (☎ 800/435-9792), and United (☎ 800/241-6522). At the airport you'll find car-rental desks, regularly scheduled shuttle vans to

Tucson at a Glance

ARIZONA

Tucson

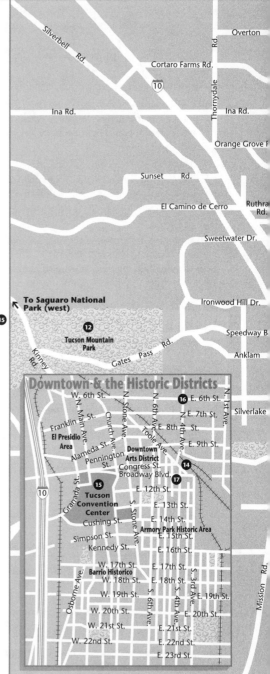

Overton

Cortaro Farms Rd.

Silverbell Rd.

10

Thornydale

Ina Rd.   Ina Rd.

Orange Grove F

Sunset   Rd.

El Camino de Cerro   Ruthra
                                     Rd.

Sweetwater Dr.

Ironwood Hill Dr.

To Saguaro National
Park (west)   12

                          Tucson Mountain
                               Park

Speedway B

Anklam

Kinney Rd.   Gates Pass Rd.

Downtown & the Historic Districts

W. 6th St.   16 E. 6th St.

N. Main Ave.   N. Stone Ave.   N. 6th Ave.   N. 4th Ave.   N. 1st Ave.

E. 7th St.   Silverlake

Franklin St.   E. 8th St.

El Presidio
Area   Alameda St.   E. 9th St.

Pennington   Downtown
St.   Arts District

Congress St.   14

Broadway Blvd.   17

10   E. 12th St.

Granada St.   15   E. 13th St.

                  Tucson
                  Convention   S. Stone Ave.
                  Center   E. 14th St.

Cushing St.   Armory Park Historic Area

Simpson St.   E. 15th St.

Kennedy St.   E. 16th St.

W. 17th St.   Barrio Historico E. 17th St.

Osborne Ave.   W. 18th St.   E. 18th St.   S. 3rd Ave.   S. 4th Ave.

                  W. 19th St.   E. 19th St.

                  W. 20th St.   E. 20th St.

                  S. 6th Ave.

                  W. 21st St.   E. 21st St.

                  W. 22nd St.   E. 22nd St.

                                   E. 23rd St.

Mission Rd.

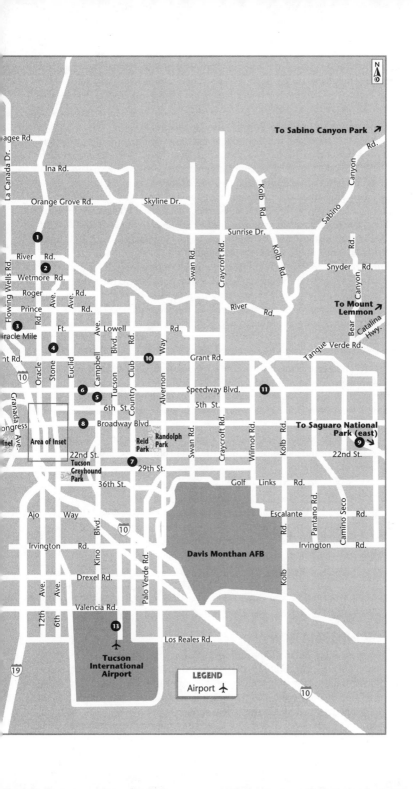

downtown, and taxis. In the baggage-claim area are two **visitor information centers** (open Monday through Saturday from 7am to 11pm and on Sunday from 8:30am to 11pm) where you can pick up brochures about Tucson and reserve a hotel room if you haven't done so already.

Transportation to and from Town   Many resorts and hotels in Tucson provide airport shuttle service and will pick you up and return you to the airport either for free or for a competitive fare, so check with your hotel. **Arizona Stagecoach** (☎ 602/889-1000) operates a daily 24-hour van service to downtown Tucson and the foothills resorts. You'll find their vans outside the center of the baggage-claim area. Fares range from $11 to downtown up to $17 to the foothills resorts. To return to the airport, be sure to call at least a day before your scheduled departure.

You'll also find taxis waiting in the same area or you can call **City Cab** (☎ 520/792-2028), **Yellow Cab** (☎ 520/624-6611) or **Allstate Cab** (☎ 520/798-1111). A taxi to downtown costs around $15.

Sun Tran (☎ 520/792-9222), the local public transit, operates a bus service to and from the airport, though you'll have to make a transfer to reach downtown. The bus at the airport is no. 25 (ask for a transfer when you board); at the Roy Laos Transit Center you should transfer to no. 16 for downtown. The fare is 75¢. Route 25 from the airport operates daily: Monday through Friday between about 7am and 8pm, on Saturday between about 8am and 7pm, and on Sunday between about 9am and 7pm. Departures are every hour.

BY CAR   **I-10,** the main east-west Interstate across the southern United States, passes through Tucson as it swings north to Phoenix. **I-19** connects Tucson with the Mexican border at Nogales. **Arizona 86** heads southwest into the Papago Indian Reservation and **U.S. 89** leads north toward Florence and eventually connects with **U.S. 60** into Phoenix.

If you're headed downtown, take the Congress Street exit off I-10. If you're headed for one of the foothills resorts north of downtown, you'll probably want to take the Ina Road exit.

BY TRAIN   Tucson is served by **Amtrak** passenger rail service (☎ 800/872-7245 in the U.S. and Canada). The *Sunset Limited,* which runs between Miami and Los Angeles, stops in Tucson. The **train station** is at 400 E. Toole Ave. (☎ 520/623-4442) in the heart of downtown Tucson and is within walking distance of the Tucson Convention Center, the El Presidio Historic District, and a few hotels. You'll find taxis waiting to meet the train.

BY BUS   **Greyhound Lines** (☎ 520/792-3475, or 800/231-2222) connects Tucson to the rest of the United States through its extensive system. The bus station is at 2 S. Fourth Ave., across the street from the Hotel Congress in the Downtown Arts District. For fare and schedule information, call 520/792-0972.

VISITOR INFORMATION

The **Metropolitan Tucson Convention & Visitors Bureau,** 130 S. Scott Ave., Tucson, AZ 85701 (☎ 520/624-1817 or 800/638-8350), is an excellent source of information on Tucson and environs. You can contact them before leaving home or stop at their visitor center, which is stocked with brochures and has helpful people at the desk to answer your questions. The visitor center is open Monday through Friday from 8am to 5pm and on Saturday and Sunday from 9am to 4pm.

CITY LAYOUT

MAIN ARTERIES & STREETS   Tucson is laid out on a grid that's fairly regular in the downtown areas but becomes less orderly the farther you go from the city center. In the foothills, where Tucson's most recent growth has occurred, the grid system breaks down completely because of the hilly terrain. Major thoroughfares are spaced at 1-mile intervals, with smaller streets filling in the squares created by the major roads.

The **main east-west roads** are (from south to north) 22nd Street, Broadway Boulevard, Speedway Boulevard, Grant Road (with Tanque Verde Road as an extension), and Ina Road/Skyline Drive. The **main north-south roads** are (from west to east) Miracle Mile/Oracle Road, Stone/Sixth Avenue, Campbell Avenue, Country Club Road, and Alvernon Road. **I-10** cuts diagonally across the Tucson metropolitan area from northwest to southeast.

In **downtown Tucson,** Congress Street and Broadway Boulevard are the main east-west streets and Stone Avenue, Fourth Avenue, and Sixth Avenue are the main north-south streets.

FINDING AN ADDRESS   Because Tucson is laid out on a grid, finding an address is relatively easy. The zero (or starting) point for all Tucson addresses is the corner of Stone Avenue, which runs north and south, and Congress Street, which runs east and west. From this point, streets are designated either north, south, east, or west. Addresses usually, but not always, increase by 100 with each block, so that an address of 4321 East Broadway Boulevard should be 43 blocks east of Stone Avenue. In the downtown area, many of the streets and avenues are numbered, with numbered streets running east and west and numbered avenues running north and south.

STREET MAPS   The best way to find your way around Tucson is to pick up a detailed map at the visitor information center at the airport, or at the Metropolitan Tucson Convention & Visitors Bureau (see "Visitor Information," above) for $2. The visitors bureau also offers a free map in the *Tucson Official Visitors Guide.* The maps handed out by car-rental agencies are not very detailed, but will do for some purposes. Local gas stations also sell detailed maps.

NEIGHBORHOODS IN BRIEF

El Presidio Historic District   Named for the Spanish military garrison that once stood on this site, the neighborhood is bounded by Alameda Street on the south, Main Avenue on the west, Franklin Street on the north, and Church Avenue on the east. The El Presidio District was the city's most affluent neighborhood in the 1880s, and many large homes from that period have been restored and now house restaurants, arts-and-crafts galleries, and a bed-and-breakfast inn. The Tucson Museum of Art anchors the neighborhood.

Barrio Historico District   Another 19th-century neighborhood, the Barrio Historico, is bounded on the north by Cushing Street, on the west by the railroad tracks, on the south by 18th Street, and on the east by Stone Avenue. The Barrio Historico is characterized by Sonoran-style adobe row houses that directly abut the street with no yards, a style typical in Mexican towns. Although a few restaurants and art galleries dot the neighborhood, most restored buildings serve as offices. This is still a borderline neighborhood with restoration a slow, ongoing process, and is best avoided late at night.

Armory Park Historic District   Bounded by 12th Street on the north, Stone Avenue on the west, 19th Street on the south, and Second Avenue and Third Avenue on the east, the Armory Park neighborhood was Tucson's first historic district. Today this area is undergoing a renaissance but isn't yet an entirely safe place to wander around in after dark.

Downtown Arts District   This neighborhood encompasses a bit of the Armory District, a bit of the El Presidio District, and the stretch of Congress Street and Broadway Boulevard west of Toole Avenue. Home to galleries, boutiques, nightclubs, and hip cafés, it's Tucson's liveliest neighborhood on weekends of Downtown Saturday Night activities. Other nights it's the realm of the young and the homeless.

Fourth Avenue   Running from University Boulevard in the north to Ninth Street in the south, Fourth Avenue is Tucson's hippest shopping district (although a little run-down and not tending upward as one would expect), with boutiques selling ethnic clothing and shops offering handcrafted items from around the world. Twice a year, in spring and fall, the street is closed to traffic for a colorful street fair. With plenty of bars and restaurants, this street sees a lot of after-dark foot traffic that keeps it pretty safe.

The Foothills   Encompassing a huge area of northern Tucson, the foothills contain the city's most affluent neighborhoods. Elegant shopping plazas, modern malls, world-class resorts, golf courses, and expensive residential neighborhoods are surrounded by hilly desert at the foot of the Santa Catalina Mountains.

2 Getting Around

BY PUBLIC TRANSPORTATION

BY BUS   Operating over much of the Tucson Metropolitan area, **Sun Tran** (☎ 520/792-9222) public buses cost only 75¢ for adults, 50¢ for students, 30¢ for senior citizens, and are free for children 5 and under. Bus stops are marked by signs that provide information on which buses stop there, the major streets they serve, and their final destinations. The **Downtown-Ronstadt Transit Center** at the corner of Congress Street and Sixth Avenue is served by nearly 30 regular and express bus routes to all parts of Tucson. Monthly bus passes and 20-ride coupon booklets are available.

The bus system does not extend to such tourist attractions as the Arizona–Sonora Desert Museum, Old Tucson, Saguaro National Park, or the foothills resorts, and consequently is of limited use to visitors.

BY TROLLEY   Though they don't go very far, the restored electric streetcars of **Old Pueblo Trolley** (☎ 520/792-1802) provide a fun way to get from the Fourth Avenue shopping district to the University of Arizona. The trolleys operate Monday through Friday from 11am to 2pm, on Friday from 6pm to midnight, on Saturday from 10am to midnight, and on Sunday from noon to 6pm. The fare is $1 for adults and 50¢ for children 6 to 12; Children under 5 ride free. All day passes are $2.50 for adults and $1.25 for children.

BY CAR

RENTALS   Unless you plan to stay by the pool or on the golf course at one of Tucson's world-class resorts, you'll probably want to rent a car to get around town.

See "Getting Around" in Chapter 3 for details on renting a car in Arizona. Luckily, rates are fairly economical, especially if you can skip the collision-damage waiver. You can usually rent a subcompact for $115 to $140 per week or $25 to $35 per day.

The **rental-car agencies** below have offices at Tucson International Airport: Alamo (☎ 800/327-9633), Avis (☎ 800/331-1212), Budget (☎ 800/527-0700), Hertz (☎ 800/654-3131), National (☎ 800/227-7368), and Thrifty (☎ 800/367-2277). Several companies have offices in other parts of the city as well, so be sure to ask if they have a more convenient location for pickup or drop-off of your car.

PARKING Downtown Tucson is still a relatively easy place to find a parking space, and parking fees are low. There are two huge parking lots at the south side of the Tucson Convention Center, a couple of small lots on either side of the Tucson Museum of Art (one at Main Avenue and Paseo Redondo, south of the El Presidio Historic District, and one at the corner of Council Street and Court Avenue) where it will cost you $1.50 to park for up to 12 hours, and parking garages beneath the main library and El Presidio Park. You'll also find plenty of metered parking on the smaller downtown streets. Almost all Tucson hotels and resorts provide free parking.

DRIVING RULES Lanes on several major avenues in Tucson change direction at rush hour to facilitate traffic flow, so pay attention to signs hung over the street. These tell you the time and direction of traffic in the lanes.

BY TAXI

If you need a taxi, you'll have to phone for one. **City Cab** (☎ **520/792-2028**), **Yellow Cab** (☎ **520/624-6611**), and **Allstate Cab** (☎ **520/798-1111**) provide service throughout the city. Fares start at $1 and increase by $1.40 per mile. Although distances in Tucson are not as great as those in Phoenix, it's still a good 10 or more miles from the foothills resorts to downtown Tucson, so expect to pay at least $10 for any taxi ride. Most resorts offer or can arrange taxi service to the major tourist attractions around Tucson.

Shoppers should keep in mind that several Tucson shopping malls offer free shuttle service from hotels and resorts. Be sure to ask at your hotel before paying for a ride to a mall.

ON FOOT

Downtown Tucson is compact and easily explored on foot. Many old streets in the downtown historic neighborhoods are narrow and much easier to appreciate if you leave your car in a parking lot. On the other hand, several major attractions, including the Arizona–Sonora Desert Museum, Old Tucson Studios, Saguaro National Park, and Sabino Canyon, require quite a bit of walking, often on uneven footing, so be sure to bring a good pair of walking shoes.

FAST FACTS: Tucson

American Express The local American Express representative in the Tucson area is Bon Voyage Travel. They have nine offices, the most convenient located at 990 E. University Blvd. (☎ 520/622-5842), open Monday through Friday from 8:30am to 5:30pm.

Area Code   The telephone area code is 520.

Babysitters   Most hotels can arrange a babysitter for you, and many resorts feature special programs for children on weekends and throughout the summer. If your hotel can't help, call A-1 Messner Sitter Service (☎ 520/881-1578), which will send a sitter to your hotel.

Business Hours   See "Fast Facts: Arizona," in Chapter 3.

Camera Repair   See "Photographic Needs," below.

Car Rentals   See "Getting Around," earlier in this chapter.

Climate   See "When to Go," in Chapter 3.

Dentist   Call the Dentist Information Service (☎ 520/790-8827) for dentist referral.

Doctor   Call the Tucson Medical Center (☎ 520/324-2000) for doctor referral. Or for answers to health questions, call Ask-A-Nurse (☎ 520/544-2000).

Driving Rules   See "Getting Around," earlier in this chapter.

Drugstores   See "Pharmacies," below.

Embassies/Consulates   See "Fast Facts: For Foreign Visitors," in Chapter 4.

Emergencies   For fire, police, or medical emergency, phone **911.**

Eyeglasses   Alvernon Optical has several stores around town where you can have your glasses repaired or replaced. Locations include 440 N. Alvernon Way (☎ 520/327-6211), 7043 N. Oracle Rd. (☎ 520/297-2501), and 7123 E. Tanque Verde Rd. (☎ 520/296-4157).

Hospitals   The Tucson General Hospital is at 3838 N. Campbell Ave. (☎ 520/327-5431), the Tucson Medical Center is at 5301 E. Grant Rd. (☎ 520/327-5461), and the University Medical Center is at 1501 N. Campbell Ave. (☎ 520/694-0111).

Information   See "Visitor Information" in "Orientation," earlier in this chapter.

Libraries   Tucson's main library is a large modern building in the center of downtown at 101 N. Stone Ave. (☎ 520/791-4010).

Lost Property   If you've lost something and you don't know where, try the Tucson Police Department Found-Recovered Property office (☎ 520/791-4458). If you lost something at the airport, call 520/573-8156; if you lost something on a Sun Tran bus, call 520/792-9222.

Luggage Storage/Lockers   You'll find baggage-storage lockers at the Greyhound bus station, 2 S. Fourth Ave. (☎ 520/792-3475).

Newspapers/Magazines   The *Arizona Daily Star* is Tucson's morning daily and the *Tucson Citizen* is the afternoon daily. The *Tucson Weekly* is the city's weekly news-and-arts journal; it's published on Thursday. The Crescent Smoke Shop Newsstand, 216 E. Congress St. (☎ 520/622-1559), carries newspapers from all over the country.

Pharmacies   Walgreens has stores all over Tucson. Call 800/WALGREENS for the Walgreens pharmacy that's nearest you or that's open 24 hours a day.

Photographic Needs   NuArt Photo, with three locations—at 3954 E. Speedway Blvd. (☎ 520/326-9606), 7000 E. Tanque Verde Rd. (☎ 520/290-1266), and El Con Mall, 3601 E. Broadway Blvd. (☎ 520/327-7062)—can supply camera needs or repairs.

Police In case of an emergency, phone 911.

Post Office The main Tucson post office is at 141 S. Sixth Ave. (☎ 520/ 622-8454), open Monday through Friday from 8:30am to 5pm and on Saturday from 9am to noon.

Radio KXCI (91.3 FM) has an eclectic mix of programming and is a favorite with local Tucsonians, while KUAT (90.5 FM) has all-classical programming and is a good station for news.

Safety Tucson is surprisingly safe for a city of its size. However, the Downtown Arts District isn't all that lively after dark and you should be particularly alert in this area if you're down here for a performance of some sort. An exception is on the nights of Downtown Saturday Night festivities. Just to the south of downtown Tucson lies a poorer section of the city that's best avoided after dark unless you are certain of where you're going. Otherwise, take the same precautions you would in any other city.

When driving, be aware that many streets in the Tucson area are subject to flooding when it rains. Heed warnings about possible flooded areas and don't try to cross a low area that has become flooded. Find an alternative route instead.

Taxes In addition to the 5% state sales tax, Tucson levies a 2% city sales tax. The hotel room tax is 9.5%.

Taxis See "Getting Around," earlier in this chapter.

Television You can get Channels 4 (NBC), 6 (PBS), 9 (ABC), 11 (Fox), 13 (CBS), 14 (Independent), 18 (Independent), and 52 (Independent). Several other stations broadcast in Spanish.

Transit Information For information on Sun Tran public buses, phone 502/ 792-9222; for the Amtrak station, call 502/623-4442; and for the Greyhound bus station, phone 502/792-3475. See "Arriving" in "Orientation," earlier in this chapter, for phone numbers of airlines serving Tucson.

Weather Phone 502/881-3333 for the local weather forecast.

3 Accommodations

Though Phoenix still holds the title of "Resort Capital of Arizona," Tucson is also rapidly becoming known as a resort destination. We personally think that the settings of these Tucson resorts are much more spectacular than those of comparable resorts in Phoenix and Scottsdale.

As far as nonresort accommodations go, Tucson has a wider variety of accommodations than Phoenix. This is in part due to the fact that several historic neighborhoods around Tucson are becoming home to bed-and-breakfast inns, and also to the presence of several guest ranches within a 20-minute drive of Tucson. Business and budget travelers are well served with downtown all-suite and conference hotels and budget chain motels.

If you're looking to stay in a bed-and-breakfast inn while in Tucson, you can contact several agencies. The **Arizona Association of Bed & Breakfast Inns,** P.O. Box 7186, Phoenix, AZ 85011 (☎ **520/277-0775**), has several members in Tucson. **Old Pueblo Homestays,** P.O. Box 13603, Tucson, AZ 85732

Tucson Accommodations

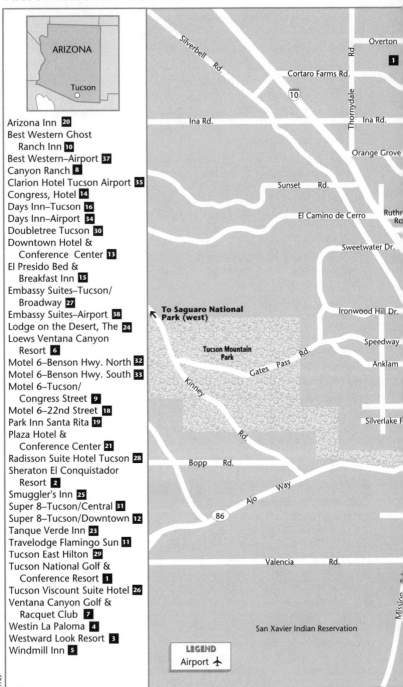

1749

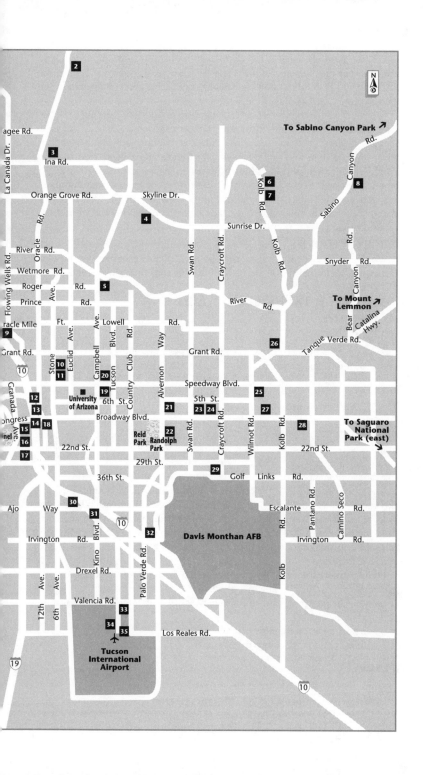

(☎ **520/790-0030** or 800/333-9776), will book you into one of its many homestays in the Tucson area. **Mi Casa–Su Casa,** P.O. Box 950, Tempe, AZ 85280-0950 (☎ **520/990-0682** or 800/456-0682), has accommodations in the Tucson area, as well as all over the Southwest.

Something else to consider when planning a trip to Tucson is that summer room rates, usually in effect from May to September or October, are roughly half what they are in winter at the more expensive hotels and resorts. Temperatures usually aren't unbearable in May or September, which makes these good times to visit. Hotels change their rates on different dates, so always ask when rates go up or down. Most hotels also offer special packages, weekend rates, various discounts, and free accommodations for children, so it also helps to ask when you reserve. Also keep in mind that nearly all hotels have no-smoking and wheelchair-accessible rooms.

PRICE CATEGORIES   The following price categories are used in the listings below, based on the cost of a standard double: "Very Expensive," over $125; "Expensive," $90 to $125; "Moderate," $60 to $90; and "Inexpensive," under $60.

DOWNTOWN & THE UNIVERSITY AREA
VERY EXPENSIVE

✪ Arizona Inn
2200 E. Elm St., Tucson, AZ 85719. ☎ **520/325-1541** or 800/933-1093. Fax 520/881-5830. 66 rms, 15 suites, 2 houses. A/C TV TEL. Jan–May, $165–$195 double; from $200 suite. May–Sept, $85–$100 double; from $100 suite. Sept–Dec, $114–$172 double; from $184 suite. AE, MC, V.

The Arizona Inn, opened in 1930, is one of the only historic inns in Arizona and the most unique resort in Tucson. Its Old Arizona atmosphere attracts a loyal clientele, many of whom return yearly. The ever-peaceful grounds are a welcome oasis from hectic city life. Just off the lobby is a large high-ceilinged library lounge where guests can sit back with a newspaper or good book and relax in the grand style, and the swimming pool is surrounded by a flower-scented private courtyard.

The guest rooms are all in pink stucco buildings surrounded by mature gardens, and are individually decorated, often with furniture made more than 60 years ago by disabled World War I veterans. Although the bathrooms are small and have their original fixtures, the guest rooms themselves are often very spacious, and most suites have private patios or enclosed sunporches, as well as sitting rooms. Some also have fireplaces.

Dining/Entertainment: The restaurant's main dining room is a casually elegant hall with French doors leading to a dining terrace. Continental cuisine is served at dinner. The lounge is filled with greenery and Audubon prints, and a pianist performs in the evening.

Services: Concierge, room service.

Facilities: Outdoor pool, two tennis courts, croquet court.

EXPENSIVE

Doubletree Tucson
445 S. Alvernon Way, Tucson, AZ 85711. ☎ **520/881-4200** or 800/222-TREE. Fax 520/323-5223. 295 rms, 11 suites. A/C TV TEL. Jan–Apr, $175 double; $220–$325 suite. Apr–May and Sept–Jan, $115–$135 double; $180–$300 suite. July–Sept, $74–$110 double; $160–$240 suite. AE, DC, DISC, MC, V.

Located directly across the street from the Randolph Park public golf course, the Doubletree is midway between the airport and downtown Tucson. Although the hotel does much convention business and sometimes feels quite crowded, the gardens, with their citrus trees and roses, are almost always tranquil. The rooms are divided between a nine-story building that offers views of the valley and a two-story building with patio rooms overlooking the quiet garden and pool area. All rooms are comfortably appointed with contemporary furnishings and have been recently renovated.

Dining/Entertainment: The Cactus Rose Restaurant serves southwestern cuisine, and the Javelina Cantina, a more lively place, serves Mexican food and mega-margaritas. There's also a quieter lobby lounge.

Services: Room service, valet service, car-rental desk.

Facilities: Outdoor pool, whirlpool, exercise room, three tennis courts.

MODERATE

⊛ Best Western Ghost Ranch Lodge

801 W. Miracle Mile, Tucson, AZ 85705. ☎ **520/791-7565** or 800/456-7565. Fax 520/791-3898. 83 rms. A/C TV TEL. Jan–Apr, $68–$98 double. Apr–July and Oct–Dec, $46–$80 double. July–Oct, $39–$76 double. AE, CB, DC, DISC, MC, V.

Although Miracle Mile was once Tucson's main drag, today it's looking a bit shabby. One exception is the Ghost Ranch, which opened back in 1941 and was for many years one of Tucson's desert resorts catering to northern visitors who stayed for the winter. Situated on 8 acres, the lodge has a justly famous cactus garden, orange grove, and extensive lawns that together create an oasis atmosphere. The guest rooms have all been recently refurbished but still have a bit of western flavor to them, with high beamed ceilings, painted brick walls, and patios covered by red-tile roofs. If you're looking for affordable Old Tucson, this is it. The lodge's dining room serves southwestern-style meals and offers dining on a poolside patio or inside with a view of the Santa Catalina Mountains. Facilities at the Ghost Ranch include a small pool, a whirlpool, and a games room.

Downtown Hotel & Conference Center

475 N. Granada Rd., Tucson, AZ 85701. ☎ **520/622-3000** or 800/446-6589. Fax 520/623-8922. 297 rms, 10 suites. A/C TV TEL. Jan–May, $56–$99 double. May–Sept, $47–$65 double. Sept–Dec, $56–$70 double. AE, CB, DC, DISC, MC, V.

Formerly a Ramada Inn, this downtown hotel was in the midst of changing names at press time. Pink stucco walls, red-tile roofs, and arched windows give the hotel

---

🏔 Family-Friendly Hotels

The Lodge on the Desert *(see p. 278)*   This economical and old-fashioned desert resort offers pleasant grounds and plenty for the kids to do, including table tennis, a pool, shuffleboard, and croquet.

The Westin La Paloma *(see p. 282)*   Kids get their own lounge and games room, and in summer and during holiday periods there are special programs for the kids so parents can have a little free time.

Guest Ranches *(see p. 284)*   Tucson has several guest ranches, most of which are family oriented. Kids can play cowboy to their heart's content, riding the range, singing songs by the campfire, or whatever.

a classic Spanish colonial flavor. Located just off I-10 and only a few blocks from the El Presidio Historic District and Tucson Museum of Art, this is an good choice for anyone who wants to be close to Tucson's past as well as its present arts district. The guest rooms are comfortable enough, but be sure to request one away from the freeway. The Olympic-size pool is the hotel's best feature. There's a restaurant on the premises.

Plaza Hotel & Conference Center

1900 E. Speedway Blvd., Tucson, AZ 85719. ☎ **520/327-7341** or 800/843-8052, 800/654-3010 in Arizona. Fax 520/327-0276. 150 rms. A/C TV TEL. Sept–May, $61–$85 double. June–Aug, $49 double. AE, CB, DC, MC, V.

Though this seven-story hotel is quite plain looking, it's conveniently located across the street from the University of Arizona campus and a five-minute drive from downtown. The upper rooms on the north side offer the best views, so try to get one of these. There's a casual café dining room in the lobby, as well as a lobby bar. A pool and whirlpool round out the offerings here.

A Bed & Breakfast

✪ El Presidio Bed & Breakfast Inn

297 N. Main Ave., Tucson, AZ 85701. ☎ **520/623-6151.** 3 suites. TEL. $85–$105 suite for two. Rates include full breakfast. No credit cards.

Built in 1886, El Presidio is a merger of Victorian and adobe architectural styles and is only steps away from the Tucson Museum of Art, Old Town Artisans, and Janos, one of Tucson's best restaurants. Owners Patti and Jerry Toci spent many years restoring the old house, and today it's a little oasis with lush gardens, fountains, and a courtyard filled with birds. The guest rooms are arranged around the courtyard, and two of the three suites have little kitchens. All are decorated with antiques and original art (some by Jerry). In addition to the filling breakfast in the sunroom, there are complimentary drinks, fruit, and treats in the afternoon and evening.

INEXPENSIVE

In addition to the three budget hotels listed below, you'll find dozens of budget chain motels along I-10 as it passes through downtown Tucson. Among the better choices are the following (rates are for the high season; see the Appendix for toll-free phone numbers): **Days Inn Tucson,** 222 S. Freeway (Exit 258), Tucson, AZ 85745 (☎ **520/791-7511**), charging $45 to $69 double; **Motel 6–Tucson/Congress Street,** 960 S. Freeway (Exit 258), Tucson, AZ 85745 (☎ **520/628-1339**), and **Motel 6–Tucson/22nd Street,** 1222 S. Freeway (Exit 259), Tucson, AZ 85713 (☎ **520/624-2516**), both charging $43 double; and **Super 8–Tucson/Downtown,** 1248 N. Stone St. (Exit 257), Tucson, AZ 85705 (☎ **520/622-6446**), charging $42 to $85 double.

ⓢ Hotel Congress

311 E. Congress St., Tucson, AZ 85701. ☎ **520/622-8848** or 800/722-8848. Fax 520/792-6366. 40 rms. TEL. $28–$39 double. Student discount available. Lower rates for shared hostel rooms. AE, MC, V.

Located in the heart of Tucson's downtown arts district, the Hotel Congress is a historic hotel that once played host to John Dillinger and now operates as a youth hostel and budget hotel. Conveniently located near the Greyhound and Amtrak stations, this hotel is popular with students and European backpack travelers. Although the hotel is far from luxurious, the lobby has been restored to its original southwestern elegance. The guest rooms get a lot of hard use and aren't in great shape, but the young crowd that stays here doesn't seem to mind. Some bathrooms have bathtubs only and others have showers only. There's a popular café off the lobby, as well as a properly western bar. At night the Club Congress is a popular and loud dance club. Guests can pick up free earplugs at the front desk if they want to sleep through the noise.

Park Inn Santa Rita

88 E. Broadway Blvd., Tucson, AZ 85701. ☎ **520/622-4000** or 800/437-7275. Fax 520/620-0376. 163 rms, 8 suites. A/C TV TEL. $47–$65 double; $67–$77 suite. AE, DISC, MC, V.

Almost across the street from the convention center and around the corner from the arts district and the El Presidio Historic District, this high-rise hotel is surprisingly inexpensive for such an excellent location. The guest rooms are done in Spanish colonial decor and aren't in the best of shape, but many are quite large. The hotel's Cafe Poca Cosa is a wildly painted café that serves some of the best Mexican food in town. The hotel offers complimentary breakfast and evening cocktails. Facilities include a pool and saunas.

☉ Travelodge Flamingo Sun Motel

1300 N. Stone Ave., Tucson, AZ 85705. ☎ **520/770-1910** or 800/300-3533. Fax 520/770-0750. 79 rms. A/C TV TEL. Dec–May, $68–$85 double. May–Dec, $35–$40 double. Rates include continental breakfast. AE, DC, MC, V.

It would be easy to pass this off as just another nondescript old motel, but a recent renovation turned the Flamingo Sun into a great budget motel deal. All the rooms have new carpets, furniture, TVs, and bathroom fixtures, and are kept quite clean. There's also a swimming pool and whirlpool. The location is convenient to both downtown and the university.

EAST TUCSON
EXPENSIVE

Embassy Suites–Tucson/Broadway

5335 E. Broadway Blvd., Tucson, AZ 85711. ☎ **520/745-2700** or 800/EMBASSY. Fax 520/790-9232. 142 suites. A/C TV TEL. Jan–May, $99–$129 suite for two. May–Oct, $79–$119 suite for two. Sept–Dec, $95–$115 suite for two. Rates include full breakfast. AE, DC, DISC, MC, V.

For the traveler who needs plenty of room, Embassy Suites offers an all-suite hotel close to East Tucson businesses and restaurants. Mission-revival decor sets the tone for the hotel, with red-tile floors and huge carved ceiling beams in the lobby. The suites are arranged around two courtyards, one containing a small pool and the other a three-story atrium garden. French doors and a wall of glass let plenty of light into each suite. There are suites with kitchenettes.

Dining/Entertainment: There's no restaurant on the premises, but a full breakfast is served. In the evening there's a two-hour complimentary happy hour in the hotel's lounge.

Services: Concierge, room service, complimentary health club passes, valet service.

Facilities: Outdoor pool, sauna, whirlpool.

Radisson Suite Hotel Tucson

6555 E. Speedway Blvd., Tucson, AZ 85710. ☎ **520/721-7100** or 800/333-3333. 304 suites. A/C TV TEL. Feb–Apr, $105–$160 suite for two. May–Oct, $49–$69 suite for two. Nov–Jan, $59–$89 suite for two. Rates include full breakfast. AE, CB, DC, DISC, MC, V.

With surprisingly reasonable rates throughout the year, this all-suite hotel is a good choice both for those who need plenty of space and for those who want to be in the east-side business corridor. The five-story brick building is arranged around two long courtyards, one of which has a small pool and whirlpool. The lobby is small but attractively decorated in contemporary southwestern style. The guest rooms also feature contemporary furnishings and the glass blocks over the wet bars add a vaguely art deco touch. All rooms have refrigerators and coffeemakers.

Dining/Entertainment: The hotel's restaurant recently changed hands, but the menu is rather unimpressive and basic.

Services: Room service (24-hour), complimentary cocktail hour, valet/laundry service.

Facilities: Pool, whirlpool, exercise room.

Tucson East Hilton

7600 E. Broadway Blvd., Tucson, AZ 85710. ☎ **520/721-5600** or 800/648-7177. Fax 520/721-5696. 232 rms, 8 suites. A/C TV TEL. Oct–Apr, $119–$174 double; $195–$315 suite. May–Sept, $74–$104 double; $165–$215 suite. AE, DC, DISC, MC, V.

Located in the east-side business corridor, this is a high-rise business hotel with unobstructed views across the valley. The lobby is large and bright; the view through the seven-story wall of glass serves as the focal point. Most rooms have just been remodeled, but even those that haven't still look good. There are floors for frequent Hilton customers as well as concierge floors with extra amenities. Some of the suites have large sundecks.

Dining/Entertainment: A casual restaurant serves continental cuisine with a hint of southwestern flavoring, and has an outstanding view of the mountains. The adjacent lounge is a lively sports bar.

Services: Room service, executive floor, passes to nearby fitness center, complimentary shuttle to within 3 miles.

Facilities: Outdoor pool, whirlpool.

Tucson Viscount Suite Hotel

4855 E. Broadway Blvd., Tucson, AZ 85711. ☎ **520/745-6500** or 800/527-9666. 215 suites. A/C TV TEL. $79–$145 suite for two. Rates include full breakfast. AE, CB, DC, DISC, MC, V.

The all-suite business hotel is centrally located in east Tucson and only a few minutes from downtown. The suites, which feature a mix of contemporary and classic furnishings, are arranged around a four-story garden atrium in which breakfast is served. Some suites have refrigerators or microwaves. Large windows let sunshine flood the bedrooms.

Dining/Entertainment: Breakfast and complimentary afternoon cocktails are served in the atrium. For more formal dining there's the Oxford Club Restaurant. Wilbur's is a sports bar named after the University of Arizona mascot.

Services: Concierge, room service, shopping shuttle.

Facilities: Outdoor pool, whirlpool, sauna, exercise room.

MODERATE

✪ The Lodge on the Desert

306 N. Alvernon Way (P.O. Box 42500), Tucson, AZ 85733. ☎ **520/325-3366** or 800/456-5634. Fax 520/327-5834. 37 rms. A/C TV TEL. Nov–May, $92–$139 double. June–Oct, $58–$105 double. Rates include continental breakfast. AE, CB, DC, DISC, MC, V.

A sort of poor man's Arizona Inn, the Lodge on the Desert offers the same adobe-style buildings in a garden compound. This older resort offers affordable rates, and is still owned by the same family that founded it in 1936. The lodge's greatest draw is its old-world charm and hacienda styling, where manicured lawns and flower gardens offer a relaxing retreat. Several guest rooms are housed in buildings made of adobe blocks, and some have beamed ceilings or fireplaces. Larger rooms have Mexican tile floors rather than carpeting, and one room has a private swimming pool. All meals are served in the lodge's dining room, one section of which has a fireplace and a bench built into the adobe wall. Among the lodge's other features are a pool with a view of the Santa Catalina Mountains, a shuffleboard court, table tennis, a croquet court, and a library.

Smuggler's Inn

6350 E. Speedway Blvd. (at Wilmot), Tucson, AZ 85710. ☎ **520/296-3292** or 800/ 525-8852. Fax 520/722-3713. 121 rms, 28 suites. A/C TV TEL. Jan–May, $99–$109 double; $125–$135 suite. May–Sept, $56–$63 double; $96 suite. Sept–Dec, $66–$73 double; $96 suite. AE, CB, DC, DISC, MC, V.

The Smuggler's Inn is a very comfortable and economically priced hotel built around an attractive garden and pond. Neatly trimmed lawns and tall palm trees give the garden a tropical look. The guest rooms are spacious and all have modern furnishings and a balcony or patio. The inn's restaurant sports a Caribbean nautical theme both in decor and on the menu, which features good fish dishes. There's also a cocktail lounge. The inn offers room service, a complimentary morning newspaper, and golf and health club privileges. Its facilities include a pool, whirlpool, and putting green.

Tanque Verde Inn

7007 E. Tanque Verde Rd., Tucson, AZ 85715. ☎ **520/298-2300** or 800/882-8484. Fax 520/298-6756. 89 rms, 2 suites. A/C TV TEL. Feb–Mar, $80–$125 double; $130 suite. Apr–May and Oct–Jan, $55–$100 double; $100 suite. June–Sept, $45–$65 double; $85 suite. Rates include continental breakfast. AE, CB, DC, DISC, MC, V.

Though it looks rather stark from the outside, the Tanque Verde Inn is surprisingly pleasant inside. This modest motel is built around four tranquil and lushly planted garden courtyards that have bubbling fountains and tile benches. Most rooms are quite large, and some have kitchenettes. There's no restaurant on the premises, but numerous excellent restaurants are nearby. The inn provides complimentary evening cocktails and health club privileges. Facilities include a pool, whirlpool, and coin-operated laundry.

THE FOOTHILLS
VERY EXPENSIVE

✪ Canyon Ranch

8600 E. Rockliff Rd., Tucson, AZ 85715. ☎ **520/749-9000** or 800/742-9000. Fax 520/ 749-7755. 180 rms. A/C TV TEL. Sept–June, $660–$1,140 double. June–Sept, $480–$720 double. Rates include all meals. AE, DISC, MC, V.

Canyon Ranch is one of America's premier health spas, and offers the sort of complete spa experience that's only available at a few places around the country (and then only to those who can afford it). On staff are doctors, nurses, psychotherapists and counselors, fitness instructors, tennis and racquetball pros, and massage therapists. There are a variety of spacious and very comfortable accommodations. So that guests are assured of a tranquil visit, children under 14 are not allowed, with the exception of infants in the care of nannies (babysitting services are not available).

Dining/Entertainment: Three gourmet low-calorie meals are served daily with options for total daily caloric intake. Because this is a health spa, no alcoholic beverages are served.

Services: Health and fitness assessments; health, nutrition, exercise, and stress-management consultations, seminars, presentations, and evaluations; fitness classes and activities; massage therapy; herbal and aroma wraps; facials, manicures, pedicures, haircuts, and styling; private sports lessons; makeup consultations; cooking demonstrations; art classes; concierge.

Facilities: 62,000-square-foot spa complex that includes seven gyms, aerobics and strength-training rooms, squash and racquetball courts, yoga/meditation room, saunas, steam rooms, inhalation rooms, whirlpools, cold plunges, private sunbathing areas, and skin care and beauty salons. Additional facilities include four pools (one indoors), eight tennis courts, and a basketball court.

✪ Loews Ventana Canyon Resort

7000 N. Resort Dr., Tucson, AZ 85715. ☎ **520/299-2020** or 800/234-5117. Fax 520/299-6832. 371 rms, 27 suites. A/C TV TEL. Jan–June, $285–$355 double; $650–$2,000 suite. June–Sept, $115–$145 double; $195–$1,050 suite. Sept–Dec, $215–$290 double; $500–$1,750 suite. AE, CB, DC, DISC, ER, JCB, MC, V.

The rugged Santa Catalina Mountains rise up in rugged contrast to the genteel comforts of this haven of luxury. Outside the grand entrance to the resort lie a small lake and the golf course, while up a nature trail you'll find a cascading waterfall. Flagstone floors in the lobby and tables with boulders for bases give the resort's public rooms a rugged but luxurious appeal. Spectacular setting aside, most guests come to avail themselves of the two golf courses, tennis courts, and other sports facilities.

The guest rooms are designed to impress. Beds angle out from corners and drapes hang from headboards. Private balconies overlook either the city lights or the mountains, and some rooms have fireplaces. The bathrooms are designed for convenience and comfort, with tiny televisions, hairdryers, telephones, travertine floors, and bathtubs built for two.

Dining/Entertainment: The Ventana Room is one of the finest restaurants in Tucson and serves new American cuisine amid views of the city lights. A casual café offers a view of the waterfall. For lakeside terrace dining there's another informal dining room. The lobby lounge serves afternoon tea and then becomes an evening piano bar.

Services: Concierge, room service (24-hour), valet/laundry service, free shopping shuttle, massages, bike rentals, car-rental desk, tour desk.

Facilities: Two 18-hole golf courses, two pools with mountain views, whirlpools, 10 tennis courts, croquet court, health spa (including a lap pool, aerobics room, exercise machines and free weights, steam rooms, saunas), beauty salon.

✪ Sheraton El Conquistador Resort & Country Club

10000 N. Oracle Rd., Tucson, AZ 85737. ☎ **520/544-5000** or 800/325-7832. Fax 520/544-1228. 432 rms, 100 suites. A/C MINIBAR TV TEL. Jan–May, $240–$280 double; $265–$1,200 suite. May–Sept, $85–$155 double; $120–$1,200 suite. Sept–Jan, $170–$210 double; $195–$1,200 suite. AE, CB, DC, DISC, ER, JCB, MC, V.

Located 14 miles north of downtown and with the Santa Catalina Mountains rising up behind it, this resort can boast one of the most spectacular settings in the state. The majority of the guest rooms are built around a central courtyard with a large pool and manicured lawns. However, this area is often taken over by conventions and those seeking peace and quiet may want to opt for a room in the separate casitas area, which has its own pool. If you're a golfer, though, you're not likely to get much rest at the resort, since it boasts three courses to keep you busy. Nongolfers have plenty of options, too, including 31 tennis courts, racquetball courts, and two health clubs. The guest rooms feature southwestern-influenced contemporary furniture, including television armoires reminiscent of old Mexican cabinets. All rooms have a balcony or patio, and there are fireplaces in most suites. The bathrooms are spacious.

Dining/Entertainment: A small, contemporary dining room serves new American cuisine with a hint of the Southwest. In the lively Mexican restaurant strolling mariachis entertain, while in the steakhouse cowboy vittles and music are the order of the day. A casual café offers patio dining and moderate prices. The country club's restaurant capitalizes on its outstanding view and serves continental and southwestern dishes.

Services: Concierge, room service (24-hour), valet/laundry service, shopping shuttle, babysitting, rental-car desk, tour desk, massages, horseback riding.

Facilities: Three golf courses (45 holes total), 31 lighted tennis courts, seven indoor racquetball courts, four pools, whirlpools, sauna, two health clubs, jogging paths, volleyball and basketball courts, rental bikes.

Tucson National Golf & Conference Resort

2727 W. Club Dr. (off Magee Rd.), Tucson, AZ 85741. ☎ **520/297-2271** or 800/528-4856. Fax 520/297-7544. 167 rms. A/C MINIBAR TV TEL. Jan–May, $265–$350 double. May–Sept, $85–$120 double. Sept–Jan, $150–$225 double. AE, CB, DC, MC, V.

As the resort's name implies, golf is the driving force behind most stays at this self-styled boutique golf resort in the foothills of north Tucson. However, the full-service health spa is one of the best in Arizona and makes for very relaxing visits. Still, if you haven't got your own set of clubs, you might feel out of place here.

The guest rooms here are mostly in two-story buildings and all are spacious and have their own patio or balcony. Hand-carved doors and Mexican hand-painted tile counters in the bathrooms give the rooms a Spanish colonial feel. For convenience there are two sinks and large dressing areas in all the rooms.

Dining/Entertainment: An ongoing renovation and expansion recently added a clublike gourmet dining room as well as a similar, though more casual, bar and grill. A third restaurant, downstairs from the lobby, serves reasonably priced southwestern fare. A lobby lounge provides distant views of the Santa Catalina Mountains.

Services: Room service (24-hour), valet parking, valet/laundry service.

Facilities: 27-hole golf course, two tennis courts, pool, basketball and volleyball courts, pro shop, and full-service health spa with exercise machines, free weights, an aerobics room, steam rooms, saunas, whirlpools, and numerous skin and body treatments.

Ventana Canyon Golf & Racquet Club

6200 N. Clubhouse Lane, Tucson, AZ 85715. ☎ **520/577-1400** or 800/828-5701, 800/233-4569 in Arizona. Fax 520/577-4063. 49 suites. A/C TV TEL. Jan–Apr, $295–$410 suite for two. Apr–June, $195–$290 suite for two. June–Sept, $115–$210 suite for two. Sept–Dec, $260–$340 suite for two. AE, MC, V.

Golf is the raison d'être of this country club–like resort. However, even the nongolfer will be impressed by the spectacular setting at the foot of the rugged Santa Catalina Mountains. Small size with big-resort amenities—like 12 tennis courts and good exercize facilities—is what makes this gated resort so appealing.

The accommodations are in spacious suites, most with walls of windows so you can enjoy the views from the comfort of your room. All include small kitchens, and some have balconies, cathedral ceilings, and spiral stairs that lead to sleeping lofts. All feature large bathrooms with oversize tubs, two sinks, and separate changing rooms.

Dining/Entertainment: The dining room, a few steps from the lobby, offers fine dining with a view of the Santa Catalinas. Drinks are served in two lounges, and there's also a poolside snack bar.

Services: Concierge, room service, golf and tennis lessons, massages, babysitting, valet/laundry service, complimentary daily newspaper, free shuttle to Loews Ventana Canyon Resort.

Facilities: Two 18-hole golf courses, 12 tennis courts, pool, whirlpools, exercise room, aerobics room, steam rooms, saunas, beauty salon, pro shop.

Westin La Paloma

3800 E. Sunrise Dr., Tucson, AZ 85718. ☎ **520/742-6000** or 800/876-3683. Fax 520/577-5878. 487 rms, 41 suites. A/C MINIBAR TV TEL. Jan–May, $280–$360 double; from $475 suite. June–Sept, $79–$190 double; from $300 suite. Sept–Dec, $220–$300 double; $425 suite. AE, CB, DC, DISC, ER, JCB, MC, V.

La Paloma (The Dove) sits in the middle of Tucson's prestigious foothills neighborhoods and offers sweeping panoramas from its hilltop perch. The resort's mission-revival architecture in a sunset pink gives it a timeless feel. The golf course, which surrounds the resort, offers great views of both the city and the Santa Catalinas. The resort's associated country club, with tennis courts and extensive exercise facilities, also keeps active guests busy. Guest rooms are situated in 27 three-story buildings and display such accents as textured cotton upholstery, woven raffia headboards, and verdigris-finished metal-and-glass tables. The bathrooms are extremely spacious, with separate tubs and showers, two sinks, telephones, and bathrobes.

Dining/Entertainment: New American cuisine is highlighted in the formal clubhouse dining room, while a dining room with views of the mountains provides a more casual setting. Another fine dining room is set in its own hacienda and is well known for its delicious fish dishes and view of the city. Snack bars are convenient to tennis and golf. There's also a swim-up bar that serves light meals. The lobby lounge provides great views and evening piano music. Golfers have their own bar at the 19th Hole.

Services: Room service (24-hour), valet service, massages, day-care center, bike rentals, shopping shuttle.

Facilities: 27-hole golf course, free-form swimming pool with water slide, 12 tennis courts, racquetball court, three whirlpools, golf and tennis pro shops, volleyball and croquet courts, children's lounge, shopping arcade, beauty salon, health club with exercise machines and aerobics room.

⑤ Westward Look Resort

245 E. Ina Rd., Tucson, AZ 85704. ☎ **520/297-1151** or 800/722-2500. Fax 520/297-9023. 244 rms, 8 suites. A/C MINIBAR TV TEL. Jan–Apr, $130 double; $190 suite. Apr–May, $95 double; $190 suite. June–Aug, $70 double; $140 suite. Sept–Jan, $90 double; $170 suite. AE, CB, DC, DISC, ER, JCB, MC, V.

Opened in 1929 as a dude ranch, the Westward Look has since become one of Tucson's most reasonably priced resorts. Offering quiet, traditional luxury in the foothills of the Santa Catalina Mountains, the resort is surrounded by desert and attracts a varied clientele. There is no golf course here, but guests enjoy tennis courts, a fitness center, and jogging trails. The guest rooms, all of which were recently renovated, are quite large and have private patios or balconies. Many also have exposed-beam ceilings and great views of the city.

Dining/Entertainment: The main dining room features walls of glass that provide sweeping views of Tucson and serves reliably excellent continental cuisine. A casual bar and grill benefits from the same views.

Services: Room service, massages, tennis lessons.

Facilities: Three pools, eight tennis courts, three whirlpools, basketball and volleyball courts, horseshoe pits, jogging trail, pro shop, fitness center with free weights, an aerobics room, and exercise machines.

MODERATE

⑤ Windmill Inn at St. Philip's Plaza

4250 N. Campbell Ave., Tucson, AZ 85718. ☎ **520/577-0007** or 800/547-4747. Fax 520/577-0045. 122 suites. A/C TV TEL. Nov–Apr, $93–$103 suite for two. May, $76–$86 suite for two. June–Oct, $53–$89 suite for two. Rates include continental breakfast. AE, DC, DISC, MC, V.

Located in St. Philip's Plaza, which has a couple of great restaurants and an array of upscale shops, this hotel offers both a great location and spacious accommodations. All the rooms are suites and have couches, work desks, two TVs, three telephones (one in the bathroom), double vanities, wet bars, small refrigerators, and microwaves. Basically there's everything to make the business traveler or vacationer comfortable for a long stay, and local phone calls are free.

Services: Lending library, complimentary use of bicycles, dry-cleaning service, complimentary morning newspaper.

Facilities: Pool, whirlpool, guest laundry.

NEAR THE AIRPORT
VERY EXPENSIVE

Embassy Suites–Tucson International Airport

7051 S. Tucson Blvd., Tucson, AZ 85706. ☎ **520/573-0700** or 800/262-8866. Fax 520/741-9645. 204 suites. A/C TV TEL. Jan–May, $139 suite for two. May–Sept, $69–$99 suite for two. Sept–Dec, $109 suite for two. Rates include full breakfast. AE, CB, DC, DISC, MC, V.

This all-suite hotel is conveniently located just outside the airport exit, and offers spacious suites that all have kitchenettes, two phones, and two TVs. The courtyard pool area is attractively planted, which makes this a great (if a bit noisy) escape at the end of the day.

Dining/Entertainment: A restaurant serves a combination of Mexican and American dishes at reasonable prices, and in the lounge you'll find a big-screen TV and pool table. Complimentary evening cocktails and hors d'oeuvres are served.

Services: Room service, complimentary airport shuttle, free morning newspaper, car-rental desk, valet service.

Facilities: Outdoor pool, whirlpool, fitness center, business center, guest laundry.

EXPENSIVE

Clarion Hotel Tucson Airport

6801 S. Tucson Blvd., Tucson, AZ 85706. ☎ **520/746-3932** or 800/526-0550 or 800/526-0550. 191 rms. A/C TV TEL. Jan–Apr, $115–$125 double. May–Sept, $60–$110 double. Sept–Dec, $85–$120 double. Rates include a full breakfast. AE, CB, DC, DISC, MC, V.

Located just outside the airport exit, this low-rise hotel provides convenience and some great amenities, including a nightly complimentary cocktail reception and late-night snacks. The rooms are generally quite large, and the "king" rooms are particularly comfortable. The poolside rooms, in addition to being convenient for swimming and lounging, also have small refrigerators.

Dining/Entertainment: The restaurant offers moderately priced meals in casual surroundings. There's also an adjacent lounge.

Services: Concierge, room service, valet service, complimentary airport shuttle, shopping shuttle.

Facilities: Pool, whirlpool, exercise room.

MODERATE

⑤ Best Western Inn at the Airport

7060 S. Tucson Blvd., Tucson, AZ 85706. ☎ **520/746-0271** or 800/528-1234. Fax 520/889-7391. 147 rms. A/C TV TEL. Sept–Jan, $71–$84 double. Feb–Mar, $84–$99 double. Apr–Sept, $61–$74 double. Rates include a full breakfast. AE, CB, DC, DISC, MC, V.

This hotel is about the first you'll come to as you leave the airport and is a good choice for anyone planning on arriving late at night or who just needs the convenience of being close to the airport. In addition to the buffet breakfast, evening cocktails and late-night snacks are also complimentary. The rooms are comfortable and have small refrigerators and hairdryers. The restaurant and the lounge assure that guests don't go hungry or thirsty. There's a small courtyard pool and a whirlpool, as well as a fitness room and a tennis court. In fact, you get a great range of amenities here at surprisingly reasonable rates. The one drawback is, unfortunately, the airport noise.

INEXPENSIVE

There are numerous budget motels near the Tucson Airport. These include the following (rates are for high season; see the Appendix for toll-free phone numbers): **Days Inn–Palo Verde,** 3700 E. Irvington Rd. (Exit 264), Tucson, AZ 85714 (☎ **520/571-1400**), charging $60 to $70 double; **Motel 6,** 755 E. Benson Hwy. (Exit 262), Tucson, AZ 85713 (☎ **520/622-4614**), charging $40 double; **Motel 6,** 1031 E. Benson Hwy. (Exit 262), Tucson, AZ 85713 (☎ **520/628-1264**), charging $41 double; and **Super 8–Tucson/East,** 1990 S. Craycroft Rd. (Exit 265), Tucson, AZ 85711 (☎ **520/790-6021**), charging $50 to $58 double.

OUTSIDE THE CITY
GUEST RANCHES

⑤ Lazy K Bar Ranch

8401 N. Scenic Dr., Tucson, AZ 85743. ☎ **520/744-3050** or 800/321-7018. Fax 520/744-7628. 19 rms, 4 suites. A/C. $180–$260 double; $220–$280 suite. Rates include all meals. AE, DISC, MC, V.

Homesteaded in 1933 and converted to a dude ranch in 1936, the Lazy K Bar Ranch covers 160 acres adjacent to Tucson Mountain Park. There are plenty of nearby hiking and riding trails, and if you have a hankering for city life, it isn't difficult to reach downtown (20 minutes away). The guest rooms vary in size and comfort level. The newest are the most comfortable, with exposed brick walls and sliding glass doors that open onto a patio. We prefer the corner rooms with windows on two sides. The ranch-oriented activities at the Lazy K include horseback riding twice daily, hayrides, lunch rides, cookouts, and square dances.

Dining/Entertainment: Meals are served family style in a dining room that features Mexican tile floors and an open-pit fireplace. The food is hearty American ranch style with cookouts some nights. Each evening there's a happy hour at the ranch's BYOB bar.

Services: Complimentary airport transfer, Sunday shuttle to Old Tucson and the Arizona–Sonora Desert Museum,

Facilities: Pool, whirlpool, two tennis courts, volleyball and basketball courts, horseshoe pits, stables.

Tanque Verde Ranch

14301 E. Speedway Blvd. (Rte. 8, Box 66), Tucson, AZ 85748. ☎ **520/296-6275** or 800/234-DUDE. Fax 520/721-9426. 67 rms. A/C TEL. Dec–Apr, $28–$340 double. May–Sept, $230–$270 double. Oct–Dec, $245–$280 double. Rates include all meals. AE, DISC, MC, V.

Far and away the most luxurious guest ranch in Tucson, the Tanque Verde Ranch, founded in 1860, is very popular with both Americans and Europeans who come to live their cowboy dreams in the Old West. The ranch, which still has some of its original buildings, borders both Saguaro National Park and the Coronado National Forest, which assures plenty of room for guided horseback rides. The guest rooms are spacious and comfortable, but don't expect a television here—ranch policy encourages guests to participate in various activities. Many rooms have fireplaces and patios, and the bathrooms are large.

Dining/Entertainment: The large dining room, which overlooks the Rincon Mountains, sets impressive buffets. There are also breakfast horseback rides, poolside luncheons, and cookout rides. An old foreman's cabin now houses a cantina.

Services: Complimentary riding and tennis lessons, children's programs, evening lectures and performances, nature and bird-banding hikes.

Facilities: Indoor and outdoor pools, riding stables, five tennis courts, exercise room, saunas, whirlpool, horseshoes, basketball and volleyball courts, tennis pro shop, rodeo arena.

White Stallion Ranch

9251 W. Twin Peaks Rd., Tucson, AZ 85743. ☎ **520/297-0252** or 800/782-5546. Fax 520/744-2786. 20 rms, 10 suites. Oct–Dec, $204–$224 double; $238–$268 suite. Dec–Apr, $224–$248 double; $268–$310 suite. Rates include all meals. Weekly rates available. Four-night minimum stay in winter. No credit cards. Closed May–Sept.

Set on 3,000 acres of desert just over the hill from Tucson, the White Stallion Ranch is perfect for those who crave wide-open spaces. Operated for nearly 30 years by the True family, this spread has a more authentic ranch feel than any other guest ranch in the area. Two fast rides and two slow rides are offered daily. A petting zoo keeps kids entertained. The guest rooms vary considerably in size and comfort from the tiny, spartan single rooms to suites with beamed ceilings, ceiling fans, modern bathrooms, and patios.

Dining/Entertainment: All meals are served family style in the main dining room, which is housed in a 90-year-old building. There's also an honor bar with cowhide stools and a longhorn steer head on the wall.

Services: Airport pickup, hayrides, guided nature walks and hikes, car-rental desk; tours available at additional charge.

Facilities: Outdoor pool, indoor hot tub, tennis courts, basketball and volleyball courts.

A BED & BREAKFAST INN

✪ Casa Tierra

11155 W. Calle Pima, Tucson, AZ 85743. ☎ **520/578-3058.** 3 rms. $75–$85 double. Rates include a full breakfast. No credit cards. Closed June–Aug.

If you've come to Tucson to be in the desert and you really want to be a part of the desert, then there's no doubt about where you should stay. Casa Tierra, a modern adobe home surrounded by 5 acres of cactus and palo verde, is situated on the west side of Saguaro National Park West, and has fabulous views of a desert full of saguaros. There are also stunning sunsets and views of the mountains to the north. The owners are a young couple who built this home to look as if it has been here since the days when the area was under Spanish rule. Surrounding a central courtyard with a desert garden is a covered seating area where guests congregate. The rooms open off this covered patio and have queen-size beds, brick floors, and private patios. The outdoor whirlpool spa makes a perfect stargazing spot at night.

4 Dining

A few years back Tucson's mayor declared the city the Mexican restaurant capital of the universe. Though Mexico City might want to contest the claim, it isn't far off the mark. There's historic Mexican at El Charro, nouveau Mexican at Café Poca Cosa, Mexico City Mexican at La Parilla Suiza, family-style Mexican at Casa Molina, and upscale Mexican at La Placita Cafe. If you like Mexican food, you'll be in heaven; if you don't, there are dozens of other restaurants serving everything from the finest French cuisine to innovative American to Italian to southwestern. Be sure to take one of your first meals here in a southwestern-style restaurant. This cuisine can be brilliantly creative, and after trying it you may want all your meals to be southwestern. Keep in mind, however, that southwestern cuisine tends to be a bit pricey. If you're in town during the summer, be on the lookout for early-bird dinners and summer sampler plates such as those served at Janos.

PRICE CATEGORIES   In the following listings, "Very Expensive" are those where the bill for dinner (without wine) will exceed $35 per person, "Expensive" are those ranging from $25 to $35, "Moderate" are those charging between $15 and $25, and "Inexpensive" restaurants are those where dinner for one costs less than $15.

DOWNTOWN & THE UNIVERSITY AREA
EXPENSIVE

✪ Arizona Inn

2200 E. Elm St. ☎ **520/325-1541.** Reservations recommended. Main courses $14.25–$20; lunch $4.75–$9.50. AE, MC, V. Mon–Sat 7–10:30am, 11:30am–2pm, and 5–10pm; Sun 7–10:30am, 11am–2pm (brunch), and 5–10pm. SOUTHWESTERN.

Opened in 1930, the Arizona Inn is one of the state's first resorts, and the dining room has established itself as a consistently excellent restaurant with reasonable prices. The rose-pink stucco pueblo-style buildings of the resort are surrounded by neatly manicured gardens that have aged gracefully, and it's a treat to dine on the terrace overlooking the garden and croquet lawn. The menu is not extensive, but every dish, such as mesquite-smoked quail with cider glaze and chestnut and wild rice stuffing, is perfectly prepared. Flavors are predominantly southwestern, with hints of continental. The fixed-price dinner, which changes daily, is an excellent value at $19.95. In the winter season there's live music in the evening. Lunches tend toward a wide variety of salads and sandwiches.

Daniel's Restaurant and Trattoria

In St. Philip's Plaza, 4340 N. Campbell Ave. ☎ **520/742-3200.** Reservations recommended. Main courses $16–$26.50. AE, DC, MC, V. Daily 5–9pm. NORTHERN ITALIAN.

A dramatic atmosphere predominates here, with large floral arrangements; ivory, black, and gold accents; and art deco touches—but what's most outstanding is the contemporary northern Italian cuisine. Service is personable and attentive—a basket of bread appears as soon as you're seated, including fresh baked focaccia and breadsticks, with basil-flavored olive oil or whipped mascarpone cheese. For an antipasto, we recommend the intriguing flavors of grilled shrimp with Gorgonzola cheese and spinach, pine nuts, and prosciutto in olive oil. The roast duck is done well here and comes treated with the likes of cranberry-basil sauce. The pastry chef has a creative flair with fruits and chocolates, so save room for a dessert such as Italian chocolate torte with dark-chocolate glaze and apricot sauce. An outstanding wine list, with an emphasis on Italian wines, and a single-malt-scotch list offer many choices.

✪ Janos

150 N. Main St. ☎ **520/884-9426.** Reservations highly recommended. Main courses $19–$32; summer sampler $12.95. AE, DC, MC, V. Mon–Thurs 5:30–8:30pm, Fri–Sat 5:30–9:30pm. Closed Sun–Mon in summer. SOUTHWESTERN/FRENCH.

Across the courtyard from the Tucson Museum of Art, and located in one of the El Presidio Historic District's beautifully restored old adobe homes, is one of Tucson's best restaurants. Janos owes its popularity as much to its setting as to its stellar cuisine. This is a spot for the well-heeled to dine before attending the theater, and is at once traditional and contemporary. The menu changes both daily and seasonally. Chef Janos shows his enthusiasm in creating such dishes as blue-corn fritters garnished with shrimp, scallops, and salmon, served on lobster sauce with three salsas (award-winning, to be sure) and tournedos of veal with foie gras potato pancakes and pink peppercorn sauce. At least one sophisticatedly embellished vegetarian entree appears on the menu nightly. Even those on a limited budget can enjoy Janos in the summer, when an amazingly low-priced sampler menu represents one of the best restaurant values in Tucson.

Penelope's

3071 N. Swan Rd. ☎ **520/325-5080.** Reservations recommended. Six-course prix fixe dinner $29.50 without wine, $42.50 with wine; lunch dishes $10–$15. MC, V. Tues–Fri 11:30am–2pm and 5:30–8pm, Sat–Sun 5:30–8pm. FRENCH.

Penelope's, located in a converted 1910 house with a small garden and country French decor, is a favorite place with the older Tucson set. It's set back from the road behind a weedy lot. On our last visit, dinner began with a pâté maison followed by a choice of tomato-tarragon or onion soup. There was a choice of four dishes including poached salmon with dill-cream sauce and filet mignon with red-wine and shallot sauce. This was followed by salad and cheese courses, and then a dessert of either dark- and white-chocolate mousse torte or crème caramel. For those who want to include wine with their meal, there are appropriately chosen selections for each course and each dish. If you can't afford dinner, you can stop by for lunch.

Tucson Dining

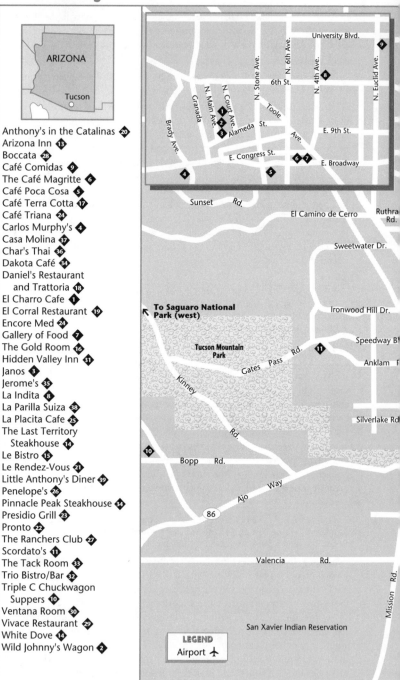

1750

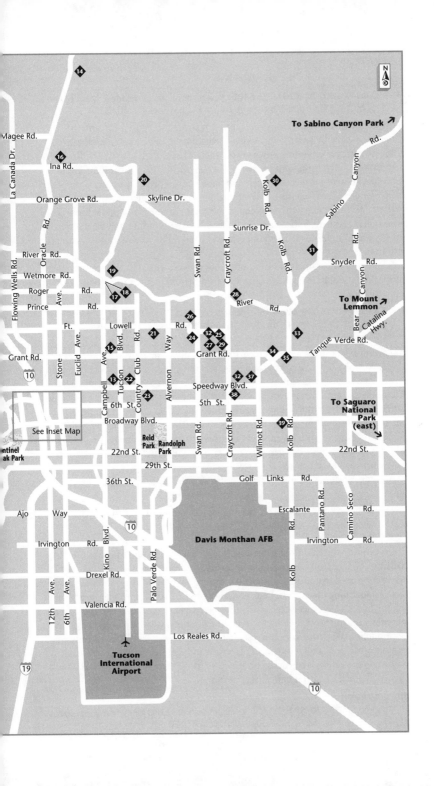

MODERATE

✪ Café Poca Cosa

88 E. Broadway Blvd. ☎ **520/622-6400.** Reservations recommended. Main courses $6.50–$15. MC, V. Mon–Thurs 11am–9pm, Fri–Sat 11am–10pm. MEXICAN.

This is not just *any* Mexican food, but Mexican food that's imaginative and different, created by owner-chef Suzana Davila. Poca Cosa is located on the ground floor of a rather common downtown hotel, where it's a surprise to find this atmosphere of rich red-and-purple walls and Mexican/southwestern artwork. The cuisine here—which has been compared to the dishes dreamed up in *Like Water for Chocolate*—consists of dishes such as beef marinated in tequila and then grilled, and chicken with a green mole sauce made with pistachios. The menu changes daily, and you never know what the offerings will be. However, every meal is accompanied by tasty rice and beans. The service staff is courteous and friendly.

There's another (smaller) Café Poca Cosa downtown at 20 S. Scott St., open for breakfast and lunch Monday through Friday from 7:30am to 2:30pm.

Carlos Murphy's

419 W. Congress St. ☎ **520/628-1958.** Main courses $7–$12. AE, DISC, MC, V. Mon–Thurs 11am–10pm, Fri–Sat 11am–11pm, Sun 11am–10pm (lounge stays open until 1am). BAJA-MEXICAN.

If you think you made a wrong turn and ended up at the train station instead of Carlos Murphy's, you're right . . . and you're wrong. It is, make that *was,* the train station but now it's a cavernous Mexican restaurant with a sense of humor. To the left inside the restaurant is Carlos's sports bar, complete with a red, white, and blue canoe hanging from the ceiling. Popular things to fill up on here include red-hot chicken wings with bleu-cheese dressing and sizzling fajitas made with sirloin, chicken, or shrimp. Sunday through Thursday, a child accompanied by an adult who purchases a meal can get a meal from the children's menu and pay just a penny per each pound of the child's weight.

Another location is at 410 N. Wilmot Rd. (☎ **520/751-0050**).

✪ El Charro Cafe

311 N. Court Ave. ☎ **520/622-1922.** Reservations recommended for dinner. Main courses $4.25–$15.50. AE, MC, V. Sun–Thurs 11am–9pm, Fri–Sat 11am–10pm (Sat–Sun brunch 11am–2pm). MEXICAN.

El Charro, located in an old stone building in the El Presidio Historic District, claims to be Tucson's oldest family-operated Mexican restaurant. A front porch has been glassed in for a greenhouselike dining area overlooking the street, and there's also dining downstairs. Look at the roof of El Charro as you approach, and you might see a large metal cage containing beef drying in the sun. This is the main ingredient in carne seca, El Charro's well-known specialty, which is oft copied but never duplicated at other Mexican restaurants around town. You'll rarely find carne seca on a Mexican menu outside Tucson, so indulge in it while you're here. A warning—the café can be packed at lunch, so arrive early or late. The family has opened ¡Toma!, a colorful bar/cantina next door.

Gallery of Food

256 E. Congress St. ☎ **520/884-5033.** Reservations recommended for dinner. Main courses $8.50–$15. MC, V. Mon–Sat 11am–9:30pm. INTERNATIONAL.

This restaurant boasts a warm, artistic ambience created through the use of flowers, candles, and Monet-esque paintings hung in a narrow high-ceilinged space. The carefully crafted meals, often garnished with bright splashes of flowers, may take a while to prepare, but the wait is worth it. Recent offerings have included saffron pasta filled with cardamom-seasoned potato and served with a pine-nut sauce, and smoked salmon with capers, sweet peppers, and cream cheese. We highly recommend the crème brûlée here, made with rose water—a velvety, buttery delight.

Le Bistro

2574 N. Campbell Ave. ☎ **520/327-3086.** Reservations recommended for dinner. Main courses $8–$17. DISC, MC, V. Mon–Fri 11am–2:30pm and 5–10pm, Sat–Sun 5–10pm. FRENCH/EUROPEAN.

Etched mirrors, lace, and live trees full of twinkling lights set the scene for some casual bistro cuisine. European specialties include the likes of duck pâté, roast quail, and bouillabaisse. However, what really catches the eye is the showcase of extravagant desserts, in all manner of shapes and textures, with names such as Tuxedo (a double-chocolate mousse) and Opera (a creation with hazelnut and mocha crème). You could come here just for one of the airy, delicious desserts.

Presidio Grill

3352 E. Speedway Blvd. ☎ **520/327-4667.** Reservations recommended for dinner. Main courses $6.25–$9 at lunch, $8–$19 at dinner. AE, MC, V. Mon–Thurs 11am–10pm, Fri–Sat 11am–midnight, Sun 8am–10pm. SOUTHWESTERN/MEDITERRANEAN.

This ever-trendy restaurant, modern in both cuisine and interior design, is located in Rancho Center, along busy Speedway Boulevard. The Sonoran Caesar salad, made with grilled shrimp, roasted peppers, and a spicy dressing, is a novel twist on an old standard. Whether you want pizza, pasta, or something from the grill, the dishes here show a variety of international influences; however, sometimes the decor is more creative than the cuisine. Sunday breakfast is served from 8am to 2pm, when you can choose from the long menu which includes many breakfast items. When we last visited, service was friendly but very slow. A good selection of wines and liquors can be found here.

Vivace Restaurant

4811 E. Grant Rd. ☎ **520/795-7221.** Reservations recommended. Main courses $9–$16. MC, V. Mon–Sat 11:30am–10:30pm, Sun 4–10:30pm. NORTHERN ITALIAN.

Run by the same folks who gave you Tucson Scordato's, this Italian restaurant serves reasonably priced creative dishes in a casual but upscale setting. The restaurant can be noisy at times, owing to its popularity and the open interior design which includes a wall of glass. The menu is contemporary, reflecting current trends. Dishes such as penne pasta baked with sausage, roasted pepper sauce, and fontina cheese, and grilled eggplant with rosemary–balsamic vinegar sauce demonstrate that Italian food can be both simple and yet complexly flavored. There's a respectable wine list, and at lunch, several dinner dishes show up at reduced prices.

INEXPENSIVE

Cafe Comidas

874 E. University Blvd. ☎ **520/623-7507.** Tapas $2.50–$14.25. AE, MC, V. Tues–Sat 9am–11pm, Sun 8am–10pm. SPANISH.

Tapas means appetizers in Spanish, and here you can get a variety of them and share bites between conversation in the large front garden or the intimate back room. We ordered Manchego cheese with apricots and baguettes, peasant garlic soup, and quail wrapped in prosciutto and grape leaves, but had to call a halt at the chocolate fondue. There are also pastries, and Spanish-influenced breakfasts. Sunday brunch is served from 8am to 2pm, and paella, both the traditional seafood and a vegetarian version, is served after 5pm at this colorful little café.

⑤ The Café Magritte

254 E. Congress St. ☎ **520/884-8004.** Reservations recommended for dinner. Main courses $7–$9.50. Tues–Thurs and Sun 11am–11pm, Fri–Sat 11am–midnight. INTERNATIONAL.

The Café Magritte is a cubbyhole of the surreal in a downtown neighborhood that in recent years has experienced a cultural renaissance as the young, hip, and artistic area of town. Shoulder to shoulder with galleries, nightclubs, and curious boutiques, this trendy café serves up inexpensive, creative meals amid a thoroughly urban atmosphere, with changing works of cutting-edge art by local artists. One of the best dishes we've had here lately was the Sonoran tortellini with toasted pistachios, olives, feta cheese, and roasted red peppers. You'll also find live music here occasionally, and some very interesting bathrooms—a surreal doff of the bowler to the artist Magritte.

La Indita

622 N. Fourth Ave. ☎ **520/792-0523.** Main courses $2.75–$8. DISC, MC, V. Mon–Fri 11am–9pm, Sat 6–9pm, Sun 9am–9pm. MEXICAN.

It's just a little family-run business serving Tohono-Tarascan-Mexican-style food, but the home cooking here is cheap and authentic. House and daily specials such as chiles rellenos, chicken mole, and chicken enchiladas with green sauce are all popular.

Another La Indita is at 8578 E. Broadway Blvd. (☎ **520/886-9191**).

⑤ Pronto

2955 E. Speedway Blvd. ☎ **520/326-9707.** Soups, salads, and sandwiches $2.50–$5.50. MC, V. Sun–Thurs 11am–9pm, Fri–Sat 11am–10pm. INTERNATIONAL.

This restaurant is a good example of what can be done to recycle a fast-food establishment. It still retains the walk-up counter, but now boasts an international menu and hip decor. You'd come here if you want food fast good and cheap. You can get not only burgers and lots of other sandwiches, but favorites such as lasagne, pizza, chicken satay, and fettuccine with wild-mushroom sauce.

Wild Johnny's Wagon

150 N. Main Ave. (on the back patio of the Corbett House near the Tucson Museum of Art). ☎ **520/884-9426.** Sandwiches $4–$5.50. No credit cards. Mon–Fri 11am–2:30pm. SOUTHWEST.

It looks like chef Janos Wilder of Janos restaurant has pulled his chuck wagon (actually a catering van) right up into downtown Tucson. He's now dishing out sandwiches, pastas, and salads that show off his talents with creative finger foods to dedicated lunch crowds. Lucky for Tucson that this food is within such easy reach. You can saunter on down to his mobile restaurant and order a blue fish taco with chili-lime paste and cilantro slaw, or, our favorite, grilled chicken with cilantro pesto on focaccia with spicy black-bean spread. There are tables under the trees where you can sit and enjoy your victuals.

EAST TUCSON
EXPENSIVE

Jerome's

6958 E. Tanque Verde Rd. ☎ **520/721-0311.** Reservations recommended. Main courses $11–$20; Sun brunch $16.95. AE, CB, DC, DISC, MC, V. Winter, daily 5–10pm; summer, daily 5–8:30pm; Sun brunch (Thanksgiving–Mother's Day) 11am–2pm. CAJUN/SEAFOOD.

Although you may not be thinking of seafood in the middle of the desert, there are those who tire of southwestern fare and crave some fish. For those people there's Jerome's, preparing contemporary seafood and New Orleans specialties. Located in the middle of Tucson's restaurant row in an adobe-style building, Jerome's is dark with wood paneling, making it a good choice for either romantic dinners or business lunches. Appetizers includes such standout dishes as calamari ceviche—a sort of Mexican sushi in that the calamari is not cooked, but marinated in a spicy lime dressing. Mesquite grilling is a specialty, and the grilled shrimp with tomatillo relish is always delicious. Early-bird dinners are served nightly from 5 to 6pm, and the Sunday New Orleans buffet (limited season) is an extravaganza of Créole and Cajun dishes.

The Ranchers Club

In the Hotel Park Tucson, 5151 E. Grant Rd. ☎ **520/321-7621.** Reservations recommended. Main courses $17–$54. AE, CB, DC, MC, V. Mon–Fri 11:30am–2pm and 5:30–10pm, Sat 5:30–10pm. STEAK/SEAFOOD.

There's no question as to where to get the best steak in Tucson—the Ranchers Club. But before you saddle up the palomino and trot over, be sure you're prepared for the hefty tab. And if you're offended by stuffed animal heads, you might want to pass it by as well. The Ranchers Club glorifies the Old West with its decor of old saddles, chaps, and steer horns, while antiques and brocade chairs lend the dining room a touch of elegance. Hefty aged prime beef is grilled over aromatic mesquite, hickory, sassafras, and cherrywood fires, adding subtle flavors to the meats. About 20 sauces and condiments such as horseradish cream, wild-mushroom sauce, and shallot butter are offered to complement the meat. Mesquite-grilled seafood is offered as well.

MODERATE

⑤ Dakota Café

6541 E. Tanque Verde Rd. (at Traildust Town near the Pinnacle Peak Steakhouse). ☎ **520/ 298-7188.** Reservations recommended on weekends. Main courses $7.50–$15. AE, DC, MC, V. Sun–Thurs 11am–9pm, Fri–Sat 11am–10pm. INTERNATIONAL.

A bold paint job and halogen lighting are an unexpected surprise at this mock–cow town location that, combined with creative dishes, have been luring a more sophisticated crowd to what was once strictly a family outing spot. We started our meal with the fruity apricot iced tea (very refreshing on a hot day) and tempura-battered Sonoran chiles stuffed with creamed cheese and served with roasted pepper aïoli. The grilled-eggplant sandwich with smoked mozzerella on French bread with pesto sauce was tasty and well textured, and came with a generous pasta salad. The chicken Caesar salad is also recommendable. The food here is hearty yet inventive enough to try on a regular basis. The prices are reasonable, and the comfortable atmosphere adds greater value.

INEXPENSIVE

Casa Molina

6225 E. Speedway Blvd. (near the northwest corner with Wilmot Rd.). ☎ **520/886-5468.**
Reservations recommended. Dinners $11–$16.50. AE, DC, DISC, MC, V. Daily 11am–10pm.
MEXICAN.

For years this has been Tucson's favorite family-run Mexican restaurant. You can't miss it—just watch for the larger-than-life-size bull and bullfighter in front. Casa Molina sports a festive atmosphere, and is usually abuzz with families, groups, and couples. The margaritas are some of the best in town, and the carne seca (sun-dried beef) shouldn't be missed. Lighter eaters will enjoy a layered topopo salad made with tortillas, refried beans, chicken, lettuce, celery, avocado, tomato, and jalapeños. The food is good and the service is efficient; the only complaint here is that prices are a little on the high side for Mexican cookery.

Other locations include 3001 N. Campbell Ave. (☎ **520/795-7593**) and 4240 E. Grant Rd. (☎ **520/326-6663**).

Char's Thai

5039 E. Fifth St. (at Rosemont). ☎ **520/795-1715.** Main courses $4.55–$12. AE, MC, V.
Mon–Thurs 11am–3pm and 5–9:30pm, Fri 11am–3pm and 5–10pm, Sat 5–10pm, Sun
5–9:30pm. THAI.

The most notable feature in this restaurant located in an older strip mall is the large and colorful mural of a Thai temple in the desert, which sets the scene for some vivid Thai flavors. Mee krob, with crunchy and sweet noodles, and tom yum soup, flavored with lime juice and lemongrass, make good starters, followed up by a spicy and fragrant pla lad prig, basil leaves and chili over deep-fried trout. The main menu is quite lengthy, and there's also a menu to accommodate vegetarians.

La Parilla Suiza

5602 E. Speedway Blvd. ☎ **520/747-4838.** Main courses $6–$13. AE, DISC, MC, V.
Sun–Thurs 11am–10pm, Fri–Sat 11am–11pm. MEXICAN.

Most Mexican food served in the United States is limited to Sonoran style, originating just south of the border. However, the cuisine of Mexico is nearly as varied as that of China, and the meals served at La Parilla Suiza are based on the style popular in Mexico City, where most of the chain's restaurants are located. Many menu items are sandwiched between two flour tortillas, much like a quesadilla, but the charcoal broiling of meats and cheeses lends the sandwiches special status.

There's another La Parilla Suiza at 2720 N. Oracle Rd. ☎ **520/624-4300.**

Little Anthony's Diner

7010 E. Broadway Blvd. ☎ **520/296-0456.** Burgers and sandwiches $3.25–$5.20. MC, V.
Mon–Thurs 11am–10pm, Fri 11am–11pm, Sat 8am–11pm, Sun 8am–10pm. AMERICAN.

This is a place for kids, although big kids like us also enjoy the 1950s music and decor. The staff is good with children, and there's a video-games room and a rocketship outside to ride. How about a jailhouse rock burger or hound dog hot dog with a tower of onion rings? Daily specials and bottomless soft drinks make feeding the family fairly inexpensive. Beer and wine is also served, and most nights after 5pm there's a DJ along with the dinner. The gaslight melodrama theater next door makes a perfect night out for the family.

NORTH TUCSON
EXPENSIVE

Anthony's in the Catalinas

6440 N. Campbell Ave. ☎ **520/299-1771.** Reservations recommended. Main courses $16–$27. AE, CB, DC, MC, V. Mon–Sat 11:30am–2:30pm and 5:30–10pm, Sun 5:30–10pm. SOUTHWESTERN/CONTINENTAL.

If you head north on Campbell Avenue up into the foothills of the Catalinas, you'll reach a modern hacienda-style building overlooking the city. Anthony's exudes southwestern elegance from the moment you drive under the portico and let the valet park your car. The waiters are smartly attired in tuxedos and the guests are almost as well dressed. Quiet classical music plays in the background, and the lights of the city below twinkle through the window of the main dining room. In such a rarefied atmosphere you'd expect only the finest meal, and that's what you get. Seared quail with polenta is a fitting beginning, followed by a southwestern-inspired pork tenderloin with prickly-pear sauce. The pastry cart may tempt you, but you'd miss out on the best part of a meal if you didn't order the day's soufflé (order early).

❸ Boccata

In River Center, 5605 E. River Rd. ☎ **520/577-9309.** Reservations recommended. Main courses $11–$24. AE, DC, MC, V. Sun–Thurs 5:30–9pm, Fri–Sat 5–10pm. MEDITERRANEAN.

You'll find this casually elegant restaurant at the back of the River Center complex in the foothills. Large windows frame the panoramic view of Tucson in the valley below. Marble floors, rich colors, and works of contemporary art add the finishing touches. In the summer a theme atmosphere prevails, with a culinary focus on a particular country. The menu changes seasonally, but usually includes such house specialties as bifteck à la folie, New York sirloin with a green-peppercorn and burnt-cognac sauce, and, our favorite, penne ciao bella, made with grilled chicken, roasted peppers, artichoke hearts, pine nuts, and a cream sauce with white wine, chives, and Gorgonzola. Save room for dessert. The profiteroles au chocolat—cream puffs filled with vanilla ice cream and topped with chocolate sauce and whipped cream—are absolutely heavenly.

Café Terra Cotta

4310 N. Campbell Ave. (at River Rd.). ☎ **520/577-8100.** Reservations recommended. Main courses $11.50–$18.95. AE, DC, DISC, MC, V. Summer, Sun–Thurs 11am–10pm, Fri–Sat 11am–11pm; winter, Mon–Sat 7am–10pm. SOUTHWESTERN.

Located in the upscale St. Philip's Plaza shopping center, Café Terra Cotta is one of Tucson's most highly acclaimed restaurants—and although the food usually is good, we have found it at times uneven. A casual atmosphere and creative south-western cooking are a combination that appeals to trendy Tucsonans, who stop by both for dinner at the restaurant or to pick up gourmet food to go. A large brick oven is used to make imaginative pizzas. How about a pizza with chicken grilled with rosemary, feta cheese, black olives, crushed chiles, and roasted garlic? With salads, small plates, and main dishes as well, it's often very difficult to make a choice, but we can recommend the grilled-chicken sandwich with salsa mayonnaise and marinated vegetables. For dessert, we like Divine Madness with espresso ice cream.

⊕ Family-Friendly Restaurants

Pinnacle Peak Steakhouse *(see p. 300)*   Dinner here is a Wild West event, with an entire western town outside and a carousel. Kids love it.

Carlos Murphy's *(see p. 290)*   Situated in Tucson's former train station, this trendy Mexican place features a mock-up of a Mexican air force biplane hanging from the ceiling.

Encore Med

2959 N. Swan Rd. (at Fort Lowell Rd.). ☎ **520/881-6611.** Reservations recommended. Main courses $13.50–$23.50. AE, DC, MC, V. Sun–Thurs 5:30–10:30pm, Fri–Sat 5:30–11:30pm. SPANISH.

More formal than its companion restaurant Café Triana, the dining room here is lit through pale stained-glass windows. It has a staid elegance popular with retirees. In his preparations of seafood, fowl, and beef, the restaurant's Spanish chef chooses from a long repetoire of Spain's regional sauces, such as a lobster-based sauce with brandy, crushed almonds, and cayenne pepper. A dish that caught our eye when we last visited was filet of lamb with eucalyptus-honey sauce. You'll also find continental preparations, such as sole meunière and filet mignon with béarnaise sauce.

The Gold Room

In the Westward Look Resort, 245 E. Ina Rd. ☎ **520/297-1151.** Reservations recommended. Main courses $14.50–$27.50. AE, CB, DC, DISC, MC, V. Mon–Sat 7–10:30am, 11:30am–2pm, and 5:30–9:30pm; Sun 7–10:30am, 11am–2pm (brunch), and 5:30–9:30pm. CONTINENTAL.

For more than 20 years the Gold Room has been one of the best hotel dining rooms in Tucson. Located in the Westward Look Resort, which opened in 1929 as a dude ranch, the Gold Room is a casual restaurant featuring southwestern ranch decor that includes stucco walls, viga beams in the ceiling, and large comfortable booths. There are views of the city through two walls of glass and a terrace for al fresco dining. Despite the casual decor, the place settings are elegant and the service is very professional. There's a distinct seafood slant to the hors d'oeuvres list, including crab cakes, salmon, and oysters in various guises. Although it's possible to order classics such as chateaubriand and roast rack of lamb, our personal favorite on a recent visit was the loin of venison marinated with poached pear and red-currant sauce.

❂ Le Rendez-Vous

3844 E. Fort Lowell Rd. (at Alvernon Way). ☎ **520/323-7373.** Reservations highly recommended. Main courses $14.25–$25.50. AE, DC, DISC, MC, V. Tues–Fri 11:30am–2pm and 6–10pm, Sat–Sun 6–10pm. FRENCH.

Le Rendez-Vous has become legendary among the gustatory cognoscenti of Tucson for its phenomenal duck à l'orange. Consequently, patrons are almost exclusively locals who return again and again for the duck, mussels cooked in white wine, and the ultimate spinach salad. If it's hot out, cool off with a bowl of creamy vichyssoise. If you're inclined to expand your own culinary horizons, you won't go wrong with the veal sweetbreads with mushrooms dijonnaises. You might expect such rich and savory fare to be served amid rarefied elegance, but instead

Le Rendez-Vous is housed in an unpretentious little stucco cottage. The waiters are dressed in black tie, but aside from this little concession the atmosphere is strictly bistro. When the pastry cart comes around, try one of the tempting, airy desserts.

✪ The Tack Room

2800 N. Sabino Canyon Rd. ☎ **520/722-2800.** Reservations recommended. Main courses $24.50–$34. AE, CB, DC, DISC, JCB, MC, V. May to mid-Jan, Tues–Sun 6–11pm; late Jan to Apr, daily 6–11pm. SOUTHWESTERN/CONTINENTAL.

The Tack Room is the city's most prestigious restaurant, housed in an older southwestern-style hacienda with an atmosphere of casual elegance in which a bevy of waiters in tuxedos attend to your every need. The longtime staff have had the opportunity to hone their professional service to a high art, and made us feel pleasingly pampered. From the time we sat down to the little bites of marinated salads that appeared on the table to the moment the last bit of chocolate was savored from the bottom of our crème brûlée, the service was attentive and discreet. We could recite a list of all the tastes we experienced, but will recall just a few, in the plump guaymas shrimp subtly seasoned with orange zest and garlic, salmon with papaya salsa perfectly grilled (crusty on top and moist on the inside), and crispy yet succulent duck, topped with pistachios and sitting on a pile of not-too-sweet fig-and-orange chutney. Coffee came with a condiment tray that included whipped cream and crumbled Belgian chocolate. Of course, you'll pay for it, but this dining experience leaves one truly satisfied.

✪ Ventana Room

In Loews Ventana Canyon Resort, 7000 N. Resort Dr. ☎ **520/299-2020.** Reservations highly recommended. Main courses $18–$27. AE, CB, DC, MC, V. Daily 6–10:30pm. NOUVELLE AMERICAN.

With the spectacular setting and waterfall at the head of Ventana Canyon, it would be worth eating at the Ventana Room even if the food weren't so good. *Ventana* means "window" in Spanish, and the views are emphasized here. The twinkling lights of the city in the valley below and the strains of ethereal harp music set the mood. The menu, which changes daily, is not long, but its memorable quality compensates for its lack of variety. Appetizers tend toward continental, with a ragoût of escargots outstanding. Venison, lamb, veal, and quail make regular appearances; on our last visit, grilled venison with green beans and dried cherry sauce was especially appealing. Don't let the dessert cart pass you by.

White Dove

At the Sheraton El Conquistador, 10000 N. Oracle Rd. ☎ **520/544-5000.** Reservations recommended. Main courses $16–$23; pastas $10–$13. AE, CB, DC, DISC, MC, V. Tues–Sun 5:30–10pm. SOUTHWEST/ITALIAN.

The predominant feature of the White Dove is the black wrought-iron design elements which contrast with the pale and neutral color scheme. The lamps cast playful shadows reminiscent of Mexican luminárias on the walls, creating a feeling of the southwest that's sophisticatedly spare yet inviting. In the kitchen, chef John Orsino blends a melange of ingredients that conjure up an Italian bistro in the Southwest, with offerings that are as casual as pizzas with marinated artichoke, mushroom, and fennel to more substantial main dishes of grilled antelope, salmon, or chipotle glazed chicken breast. A choice of interesting accompaniments to the entree include quinoa and dried-cherry pilaf or spinach and escarole sauté.

MODERATE

Café Triana

2959 N. Swan Rd. (at Fort Lowell Rd.). ☎ **520/881-6611.** Reservations recommended on weekends. Main courses $6.50–$13.50. AE, DC, MC, V. Daily 11am–10:30pm. SPANISH.

Café Triana specializes in *tapas* (Spanish appetizers), served in a bright and airy interior. A tempting display case in front primed our appetites, so we tried an assortment of tapas including Spanish sausage in sherry, green olives stuffed with anchovies, and mussels in a Basque-style sauce of white wine with peas, garlic, and parsley—which was pleasantly garlicky. The menu ranges from something as simple as the stuffed olives to a couple of different types of paella. The service staff was efficient and professional. If Muzak irritates you, you might want to pass—but otherwise, the food is enjoyable.

La Placita Cafe

In the Plaza Palomino, 2950 N. Swan Rd. ☎ **520/881-1150.** Reservations recommended on weekends. Main courses $5–$15. AE, DISC, MC, V. Mon–Sat 11:30am–2:30pm and 5–9:30pm, Sun 5–9:30pm. MEXICAN.

The Plaza Palomino is an upscale, modern shopping center in northern Tucson, and La Placita is a rather upscale Mexican restaurant. The decor is pastel with a few Mexican crafts on display, not your usual garish Mexican hacienda design. The varied menu includes not only dishes from around Mexico, but also some gringo fare. The menu offers four soups, including menudo, the classic Mexican hangover cure. There are all the usual tacos, enchiladas, burritos, tostadas, and tamales, but you'd do well to try one of the special dinners. Mole oaxaqueño is our favorite. It's served in a spicy chocolate-based sauce.

✪ Trio Bistro/Bar

In the Plaza Palamino, 2990 N. Swan Rd. ☎ **520/325-3333.** Reservations recommended on weekends. Main courses $11–$17. AE, MC, V. Daily 11:30am–2:30pm and 4:30–9:30pm,. Lounge open until midnight. MEDITERRANEAN/ASIAN/LATIN.

The idea here is to present cuisine from three separate places on the globe, and although this would seem to result in chaos, it actually works. The ingredients are not "fused," so each dish retains its cultural integrity. The bread basket delivered spicy East Indian papadams and chewy focaccio. As you might imagine, the flavors here run quite the gamut, from warm and rich roasted corn and poblano chowder to zesty Greek salad to piquant Moroccan vegetables with spicy Tunisian sauce, most prepared with a health-conscious attitude. And for dessert there's even black sticky rice with mango (but be sure, however, to ask if the mango is ripe and sweet). The use of mechanized palm leaf ceiling fans are a whimsical addition to the decor.

INEXPENSIVE

⑤ El Corral Restaurant

2201 E. River Rd. ☎ **520/299-6092.** Reservations not accepted. Complete dinner $7–$11.25. AE, DC, DISC, MC, V. Daily 5–10pm. STEAKS.

Owned by the same folks who brought you Tucson's Pinnacle Peak Steakhouse, El Corral is another inexpensive steakhouse, and very popular with retirees and families. The restaurant doesn't accept reservations, so expect long lines. The hacienda building has flagstone floors and wood paneling that make it dark and cozy, while outside in the bright sunlight a cactus garden flourishes. In keeping with the name, there's a traditional corral fence of mesquite branches around the restaurant parking lot. Prime rib is the house specialty, but there are also steaks, pork ribs, chicken, and burgers for the kids.

WEST TUCSON

Scordato's

4405 W. Speedway Blvd. ☎ **520/792-3055.** Reservations highly recommended. Main courses $16–$21. AE, CB, DC, DISC, MC, V. Tues–Thurs 5–9pm, Fri–Sat 5–10pm, Sun 4–9pm. ITALIAN.

It's a long way out to Scordato's, but that doesn't bother the loyal clientele who enjoy the setting near Saguaro National Park. The restaurant looks a bit like a lost Italian villa searching for the Mediterranean coast, with saguaros standing next to cypresses out front. Inside, plush carpets, comfortable brocade chairs, and big windows allow diners to enjoy desert views in comfort. Despite the crystal chandeliers and tapestries on the walls, you don't have to dress up for dinner here, where you'll find both families and business types. The menu contains many tempting choices, although it's difficult to move beyond the variety of veal dishes. Veal stresa is our favorite—it's stuffed with prosciutto and mozzarella and then sautéed in marsala and white-wine sauce. For an appetizer, we like the scampi sauté. The extensive wine list will satisfy the wine connoisseur.

SPECIALTY DINING
DINING WITH A VIEW

Virtually all the foothills resorts offer dining with a view, including the **Ventana Room** and the **Gold Room,** both discussed above. Outside the foothills resorts, there are many additional choices. **Anthony's in the Catalinas, Boccata, Scordato's,** and **The Tack Room** offer superb views of the city's twinkling lights or the jagged mountains surrounding the valley. These restaurants are listed above.

COWBOY STEAKHOUSES

Hidden Valley Inn

4825 N. Sabino Canyon Rd. ☎ **520/299-4941.** Main courses $10–$18. MC, V. Mon–Sat 11:30am–3pm and 5–10pm, Sun 4:30–10pm. STEAKS.

This steakhouse is the kind of place where people come to celebrate a family birthday and inevitably leave with large doggie bags. Cowpuncher-size steaks and barbecued ribs are the main attraction. The back room is cavernous, with kerosene lamps on the tables and live western music.

The Last Territory Steakhouse & Music Hall

In the Sheraton El Conquistador, 10000 N. Oracle Rd. ☎ **520/544-1738.** Reservations recommended. Main courses $10–$29. AE, CB, DC, DISC, MC, V. Daily 5–10pm. STEAKS.

A resurgence of interest in red meat has been prompting individuals to seek out restaurants where only the best is offered. The Last Territory, which serves wet-aged premium beef cooked over mesquite-wood fires, is one of them. The quality of the steaks (accompanied by a baked potato, generous salad, and other cowboy fixin's), a live musical revue on weekends, and a big hall in which to eat your steak and throw your peanut shells on the floor make the trip out to this resort worth it.

✪ L'il Abner's Steakhouse

8500 N. Silverbell Rd. ☎ **520/744-2800.** Reservations accepted Fri–Sat. Main courses $11–$22. MC, V. Sun–Thurs 5–10pm, Fri–Sat 5–11pm. Take I-10 to the Cortaro Farms Road exit, then go west on Cortaro Farms Road and north on Silverbell Road. STEAKS.

This steakhouse, which used to be an old stagecoach stop, is still beyond the city lights, and almost as rustic as in the days of the Wild West. The steaks are cooked over a mesquite fire and eaten (with all the beans, bread, and salsa your heart desires) at picnic tables. Friday and Saturday nights are extra-lively with country music and dancing.

Pinnacle Peak Steakhouse

6541 E. Tanque Verde Rd. ☎ **520/296-0911.** Main courses $4–$13. AE, DC, DISC, MC, V. Nov–May, Mon–Thurs 5–10pm, Fri–Sun 4:30–10pm; June–Oct, daily 5–10pm. STEAKS.

Located in the Trail Dust Town, a Wild West–themed shopping and dining center, the Pinnacle Peak Steakhouse specializes in family dining in a fun cowboy atmosphere. Be prepared for crowds—this place is very popular with tour buses. Stroll the wooden sidewalks past the opera house and saloon to the grand old dining rooms of the Pinnacle Peak Steakhouse. You'll be surprised at the authenticity of the restaurant, which really resembles a dining room in Old Tombstone or Dodge City.

Triple C Chuckwagon Suppers

8900 Bopp Rd. ☎ **520/883-2333.** Reservations recommended. Complete meal 12–$17 adults, $6–$11 children. AE, MC, V. Thanksgiving–Apr, daily 7–10pm. Closed May–Thanksgiving. Take Ariz. 86 west to San Joaquin Road. WESTERN.

This restaurant is located on an old cattle ranch. Dinner, which consists of cowboy fare such as barbecued beef or chicken and baked beans is dished up chuck-wagon style (in a serving line), and there are nightly western-music performances.

CAFÉS, COFFEEHOUSES & A BAKERY

For a light meal with a Mediterranean theme and a high-tech/rustic ambience to go with your coffee, visit **Milagro,** 3073 N. Campbell Ave. (☎ **520/795-1700**). A student hangout near Park Avenue and the University of Arizona, **Pony Espresso,** 911 E. University Blvd. (☎ **520/624-5112**), serves great vanilla lattès, and the nearby **Café Paraíso,** 820 E. University Blvd. (☎ **520/624-1707**), has a shady and cool patio, easy chairs, and delectable pastries. **Cuppuccinos,** 3400 E. Speedway Blvd. (☎ **520/323-7205**), bills itself as a Seattle-style coffeehouse, and **The Epic Café,** 745 N. Fourth Ave. (☎ **520/624-6844**), is a good hangout place with wild artwork, delicious pastries, and salads. Look for the mural out front.

With cookies from chocolate chip to white-chocolate/macadamia nut, **Stacia's Bakery Café,** 3022 E. Broadway Blvd. (☎ **520/325-5549**), has the most delectable cookies in Tucson.

5 Attractions

SUGGESTED ITINERARIES

If You Have 1 Day

Start your day at the Arizona–Sonora Desert Museum, then drive through Saguaro National Park. After lunch, visit Old Tucson Studios if you're a fan of western movies, then head downtown to the El Presidio Historic District. Have drinks or dinner at one of the foothills resorts and enjoy the view.

If You Have 2 Days

Spend your first day as suggested above. Start your second day at the Arizona Historical Society Tucson Museum, then cross the street to the Arizona State Museum. After lunch, visit the University of Arizona Museum of Art, then head out to Sabino Canyon to experience a desert oasis.

If You Have 3 Days

Spend your first two days as suggested above. On Day 3, head south to visit Mission San Xavier del Bac, and then continue south to Tubac and Tumacacori.

If You Have 5 Days or More

For Days 1 to 3, see the suggestions above. Start your fourth day with a hike or some horseback riding;, later in the day, head up to Mount Lemmon to see how close the mountains are to downtown Tucson. On Day 5, drive to Tombstone and Bisbee for the day (or start on Day 4 and make it an overnight trip). Alternatively, you can do some golfing, play tennis, or lay by the pool for a couple of relaxing days.

THE TOP ATTRACTIONS

✪ Arizona–Sonora Desert Museum

2021 N. Kinney Rd. ☎ **520/883-2702** or 502/883-1380. Admission $8.95 adults, $1.75 children 6–12, free for children 5 and under. Oct–Feb, daily 8:30am–5pm; Mar–Sept, daily 7:30am–6pm. From downtown Tucson, go west on Speedway Boulevard, which becomes Gates Pass Boulevard, and follow the signs.

Don't be fooled by the name. This is a zoo, and it's one of the best in the country. Don't be surprised to find yourself spending more hours here than you intended. The Arizona–Sonora Desert Museum is located 14 miles west of Tucson between Tucson Mountain Park and Saguaro National Park West.

The Sonora Desert is the arid region that encompasses much of central and southern Arizona as well as parts of northern Mexico. In this desert are not only arid lands but also forested mountains, springs, rivers, and streams. The full spectrum of Sonora Desert life—from plants to insects to fish to reptiles to

---

❓ Did You Know?

- The University of Arizona was established in Tucson to appease the citizenry after the territorial capital was moved to Phoenix.
- Mount Lemmon, named for the woman who first climbed it, is the site of the southernmost ski area in the continental United States.
- Tucson is the sunniest city in the country.
- The Sonora Desert is the only place in the world where the saguaro cactus grows, and Saguaro National Park outside Tucson has the greatest concentration of these plants.
- Singer Linda Ronstadt is part of a Tucson family very active in local politics; a public bus station is named for one of the Ronstadts.
- More astronomical observatories are within a 50-mile radius of Tucson than in any other area of comparable size in the world.

Tucson Attractions

Arizona Historical Society
  Tucson Museum ❾
Arizona-Sonora Desert
  Museum ❶
Arizona State Museum ❿
Center for Creative
  Photography ❼
De Grazia Gallery
  in the Sun ⓳
El Tiradito ⓮
Flandrau Science
  Center & Planetarium ⓫
The International
  Wildlife Museum ❸
Mission San
  Xavier del Bac ⓲
Old Tucson Studios ❷
Pima Air Museum ⓱
Reid Park Zoo ⓰
Sabino Canyon Park ❺
Sosa-Carillo Fremont
  House Museum ⓭
Tohono Chul Park ❹
Tucson Botanical
  Gardens ❻
Tucson Children's
  Museum ⓯
Tucson Museum of Art ⓬
University of Arizona
  Museum of Art ❽

ARIZONA

Tucson

Silverbell Rd.

Overton

Cortaro Farms Rd.

Thornydale Rd.

10

Ina Rd.

Ina Rd.

Orange Grove R

Sunset   Rd.

El Camino de Cerro   Ruthrau
                          Rd.

Sweetwater Dr.

To Saguaro National
Park (west)

Ironwood Hill Dr.

❶

❸

Tucson Mountain
Park

Speedway Blv

❷

Gates Pass Rd.

Anklam Rc

Kinney

Rd.

Silverlake Rd.

Bopp   Rd.

Ajo   Way

86

Valencia   Rd.

Mission Rd.

San Xavier Indian Reservation

LEGEND
Airport ✈

1751

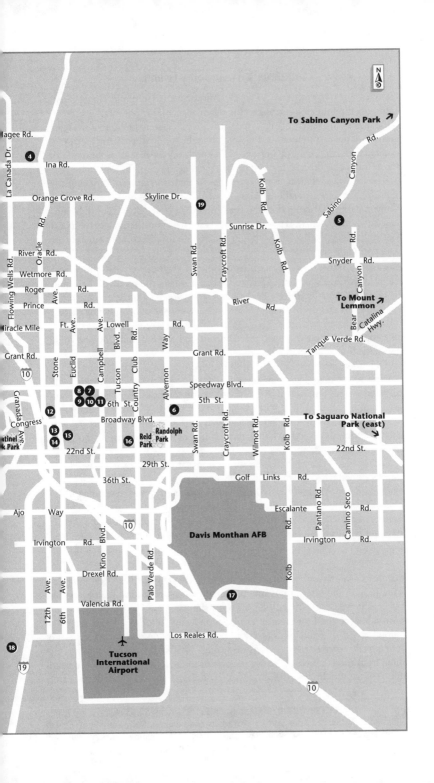

Saguaros & Their Spiny Friends

Cacti (cactuses is correct, too) are the most distinctive feature of the Sonora desert. From the diminutive hedgehog to the stately saguaro, the Sornora Desert supports an amazing variety of cactus species. Cacti can be seen throughout the state, and one of the best times to cactus-watch is in the spring when many species are covered with large, colorful flowers. May is probably the best all-around month for seeing cactus flowers, but you can see them in April and June as well.

The best natural areas to see cactus are in Saguaro National Park (outside Tucson), Organ Pipe National Monument (100 miles west of Tucson), Sabino Canyon Park (in Tucson), Picacho Peak (near Casa Grande), and South Mountain Park (in Phoenix). To learn more about cacti, visit the Desert Botanical Garden in Phoenix, Boyce Thompson Southwestern Arboretum in Superior, or Tucson Botanical Gardens.

Saguaro Cactus   The saguaro (pronounced "sa-*hwah*-ro") is the largest cactus of Arizona's Sonora Desert and grows nowhere else on earth. Reaching heights of as much as 50 feet, saguaros are the redwoods of the desert, and often grow in dense stands that resemble forests. Saguaros are a slow-growing cactus; a 10-year-old may be as little as 6 inches tall, and it can take 75 years for a saguaro to sprout its first branch. The oldest-known saguaros are around 200 years old, and some have more than 40 arms.

To support their great size in such an arid environment, saguaros have a highly efficient root system that can be as large as 100 feet in diameter. These roots soak up water quickly and store it in the spongy interior of the cactus. The exterior of a saguaro is pleated so that it can expand and contract as it takes up and loses water. After a rainstorm, a mature saguaro can weigh as much as 7 tons and can survive for up to two years without another drop of water. Supporting this great mass is an internal framework of sturdy ribs.

Each spring, waxy white flowers sprout from the tips of saguaro arms. These flowers are pollinated by white-winged doves and lesser long-nosed bats that come from hundreds of miles away in Mexico just for saguaro flowering season. Other animals that rely on saguaros include gila woodpeckers and elf owls that nest in holes in saguaro trunks. When a bird pecks a hole into a saguaro, the cactus responds by forming a tough scab around the interior of the hole.

mammals—is on display in natural settings. There are black bears and mountain lions, beavers and otters, frogs and fish, tarantulas and scorpions, prairie dogs and javelinas (a wild pig). In addition, there's a simulated cave with exhibits on prehistoric desert life. Our favorite exhibit is an aviary holding a dozen species of hummingbird. The tiny birds buzz past your ears and stop only inches in front of your face. A separate aviary contains many other bird species. Guides explain everything from the life cycle of the saguaro cactus to the feeding habits of the tarantula. A restaurant, Ironwood Terraces, serves excellent food and is well worth a stop.

Old Tucson Studios

201 S. Kinney Rd. ☎ **520/883-0100.** Admission $11.95 adults, $7.95 children 4–11, free for children 3 and under; after 5pm, $7.95 adults and children. Daily 9am–9pm. Closed Thanksgiving and Dec 25. Take Speedway Boulevard west, continuing in the same direction when it becomes Gates Pass Boulevard, and turn left on South Kinney Road.

The Tohono O'odham natives of the Sonora Desert have long relied on saguaro cactus fruit as an important food source, and in fact the Tohono O'odham year begins with the saguaro harvest. The Saguaro fruit, with its red, seedy pulp, is made into a wine that's used in traditional ceremonies.

Organ Pipe Cactus   This close relative of the saguaro takes its name from its many trunks, which give it the appearance of an old pipe organ. The organ pipe cactus is even more frost sensitive than the saguaro and lives only in an area 100 miles west of Tucson on either side of the Mexican border. This population of stately cacti has also been preserved as a national monument.

Barrel Cactus   When mature, these cacti look much as their name implies and can be confused with young saguaros. However, the barrel cactus can be distinguished by its fishhook-shaped spines which are usually yellow or red in color. This is the cactus that for years has been touted as a source of life-giving water to anyone lost in the desert. The liquid in this cactus's spongy interior is actually quite bitter and fowl tasting. However, the same spongy pulp, when cooked in sugar water, becomes very tasty.

Cholla Cactus   The cholla (pronounced "*choi*-yah") is the most dreaded of all the Arizona cacti. Its spines are long, plentiful, sharp, and brittle. To brush up against a cholla is to know certain pain. There are several species of this cacti, which resemble small trees, in Arizona. They go by such graphic names as jumping cholla, which is said to throw pieces of its spiny branches at unwary passersby; teddy bear cholla, which is so covered with spines that it looks fuzzy; and the chain-fruit cholla, on which fruit hang in fragile, spiny chains. The chollas are favored nesting spots of cactus wrens and doves. Give them a wide birth.

Prickly Pear Cactus   This is one of the largest and most widespread families of cacti and can be found throughout the United States, not just in the desert. They are also among the most commercially important cacti. The flat stems or pads (known as *nopales* in Spanish) of one species are used in Mexican cooking and can be found both fresh and canned in markets in Arizona. The fruit of prickly pears is also edible and is relished by both humans and animals. Here in Arizona, it's possible to find prickly pear jams and jellies, as well as prickly pear ice cream.

This is not the genuine old Tucson, but rather a western town originally built as the set for the 1939 movie *Arizona*. In the years since then, Old Tucson has been used during the filming of John Wayne's *Rio Lobo, Rio Bravo,* and *El Dorado;* Clint Eastwood's *The Outlaw Josey Wales;* Kirk Douglas's *Gunfight at the O.K. Corral;* Paul Newman's *The Life and Times of Judge Roy Bean;* and, more recently, *Tombstone* and *Geronimo.*

Today, however, Old Tucson is far more than just a movie set. In addition to serving as a film site for frequent film, TV, and advertising productions, it has become a Wild West theme park with diverse family-oriented activities and entertainment. Throughout each day there are staged shoot-outs in the streets, stunt shows, cancan performances, medicine shows, and other performances. There are also train rides, stagecoach rides, kiddie rides, video games, restaurants, a kachina museum, and gift shops.

A fire destroyed much of Old Tucson in early 1995 and many of the original buildings were lost. However, the town has been rebuilt and though it isn't quite the same Old Tucson it once was, movie sets can look pretty authentic.

✪ Saguaro National Park

3693 S. Old Spanish Trail. ☎ **520/733-5100.** Admission $4 per car (east section only). Park, daily 7am–sunset; visitor centers, daily 8am–5pm. To reach the west section, take Speedway Boulevard west from downtown Tucson (it becomes Gates Pass Boulevard); to reach the east section, take Speedway Boulevard east, then head south on Freeman Road to Old Spanish Trail.

The saguaro cactus has been called the monarch of the desert and is the quintessential symbol of the American desert. Coyotes, foxes, squirrels, and javelinas all eat the sweet fruit and seeds of the saguaro, as have the Tohono O'odham for centuries.

Since 1933 the two sections of Saguaro National Park have protected the saguaro and all the other inhabitants of this section of the Sonora Desert. The west section is the more popular because of its proximity to both the Arizona–Sonora Desert Museum and Old Tucson Studios. In the area near the Red Hills Information Center is a water hole that attracts wild animals, which you're most likely to see at dawn, dusk, or at night. The east section of the park contains an older area of forest at the foot of the Rincon Mountains. This section is popular with hikers because most of it has no roads. There's also a visitor center here. Both sections have loop roads, nature trails, hiking trails, and picnic grounds.

Arizona Historical Society Tucson Museum

949 E. Second St. ☎ **520/628-5774.** Admission free or by donation. Mon–Sat 10am–4pm, Sun noon–4pm. Closed major holidays. Bus: 1.

As Arizona's oldest historical museum, this repository of all things Arizonan is a treasure trove for the history buff. If you've never explored a real mine, you can do the next best thing by looking at the museum's full-scale reproduction of an underground mine tunnel. You'll also see an assayer's office, miner's tent, stamp mill, and blacksmith's shop in the mining exhibit. Transportation through the years is another interesting exhibit, with silver-studded saddles of Spanish ranchers, steam locomotives that opened Arizona to the world, and "horseless carriages" that revolutionized life in the Southwest. The museum has a research library and a good gift shop.

Tucson Museum of Art and Historic Block

140 N. Main Ave. ☎ **520/624-2333.** Admission $2 adults, $1 students and seniors, free for children 12 and under; free for everyone Tues. Mon–Sat 10am–4pm, Sun noon–4pm. Closed all national holidays. All downtown-bound buses.

The **Tucson Museum of Art** is situated in a large modern building surrounded by historic adobes and a spacious plaza frequently used to display sculpture. The museum boasts an excellent collection of pre-Columbian art representing 3,000 years of life in Mexico and Central and South America, and a large collection of western art depicting cowboys, horses, and the wide-open spaces of the American West. In addition, the museum always hosts temporary exhibitions, such as the annual "American Women Artists and the West."

The restored homes on the block bordering the museum date from 1850 to 1907 and are all built on the former site of the Tucson presidio. **La Casa Cordova,** the oldest house on the block, is one of the city's earliest. It serves as a Mexican Heritage Museum. The **Leonardo Romero House** is now part of the museum's

Frommer's Favorite Tucson Experiences

Seeing the Arizona–Sonora Desert Museum. One of the world's finest zoos, the museum focuses exclusively on the animals and plants of the Sonora Desert of southern Arizona and northern Mexico.

Taking a Full-Moon Desert Hike. There's no better time to explore the desert than at night (when the desert comes alive) under a full moon. Drive to the east or west section of Saguaro National Park for your hike.

Making the Drive to Mount Lemmon. From the desert, the road twists and turns up into the Santa Catalina Mountains, with cactus and palo verde gradually replaced by pine and juniper. You'll have breathtaking views of Tucson along the way.

Taking in Downtown Saturday Night. On the first and third Saturday of each month Tucson's Downtown Arts District abounds in open art galleries, boutiques, crafts shops, street performers, and free entertainment in hip cafés.

Spending a Day in Tubac. As the first European settlement in what would later become Arizona, Tubac has a long history now complemented by nearly 100 arts and crafts studios, galleries, and shops. A day here is a great outing.

art school, the **Stevens House** is home to Janos, one of the best restaurants in Tucson, and the **Fish House** will contain the museum's western collection. A map and descriptive brochures about the houses are available at the museum's front desk. Free guided tours of the galleries and historic block are available.

University of Arizona Museum of Art

Park Ave. and Speedway Blvd. ☎ **520/621-7567.** Admission free. Late Aug to mid-May, Mon–Fri 9am–5pm, Sun noon–4pm; mid-May to late Aug, Mon–Fri 10am–3:30pm, Sun noon–4pm. Closed major holidays. Bus: 1.

Established in 1955, this art museum has a more extensive and diverse collection than the Tucson Museum of Art. The collection includes European and American works from the Renaissance to the 20th century, notably by Tintoretto, Rembrandt, Piranesi, Picasso, O'Keeffe, Warhol, and Rothko. Another attraction is the *Retable of Ciudad Rodrigo,* which consists of 26 paintings from 15th-century Spain. The retable was originally above a cathedral altar. The museum also has an extensive collection of 20th-century sculpture that includes more than 60 clay and plaster models and sketches by Jacques Lipchitz.

Arizona State Museum

On the University of Arizona campus, University Blvd. and Park Ave. ☎ **520/621-6302.** Admission free. Mon–Sat 10am–5pm, Sun noon–5pm. Closed major holidays. Bus: 1.

Founded in 1893, the Arizona State Museum houses an extensive collection of artifacts from prehistoric and contemporary Native American cultures of the Southwest. A Paleo-Indian exhibit displays 12,000-year-old spear points that were found embedded in the bones of mammoths, now long extinct. A large exhibit covers the Hohokam, an ancient farming culture that lived in the desert and built extensive networks of irrigation canals until it disappeared mysteriously around 1450. Across the street in the North Building, an exhibit explores the lifestyles and cultural traditions of Native American peoples living in Arizona today. Excellent temporary exhibits, such as one on Mexican fiesta masks, appear here.

The Shrine That Stopped a Freeway

The southern Arizona landscaped is dotted with roadside shrines, symbols of the region's Spanish and Roman Catholic heritage. Most are simple crosses decorated with plastic flowers and dedicated to people who have been killed in auto accidents. However, only Tucson's **El Tiradito** (The Castaway), a shrine dedicated to a sinner, has stopped a freeway.

El Tiradito, located on South Granada Avenue at West Cushing Street, is the only shrine in the United States dedicated to a sinner buried in unconsecrated soil. Several stories tell of how this shrine came to be, but the most popularly accepted tells of a young shepherd who fell in love with his mother-in-law some time in the 1880s. When the father-in-law found his wife in the arms of this young man, he shot the son-in-law. The young shepherd stumbled from his in-laws' house and fell dead beside the dusty street. Because he had been caught in the act of adultery and died without confessing his sins, his body could not be interred in the church cemetery, so he was buried where he fell.

The people of the neighborhood soon began burning candles on the spot to try to save the soul of the young man, and eventually people began burning candles in hopes that their own wishes would come true. They believed that if the candle burned through the night their prayers would be answered. The shrine eventually grew into a substantial little structure, and in 1927 was dedicated by its owner to the city of Tucson. In 1940 the shrine became an official Tucson monument.

However, such status was not enough to protect the shrine from urban renewal, and when the federal government announced that it would level the shrine when it built a new freeway through the center of Tucson, the city's citizens were outraged. Their activities and protest led the shrine to be named to the National Register of Historic Places. Thus protected, the shrine could not be destroyed, and the freeway was moved a few hundred yards to the west.

To this day, devout Catholics from the surrounding neighborhood still burn candles at the shrine that stopped a freeway.

Sabino Canyon

5900 N. Sabino Canyon Rd. ☎ **520/749-2861.** Admission free. Tram ride, $5 adults, $2 children 3–12, free for children 2 and under. Daily, dawn–dusk. Tram rides, daily 9am–4:30pm (more limited in summer). Take Grant Road east to Tanque Verde Road, continuing east; at Sabino Canyon Road, turn north and watch for the sign.

Located in the Santa Catalina Mountains of Coronado National Forest, Sabino Canyon is a desert oasis that has attracted people and animals for thousands of years. Along the length of the canyon are waterfalls and pools where you can swim. For those who prefer just to gaze at the beauty of crystal-clear water flowing over rock, there's a narrated tram ride through the lower canyon leaving frequently every day. There are also many trails and picnic tables. Moonlight tram rides take place three times each month between April and December (phone 520/749-2327 for reservations).

MORE ATTRACTIONS
CHURCHES & SHRINES

In addition to Mission San Xavier del Bac, Tucson has a small shrine—El Tiradito—with an interesting history. See the accompanying box to learn about this unusual spot.

Mission San Xavier del Bac

1950 San Xavier Rd. ☎ **520/294-2624.** Admission free. Daily 9am–6pm. Take I-19 south about 9 miles to the Valencia Road exit and follow the signs.

Called the White Dove of the Desert and considered the finest example of mission architecture in the United States, Mission San Xavier del Bac incorporates Moorish, Byzantine, and Mexican Renaissance architectural styles into a single beautiful church. Brilliantly white in the desert sun, the church serves the residents of the surrounding San Xavier Indian Reservation. Although a church had existed near here as early as 1700, the existing structure was built between 1783 and 1797. Why only one church tower was completed is a mystery, but you'll immediately notice the missing dome of the right-hand tower. The building is constructed of adobe brick, and faded murals cover the walls. A statue of St. Francis Xavier, the mission's patron saint, is to the left of the ornate main altar. Outside, a small hill just east not only affords an interesting view of the church but is also the site of a replica of the famous grotto in Lourdes, France. The mission is an active Roman Catholic church. Masses are held Monday through Friday at 8:30am, on Saturday at 8:30am and 5:30pm, and on Sunday at 8am, 9am, 11am, and 12:30pm. For the past few years the mission has been undergoing restoration, and much of the elaborate interior decoration has taken on a new luster.

OUTDOOR ART

Tucson abounds in outdoor murals. For a guide and map to the most notable, stop by the **Tucson/Pima Arts Council,** 240 N. Stone Ave. (☎ **520/624-0595**), which is located adjacent to the Tucson Museum of Art. Of particular interest is the mural of Farmer John Meats, at 1102 W. Grant Rd.

HISTORIC BUILDINGS/MONUMENTS

Sosa-Carillo Frémont House Museum

151 S. Granada Ave. (between Broadway Blvd. and Cushing St.). ☎ **520/622-0956.** Admission free. Wed–Sat 10am–4pm. Closed all major holidays. All downtown-bound buses.

Located on the shady grounds of the modern Tucson Convention Center, the Sosa-Carillo Frémont House is a classic example of Sonoran Mexican adobe architecture. Originally built in 1858 as a small adobe house, the structure was enlarged after 1866. In 1878 it was rented to territorial governor John Charles Frémont, who had led a distinguished military career as an explorer of the West. It's to this period that the building has been restored, with the living room and bedrooms opening off a large central hall known as a *zaguán;* all rooms are decorated with period antiques. The flat roof is made of pine beams called *vigas,* covered with saguaro cactus ribs and topped by a layer of hard-packed mud.

MUSEUMS/GALLERIES

✪ Center for Creative Photography

East of the corner of Park Ave. and Speedway Blvd. ☎ **520/621-7968.** Admission free. Mon–Fri 11am–5pm, Sun noon–5pm. Bus: 1.

Have you ever wished you could see an original Ansel Adams print up close, or perhaps an Edward Weston or a Richard Avedon? You can at the Center for Creative Photography. Originally conceived by Ansel Adams, the center now holds more than 500,000 negatives, 200,000 study prints, and 60,000 master prints by the world's greatest photographers, making it one of the best and largest collections in the world. Although the center mounts excellent photography exhibits year-round, it's also a research facility that preserves the complete photographic archives of various photographers, including Adams. Prints may be examined in a special room. It's highly recommended that you make an appointment and decide beforehand whose works you'd like to see. You're usually limited to two photographers per visit.

De Grazia Gallery in the Sun

6300 N. Swan Rd. ☎ **520/299-9191.** Admission free. Daily 10am–4pm.

Southwestern artist Ettore "Ted" De Grazia is a Tucson favorite son, and his gallery, set in an adobe home in the foothills, is a Tucson landmark. De Grazia is said to be the most reproduced artist in the world because many of his impressionistic images are found on greeting cards from the 1950s to 1960s and numerous other places. Connected to the gallery is a small adobe chapel that De Grazia built in honor of the missionary explorer Fr. Eusebio Kino. No original works are for sale, but there are many reproductions and other objects with De Grazia images.

The International Wildlife Museum

4800 W. Gates Pass Rd. ☎ **520/624-4024** or 520/629-0100. Admission $5 adults, $3.75 seniors and students, $1.50 children 6–12, free for children 5 and under. Daily 9am–5pm. Take Speedway Boulevard west from downtown.

This castlelike building on the road that leads to the Arizona–Sonora Desert Museum is a natural-history museum filled with stuffed animals in lifelike poses and surroundings. Animals from all over the world are displayed.

Pima Air Museum

6000 E. Valencia Rd. ☎ **520/574-9658** or 520/574-0646. Admission $5 adults, $4 seniors and military, $3 children 10–17, free for children 9 and under. Daily 9am–5pm. Closed Dec 25. Take the Valencia Road exit from I-10 and then drive east 2 miles to the museum entrance.

Located just south of Davis Monthan Air Force Base, reachable from I-10, the Pima Air Museum displays more than 200 aircraft covering the evolution of American aviation. This is the third-largest collection of historic aircraft in the world. A 20,000-square-foot building houses part of the collection, though most of the aircraft are outside. The collection includes replicas of the Wright brothers' 1903 Wright Flyer and the X-15, the world's fastest aircraft. World War II bombers and later jet fighters are popular attractions.

The Pima Air Museum also operates the **Titan Missile Museum** in nearby Green Valley. This is the only intercontinental ballistic missile (ICBM) complex in the world open to the public. Hours and admission fees are the same as for the Pima Air Museum.

PARKS & GARDENS

Reid Park Zoo

Lake Shore Lane and 22nd St. (between Country Club Road and Alvernon Way). ☎ **520/791-4022.** Admission $3.50 adults, $2.50 seniors, 75¢ children 5–14, free for children 4 and under. Daily 9am–4pm. Closed Dec 25. Bus: 14.

Although small and overshadowed by its neighbor, the Arizona–Sonora Desert Museum, the Reid Park Zoo is an important breeding center for several endangered species. Among the animals in the zoo's breeding programs are giant anteaters, white rhinoceroses, tigers, ruffed lemurs, and zebras. There's also a good playground at the park here.

✪ Tucson Botanical Gardens

2150 N. Alvernon Way. ☎ **520/326-9255.** Admission $3 adults, $2 seniors, free for children 11 and under. Daily 8:30am–4:30pm. Closed Jan 1, July 4, Thanksgiving, and Dec 24–25. Bus: 11.

These gardens form an oasis of greenery in suburban Tucson. On the 5 1/2-acre grounds are several small gardens and a cactus garden that not only have visual appeal but are also historic and educational. If you live in the desert, you'll benefit from a visit when you learn about harvesting rainfall for the desert garden and designing a water-conserving landscape. The sensory garden stimulates all five senses, while in another garden traditional southwestern crops are grown for research purposes.

Tohono Chul Park

7366 N. Paseo del Norte. ☎ **520/575-8468.** Admission by suggested donation, $2. Grounds, daily 7am–sunset. Exhibit house, Mon–Sat 9:30am–5pm, Sun 11am–5pm. Tea room, daily 8am–5pm.

Though this public park is fairly small, it provides an excellent introduction to the plant and animal life of the desert. The park includes an ethnobotanical garden; a garden for children that encourages them to touch, listen, and smell; a demonstration garden; natural areas; an exhibit house for art displays; and a tea room and café that are great for breakfast, lunch, or afternoon tea.

A PLANETARIUM

Flandrau Science Center & Planetarium

Cherry Ave. and University Blvd. ☎ **520/621-STAR** or 520/621-4515. Admission to exhibits, $2 adults; one child with an adult is free; free for everyone Wed. Telescope viewing free. Theater, $3–$5. Daytime, Mon–Fri 10am–5pm, Sat–Sun 1–5pm; evenings, Wed–Thurs 7–9pm, Fri–Sat 7pm–midnight. Closed major holidays. Bus: 1.

Located on the campus of the University of Arizona, the Flandrau Planetarium offers stargazers a chance to learn more about the universe. The planetarium theater presents programs on the stars as well as very popular laser shows set to music. Exhibit halls contain hands-on science exhibits for people of all ages, and a mineral museum. On clear nights, you can gaze through the planetarium's 16-inch telescope. (Arizona has become a magnet for stargazers, and several famous telescopes are near Tucson. See "Easy Excursions from Tucson," later in this chapter, for information on the Kitt Peak National Observatory.)

ESPECIALLY FOR KIDS

Tucson Children's Museum

200 S. Sixth Ave. ☎ **520/884-7511.** Admission $3 adults, $1.50 seniors and children 3–16, free for children 2 and under; free for everyone on the third Sun of each month. Wed 10am–6pm, Thurs–Fri 9am–1pm, Sat 10am–5pm, Sun noon–5pm. Closed Jan 1, Memorial Day, July 4, Labor Day, Thanksgiving, Dec 25. All downtown-bound buses.

This museum is located in the old Carnegie Library in downtown Tucson and is filled with hands-on activities that are fun and educational. Exhibits change every year or so, but have included a doctor's office, a fire station, and a bubble factory. Weekends generally include special performances and programs.

SPECIAL & FREE EVENTS

Because of the excellent weather year-round, Tucson hosts numerous outdoor festivals, celebrations, and events. Many are free and are held downtown and in the city's parks. See "Tucson Calendar of Events" in Chapter 3 for details.

One year-round favorite free event is **Downtown Saturday Night,** a celebration of the Downtown Arts District held on the first and third Saturday of each month. From 7 to 10pm on these nights, the district—which includes East Pennington Street, East Congress Street, and East Broadway Boulevard between Fourth Avenue and Stone Avenue—comes alive with music performances on the street and in cafés, art gallery openings, and late-evening shopping. For more information, call the Tucson Arts District Partnership at 520/624-9977. You'll also hear live music if you wander over to the Old Town Artisans crafts market in the El Presidio Historic District.

WALKING TOUR 1
The El Presidio Historic District

Start: The Fish House.
Finish: Pima County Courthouse.
Time: Three hours.
Best Times: Weekends, when restaurants aren't packed at lunch.
Worst Times: The summer, when it's just too hot to do any walking.

Tucson has a long and varied cultural history, which is most easily seen on a walking tour of the city's downtown historic districts.

Start your tour at the corner of Alameda Street and Main Avenue. With your back to the modern high-rise office buildings of downtown Tucson, you'll be facing the El Presidio Historic District, which is named for the Presidio of San Augustín del Tucson (1775), the Spanish garrison that once stood here to protect the San Xavier del Bac Mission from the Apache. For many years this was the heart of Tucson. No original building still stands, and those you'll see date from the mid-19th century. The building directly in front of you is the:

1. **Fish House,** 120 N. Main Ave., built in 1868 in the Sonoran architectural style and named for Edward Nye Fish, a local merchant. Next along Main Avenue is the:

2. **Stevens Home,** 150 N. Main Ave. Together with the Fish House, this was the cultural heart of Tucson in the latter 19th century. It now houses Janos, one of Tucson's best restaurants.

   From Janos, take a right onto Washington Street and then another right onto Meyer Avenue, where you'll see the:

3. **Romero House.** Built in 1868, it now contains the Tucson Museum of Art School. Next door is:

4. **La Casa Cordova,** 175 N. Meyer Ave., which dates to about 1848 and is one of the oldest buildings in Tucson. As a part of the art museum, it's furnished in the style of the period and is dedicated as a Mexican Heritage Museum.

   Diagonally across Meyer Avenue is Tucson's premier crafts market:

5. **Old Town Artisans,** 186 N. Meyer Ave. In this adobe building dating from 1862 are several rooms full of handmade southwestern crafts (see "Savvy

Walking Tour 1—The El Presidio Historic District

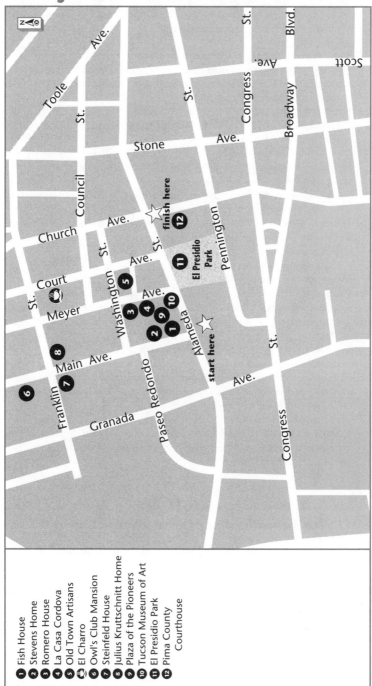

1. Fish House
2. Stevens Home
3. Romero House
4. La Casa Cordova
5. Old Town Artisans
6. El Charro
7. Owl's Club Mansion
8. Steinfeld House
9. Julius Kruttschnitt Home
10. Plaza of the Pioneers
11. Tucson Museum of Art
12. El Presidio Park
13. Pima County Courthouse

Shopping," later in this chapter, for details). You could spend hours browsing through the amazing assortment of crafts.

☕ **TAKE A BREAK** If you started your tour late in the morning you're probably hungry by now, so head up Court Avenue to **El Charro,** Tucson's oldest Mexican restaurant. Be sure to order carne seca. (See "Dining," earlier in this chapter, for complete information.)

Continue up Court Avenue, turn left on Franklin Street, and then right on Main Avenue to reach the:

6. Owl's Club Mansion, 378 N. Main Ave., built in 1901 as a gentlemen's club for some of Tucson's most eligible bachelors. At the southwest corner of Franklin and Main is the:

7. Steinfeld House, 300 N. Main Ave., built in 1899 in Spanish mission-revival style. This was the original Owl's Club. Directly across the street is the:

8. Julius Kruttschnitt Home, 297 N. Main Ave., which now serves as the El Presidio Bed and Breakfast Inn. Victorian trappings disguise the adobe origins of this unique home.

Continue down Main Avenue to the archway between the Fish and Stevens homes, turn left, and cross the:

9. Plaza of the Pioneers, with fountains and sculptures. The plaza is the site of summer-evening jazz concerts. Across the plaza is the entrance to the:

10. Tucson Museum of Art (see "The Top Attractions," above, for complete information). This modern building houses collections of pre-Columbian and western art, as well as contemporary exhibits.

Cross Alameda Street to:

11. El Presidio Park, once the parade ground for the presidio and now a shady gathering spot for homeless people and downtown office workers. Just to the east of the park is the very impressive:

12. Pima County Courthouse, 155 N. Church St. Built in 1928, the courthouse incorporates Moorish, Spanish, and southwestern architectural features, including a colorful tiled dome. A portion of the original presidio wall is in a glass case on the second floor.

WALKING TOUR 2
The Barrio Historico & Downtown Arts District

Start: The Tucson Convention Center.
Finish: Congress Hotel.
Time: Four hours.
Best Times: Daytime, when there are people on the street and it's safer to walk around.
Worst Times: After dark or in the summer heat.

When the Tucson city council decided to raze its historic districts in the name of urban renewal, they didn't realize that the old homes in the neighborhood were actually worth saving and an important part of Tucson's history and culture. About half of the downtown was razed before the voices for preservation and restoration were finally heard. And if it had not been for the activism of the residents of the Barrio Historico, Interstate 10 would now run right through much of this area.

Walking Tour 2—
The Barrio Historico & Downtown Arts District

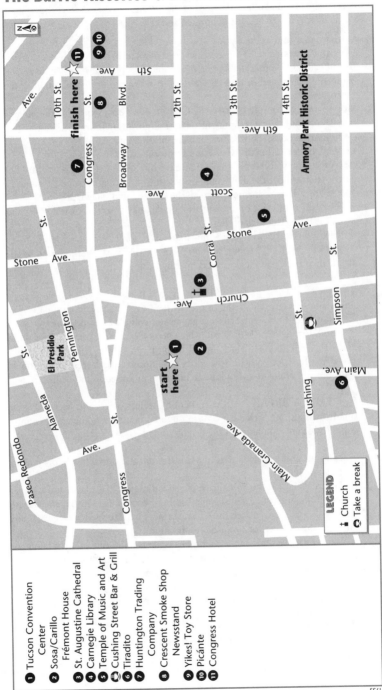

N

start here

finish here

Armory Park Historic District

El Presidio Park

LEGEND
✝ Church
🔄 Take a break

Streets: 5th Ave., 5th St., 10th St., 12th St., 13th St., 14th St., 6th Ave., Congress St., Broadway Blvd., Scott Ave., Stone Ave., Corral St., Church Ave., Simpson St., Cushing St., Main Ave., Main-Granada Ave., Pennington St., Alameda St., Paseo Redondo, Congress Ave.

1. Tucson Convention Center
2. Sosa/Carillo Frémont House
3. St. Augustine Cathedral
4. Carnegie Library
5. Temple of Music and Art
6. Cushing Street Bar & Grill
7. Tiradito
8. Huntington Trading Company
9. Crescent Smoke Shop Newsstand
10. Yikes! Toy Store
11. Picánte
12. Congress Hotel

1753

Lying just to the east of the Tucson Convention Center, the Congress Street commercial neighborhood is now the heart of the Downtown Arts District and is home to several art galleries, eclectic boutiques, and cafés.

Start your tour at the:

1. Tucson Convention Center, a sprawling complex that includes a sports arena, grand ballroom, concert hall, theater, pavilions, meeting halls, gardens, craft and souvenir vendors, and, near the fountains in the center of the complex, the historic:

2. Sosa-Carillo Frémont House, 151 Granada Ave., an adobe structure built in the 1850s and later the home of territorial governor John C. Frémont (see "More Attractions," above, for complete information).

Walk back to Church Avenue and across the street you'll see:

3. St. Augustine Cathedral. The entrance is from Stone Avenue, so walk around to the front. Above the door you'll see a statue of St. Augustine and symbols of the Arizona desert—the horned toad, the saguaro, and the yucca.

From the south side of the cathedral, walk a block east on Corral Street and you'll be facing the back of the:

4. Carnegie Library, which now houses the Tucson Children's Museum (see "Especially for Kids," above, for complete information). Walk around to the front, then back one block toward St. Augustine's, turn left, and you'll come to the:

5. Temple of Music and Art, 330 S. Scott Ave. It was built in 1927 as a movie and stage theater, and is the home of the Arizona Theatre Company (see "Tucson After Dark," later in this chapter, for complete information).

If you turn right on 14th Street, which becomes Cushing Street in one block, and then walk another block, you'll be on the northern edge of the Barrio Historico District with its 150 adobe row houses, the largest collection of 19th-century Sonoran-style adobe architecture preserved in the United States.

☕ **TAKE A BREAK**   At the corner of Cushing Street and Meyer Avenue stands the Cushing Street Bar & Grill, housed in an old home and a country store. Inside are old photos of the neighborhood.

Continue another block west to Main Avenue and turn left. On the far side of the street stands:

6. El Tiradito. This is the only shrine in the United States dedicated to a sinner buried in unconsecrated soil. People still light candles here in hope of having their wishes come true (see the "The Shrine That Stopped a Freeway" box earlier in this chapter for complete information).

Wander a while through the Barrio Historico District admiring the Sonoran-style homes that are built right out to the street. Many of these homes sport colorfully painted facades, signs of the ongoing renovation of this neighborhood.

Head back up Church Avenue when you're ready and turn right on Congress Street. As you walk along this street, you'll see many interesting shops and art galleries, including the:

7. Huntington Trading Company, 111 E. Congress St.(☎ 520/628-8578), specializing in Mexican and Native American art. Cross the street, and in the next block, you'll come to the:

8. Crescent Smoke Shop Newsstand, 216 E. Congress St., an old-fashioned smoke shop with cigars, magazines, and newpapers from all over the country. In the next block is:

9. Yikes! Toy Store, 302 E. Congress St. (☎ 520/622-8807), a wacky toy store filled with rubber dinosaurs, plastic spiders, and other inexpensive, offbeat items that appeal as much to adults as they do to children. Next door is:

10. Picánte, 306 E. Congress St. (☎ 520/622-8807), which has a plethora of Hispanic-themed icons and accessories, including milagros and Day of the Dead skeletons.

Just before the end of Congress Street, you'll come to the:

11. Congress Hotel, 311 E. Congress St. The famous gangster John Dillinger stayed here shortly before he was captured. The Congress Hotel was recently renovated and now houses a youth hostel and budget hotel. Be sure to look around the lobby.

6 Organized Tours

To get a thorough overview of Tucson, you can take a 6¹/₂-hour tour with **Old Pueblo Tours** (☎ **520/575-1175**). The tour includes visits to A Mountain, the downtown historic districts, De Grazia's Gallery in the Sun, the Arizona Historical Society Tucson Museum, and Mission San Xavier del Bac. The tour is $32 for adults and $15 for children 16 and under. **Tucson Tours** (☎ **520/297-2911**) offers 1¹/₂-hour guided city tours for $15. The tours head up to the top of A Mountain for an overview of the city, then visit the three downtown historic districts and the University of Arizona. The same company also offers a shuttle service to the Arizona–Sonora Desert Museum and Old Tucson Studios, and tours to Mission San Xavier del Bac.

To learn more about the history of Tucson, see if you can attach yourself to one of **Ken Scoville's Presentation** (☎ **520/323-9290**) walking tours of downtown (he usually does tours for groups only). Mr. Scoville has a wealth of knowledge about the city and can make the historic districts come alive. These two-hour tours cost $10 and are offered November to April; call for a reservation first.

If you'd like to learn more about people who lived in the Tucson area hundreds of years ago, take a tour with the **Center for Desert Archeology** (☎ **520/ 881-2244**). A nonprofit educational and research organization, it can take you to view petroglyphs near Tucson and ruins of the Hohokam people in Catalina State Park. Tours cost $40 for a half day and $70 for a full day.

For getting out into wild nature or a taste of pioneer history, **High Desert Convoys** (☎ **520/323-3386** or 800/93-TOURS) offers a hike to a cave, bird- and animal watching, and an excursion to ghost towns. Prices range from $45 to $60.

7 Outdoor Activities

BALLOONING   **Balloon America** (☎ **520/299-7744**) offers breakfast flights over the foothills of the Santa Catalina Mountains with free pickups at most resorts. The ballooning season runs only from October to June. Flights cost $110 to $195 per person, depending on flight duration.

BICYCLING   You can explore the Arizona backcountry with a rental bicycle from **Bargain Basement Bike,** 428 N. Fremont Ave., near the university

(☎ **520/628-1015**), or **Broadway Bicycles,** 140 S. Sarnoff Dr. (☎ **520/296-7819**). Mountain bikes rent for about $18 to $20 per day.

Places for biking include the **Rillito River Park,** a 4-mile trail that runs along the riverbed between Campbell Avenue and La Cholla Boulevard; and the **Santa Cruz River Park,** from West Grant Road to 29th Street, 4 miles with a view of the Santa Cruz River. But the best place for biking is in **Sabino Canyon** (see "The Top Attractions," above), where bicycles are allowed after 5pm and before 9am every day except Wednesday and Saturday.

GOLF Golf is extremely popular in Arizona, and golf courses abound in Tucson. Tucson Parks & Recreation operates five public golf courses: **Randolph North and Randolph South,** 600 S. Alvernon Way (☎ **520/325-2811**); **El Rio,** 1400 W. Speedway Blvd. (☎ **520/791-4229**); **Silverbell,** 3600 N. Silverbell Rd. (☎ **520/791-5235**); and **Fred Enke,** 8251 E. Irvington Rd. (☎ **520/296-8607**). Greens fees range from a summer weekday low of $12.50 for 9 holes to a high of $21 for 18 holes. Golf carts are available for $9 to $14.

In addition to the public links, resort courses open to the public include the **Sheraton El Conquistador Resort & Country Club,** 10555 N. La Cañada Blvd. (☎ **520/544-1800**), and the **Ventana Canyon Golf & Racquet Club,** 6200 N. Clubhouse Lane (☎ **520/577-6258**). Greens fees at these clubs vary with the season, and are about $70 to $125 for 18 holes in winter, less in summer.

HIKING Tucson is nearly surrounded by mountains that are protected as city and state parks, a national forest, and a national monument. Within these areas are hundreds of miles of hiking trails.

Sections of **Saguaro National Park** are off Old Spanish Trail east of Tucson and past the end of Speedway Boulevard west of the city. In these areas you can observe Sonora Desert vegetation and wildlife and hike among the huge saguaro cacti for which the park is named.

Tucson Mountain Park, also at the end of Speedway Boulevard, is adjacent to Saguaro National Park and preserves a similar landscape.

Sabino Canyon, off Sabino Canyon Road, is Tucson's most popular recreation area. A cold mountain stream here cascades over waterfalls and forms pools that make great swimming holes. The most popular trail is the 4¹/₂-mile-long Seven Falls Trail, which follows the canyon deep into the mountains.

Catalina State Park, north of the city on North Oracle Road, is set on the rugged northwest face of the Santa Catalina Mountains, between 2,500 and 3,000 feet high. Hiking trails beginning in the park lead into the Pusch Ridge Wilderness.

The **Mount Lemmon Recreation Area,** at the end of the Catalina Highway, is set amid high alpine forests on this 8,250-foot mountain. The cool air at this elevation makes this a popular summertime retreat.

HORSEBACK RIDING If you want to play cowboy or just go for a leisurely ride through the desert, there are plenty of stables around Tucson where you can saddle up. In addition to renting horses and providing guided trail rides, all the stables below also offer sunset rides with cookouts. Though reservations are not always required, they're a good idea.

Pusch Ridge Stables, 13700 N. Oracle Rd. (☎ **520/825-1664**), is adjacent to Catalina State Park and Coronado National Forest. Rates are $15 for 1 hour, $22 for 2 hours, and $20 for a 1¹/₂-hour sunset ride.

El Conquistador Stables, 10000 N. Oracle Rd. (☎ **520/742-4200**), is part of the Sheraton El Conquistador Resort, but the public is welcome. Rates are $14 for 1 hour, $22 for 2 hours, and $18 for a 1¹/₂-hour sunset ride. Reservations are required.

Desert–High Country Stables, 6501 W. Ina Rd. (☎ **520/744-3789**), is located 2 miles west of I-10 and offers a variety of rides in the Tucson Mountains and Saguaro National Park West. Rates range from $15 for 1¹/₂ hours to $60 for a full day. Reservations are requested.

IN-LINE SKATING   You can rent in-line skates at **Peter Glen's,** 5626 E. Broadway Blvd. (☎ **520/745-4514**), for $4 per three hours or $12 per day, including protective equipment. Good places to skate include Reid Park, the University of Arizona Campus, and the Rillito River Wash between North Campbell Avenue and North Oracle Road.

JOGGING   McCormick Park, 2950 N. Columbus Blvd., has a 1-mile jogging course, and **Fort Lowell Park,** 2900 N. Craycroft Rd., has a 1¹/₂-mile course. Both are open from sunup to sundown.

SKIING   One hour (35 miles) from Tucson, **Mount Lemmon Ski Valley** (☎ **520/576-1400**) offers 15 slopes for experienced downhill skiers as well as beginners. This is the southernmost ski area in the continental United States, and at times there's insufficient snow for good skiing. Be sure to call ahead before driving here. The ski season runs from December to April. Lift tickets are $25 for adults, $10 for children.

TENNIS   Tucson boasts more than 220 public tennis courts, many lighted for night playing. The **Randolph Tennis Center,** 100 S. Alvernon Way (☎ **520/791-4896**), convenient to downtown, offers 25 courts, 11 lighted. Many of the city's hotels and resorts provide courts for guest use.

8 Spectator Sports

For most sporting events, call the numbers in the listings below for ticket information. However, tickets for special sporting events at the **Tucson Convention Center Arena** are sold by Dillard's department store box offices (☎ **800/638-4253**).

AUTO RACING   Stock cars race at **Tucson Raceway Park,** 12500 S. Houghton Rd., Vail (☎ **520/762-5885**). Tickets range from $9 to $16.

BASEBALL   The **Colorado Rockies** (☎ **520/327-9467**) pitch spring training camp in March at Hi Corbett Field in Reid Park, at South Country Club Road and East 22nd Street. Tickets are $1 to $5. This is also where you can watch the **Tucson Toros** (☎ **520/325-2621**), the Houston Astros AAA team in the Pacific Coast League. The season runs from April to August, and tickets are $4 to $5 for adults and $3 for children 6 to 16, free for children 5 and under.

FOOTBALL   The **University of Arizona Wildcats** (☎ **520/621-2411**), a PAC-10 team, play at the U of A's Wildcat Stadium, and between Christmas and New Year's Day each year, two of the nation's top NCAA teams play each other in the Weiser Lock Copper Bowl game.

GOLF TOURNAMENTS   Women golfers compete for big prizes at the **Ping/Welch's Championship** (☎ **520/791-5742**), an LPGA tournament held in mid-March at the Randolph North Golf Course. The **Northern Telecom Open** (☎ **800/882-7660**), Tucson's main PGA tournament, is held in early January at the Tucson National Golf & Conference Resort.

GREYHOUND RACING   Greyhounds race year-round at **Tucson Greyhound Park,** 2601 S. Third Ave. (☎ **520/884-7576**). Admission ranges from $1.25 for general admission to $3 for the clubhouse.

TENNIS TOURNAMENTS   The **CIGNA Beau Bridges Celebrity Tennis Classic** (☎ **520/623-6165**) takes place at the Randolph Tennis Center at Randolph Park in late April, when more than 40 celebrity tennis players take on local tennis players.

9 Shopping

Tucsonans have a very strong sense of their place in the Southwest, and this is reflected in the city's shopping scene. Southwestern clothing, food, crafts, furniture, and art abound (and often at reasonable prices), as do shopping centers built in a southwestern architectural style.

THE SHOPPING SCENE

Although Tucson is overshadowed by Scottsdale and Phoenix, the city provides a very respectable diversity of merchants. Its population center has moved steadily northward for some years, and you'll find the most expensive shops selling the best-quality merchandise as well as large enclosed shopping malls in the northern foothills.

Aside from the foothills, there are plenty of new, hip, and unusual shops downtown. On Fourth Avenue, between Congress Street and Speedway Boulevard, are more than 100 shops, galleries, and restaurants in the **North Fourth Avenue historic shopping district.** The buildings here were built in the early 1900s, and a drive to keep the neighborhood humming has helped maintain Tucson's downtown vitality. Through the underpass at the south end of Fourth Avenue is Congress Street, the heart of the **Downtown Arts District.** Here you'll find numerous galleries specializing in contemporary art, avant-garde boutiques, and a few trendy eating establishments. However, neither of these neighborhoods seem to be catching on very fast with Tucson shoppers, and they continue to be a bit seedy.

The **El Presidio Historic District** around the Tucson Museum of Art is the city's center for crafts shops. Here are Old Town Artisans and the Tucson Museum of Art museum shop. The **"Lost Barrio"** on the corner of Southwest Park Avenue and 12th Street near downtown Tucson is a group of warehouses that sells Mexican imports and other imported crafts at good prices.

SHOPPING A TO Z
ANTIQUES

Saguaro Moon Antiques Co-Op
45 S. Sixth Ave. ☎ **520/623-5393.**

Several dealers of antiques and collectibles inhabit this downtown shop. You'll find old Mexican sombreros, racks of old *Life* magazines, vintage telephones and radios, and the like.

Unique Antique
5000 E. Speedway Blvd. ☎ **520/323-0319.**

This mall has 90 dealers and claims to be the largest antiques mall in southern Arizona. For sale are all manner of collectibles and antiques.

ART

America West Primitive and Modern Art
363 S. Meyer Ave. ☎ **520/623-4091.**

Although this gallery specializes in works by Native Americans, you'll also find pre-Columbian art and pieces from Africa, Oceania, and Asia. An appointment is requested.

Dinnerware Artists Cooperative Gallery
135 E. Congress St. ☎ **520/792-4503.**

This gallery is a venue for American contemporary art which often is oriented toward radical youth culture themes.

Eleanor Jeck Galleries
4280 N. Campbell Ave. (at River Rd. in St. Phillip's Plaza). ☎ **520/299-2139.**

Featuring brilliant contemporary paintings, this gallery also carries art glass, sculpture, painted furniture, large-format ceramics, and art jewelry.

El Presidio Gallery
7000 E. Tanque Verde Rd. (at Santa Fe Sq.). ☎ **520/733-0388.**

This gallery deals primarily in traditional paintings of the Southwest, although some contemporary works are also available.

A second location is at St. Phillip's Plaza, 4340 N. Campbell Ave. (☎ **520/529-1220**).

Etherton Gallery
135 S. Sixth Ave. ☎ **520/624-7370.**

For more than 20 years this gallery has been presenting Tucson with some of the finest new art to be found in this city, including contemporary and historic photographs of the American West.

Philabaum Gallery
711 S. Sixth Ave. ☎ **520/884-7404.**

Visitors can stop by Tom Philabaum's glass studio and watch vases, perfume bottles, and bowls being blown, then browse the gallery full of these lovely art glass pieces.

BOOKS

The Book Mark
5001 E. Speedway Blvd. ☎ **520/881-6350.**

This plain-looking storefront doesn't hint at what lies behind it. What you'll find are shelves of densely packed books and books piled on the floor that offer a huge selection, including local authors.

✪ Coyote's Voice
16 S. Eastbourne Ave. (at Broadway Blvd. and Country Club Rd.). ☎ **520/327-6560.**

Located in the Broadway Village, Coyote's Voice specializes in books on Hispanic writers, Mexican fiction and history, and southwestern architecture. It has an active schedule of readings and signings by regional authors.

CRAFTS

✪ Berta Wright Gallery
260 E. Congress St. ☎ **520/882-7043.**

A rich assemblage of imported crafts including Huichol beadwork, southwestern and Mexican jewelry, sculpture, figurines, and a smattering of ethnic clothing here are all selected by the scrutinizing eye of Berta Wright.

Obsidian Gallery

4340 N. Campbell Ave. (at River Rd. in St. Phillip's Plaza). ☎ **520/577-3598.**

Contemporary crafts by artists of national renown fill this gallery. You'll find luminous art glass, unique jewelry, imaginative ceramics, and much more.

✪ Old Town Artisans

186 N. Meyer Ave. ☎ **520/623-6024.**

Housed in a restored 1850s adobe building covering an entire city block of the El Presidio Historic District are 15 rooms brimming with the best of southwestern arts and crafts. You'll find traditional and contemporary designs by more than 400 artisans.

Pink Adobe Gallery

222 E. Congress St. ☎ **520/623-2828.**

This contemporary crafts gallery sells works produced by artists from all over the United States. On a recent visit there were hand-tinted photos, painted-tin folk art, ceramics, one-of-a-kind pieces of furniture, and cases full of unique jewelry.

Tucson Museum of Art Shop

140 N. Main Ave. (in downtown Tucson's Historic District). ☎ **520/624-2333.**

The museum's gift shop offers a colorful and changing selection of southwestern arts and crafts, mostly by local and regional artists.

FASHIONS

Western Wear

Arizona Hatters

3600 N. First Ave. ☎ **520/292-1320.**

If you've decided to outfit yourself in proper Arizona cowboy or cowgirl attire, this is the place to start for the essential cowboy hat by Stetson or any of the other less well known makers.

The Corral Western Wear

4525 E. Broadway Blvd. ☎ **520/322-6001.**

Standard cowboy gear and accoutrements for the more flamboyant wrangler such as turquoise cowboy hats and brightly colored cowboy boots are stocked here.

Western Warehouse

3030 E. Speedway Blvd. ☎ **520/327-8005.**

If you want to put together your western-wear ensemble under one roof, this is the place. It's the largest western-wear store in Tucson and can deck you out in jeans, hats, boots, and Native American jewelry.

There are also branches at 3719 N. Oracle Rd. (☎ **520/293-1808**) and 6701 E. Broadway Blvd. (☎ **520/885-4385**).

Men's & Women's

The Buffalo Exchange

2001 E. Speedway Blvd. ☎ **520/795-0508.**

It's fun to visit the Buffalo Exchange and browse through racks of resale and new clothing at fairly reasonable prices. You'll find a very large selection of things recently in style.

There's another Buffalo Exchange at 7045 E. Tanque Verde Rd. (☎ **520/ 885-8302**).

Men's

Franklin's

5420 E. Broadway Blvd. ☎ **520/747-0680.**

From casual attire such as Hawaiian shirts to business suits, all here is good quality and a favorite place for local guys to shop.

Individual Man

In St. Philip's Plaza, 4320 N. Campbell Ave. ☎ **520/577-2121.**

Unique ties, silk and other natural-fiber shirts, and cotton slacks are colorful and casual, with styles by American and Italian designers.

Women's

Jasmine

423 N. Fourth Ave. ☎ **520/629-0706.**

Fine natural fibers, including washable silks, are the specialty here. The styles range from classic to exotic and fabrics are often hand-loomed. There are southwestern accessories and jewelry to go with the clothes.

Maya Palace

In Plaza Palomino, 2960 N. Swan Rd. ☎ **520/325-6411.**

This small shop features lushly ethnic but very wearable women's clothing in natural fabrics.

A second shop is at El Mercado de Boutiques, 6332 E. Broadway Blvd. (☎ **520/748-0817**).

✪ Rochelle K

5350 E. Broadway Blvd. ☎ **520/745-4600.**

With everything from the latest in the little black dress to casual and drapey silks and linens, Rochelle K attracts a well-heeled clientele. There are also beautiful accessories and jewelry.

Urbane Cowgirl

303 E. Congress St. ☎ **520/882-2822.**

This is the place for citified cowgirl getups. From arty cowgirl boots to crushed-velvet dresses and blouses to Victorian dresses made from tablecloth lace, you'll find it here. Designer/owner Martin McCrea is the creator of some of these fashions.

Gifts/Souvenirs

B&B Cactus Farm

11550 E. Speedway Blvd. ☎ **520/721-4687.**

This plant nursery is devoted exclusively to cacti and succulents. The store can pack your purchase for traveling or can ship it anywhere in the United States. The farm is worth a visit just to see the amazing variety of cactus on display.

Picánte

306 E. Congress St. (downtown). ☎ **520/622-8807.**

There's a lot of things to look at and buy in this tiny shop, which has a plethora of Hispanic-theme icons and accessories, including milagros, Day of the Dead skeletons, Mexican crosses, jewelry and greeting cards.

Señor Coyote
In the Tucson Mall, 4500 N. Oracle Rd. ☎ **520/888-8884.**

The bright colors of contemporary southwestern art have become all the rage recently, and at Señor Coyote you'll find those great colors in T-shirts, sweatshirts, hats, and posters. Howling coyotes and cow skulls are very popular designs.

JEWELRY

Beth Friedman Jewelry
186 N. Meyer Ave. ☎ **520/622-5013.**

Located in the Old Town Artisans complex, this shop sells jewelry from southwestern Native American and international designers.

✪ Thunderbird Shop
In the Broadway Village, 3000 E. Broadway Blvd. ☎ **520/795-0086.**

In business since 1927, this shop specializes in high-quality Native American jewelry as well as creating its own contemporary designs. It also has loose stones and will create custom jewelry for you.

Turquoise Door
In St. Phillip's Plaza, 4330 N. Campbell Ave. (at River Rd.). ☎ **520/299-7787.**

The southwestern contemporary jewelry here is among the most stunning in the city and is made with opals, diamonds, lapis lazuli, amethyst, and the ubiquitous turquoise. There are also baskets, sculptures, bronzes, rugs.

Another location is at 5675 N. Swan Rd. (☎ **520/299-7551**).

The Turquoise Land
In the Park Mall, 5870 E. Broadway Blvd. ☎ **520/745-1383.**

Masses of Native American turquoise-and-silver jewelry at reasonable prices make this a good stop for anyone looking to accessorize à la Southwest. Most of the materials used are natural.

MALLS/SHOPPING CENTERS

Broadway Village
Broadway Blvd. and Country Club Rd.

Broadway Village is the oldest shopping center in Tucson, as evidenced by the lettering painted on the brick walls. Stacia's Cafe and Coyote's Voice Bookstore, along with other small shops, are housed here.

El Con Mall
3601 E. Broadway Blvd. ☎ **520/795-9958.**

With more than 140 establishments, including major department stores, theaters, and restaurants, this is Tucson's oldest regional shopping mall.

El Mercado
6336 E. Broadway Blvd. ☎ **520/747-4100.**

This small Mexican-style *mercado* (market) contains 19 interesting shops and several restaurants, including the popular Good Earth Restaurant.

Park Mall Shopping Center
5870 E. Broadway Blvd. (at Wilmot Rd.). ☎ **520/748-1222.**

Offering everything from department stores to a post office, this mall has 120 shops and provides a courtesy hotel shuttle.

Plaza Palomino
2970 N. Swan Rd. ☎ **520/795-1177.**

This small shopping plaza is built in the style of a Spanish hacienda with a courtyard and fountains, and is home to some of Tucson's little boutiques, specialty shops, galleries, and restaurants.

✪ St. Philip's Plaza
4300 N. Campbell Ave. (at River Rd.). ☎ **520/529-2775.**

This *yup*scale southwestern-style shopping center includes two excellent restaurants, a luxury beauty salon, and numerous shops and galleries, including Bahti Indian Arts and Turquoise Door jewelry.

The Tucson Mall
4500 N. Oracle Rd. ☎ **520/293-7330.**

The foothills of northern Tucson have become shopping center central, and this is the largest of the malls. You'll find more than 200 merchants in this busy two-story skylit complex.

NATIVE AMERICAN ARTS & CRAFTS

Bahti Indian Arts
In St. Philip's Plaza, 4300 N. Campbell Ave. ☎ **520/577-0290.**

Family owned for more than 40 years, this store sells fine Native American arts and crafts. You'll find jewelry, baskets, sculpture, paintings, books, weavings, kachina dolls, and much more.

✪ Huntington Trading Company
111 E. Congress St. (downtown). ☎ **520/628-8578.**

Grotesque and humorous Yaqui masks glare at you from the walls of this store specializing in American and Mexican tribal arts and crafts. There are also Tohono O'odham and Tarahumara baskets, Huichol bead sculptures, Casas Grandes and Oaxacan pottery, and paintings and sculptures by various artists.

✪ Indian Territory
5639 N. Swan Rd. (on the northwest corner with Sunrise Dr.). ☎ **520/577-7961.**

Despite the location in the foothills in a mall, it's a bit like an old museum in here, with hardwood floors and antique display cases full of Plains and Southwest Native American arts and crafts and regalia. Though much of the store is devoted to new works, you'll also find rare old pieces.

✪ The Kaibab Shops
2841–43 N. Campbell Ave. ☎ **520/795-6905.**

This store has been in business for almost 50 years and offers one of the best selections of Native American arts and crafts in Tucson. This is a complex of shops where you can also find high-quality jewelry, Mexican pottery, home furnishings, glassware, kachinas, and antique retablos.

Medicine Man Gallery
In Santa Fe Center, 7000 E. Tanque Verde Rd. ☎ **520/722-7798.**

If you've decided you want to take home a Navajo rug, this is a place to do your shopping in Tucson. There are also Mexican and other Hispanic textiles, Acoma pottery, and other Indian crafts.

✪ Morning Star Traders
2020 E. Speedway Blvd. (next door to the Plaza Hotel). ☎ **520/881-5694.**

With hardwood floors and a museumlike atmosphere, this store features museum-quality goods in the way of antique Navajo rugs, kachinas, furniture, and a huge selection of jewelry.

Silverbell Trading
In Casa Adobes Plaza, 7007 N. Oracle Rd. ☎ **520/797-6852.**

Not your usual run-of-the-mill crafts store, this shop carries unique items that the shopkeeper has obviously sought out. Small items such as stone Navajo corn maidens and animals carved from sandstone caught our eye.

Another store is next to Lil Abner's Steakhouse, far northwest of the city, at 8501 N. Silverbell Rd. (☎ **520/744-3443**).

OUTDOOR EQUIPMENT

Bob's Bargain Barn
2230 N. Country Club Rd. (south of Grant Rd.). ☎ **520/325-3409.**

From that last-minute camping necessity to lightweight desert clothing to a major purchase like hiking boots, Bob's has what you need at good prices.

10 Tucson After Dark

Tucson after dark is a much easier landscape to negotiate than the vast cultural sprawl of the Phoenix area. Instead of having numerous performing arts centers all over the suburbs as in the Valley of the Sun, Tucson has a more centralized nightlife scene. The **Downtown Arts District** is the center of all the action, with the Temple of Music and Art, the Tucson Convention Center Music Hall, a small avant-garde theater, and several nightclubs. The **University of Arizona campus,** only a mile away, is another hot spot for entertainment.

The best place to look for entertainment listings is in the *Tucson Weekly.* Here you'll find thorough listings of concerts, theater and dance performances, and club offerings. The newspaper is free and can be picked up in convenience stores and record stores, among other places. For information on the current week's music performances on the University of Arizona campus, call the **MusiCall hotline** (☎ **520/621-2998**).

Tickets to many concerts and theater performances are available at **Dillard's** department store box offices or by calling the Dillard's telephone reservation line (☎ **800/638-4253**). **TicketMaster** (☎ **520/321-1000**) also sells tickets to some Tucson performances, but they don't have any sales outlets here. Students can get $6 rush tickets to performances of the Arizona Theatre Company at the Temple of Music and Art. For more information, call 520/622-2823.

THE PERFORMING ARTS

To a certain extent, Tucson is a clone of Phoenix when it comes to the perform-ing arts. Three of Tucson's major performance companies—the Arizona Opera

Company, Ballet Arizona, and the Arizona Theatre Company—spend half their time in Phoenix. This means that whatever gets staged in Phoenix also gets staged in Tucson. This city does, however, have its own symphony, and Tucson manages to sustain a more diversified theater scene as well, with more experimental theater getting staged here.

CLASSICAL MUSIC, OPERA & DANCE

The **Tucson Symphony Orchestra** (☎ **520/792-9155** for information, 520/882-8585 for tickets), which performs at the Tucson Convention Center Music Hall, 260 S. Church Ave., is the oldest continuously performing symphony in the Southwest; tickets run $7 to $26.

Opera fans can catch the **Arizona Opera Company** (☎ **520/293-4336**), performing at the Tucson Convention Center Music Hall, 260 S. Church Ave. Tickets go for $12 to $56. This company performs both in Phoenix and Tucson.

Tucson's dance scene is dominated by **Ballet Arizona** (☎ **520/882-5022**), which splits its season between Tucson and Phoenix. Productions usually include well-known ballets as well as new works by regional choreographers, and performances are at different venues around town. Tickets are $16 to $65.

THEATER

Tucson doesn't have a lot of theater companies, but what few it does have stage a surprisingly diverse sampling of both classic and contemporary plays.

The **Arizona Theatre Company (ATC)** (☎ **520/622-2823**), which performs at the Temple of Music and Art, 330 S. Scott Ave., splits its time between here and Phoenix and is the state's top professional theater company. Each season sees a mix of comedy, drama, and Broadway-style musical shows; tickets cost $17 to $26.

Performing primarily Broadway musicals, the **Southern Arizona Light Opera Company** (☎ **520/323-7888**), which performs at the Tucson Convention Center Music Hall, 260 S. Church Ave., is a community theater company. Tickets run $15 to $30.

If you enjoy new works by unknown playwrights, check the schedule of the **A.K.A. Theatre,** 125 E. Congress St. (☎ **520/623-7852**), a company that often stages plays by local playwrights. This company also does late shows on Friday and Saturday nights. Tickets cost $7 to $10.

For yet more daring and experimental theater, there's the **Invisible Theatre,** 1400 N. First Ave. (☎ **520/882-9721**), a tiny theater in a converted laundry building that has been home to Tucson's most experimental theater for 25 years. Tickets here go for $10 to $20.

The West just wouldn't be the West without good old-fashioned melodramas, and the **Gaslight Theatre,** 7010 E. Broadway Blvd. (☎ **520/886-9428**), is where evil villains, stalwart heroes, and defenseless heroines pound the boards in Tucson. You can boo and hiss, cheer and sigh as the predictable stories unfold on stage. It's all great fun for kids and adults. Tickets are $12.95 for adults, $10.95 for students and senior citizens, and $6 for children.

PERFORMING ARTS CENTERS & HALLS

Tucson's largest performance venue is the **Tucson Convention Center Music Hall,** 260 S. Church Ave. (☎ **520/791-4266**). It's the home of the Tucson Symphony Orchestra and is where the Arizona Opera Company and Ballet Arizona usually perform when they're in town. This hall also hosts many touring companies. The box office is open Monday through Saturday from 10am to 6pm; tickets run $10 to $65.

However, the **Temple of Music and Art,** 330 S. Scott Ave. (☎ **520/622-2823** or 520/884-8210), a restored historic theater dating back to 1927, is the centerpiece of the Tucson theater scene. The 605-seat Alice Holsclaw Theatre is the Temple's main stage, but there's also the 90-seat Cabaret Theatre. You'll also find an art gallery and a restaurant here. Free tours of the Temple of Art and Music are given on Monday and Saturday mornings. The box office is open Monday through Friday from 10am to 6pm, on Saturday from 10am to 5pm, and on Sunday from 10am to 2pm. Tickets range from $7 to $30.

Located on the campus of the University of Arizona, **Centennial Hall,** at University Boulevard and Park Avenue (☎ **520/621-3341**), is one of Tucson's main venues for touring national musical acts, international performance companies, and Broadway shows. A large stage and excellent sound system permit large-scale productions. The box office is open Monday through Friday from 10am to 5pm and 1$\frac{1}{2}$ hours before curtain time. Tickets go for $15 to $45.

The **Center for the Arts,** Pima Community College (West Campus), 2202 W. Anklam Rd. (☎ **520/884-6456**), is another good place to check for performances. It offers a wide variety of shows, including the occasional name act, with tickets priced at $4 to $15.

OUTDOOR VENUES & SERIES

Between April and October, Tucsonans head to Reid Park's **DeMeester Outdoor Performance Center,** at Country Club Road and East 22nd Street (☎ **520/ 791-4079**), for performances under the stars. This amphitheater is the site of performances by the Parks and Recreation Community Theatre and other production companies, as well as frequent music performances.

The **Tucson Jazz Society** (☎ **520/743-3399**), which books a few well-known jazz musicians each year, sponsors different outdoor music series throughout the year, sometimes at St. Philip's Plaza shopping center and sometimes downtown at the Plaza of the Pioneers next to City Hall. The society manages to book quite a few well-known jazz musicians.

THE CLUB & MUSIC SCENE

Check the "Big Noise" section of the *Tucson Weekly* for club listings. You can pick up the *Tucson Weekly* at convenience stores.

A COMEDY CLUB

Laffs Comedy Caffè

The Village, 2900 E. Broadway Blvd. ☎ **520/323-8669.** Cover $5–$8.

This stand-up comedy club has professional comedians from around the country performing Wednesday through Sunday nights.

COUNTRY

Cactus Moon Café

5470 E. Broadway Blvd. (on the east side of town at the corner of Craycroft Rd.). ☎ **520/ 748-0049.** Cover $3 Fri–Sat.

A younger to middle-aged crowd frequents this large and glitzy nightclub for top 40 and rock, but mostly for country music (free dance lessons in the early part of the week) and drink specials.

The Maverick
4702 E 22nd. St. (at Swan Rd.) ☎ **520/748-0456.** Cover $2 Fri–Sat.

Compared to a club like Wild Wild West, this country-and-western place is small and more personable. Basically it attracts an older crowd, but there's usually a mix of people. Occasionally live bands play.

Wild Wild West
4385 W. Ina Rd. ☎ **520/744-7744.** Cover $3 Fri–Sat.

This country-music club used to be a bowling alley, and since the conversion it has the biggest and best dance floor in Tucson. In fact there's an acre of floorboard for all you two-steppers. The crowd is mixed ages and dance lessons are available. Closed Monday.

ROCK, JAZZ & BLUES

Berky's Bar
5769 E. Speedway Blvd. ☎ **520/296-1981.** Cover $3 after 8pm.

The blues wail seven nights a week at this dark and smoky bar.

Berky's on Fourth
424 N. Fourth Ave. ☎ **520/622-0376.** Cover $1–$3.

Most of what you'll hear here is great live blues, but alternative music and jam sessions happen regularly.

Chicago Bar
5954 E. Speedway Blvd. ☎ **520/748-8169.** Cover $3 Wed–Sat.

Transplanted Chicagoans love to watch their home teams on the TVs here at this neighborhood bar, but there's also live music ranging from the house blues band to reggae six nights a week.

Club Congress
311 E. Congress St. ☎ **520/622-8848.** Cover $1–$15.

Just off the lobby of the restored Hotel Congress (now a youth hostel), Club Congress is one of Tucson's main alternative-music venues. There are usually a couple of nights of live music each week.

Cushing Street Bar & Restaurant
343 S. Meyer Ave. ☎ **520/622-7984.** Cover $2–$15.

The building may be 100 years old, but the music at this club in the Barrio Historico District is certainly up-to-the-minute. Live rock, blues, and folk music by local and national acts can be heard nightly.

MARIACHI MUSIC

El Mariachi Restaurant
106 W. Drachman St. ☎ **520/791-7793.** No cover.

Although the view of the stage is better and the music is just as good, El Mariachi just doesn't have the atmosphere you'll find at La Fuente (see below). The band International Mariachi America performs Wednesday through Sunday night and the menu features steaks, shrimp, and Mexican food in the $9 to $17 range. Shows are at 7, 8:30, and 10pm. Reservations are recommended.

La Fuente
1749 N. Oracle Rd. ☎ **520/623-8659.** No cover.

La Fuente is Tucson's most popular spot to catch Mexico's most popular traditional music. The music starts after 6pm Wednesday through Sunday night. La Fuente is the largest Mexican restaurant in Tucson and serves up good food as well as music. If you just want to listen to the music, you can sit in the lounge.

DANCE CLUBS/DISCOS

The Cage
5851 E. Speedway Blvd. ☎ 520/885-3030. Cover $4.

The youngish crowd here turns out for the drink specials, pounding industrial and techno rock, and the 10-foot video screen. It's very casual and very big.

THE BAR & PUB SCENE

The Arizona Inn
2200 E. Elm St. ☎ 520/325-1541.

If you're looking for a quiet and comfortable scene, the piano music in the Audubon Lounge at the Arizona Inn is sure to soothe your soul. The gardens here are beautiful.

The Bum Steer
1910 N. Stone Ave. ☎ 520/884-7377.

This huge red barn is a hit with the college crowd and has stuff hanging from every inch of wall and ceiling space in the joint. There's a volleyball court out back for those who want to pretend this is the beach.

Gentle Ben's Brewing Co.
At the corner of Tyndall Ave. and University Blvd. ☎ 520/624-4177.

Gentle Ben's is Tucson's favorite microbrewery, with daily food and drink specials. The crowd is young and active.

¡Toma! Bar
311 N. Court Ave. (in the El Presidio Historic District). ☎ 520/622-1922.

Owned by the family who operates El Charro Café next door, this café has a humorous and festive atmosphere with a Mexican hat sculpture in the courtyard. Happy hour is Friday from 5 to 8pm, and Latino and salsa music happens Friday and Saturday nights.

COCKTAILS WITH A VIEW

Just about all the best vistas in town are at foothills resorts, but luckily they don't mind sharing with nonguests.

Desert Garden Lounge
In the Westin La Paloma, 3800 E. Sunrise Dr. ☎ 520/742-6000.

If you'd like to gaze up at the Santa Catalina Mountains, head over to the Desert Garden Lounge, where there's live entertainment and southwestern decor.

✪ Flying V Bar and Grill
In Loews Ventana Canyon Resort, 7000 N. Resort Dr. ☎ 520/299-2020.

If you can't afford the lap of luxury, at least you can pull up a chair next to the large waterfall at this popular watering hole. The view over the golf course to the lights of Tucson far below is one of the best in the city, although trees have grown up to partially obscure the view.

Lookout Lounge
In the Westward Look Resort, 245 E. Ina Rd. ☎ **520/297-1151.**

The Westward Look is one of Tucson's oldest resorts and took to the hills long before it became the fashionable place to be. The nighttime view of twinkling city lights and stars is unmatched. There's live music Thursday through Saturday nights.

SPORTS BARS

Famous Sam's
3620 N. First Ave. ☎ **520/292-0314.**

With 10 locations around the city, Famous Sam's keeps a lot of Tucson's sports fans happy. Other convenient locations include 1830 E. Broadway Blvd. (☎ **520/884-0119**), 7930 E. Speedway Blvd. (☎ **520/290-9666**), and 4801 E. 29th St. (☎ **520/748-1975**).

Trophies
In the Hotel Park Tucson, 5151 E. Grant Rd. ☎ **520/323-6262.**

On weekends and any time there's an Arizona sports team playing, this place gets packed. If you want some sports camaraderie, check it out.

GAY BARS

Ain't Nobody's Bizness
2900 E. Broadway Blvd. ☎ **520/318-4838.**

This bar, located in a mall, has a couple of pool tables and a dance floor and caters to lesbians and their friends.

Club 2520
2520 N. Oracle Rd. ☎ **520/882-5799.**

If you want to listen to some country music and learn a bit of line dancing, this is the best place in town.

Hours
3455 E. Grant Rd. ☎ **520/327-3390.**

With a pool table and dance floor, this casual neighborhood bar is one of Tucson's most popular gay and lesbian hangouts, but straight people come here too.

MORE ENTERTAINMENT
A MOVIE HOUSE

The Loft Cinema
3233 E. Speedway Blvd. ☎ **520/795-7777.**

This film house shows foreign films, independent features, and other non-mainstream films.

11 Special & Free Events

Because of the excellent weather year-round, Tucson hosts numerous outdoor festivals, celebrations, and events. Many are free and are held downtown and in the city's parks. See "Tucson Calendar of Events" in Chapter 3 for a complete list.

One year-round favorite free event is **Downtown Saturday Night,** a celebration of the Downtown Arts District held on the first and third Saturday of each month. From 7 to 10pm on these nights, the district—which includes East Pennington Street, East Congress Street, and East Broadway Boulevard between Fourth Avenue and Stone Avenue—comes alive with art gallery openings, late-evening shopping, and music performances on the street and in the cafés. For more information, call the Tucson Arts District Partnership at 520/624-9977. You'll also hear live music if you wander over to the Old Town Artisans crafts market in the El Presidio Historic District.

TUCSON CALENDAR OF EVENTS

January
- **Northern Telecom Open Golf Tournament,** Tucson National Golf Course. Call 800/882-7660 for information. Mid-January.

February
- **Indian Arts Benefit Fair,** Old Town Artisans. Craft sales and entertainment. For more information, phone 520/623-6024. Early February.
- **Tucson Gem & Mineral Show,** Tucson Convention Center. This huge show is open to the public as well as to wholesalers. For details, call 520/322-5773. Early to mid-February.
- **Tucson Rodeo Parade,** Tucson Rodeo Grounds. The world's largest nonmotorized parade. Phone 520/741-2233 for information. Late February.
- **La Fiesta de los Vaqueros,** Tucson Rodeo Grounds. Cowboy festival and rodeo. Call 520/741-2233 for details. Late February.

March
- **Wa:k Powwow,** Mission San Xavier del Bac. Tohono O'odham celebration featuring many southwestern Native American groups. Call 520/294-5727 for more information. Early March.
- **Yaqui Easter Lenten Ceremony,** Old Pasqua Village. Religious ceremonies blending Christian and Yaqui Native American beliefs. For further information, phone 520/791-4609. Holy Week.

April
- **San Xavier Pageant & Fiesta,** Mission San Xavier del Bac. A celebration of the mission's founding. For details, call 520/624-1817, or 800/638-8350. The Friday after Easter.
- **Tucson International Mariachi Conference,** citywide. Mariachi bands from all over come to compete. Call 520/884-9920, ext. 243, for more information. Mid- to late April.

May
- **Cinco de Mayo,** Kennedy Park. Mexican food, music, and dancing. Phone 520/623-8344 for more details. May 5–6.
- **Mountain Lemmon Summer Music Festival,** Mount Lemmon Ski Area. A series of open-air concerts. Call 520/576-1321 schedule and ticket information. Weekends mid-May to mid-July.
- **Summerset Suite,** Tucson Museum of Art. Open-air jazz concerts. For details, call 520/743-3399. May to July.

July
- **Independence Day.** Fireworks on "A Mountain" and a celebratory parade downtown. Call 520/791-4860 or 520/791-4873 for information. July 4.

August
- **La Fiesta de San Agustín,** Arizona Historical Society. Celebration to honor the patron saint of Tucson. For more information, phone 520/628-5774. Late August.

October
- **Tucson Heritage Experience Festival (T.H.E.),** El Presidio Park. Celebration of Tucson's ethnic diversity. Phone 520/888-8816 for details. Mid-October.
- **Fiesta de los Chiles,** Tucson Botanical Gardens. Lots of hot chiles, crafts, and music. For more information, call 520/326-9686. Mid- to late October.
- **Tucson Blues Festival,** Reid Park. Local, regional, and national blues masters perform. Call 520/791-4873 for more details. Mid-October.

November
- **Western Music Festival,** varying locations. Concerts and workshops by western music performers. Phone 520/323-3311 for details. Mid-November.
- **Indian Arts Show & Benefit,** Old Town Artisans. Handcrafts and entertainment. For more information, phone 520/623-6024. Mid- to late November.

December
- **Lumináría Nights,** Tucson Botanical Gardens. A glowing display of holiday lights. For details, call 520/326-9255. Early December.
- **Fourth Avenue Street Fair,** Fourth Avenue. Outdoor arts-and-crafts festival. Phone 520/624-5004 for more information. Early December.
- **Fiesta de Guadalupe,** De Grazia Gallery in the Sun. Celebration of Mexico's patron saint. For further information, call 520/299-9192. Early December.
- **Las Posadas,** varying locations. A tradition from Mexico where children reenact Joseph and Mary's search for an inn. Phone 520/622-6911 for details. Mid-December.

12 Easy Excursions from Tucson

NORTH OF TUCSON

Biosphere 2 Visitor Center
Ariz. 77, mile marker 96.5. ☎ **520/896-6200.** Admission $12.95 adults, $10.95 seniors, $6 children 6–17, free for children 5 and under. Daily 9am–5pm. Closed Dec 25. Take Oracle Road north out of Tucson and continue north on U.S. 89 and Ariz. 77 until you see the Biosphere sign.

For two years, beginning in September 1991, four men and four women were locked inside this airtight, 3-acre greenhouse in the desert 35 miles north of Tucson near the town of Oracle. During their tenure in Biosphere 2 (earth is considered Biosphere 1) they conducted experiments on how the earth, basically a giant greenhouse, manages to support all the planet's life forms. Similar experiments continue to be undertaken at Biosphere 2, but today this giant science project is also a major tourist attraction. Tours of the facility are offered daily. Although you aren't allowed into Biosphere 2 itself, you can learn about the project at an orientation center and then take a guided tour around the outside of the main buildings. Tours also take you through the Biome Ecology Laboratories, which give you an idea of what it's like inside Biosphere 2, as does a video presentation. An interactive display area provides entertainment for children. Whether you see it as science or a tourist attraction, there's plenty to see and do here. Also on the grounds are a hotel, restaurant, café, bookstore, and gift shop.

WEST OF TUCSON

Kitt Peak National Observatory

Off Ariz. 86. ☎ 520/325-9200. Admission $2 donation. Daily 9am–4pm. Closed Jan 1, Thanksgiving, and Dec 24–25. Take Ariz. 86 southwest from Tucson; in about 40 miles you'll see the turnoff for Kitt Peak.

Southern Arizona likes to brag about how many sunny days it has each year, and the nights are just as clear. The starry skies have lured more astronomical observatories to the Tucson vicinity than to any other region of the world. Southern Arizona has come to be known as the "Astronomy Capital of the World," and the largest of the astronomical observatories here is the famous Kitt Peak National Observatory. Located in the Quinlan Mountains, 56 miles southwest of Tucson, the observatory is atop 6,882-foot Kitt Peak. The lack of lights in the surrounding Tohono O'odham Reservation makes the night sky here as brilliant as anywhere on earth.

There are five major telescopes operating at Kitt Peak. The McMath telescope is the world's largest solar telescope. Its system of mirrors channels an image of the sun deep into the mountain before reflecting it back up to the observatory where scientists study the resulting 30-inch-diameter image. The 158-inch Mayall telescope features a 30,000-pound quartz mirror and is used for studying distant regions of the universe.

Guided tours are given daily. There's also a visitor center and museum. There's no restaurant at the observatory, but there is a picnic area.

Organ Pipe Cactus National Monument

Ariz. 85, Ajo. ☎ 520/387-6849. Admission $4 per car; $8 per night for camping. Visitor center, daily 8am–5pm. Take Ariz. 86 West to Ariz. 85 South.

Located 145 miles west of Tucson, Organ Pipe Cactus National Monument is a preserve for the rare organ pipe cactus. This massive cactus resembles the saguaro in many ways, but instead of forming a single main trunk, it forms many trunks, some 20 feet tall, that resemble organ pipes. This is a rugged region with few towns or services. Be sure to gas up your car before leaving Ajo. Inside the park there's only one campground, and the only roads other than Ariz. 85 are gravel. In the western section of the national monument, 15 miles down a gravel road, is Quitobaquito Spring, which was relied on by Native Americans and pioneers as the only reliable source of water for miles around.

EAST OF TUCSON

Colossal Cave Mountain Park

Vail. ☎ 520/647-7275. Admission $6.50 adults, $5 children 11–16, $3.50 children 6–10, free for children 5 and under. Mar 16–Sept 15, Mon–Sat 8am–6pm, Sun and holidays 8am–7pm; Sept 16–Mar 15, Mon–Sat 9am–5pm, Sun and holidays 9am–6pm.

Located 22 miles east of Tucson off I-10, Colossal Cave may once have served as a bandit hangout. Today, tours through the cave combine a bit of history with a bit of geology. This is a dry cave, where the stalactites, stalagmites, and other formations are no longer actively growing. The 45-minute tours of the cave cover about half a mile, and the temperature is a comfortable 70° to 72°F.

SOUTH OF TUCSON
A MISSILE MUSEUM
Titan Missile Museum
Duval Mine Rd., Green Valley (Exit 69 from I-19). ☎ **520/625-7736.** Admission $5 adults, $4 seniors, $3 children 10–17, free for children 9 and under. May–Oct, Wed–Sun 9am–5pm; Nov–Apr, daily 9am–5pm.

This museum is a deactivated ballistic missile silo and is the only such museum in the country. Tours lead you down into the silo itself so you can get a firsthand look at what it would be like to have your finger on the button.

TUBAC & TUMACACORI

Before Phoenix and Tucson there was Tubac. First settled by the Spanish in 1691 when Fr. Eusebio Francisco Kino established the nearby Tumacacori mission, Tubac was the first European settlement in what is today Arizona. However, the Tubac area had long been home to Native Americans. Archeologists have found evidence that there have been people living along the nearby Santa Cruz River for nearly 10,000 years. The Hohokam dwelt in the area from about A.D. 300 until their mysterious disappearance around 1500. Between 1691 and the present, seven different flags have flown over Tubac, including those of Spain, Mexico, the New Mexico Territory, the Confederacy, the U.S. Territory of Arizona, and the State of Arizona.

Located 60 miles due south of Tucson on I-19, Tubac is today one of Arizona's largest arts communities (others include Sedona, Jerome, and Bisbee). The town's old buildings house more than 80 shops selling fine arts, crafts, and unusual gifts. This amazing collection of artists' studios and galleries makes Tubac one of southern Arizona's most popular destinations, and a small retirement community is beginning to develop in the area. After visiting Tubac Presidio State Historic Park and Tumacacori National Monument to learn about the area's history, you'll probably want to spend some time browsing through these interesting shops. Keep in mind, however, that many of the local artists leave town during the summer, so it's best to visit on weekends then. The busy season is from October to May, and during these months shops are open daily.

The **Tubac Festival of the Arts** is held each year in February. Artists from all over the country participate. In October, **De Anza Days** commemorate Capt. Juan Bautista de Anza's 1775 trek to found San Francisco.

Also, keep in mind that you can also combine a visit to Tubac and Tumacacori with a trip south of the border to Nogales, Mexico.

What to See & Do
In addition to the attractions listed below and the many shops and galleries right in Tubac, there's an interesting store near Tumacacori National Historical Park. **Santa Cruz Chile & Spice Co.** (☎ **520/398-2591**) is a combination store and packing plant. You'll find all things hot (chiles, hot sauces, salsas) arranged on the store's shelves. There's also an amazing assortment of familiar and obscure spices for sale. In the back, you can see various herbs being prepared and packaged.

Tumacacori National Historical Park
Frontage Rd. ☎ **520/398-2341.** Admission $2 per person, free for children 16 and under. Daily 8am–5pm. Closed Thanksgiving and Dec 25. Take I-19 to Exit 29; you'll find Tumacacori 3 miles south of Tubac.

Impressions

It has a melancholy appearance. The walls of the church still stand, no roof, and only the upright piece of the cross. It looks desolate indeed.
      —A traveler named Hays, upon seeing the ruins of Tumacacori in 1849

We in the United States often forget our Spanish heritage, but these mission ruins are a silent reminder of the role that Spanish missionaries played in settling the Southwest. The Tumacacori mission was founded by Jesuit missionary and explorer Fr. Eusebio Francisco Kino in 1691 to convert the Pima. Much of the old adobe mission church still stands, and the Spanish architectural influence can readily be seen. A small museum contains exhibits on mission life and the history of the region. On weekends Native American and Mexican craftspeople give demonstrations of native arts. The **Tumacacori Fiesta,** a celebration of Native American, Hispanic, and Anglo cultures, is held in early December.

Tubac Presidio State Historic Park

Presidio Dr. ☎ **520/398-2252.** Admission $2 adults, $1 children 12–17, free for children 11 and under. Daily 8am–5pm. Closed Dec 25.

The Tubac Presidio has a long and fitful history. Though the Tumacacori mission had been founded in 1691, it was not until 1752 that the Tubac Presidio was established in response to a Pima uprising. In 1775 the presidio's military garrison was moved to Tucson and, with no protection from raiding Apache, most of Tubac's settlers also left the area. A military presence was reestablished in 1787, but after Mexican independence in 1821 insufficient funds led to the closing of the presidio. Villagers once again abandoned Tubac because of Apache attacks. After the Gadsden Purchase, Tubac became part of the United States and was again resettled.

Though little but buried foundation walls remains of the old presidio, Tubac Presidio State Historic Park has exhibits that explain the history of Tubac. There are displays on the Spanish soldiers, Native Americans, religion, and contemporary Hispanic culture in southern Arizona.

Tubac Center of the Arts

Plaza Rd. ☎ **520/398-2371.** Admission free. Sept–May, Tues–Sat 10am–4:30pm, Sun 1–4:30pm. Closed June–Aug.

Tubac is an arts community, and this Spanish colonial building serves as its center for cultural activities. Throughout the season there are workshops, traveling exhibitions, juried shows, an annual craft show, theater and music performances, and a gift shop.

Where to Stay

Tubac Golf Resort

1 Otero Rd. (P.O. Box 1297), Tubac, AZ 85646. ☎ **520/398-2211,** 520/624-5857 in Tucson, or 800/848-7893. 16 rms, 16 casitas. A/C TV TEL. $64–$109 single or double; $77–$143 casita. AE, MC, V.

The Tubac Golf Resort is built on the Otero Ranch, which, in 1789, became the first Spanish land grant in the Southwest. The old ranch stables, which now house the resort's restaurant, are the ranch's oldest buildings and date back to the turn of the century. Red-tile roofs and brick archways remind you that this was once a Spanish hacienda. The guest rooms come in two sizes, but all have brick walls and shuttered windows. The casitas have two patios, tile bathroom counters, beamed ceilings, and beehive fireplaces.

The dining room, in the old ranch stables, has booths that resemble horse stalls, and the menu focuses on mesquite-broiled steaks and seafood. A wall of glass looks out from the lounge to the golf course and mountains beyond. Facilities include an 18-hole golf course, a swimming pool, and a pro shop.

MADERA CANYON

Located in the Coronado National Forest about 40 miles south of Tucson, **Madera Canyon** (☎ **520/281-2296**) is one of southern Arizona's prime bird-watching spots. Because of the year-round water to be found here, Madera Canyon attracts a surprising variety of bird life, and in recent years has also been attracting a surprising number of bird-watchers as well. Avid birders flock to this canyon from around the country in hopes of spotting more than a dozen species of hummingbirds, an equal number of flycatchers, warblers, tanagers, buntings, grosbeaks, and many rare birds that are not found in any other state.

However, before birding became a hot activity, this canyon was popular with families looking for a way to escape the heat down in Tucson. The shady picnic areas and trails still get a lot of use by those who don't carry binoculars. If you're heading out here for the day, arrive early—parking is very limited. To reach Madera Canyon, take Exit 39 from I-19; from the exit, it's another 12 miles southeast. Admission is a $2 donation and the canyon is open daily from dawn to dusk.

Where to Stay

Santa Rita Lodge Nature Resort
HC 70, Box 5444, Sahuarita, AZ 85629. ☎ **520/625-8746.** 8 rms, 4 cabins. $68 single or double in the lodge, $78 single or double in cabins. MC, V.

Located in the shade of Madera Canyon, this lodge is used almost exclusively by bird-watchers, and natural history programs and guided bird walks are offered. The rooms and cabins are large and fairly comfortable.

10 | Southeastern Arizona

Southeastern Arizona—the land between the Mexican border and Interstates 8 and 10 and between New Mexico and Interstate 19—is a region of Arizona that's rapidly gaining national recognition. Much of the region lies around a mile high, which means that the climate is quite temperate. This good weather has attracted thousands of retirees to the area in recent years. However, a century ago it was gold and silver that lured prospectors and fortune seekers to what was then considered a godforsaken wasteland. Tombstone, "the town too tough to die," was the most infamous of the region's mining towns, but others such as Bisbee, which has recently become a popular weekend destination, survived long after the mines shut down in Tombstone. In the past few years yet another type of visitor has discovered this region—bird-watchers. The mountains of southeastern Arizona are home to more than a dozen species of hummingbirds, as well as many other species of birds that are found nowhere else in the United States. Aside from Tucson, which can be considered part of southeastern Arizona but is so large that it was given its own chapter (see Chapter 9), this region is without any major cities. Giant saguaro cacti cover the slopes of the Sonora Desert throughout much of southeastern Arizona. However, numerous mountain ranges also rise up above the desert. Cacti give way to pines in the cool mountains, where passing clouds bring snow and rain. Narrow canyons and broad valleys, fed by the rain and snow melting on the high peaks, provide habitats for birds and other wildlife unique to the region.

Many of the high valleys between the mountain ranges receive enough rain to support some of the best grasslands in the country. This is prime grazing land, and huge ranches have sprawled across the landscape for more than a century.

Perhaps because of this prime ranchland, it was here that much of America's now-famous western history took place. Wyatt Earp and the Clantons shot it out at Tombstone's O.K. Corral, and Doc Holiday played his cards. Cochise and Geronimo staged the last Native American rebellions from strongholds in the rugged mountains of this region, cavalries charged against the Apache, and prospectors scoured the wastelands in search of mineral wealth, leaving behind them a string of ghost towns.

What's Special About Southeastern Arizona

Natural Spectacles
- The rocks of Chiricahua National Monument.

Bird-Watching
- Ramsey Canyon Preserve, home to 14 species of hummingbirds.
- Patagonia–Sonoita Creek Sanctuary, home to more than 200 species of birds.

Monuments
- The Coronado National Memorial, commemorating the early Spanish explorer Francisco Vásquez de Coronado.
- Cochise Stronghold, the rugged mountains where this Apache chief and his men hid from U.S. troops.

Buildings
- The Gadsden Hotel in Douglas, featuring a classic grand lobby.

Museums
- The Amerind Foundation, in Texas Canyon near Willcox, with an outstanding collection of art and artifacts from Native American cultures.

Great Towns/Villages
- Bisbee, a former copper-mining town that has become an artists' community.
- Tombstone, "the town too tough to die," home of the O.K. Corral.

Shopping
- Nogales, Mexico, where Mexican crafts are available at low prices.

The very first Spanish expedition into the American Southwest, led by Francisco Vásquez de Coronado in 1540, marched up the San Pedro River valley past present-day Sierra Vista, where a national memorial commemorates his unfruitful search for the Seven Cities of Cibola. These cities were rumored to be filled with gold and precious jewels, but all Coronado found were poor Native American pueblos. Nearly 150 years later Fr. Eusebio Francisco Kino would found a string of Jesuit missions across the Pimeria Alta, a region that would later become northern Mexico and southern Arizona. Converting the Native Americans and building mission churches, Father Kino left a long-lasting mark on this region. Today two of the missions founded by Father Kino—San Xavier del Bac and San José de Tumacacori—still stand (see "Attractions" and "Easy Excursions," in Chapter 9 on Tucson).

Native Americans still make their homes here in southern Arizona, and the Papago Indian Reservation covers a vast expanse south of Casa Grande and west of Tucson. This reservation belongs to the Tohono O'odham tribe, who were formerly known as the Papagos. Well known for their basketry, the Tohono O'odham also sponsor one of the largest annual Native American festivals in the country. The O'odham Tash is held each February in Casa Grande and attracts dozens of tribes, who participate in rodeos, parades, arts and crafts exhibits, and dance performances. Near Willcox, the Amerind Foundation, one of the state's finest museums dedicated to the cultures of Southwest peoples, provides insightful exhibits on Native American culture.

1 Nogales

175 miles S of Phoenix, 63 miles S of Tucson, 65 miles W of Sierra Vista

Situated on the Mexican border 63 miles south of Tucson, the twin towns of Nogales, Arizona, and Nogales, Sonora, Mexico, (known jointly as Ambos Nogales) together form a bustling border town. All day long U.S. citizens cross into Mexico to shop for bargains on handcrafted items and duty-free imports from around the world, while Mexican citizens cross into the United States to buy products not available in their own country. Nogales is also the busiest produce port in the world. During the harvest season more than 700 truckloads of produce daily cross into the United States from Mexico.

ESSENTIALS
GETTING THERE

By Bus   Citizens/Grayline Bus has service between Nogales and Tucson. There's also bus service from Mexico. The bus station is at 35 N. Terrace Ave. Call 520/287-5628 for schedules and rates.

By Car   Nogales is the last town on I-19 before the Mexican border. Arizona 82 leads northeast from town toward Sonoita and Sierra Vista.

VISITOR INFORMATION

For further information on Nogales, contact the **Nogales–Santa Cruz County Chamber of Commerce,** Kino Park, Nogales, AZ 85621 (☎ **520/287-3685**).

WHAT TO SEE & DO

Most people who visit Nogales, Arizona, are here to cross the border to Nogales, Mexico. The favorable exchange rate makes shopping in Mexico very popular with Americans, though most of the items for sale in Mexico are cheaper in Tucson. If you'd like to learn more about the history of this area, stop by the **Pimeria Alta Historical Society,** at the corner of Grand Avenue and Crawford Street (☎ **520/287-4621**), near the border crossing in downtown Nogales. The historical society maintains a small museum, library, and archives on this region of northern Mexico and southern Arizona, which was once known as Pimeria Alta. It's open Tuesday through Friday from 10am to 5pm and on Saturday from 10am to 4pm, and is free to visit.

Just a couple of miles outside Nogales on the road to Patagonia, you'll see signs for the **Arizona Vineyard Winery** (☎ **520/287-7972**). You may not think of Arizona as wine country, but the Spanish began growing grapes and making wine as soon as they arrived in the area several centuries ago. You can taste free samples of white burgundy, Grand Canyon White, Desert Dust, and Rattlesnake Red, among others.

SHOPPING

As you can probably guess, Nogales, Mexico, is a typical border town filled with tiny shops selling Mexican crafts and souvenirs, and dozens of restaurants serving simple Mexican food. Some of the better deals are on wool rugs, which cost a small fraction of what a Navajo rug will cost, but also are not nearly as well made. Pottery is another popular buy, though our personal favorite items are the handblown drinking glasses and pitchers.

Southeastern Arizona

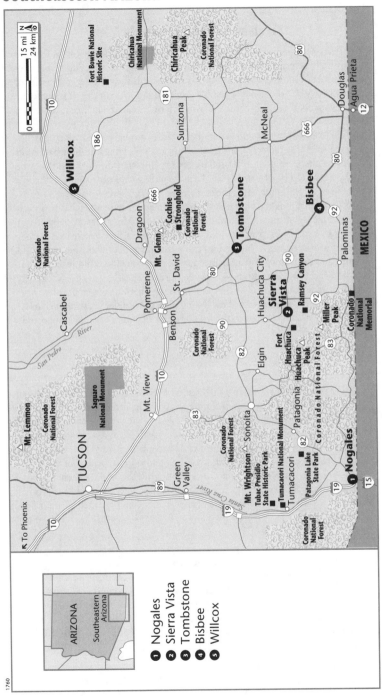

- **1** Nogales
- **2** Sierra Vista
- **3** Tombstone
- **4** Bisbee
- **5** Willcox

Tumbleweed, an Undesirable Alien

The first ones snuck into the country with a load of wheat from Russia. Farmers unwittingly helped these new aliens move around the country, and before anyone realized it an invasion was under way. Though there are several species of plants that go by the name of tumbleweed, it's the Russian thistle (*Salsola kali* var. *tenuifolia*) that has become the bain of farmers and the mainstay of many a western movie.

Able to live on next to no water, these scruffy annual plants, which grow to about 3 feet in diameter, colonize seemingly any soil, no matter how bad. After maturing and setting up to 50,000 seeds per plant, they die down and become dry and brittle. The first strong wind can snap their weakened stems and send a tumbleweed rolling off across the landscape.

With good winds and with miles of treeless plains, tumbleweed has traditionally had plenty of room to roam. But the West is no longer as wide open as it once was. Fences crisscross the land, and when tumbleweeds meet fences they pile up into deep drifts. Sometimes the wind fills gullies with these wayward plants, and the unfortunate homesteader who happened to build his house out of the wind sometimes found his abode buried beneath many feet of thorny tumbleweeds. These days it's drivers on Interstate highways who more often have unfortunate encounters with these rolling plants. Tumbleweeds trapped under cars have been known to catch fire from the heat of a muffler or an inopportune spark.

All the shops and restaurants in Nogales, Mexico, are within walking distance of the border, so unless you're planning to continue farther into Mexico, it's not a good idea to take your car across the border. There are numerous pay parking lots and garages on the U.S. side of the border where your car will be secure for the day. If you should take your car into Mexico, be sure to get Mexican auto insurance before crossing the border—your U.S. auto insurance is not valid. There are plenty of insurance companies set up along the road leading to the border.

Most shops and restaurants in Nogales, Mexico, accept U.S. dollars. You may bring back $400 worth of merchandise duty free, including 1 liter of liquor (if you are 21 or older).

WHERE TO STAY

In addition to the golf resort listed below, you'll find numerous budget chain motels in Nogales. These include the following (see the Appendix for toll-free phone numbers): **Best Western Time Motel,** 921 N. Grand Ave., Nogales, AZ 85621 (☎ **520/287-4627**), charging $36 to $50 double; **Motel 6,** 141 W. Mariposa Rd., Nogales, AZ 85621 (☎ **520/281-2951**), charging $38 double; and **Super 8 Motel,** 543 W. Mariposa Rd., Nogales, AZ 85621 (☎ **520/281-2242**), charging $46 to $51 double.

Rio Rico Resort & Country Club

1069 Camino Caralampi, Rio Rico, AZ 85648. ☎ **520/281-1901** or 800/288-4746. Fax 520/281-7132. 180 rms, 15 suites. A/C TV TEL. $85–$105 double; $100–$155 suite. AE, CB, DC, DISC, MC, V.

A few miles north of Nogales, Rio Rico is the site of a secluded and little-known golf resort that through recent improvements is hoping to siphon off a bit of Tucson's resort business. For now, however, guests tend to be golfing senior citizens contemplating a move to this area. The hotel is built atop a low hill, and all the guest rooms have excellent views over the golf course and desert. The rooms have sliding glass doors that open onto patios or balconies. The resort's dining room sports southwestern decor and features great views and primarily Italian dishes. The adjacent lounge offers the same views. The resort also offers horseback riding, a Mexico shopping shuttle, an 18-hole golf course, pool, whirlpool, sauna, exercise room, four tennis courts, and pro shop.

WHERE TO DINE

✪ La Roca Restaurant

Calle Elias 91, Nogales, Mexico. ☎ **(52)631/2-07-60.** Main courses $7–$14.50. MC, V. Daily 11am–midnight. MEXICAN.

After you pass through the border checkpost, walk 100 feet or so, cross over the railroad tracks on your left, and continue walking away from the border. Within a block, you'll see a narrow street angling toward the big rock wall to your left. La Roca is built into this rock, and is as cool as a cave. Folk art and large paintings in the spacious rooms seem to make the interior glow, and at night the place is lit with candles ensconced on the stone walls. The setting speaks of colonial Spain and is far from the usual picture of a border-town eatery. We selected Guaymas shrimp and chicken mole from the chalkboard menu presented by a professional white-jacketed waiter. The shrimp were exceptionally succulent, and the mole sauce was a brilliantly flavorful balance between chile and chocolate. The margaritas here are delicious—zesty with lime and full of tequila.

Las Vigas Steak Ranch

180 W. Loma St. ☎ **520/287-6641.** Main courses $4.75–$10.50. MC, V. Mon 10am–3pm, Tues–Sun 10am–10pm. Head down Grand Avenue toward the border; before you get to downtown Nogales, watch for Arroyo Boulevard, which forks to the right; Las Vigas is just past the fork. STEAK/MEXICAN.

This is a western-style building with a covered sidewalk in front and old photos of Mexican men and women inside. Animal heads and skins on the walls give Las Vigas a very rustic feel. Meals are inexpensive and filling, and there are daily specials.

Mr. C's Supper Club

282 W. View Point Dr. (off Mariposa Rd.). ☎ **520/281-9000.** Reservations recommended. Main courses $13–$20. DISC, MC, V. Daily 11:30am–midnight. Closed hols. CONTINENTAL.

Located atop a hill on the north side of town, Mr. C's is Nogales's best restaurant. The menu leans heavily toward fresh fish dishes, with the day's menu written over the salad bar. There are fat Guaymas shrimp, escargots, salmon, and tender steaks. Early diners can take advantage of the early-bird specials for $10 to $13. On Thursday and Friday nights there's karaoke in the smoky lounge.

2 Patagonia/Sonoita

Patagonia: 171 miles SE of Phoenix, 60 miles SE of Tucson, 50 miles SW of Tombstone, 19 miles NW of Nogales

The two small communities of Patagonia and Sonoita have become a favorite weekend getaway for Tucsonans. The mild climate, bed-and-breakfast inns, and wineries are the main attractions for many. However, it's Sonoita Creek that manages to attract visitors from all over the country. This creek is one of only a few in the region that flows throughout the year, and consequently attracts an amazing variety of birdlife and bird-watchers.

ESSENTIALS
GETTING THERE
By Car   Sonoita is at the junction of Ariz. 83 and Ariz. 82. Patagonia is 12 miles southwest of Sonoita on Ariz. 82.

VISITOR INFORMATION
For further information on Patagonia and Sonoita, contact the Patagonia Community Association, **Patagonia Visitors Center,** P.O. Box 241, Patagonia, AZ 85624 (☎ **520/394-0060**), which is located in the center of town.

WHAT TO SEE & DO
Patagonia, 18 miles north of Nogales on Ariz. 82, is a historic old mining and ranching town 4,000 feet up in the Patagonia Mountains. Surrounded by higher mountains, the little town has for years been popular with film and television crews. Among the films that have been shot here are *Oklahoma, Red River, A Star Is Born,* and *David and Bathsheba.* Television programs filmed here have included "Little House on the Prairie," "Red Badge of Courage," and "The Young Riders." Today, however, it's bird-watching and tranquillity that are attracting people to this remote town.

The **Patagonia–Sonoita Creek Sanctuary** is a nature preserve owned by the Nature Conservancy and protects a mile and a half of Sonoita Creek riparian (riverside) habitat, which is important to migratory birds. More than 250 species of birds have been spotted on the preserve, which makes this a very popular spot with birders from all over the world. Among the rare birds that may be seen here are 22 species of flycatchers, kingbirds, and phoebes, and the Montezuma quail. A forest of cottonwood trees, some of which are 100 feet tall, lines the creek and is one of the best examples of such a forest left in southern Arizona. At one time forests such as this grew along all the rivers in southern Arizona. The sanctuary is located just outside Patagonia on a dirt road that parallels Ariz. 82.

Patagonia Lake State Park (☎ **520/287-6965**), a popular boating and fishing lake formed by the damming of Sonoita Creek, is 11 miles south of Patagonia. The lake is 2¹/₂ miles long and has been stocked with bass, crappie, bluegill, and catfish. Park facilities include a picnic ground, a campground, and a swimming beach.

Sonoita proper is little more than a crossroads with a few shops and restaurants. Surrounding the community are miles of rolling grasslands that are primarily cattle ranches. However, recent years have seen the planting of several wine vineyards in the area and the Sonoita area is slowly becoming Arizona's wine country. The **R. W. Webb Winery** (☎ **520/762-5777**) is the most accessible of the area's wineries and is located 27 miles north of Sonoita at Exit 281 off I-10. Two miles south of the ghost town of Elgin on Canelo Road, you'll find **Sonoita Vineyards** (☎ **520/455-5893**). Also in the area is the **Santa Cruz Winery** (☎ **520/455-5373**), which at press time was in the process of moving to an as yet undetermined new location (call for directions to wherever they're doing tastings currently).

WHERE TO STAY

Duquesne House

357 Duquesne St., Patagonia, AZ 85624. ☎ **520/394-2732.** 3 suites. $65 suite for two. No credit cards.

This adobe building with a long shady porch across the front was built at the turn of the century as a miner's boarding house and was recently renovated and converted into a B&B. Each guest room has its own entrance off the front porch, and all have sitting rooms and bedrooms. At the back of the house is a screened porch that overlooks the garden and a fish pond.

Rothrock Cottage and Adobe

325 Pennsylvania St., Patagonia, AZ 85624. ☎ **520/394-2952.** 2 cottages. $75 cottage for two. No credit cards.

These two cottages, one an adobe, on a quiet side street in the center of Patagonia have been renovated and now provide guests with cozy rooms to return to after a day of exploring the area. Both cottages come with full kitchens that are stocked with all the ingredients needed to fix your own breakfast. The adobe has two bedrooms, which makes it ideal for two couples traveling together. Both cottages have comfortable living rooms. The shade trees surrounding help keep the rooms cool.

WHERE TO DINE

So far there aren't very many good places to eat in this area. However, for breakfasts, snacks, and light lunches, most people head for **The Ovens of Patagonia** (☎ 520/394-2483), which bakes delicious, if expensive, muffins, breads, stuffed focaccios, and the like. You'll find this bakery right on Ariz. 82 in Patagonia.

Karen's Wine Country Café

Elgin. ☎ **520/455-5282.** Reservations highly recommended. Main courses $14–$15. No credit cards. Thurs and Sun 10am–4pm, Fri–Sat 10am–8pm. SOUTHWESTERN.

This café appears to be all alone in the middle of a vast rolling plain (Elgin is still something of a ghost town), but what a surprise when you walk through the front door. Instead of dusty, beer-drinking cowboys, there are well-dressed urbanites sipping wine and eating focaccia. Karen's is currently an "in" place to eat and there's often a wait for one of the four or five tables inside or maybe twice that many on the cool screened porch. You can order black-bean and jack-cheese ravioli topped with tomatillo sauce and roasted peppers, soups, quiche, and pasta. Our salad was good, but drenched in too much dressing (which is a specialty here). This being wine country, local wines are available.

3 Sierra Vista

189 miles SE of Phoenix, 70 miles SE of Tucson, 33 miles SW of Tombstone, 33 miles W of Bisbee

At 4,620 feet above sea level, surrounded by deserts and mountains, Sierra Vista is blessed with the perfect climate—never too hot, never too cold. However, because it's a long way from any population centers and is not on an Interstate highway, few people know about Sierra Vista. If it weren't for the U.S. Army's Fort Huachuca, it's likely that no one would have ever settled here, but when Camp Huachuca (later to become Fort Huachuca) was founded in 1877, the seeds of Sierra Vista were sown. Today, however, retirees, free from the necessity of living where there are jobs available, have discovered the climate and settled down here.

Though the town itself is modern and has very little character, the surrounding countryside has much to offer. Within a few miles' drive of town are a national conservation area, a national memorial, and a Nature Conservancy preserve. No other area of the United States attracts more attention from birders, who come for the 300 bird species in southeastern Arizona. With its many inexpensive motels, Sierra Vista makes a good base for exploring all of this region.

ESSENTIALS
GETTING THERE

By Plane   America West has regular flights from Phoenix to the Fort Huachuca Airport, 2100 Airport Dr. Call 800/235-9292 for schedules and fares.

By Bus   Bridgewater Bus Lines provides service to Sierra Vista. The station is on 28 Fab Ave.; phone 520/458-3471 for fares and schedules.

By Car   Sierra Vista is located at the junction of Ariz. 90 and Ariz. 92 about 35 miles south of I-10.

VISITOR INFORMATION

For further information on Sierra Vista, contact the **Sierra Vista Chamber of Commerce,** 77 S. Calle Portal, Suite A-140, Sierra Vista, AZ 85635 (☎ **520/ 458-6940,** or 800/288-3861).

WHAT TO SEE & DO
NATURAL AREAS & BIRD-WATCHING

✪ Ramsey Canyon Preserve

Ariz. 92. ☎ **520/378-2785.** Admission $5 suggested donation (free for Nature Conservancy members). Daily 8am–5pm.

A buzzing fills the air in Ramsey Canyon, but it's not the buzzing of mosquitoes. Instead it's the buzzing of curious hummingbirds. Wear bright red clothing when you visit this preserve and you're certain to attract the curious little avian dive bombers, which will mistake you for the world's largest flower. Located 5 miles south of Sierra Vista off Ariz. 92, this wildlife preserve is owned by the Nature Conservancy and is internationally known as home to 14 species of hummingbirds—more than anywhere else in the United States.

Covering only 280 acres, the preserve is situated in a wooded gorge in the Huachuca Mountains. A short nature trail leads through the canyon, with an explanatory guidebook that points out the reasons for and difficulties in preserving Ramsey Canyon; a second trail leads higher up the canyon. There are guided walks as well. Ramsey Creek is a year-round stream, a rarity in this region, and attracts a wide variety of wildlife, including bears, bobcats, and nearly 200 species of birds.

Because the preserve has become very popular and has only a few parking spaces, a parking reservation is required on weekends. During the week, parking is first come, first served. April and May are the busiest time of year here and August and May are the best times to see hummingbirds. To avoid parking problems, you can stay in a cabin at the preserve (see "Where to Stay," below, for details).

Coronado National Memorial

Montezuma Canyon Rd. ☎ **520/458-9333** or 520/366-5515. Admission free. Daily 8am–5pm.

About 20 miles south of Sierra Vista is a 5,000-acre memorial dedicated to Francisco Vásquez de Coronado, the first European to explore this region. Coronado, leading more than 700 people, left Compostela, Mexico, on February 23, 1540, in search of the fabled Seven Cities of Cibola. These cities were said to be rich in gold and jewels, and Coronado had dreams of becoming wealthy from his expedition. Coronado led his band of weary men and women up the valley of the San Pedro River sometime between 1540 and 1542. The forested Montezuma Pass, in the center of the memorial, is situated at 6,575 feet and provides far-reaching views of Sonora, Mexico, to the south, the San Pedro River to the east, and several mountain ranges and valleys to the west. A visitor center tells the story of Coronado's fruitless quest for riches, and features a wildlife observation area where you might see some of the memorial's 140 or more species of birds.

San Pedro Riparian National Conservation Area

Ariz. 90. ☎ **520/458-3559.** Admission free. Daily 24 hours.

Located 8 miles east of Sierra Vista, the San Pedro Riparian National Conservation Area is a rare example of a natural riparian (riverside) habitat. Over the past 100 years the southwestern landscape has been considerably altered by the human hand. Most deleterious of these changes has been the loss of 90% of the region's free-flowing year-round rivers and streams that once provided water and protection to myriad plants and animals, including humans. Fossil findings from this area indicate that people were living along this river 11,000 years ago. At that time this area was not a desert but a swamp, and the San Pedro River is all that remains of this ancient wetland (today there isn't much water on the surface because most of the river water has flowed underground since an earthquake a century ago). The conservation area is particularly popular with birders, who have a chance of spotting more than 300 species of birds here. Also living along the river are 80 species of mammals, 14 species of fish, and 40 species of amphibians and reptiles.

There are three main parking areas for the conservation area, at the bridges over the San Pedro River on Ariz. 92, Ariz. 90, and Ariz. 82. This last parking area is at the ghost town of Fairbank, which now is the site of the conservation area's headquarters. The headquarters building, open Monday through Friday from 7:45am to 4:15pm, has handouts and maps of the area. At the Ariz. 90 parking area, the San Pedro House, a 1930s ranch, operates as a visitor center and bookstore. It's open daily from 9:30am to 4:30pm.

A HISTORIC SITE

Fort Huachuca Museum

Inside the Fort Huachuca U.S. Army base, Grierson Rd. ☎ **520/533-5736.** Admission free. Mon–Fri 9am–4pm, Sat–Sun 1–4pm.

Fort Huachuca, an army base located at the mouth of Huachuca Canyon northeast of Sierra Vista, was established in 1877 and, though it has been closed a couple of times, is still active today. The buildings of the old post have been declared a

National Historic Landmark and one is now a museum dedicated to the many forts that dotted the Southwest in the latter part of the 19th century. Near the museum stands a row of Victorian officers' quarters.

Though not exactly a part of the museum, the B Troop, 4th Regiment, U.S. Cavalry (Memorial) is one of Sierra Vista's most famous attractions. The original B Troop was formed in 1855 and saw action at Little Big Horn. To celebrate the horseback days of the cavalry, the new B Troop memorial was formed. The troop of about 30 members, who dress in the blue-and-gold uniforms of the 1880s, has made appearances across the country, including at the Tournament of Roses Parade, and can often be seen right here in Sierra Vista. Phone 520/533-2622 to find out if they'll be riding while you're in town.

WHERE TO STAY
MODERATE

Ramada Inn–Sierra Vista

2047 S. Ariz. 92, Sierra Vista, AZ 85635. ☎ **520/459-5900** or 800/825-4656. Fax 520/458-1347. 149 rms, 3 suites. A/C TV TEL. $63–$86 double; $95–$110 suite. Rates include full breakfast. AE, CB, DC, DISC, JCB, MC, V.

This modern three-story motel on the south side of town is one of Sierra Vista's best lodgings and one of the closest motels to Ramsey Canyon. The guest rooms feature contemporary furnishings, coffeemakers, large closets, and plenty of counter space in the bathrooms. There's a casual restaurant, a lounge, an outdoor pool, and a whirlpool. The hotel also offers room service, complimentary evening cocktails, and access to a health club.

✪ Ramsey Canyon Inn

31 Ramsey Canyon Rd., Hereford, AZ 85615. ☎ **520/378-3010.** 6 rms, 2 cottages. $90–$105 double (including full breakfast); $95–$115 cottage for two. No credit cards.

Located just outside the gates of the Nature Conservancy's Ramsey Canyon Preserve, the Ramsey Canyon Inn is a pleasant bed-and-breakfast inn that offers less rustic accommodations than are available in the preserve. Located on both sides of Ramsey Creek, the inn has rooms in the main building and small cabins that are reached by a footbridge over the creek. Hummingbird feeders set up on the inn's front porch attract 14 species of hummers throughout the year. A large country breakfast is served in the morning, and in the afternoon you're likely to find a fresh pie made with fruit from the inn's orchard. Breakfast is not included in the cottage rates because they have their own kitchens.

Ramsey Canyon Preserve

27 Ramsey Canyon Rd., Hereford, AZ 85615. ☎ **520/378-2785.** 6 cabins. $75–$85 cabin for two. MC, V.

Located on the banks of Ramsey Creek within the Nature Conservancy's preserve, these very basic cabins stay filled most of the year with avid bird-watchers. Each cabin is different, but all have kitchens where you can fix your own meals. There are also patio chairs and barbecue grills. If you're used to roughing it, these cabins should be fine for you. You can be out birding at dawn and dusk when the birds are most active. If you're planning to visit during the summer, you should make a reservation at least a year in advance. You can bring your own food, but there are also restaurants within 5 miles of the preserve.

INEXPENSIVE

In addition to the cabins listed below, you'll find numerous budget chain motels in Sierra Vista. These include the following (see the Appendix for toll-free phone numbers): **Motel 6,** 1551 E. Fry Blvd., Sierra Vista, AZ 85635 (☎ **520/ 459-5035**), charging $31 double; and **Super 8 Motel,** 100 Fab Ave., Sierra Vista, AZ 85635 (☎ **520/459-5380**), charging $42 to $46 double.

WHERE TO DINE

ⓈBunbuku

297 W. Fry Blvd. ☎ **520/459-6993.** Main courses $5.75–$14.50. MC, V. Daily 11am– 2:30pm and 4:30–9pm. JAPANESE.

Because Sierra Vista is home to a military base and many of the servicemen have Asian wives, the town supports quite a number of excellent Asian restaurants. Serving good Japanese meals, this place is packed at lunch when everyone from the base heads into town to eat, but at dinner there's usually no problem getting a seat. Katsu donburi (pork cutlets), yakitori (chicken on a skewer), tempura, sushi, and sashimi are all available. Prices at lunch are quite low.

The Outside Inn

4907 S. Ariz. 92. ☎ **520/378-4645.** Reservations recommended on weekends. Main courses $11–$22. AE, MC, V. Mon–Fri 11am–1:30pm and 5–9pm, Sat 5–9pm, Sun 5–8pm. STEAK/SEAFOOD.

Located south of town near the turnoff for Ramsey Canyon, the Outside Inn is a culinary oasis in southern Arizona. The restaurant is a casual place with a bright, tile-floored main dining room and a patio area. The dinner menu includes such well-prepared fare as salmon baked in parchment and chicken topped with prosciutto ham and fontina cheese. The lunch menu offers a variety of salads and sandwiches.

4 Tombstone

181 miles SE of Phoenix, 70 miles SE of Tucson, 24 miles N of Bisbee

"The town too tough to die" is today one of Arizona's most popular tourist attractions, though we'll leave it up to you to decide whether the town deserves its reputation (either as a tough town or as a tourist attraction). Although the name Tombstone alone would be enough to interest most visitors, this old mining town's claim to fame is that of the Wild West—"cowboys and Indians," and the cavalry. It was here in Tombstone that once stood a livery stable known as the O.K. Corral; and when Wyatt Earp, his brothers Virgil and Morgan, and Doc Holiday took on the outlaws Ike Clanton and Frank and Tom McLaury on October 26, 1881, the ensuing gun battle sealed the fate of this town.

Tombstone was named by Ed Schieffelin, a silver prospector who had been warned against venturing into this region, which at the time was home to Apache tribes who were fighting to preserve their homeland. Schieffelin was warned that the land would be his tombstone, so when he discovered a mountain of silver here, he named it Tombstone. Within a few years Tombstone was larger than San Francisco. Between 1880 and 1887 an estimated $37 million worth of silver was mined here. Such wealth created a sturdy little town, and as the Cochise County seat of the time, Tombstone boasted a number of imposing buildings, including the county courthouse, which is now an Arizona state park. In 1887 the silver mines were flooded by an underground river. Despite attempts to pump the water out, the mines were never reopened, and the population rapidly dwindled.

Today the historic district consists of both original buildings built after the town's second fire and newer buildings built in keeping with the architectural styles of the time. Most of the buildings are souvenir shops and restaurants, which should give you some indication that this is a classic tourist trap, but kids (and adults raised on Louis L'Amour and John Wayne) love it, especially when the famous shootout is reenacted on alternate Sundays, at 2pm.

ESSENTIALS
GETTING THERE

By Car   From Tucson, take I-10 east to Benson, from which U.S. 80 heads south to Tombstone. From Sierra Vista, take Ariz. 90 north to Ariz. 82 heading east.

VISITOR INFORMATION

For more information on Tombstone, contact the **Tombstone Office of Tourism,** P.O. Box 917, Tombstone, AZ 85638 (☎ **520/457-2211**). There's also a **visitor information center** on the corner of Allen Street and Fourth Street that's run by the Tombstone Chamber of Commerce (☎ **520/457-3929**).

WHAT TO SEE & DO

The shootout has come to epitomize the Wild West in western novels, movies, and television shows of the 1950s and 1960s. All over Arizona there are regular reenactments of gunfights, with the sheriff in his white hat always triumphing over the bad guys in their black hats. But nowhere is this great American phenomenon more glorified than here in Tombstone, where the star attraction is the famous **O.K. Corral,** site of a brief gun battle that has taken on mythic proportions. Six days a week you'll have to be content to view the lifelike figures posed in the corral in the position they were in when the fighting started, but the first and third Sunday of each month at 2pm there's a live reenactment of the famous shoot-out. Other opportunities to see shoot-outs are provided by the Boothill Gunslingers who knock each other down Monday through Saturday at 2pm and on Friday and Saturday at 5:30pm; and the Vigilantes, who blaze away on the second, fourth, and fifth Sundays of the month.

When the shooting was over, three men lay dead. They were later carted off to the **Boot Hill Graveyard** on the edge of town. The cemetery is open to the public and is entered through a gift shop on U.S. 80 just north of town. The graves of Clanton and the McLaury brothers, as well as those of others who died in gunfights or by hanging, are well marked.

When the residents of Tombstone weren't shooting each other in the streets, they were likely to be found in the saloons and bawdy houses that lined Allen Street. The most famous of these is the **Bird Cage Theatre,** so named for the large cagelike cribs that hang from the ceiling. These velvet-draped cages were used by prostitutes to ply their trade. The town's other famous drinking and gambling emporium is the **Crystal Palace,** at the corner of Allen Street and Fifth Street. The high-ceilinged saloon, built in 1879, has been completely restored and is a hangout for costumed members of the Wild Bunch, the local group that stages the Sunday shoot-out at the O.K. Corral.

On a much lighter note is the **Rose Tree Inn Museum** at Fourth Street and Toughnut Street. The museum claims to have the world's largest rosebush growing on its grounds. The shrub is indeed impressive as it sprawls across an arbor and covers 8,000 square feet. Inside the museum you'll see antique furnishings from Tombstone's heyday in the 1880s.

The most imposing building in town is the **Tombstone Courthouse State Park,** at the corner of Third Street and Toughnut Street. Built in 1882, the courthouse is now a state historic park and museum, containing artifacts, photographs, and newspaper clippings chronicling Tombstone's lively past. In the courtyard, the gallows that once ended the lives of outlaws and bandits still stands.

Tombstone was once well known for its saloons, and a couple of historic drinking establishments are still in business. The Crystal Palace, at the corner of Allen Street and Fifth Street, was built in 1879, and has been fully restored to the way it might have looked on the day of the famous shoot-out.

Tombstone's biggest annual celebrations are **Territorial Days,** held the first weekend of March; **Wyatt Earp Days,** held Memorial Day weekend; and **Helldorado Days,** held in late October. The latter celebrates the famous gunfight at the O.K. Corral and includes countless shoot-outs in the streets, mock hangings, a parade, and contests.

AN EXCURSION TRAIN

Railroad buffs and anyone else who wants to see this from a different perspective may want to check out the **San Pedro & Southwestern Railroad** (☎ **520/ 586-2266**), which operates excursion trains between Benson and Charleston. Along the route, the train passes many abandoned ranches and ruins of a Spanish outpost. Much of the trip is within the San Pedro Riparian National Conservation Area. Round-trip tickets for the 3 1/2-hour rides are $24 round-trip for adults, $21 for seniors, and $15 for children 2 to 12. Call ahead for the current schedule and for directions to the depot.

WHERE TO STAY

Adobe Lodge Motel

505 Fremont St. (P.O. Box 718), Tombstone, AZ 85638. ☎ **520/457-2241.** 20 rms. A/C TV TEL. $55–$60 double. AE, DISC, MC, V.

Located in the heart of Tombstone only a block off historic Allen Street, the Adobe is a small motel with clean, no-frills rooms. If you prefer being close to the historic district, where you can walk back to your room after dinner or a nightcap, this is a good choice.

Best Western Lookout Lodge

U.S. 80 West (P.O. Box 787), Tombstone, AZ 85638. ☎ **520/457-2223** or 800/652-6772. 40 rms. A/C TV TEL. $55–$65 double. Rates include continental breakfast. AE, CB, DC, DISC, MC, V.

The biggest motel in Tombstone is located 1 mile north of town. Stone walls, porcelain doorknobs, Mexican tiles in the bathrooms, and old-fashioned "gas" lamps give the spacious rooms an Old West feel, and all overlook the Dragoon Mountains. The rooms come with king- or queen-size beds. In summer the pool is very welcome after a long hot day.

Priscilla's Bed and Breakfast

101 N. Third St. (P.O. Box 700), Tombstone, AZ 85638. ☎ **520/457-3844.** 3 rms (none with bath). $55 double. Rates include full breakfast. AE.

Located two blocks from the O.K. Corral, this small Victorian farmhouse has been completely restored and is set behind its original white picket fence. Built in 1904, this home reflects a less notorious period of Tombstone's past, a time when lawyers could build houses such as this. Lace curtains hang in the windows and, throughout the house, oak trim and oak furniture set a Victorian mood.

WHERE TO DINE

Bella Union Restaurant

401 E. Fremont St. ☎ **520/457-3656.** Reservations recommended on weekends. Main courses $7–$19. AE, CB, DC, DISC, JCB, MC, V. Mon–Thurs 6am–9pm, Fri–Sun 6am–9:30pm. STEAK/SEAFOOD.

Huge dining rooms, long drapes, a stamped-tin ceiling, and a bar in the front room contribute to the authenticity of this restaurant, which has been around almost as long as Tombstone has. It's open early for breakfast, and dinner choices include chicken, pork, and lamb as well as juicy steaks and seafood. The Saturday-night special is prime rib for $10.95.

5 Bisbee

205 miles SE of Phoenix, 94 miles SE of Tucson, 24 miles NW of Douglas

Arizona abounds in ghost towns that boomed on mining profits but then quickly went bust when the mines played out. Between 1880 and 1975 the mines in Bisbee produced $6.1 *billion* worth of metals, but when the Phelps Dodge Company shut down its copper mines here, Bisbee nearly went the way of other abandoned mining towns. However, because Bisbee is the county seat of Cochise County, it was not fated to disappear into the dust of the Southwest desert. And because the town stopped growing in the early part of this century, today it's one of the best-preserved turn-of-the-century towns anywhere in the Southwest. Old brick buildings line the narrow winding streets of the old section of town. Television and movie producers have discovered these well-preserved streets and in recent years Bisbee has doubled as New York City, Spain, Greece, Italy, and, of course, the Old West.

The rumor of silver in "them thar hills" is what first attracted prospectors to the area in 1877, and within a few years the diggings attracted the interest of some San Francisco investors, among them the Judge DeWitt Bisbee for whom the town is named. However, it was copper and other less-than-precious metals that would make Bisbee's fortune. With the help of outside financing, large-scale mining operations were begun in 1881 by the Phelps Dodge Company. By 1910 the population had climbed to 25,000 and Bisbee was the largest city between New Orleans and San Francisco. The town boasted that it was the liveliest spot between El Paso and San Francisco—and the presence of nearly 50 saloons and houses of prostitution along Brewery Gulch backed up the boast.

Tucked into a narrow valley surrounded by red hills a mile high in the Mule Mountains, Bisbee today has a very cosmopolitan air about it. Many artists now call the town their home, and urban refugees have been dropping out of the rat race to restore the town's old buildings and open small inns, restaurants, and art galleries. Between the rough edges left over from its mining days and this new cosmopolitan atmosphere, Bisbee is rapidly becoming one of Arizona's most interesting towns.

ESSENTIALS
GETTING THERE
By Car Bisbee is on U.S. 80, which begins at I-10 in the town of Benson, 45 miles east of Tucson.

VISITOR INFORMATION
For further information on Bisbee, contact the **Bisbee Chamber of Commerce,** 7 Main St. (P.O. Box BA), Bisbee, AZ 85603-0560 (☎ **520/432-5421**).

WHAT TO SEE & DO
At the Bisbee Chamber of Commerce visitor center, located in the middle of town, you can pick up walking-tour brochures that will lead you past the most important buildings and sites in town. Along the way you can stop at the **Muheim Heritage House,** 207B Youngblood Hill (☎ **520/432-7071**), which was built between 1902 and 1915 and has an unusual semicircular porch. Inside is period furniture. You'll find the historic home up Brewery Gulch. The Muheim House is open Friday through Monday from 10am to 4pm (longer hours in summer), and admission is a suggested $2 donation.

If you climb up to the top of **OK Street,** there's a path that will take you up to a hill above town for an excellent panorama of the jumble of old buildings. After you've seen the old town, you might want to drive out to the Warren district, where the wealthier citizens of old Bisbee built their homes.

If you want to learn more about Bisbee's history both above and below ground, stop in at the **Bisbee Mining and Historical Museum,** 5 Copper Queen Plaza (☎ **520/432-7071**), which is housed in the 1897 Copper Queen Consolidated Mining Company office building. This small museum features several rooms of old mining equipment, mineral displays, and exhibits on the history of the town itself. The museum is open daily from 10am to 4pm, and admission is $3 for adults, $2.50 for seniors, and free for anyone 17 and under.

You can also see what it was like to work inside one of Bisbee's copper mines by taking one of the **Queen Mine Tours** (☎ **520/432-2071**). You can choose either the underground Queen Mine tour or the surface mine and historic tour. Tours are offered daily from 9am to 3:30pm. Underground Queen Mine tours cost $8 for adults, $3.50 for children 7 to 11, $2 for children 3 to 6; surface mine and historic tours cost $7 per person. You'll find the ticket office and mine just south of the old Bisbee business district at the U.S. 80 interchange.

If you have an interest in the plants of the desert, stop by **Arizona Cactus's Botanical Garden,** which is located at Arizona Cactus & Succulent Research, 8 S. Cactus Lane (☎ **520/432-7040**), 6 miles south of Bisbee at Bisbee Junction. Guided tours are available.

SPECIAL EVENTS
Bisbee's population of artists, writers, and other creative souls demand an active cultural life, so throughout the year you can enjoy classical music performances, gallery exhibits, comedy nights, theater performances, and that old western standby, the melodrama. To find out about gallery openings, call the **Bisbee Gallery Association** (☎ **520/432-3660**) and join others in celebrating local talent. **Other events** include the Vuelta de Bisbee bicycle race, Mule Mountain Marathon, and Mile High Chili Cookoff, in April; the Bisbee Wine Festival, in May;

a Poetry Festival, in August; Brewery Gulch Days, in September; a Gem and Mineral Show, in October; and a Fiber Arts Festival, in November. Visit the Bisbee Chamber of Commerce at 7 Main St. for specific information.

SHOPPING

Shopping is one of Bisbee's main attractions. There are many art galleries selling both traditional western art and avant-garde contemporary works by artists from Bisbee and around the state. There are also a number of antiques stores, the largest of which is **Main St. Antiques,** 67 Main St. (☎ 520/432-4104). Several jewelry makers in town work with turquoise and malachite mined in Bisbee. Visit **Gloria's Jewelry & Gemstones,** 86 Main St. (☎ 520/432-2179), for a look at some of the best local jewelry.

Bisbee's most famous shop has to be the **One Book Bookstore** (☎ 520/432-5512), 30 Main St., operated by Walter Swan. The store now sells several books, all of which were written by Swan and his wife, Deloris. The down-home flavor and the fascinating tidbits of historical information have made these books very popular. In fact, after Swan published his first book and opened his bookstore to sell it, he found himself garnering national attention and making television talk-show appearances.

EVENING ENTERTAINMENT

Once home to more than 50 saloons, Bisbee now has only a handful of authentic Old West saloons. The **Bisbee Grand Saloon,** at 57 Main St. (☎ 520/432-5900), boasts a bar from Tombstone and has a couple of billiard tables.

WHERE TO STAY
MODERATE

✪ Copper Queen Hotel

11 Howell Ave. (P.O. Drawer CQ), Bisbee, AZ 85603. ☎ **520/432-2216** or 800/247-5829. 43 rms. TV TEL. $67–$115 double. AE, DC, MC, V.

Located in the center of Bisbee, the Copper Queen Hotel was built just after the turn of the century by the Copper Queen Mining Company. At that time Bisbee was a booming mining town and the "Queen" played hostess to such notables as Teddy Roosevelt and Gen. "Black Jack" Pershing.

The atmosphere here is casual and authentic. The old safe behind the check-in desk has been there for years, as has the oak rolltop desk. Spacious halls, with their own lounges, lead to guest rooms furnished with antiques. The hotel's dining room, through swinging screen doors off the lobby, serves continental and southwestern fare, and out front there's a terrace for al fresco dining. And what would a mining town hotel be without its saloon? For cooling off, there's even a swimming pool.

✪ High Desert Inn

8 Naco Rd. (P.O. Box 145), Bisbee, AZ 85603-9998. ☎ **520/432-1442** or 800/281-0510. 6 rms. A/C TV TEL. $60–$90 double. DISC, MC, V.

Though small, this is Bisbee's most luxurious hotel and is housed in the former Cochise Country Jail (ca. 1901). The guest rooms vary in size, but all feature high ceilings, new carpets, and contemporary furnishings including wrought-iron headboards on the beds. The small bathrooms have lace shower curtains and modern fixtures. The inn's dining room is one of the best restaurants in town.

INEXPENSIVE

ⓢ Bisbee Grand Hotel

61 Main St. (P.O. Box 825), Bisbee, AZ 85603. ☎ **520/432-5900** or 800/421-1909. 8 rms, 4 with bath; 3 suites. $52 double without bath; $55–$78 double with bath; $95–$105 suite. DISC, MC, V.

The Bisbee Grand Hotel is the sort of hotel you'd expect Wyatt Earp and his wife to patronize. At street level there's a historic saloon with a high pressed-tin ceiling and an 1880s back bar from Tombstone. Upstairs are beautifully decorated turn-of-the-century guest rooms. The Oriental Suite has a ceiling fan, brass bed, claw-foot tub, and skylight, and the Victorian Suite has a red-velvet canopy bed. Other rooms are equally attractive and sport their own themes, such as the cherub room. Though only half the rooms have private bathrooms, they all have sinks.

The Inn at Castle Rock

112 Tombstone Canyon Rd. (P.O. Box 1161), Bisbee AZ 85603. ☎ **520/432-4449** or 800/566-4449. Fax 520/432-7195. 15 rms. $50–$80 double. Rates include full breakfast. MC, V.

This funky B&B right on the main road into Bisbee was built in 1890 as a miners' boarding house. Today the two-story inn, with its verandas on both floors, attracts a young and artistic clientele who appreciate the owners' unusual sense of style. The rooms are small and affect such themes as a sultan's harem.

School House Inn Bed & Breakfast

818 Tombstone Canyon (P.O. Box 32), Bisbee, AZ 85603. ☎ **520/432-2996** or 800/537-4333. 9 rms. $45–$65 double. Rates include full breakfast. AE, DC, DISC, MC, V.

Located on a hillside overlooking Bisbee, this old schoolhouse dates back to 1918. The original hardwood floors still creak underfoot, and the bathrooms date to when the building was converted into apartments. The rooms on the front side of the B&B have the best views, but all the rooms are fairly comfortable. The rooms are filled with an eclectic mix of antique and newer furniture. On warm days, breakfast is served on the terrace beneath a big, old shade tree.

WHERE TO DINE

Café Cornucopia

14 Main St. ☎ **520/432-3364.** Sandwiches, juices, and smoothies $3–$5. No credit cards. Tues–Sat 6:30am–4:30pm. SANDWICHES/JUICES.

Every town should have an atmospheric juice bar, and luckily there's one in Bisbee. Not only do they serve intoxicating smoothies such as the Mango Tango, a blend of mango, cantaloupe, and banana, but quiches and sandwiches on delicious home-made bread are also available. You can get an early breakfast here.

ⓢ Café Roka

35 Main St. ☎ **520/432-5153.** Reservations recommended. Main courses $8.50–$15.50. MC, V. Wed–Sat 5–9pm. MEDITERRANEAN/SOUTHWESTERN.

This restaurant offers good value, as well as imaginatively prepared food. Every main course comes with a soup, salad, and sorbet, and the presentation is quite elegant. You'll find an interesting mix of locals and out-of-towners here having dinner or sitting at the bar in the middle of the room. It's all very sophisticated and a surprising find in out-of-the-way Bisbee.

High Desert Inn Restaurant

8 Naco Rd. ☎ **520/432-1442.** Reservations recommended. Main courses $9.50–$13.50. DISC, MC, V. Wed–Sat 5:30–9pm, Sun 9am–3pm (brunch) and 5:30–9pm. INTERNATIONAL.

Along with Café Roka, this is the most upscale/uptown restaurant in Bisbee. It's housed in what was formerly a courthouse—the back patio used to be the jail cells. In a genteel, romatically lit ambience, you may dine here on food that draws its inspiration from around the globe, such as ahi tuna seared with Cajun spices, fruit salsa, and saffron rice, Cornish game hen with herbed goat cheese, and Indian curry with cucumber raita and peach chutney.

Stenzels

207 Tombstone Canyon Rd. ☎ **520/432-7611.** Reservations recommended on weekends. Main courses $8–$16. MC, V. Mon–Tues and Thurs–Fri 11:30am–10pm, Sat–Sun 5–10pm. STEAK/SEAFOOD.

It seems strange to think about fish in the middle of the desert, but seafood is the primary attraction in this small café. There are plenty of succulent dishes to choose from, including steamed mussels, mahimahi, and shrimp sautéed with oysters. If it's on the menu, try the Vidalia onion and green-chile soup. The appearance of Stenzels might put you off: an old converted house that has seen better days.

6 Cochise Country

Willcox: 192 miles SE of Phoenix, 81 miles E of Tucson, 74 miles N of Douglas

This is the land that Apache chief Cochise once called home and that he and his men fought hard to keep. The region's high plains early on attracted cattle ranchers and to this day cattle ranching is still a mainstay of the local economy. However, these days it's the spectacular scenery of the Chiricahua and Dragoon mountains that lure many visitors. Others come to add to their bird-watching life lists.

In the southern part of this region lies the town of Douglas, which is an important gateway to Mexico. Unless you're heading to Mexico, there aren't many reasons to visit Douglas. However, if you're passing through town, be sure to stop in at the historic Gadsden Hotel. Just across the border from Douglas is Agua Prieta, Sonora, where Pancho Villa lost his first battle. Whitewashed adobe buildings, old churches, and sunny plazas provide a contrast to Douglas. Curio shops and Mexican restaurants abound.

ESSENTIALS
GETTING THERE

By Bus   Willcox is served by Greyhound Lines. The station is at 144 S. Haskell Ave. Phone 520/384-2183 for rates and schedules.

By Car   Willcox is located on I-10, with Ariz. 186 heading southeast toward Chiracahua National Monument.

VISITOR INFORMATION

For more information on this area, contact the **Willcox Chamber of Commerce & Agriculture,** 1500 N. Circle I Rd., Willcox, AZ 85643 (☎ **520/384-2272**).

WHAT TO SEE & DO
NATURAL AREAS & BIRD-WATCHING

Sea Captain, China Boy, Duck on a Rock, Punch and Judy—these may not seem like appropriate names for landscape features, but **Chiricahua National Monument** (☎ **520/824-3560**) is no ordinary landscape. These gravity-defying rock formations—called "the land of the standing-up rocks" by the Apache and the "wonderland of rocks" by the pioneers—are the equal of any of Arizona's many amazing rocky landmarks. Rank upon rank of monolithic giants seem to have been turned to stone as they marched across the forested Chiricahua Mountains. Big Balanced Rock and Pinnacle Balanced Rock threaten to come crashing down at any moment. Formed about 25 million years ago by a massive volcanic eruption, these rhyolite badlands were once the stronghold of renegade Apache. If you look closely at Cochise Head peak, you can even see the famous chief's profile.

Within the monument are a campground, picnic area, visitor center (open daily from 8am to 5pm), many miles of hiking trails, and a scenic drive that provides views of many of the most unusual rock formations. Admission is $4 per vehicle. To reach Chiricahua National Monument, take Ariz. 186 southwest from Willcox for about 30 miles and watch for the signs.

The Chiricahuas are still an important refuge, but now they're a refuge for nature. Many species of birds, mammals, and plants that are normally found only in Mexico have found just the right climate to survive here in the Chiricahuas. To the east of the monument, on the far side of the Chiricahuas, is **Cave Creek Canyon,** one of the most important bird-watching spots in America. It's here that the colorful elegant trogon reaches the northern limit of its range. Other rare birds that have been spotted here include sulfur-bellied flycatchers and Lucy's, Virgina's, and black-throated gray warblers. To reach Cave Creek Canyon in summer you can drive over the Chiricahuas from the national monument on graded gravel roads. However, in the winter you'll have to drive around the mountains, which entails going south to Douglas or north to I-10.

Another great bird-watching spot in this region is the **Willcox sewage-recycling ponds** areas just past the golf course on the south side of town, where bird-watchers can see a wide variety of waterfowl including avocets and sandhill cranes. To find the ponds, head south out of Willcox on Ariz. 186.

Across the Sulphur Springs Valley from the Chiricahuas is **Cochise Stronghold,** a rugged section of the Dragooon Mountains that's almost as spectacular as Chiricahua National Monument. Here you'll find hiking trails, a campground, and a picnic area, and a hike among the spectacular rock formations is an opportunity to muse on the history of this area.

The Apache peoples first moved into this region of southern Arizona sometime in the early 16th century. They pursued a hunting and gathering lifestyle that was supplemented by raiding neighboring tribes for food and other booty. When the Spanish arrived in the area, the Apache acquired horses and became even more efficient raiders. They continued to attack Spanish, Mexican, and eventually American settlers, and despite repeated attempts to convince them to give up their hostile way of life, the Apache refused to change. Not long after the Gadsden Purchase of 1848 made Arizona U.S. soil, more people than ever before began settling in the region. The new settlers immediately became the subject of Apache raids, and eventually the U.S. Army was called in to put an end to the attacks.

By the mid-1880s only Cochise and Geronimo and their Chiracahua Apache were continuing to attack settlers and fight the U.S. Army. Cochise used this rugged section of the Dragoon Mountains as his hideout, and managed to elude capture for years because the granite boulders and pine forests made it impossible for the army to track Cochise and his followers. Cochise eventually died and was buried at an unknown spot somewhere in the area now called Cochise Stronghold.

HISTORIC SITES & A MUSEUM

Fort Bowie National Historic Site

Off Ariz. 186. ☎ **520/847-2500.** Admission free. Ranger station, daily 8am–5pm; grounds, daily dawn–dusk. Drive southeast from Willcox on Ariz. 186, and after about 20 miles, watch for the signs; it's another 6 miles up a dirt road and then a 1¹/₂-mile hike to the fort.

The Butterfield Stage, which carried mail, passengers, and freight across the Southwest in the mid-1800s, followed a route that passed through the heart of Apache territory in the Chiricahua Mountains. Fort Bowie was established in 1862 near the mile-high Apache Pass to protect the slow-moving stage as it traversed this difficult region. It was from Fort Bowie that federal troops battled Geronimo until the Apache chief finally surrendered in 1886. Today there's little left of Fort Bowie but some crumbling adobe walls.

Slaughter Ranch State Park

☎ **520/558-2474.** Admission $3 adults, 50¢ children. Wed–Sun 10am–3pm. From Douglas, go east on 15th Street, which runs into Geronimo Trail; keep going east.

About 15 miles east of Douglas on a gravel road is the verdant San Bernardino Valley. In 1884, former Texas Ranger John Slaughter bought the valley and turned it into a cattle ranch, one of the finest in the West. Slaughter later went on to become the sheriff of Cochise County and helped rid the region of the unsavory characters who had flocked to the many mining towns of this remote part of the state. Today the ranch is a National Historic Landmark and has been restored to its turn-of-the-century look. Long shady porches, whitewashed walls, and dark green trim give the ranch a well-manicured look, while inside, antique furnishings present a picture of a very comfortable life.

✪ Amerind Foundation Museum

☎ **520/586-3666.** Admission $3 adults, $2 seniors and children 12–18, free for children 11 and under. Sept–May, daily 10am–4pm; June–Aug, Wed–Sun 10am–4pm. Closed major holidays. See the text below for directions.

It may be out of the way and difficult to find, but this museum is well worth seeking out. Established in 1937, the Amerind Foundation is dedicated to the study, preservation, and interpretation of prehistoric and historic Native American cultures. To that end the foundation has compiled the nation's finest private collection of Native American archaeological artifacts and contemporary items. There are exhibits about the dances and religious ceremonies of the major southwestern tribes, including the Navajo, Hopi, and Apache, and exhibits that contain archaeological artifacts amassed from the numerous Amerind Foundation excavations over the years. Many of the pieces came from right here in Texas Canyon. Other exhibits contain fascinating ethnology displays, including amazingly intricate beadwork from the Plains tribes, a case full of old Zuñi fetishes, Pima willow baskets, old kachina dolls, 100 years of southwestern tribal pottery, and Navajo weavings. The art gallery contains works by 19th- and 20th-century American artists, such as Frederic Remington, whose works focused on the West. The museum store is small but has a surprisingly good selection of books and Native American crafts and jewelry.

The Amerind Foundation is located 64 miles east of Tucson in the heart of Texas Canyon, a small but rugged canyon strewn with huge rounded boulders. To reach the museum, take the Triangle T–Dragoon exit (Exit 318) from I-10 between Benson and Willcox. There's no museum sign on the highway so you must pay attention. The museum entrance is 1 mile east.

OTHER ATTRACTIONS & ACTIVITIES

If you're a fan of old-time singing cowboys, you may want to visit Willcox's **Rex Allen Museum,** Rail Road Avenue (☎ **520/384-4583**). It was Rex Allen who made famous the song "Streets of Laredo." The museum houses Rex Allen memorabilia and a Cowboy Hall of Fame exhibit. Each year in October, Willcox celebrates Rex Allen Days. The museum is open daily from 10am to 4pm, and admission is $2 per person or $5 per family.

If you want to learn more about the history and geology of southeastern Arizona, stop by the **Museum of the Southwest,** a small museum housed in the same buildings as the Willcox Chamber of Commerce Visitor Center at 1500 N. Circle I Rd. (☎ **520/384-2272**). The museum is located just off the Interstate at the Rex Allen Drive exit (Exit 340) and is open Monday through Saturday from 9am to 5pm and on Sunday from 1 to 5pm. Admission is free.

Right next door, you'll find **Stout's Cider Mill** (☎ **520/384-3696**), off I-10 at Exit 340. It makes delicious concoctions with apples, including cider, cider floats, cidersicles, apple cake, and the biggest (and contender for the best) apple pie in the world here. They're open daily 9am to 6pm.

While in the Willcox area, you can visit the **Kokopelli Winery,** north of town at 961 N. Haskell Ave. (☎ **520/384-3800**), which makes several distinctive and very reasonably priced wines. The tasting room is open Friday through Sunday from 11am to 5pm. Call for directions and to be sure they'll be open.

WHERE TO STAY
DOUGLAS

Gadsden Hotel

1046 G Ave., Douglas, AZ 85607. ☎ **520/364-4481.** 150 rms, 6 suites. A/C TV TEL. $32–$43 double; $70–$85 suite. AE, DC, MC, V.

There aren't many reasons to stay in Douglas, but this hotel is one of them. Built in 1907, the Gadsden bills itself as "the last of the grand hotels," and its listing on the National Register of Historic Places backs up that claim. The marble lobby, though dark, is a classic. Vaulted stained-glass skylights run the length of the ceiling, and above the landing of the wide Italian marble stairway is a genuine Tiffany stained-glass window. Though the carpets in the halls are well worn, many of the rooms have been renovated and refurnished in various styles. The bathrooms are also a bit worse for the wear. The lounge is a popular local hangout, with more than 200 cattle brands painted on the walls. The dining room serves Mexican and American food, and there's also a coffee shop.

PEARCE

✪ Grapevine Canyon Ranch

P.O. Box 302, Pearce, AZ 85625. ☎ **520/826-3185** or 800/245-9202. Fax 520/826-3636. 3 cabins, 9 casitas. Mar–May and Sept–Nov, $280 cabin for two; $320 casita for two. Dec–Feb and June–Aug, $240 cabin for two; $280 casita for two. Rates include all meals. AE, DISC, MC, V.

This ranch is located in the Dragoon Mountains about 35 miles southwest of Willcox and can be either a quiet hideaway where you can enjoy the natural setting or a place to experience traditional ranch life—horseback riding, rounding up cattle, mending fences. The comfortably furnished small cabins with showers only in their bathrooms and larger casitas with combination baths are set under groves of manzanita and oak trees, and there are decks where you can view wildlife and the night sky. There's a swimming pool, and if you don't care to go horseback riding, complimentary sightseeing is included.

PORTAL

Portal Peak Lodge

P.O. Box 364, Portal, AZ 85632. ☎ **520/558-2223.** 16 rms. A/C TV. $65 double. AE, DISC, MC, V.

This birders' lodge is located behind the general store and café in the hamlet of Portal, which lies just east of the Chiricahua Mountains and Cave Creek Canyon, a nesting area for the rare elegant trogon. The guest rooms are new and face each other across a wooden deck. All have two double beds and coffeemakers. Meals are available in the adjacent café.

WILLCOX

Budget chain motels are the only options in Willcox. These include the following (see the Appendix for toll-free phone numbers): **Best Western Plaza Inn,** 1100 W. Rex Allen Dr., Willcox, AZ 85643 (☎ **520/384-3556**), $55 to $80 double; **Motel 6,** 921 N. Bisbee Ave. (off I-10 at Exit 340), Willcox, AZ 85643 (☎ **520/384-2201**), $33 double; and **Econo Lodge,** 724 N. Bisbee Ave. (off I-10 at Exit 340), Willcox, AZ 85643 (☎ **520/384-4222**), $46 to $78 double.

WHERE TO DINE
WILLCOX

Historic Saxon House

308 S. Haskell Ave. (Bus. Rte. 10). ☎ **520/384-4478.** Reservations recommended on weekends. Main courses $7.25–$13. MC, V. Wed–Sat 5–9pm; plus Wed–Sun 11am–2pm in the summer. STEAK/SEAFOOD.

The Saxon house is a former home of Henry Saxon, a cowboy rancher who used it as his "city house" during the 1920s. Period furnishings and racehorse photos add to the sense of history here. The menu is simple and straightforward, with traditional favorites such as lasagne, shrimp scampi, and steaks; lunch options include sandwiches, salads, and some main courses for less than $6.

The Sonora Express

130 E. Maley St. ☎ **520/384-0036.** Reservations not accepted. Main courses $1.50–$7.50. No credit cards. Mon–Sat 11am–8pm, Sun 11am–3pm. MEXICAN.

Housed in an old railroad car on the edge of downtown Willcox, this cheery Mexican restaurant is the place to come for large servings of burritos, fajitas, and chimichangas. You'll find huevos rancheros or huevos con chorizo here for breakfast. Service is fast and friendly.

Western Arizona 11

They call it Arizona's West Coast, and for all intents and purposes that's exactly what it is: a 340-mile-long coast bordering the Colorado River and the string of lakes formed by the damming of the river—Lake Havasu, Lake Mohave, and Lake Mead—which in themselves offer thousands more miles of shoreline. In some ways Arizona's West Coast is better than the Pacific coast of California. Though there aren't any waves, the weather and the water are warmer, the fishing is some of the best in the country, and sailboarding, Jet Skiing, and waterskiing are popular on all the lakes.

In addition to the lakefront resorts, hotels, and campgrounds on all three lakes, there are also houseboats, which are perfect for family or group vacations. When you find a remote cove, the best fishing, or the most spectacular views, you can just anchor for a few days. You can even houseboat to the London Bridge on Lake Havasu.

A hundred years ago, rugged individuals ventured into this sunbaked landscape hoping to strike gold in the mountains. Some did hit pay dirt, and mining towns flourished briefly, only to be abandoned when the gold played out. Today, Oatman is the most famous of these towns, though it has a few too many people (and wild burros) to be a true ghost town. People are still venturing into this region in hopes of striking it rich, but now they head for the casinos in the boomtown of Laughlin, Nevada, just across the Colorado River from Bullhead City, Arizona.

1 Kingman

90 miles SE of Las Vegas, 180 miles SW of Grand Canyon Village, 150 miles W of Flagstaff, 30 miles E of Laughlin

Though Lt. Edward Fitzgerald Beale, leading a special corps of camel-mounted soldiers, passed through this area in 1857, Kingman was not founded until 1882, by which time the railroad had come to this region. Gold and silver were discovered in the nearby mountains in the 1870s and mining successfully continued well into the 1920s, until the mines eventually became unprofitable and were abandoned.

During the 1930s Kingman was a stop on the road to the promised land of California, as tens of thousands of unemployed people

What's Special About Western Arizona

Beaches
- Lakes Mead, Mohave, and Havasu, all with numerous beaches along their shores.

Activities
- Fishing for striped bass in Lake Mohave.
- Houseboating on Lakes Mead, Mohave, or Havasu.
- Gambling in Laughlin, Nevada, across the Colorado River from Bullhead City, Arizona.

Ace Attractions
- The London Bridge, which was moved to Lake Havasu City before falling down.
- Hoover Dam, one of the tallest in the world.

Great Towns/Villages
- Oatman, an old mining town where wild burros roam the streets.

followed U.S. 66 from the Midwest to Los Angeles. The old Route 66 has since been replaced by I-40, but the longest-remaining stretch of the old highway runs between Kingman and Seligman. Over the years old Route 66 has taken on legendary qualities. Today people come from all over the country searching for pieces of this highway's historic past.

Remember Andy Devine? No? Well, Kingman is here to tell you all about its squeaky-voiced native-son actor. Devine starred in hundreds of short films and features in the silent-screen era, but he's perhaps best known as cowboy sidekick Jingles on the 1950s television western "Wild Bill Hickok." In the 1960s he played Captain Hap on the popular program "Flipper." Devine died in 1977, but here in Kingman his memory lives on—in a room in the local museum, on an avenue named after him, and, every October, when the town celebrates Andy Devine Days.

ESSENTIALS
GETTING THERE

By Plane   America West Express flies between Phoenix and Kingman Airport. A one-way ticket is about $124. Call 800/235-9292 for fare and schedule information.

By Train   There is Amtrak passenger service to Kingman from Chicago and Los Angeles. The train stops along Andy Devine Avenue downtown. Phone 800/872-7245 for fares and schedules.

By Bus   Greyhound Lines provides service to Kingman Station, 3264 E. U.S. 66. Call 800/231-2222 for Greyhound and 520/757-8400 for the station.

By Car   Kingman is on I-40 at the junction with U.S. 93 from Las Vegas. One of the last sections of old Route 66 (U.S. 66) connects Kingman with Seligman, Arizona.

Western Arizona

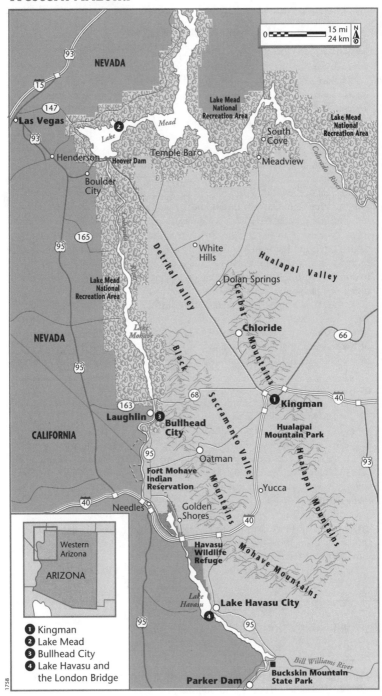

0   15 mi
0   24 km

N

NEVADA

93

15

147

93

● Las Vegas

○ Henderson

Boulder
City

95

165

95

NEVADA

CALIFORNIA

Lake Mead National Recreation Area

Lake *Mead*

Hoover Dam

Temple Bar

South
Cove

○ Meadview

Lake Mead
National
Recreation Area

Colorado River

White
Hills

○ Dolan Springs

Hualapai Valley

Lake Mead
National
Recreation Area

Lake
Mohave

Detrital Valley

Cerbat Mountains

Chloride

66

Black

163

Laughlin

95

2 Lake Mead

3 Bullhead
City

68

Sacramento Valley

● Kingman

40

Hualapai
Mountain Park

93

Oatman ○

Fort Mohave
Indian
Reservation

Mountains

○ Yucca

Hualapai Mountains

95

Needles

Golden
Shores

40

Mohave Mountains

Havasu
Wildlife
Refuge

Lake
Havasu

4 Lake Havasu City

95

95

Bill Williams River

Parker Dam

Buckskin Mountain
State Park

Western
Arizona

ARIZONA

1 Kingman
2 Lake Mead
3 Bullhead City
4 Lake Havasu and
   the London Bridge

1758

Get Your Kicks on Route 66

It was the Mother Road, the Main Street of America. Route 66 meandered across northern Arizona on the last leg of its journey from Chicago to California, and for thousands of midwesterners devastated by the dust bowl days of the 1930s it was the road to a better life. Officially dedicated in 1926, Route 66 was the first highway in America to be uniformly signed from one state to the next. Less than half of the highway's 2,200-mile route was paved, and in those days the stretch between Winslow and Ashfork was so muddy in winter that drivers had their cars shipped by railroad between those two points. By the 1930s, however, the entire length of Route 66 had been paved, and the westward migration that characterized the Great Depression was under way.

The years following World War II saw Americans take to Route 66 in unprecedented numbers, but this time for a different reason. Steady jobs, a new prosperity, and reliable cars made travel a pleasure, and Americans set out to discover the West—many on the newly affordable family vacation. Motor courts, cafés, and tourist traps sprang up along its length, and these businesses turned to increasingly more eye-catching signs and billboards in order to lure passing motorists. Neon lights also abounded, looming out of the dark western nights on lonely stretches of highway.

By the 1950s Route 66 just couldn't handle the amount of traffic it was seeing. With President Eisenhower's initiation of the National Interstate Highway System, Route 66 was eventually replaced by a four-lane divided highway. Many of the towns along the old highway were bypassed, and motorists stopped frequenting such roadside establishments as Pope's General Store and the Oatman Hotel. Many closed, and others were replaced by their more modern equivalents. Some, however, have managed to survive, and they appear along the road like strange time capsules from another era, vestiges of Route 66's legendary past.

Our personal favorite Route 66 landmark is the Wigwam Motel. For many miles out from the town of Holbrook, billboards along I-40 beckon weary motorists with the chance to sleep in a wigwam. The wigwams in question (circa 1940) are made of concrete and still contain many of their original furnishings. Also in Holbrook are several rock shops with giant signs—and life-size concrete dinosaurs—that date from Route 66 days. Nighttime here comes alive with vintage neon.

Continuing west, between Winslow and Flagstaff, you'll find a landmark that even made it into the movie *Forrest Gump*. The Twin Arrows truck stop, now little more than an old café just off the Interstate, has as its symbol two giant arrows constructed from telephone poles.

Flagstaff, the largest town along the Arizona stretch of Route 66, became a major layover spot. Motor courts flourished on the road leading into town from

Visitor Information

For more information about Kingman, contact the **Kingman Area Chamber of Commerce,** 333 W. Andy Devine Ave. (P.O. Box 1150), Kingman, AZ 86402-1150 (☎ **520/753-6106**). The **Kingman Visitor & Convention Bureau** (☎ **520/753-5001**) is at the same address.

the east. Today this road has been officially renamed Route 66 by the city of Flagstaff, and many of the old motor courts remain. Though we wouldn't want to stay in many of these old motels, their neon signs were once beacons in the night for tired drivers. Downtown Flagstaff has quite a few shops where you can pick up Route 66 memorabilia, and the first weekend in June, the town stages a Route 66 Festival complete with a classic car show.

About 65 miles west of Flagstaff begins the longest remaining stretch of old Route 66. Extending for almost 100 miles from Ashfork to Kingman, this lonely blacktop passes through some of the most remote country in Arizona. There are no real towns to speak of along this stretch, but in the community of Seligman you'll find the Snow Cap Drive-In, a classic burger joint with some outrageous decor. You can't miss it. You might also want to stop in at Angel's Barber Shop and Pope's General Store.

After leaving Seligman, the highway passes through such waysides as Peach Springs, Truxton, Valentine, and Hackberry. Before reaching Peach Springs, you'll come to Grand Canyon Caverns, once a necessary stop for families traveling Route 66. At Valle Vista, near Kingman, the highway goes into a curve that continues for 7 miles. Some people claim it's the longest continuous curve on a U.S. highway.

After driving through the wilderness west of Seligman, Kingman feels like a veritable metropolis, and its bold neon signs once brought a sigh of relief to the tired and the hungry. Today there are dozens of modern motels in Kingman, but our favorite is the Quality Inn on Andy Devine Avenue. The lobby here is filled with Route 66 memorabilia and a breakfast room is done up like a 1950s malt shop. Mr. D'z Route 66 Diner, a modern rendition of a 1950s diner, serves burgers and blue plate specials and has a collection of classic cars parked out front. Each April, Kingman is the site of the Route 66 Classic Car Rally and Show. This is also the headquarters of the Historic Route 66 Association of Arizona, which has its information desk at the Kingman Visitor & Convention Bureau, 333 W. Andy Devine Ave. (520/753-5001).

The last stretch of Route 66 in Arizona heads southwest out of Kingman through the rugged Sacramento Mountains. This stretch of original 66 passes through Oatman, once almost a ghost town after the local mining industry collapsed and the new interstate pulled money out of town. Today mock gunfights and friendly wild burros entice motorists to stop, and shops playing up Route 66 heritage line the wooden sidewalks.

Dropping down out of the mountains, the road once crossed the Colorado River on a narrow metal bridge. The bridge is still there, but now it carries a pipeline instead of traffic, and cars must return to the bland I-40 to continue their journey into the promised land of California.

WHAT TO SEE & DO

There isn't much to do in Kingman, but while you're in town, you can learn more about local history at the **Mohave Museum of History and Arts,** 400 W. Beale St. (☎ **520/753-3195**). There's also plenty of Andy Devine memorabilia on display. The museum is open Monday through Friday from 10am to 5pm and on

Saturday and Sunday from 1 to 5pm. Admission is $2. Nearby is the historic **Bonelli House,** 430 E. Spring St., a two-story stone home that was built in 1915 and is now furnished much as it may have been when it was constructed. The house is open to the public Thursday through Monday from 1 to 5pm. Admission is by donation.

If you're tired of the heat and want to cool off, you can head southeast of Kingman to **Hualapai Mountain Park,** on Hualapai Mountain Road (☎ 520/ 757-0915), which is at an elevation of 7,000 feet and offers picnicking, hiking, camping, and rustic rental cabins that were built in the 1930s by the Civilian Conservation Corp.

Located 30 miles southwest of Kingman on what was once Route 66 is the busy little ghost town of **Oatman.** Founded in 1906 when gold was discovered here, Oatman quickly grew into a lively town of 12,000 people, and was an important stop on Route 66—even Clark Gable and Carole Lombard once stayed here. However, when the U.S. government closed down many of Arizona's gold-mining operations in 1942 because gold was not essential to the war effort, Oatman's population plummeted. Today there are fewer than 250 inhabitants, and the once-abandoned old buildings have been preserved as a ghost town. The historic look of Oatman has attracted filmmakers for years, and among the movies filmed here was *How the West Was Won.*

One of the biggest attractions of Oatman is its population of almost-wild burros. These animals, which roam the streets of town begging for handouts, are descendants of burros used by gold miners.

On weekends there are staged shootouts in the streets and dancing to western music in the evening. Three saloons, three restaurants, and a couple of very basic hotels provide food and lodging if you decide you'd like to stay in Oatman for a while.

Not exactly a ghost town, **Chloride** is located about 20 miles northwest of Kingman. The town was founded in 1862 when silver was discovered in the nearby Cerbat Mountains, and is named for a type of silver ore that was mined here. By the 1920s there were 75 mines and 2,000 people in Chloride. When the mines shut down in 1944 the town lost most of its population. Today there are about 300 residents.

Much of the downtown area has been preserved as a historic district and includes the oldest continuously operating post office in Arizona, the old jail, the Silverbelle Playhouse, and the Jim Fritz Museum. Many of the downtown buildings now serve as studios and shops for artists and craftspeople. Melodramas are performed at the Silverbelle Playhouse and the VFW hall on the first and third Saturday of every month, and on the last Saturday of June the town celebrates Old Miners Day with a parade, shoot-outs, melodramas, music, and dancing.

For more information about Chloride, contact the **Chloride Chamber of Commerce,** P.O. Box 268, Chloride, AZ 86431 (☎ 520/565-2204).

WHERE TO STAY

In addition to the motel listed below, most of the budget chain motels have lodgings in Kingman. These include the following (see the Appendix for toll-free phone numbers): **Days Inn–Kingman,** 3023 E. Andy Devine Ave., Kingman, AZ 86401 (☎ 520/753-7500), charging $50 to $65 double; **Motel 6,** 3351 E. Andy Devine Ave., Kingman, AZ 86401 (☎ 529/757-7151), charging $29 double;

and **Super 8 Motel,** 3401 E. Andy Devine Ave., Kingman, AZ 86401 (☎ **520/ 757-4808**), charging $37 double.

Quality Inn–Kingman

1400 E. Andy Devine Ave., Kingman, AZ 86401. ☎ **520/753-4747,** or 800/221-2222. 98 rms. A/C TV TEL. $65–$69 double. Rates include continental breakfast. AE, CB, DC, DISC, MC, V.

Andy Devine Avenue used to be the famous Route 66, and this motel, located 2 miles south of I-40, cashes in on the fame of the former highway with antique gas pumps and other Route 66 memorabilia in the motel lobby and a breakfast room done up like a 1950s soda shop. The rooms here are a bit cramped, but are clean and have coffeemakers and two sinks in the bathrooms. The hotel also offers an outdoor pool, whirlpool, sauna, and fitness room.

WHERE TO DINE

Dam Bar & Steak House

1960 E. Andy Devine Ave. ☎ **520/753-3523.** Main dishes $8.50–$25. AE, DC, MC, V. Mon–Sat 4–10pm. STEAK.

It's hard to miss the Dam Bar—just watch for the steer on the roof of a rustic wooden building as you drive along Andy Devine Avenue. Inside, the atmosphere is very casual, with sawdust on the floor and wooden booths. Mesquite-broiled steaks are the name of the game here. Locals claim they're the best in town.

Mr. D'z

105 E. Andy Devine Ave. (at Rte. 66 and First St.). ☎ **520/298-7188.** Sandwiches $3–$6; blue plate specials $7–$9. MC, V. Mon–Thurs 7am–10pm, Fri–Sat 7am–11pm. AMERICAN.

This 1990s version of the vintage diner is where car enthusiasts traveling Route 66 like to stop, probably because of the good burgers and the highly polished vintage cars in the parking lot. We tried the Corvette burger, with honey-barbecue sauce, and if we didn't care about the calories, we would have ordered a root-beer float to go along with it. Blue plate specials include meatloaf and turkey plates, with gravy of course. The retro lunch counter and pink-and-turquoise booths are fun.

2 Lake Mead National Recreation Area

30 miles SE of Las Vegas, 70 miles NW of Kingman, 256 miles NW of Phoenix

Encompassing both Lake Mead and Lake Mohave, and separating Arizona and Nevada for most of its length, the Lake Mead National Recreation Area is one of Arizona's favorite recreation areas, and annually more than eight million people visit the lake to boat, ski, fish, swim, and camp.

Both of the recreation area's lakes have been formed by dams across the Colorado River—Hoover Dam and Davis Dam. However, it's the **Hoover Dam** that's the more noteworthy of the two. Constructed between 1931 and 1935, Hoover Dam was the first major dam on the Colorado River, and by providing huge amounts of electricity and water to Arizona and California, it set the stage for the phenomenal growth that this region has experienced in the second half of this century. At 726 feet from bedrock to the roadway atop the dam, this is the highest concrete dam in the western hemisphere. The dam tapers from a thickness of 660 feet at its base to only 45 feet thick at the top. Lake Mead, the reservoir formed by Hoover Dam, is 110 miles long, has more than 550 miles of shoreline, and is the largest man-made lake in the United States. U.S. 93 runs right across the top of the dam, and there's a visitor center here that chronicles the dam's construction.

Fishing for monster striped bass is one of the most popular activities on the lakes, but waterskiing, board-sailing, and Jet Skiing are also popular. Despite the area's decided water orientation, there's also quite a bit of mountainous desert here, land that's home to bighorn sheep, roadrunners, and other wild animals. This land was also once home to several Native American tribes who left reminders of their presence in petroglyphs.

There are a number of marinas on both the Arizona and Nevada sides of the lake offering boat rentals, resorts, and campgrounds. Temple Bar is the easiest marina to reach on the Arizona side, while on the Nevada side, Boulder Beach and Echo Bay are the most easily accessible. On nearby Lake Mohave, Katherine Landing, just outside Bullhead City, Arizona, provides all amenities.

ESSENTIALS
GETTING THERE

By Car   U.S. 93, which runs between Las Vegas and Kingman, crosses over the Hoover Dam, which forms Lake Mead. Several small secondary roads lead to various marinas on the lake.

VISITOR INFORMATION

For more information, contact the **Lake Mead National Recreation Area,** 601 Nevada Hwy., Boulder City, NV 89005 (☎ **702/293-8906**). The **telephone area code** for Nevada is 702.

WHERE TO STAY & DINE
HOUSEBOATS

Seven Crown Resorts
P.O. Box 16247, Irvine, CA 92713-0068. ☎ **800/752-9669.** A/C. $1,250–$1,850 per week. DISC, MC, V.

Why pay extra for a lake-view room when you can rent a houseboat that always has a 360° water view? There's no better way to explore Lake Mead than on a houseboat. You can cruise for miles, tie up at a deserted cove, and have a wilderness adventure with all the comforts of home. Houseboats come complete with full kitchens, air-conditioning, and room to sleep up to 10 people. The scenery here isn't quite as spectacular as on Lake Powell, Arizona's other major houseboating lake.

LAKE RESORTS

Lake Mohave Resort
Katherine Landing, Bullhead City, AZ 86430. ☎ **520/754-3245** or 800/752-9669. 53 rms. A/C TV TEL. $60–$83 double. MC, V.

Just up Lake Mohave from Davis Dam and only a few minutes outside Bullhead City, the Lake Mohave Resort is an older motel, but the huge rooms are ideal for families on vacation. About half the rooms have limited views of the lake, which is across the road from the motel. Tail O' the Whale, the resort's nautical-theme restaurant and lounge, overlooks the marina. The resort also offers boat rentals, a convenience store, and a tackle-and-bait store.

Temple Bar Resort
Temple Bar, AZ 86443. ☎ **520/767-3211** or 800/752-9669. 40 rms. A/C TV TEL. $43–$89 double. DISC, MC, V.

Though basically just a motel, the Temple Bar Resort has a wonderfully remote setting with a beach that makes it an excellent getaway, especially if you enjoy waterskiing or fishing. Waterskiers in particular like Temple Bar because it offers 20 miles of unobstructed skiing in either direction. Directly across from Temple Bar is the huge Temple monolith from which this area gets its name. A restaurant and lounge overlook the lake and provide economical meals. The resort offers ski rentals, powerboat rentals, shuffleboard, bocce, horseshoes, and a convenience store.

The same company that operates this resort also operates two others on the Nevada side of the lake. Contact the above toll-free number for more information.

3 Bullhead City & Laughlin, Nevada

30 miles W of Kingman, 216 miles NW of Phoenix, 60 miles N of Lake Havasu City

You may find it difficult at first to understand why anyone would ever want to live in Bullhead City. According to the U.S. Weather Service, this is the hottest town in the country, with temperatures regularly topping 120° Fahrenheit during the summer. However, to understand Bullhead City, you need only gaze across the Colorado River at the Emerald City—the promised land of Laughlin, Nevada, where the slot machines are always in action and the gaming tables are always as hot as the air outside (well, sometimes). Laughlin, Nevada, is the southernmost town in Nevada, and is therefore the closest place to Phoenix to do some serious gambling. This makes Bullhead City one of the busiest little towns in Arizona.

Laughlin is a perfect miniature of Las Vegas. High-rise hotels loom above the desert like so many glass mesas. Miles of neon lights turn night into day. Acres of asphalt are always covered with cars and RVs as hordes of hopeful gamblers go searching for Lady Luck. Cheap rooms and cheap meals lure people into spending on the slot machines what they save on food and a bed. It's a formula that works well. Why else would anyone endure the heat of this remote desert?

ESSENTIALS
GETTING THERE

By Plane   The Bullhead City–Laughlin Airport is in Bullhead City and is served by United Express (☎ 800/241-6522) and America West Express (☎ 800/235-9292). Car rentals are available in Bullhead City and Laughlin from Avis (☎ 800/831-2847), Budget (☎ 800/527-0700), and Hertz (☎ 800/654-3131).

By Bus   Greyhound Lines (☎ 800/231-2222) provides service to Bullhead City. The station is at 1010 Ariz. 95 (☎ 520/754-4655).

By Car   From Phoenix, take U.S. 60, which becomes U.S. 93, northwest to I-40. From Kingman, take Ariz. 68 west to Bullhead City.

VISITOR INFORMATION

For more information on Bullhead City and Laughlin, Nevada, contact the **Bullhead Area Chamber of Commerce,** 1251 Ariz. 95, Bullhead City, AZ 86430 (☎ **520/754-4121**).

WHAT TO SEE & DO

There are only a couple of reasons to venture into this rugged and remote corner of Arizona. You're either headed for Lake Mohave to do some fishing or houseboating, or you're here to do some gambling. We'll bet money that you're here to gamble.

Laughlin is a very popular weekend destination for Phoenicians and other Arizonans, who have limited gambling in their own state. The casinos of Laughlin are known for having liberal slots—that is, the slot machines pay off frequently. There's also keno, blackjack, poker, craps, off-track betting, and sports betting. If you want to learn how to play a game that requires a bit more thinking than slot machines, you can take a lesson in poker, blackjack, or craps at most of the casinos. To help you spread your wealth around, there's a free casino shuttle, and free ferries also shuttle gamblers across the Colorado River.

If you'd like to see a bit more of the Colorado, there are daily cruises on the paddlewheelers *Little Belle* (☎ 702/298-1047), which leaves from the Edgewater Casino, and *Fiesta Queen* (☎ 702/298-1047), which leaves from the Gold River Hotel.

If you'd rather take the helm yourself, you can **rent ski boats, fishing boats, and patio boats** at the Lake Mohave Resort (☎ 520/754-3245). Rates range from $60 to $225 per day. There are also numerous watercraft-rental places along the waterfront behind the casinos. You can also check with **Riverfront Water Sports,** 1631 Ariz. 95, Bullhead City (☎ 520/763-3533).

Fishermen will be interested to know that Lake Mohave is home to awesome striped bass that really put up a fight. If you'd like to find out more about why Lake Mohave is there for you to play in, stop by the Davis Dam for a free self-guided tour. The dam is just north of town and open to the public daily from 7:30am to 3:30pm.

Golfers can play a round at the **Emerald River Golf Course** (☎ 702/298-0061), which is 2¹/₂ miles south of Harrah's.

If you'd like to learn more about the history of this area, visit the **Colorado River Museum** (☎ 520/754-3399), which is located half a mile north of the Laughlin Bridge.

EVENING ENTERTAINMENT

All the hotels in Laughlin offer live entertainment of some sort, including occasional name entertainment, but gambling is still the main event as far as evening entertainment is concerned.

WHERE TO STAY & DINE
BULLHEAD CITY

In addition to the moderately priced hotel listed below, Bullhead City has numerous budget chain motels, including the following (see the Appendix for toll-free phone numbers): **Days Inn,** 2200 Karis Dr., Bullhead City, AZ 86442 (☎ 520/758-1711), charging $48 to $97 double; **Econo Lodge,** 1717 Ariz. 95, Bullhead City, AZ 86442 (☎ 520/758-8080), charging $28 to $95 double; **Motel 6.** 1616 Ariz. 95, Bullhead City, AZ 86442 (☎ 520/763-1002), charging $20 to $30 double; and **Super 8,** 320 Lee St., Bullhead City, AZ 86430 (☎ 520/754-4651), charging $44 to $46 double.

LAUGHLIN, NEVADA

Laughlin, Nevada, currently has nine huge hotel-and-casino complexes, eight of which are on the west bank of the Colorado River. All offer incredibly cheap rooms to lure potential gamblers. In addition to huge casinos with hundreds (even thousands) of slot mach-ines and every sort of gaming table, these hotels all have several restaurants each (with ridiculously low prices in at least one restaurant), bars and lounges (usually with live country or pop music nightly), swimming pools, video arcades for kids, ferry service, valet parking, room service, car-rental desks, airport shuttles, gift shops, and gaming classes. The only real difference between most of these places is the theme each has adopted for its decor.

All the hotels here also have plenty of RV parking areas, and in addition, there's the **Riverside RV Park** (☎ 702/298-2535, or 800/227-3849) across from the Riverside Resort Hotel.

Best Western Riverside Resort Hotel & Casino

1650 S. Casino Dr. (P.O. Box 500), Laughlin, NV 89029. ☎ **702/298-2535** or 800/ 227-3849. 1,405 rms, 124 suites. A/C TV TEL. $19–$49 double Sun–Thurs, $29–$69 Fri–Sat; $51–$91 suite. AE, CB, DC, DISC, MC, V.

This is Don Laughlin's original Laughlin casino and hotel, and offers as many entertainment and dining options as you'll find under any one roof in Laughlin. The guest rooms are spacious and modern.

Colorado Belle Hotel & Casino

2100 Casino Dr. (P.O. Box 2304), Laughlin, NV 89029. ☎ **702/298-4000** or 800/ 458-9500. 1,238 rms, 8 suites. A/C TV TEL. $21–$39 double Sun–Thurs, $45–$60 Fri–Sat; $75–$120 suite. AE, CB, DC, DISC, MC, V.

Nevada gambling casinos and hotels have always been given over to Disneyesque flights of fancy when it comes to architectural themes, and Laughlin is no exception. The Colorado Belle is built to resemble a Brobdingnagian paddle-wheel riverboat, complete with smokestacks and eight-story paddle wheels. Of course the guest rooms are all done in nautical themes as well.

Edgewater Hotel & Casino

2020 S. Casino Dr. (P.O. Box 30707), Laughlin, NV 89028. ☎ **702/298-2453** or 800/ 677-4837. 1,450 rms, 4 suites. A/C TV TEL. $14–$24 double Sun–Thurs, $40–$55 Fri–Sat; $75–$120 suite. AE, CB, DC, DISC, MC, V.

Riverfront rooms here are slightly more expensive than other rooms, but there really isn't an expensive room in the house. The Edgewater is one of the largest of the Laughlin hotels and is conveniently located right in the middle of all the action. The riverfront walk behind the hotel can connect you to other casinos.

Flamingo Hilton

1900 S. Casino Dr., Laughlin, NV 89029. ☎ **702/298-5111** or 800/HILTONS or 800/ FLAMINGO. 2,000 rms, 30 suites. A/C TV TEL. $19–$29 double Sun–Thurs, $39–$69 Fri–Sat; $200–$600 suite. AE, CB, DC, DISC, MC, V.

Two shimmering glass towers reflect all the neon in Laughlin at night and make the Flamingo impossible to miss. The guest rooms are attractively decorated and feature modern furnishings.

Gold River Resort & Casino

2700 S. Casino Dr. (P.O. Box 77700), Laughlin, NV 89029-7770. ☎ **702/298-2242** or 800/835-7904. 1,005 rms, 8 suites. A/C TV TEL. $15–$25 double Sun–Thurs, $35–$55 Fri–Sat; $125–$300 suite. AE, CB, DC, DISC, MC, V.

This high-rise hotel is done up to look like an old mine building with a copper roof and open beams. Often, the Gold River has the lowest room rates in town. You'll also find a health spa here.

Golden Nugget

2300 S. Casino Dr., Laughlin, NV 89029. ☎ **702/298-7222** or 800/950-7700. 304 rms, 4 suites. A/C TV TEL. $21–$49 double Sun–Thurs; $35–$65 Fri–Sat; $150 suites. AE, CB, DC, DISC, MC, V.

Here in the lobby of the Golden Nugget, the desert is turned into the jungle, with lush plantings of tropical plants and waterfalls. Tarzan's Lounge, Jane's Grill, and Cheetah's Bar also reflect this jungle theme.

Harrah's Laughlin

2900 S. Casino Dr., Laughlin, NV 89029-9010. ☎ **702/298-4600** or 800/447-8700. 1,600 rms. A/C TV TEL. $23–$38 double Sun–Thurs; $55–$65 Fri–Sat. AE, CB, DC, DISC, MC, V.

This is one of the biggest and glitziest of the Laughlin hotels, and sits on the bluff at the south end of town. The hotel even has its own sand beach. There are also boat rentals, a health club, and two pools. The hotel is done up in a Mexican hacienda style throughout.

Pioneer Hotel & Gambling Hall

2200 Casino Dr. (P.O. Box 29664), Laughlin, NV 89028-9664. ☎ **702/298-2442** or 800/634-3469. 414 rms. A/C TV TEL. $28–$75 double Sun–Thurs; $39–$75 Fri–Sat. AE, CB, DC, DISC, MC, V.

This smaller (by Laughlin standards) hotel is done up to resemble an old western town, and in true Las Vegas fashion, features a giant, waving neon cowboy. Many of the rooms are quite close to the water.

Ramada Express

2121 S. Casino Dr. (P.O. Box 77771), Laughlin, NV 89028. ☎ **702/298-4200** or 800/2RAMADA. 1,501 rms, 48 suites. A/C TV TEL. $21–$25 double Sun–Thurs; $29–$34 Fri–Sat; $59–$89 suite. AE, DC, DISC, MC, V.

This is the only hotel in Laughlin that isn't on the water. The hotel sports a railroad theme and is designed to resemble a turn-of-the-century railway station. There's even a small train that provides free rides around the grounds. The hotel has tennis courts and a locomotive-shaped swimming pool.

4 Lake Havasu & the London Bridge

200 miles NW of Phoenix, 60 miles S of Bullhead City, 61 miles S of Kingman, 150 miles S of Las Vegas

Once upon a time London Bridge really was falling down, but that was before Robert McCulloch, founder of Lake Havasu City, hit upon the brilliant idea of buying the bridge and having it shipped to his under-touristed little town in the middle of the Arizona desert. Today the London Bridge sits like a mirage on the banks of Lake Havasu in this hot and dusty desert town. An unlikely place for a bit of British heritage it's true, but Lake Havasu City and the London Bridge have become the second-most-popular tourist destination in Arizona. Only the Grand Canyon attracts more visitors.

Lake Havasu was formed in 1938 by the building of the Parker Dam, but it wasn't until 1963 that the town of Lake Havasu City was founded by McCulloch. Not too many people were keen on spending time out in this remote corner of the desert, where summer temperatures are often over 110° Fahrenheit. Despite its name, Lake Havasu City was little more than an expanse of desert with a few mobile homes on it. It was then that McCulloch began looking for ways to attract more people to his little city on the lake. His solution proved to be a stroke of genius.

WHAT TO SEE & DO

LONDON BRIDGE   In the mid-1960s the British government decided to sell the London Bridge, which was indeed falling down—or, more correctly, sinking—into the Thames River because of too much heavy car and truck traffic. McCulloch and his partner paid $2,460,000 for the famous bridge and had it shipped 10,000 miles to Long Beach, California, and then trucked it to Lake Havasu City. Reconstruction of the bridge was begun in 1968 and the grand reopening was held in 1971. Oddly enough, the 900-foot-long bridge was not built over water. It connected only desert to more desert on a peninsula jutting into Lake Havasu. It wasn't until after the bridge was rebuilt that a 1-mile-long channel was dredged through the base of the peninsula, thus creating an island offshore from Lake Havasu City.

The London Bridge has a long history, though the bridge that now stands in Arizona is not very old by British standards. The first bridge over the Thames River in London was probably a pontoon bridge built by the Romans in A.D. 43. However, the first written record of a London Bridge comes from the mention of a suspected witch being drowned at the bridge in 984. In 1176 the first stone bridge over the Thames was built. They just don't build 'em like that bridge anymore—it lasted for more than 600 years, but was eventually replaced in 1824 by the bridge that now stands in Lake Havasu City.

At the base of the bridge you'll find **English Village,** which is done up in proper English style and has shops, restaurants, and a waterfront promenade. It's here that you'll find several cruise boats and small-boat rental docks.

BOAT TOURS   There are several companies offering different types of boat tours on Lake Havasu. **Blue Water Charters** (☎ 520/855-7171) offers jet-boat tours that leave from the London Bridge and spend two hours cruising up the Colorado River to the Topock Gorge, a scenic area 25 miles from Lake Havasu City. The tours cost $18.50 for adults, $10 for children 6 to 12, and are free for children 5 and under. **Miss Havasupai Boat Tours** (☎ 520/855-7979) provides a more leisurely narrated pontoon-boat tour of the island that was formed when the London Bridge was built. You can also cruise on the *Dixie Belle* (☎ 520/453-6776), a small replica paddle-wheel riverboat. Cruises are $12 for adults and $5 for children 6 to 12; children 5 and under ride free.

WATER SPORTS   After the London Bridge, water sports on 45-mile-long Lake Havasu are the most popular local attraction. If you didn't bring your own boat, you can rent one at **Resort Boat Rentals,** in the English Village beside the bridge (☎ 520/453-9613). They offer half- and full-day rentals of ski, pontoon, and nordic boats. Rental rates start at $45 an hour for a pontoon boat or runabout. They also rent waterskiing equipment for $25 a day.

Two- and three-passenger Waverunners are available from **Arizona Jet Ski Rentals,** 635 Kiowa Ave. (☎ 520/453-5558). Rates range from $35 to about $45 an hour.

If you prefer a cheaper mode of transportation and don't mind using a little muscle power, stop by the **Fun Center** (☎ 520/453-4FUN) in the English Village. They have paddle boats, canoes, and aqua cycles for $10 an hour, as well as Waverunners for $40 to $55 an hour. They also offer parasailing for $35 to $45.

GOLF   And what would an Arizona desert community be without its golf course? Lake Havasu City has four, all of which are open to the public. They are the **Queens Bay Golf Course,** 1480 Queen's Bay (☎ 520/855-4777), at the London Bridge Resort; **London Bridge Golf Club,** 2400 Clubhouse Dr. (☎ 520/855-2719); the **Nautical Inn Resort,** 1000 McCulloch Blvd. (☎ 520/855-2141); and the **Stonebridge Golf Course,** 2400 Clubhouse Dr. (☎ 520/855-2719).

WHERE TO STAY
HOTELS & MOTELS

Bridgeview Motel

101 London Bridge Rd., Lake Havasu City, AZ 86403. ☎ **520/855-5559.** Fax 520/855-5564. 37 rms. A/C TV TEL. $30–$50 double. Rates higher on holidays. MC, V.

If you're just looking for a clean and inexpensive place to stay in town, this motel fits the bill and offers a view of the bridge. It's also quiet here and there's a small pool.

Island Inn Resort

1300 W. McCulloch Blvd., Lake Havasu, AZ 86403. ☎ **520/680-0606** or 800/243-9955. Fax 520/680-4218. 117 rms, 2 suites. A/C TV TEL. $65–$110 double; $125–$175 suite. AE, DC, DISC, MC, V.

This is one of the newest hotels in Lake Havasu City, and is located across the London Bridge from downtown. Though it's not right on the water, the Island Inn is close to the area's best public beach. The rooms are large and spartan, though they do have large TVs. Most rooms have balconies, and those on the upper floors have the better views. The lobby restaurant serves moderately priced Mexican food. There's also a bar adjacent to the restaurant. Facilities include an outdoor pool and a whirlpool.

✪ London Bridge Resort

1477 Queens Bay, Lake Havasu City, AZ 86403. ☎ **520/855-0888** or 800/624-7939. Fax 520/855-9209. 170 rms, 14 suites. A/C TV TEL. $59–$79 double Sun–Thurs, $79–$159 Fri–Sat; $169–$250 suite. Higher rates on holidays. AE, DC, DISC, MC, V.

It doesn't take much to figure out that this resort was built after the London Bridge made its historic move to the Arizona desert. Merrie Olde England was once the theme here, with Tudor half-timbers jumbled up with turrets, towers, ramparts, and crenellations. However, England is giving way to the tropics and the desert as the resort strives to please its young, partying clientele. Though the bridge is just out the hotel's back door, and inside the lobby is a replica of Britain's gold State Coach, guests are more interested in the three pools, the tropical-theme outdoor nightclub, and the Mexican cantina. Even the English dining room now serves southwestern food. The rooms are large, but even the view rooms have only small windows and the furnishings date from the dark ages of the 1970s. In addition to the three pools, recreational options here include an executive golf course, tennis courts, whirlpools, and a beach.

HOUSEBOATS

Havasu Springs Resorts

Rte. 2, Box 624, Parker, AZ 85344. ☎ **520/667-3361.** Mar–Sept, $1,750–$2,295 per week. Oct–Feb, $1,100–$1,595 per week. MC, V.

One of the most popular ways to enjoy Lake Havasu is on a rented houseboat. You can spend your days motoring from one good fishing or swimming spot to the next, and there are beaches and secluded coves where you can drop anchor and stay for days. If you feel like doing a bit of sightseeing or shopping, you can cruise right up to the London Bridge. Houseboats come in four sizes, with the large boats providing much more luxury (such as air-conditioning). Boats sleep 10 to 12 people and are very popular with families.

WHERE TO DINE

Allee Café

1530 El Camino Way (1 mile north of London Bridge). ☎ **520/680-1011.** Reservations recommended. Main courses $9–$21. MC, V. Tues–Sat 11am–2pm and 5–10pm, Sun 10am–2pm (brunch) and 5–10pm. CONTINENTAL.

In this dark-interiored cube of a building, European chef Horst Finke turns out favorites with both traditional and innovative flair, such as prosciutto with melon, chicken Kiev, swordfish with raspberry sauce, German schnitzel, and the occasional coconut shrimp. The dining room isn't big on atmosphere, but the meals are some of the best around Lake Havasu.

London Arms Pub & Restaurant

422 English Village. ☎ **520/855-8782.** Reservations recommended. Main courses $7–$18. AE, DISC, MC, V. Sun–Thurs 11:30am–9pm, Fri–Sat 11:30am–10:30pm. PUB.

A British pub atmosphere reigns here, with a Tudor-style interior and Welsh rarebit, steak-and-mushroom pie, and bangers and mash on the menu. It's a cool retreat from the blazing sun, and kind of an odd place to find oneself (since this *is* the desert). But take heart—if you desire some good American fare, they also serve garden burgers and Cajun-seasoned halibut steak. For dessert, we wouldn't pass up the trifle, and yes, they have imported British beers, served cold. The patio with striped umbrellas is an airy alternative.

Shugrue's

1425 McCulloch Blvd. ☎ **520/453-1400.** Reservations recommended. Main courses $7–$23. AE, MC, V. Mon–Thurs 11am–3pm and 5–10pm, Fri–Sat 11am–3pm and 5–11pm, Sun 10am–3pm and 5–10pm. CONTINENTAL.

Located just across the London Bridge from the English Village shopping complex, Shugrue's offers flavorful food at very reasonable prices. The large restaurant has been built with many windows, so most diners get a view of the London Bridge. In addition to the seafood, prime rib, wok specialties, and pasta, there's a short list of Cajun favorites. Dieters, and those who like to save room for dessert, may want to choose from the menu of lighter fare.

Versailles

357 S. Lake Havasu Ave. ☎ **520/855-4800.** Reservations recommended. Main courses $8–$22. MC, V. Mon–Thurs 5–9pm, Fri–Sat 5–10pm. Closed Mon June–Aug. CONTINENTAL.

This building looks a little shabby on the outside but the inside is surprisingly elegant, if not a little fussy—it's definitely not the kind of place to come wearing your cutoffs. The view from the dining room overlooks the highway and the lake beyond, while a sophisticated bar is a comfortable spot to try a selection from the long wine list. An oversize menu full of traditional choices offers such dishes as escargots with garlic sauce, surf and turf, veal marsala, frogs' legs with herb butter, and coquilles St-Jacques. Live organ music creates a lounge ambience on weekend evenings.

EN ROUTE TO YUMA

The population of the desert community of **Quartzsite** each winter swells tremendously with the annual influx of RVing retirees, and from early January to mid-February the community holds several gem-and-mineral shows that attract more than a million rock hounds. If you're passing through during these months, you might want to check out one of these shows. For more information, contact the **Quartzsite Chamber of Commerce,** P.O. Box 85, Quartzsite, AZ 85346 (☎ 520/927-5600).

Also in Quartzsite is the pyramid-shaped stone monument and **tomb of Hadji Ali,** the Syrian camel driver who tended the camels of the U.S. Army's experimental camel corps from 1856 to 1864.

5 Yuma

180 miles SW of Phoenix, 180 miles E of San Diego, 240 miles W of Tucson

Though you may never have heard of Yuma, Arizona, it was once one of the most important towns in the Southwest. Founded on a shallow spot along the Colorado River, Yuma was once the Rome of the Southwest, for all roads led to the river crossing, and through it passed Quechan peoples, Spanish missionaries and explorers, Kit Carson and his mountain men, '49ers heading for the goldfields of California, pioneers, and soldiers. Despite its location in the middle of the desert, Yuma was a busy port town when shallow-draft steamboats began traveling up the Colorado River from the Gulf of California in the 1850s. From here military supplies were transported overland to the many forts and camps throughout the Southwest during the Apache wars of the 1870s and 1880s. When the railroad pushed westward into California in the 1870s, it also passed through Yuma. Even today I-8, which connects San Diego with Tucson and Phoenix, crosses the Colorado at Yuma.

Hotter than Phoenix, Yuma's summer temperatures regularly top 120° Fahrenheit, and the U.S. Weather Service says that Yuma is the sunniest city in the United States. Yuma is gloriously warm and sunny in the winter and has become the winter home of tens of thousands of "snowbirds" (winter visitors from up north), who drive their RVs down from as far away as Canada.

Yuma is also well known among rock hounds. Within 80 miles of here are numerous **gem fields** where it's possible to search for such interesting minerals and semiprecious stones as garnet, tourmaline, magnetite, jasper, rhyolite, pyrite, agate, and chalcedony roses. Contact the Yuma Convention and Visitors Bureau for information on getting to some of these gem fields.

ESSENTIALS
VISITOR INFORMATION

For more information about Yuma, contact the **Yuma Convention and Visitors Bureau,** 488 S. Maiden Lane (P.O. Box 10831), Yuma, AZ 85366-8831 (☎ 520/783-0071).

Southwestern Arizona

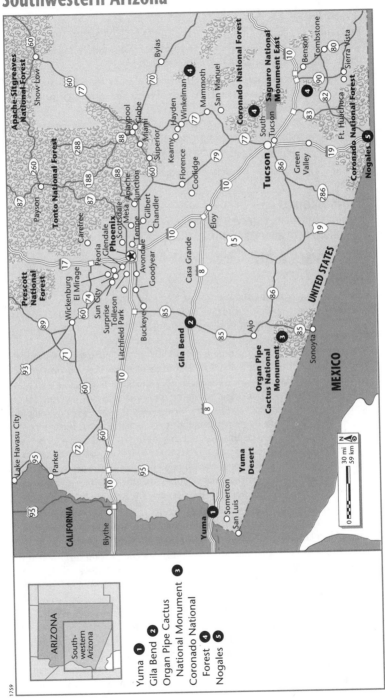

Yuma **1**
Gila Bend **2**
Organ Pipe Cactus National Monument **3**
Coronado National Forest **4**
Nogales **5**

ARIZONA
Southwestern Arizona

GETTING THERE

By Plane   The Yuma Airport is at 2191 32nd St.; call 520/726-5882 for flight information. It's served by Skywest and America West; for fares and schedules, phone 800/453-9417 and 800/235-9292, respectively.

By Train   There's Amtrak passenger service to Yuma from Los Angeles and New Orleans. The station is on Gila Street. Phone 800/872-7245 for fares and schedules.

By Bus   Greyhound Lines buses stop in Yuma on their way between San Diego and Phoenix; call 800/231-2222 for fare and schedule information. The station is at 170 E. 17th Place; phone 520/783-4403 for arrival/departure information.

By Car   Yuma is on I-8, which runs from San Diego, California, to Casa Grande, Arizona.

GETTING AROUND

For a taxi, call **Yuma Cab** (☎ **520/782-0111**). Rental cars are available in Yuma from **Budget** (☎ **800/527-0700**).

WHAT TO SEE & DO
HISTORICAL SITES

Yuma Crossing Quartermaster Depot Historic Site
221 N. Second Ave. (Fourth Ave. and the Colorado River). ☎ **520/329-0404.** Admission $3 adults, $2.50 senior citizens, $2 children 6–17, free for children 5 and under. Daily 10am–5pm. Closed Dec 25.

Yuma was a busy river port during the mid-19th century and a depot for military supplies shipped from California. After unloading in Yuma, supplies were shipped to military posts throughout the region. In 1877 the railroad arrived in Yuma and the Quartermaster Depot began losing its importance in the regional supply network. By 1883 the depot had been closed. Today the large wooden buildings are set back a bit from the new channel of the Colorado River, but it's easy to imagine being stationed at this hot and dusty outpost in the days before air-conditioning. Exhibits tell the story of the people who lived and worked at Yuma Crossing. Costumed guides happily answer questions about the depot and its role in Arizona history. A short video documentary tells the story of Yuma Crossing, when it acted as a stopover point for travelers heading for southern California.

Yuma Territorial Prison State Historic Park
209 N. Penitentiary Ave. ☎ **520/783-4771.** Admission $3 adults, $2 children 12–17, free for children 11 and under. Daily 8am–5pm. Closed Dec 25.

Yuma is one of the hottest places in the world, so it comes as no surprise that the Arizona Territory chose this bleak spot for a prison (although there is a view of the confluence of the Gila and Colorado rivers from Prison Hill). The prison first closed its doors on convicts in 1876 and operated for only 33 years before being replaced by a larger prison. Despite the stone walls (albeit thick ones) and iron bars, this prison was considered a model penal institution in its day. It even had its own generating plant for electricity and a ventilation system. The prison museum has some interesting displays, including photos of many of the 3,069 prisoners who were incarcerated at Yuma over the years; 29 were women. After the prison was shut down, the building served as a high school and as housing for the homeless during the Depression.

OTHER ATTRACTIONS & ACTIVITIES

Downtown Yuma isn't exactly a bustling place, but it's well worth a visit for its south-of-the-border atmosphere. Huge well-shaped ficus trees provide deep shade, and at the center of the shopping district is a plaza similar to those found in towns all over Mexico. Funky and inexpensive craft shops occupy an occasional storefront. An alleyway of shops off Main Street (at 224 Main St., across from Lutes Casino) has a potpourri of small tourist-oriented stores.

If you'd like to find out more about the life of a pioneer Yuma merchant, visit the **Arizona Historical Society Century House Museum** at 240 S. Madison St. (☎ 520/782-1841). This territorial-period home is full of historical photographs and artifacts and is surrounded by palm trees and lush gardens. The museum is open Tuesday through Saturday from 10am to 4pm and admission is free.

Cross the river to California to find displays of tribal arts and crafts and historic photos and artifacts covering both the past and present of the Quechan culture at the **Quechan Indian Museum,** Indian Hill Road (☎ 619/572-0661). The Quechan were one of eight tribes living and farming along the Colorado River when the Spanish first arrived in this region in 1540. The museum is open Monday through Friday from 8am to noon and 1 to 5pm and admission is $1.

A hundred years ago there used to be camels wandering the deserts near here. No, they weren't native camels, they were just some the army turned loose after an experimental camel corps was disbanded. Today there are still camels in Yuma at the **Saihati Camel Farm,** 15672 S. Avenue 1E (☎ 520/627-2553), which keeps a large camel herd, as well as other interesting wildlife of the desert. Guided tours are offered October to May (reservations recommended), Monday through Saturday at 10am and 2pm and on Sunday at 2pm; June to September (reservations required), Monday through Saturday at 10am. Admission is $3.

The Colorado River has been the life blood of the southwestern desert, and today there's a wealth of history along its banks. **Yuma River Tours,** 1920 Arizona Ave. (☎ 520/783-4400), operates narrated jet-boat tours of varying lengths between Yuma and the Imperial Wildlife Refuge to the north. Along the way, you'll learn about the homesteaders, boatmen, Native Americans, and miners who relied on the Colorado River. Tours cost $25 to $75.

Golf courses cater to the "snowbirds" who descend on this area every winter. The **Mesa del Sol Golf Resort,** 10583 Camino del Sol (☎ 520/342-1817), off I-8 at the Fortuna Road exit, is the most challenging local course open to the public. Others include the **Arroyo Dunes Golf Course,** 32nd Street and Avenue A (☎ 520/726-8350); the **Desert Hills Municipal Course,** 1245 Desert Hills Dr. (☎ 520/344-4653); and the **Cocopah Bend RV Resort,** 6800 Strand Ave. (☎ 520/343-1663).

WHERE TO STAY
MODERATE

Best Western Inn Suites
1450 S. Castle Dome Ave., Yuma, AZ 85365. ☎ **520/783-8341** or 800/922-2034. Fax 520/783-1349. 166 studios and suites. A/C TV TEL. Summer, $74–$99 studio or suite for two. Winter, $89–$139 studio or suite for two. Rates include continental breakfast. AE, DC, DISC, MC, V.

If you've come to Yuma to escape the cold weather up north and want to enjoy some active sports, this hotel may be just what you're looking for. They've got a pool, whirlpool, exercise room, and tennis courts, and there's a golf course nearby. The rooms are divided between studios and one-bedroom suites, and all have microwave ovens, coffeemakers, refrigerators, and hairdryers. P.J.'s Poolside Café serves breakfast, sandwiches, snacks, and cocktails, and Wednesday nights there's a free barbecue for guests. The hotel also offers complimentary afternoon cocktails and morning newspaper.

La Fuente Inn

1513 E. 16th St., Yuma, AZ 85365. ☎ **520/329-1814,** or 800/841-1814. 96 rms, 46 suites. A/C TV TEL. $53–$80 double; $63–$95 suite. Rates include continental breakfast. AE, DC, DISC, MC, V.

Conveniently located just off the Interstate at 16th Street, this appealing hotel is done in Spanish colonial style with red-tile roof, pink stucco walls, and a fountain out front. In the lobby the theme is continued with rustic furnishings and a tile floor. French doors open onto the pool terrace and a large courtyard, around which the guest rooms are arranged. These rooms feature modern motel furnishings. Suites offer much more space and are well designed. The hotel also offers complimentary newspapers, evening happy hour, whirlpool, fitness room, coin laundry, and poolside gas barbecue grills.

Shilo Inn Hotel

1550 S. Castle Dome Rd., Yuma, AZ 85365. ☎ **520/782-9511,** or 800/222-2244. 134 rms, 10 suites. A/C TV TEL. $79–$105 double; $200 suite. AE, CB, DC, DISC, ER, JCB, MC, V.

Located on the edge of town overlooking farmland and desert, the Shilo Inn is Yuma's most luxurious hotel. The gardens are neatly manicured and provide an oasis of greenery in this dry landscape. The bright guest rooms have comfortable chairs, couches, and patios. In the tile bathrooms you'll find plenty of counter space. The hotel's more expensive rooms are those with a view of the desert. For long-term stays, there are also suites with kitchenettes. The hotel's spacious dining room offers both indoor and terrace dining, and to one side of the dining room is a lounge. The hotel also offers complimentary newspaper and coffee, room service, a large pool, whirlpool, exercise room, sauna, and steam room.

INEXPENSIVE

In addition to several older budget motels, Yuma has several newer budget chain motels. These include the following (see the Appendix for toll-free phone numbers): **Motel 6,** 1445 E. 16th St., Yuma, AZ 85365 (☎ **520/782-9521**), charging $33 to $42 double; and **Travelodge,** 2050 S. Fourth Ave., Yuma, AZ 85364 (☎ **520/783-3831**), charging $37 to $87 double.

WHERE TO DINE

Hungry Hunter

2355 S. Fourth Ave. ☎ **520/782-3637.** Reservations recommended. Main courses $12–$18. AE, MC, V. Mon–Thurs 11am–2:30pm and 5–9:30pm, Fri 11am–2:30pm and 5–10pm, Sat 5–10pm, Sun 3–9pm. STEAK/SEAFOOD.

Yuma's poshest restaurant sports an Eddie Bauer hunt-club decor with duck images everywhere. Frosted-glass dividers, liberal use of brass and oak, and a rich forest green color scheme may have you expecting a cool forest when you step outside. All meals are served with a cup of soup, fresh bread, a potato or rice pilaf, and a lazy Susan salad bar that's brought to your table. If this isn't enough to satisfy your hunger, you may want to precede your meal with an appetizer of spicy shrimp, crab cake, or crab-stuffed mushrooms, or top off your meal with a towering mud pie made with two ice creams, Grand Marnier, hot fudge, and whipped cream. In between, save room for some of their excellent prime rib.

✪ Garden Cafe

250 Madison Ave. ☎ **520/783-1491.** All items $4–$7.25. AE, MC, V. Tues–Fri 9am–2:30pm, Sat–Sun 8am–2:30pm. SANDWICHES/SALADS.

In back of the Century House Museum you'll find Yuma's favorite breakfast and lunch café. We had pancakes with lingonberry sauce here for breakfast that were scrumptious. Set amid quiet terraced gardens and large aviaries full of singing birds, the Garden Cafe is a cool retreat from Yuma's heat. On the hottest days, misters spray the air with a gentle fog that keeps the gardens cool. There's also an indoor dining area. The menu consists of various well-constructed sandwiches, daily special quiches, salads, and rich desserts. On Sunday there's a brunch buffet.

⑤ Lutes Casino

221 Main St. ☎ **520/782-2192.** $2.50–$3.50. No credit cards. Mon–Thurs and Sat–Sun 9am–7pm, Fri 9am–8pm. BURGERS.

You won't find any slot machines or poker tables at Lutes Casino anymore, but back in the 1920s when this place opened, gambling was legal in Arizona. Today it's a dark and cavernous pool hall and the state's only domino parlor, but it's better known as a family restaurant serving the best hamburgers in town. You don't need to see a menu—just walk in and ask for a Special, or Especial (this is a bilingual joint). What you'll get is a combination of a cheeseburger and a hot dog. Then cover your Special with Lute's own secret-recipe hot sauce to make it truly special.

Mandarin Palace

350 E. 32nd St. ☎ **520/344-2805.** Main dishes $8.50–$14. AE, CB, DC, DISC, MC, V. Sun–Thurs 11am–10pm, Fri–Sat 11am–11pm. CHINESE.

Yuma doesn't seem the sort of town to support a palace, but that's exactly what this Chinese restaurant seems to be. It's big and elegant, with a host in a tuxedo. The menu prices seem a bit high for a Chinese restaurant, but you get plenty of choices that on the whole are fairly well done, including smoked tea duck, a half or whole duck smoked in tea leaves, and a number of Szechuan dishes. At lunch on weekdays there is a buffet for $5.95.

Appendix

MAJOR AIRLINES

Alaska Airlines	800/426-0333
Aero México	800/237-6639
America West	800/235-9292
American	800/433-7300
Continental	800/525-0280
Delta	800/221-1212
Northwest	800/225-2525
Southwest	800/435-9792
TWA	800/221-2000
United	800/241-6522
USAir	800/428-4322

CAR-RENTAL COMPANIES

Alamo	800/327-9633
Avis	800/331-1212
Budget	800/527-0700
Dollar	800/800-4000
Hertz	800/654-3131
National	800/227-7368
Thrifty	800/367-2277

MAJOR CHAIN MOTELS

Best Western	800/528-1234
Comfort Inns	800/228-5150
Days Inns	800/329-7466
	(800/DAYS-INN)
Econo Lodges	800/424-4777
Embassy Suites	800/362-2779
	(800/EMBASSY)
Hampton Inns	800/426-7866
	(800/HAMPTON)
Hilton	800/445-8667
Holiday Inns	800/465-4329
	(800/HOLIDAY)
La Quinta Inns	800/531-5900
Marriott	800/228-9290
Marriott	
Residence Inn	800/331-3131
Motel 6	505/891-6161
	(no 800 number)
Quality Inns	800/228-5151
Radisson	800/333-3333
Ramada	800/272-6232
Rodeway Inns	800/424-4777
Sheraton	800/325-3535
Super 8 Motels	800/800-8000
Travelodge	800/578-7878
Wyndham	800/996-3426

Index

Now Save Money on All Your Travels by Joining

Frommer's
T R A V E L   B O O K   C L U B

The Advantages of Membership:

1. Your choice of any **TWO FREE BOOKS.**

2. Your own subscription to the **TRIPS & TRAVEL** quarterly newsletter, where you'll discover the best buys in travel, the hottest vacation spots, the latest travel trends, world-class events and festivals, and much more.

3. A **30% DISCOUNT** on any additional books you order through the club.

4. **DOMESTIC TRIP-ROUTING KITS** (available for a small additional fee). We'll send you a detailed map highlighting the most direct or scenic route to your destination, anywhere in North America.

Here's all you have to do to join:

Send in your annual membership fee of $25.00 ($35.00 Canada/Foreign) with your name, address, and selections on the form below. Or call 815/734-1104 to use your credit card.

Send all orders to:

FROMMER'S TRAVEL BOOK CLUB
P.O. Box 473 • Mt. Morris, IL 61054-0473 • ☎ 815/734-1104

YES! I want to take advantage of this opportunity to join Frommer's Travel Book Club.

[ ] My check for $25.00 ($35.00 for Canadian or foreign orders) is enclosed.
    All orders must be prepaid in U.S. funds only. Please make checks payable to Frommer's Travel Book Club.

[ ] Please charge my credit card: [ ] Visa or [ ] Mastercard

Credit card number: _____

Expiration date: ___ / ___ / ___

Signature: _____

Or call 815/734-1104 to use your credit card by phone.

Name: _____

Address: _____

City: _____ State: _____ Zip code: _____

Phone number (in case we have a question regarding your order): _____

Please indicate your choices for TWO FREE books (*see following pages*):

Book 1 - Code: _____   Title: _____

Book 2 - Code: _____   Title: _____

For information on ordering additional titles, see your first issue of the *Trips & Travel* newsletter.

Allow 4–6 weeks for delivery for all items. Prices of books, membership fee, and publication dates are subject to change without notice. All orders are subject to acceptance and availability.

AC1

The following Frommer's guides are available from your favorite bookstore, or you can use the order form on the preceding page to request them as part of your membership in Frommer's Travel Book Club.

FROMMER'S COMPLETE TRAVEL GUIDES
(Comprehensive guides to sightseeing, dining and accommodations, with selections in all price ranges—from deluxe to budget)

FROMMER'S $-A-DAY GUIDES
(Dream Vacations at Down-to-Earth Prices)

FROMMER'S COMPLETE CITY GUIDES

(Comprehensive guides to sightseeing, dining, and accommodations in all price ranges)

FROMMER'S FAMILY GUIDES

(Guides to family-friendly hotels, restaurants, activities, and attractions)

FROMMER'S WALKING TOURS

(Memorable strolls through colorful and historic neighborhoods, accompanied by detailed directions and maps)

FROMMER'S AMERICA ON WHEELS

(Guides for travelers who are exploring the U.S.A. by car, featuring a brand-new rating system for accommodations and full-color road maps)

FROMMER'S SPECIAL-INTEREST TITLES

Arthur Frommer's Branson!	P107	Frommer's Where to Stay U.S.A., 11th Ed.	P102
Arthur Frommer's New World of Travel (avail. 11/95)	P112	National Park Guide, 29th Ed.	P106
Frommer's Caribbean Hideaways (avail. 9/95)	P110	USA Today Golf Tournament Guide	P113
Frommer's America's 100 Best-Loved State Parks	P109	USA Today Minor League Baseball Book	P111

FROMMER'S BEST BEACH VACATIONS
(The top places to sun, stroll, shop, stay, play, party, and swim—with each beach rated for beauty, swimming, sand, and amenities)

California (avail. 10/95)	G100	Hawaii (avail. 10/95)	G102
Florida (avail. 10/95)	G101		

FROMMER'S BED & BREAKFAST GUIDES
(Selective guides with four-color photos and full descriptions of the best inns in each region)

California	B100	Hawaii	B105
Caribbean	B101	Pacific Northwest	B106
East Coast	B102	Rockies	B107
Eastern United States	B103	Southwest	B108
Great American Cities	B104		

FROMMER'S IRREVERENT GUIDES
(Wickedly honest guides for sophisticated travelers and those who want to be)

Chicago (avail. 11/95)	I100	New Orleans (avail. 11/95)	I103
London (avail. 11/95)	I101	San Francisco (avail. 11/95)	I104
Manhattan (avail. 11/95)	I102	Virgin Islands (avail. 11/95)	I105

FROMMER'S DRIVING TOURS
(Four-color photos and detailed maps outlining spectacular scenic driving routes)

Australia	Y100	Italy	Y108
Austria	Y101	Mexico	Y109
Britain	Y102	Scandinavia	Y110
Canada	Y103	Scotland	Y111
Florida	Y104	Spain	Y112
France	Y105	Switzerland	Y113
Germany	Y106	U.S.A.	Y114
Ireland	Y107		

FROMMER'S BORN TO SHOP
(The ultimate travel guides for discriminating shoppers—from cut-rate to couture)

Hong Kong (avail. 11/95)	Z100	London (avail. 11/95)	Z101